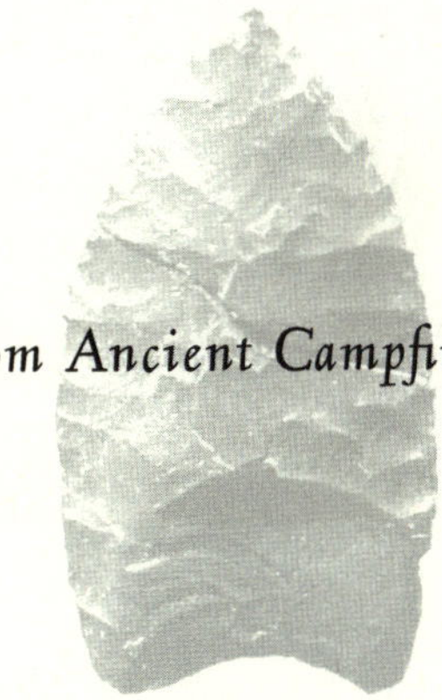

Light from Ancient Campfires

TREVOR R. PECK

Light from Ancient Campfires

ARCHAEOLOGICAL EVIDENCE FOR NATIVE LIFEWAYS ON THE NORTHERN PLAINS

AU PRESS

Published by AU Press, Athabasca University
1200, 10011 – 109 Street
Edmonton, AB T5J 3S8

Library and Archives Canada Cataloguing in Publication

Peck, Trevor R. (Trevor Richard), 1968–
Light from ancient campfires :
archaeological evidence for Native lifeways on the northern plains / Trevor R. Peck.

Includes bibliographical references and index.
Issued also in electronic format.
ISBN 978-1-897425-96-1

1. Indians of North America — Alberta — Antiquities.
2. Indians of North America — Material culture — Alberta.
3. Projectile points — Alberta.
4. Paleo-Indians — Alberta.
5. Paleo-Indians — Great Plains.
6. Indians of North America — Great Plains — Antiquities.
7. Excavations (Archaeology) — Alberta.
8. Alberta — Antiquities.
9. Great Plains — Antiquities.
I. Title.

E78.A5P43 2011 971.23004'97 C2010-905790-2

Cover and book design by Natalie Olsen, Kisscut Design.
Author photo by Wendy Unfreed.
Printed and bound in Canada by Marquis Book Printing.

This project was funded in part by the Alberta Foundation for the Arts. The author is grateful to the Archaeological Society of Alberta and to the Association of Consulting Archaeologists (Alberta) for their generous financial support.

Alberta Foundation for the Arts

ARCHAEOLOGICAL SOCIETY OF ALBERTA

In memory of Dorothea Catherine Moritz (1905–1992),

my first and finest instructor concerning the value of the past,

and

for my parents, Donna and Gurdon Peck,

my first and finest instructors.

TABLES

FIGURES

PLATES

ACKNOWLEDGEMENTS

I owe a particular debt of gratitude to my supervisors at the Heritage Division, Culture and Community Spirit. Dr. David Link, Assistant Deputy Minister (Acting), and Brian Ronaghan, Director of the Archaeological Survey, were exceedingly supportive of the project, allowing exceptional access to the Cultural Resource Management literature. As well, constructive critical comment was provided by Wendy Unfreed, Plains Archaeologist, Archaeological Survey, throughout the project.

A handful of people reviewed the document at various stages of completion. The sheer size of the volume would have frightened off most scholars. I am deeply indebted for the constructive criticism provided by four anonymous reviewers as well as by Caroline Hudecek-Cuffe, Brian Vivian, Alison Landals, and, again, Wendy Unfreed. The work was enhanced by the many, many, many suggested improvements.

Numerous colleagues generously shared copies of their theses and unpublished papers, including Brian (Barney) Reeves, Laureen Bryant, Charles (Chuck) Ramsay, Sean Webster, Alison Landals, Brian Scribe, Jennifer Tischer, Barbara Neal, Brian Kooyman, Allyson Ramsay, Benjamin Hjermstad, Grant Clarke, Karl Hutchings, Gerald Oetelaar, Jason Gillespie, Steven Kasstan, Irene (Rena) Varsakis, Mack Shortt, David Norris, Brad Himour, Dale Walde, Michael Klassen, Jean Prentice, Leslie (Butch) Amundson, Suzanne Zurburg, Riel Cloutier, Margaret Hanna, Thomas Head, Mary Malainey, and Caroline Hudecek-Cuffe.

The Royal Alberta Museum deserves special thanks for their support of this work. Jack Brink, Bob Dawe, Kristine Fedyniak, and Karen Geiring repeatedly obliged requests for access to collections. Similarly, Parks Canada, the Department of Archaeology at the University of Calgary, and Lifeways of Canada Ltd. also allowed access to collections for photography.

Permission to reproduce a number of photographs was granted by the following individuals and firms: Dale Walde (University of Calgary), Gerald Oetelaar (University of Calgary), Eugene Gryba, Lifeways of Canada Ltd., Laurie Milne, Jason Gillespie, John Brumley, Darryl Bereziuk, Michael Quigg, FMA Heritage Resources Consultants Inc., Bison Historical Services Ltd., Glenbow Museum, and ARESCO. Photographs taken on contract to the Archaeological Survey were skilfully produced by Kim Tymko, Kathy McCormick, and Jason Gillespie. Robin Woywitka plotted the sites on the maps.

Finally, I thank my family for their support for this project. My parents, Donna and Gurdon, have been supportive of my career in archaeology for over twenty years. Their enthusiasm for this project was no different despite its ambitious nature. My brother Chris and his family have provided verbal support from their home in Australia. My wife, Beth, expertly drafted all the plates with projectile points and her professional editing skills polished the draft document in its final stages. My appreciation cannot be expressed in words.

Introduction

People have lived in what is now southern Alberta for about the past 13,000 years. Archaeological evidence for Native lifeways in Alberta has been documented by ordinary citizens who find artifacts on their land, by academics conducting research at universities, and by local archaeological societies who rally to map and preserve sites. The greatest source of archaeological information, however, is Alberta's cultural resource management (CRM) community, which includes the Alberta Historic Resources Management Branch and the archaeological consultants. In accordance with the Alberta Historical Resources Act (1973), the Alberta Historic Resources Management Branch regulates all archaeological matters in the province. Among other things, the act influences when archaeological studies are required as part of land development projects. Consulting archaeologists are contracted by land developers to mitigate effects of development projects on Alberta's archaeological resources. The joint efforts of all these groups — concerned citizens, avocational archaeologists, academics, archaeological consultants and government regulators — has led to the identification of 35,500 sites in Alberta. This wealth of information provides the basis for this book.

Scope of the Book

The aim of this text is to provide a synthesis and revision of the culture-historical sequences used to organize archaeological evidence of Alberta plains prehistory (see Figure 1). To accomplish this aim, the sequence and its cultural units (traditions, complexes, and phases) are examined in a three-fold process. First, background research previously conducted for each cultural unit is summarized. Second, the vast amount of data generated by the cultural resource management community as well as other relevant sources is presented as raw data for each cultural unit. Third, a new definition of the cultural unit is offered with a synthesis of its material culture, technology, social organization and spiritual practices. The defined cultural unit is compared to similar entities in nearby Saskatchewan, Manitoba, Montana, North Dakota, South Dakota and Wyoming to determine if a broader distribution of each archaeological culture can be recognized.

The presentation of so much raw data provides opportunity for readers to interpret the data for themselves rather than simply accept the author's perspective. This is especially true given the restrained interpretation of the voluminous raw data presented in the text. Thus, the volume ends with a commentary rather than a summary to loosen the restraints on interpretation with the aim of further eliciting discussion within the discipline.

In recent years, archaeological excavations and studies in cultural resource management have dramatically increased. Many sites have been reported to the Historic Resources Management Branch in detail but the information is not widely available to the academic community or public. The first thorough synthesis of Alberta's plains prehistory was done by Reeves (1969, 1983a), with more recent critiques of the model by Vickers (1986), Brumley and Dau (1988:20–77), and Brumley and Rennie (2005). A reassessment of the prehistoric record of archaeological material on the Alberta plains is long overdue.

While the production of a new sequence is important and much attention has been paid to timing of events, the relationships between the various cultural entities that comprise the sequence still require elucidation. As stated, this text's focus is provincial, with heavy emphasis on the material culture recorded in Alberta. Additional effort has been made to pursue cultural entities into adjacent regions of the Northwestern Plains in order to provide a broader context for interpreting Alberta's past.

The text is mainly organized chronologically, based on diagnostic projectile points that define archaeological phases and complexes. With a few exceptions, only sites with diagnostic projectile points *and* associated radiocarbon dates have been included in this review. Some sites with dubious associations have been included but the issues associated with these sites are included. A few sites lacking radiocarbon dates but containing diagnostic projectile points have been included, owing to their comparability

Period	Phase / Complex	Time (BP)	Old Scheme
PROTO	One Gun	ca. 200	One Gun
	Old Women's	300–250	Old Women's
LATE	Highwood	500–300	Old Women's
	Old Women's	1100–500	
	Avonlea	1350–1100	Avonlea
TRANSITION	Sonota	1500–1350	Besant
MIDDLE	Besant	2100–1500	
	Bracken	2800–2100	Pelican Lake
	Outlook / Sandy Creek	ca. 2500	
	Pelican Lake	3600–2800	
	McKean	4200–3500	McKean
	Oxbow	4500–4100	Oxbow
	Estevan	4900–4500	Mummy Cave
	Calderwood	5200–4700	
	Maple Leaf	6300–5200	
	Mummy Cave	7300–6700	
	Country Hills	7500–7300	
TRANSITION	Lusk	8300–7500	Plains/Mountain
	Plains / Mountain	8500–7700	
EARLY	Cody	9000–8500	Cody
	Alberta	9700–9000	Agate Basin
	Agate Basin	10200–9700	
	Basally thinned	ca. 10500	Folsom
	Folsom	10900–10200	
	Clovis	11050–10800	Clovis

FIGURE I
Culture-historical models: Proposed model (left column) and current model (right column)

to known-age specimens. As is demonstrated throughout the text, the morphology of a projectile point can be misleading with respect to its age. The best way to evaluate a site is through recovery of diagnostic materials in a well-dated context.

Chronological organization of the culture-historical sequence starts with the earliest archaeological evidence for people in Alberta and proceeds to the present. As mentioned above, each part of the culture-historical sequence (i.e., phases or complexes) is discussed separately, addressing three distinct elements. First, the background research that has been previously conducted for each cultural unit is presented. Questions such as *What defines the cultural entity? Has our notion of it changed with increased information?* and *What is the current state of thought concerning this issue?* are presented in the introductory passages. Any interpretation of the archaeological record makes more sense couched in the context from which that understanding stemmed. Second, the vast amount of data generated by the cultural resource management community is rarely published in readily accessible sources; this work usually presents raw data for site type, location, amount of excavation conducted, artifacts collected, and radiocarbon dates, site by site. Lastly, a new or reviewed definition of the phase or complex is offered. A generalized synthesis of the culture's place in the past with respect to material culture, technology, social organization, and spiritual practices is presented. The defined cultural units are compared with similar material in nearby Saskatchewan, Manitoba, Montana, North Dakota, South Dakota, and Wyoming, and a broader distribution of each is suggested where continuity in material culture with adjacent regions is demonstrated.

Archaeological Systematics

In order to organize the great amount of archaeological evidence that has been gathered from the province, a consistent classification scheme is required. A number of different systems have been proposed for archaeological assemblages, with most relying on the nature of morphological change in projectile points over time. This approach is possible owing to the largely diachronic technological change in projectile points (i.e., spear to dart to arrow) known to have taken place across North America, coupled with more localized morphological variation during each technological stage. Such morphological change in the projectile points has been attributed to many phenomena, including function and stochastic variation, but ethnicity dominates most interpretations of Northern Plains cultures (e.g., Dyck 1983:132; Greaves 1982; Kehoe 1966b:839–840; Peck 1996:117–136).

Traditionally, the archaeological record in Alberta, and on the Northwestern Plains in general, has been divided into segments of time called periods. Each period is further subdivided into smaller segments of time called complexes, traditions, or phases (sometimes with subphases). As alluded to above, the periods have been differentiated based on changes in projectile point morphology, changes which have been inferred to reflect changes in hunting systems technology (e.g., Dyck 1983; Forbis 1970; Mulloy 1958:204–223; Peck 2004:2–3; Reeves 1969, 1983a:35–37; Vickers 1986:9–16; Wormington and Forbis 1965:183–198).

Mulloy (1958:204–223) proposed the first organizational scheme for archaeological materials from the Northwestern Plains. He considered archaeological material from his Early Prehistoric period, ca. 11,000–4,000 B.C., to be amongst the earliest produced by people in North America (Mulloy 1958:204–205). Interestingly, he suggested that the evidence from this time period indicates that large lanceolate points were used with spear-throwers rather than thrusting spears (Mulloy 1958:205, 208). He proposed a hiatus, ca. 4,000–1,500 B.C., between the Early Prehistoric period and the Early Middle Prehistoric period, owing possibly to climatic conditions. The Early Middle Prehistoric period, ca. 1,500 B.C.–A.D. 1, is represented by small lanceolate points and stemmed points (Mulloy 1958:209). The Late Middle Prehistoric period, (A.D. 1–500, produced corner-notched points (Mulloy 1958:209). In the Late Prehistoric period, A.D. 500–1800, small corner-notched points occurred, but small side-notched points are considered the best diagnostic along with ceramics (Mulloy 1958:211, 213). The Historic period, A.D. 1800 to the present day, differed from the previous period, as evidenced by the inclusion of European trade items in the archaeological record.

Wormington and Forbis (1965) developed the first systematic classification of archaeological material designed specifically for assemblages in Alberta. They rejected Mulloy's system because it leads to confusing terminology such as "Late Early Prehistoric" and "Early Late Prehistoric" (Wormington and Forbis 1965:13). They did recognize that the three technological-cultural stages found in the United States are found in Alberta, but instead proposed the terms *Palaeo-Indian*, *Meso-Indian*, *Neo-Indian*, and *Historic* (Wormington and Forbis 1965:13). During meetings in 1966, Forbis (1968b:44) acknowledged that "the historical outline placed before us several years ago by Mulloy is by and large still valid for Alberta. I do not imagine that we will seriously alter his general scheme. What we can do is fill in some extremely interesting details." In another proposed scheme, based on data attained in Alberta up to 1964, Forbis (1970) proposed slightly different terminology for the technological-cultural periods already established. He suggested "Early Lithic period," "Middle Lithic period," and "Late Lithic Period," with the possibility of a pre-projectile point horizon at the beginning of the sequence (Forbis 1970).

It was not until the late 1960s that Mulloy's model was accepted as the basis for the modern version of the classification scheme. Brian Reeves stated: "Following Mulloy (1958), the Post-Glacial cultural sequence may be divided into three periods: Early, Middle and Late. The following sequence is divided either into complexes when the relationship is unclear between the sequent assemblages or into phases when the relationships are discernible between the serial assemblages. The latter are linked by cultural traditions" (Reeves 1983a:19). Reeves (1969) presented the essence of the current classification with the Early Prehistoric period consisting of the Clovis, Folsom-Midland, Agate Basin/Hell Gap, Alberta-Cody, Lusk, and Frederick complexes. His Middle Prehistoric period included Mummy Cave, Oxbow, McKean-Duncan, Hanna, and Pelican Lake phases of the Tunaxa cultural tradition, and the Besant phase of the Napikwan cultural tradition. Reeves' Late Prehistoric period included the Avonlea phase of the Tunaxa cultural tradition and the Old Women's phase of the Napikwan cultural tradition. While these cultural traditions are not often recognized, and some of the complexes are now called phases, this arrangement strongly agrees with the modern classification scheme.Following Willey and Phillips (1958:72), Reeves (1983a:39) defined a phase as an archaeological unit that exhibits traits distinct enough to discern it from other units. A phase does not necessarily correlate to a locality or region; it can change through time, and may be found in two or more environmentally distinct regions. A phase must also demonstrate a discernable relationship between serial assemblages. When the relationship is unclear between the sequential assemblages, it is called a complex (Reeves 1969:19). If a sequence of phases is established based on discernable relationships between serial assemblages it is called a tradition (Reeves 1983a:40). In short, Reeves' cultural traditions articulated phases that were inferred to be related along a space-time continuum and are labelled with a specific cultural tradition title, such as Tunaxa cultural tradition.

Of course, projectile points have been used as the principle diagnostic criteria for each of the phases and complexes on the Alberta plains. Almost always, the phase or complex is named for its diagnostic projectile point type. The traditions have been labelled based on inferred ethnic identification: for example the Napikwan cultural tradition being an archaeological unit ultimately affiliated with the Blackfoot, and the Tunaxa cultural tradition reflecting the archaeological past of the Kutenia.

In Alberta, it seems fair to say that most archaeologists recognize the terms *phase*, *complex*, and *tradition* as defined here. The same cannot be said for the rest of the Northwestern Plains. For example, Dyck (1983:69) and Syms (1977:70–72) both discussed the Northern Plains in their syntheses but used different terms for archaeological entities than those used in Alberta. The diversity of meanings for the various terms can cause confusion when interregional discussions occur. The definitions delimited above will be retained for the purposes of this text.

Recently, there has been a trend to replace the term *Prehistoric period* with the term *Precontact period* in an attempt to use culturally sensitive language. This sentiment is misplaced. *Precontact* embeds the Eurocentric notion that contact with Europeans was the only significant contact event Native people have experienced (Jones 1997:64–65). This is not true, of course, as Native trade networks were known to have flourished and collapsed in many places at many times, bringing a variety of Native peoples into contact. In contrast, *prehistory* is used in archaeology to mean "prior to the keeping of written records," a definition that can be found in most dictionaries. The term has been used appropriately for a long time in Northern Plains archaeology, in no way disparagingly, and it is correctly used here.

Other concerns over terms used in Northern Plains classification have been raised by Yellowhorn (2003). He proposed that the Northern Plains match terminology used in Europe's Paleolithic period. This proposal elicited a reasonable rebuttal that the current classification system has solid historical precedent and demonstrated utility (Gillespie 2003). Again, for purposes of continuity with the Alberta literature, the terms and meanings currently in use, as described above, are retained.

Theoretical Perspective

This text explicitly pursues a culture-historical paradigm. For Alberta, culture-historical models were first sketched by Wormington and Forbis (1965) in the mid-1960s and solidified by Reeves (1969, 1983a) in the late

1960s, with updated versions in recent years (Reeves et al. 2000; Reeves 2003). This model has benefited from a number of other individuals who have slotted new sites into the appropriate archaeological cultures, such as Brumley and Dau (1988), Peck and Hudecek-Cuffe (2003), and Vickers (1986, 1994). Lyman and O'Brien (2006) revised the history and development of culture historical models by providing a novel understanding of their fundamental underpinnings. This text follows their groundbreaking effort.

Culture-historical perspectives are often viewed as being mainly interested in the chronology of archaeological phenomenon: time-space grids (Lyman and O'Brien 2006:6). Lyman and O'Brien (2006) argued that the culture-historical paradigm is evolutionary in its underlying principles. One of the oldest artifact-based chronometers used to place assemblages in order within the cultural-historic framework is the direct historical approach (Lyman and O'Brien 2006:12). The direct historical approach relies on "overlapping" to provide the measurement of time as a continuous variable between two points: "The principle of overlapping... concerns the occurrence of a cultural trait or artifact type in multiple cultural complexes or in artifact assemblages potentially of different age, and it is these shared, or overlapping, traits or types that serve as the basis for placing those complexes or assemblages adjacent to another in an ordering thought to comprise a sequence" (Lyman and O'Brien 2006:104). The assumption implicit in the direct historical approach is that the more traits shared between an historic assemblage and a protohistoric or prehistoric assemblage, the closer they are in time. "The concept of overlapping is critically important because it reveals the underpinning (and typically implicit) view of culture change as an evolutionary process minimally involving cultural transmission and inheritance, or what during the first half of the twentieth century was referred to commonsensically as persistence (Rouse 1939) or tradition (Willey 1945)" (Lyman and O'Brien 2006). Heritable/historical continuity through genetics, or cultural transmission between people, is what biologists call lineages and archaeologists call traditions. Thus temporally sequent phenomena share at least some kind of affinity. Transmission is not always precise despite cultural constraints ensuring a relatively high degree of fidelity; "descent with modification" can occur as a result of cultural innovation (i.e., "mutations") and problems in the fidelity of replication (Lyman and O'Brien 2006:22–23). A caveat to this paradigm is that the use of assemblages with the direct historical approach, or even assemblages excavated from stratigraphic sequences, should not be considered real or discrete entities, but merely chunks of the cultural continuum: there is no steady state within a culture.

Descent with modification relies on the principle of heritable continuity, which requires fidelity of replication between the "ancestor" and the "descendent." Transmission, along with its innovations and errors, and natural selection together ensure that change is constantly occurring. The direction of change cannot be determined because it is historically contingent. "What is available for transmission depends on the random — with respects to what is or might be needed among descendents — generation of innovative variants; what actually is transmitted depends on the transmission mechanisms and their operation; what is replicated depends on the size of the transmitting population and the particular sorting filters in operation at the time of transmission" (Lyman and O'Brien 2006:169).

To provide a practical application of this paradigm, I address the problem of heterogeneity and homogeneity in material culture. A major "sorting filter" affecting transmission in human life is kinship, a social structure through which much of "the way to make things" is transmitted. In a general sense, generic Plains social structure or kinship is generational or horizontal; that is, it exhibits little time depth with an extended family often centred on a sibling group. In the past, band organization was usually composite, consisting of extended family groups centered on a chief and his close relatives and followers. The composition of a band changed with the circumstances of politics and economics. Leadership was established through status and rarely through heredity. People were free to leave and seek other bands and other leaders. This configuration of social structure allowed for fluidity (e.g., Eggan 1955a, 1955b). In contrast, many groups coming on to the plains in the Historic period, especially from the east, did not exhibit this social structure (Eggan 1955b). Those exhibiting cross-cousin marriage, for example, created multiple bonds between a limited array of relatives and maintained those bonds from generation to generation. This is different than a generational kinship system that ties non-relatives together in a horizontally expanding system.

With regards to the production of material culture, the fluid nature of groups with generational systems brings together people with highly varied backgrounds in terms of heritable continuity. That is to say, transmission from parents to their children may have been produced with high fidelity, but others who have joined the group are less likely to fit within the "lineage" owing to historical contingency. So, material culture will look generally similar within the cultural group, with an overall appearance of heterogeneity. In contrast, for some of the groups coming on to the Plains, with cross-cousin marriage systems for example, transmission with high fidelity should occur, increasing the likelihood of heritable continuity. In this scenario, fewer outside social forces influence the transmission mechanisms, further promoting conformity. In short, transmission within groups with constrained filtering mechanisms (e.g., cross-cousin marriage, craft specialization, sodalities) should produce items of material culture that exhibit a strong similarity owing to the fidelity of transmission.

The following provides an example of this theoretical position from Alberta's archaeological record. In the Late Prehistoric period, the arrival of the Avonlea phase and its characteristic projectile point, the Avonlea point, is striking. Avonlea pottery is also limited in its diversity, exhibiting parallel-grooved, fabric/net-impressed, and plain surface finishes. The regularity and homogeneity of Avonlea points and pottery is well known in Northern Plains archaeology. Interestingly, the most recent research suggests the Avonlea phase has its origin on the eastern periphery of the Plains. The current model would suggest it exhibited a structured kinship system that generated bonds through generations, thus passing down the "way to make things." The Old Women's phase has produced the most heterogeneous diagnostic projectile points and pottery in Alberta's archaeological record. Importantly, there is strong evidence to link the end of the Avonlea phase to the beginning of the Old Women's phase. As well, the Old Women's phase has been linked with the ethnologically known Blackfoot through a series of convincing arguments. The Blackfoot are a classic band-oriented society. Using the model, the Avonlea phase, a group of people on the eastern periphery of the Plains, migrated across the Plains to southern Alberta, southwestern Saskatchewan, and northern Montana. There, their rigid social structure was slowly reconsidered in the face of the harsh Plains environment in favour of a more fluid band structure. Through this process, the rigid social structure that produced homogeneous Avonlea points and pottery was replaced with a more fluid structure. The result was the Old Women' phase, which exhibits heterogeneous point and pottery forms. The correlation of Old Women's phase to Blackfoot culture strongly hints at a classic band organization for the archaeological culture.

The renewed culture-historical paradigm has many profound implications for Alberta's culture-historical sequence. First, the entire cultural sequence should be revisited given the evolutionary nature of the cultural-historic models. It should be kept in mind that cultural transmission and descent with modification are the underlying principles of this perspective. Second, the sequence itself need not change but the idea of the static "phase" should now be re-interpreted as points within a continuum of culture change. Third, evidence of "overlapping" should be sought out as it indicates culture change as an evolutionary process minimally involving cultural transmission and inheritance. Lastly, social structures such as kinship should be examined as possible filtering mechanisms for transmission. As the example above suggests, it seems possible that generational kinship structures, more varied in their historical contingencies, will transmit/inherit more-varied transmissions. In contrast, cross-cousin kinship structures, very cohesive in their historical contingencies, will transmit/inherit more-succinct transmissions.

1 *Earliest Inhabitants*

PRIOR TO CA. 11,050 BP

The glacial maximum in Alberta occurred about 20,000 BP (before present, where present = A.D. 1950). Ice covered most of the province with the exception of areas in and around the Cypress Hills and a few isolated locations along the foothills of the Rocky Mountains. At this time the Cordilleran, or Montane, ice coalesced with the Laurentide ice sheet in the area of the foothills. There is some debate whether deglaciation began shortly after this as a slow process lasting until 12,000 BP or whether coalescence lasted until about 12,000 BP with a rapid deglaciation. Regardless, meltwater played an important role in shaping the Alberta landscape.

People living in such an environment would have experienced a relatively unstable and rapidly changing periglacial world. Archaeological evidence of these people would likely be quickly destroyed or buried in unusual localities and/or deep sediments (Beaudoin and Oetelaar 2003:187).

PRE-CLOVIS SITES (>CA. 11,050 BP)

Most scholars agree that the peopling of the Americas took place via the northern latitudes, across the Bering Land Bridge or along its shores. Despite the numerous lines of evidence that support this perspective, a precise route and arrival time of people to the Americas has yet to be documented. Alberta is intimately intertwined in this debate since one possible entry route would have been an inland penetration along the front range of the

Rocky Mountains; alternatively, a coastal route would have taken people along the shores of British Columbia.

The Coastal entry route would require access to now submerged palaeoshorelines along the west coast of Alaska and British Columbia. These shorelines began to submerge as ice on land melted, returning water to the oceans and causing sea levels to rise. There is evidence arguing against the coastal route. First, the earliest known sites in the coastal region date between ca. 10,500 to 10,000 BP, consisting of lanceolate points and lithic assemblages, and located between Alaska and Vancouver Island (e.g., Carlson and Magne 2008). Second, no obvious predecessor in western Beringia has been found with a marine-based culture of an appropriate age (West 1996). And third, there does not appear to be any cultural descendants of a coastal-adapted culture. The Clovis complex has possible antecedents in the technology and hunting adaptation of the Nenana complex or other large-mammal hunting people of the interior of Beringia or Alaska-Yukon. There does not appear to be any evidence of an early populating entity exhibiting any signs of a remnant coastal background. Still, the debate over the entry route taken by the first people has become progressively interesting with the increased acceptance of the Monte Verde site in south-central Chile. The Monte Verde site, dated to 12,500 BP, may provide evidence for the initial occupation of the Americas. The site consists of huts with log foundations, clay-lined pits for cooking, food remains including organics (e.g., seeds, nuts, fruits, berries, and tubers), and evidence of mastodon. Eleven consistent radiocarbon dates average about 12,500 BP (Adovasio and Pedler 1997:578). More astonishing is an older layer with chipped stone and possible fire pits dated to 33,000 BP. Many authorities accept the authenticity of Monte Verde (e.g., Adovasio and Pedler 1997; Fiedel 2000:85) while others do not (e.g., West 1996:540).

While the acceptance of Monte Verde as the oldest New World human occupation (i.e., pre-Clovis) would have profound implications for archaeology in the Americas, three important points must be acknowledged. First, internally consistent radiocarbon sequences in apparent firm association with actual artifacts *can* be a product of contamination. Second, regardless of Monte Verde's status, it has been thirty years since the discovery of the site but few if any comparable sites have come to light. When the first Folsom fluted point recoveries were made in the late 1920s, tens of additional similar finds were recorded within a decade of the original find. Thus, the site of Monte Verde may represent the *initial occupation* of the Americas, but it likely does not represent evidence for a *peopling event*. Thus, the view of Clovis technology spreading between existing groups of people (e.g. Stanford 1978b; Waters and Stafford 2007) seems improbable since there is no evidence to indicate that a substantial pre-Clovis population existed. Third, recently there have been acknowledged differences between the structural form of the radiocarbon calibration curves from the northern and southern hemispheres (McCormac et al. 2004; Landals 2008). Dates in the southern hemisphere, such as those from Monte Verde, have the potential to be incorrect, as the southern hemisphere needs to develop dendrochronologically dated wood and radiocarbon calibration curves independent of the northern hemisphere (McCormac et al. 2004; Landals 2008).

Alternatively, to enter the Americas via the inland route across the Bering Land Bridge would require the Ice-free Corridor to connect the northern land bridge or Beringia to the lands south of the mountain and continental ice sheets. The Ice-free Corridor consisted of deglaciated land along the eastern front range of the Cordilleran mountains in the Yukon, British Columbia, and Alberta. It is expected that the earliest known archaeological sites south of the ice sheets should coincide with the timing of the opening of the Ice-free Corridor, as the Cordilleran and Laurentide ice sheets separated. At present, the route is inferred to have opened by ca. 12,000 BP (e.g., Osborn et al. 2000).

The Clovis complex consists of the oldest sites of undisputed authenticity in the Americas south of the ice sheets. There are, however, sites that are as old as, if not older than, Clovis sites in the Americas of undisputed authenticity. These sites are all located north of the former North American ice sheets, in the Yukon and Alaska. Bluefish Caves is located 54 km southwest of the Old Crow settlement in the northwestern Yukon Territory. Bluefish Cave I is a multicomponent site with cultural material in levels III through V. Late Pleistocene and early Holocene-age fauna such as bison and horse were recovered from these levels. The lowest clear cultural level, level V, produced three flakes and thirty-seven micro-chips in a context expected to date about 13,000 BP (Cinq-Mars 1979:28). A microblade may occur in the overlying level and micro-chips may occur in underlying levels (Cinq-Mars 1979:28). The assemblages contained so few artifacts, however, that it is difficult to compare the material to other assemblages.

Perhaps more informative are the sites of the Nenana complex in the Alaska Range in central Alaska. Within the Nenana Valley is a series of sites — Dry Creek 1 (11,120 +/- 85 BP), Owl Ridge (11,340 +/- 150 BP), Moose Creek (11,730 +/- 250 BP), and Walker Road (11,010 +/- 230 BP; 11,170 +/- 180 BP; 11,300 +/- 120 BP; and 11,820 +/- 200 BP) — that are coeval with or predate Clovis sites (Hoffecker, Powers, and Bigelow 1996; Hoffecker, Powers, and Phippen 1996; Goebel et al. 1996; Hoffecker 1996). Goebel, Powers, and Bigelow (1991:74) noted that Nenana toolkits are virtually identical to Clovis tools, except the Nenana toolkits lack lanceolate projectile points. They suggest Nenana and Clovis may represent the northern and southern remnants of a peopling event, respectively, but they remain open to whether the peopling event was a late or early entry. A late entry about 13,000–12,000 BP would have occurred as the ice melted and allowed dispersal down the Ice-free Corridor. A much earlier entry could have had people into the Americas about 22,000–25,000 BP, before the Ice-free Corridor closed (Goebel et al. 1991:75). Recent excavations at the Yana RHS site, Siberia, have produced bifacial lithic industries and bone foreshafts that are similar to Clovis materials, dating to 27,000 BP (Pitulko et al. 2004). The recovery of materials dating to such an early time period so far north in Siberia verifies northern-adapted people were positioned for an early or late dispersal into the Americas.

Importantly, there are sites in Alaska that predate the Nenana complex. Materials from the Broken Mammoth, Swan Point, and Mead sites date to 12,000–11,500 BP. The lowest level at Swan Point produced dihedral burins, microblades, and a core tablet, and may be related to the Dyuktai culture of northeast Asia. While the context of the microblades has been questioned, Hoffecker (2001:149) noted that microblades had also been recovered from Bluefish Cave. Hoffecker (2001:149) suggested there was an early Beringian Dyuktai industry in Alaska no earlier than 11,500 BP. It was succeeded by the Nenana complex ca. 11,500–10,800 BP, which would provide a plausible source for Palaeoindian complexes entering the remainder of the Americas via the Ice-free Corridor (Hoffecker 2001:150).

The Sites

Because of the potential peopling route through the Ice-free Corridor, Alberta has enjoyed being in the spotlight for peopling studies (Beaudoin et al. 1996; Carlson 1991; Haynes 1987). A number of Alberta sites have become well known as potential early peopling sites (see Plate 1 and Figure 2).

PLATE 1
Flaked tools from Varsity Estates site. Photo credit: Jason Gillespie.

Taber Child (DlPa 4). The Taber Child site consists of fragments of an immature human skeleton that were found eroded from a steep coulee wall above the Oldman River just north of Taber. The site was discovered during a Geological Survey of Canada study conducted by Dr. A.M. Stalker in 1961. Wormington and Forbis (1965:117) and Wilson, Harvey, and Forbis (1983:180), amongst others, have called it the Stalker site and noted common confusion with the Bayrock site, which has been referred to as the Taber Early Man site (Bayrock is an Alberta phase kill site; see below).

The Taber Child skeleton is mainly represented by skull fragments, two vertebrae, a clavicle and part of a tibia (Moffat and Wainwright 1983:224). The child was estimated to be between nine months and four years of age at the time of death (Moffat and Wainwright 1983:224). Wormington and Forbis (1965:117) were the first to publicly propose great antiquity for the site based on the assessment of its geological position beneath till (Wilson et al. 1983:179).

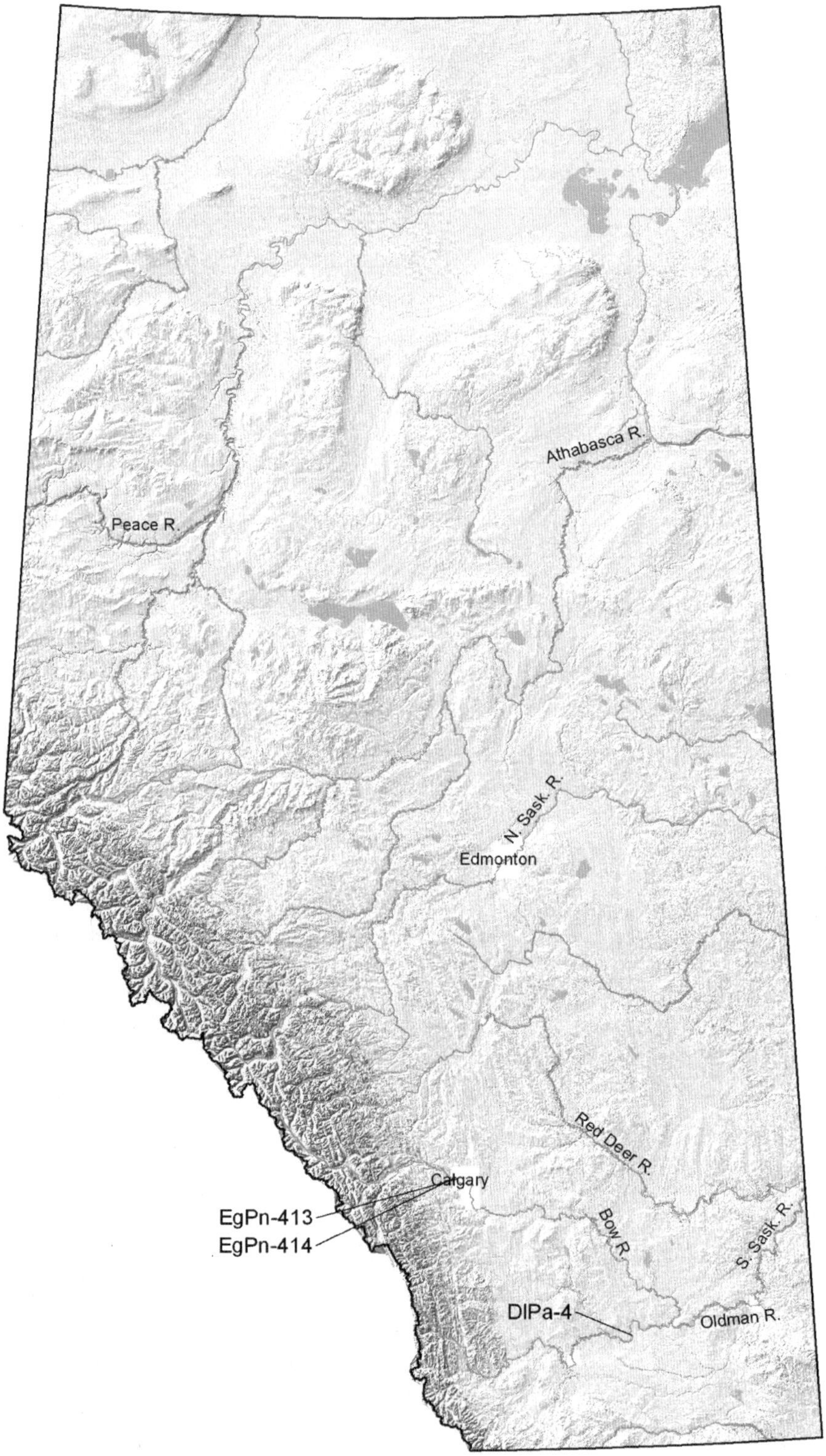

FIGURE 2
Pre-Clovis sites within Alberta

In 1977, excavations at the site set out to provide stronger evidence for the age of the skeletal material (Wilson et al. 1983:185). Evidence of Holocene mudflow deposits was observed near the Taber Child. This discovery suggested that the Taber Child bones had been recovered from orange sand deposits that were determined to date as old as 20,000 BP. X-ray diffraction analysis of matrix from the Taber Child specimen did not show evidence of the orange sand. The matrix most resembled the Holocene slope deposits when compared to baseline samples from across the slope (Wilson et al. 1983:199). The authors concluded that the skeletal material likely derived from mudflow deposits inset within the orange sand unit (Wilson et al. 1983:203–204). An infrared spectrophotometry analysis was undertaken to assess the loss of collagen. The protein content suggested that the Taber Child, in comparison with reference specimens, was consistent with those 10,000 BP or less (Moffat and Wainwright 1983:229). Similarly, accelerator ^{14}C dating of the Taber Child produced an age of 3,550 +/- 500 BP (Brown et al. 1983).

Varsity Estates (EgPn 413) and Silver Springs (EgPn 414). The Varsity Estates and Silver Spring sites are located on the north side of the Bow River on a roughly 50-metre-long escarpment of the valley in northwest Calgary. The Varsity Estates site consists of lithic artifacts eroding out of the gravel upper part of a layer of till that immediately underlies Glacial Lake Calgary sediments (Chlachula 1994a:104). The Silver Springs site consists of redeposited lithic artifacts in the upper part of some fluvial gravels of the Bow Valley till (Chlachula 1994a:104). The steep slope prohibited a large excavation but 15 m² was excavated in 1992–1993 at the Varsity Estates site and a series of 0.5-×-1.0-m units were excavated at the Silver Springs site (Chlachula 1996:298–299).

The assemblage from the Varsity Estates sites consisted of an upper and lower series. The lower series, presumably derived from an older cultural context, produced sixteen flakes "removed from the original laterally exposed face of the Bow Valley till (Unit 1) over a distance of 70–100 m in the steepest middle part of the slope" (Chlachula 1996:298). The second, or upper, series consisted of forty artifacts including cores (n = 2), side scrapers (n = 2), an end scraper, choppers (n = 2), a biface, and pieces of debitage (n = 17, with five flakes from the biface tool) recovered in roughly a 15-m² area on the till surface immediately beneath the lake (Chlachula 1994a:105, 1996:298). The Silver Springs site material (n = 31) was recovered from an eroded context. Eighteen artifacts were recovered from the till (Chlachula 2006:300–301). In short, a simple core and flake industry is said to be represented. A pollen sample from the site suggests sedge and pine were in the area (Chlachula 1994a:125). No datable macro-organic material was recovered from the site. The material was interpreted as a pre-Palaeoindian occupation in the foothills of Alberta that dates between roughly 25,000 and 21,000 BP based on chronostratigraphic correlation of the culture-bearing deposits to existing Late Quaternary temporal frameworks (Chlachula 1994a:126, 1994b, 1996:306).

Bryan and Gruhn (2007) argued that only four items recovered from the till at the Varsity Estates site were artifacts, but that the artifacts' stratigraphic position suggest a terminal Pleistocene age rather than the previously hypothesised pre-Late Wisconsinan age. The authors suggested that the artifacts were left on the surface of ice still in the area and later incorporated into the till. They argued that quarrying activity would have taken place at the site, not habitation (Bryan and Gruhn 2007:98).

Grimshaw. The Grimshaw site is located in the Grimshaw Gravel Pit, in the middle Peace River area, in gently rolling terrain about 5 km north of the town of Grimshaw in northwestern Alberta. The site consists of quartzite cobble artifacts recovered from the base of a Laurentide till exposed in a gravel operation (Chlachula and Leslie 2001).

Seventeen cobble artifacts were recovered: two observed in the lab, twelve in situ in the field, and three eroded from an exposed face (Chlachula and Leslie 2001:873). The tools include unifacial choppers (n = 7), bifacial choppers (n = 2), side scrapers (n = 2), an end scraper, a retouched flake, hammerstones (n = 3), and a cobble core (Chlachula and Leslie 2001:876). All materials were recovered from the lower till, immediately above its contact with the underlying gravels, over a distance of 30 m. The material is comparable to the Varsity Estates and Silver Springs sites (Chlachula and Leslie 2001:876). An age prior to the last glaciation is assigned to this material, presumed to be the Middle Wisconsinan (Chlachula and Leslie 2001:883).

Pre-Clovis: Still Searching for the Evidence

Unfortunately, we are not yet able to say when the first people entered the Americas, or Alberta for that matter. Such an "event" continues to be a contentious issue. Many archaeologists advocate an early peopling in order to account for sites such as Monte Verde. Others strongly support a later dispersal with the Clovis complex as the material representation of the dispersal phenomenon. The route that people traveled or populated is also controversial, with the Ice-free Corridor and a coastal migration most commonly touted.

Research within Alberta has added fuel to this debate. The announcement of the Pleistocene-age human infant skeleton near Taber produced substantial controversy at the time. Finds of exceptional antiquity are usually confronted with caution and scepticism in the archaeological community. The 1983 paper presentations on "Dating the Taber Child" in the *Canadian Journal of Archaeology* (vol. 7, no. 2) demonstrated a strong consensus that the skeleton was an Indigenous infant of modest antiquity, perhaps a few thousand years old.

The recovery of lithic artifacts in close association with glacial till has been proposed at three sites in Alberta: Varsity Estates, Silver Springs, and Grimshaw. Also, the Varsity Estates and Silver Springs sites have received substantial criticism concerning both the nature of the artifacts and the purported age of the deposits from which they came. The reconstruction of the palaeoenvironment at the Varsity Estates and Silver Springs sites has been strongly questioned. Young, Rains, and Osborn (1998) indicated that the literature suggests that a Late Quaternary ice sheet coalesced in the Calgary area, followed by glacial lake formation rather than an interval for human occupation. This assertion is further supported in subsequent research detailing the NW–SE oriented landforms that could have only been created by coalescing ice, and cosmogenic ^{36}Cl dates of 12–17 ka on foothills erratics together indicating Late Wisconsinan coalescence (Osborn et al. 2000:209–215). Furthermore, concerning the artifacts themselves, Gillespie, Tupakka, and Cluney (2004) questioned the cultural origin of the stone tools. Sixteen lithic attributes were shown to exhibit significant differences between known archaeological samples and known natural samples from a river bed. When the Varsity Estates and Silver Springs sites were evaluated using these attributes, the results indicated that the sites were most like the geological specimens or geofacts (Gillespie et al. 2004:630–631).

The Grimshaw site has received similar criticism. Driver (2001) focused his criticism on the unequivocal assignment of the lithics at the site as culturally fractured rather than naturally fractured. He felt the criteria used to distinguish humanly flaked stone were never proven to be limited to artifacts. Control specimens were never established from analogous sediments to compare to the Grimshaw artifacts. Because of this shortcoming in the analysis, "it is just as likely that the fractured Grimshaw cobbles were produced naturally as by humans, and better evidence is required to support an argument for preglacial humans in western Canada" (Driver 2001:873).

It is fair to state that there are no unequivocal pre-Clovis sites known in Alberta. That is not to say that such sites do not exist, only that they have not yet been recognized or confirmed. The task in front of researchers rests in developing reliable methods of identifying where these sites could be located and being able to distinguish their assemblages from naturally occurring materials. Both the Varsity Estates and Silver Springs sites are buried deep beneath metres of glacial and postglacial sediments. Even early Palaeoindian sites, dating later in time, are likely to be buried under substantial amounts of sediment given the highly active geomorphology at the glacial/postglacial boundary. For example, the Indian Creek Folsom occupation in the front range of the Rocky Mountains in west-central Montana is approximately 7.5 m below the surface. Its discovery was facilitated by cutbank erosion (Davis and Greiser 1992).

Early Prehistoric Period 2

CA. 11,050 BP TO 8,600 BP

Many researchers consider the coalescence of the Cordilleran and Laurentide ice sheets to have ceased around 12,000 BP (e.g., Osborn et al. 2000). Following this, the exposed land between the retreating ice sheets produced the so-called Ice-free Corridor. This new landscape was relatively unstable, exhibiting rapid change resulting from deglaciation. Meltwater created extensive proglacial lakes and erosional landforms. Revegetation likely occurred from plant communities to the south. Data gathered mainly from pollen records in the foothills suggests shrubby open vegetation in the mountains, open vegetation along a broad band at the foot of the mountain range, and spruce-dominated vegetation in the northeast (Beaudoin and Oetelaar 2003:196). By 11,000 BP, the ice had largely retreated from the province with the possible exception of the very northeast corner. Aeolian activity in dune fields, common in parts of Alberta, may have preserved or destroyed evidence of human activity at this time (Wolfe et al. 2006). Periglacial processes lessened as the glaciers retreated. By 10,000 BP, landforms were more stable and rivers began to incise into the terrain (Beaudoin and Oetelaar 2003:199). The dynamic environment that predominated during this time period likely played a large role in limiting the number of sites preserved and the archaeological visibility of sites from the Early Prehistoric period. The question remains whether the dynamic environment largely destroyed or deeply buried evidence of human activity.

CLOVIS PHASE (CA. 11,050 TO 10,800 BP)

The earliest widely accepted archaeological culture in the Americas is the Clovis phase of the Llano tradition. The most characteristic artifact of the phase is a large, fluted projectile point: the Clovis point. Flaked stone technology exhibiting bifacial and flake tool manufacturing is also common. Flake tools include knives, gravers, end scrapers (in some cases spurred), and large (macro-) blades (Haynes 1993). The fluted projectile points have sharp tips for initial penetration, sharp blade edges for cutting a hole to allow further penetration of the point, flutes for easy attachment to a notched foreshaft, and a narrower basal edge area than distal area for application of the binding so it does not inhibit penetration (Frison 1993b:241). As well, Clovis toolkits often contain what appear to be cylindrical, bevelled bone points, bone shaft wrenches, and rib segments with rounded and polished ends (Haynes 1993). Based on recoveries from the Anzick Burial site, ceremonial items apparently include exceptionally large and well-made Clovis points along with large bifaces, cylindrical bone rods and points, and red ochre (Haynes 1993:219). In terms of the range of sites encountered in the Clovis phase, most excavated sites have been interpreted as either kill sites or meat-processing sites, with the remainder being interpreted as burials and caches (Bradley 1993:253).

The subsistence strategy of the Clovis phase is most commonly thought of as big-game hunting. Evidence from fauna recovered at Clovis sites indicates a more complex subsistence than simply hunting of large mammals. Grayson and Meltzer (2002) reviewed the faunal assemblages from seventy-six sites and determined that only fourteen provided evidence of Clovis predation on megafauna, with twelve sites containing mammoth and two containing mastodon. Likewise, Clovis people were not preying on the full array of then-extant fauna that are now extinct, which suggests that Clovis people had little role in their extinction (Grayson and Meltzer 2002).

Delimiting the geographic extent of Clovis phase is complicated by the difficulty of differentiating Clovis points from other fluted points (Howard 1990). Clovis points are "comparatively large and heavy bifacially flaked fluted lanceolate points, lenticular to near oval in cross-section with parallel to moderately convex lateral edges" (Howard 1990:259), which are "normally fluted on both faces. Flutes are most often produced by multiple flake removals. Length and quality of flutes are greatly variable, with length usually 30 to 50 percent of overall point length" (Howard 1990:259). Importantly, the eastern fluted points do not match this description as they tend to exhibit more advanced technological refinements such as large single channel flakes produced using the Folsom technique, deep basal concavities, constricted waists, extensive basal retouch, and comparatively fine, often sequentially positioned overall flaking (Howard 1990:259). A recent continent-wide study of Early Palaeoindian points supports this classification. Buchanan and Collard (2007) used cladistic analysis on morphological attributes of Palaeoindian projectile point assemblages. The analysis was conducted on the grounds that the migration route into the Americas by a group of people could be inferred by the relationships amongst the various populations left along the route; they argued that cladistics, because it takes into account projectile point morphology, could infer the historical relationships between the groups of people (Buchanan and Collard 2007). Their data indicate that the Clovis phase was a rapidly migrating population having its origin in the Ice-free Corridor, or possibly the Northwest Coast, but not the Isthmus of Panama or an ice bridge across the mid-Atlantic (Buchanan and Collard 2007; Hamilton and Buchanan 2007). Thus, the earliest Clovis points and Clovis variant points are found on the northern and western plains; the eastern fluted material is related to Clovis but is a later derivative, more properly "Folsom-like."

The extreme rapidity with which the Clovis phase spread across the Americas from the northwest appears to be demonstrated in the aforementioned analyses by Buchanan and Collard (2007) and Hamilton and Buchanan (2007). Kelly and Todd (1988) suggested that Clovis hunters were not analogous to any modern hunter-gatherers. The apparent continual range shift would have brought these hunters into new and different environments but a primary dependence on large fauna would not have required a niche shift (Kelly and Todd 1988:234–235). As Clovis people were likely entering territory uninhabited by humans, they would have had few if any neighbouring groups to rely upon for assistance. They would have had no detailed knowledge of the terrain, thus, they would have used the landscape in a short-term and redundant fashion (Kelly and Todd 1988:235). Large Clovis bifaces of high-quality raw materials provided a transportable technology that was usable in unknown terrain for hunting-specific tasks (Kelly and Todd 1988:235). Long-term storage at successful kills would not be expected as stores reduced mobility; rather, renewed resource procurement was a less risky strategy under conditions of regionally abundant but locally unpredictable resources (Kelly and Todd 1988). An example supporting this model is Blackmar's (2001) examination of the distribution pattern of Clovis points in Kansas, Oklahoma, and Texas; it suggests that the distribution of Clovis materials represents a homogeneous occupation across the study area, possibly reflecting a subsistence strategy towards large mammals.

Traditionally the Clovis phase has been dated between ca. 11,500 BP and 10,900 BP (Frison 1991a:25). More recently, Waters and Stafford (2007) have determined a more accurate time span for the Clovis phase by obtaining and analyzing high-precision accelerator mass spectrometry ^{14}C ages from previously dated sites. Their research suggested that the Clovis phase existed between 11,050 BP and 10,800 BP. Thus, the Clovis phase would have been present over a roughly 250-year period, regardless of whether one examines radiocarbon or calendar years (Waters and Stafford 2007:1124).

In Alberta, there are no Clovis points from excavated contexts in demonstrable association with other Clovis material. The vast majority of the evidence for the Clovis occupation of Alberta has been recovered as isolated projectile points from cultivated fields and eroded areas. Comparison of the formal morphology of these projectile points to specimens of known age from adjacent regions of the United States has provided the evidence for their chronological placement. A brief historical outline of the recovery of Clovis points in Alberta follows, documenting the development of research in this area over the past few decades.

In the late 1930s, an eroded area north of Chinook produced a complete Clovis point and a point base along with other Palaeoindian artifacts. This site is called Johnston Locality 4 or EkOr 1 (Wormington and Forbis 1965:75–80, especially 77, fig. 20b; Gryba 1988:A3-33 to 35). In 1955, when William Mulloy of the Glenbow Foundation investigated the location, he noted that the area had likely been destroyed by erosion (Wormington and Forbis 1965:75). In the early 1950s, Armin Dyck found a Clovis point in the bottom of a trench while serving on a city road construction crew in Lethbridge (Wormington and Forbis 1965:135, fig. 55). Wormington and Forbis (1965:177, fig. 77a, b) mentioned three additional locations of lanceolate points that resemble possible Clovis sites. One locale produced two lanceolate points near Clear Hill, northwest of Peace River (Wormington and Forbis 1965:176; 177, fig. 77a). A second locale, located north of Peace River, produced a cache of up to 150 flakes along with two lanceolate points (Wormington and Forbis 1965:183). E. Mott Davis tested the location, labelling it HbQi 1, with a cross-shaped trench covering 400 square feet (~37 m^2), but he recovered only a few bone fragments (Wormington and Forbis 1965:183). The third locale was a cache located southeast of North Star. The cache consisted of bifaces as large as nine inches long (~23 cm), flakes, and "arrowheads" (Wormington and Forbis 1965:180). Similar caches of bifacially flaked specimens of black stone were reported for at least two other locations in the area (Wormington and Forbis 1965:180). The large bifacial tools and lanceolate points are hallmarks of Clovis cache strategy (e.g., Gillespie 2007).

Gryba (1988) conducted an inventory of fluted point occurrences in Alberta, with the objective of bringing together, in a single source, as many occurrences of fluted and Early Prehistoric period points as possible. He recorded 150 fluted point specimens during his fieldwork, including Clovis points (n=46), multiple-fluted points (n=13), fluted points (n=21), Folsom points (n=18), Midland points (n=15), and basally thinned points (n=37), as well as Palaeoindian points (n=29) and one large biface fragment. (Gryba 1988). Gryba (1988:16) noted the heavy reliance on locally available lithic raw material in point manufacture, although some exotic materials were used. In terms of the geographic distribution of the Clovis points, Gryba (1988:17) described their almost exclusive presence in southern Alberta south of Cold Lake, as well as near Peace River, with a strong association to areas with agricultural and developed landscapes. Almost all subsequent research on fluted points has built on this significant collection of raw data.

Gillespie (2002; Gillespie et al. 2002) built upon Gryba's (1988) database, from which he produced a typology. Attributes used in the typology were restricted to those related to basal morphology as these were seen as less controlled by function than the blade; a total of eight types were created (Gillespie 2002:65–80). In comparing the Alberta fluted-point database to an American fluted-point database (Tompkins 1993), Gillespie (2002:81–97) repeatedly found the strongest similarities between Alberta fluted material, Saskatchewan fluted material, and western U.S. fluted material, rather than to eastern U.S. or South American materials. The raw materials utilized in manufacturing the Alberta fluted points were dominated by locally available quartzite, siltstone, and mudstone (64%). In total, 71 percent of the raw materials were local, 16 percent were exotic, and 13 percent were undetermined (Gillespie 2002:108–109). This extensive use of local materials is in contrast to both modelled (Kelly and Todd 1988) and observed (Lahren and Bonnichsen 1974) Clovis lithic activity to the south in the United States.

Concerning the origin of the fluted material in Alberta, Gillespie (2002:130–135) argued that entry into Alberta could not have been from the north through the Ice-free Corridor, as palaeoenvironmental and faunal evidence suggests that people could not have been supported within the corridor before 12,000 BP. Instead he proposed a northward migration into the province, based on the current lack of known human occupations in Alberta that predate fluted point sites in the United States (Gillespie 2002:138). Further, he compared the similarly undated Alaskan fluted points to the Alberta sample, as both exhibit triple fluting and heavy pressure flaking. Again he saw similarities that he interpreted as evidence of a northward migration.

The Sites

As stated above, surface finds of Clovis points are not common. It is difficult to assess the exact number of Clovis points that have been recovered from surface finds, owing to their lack of stratigraphic context, which causes them to lack key information about associated material culture. That is, there are many fluted points in Alberta that likely postdate the Clovis phase (see the Sibbald phase below) or are regional variants of the classic form (e.g., Gillespie 2002:80). Regardless, there are a number of Clovis points recovered from the surface and they are discussed below (see Plate 2 and Figure 3).

Gryba's Inventory. Gryba (1988) provided the first exhaustive inventory of fluted points in Alberta. Many of the Clovis points known today are a product of his extensive and tireless research on Palaeoindian surface finds in the province. Table 1 summarizes keys aspects of his report for Clovis point recoveries.

EfPl 93. EfPl 93 is a buried campsite at the prairie level on the east side of the Bow River about 0.8 km south of its confluence with Fish Creek in south Calgary (McIntyre 1975). Ten 2-×-2-m units were excavated at the site. Two occupations were recorded. The lower occupation produced an ash-filled elliptical hearth associated with fire-broken rock (FBR) (McIntyre 1975:15–16). The upper occupation consisted of two rock-lined hearths, a surface hearth, and concentrations of FBR with bone and a few artifacts. A Besant point was collected from the surface while the base of a Clovis point was recovered from 20 cm below surface (cm BS) (McIntyre 1975:15–17; Gryba 1988). The Clovis specimen exhibited an arced base and straight lateral margins. The occupation was interpreted as a one-time, short-term campsite likely during the Besant phase. The Clovis point base was considered to be out of context and likely redeposited by later users of the area (McIntyre 1975).

PLATE 2
Clovis points. Illustrated are specimens from the Reed collection (a); Lougheed collection (b); Haug collection (c); DhPg 8 (d, i, n, and o); Bull collection (e); Cameron collection (g and l); Dyck collection (h); Johnston collection (j); Blumhagen collection (k); and Sawyer collection (m). *Photo credit:* Eugene Gryba (a–c, e, g–h, j–m); Shayne Tolman (d, f, i, n, and o).

FIGURE 3
Clovis and Goshen sites within Alberta

TABLE I Clovis points listed in Eugene Gryba, *An Inventory of Fluted Point Occurrences in Alberta* (1988)

Collection	Find Spot	Portion	Base Shape	Lateral Margins	Raw Material	Other
Erik Andersen	Beaverlodge	complete	arced	excurvate	ironstone	reworked
Erik Andersen	Beaverlodge	complete	arced	excurvate	quartzite	reworked
Eddy Cameron	Rocky Rapids	missing tip	arced	excurvate	quartzite	reworked
Eddy Cameron	Rocky Rapids	base, missing ear	V-shaped	straight	mudstone	
Eddy Cameron	Rocky Rapids	complete	acred	straight	chert	reworked
Eddy Cameron	Rocky Rapids	complete	V-shaped	straight	mudstone	potlid fracture
Alec Allen	Stony Plain	base, missing ear	V-shaped	excurvate	quartzite	
Hugh Bower	Red Deer	complete	V-shaped	straight	Swan River Chert	
Hugh Bower	Red Deer	missing tip	arced	straight	siltstone	reworked
Hugh Bower	Red Deer	base	arced	excurvate	northern quartzite	
Philip Reed	Ponoka (?)	missing tip	arced	excurvate	mudstone (?)	
Philip Reed	Ponoka (?)	missing tip	arced	excurvate	mudstone	
Jack McIntosh	Ponoka	complete	V-shaped	excurvate	siltstone	
Gordon Freeman	Ponoka	base	V-shaped	excurvate	mudstone	
Mrs. Gordon Boehlke	Sullivan Lake	complete	arced	straight	Swan River chert	heat treated
Harold Strandberg	Sullivan Lake	complete	arced	excurvate	siltstone	reworked
Russell A. Johnston	EkOr 1	base	arced	straight	chert	
Russell A. Johnston	EkOr 1	complete	arced	straight	chert	
Russell A. Johnston	EjOt 2	complete	arced	straight	siltstone	reworked
Ms. Margaret Wood	Sibbald	complete	arced	excurvate	Swan River chert	heat treated
George Sawyer	Edgerton	complete	arced	excurvate	Swan River chert	heat treated
Val Deidrich	Bruderheim	base, mid-blade	arced	excurvate	chert	
Arthur V. Blumhagen	Battle River	complete	arced	straight	chert	reworked
Parks Canada	EhPu 1	base, mid-blade	V-shaped	straight	chert	
Robert McLeod	Cremona	base	arced	excurvate	siltstone	
James Haug	EkPq 7	complete	acred	straight	chalcedony	
Fred Kirton	Bowden	complete	arced	straight	siltstone	
Robert McLeod	Penhold	base, mid-blade	V-shaped	straight	quartzite	
Don King	EdPk 9	missing tip	arced	excurvate	siltstone	
Don King	Frank Lake	base	arced	excurvate	chert	
Lloyd Peterson	Frank Lake	missing tip, ears	V-shaped	straight	chalcedony	
Armin Dyck	Travers Reservoir	base, mid-blade	acred	straight	chalcedony	
Armin Dyck	Lethbridge	missing tip	V-shaped	excurvate	agate	
J.A. Spencer	DiPe 1	missing tip, ear	arced	excurvate	quartzite	reworked

Wally's Beach (DhPg 8). The Wally's Beach site is situated along the shoreline and in the lake bed of the St. Mary Reservoir, an impounded water body of the St. Mary River near Cardston in southwestern Alberta. The site consists of archaeological lithic and faunal surface scatters, along with palaeontological specimens and animal footprints from the end of the last glaciation, that were exposed by the erosion of 1.5 to 2 m of shoreline and lake bed during periods of high drawdown (Tolman 2001). The site was found by Shayne Tolman during a family outing in 1996 (Tolman 2001:2). A drawn-down area of the southeast shoreline has been repeatedly examined by various investigators. By 2001, approximately 5,400 culturally modified lithic specimens had been surface collected (Tolman 2001:85). Projectile points from the Early Prehistoric period to the Historic period have been found, including ten fluted points (Tolman 2001:86). Fauna recovered dated to about 11,100 BP, and included extinct horse, extinct bison, helmeted musk ox, and caribou.

The lack of context for the Early Prehistoric period points led to a protein residue analysis (i.e., crossover immunoelectrophoresis, or CIEP) to provide a link between the fluted specimens and palaeontological fauna recovered at the site (Kooyman et al. 2001). The points tested included three Clovis points, one Folsom point, and two Goshen points. The test produced positive results for protein residue on the three Clovis points: two for horse and one for bovid (i.e., bison, musk oxen, or cattle). Other Clovis sites in North America that are known to have horse are Bonfire Shelter, Colby, and Lubbock Lake.

Smuland Creek (GdQn 1). The Smuland Creek site is located in uplands southeast of Grand Prairie. Shovel testing at the site led to the recovery of a proximal portion of a quartzite fluted point, a black chert graver, and ten pieces of debitage (Bereziuk 2001). The site appears to occur along a strandline or beach ridge associated with the uppermost and earliest level of Glacial Lake Peace. All the artifacts were recovered in the top 15 cm of the sediments in an area of about 60 × 25 m. The compressed stratigraphy has foiled dating efforts at the site and it was not possible to determine associations between the artifacts (Bereziuk 2001). Still, the fluted point exhibits an arced basal edge and excurvate lateral margins, making it similar to Clovis material, while its small size likens it to the Northern Fluted points.

FgQm 59 (243R). FgQm 59 is a buried multicomponent campsite on a terrace on the north bank of the Snake Indian River in Jasper National Park (Hudecek-Cuffe 1998). The deposits consist of silts at 120–150 cm BS, overlying clay and glacial till. Seven components were excavated down to sterile glacial deposits during the 1997 University of Alberta field school. A single fluted point was recovered at 119.5 cm BS in a lens of dark reddish-brown silt. It is manufactured on a white, opaque quartzite with a single flute on one side. The basal edge is *v*-shaped. A number of small charcoal flecks were recovered between 120 and 125 cm BS but not in direct association with the point. Dates derived from the charcoal were 8,840 +/- 40 BP (CAMS 41241) and 8,410 +/- 80 BP (TO-6848). A few pieces of silicified siltstone debitage were recovered as well as a single mudstone flake from the fine screen, from 120–125 cm BS. The remaining sediments were sterile to a depth of 144 cm BS, where glacial till was encountered (Hudecek-Cuffe 1998:69). Assigning the specimen to the Sibbald phase was rejected owing to the widest part of the point apparently being located toward the tip rather than the base, and the fluting/thinning on the base is single rather than multiple (Hudecek-Cuffe 1998:371).

Clovis: An Unprecedented "Homecoming"?

There can be little doubt that Clovis material has been recovered in Alberta. Studies thus far suggest Alberta's Clovis material is largely manufactured on local material with few exotic lithics being utilized (Gryba 1988; Gillespie 2002). This is in contrast to Clovis material from the south in the United States. This difference is interesting for a number of reasons. First, entry into the Americas through Alberta would have presented Clovis people with few lithic choices. Despite Gillespie's (2002) argument, Clovis knowledge of superior southern lithics would have predisposed these "stone snobs" to travel and outfit themselves at the better quarries to the south if a northern migration had occurred. It is reasonable to infer that they failed to use southern materials because they did not know about the resources. If they had, Alberta would exhibit evidence of the use of exotic lithics within Clovis' transportable technology (Kelly and Todd 1988). The lack of a strong southern influence in the Alberta Clovis lithic material is reasonably explained by the idea that they had not reached the southern latitudes yet.

Another line of evidence supporting antiquity of Alberta's Clovis material rests in point morphology. A thorough analysis of the technological reasons for the consistent difference in base form (i.e., arced versus *v*-shaped) and lateral margin shape (i.e., straight versus excurvate) is overdue. For example, straight lateral margins, which appear to be rare to the south (e.g., Frison 1991a), might reflect an earlier Clovis technology replaced by excurvate forms that better allow haft penetration. Such technological analyses might help refine the typology, allowing Clovis material to be distinguished from other fluted material in Alberta.

Here, a discussion about the phenomenon of Northern Fluted points is appropriate. Numerous fluted points have been recovered from Alaska and the Yukon Territories. These often exhibit one, two, or, more commonly, three flutes (Clark 1984). These points are not the large Clovis points found on the plains of North America but are stouter specimens. Because of the surficial nature of most of the finds, it is unclear if the specimens are associated with the Denbigh Flint complex, the Northern Archaic tradition, the Palaeo-Arctic tradition, or the Palaeoindian tradition (Clark 1984). Loy and Dixon (1998) analyzed blood residue from thirty-four fluted points and two morphologically similar points from Eastern Beringia. Twenty-one specimens had microscopically visible residues (Loy and Dixon 1998:37). Five residues yielded mammoth crystals, two yielded modern bison, two produced sheep, one produced bear, eight yielded caribou, and one yielded musk ox (Loy and Dixon 1998:39–40). Although there are still questions to be asked of the technique, it suggests that Northern Fluted points are related to the Palaeoindian tradition that has been more fully documented to the south for the end of the Pleistocene (Loy and Dixon 1998). Some of the Alberta fluted points may be related to the Northern Fluted points, as suggested by the multiple flutes and stout size coupled with the location of the Ice-free Corridor that geographically linked the Alaska-Yukon area to Alberta.

In terms of the timing of entry into the Americas, the revised age range for Clovis sites easily allows for entry via the Ice-free Corridor, as there are hundreds of years between the separation of the glacial ice sheets and the earliest Clovis sites (Waters and Stafford 2007). The revised age range also makes sense in terms of the geographic extent of Clovis material. The work of Buchanan and Collard (2007), amongst others, has assisted in narrowing the geographic extent of the Clovis phase. Clovis material only covers the western Plains area of Canada and the United States. The fluted material to the east is distinctive in shape, and dates to slightly more recent times. Similarly, fluted fishtail material in South America is morphologically distinct and dates to slightly more recent times. Thus, the arrival of Clovis as a generalist hunter-gatherer covers a restricted time and space. Clovis likely spread from the northwestern plains and adjacent areas to the southern plains between 11,050 and 10,800 BP. Related cultural phenomena such as the Folsom phase, eastern fluted points, and fishtail fluted points appear around the time that Clovis disappears.

Clovis material is known from the provinces and states adjacent to Alberta. A brief review of this data will help place Alberta's material into perspective.

British Columbia has produced a Clovis point. The Pink Mountain site (HhRr 1) produced the base of a Clovis point (Wilson 1987:219, fig. 57). The site is 150 km northwest of Fort St. John. It is characterized by a scatter of material over a kilometre-long portion of a ridge overlooking the Sikanni Chief River (I. Wilson 1987:217). Also recovered at the site were macroblades and numerous other Palaeoindian points (Wilson 1987:217).

In Saskatchewan, a number of Clovis points are known. Kehoe (1966a:532, fig. 2) illustrated five classic specimens. He distinguished these fluted points from others based on their larger size and *v*-shaped bases. Kehoe's (1966a:534–535) atypical fluted points tend to be more stout specimens with their greatest width near the base rather than midshaft. While still very similar to Clovis specimens, without secure contexts one is just as tempted to classify them as Northern Fluted points.

A bone rod was recovered in Saskatchewan (Wilmeth 1968). It was found near Grenfel at a depth of 2.5 m during excavation of a waterhole in the early 1900s; it was donated to the National Museum of Canada (Wilmeth 1968:100). Bone rods are known from a number of sites such as Blackwater Draw Locality No. 1 (Sellards 1952), the Sheaman site (Frison and Stanford 1982), and the Anzick site (Lahren and Bonnichsen 1974). These objects are commonly interpreted as part of a hafting system for the Clovis point itself (Lahren and Bonnichsen 1974; Stanford 1996) while some have argued that they represent levered hafting wedges for tightening sinew (Lyman et al. 1998). Two Clovis points have also been reported from near Invermay, 80 km north of Yorkton (Gryba and Gryba 1980). Fluted points are not common in this portion of the Saskatchewan plains. The specimens were made on quartzite and jasper, which is atypical of local stone (i.e., chalcedony and Swan River chert), suggesting that Clovis hunters brought the materials with them when they moved into the area (Gryba and Gryba 1980:172). A number of Clovis points have been reported from surface finds in west-central Saskatchewan. Carlson (1993) conducted a survey of Palaeoindian material in collections from the Battleford and Lloydminster area. At least twenty-six fluted points were identified (Carlson 1993, see also Gryba 2001). Most were manufactured on local materials (e.g., Swan River chert, quartzite) but some exotic materials such as Knife River flint did occur (n = 3). Few Clovis specimens appear to be in the collections, but numerous shorter specimens comparable to the Northern Fluted points are present.

A number of Clovis points are known from surface finds in Manitoba. Pettipas (1970:14, fig. 9a) recorded a specimen from Mentmore. A second Clovis point was recovered from the Brookdale-Mentmore area (Pettipas 1971:8). A Clovis point was recovered from the uppermost terrace of the Pembina River south of Manitou (Pettipas 1976). The latter specimen had been reworked and exhibited pot-lid fractures, an arced base, and straight margins. It was manufactured on thin-banded limestone (Pettipas 1976:4). A Clovis point was recovered near Erickson (Saylor 1978). A revisit to the findspot led to the recovery of two more artifacts. Three 2-×-2-m units were excavated at the site. Nine additional artifacts were recovered, thought possibly to be in association with the Clovis point.

Davis (1988:25) reported that few fluted points have been found in Montana, compared to Alberta, Saskatchewan, and Wyoming. He noted that recovered specimens tended to be manufactured on a wide range of lithics including basalt, obsidian, chert, quartzite, porcellanite, chalcedony, and Knife River flint, not all of which could be found in Montana (Davis 1988:26). The highest concentration of fluted material appears to be along the eastern foothills (Davis 1988:26, fig. 1). A working hypothesis proposed that fluted material was focused in areas of high relief and/or in the proximity of freshwater springs with better access to lithic-rich gravels (Davis and Aaberg 1988; Davis et al. 1989:6). The OTL Ridge site (24DW272), in the Blue Mountain area of Dawson County in east-central Montana, produced a Goshen point base made on patinated chalcedony, along with a number of other artifacts (Davis et al. 1989:5).

A few words need to be said about Goshen. Goshen points appear to be a technology related to the Clovis phase. The Goshen material was named for Goshen County, Wyoming, and was first recognized at the Hell Gap site in southeast Wyoming (Frison 1991a:44). It was tentatively labelled "Plainview," reflecting similarity to points on the southern plains that occur post-Folsom; however, its pre-Folsom stratigraphic context suggested it was something else (Frison 1993a:7–8).

Goshen points are smaller than Clovis points and are manufactured by pressure flaking rather than percussion (Frison 1993b:241). Frison (1993b:242) suggested that the change from percussion in Clovis point manufacture to pressure flaking in Goshen point manufacture is reflected in later Folsom points, which are also manufactured by pressure flaking. The Goshen toolkit, however, resembles a Clovis toolkit, including bifaces and blade tools (Frison 1991a:45). Goshen sites are geographically located on the northwestern plains with the classic example being the Mill Iron site, in southeastern Montana (Frison 1991b). Goshen has also been found stratigraphically below Folsom at the Hell Gap site, below Folsom at the Carter/Kerr-McGee site, surficially at the Powars II site near the Hell Gap site, and in Bentzen-Kaufmann Cave near Sheridan, Wyoming (Frison 1991a:45–46). A number of Goshen surface finds have been reported from adjacent South Dakota (Sellet and Fosha 2000; Fosha and Sellet 2000).

In Alberta, there is only one possible Goshen site recovered in situ: the base of a point was recovered in association with a well-defined hearth in Operation 17, Occupation 8, at Lake Minnewanka (EhPu 1) (Landals 2008:141). A total of eighty-four lithic artifacts were recovered, representing mainly local sources. Bone fragments (n = 39) produced two pieces identified as mountain sheep. The intentional incorporation of coal in the hearth by the past inhabitants produced two unacceptably old dates (Landals 2008:145–147). A date of ca. 10,250 BP from bone around the periphery of the hearth was accepted as a limiting date (Landals 2008:114). Because of the fragmentary nature of the point, the researcher suggested that affiliation to Clovis, Goshen, or Folsom was possible. In addition, a Goshen point was recovered as a surface find in close proximity to a Folsom point surface find at the Purple Springs site (DlOx 6) (Peck et al. 2006). Gryba (1988:A1–20) illustrated what he calls a Mill Iron-style point from a surface find west of Frank Lake. It exhibits morphology strikingly similar to Goshen material. Otherwise, there are very few of these points known in Alberta.

To summarize, perhaps the most striking aspect of the Clovis phase is its unique material culture and the implications of that uniqueness: the fluted points, large bifaces, macroblades, and use of high-quality stone from greatly distant sources all suggest a highly mobile people. Only the related Folsom phase exhibits such an interesting combination of material culture designed for high mobility and efficiency. A particularly strong reason for Clovis, and Folsom for that matter, to have left behind such material records is that they were likely entering a world that was devoid or nearly devoid of people. This unusual circumstance allowed for an adaptation unlike any other time during the Holocene, as most other movements of people brought the immigrants in contact with new people. A key to deciphering this scenario may rest with Goshen materials, which appear to derive directly from the preceding Clovis phase and lead to the Folsom phase.

FOLSOM PHASE (CA. 10,900 TO 10,200 BP)

The Folsom phase of the Llano tradition is dated between ca. 10,900 and 10,200 BP (e.g., Frison 1991a:50, Haynes et al. 1992:96). Folsom material appears to derive from the preceding Clovis material, with the transition possibly occurring in less than a century (Haynes 1993). The Folsom point, with its long flute extending over two thirds of its length, is the diagnostic artifact of this phase. Ahler and Geib (2000) argued that the Folsom point provides an elegant technological solution to problems faced by mobile hunter-gatherers: "The symmetrical, bifluted form allowed a split, facial-contact haft to extend nearly to the tip, thereby controlling both location and extent of fracture and allowing many cycles of point reworking. Extreme thinness achieved by fluting facilitated leading edge sharpness for enhanced penetration. The near constant cross-section from tip to base meant no loss of leading edge acuteness upon resharpening and interchangeability of broken segments." Such an efficient use of stone was critical for hunter-gatherer groups spending substantial time without access to raw materials (Ahler and Geib 2000).

Importantly, not all Folsom points are fluted. An unfluted point called Midland, similar to the Folsom point in every other way, occurs in some Folsom sites such as the Lindenmeier, Hanson, Agate Basin, and Shifting Sands sites (Frison 1991a:50; Hofman et al. 1990). The co-occurrence of these point styles suggests there may be no justification for two separate cultural entities (Agogino 1969, Ahler and Geib 2000:817; Bamforth 1991a:313, Frison 1991a:51, 1993b:242).

The Folsom point production appears to be the result of a specialized biface manufacturing process that is derived from Clovis biface reduction method (Bradley 1993:254). Bradley (1993:254–255) states that for Folsom lithic craftsmen, "biface manufacture functioned primarily as a flake production process (especially in the early stages) and shifted over to bifacial knife manufacture as the biface became too small and thin to produced usable flakes. It is also unlikely that the end product of this process was the production of Folsom points." Despite the functional arguments for the flute on Folsom points as a way to enhance the hafting process (e.g., Ahler and Geib 2000; Frison 1993b:243; F. Roberts 1935:21), other explanations for the large flute have been put forward. For example, Bradley (1993:256) suggested fluting was a risky ritualistic activity performed as a supernatural method of prognosticating success of an upcoming event such as a hunt. Frison (1991a:51) suggested that the exquisite craftsmanship found in Folsom points was more of an art form rather than for function. Regardless, Folsom point aesthetics were a pinnacle of lithic craftsmanship on the Northern Plains.

Bone tools were also exquisitely made objects. Delicately incised bone artifacts, apparently created as decorative pieces, are known from the Agate Basin and Lindenmeier sites (Frison 1991a:51). Eyed bone needles comparable in size to modern metal needles were recovered with Folsom material at the Agate Basin site (Frison 1991a:51). Bone and antler points and punches were recovered in the Folsom components of the Agate Basin site. A bison skull decorated with a red zigzag pigment, thought to be hematite, was recovered at the Cooper site in Oklahoma (Bement 1997). It was interpreted as a ritualistic object used in preparation for a bison kill (Bement 1997:92–93).

A variety of site types were produced by the people who left behind Folsom material. Many sites are campsites such as the MacHaffie site (Forbis and Sperry 1952) and the Hell Gap site (Irwin-Williams at al. 1973). Some sites are campsites/kill sites such as the Agate Basin site (Frison and Stanford 1982) and Fowler-Parrish site (Agogino and Parrish 1971). Short-term occupations have been excavated at the Rattlesnake Pass site (Smith and McNees 1990). The Adobe site has been interpreted as a hunting stand or lookout (Hofman and Ingbar 1988). Other sites have been interpreted as small field camps, such as the Mitchell Locality of Blackwater Draw (Boldurian 1990). Quarrying and manufacturing/repair stations are also known at sites such as the Lincoln Hills site (C. Howard 1988). There appears to be a much wider range of site types than was present for the Clovis phase. This wider range of site types is inferred to represent more specialized activities and more familiarity with the region.

Bison were most commonly the target of Folsom hunters — e.g., Cooper (Bement 1997), Stewart's Cattle Guard (Jodry and Stanford 1992), Lake Theo (Buchanan 2002), Waugh (Hill and Hofman 1997), Fowler-Parrish (Agogino and Parrish 1971), and Shifting Sands (Hofman et al. 1990). The lack of mammoth remains in Folsom sites suggests that they had disappeared by the time this culture developed (Frison 1991a:47). Elk bone was recovered as part of the tool assemblage in the Folsom levels of the Agate Basin site, but there was nothing to suggest that the animals were a large part of the Folsom food supply (Frison 1991a:57). At the MacHaffie site the faunal remains included bison, deer, wolf, and rabbit (Forbis and Sperry 1952:128). Similarly, bison, wolf, fox, and rabbit were reported for the faunal assemblage at the Lindenmeier site (Roberts 1935).

Much has been written on the topic of Folsom mobility and organization. There can be little doubt that the Folsom and Midland points, themselves, were functionally designed for expedient and efficient hafting and cutting edges (e.g., Ahler and Geib 2000). In terms of Folsom mobility and lithic utilization patterns, Blackmar (2001) argued they were linked to bison. Unlike the Clovis phase, the Folsom phase exhibits a predominance of bison kill sites. There is a strong correlation between the distribution of Folsom sites and the plains-prairie ecozone rather than the woodland ecozone in the Pleistocene for the Clovis phase. The Folsom lithic organization represents a solution to bison killing in a lithic-poor area (Blackmar 2001:78): practices of stone conservation (Amick 1996), such as the use of biface cores (Boldurian 1991), multifunction stone tools, and Folsom point preforms as tools (Boldurian and Hubinsky 1994), all represent elegant adaptive responses to a lifeway of hunting bison in stone-poor areas. Still, retooling at quarries would have been necessary (Buchanan 2002). The high mobility and scale of land use by people during the Folsom phase has been argued as distinctive from modern hunter-gatherers (Amick 1996). Additionally, Walker (1982:291–294) proposed that a recovered maxilla of a canid represents evidence of a domesticated dog in a Folsom component at the Agate Basin site. The possibility of a domesticated dog during Folsom times opens the door for other avenues of mobility, which will remain supposition until additional evidence is discovered.

The Midland complex at the Hell Gap site, Locality II, produced evidence of two possible structures consisting of circular arrangements of postmoulds about 2 m in diameter or about 4 m in diameter. At the time, the authors suggested that the Midland complex exhibited a projectile point form distinct from the Folsom phase (Irwin-Williams et al. 1973:47). However, as noted above, it is generally believed these assemblages may represent a common cultural entity. Thus, the remains of early structures may be attributed to the Folsom phase.

The geographic distribution of Folsom sites is alluded to above with reference to the importance of a plains bison-oriented subsistence. Folsom points are known from as far north as northeastern British Columbia where a Midland base fragment was recovered (I. Wilson 1987). While the Midland identification may be contentious, firm identification of Folsom points from surface finds are known from as far north as the Grand Prairie area of Alberta, and from southern Alberta (e.g., Gryba 1988), southern Saskatchewan (e.g., Kehoe 1966a), and southwestern Manitoba (e.g., Boyd 2000). To the south, Folsom material has been recovered in Idaho (e.g., Campbell 1956), Montana (e.g., Forbis and Sperry 1952), North Dakota (Shifrin and William 1996; Root et al. 1996; Root et al. 1999), South Dakota (Sellet and Fosha 2000; Fosha and Sellet 2000), Wyoming (Frison and Stanford 1982; Irwin-Williams et al. 1973), Colorado (e.g., F. Roberts 1935; Agogino and Parrish 1971; Jodry et al. 1996), Oklahoma (e.g., Bement 1997; Hill and Hofman 1997), and Texas (Hester 1968; Hofman et al. 1990; Perttula 1993), as well as numerous sites observed within the plains-prairie ecozone in the states to the east (e.g., Billeck 1998; Delling 1966; Hofman 1994; Munson 1990). In essence, the distribution of Folsom sites is not unlike that of Clovis sites in terms of overall geography.

The Sites

Folsom points have not been found in situ in Alberta. Sixteen points are known from surface collections within the province (Gryba 1988; Trace 1991; Dawe 1997; Ronaghan 1993; Wormington and Forbis 1965:157). These specimens were largely recovered from the southern and southwest part of the province (see Plate 3 and Figure 4).

Gryba's Inventory. Most of the Folsom sites that are known today are due to Gryba's (1988) tireless research on Palaeoindian surface finds in the province. Keys aspects of his report are summarized in Table 2. In addition to the Folsom points, Gryba (1988) documented fifteen Midland points. Of these, worth mentioning are the Midland point at the Minnewanka site (EhPu 1) in Banff National Park and the Midland point base at the Sibbald Creek site (EgPr 2) recovered in the basal level of the site with two basally thinned triangular point specimens (Gryba 1983:66–68, 1988).

PLATE 3 Folsom points. Illustrated are specimens from the Braseth collection (a); King collection (b and n); DhPg 8 (c); Gardner collection (d); Peterson collection (e, f, and i); Baines collection (g); Payne collection (h); Plant collection (j); Johnson collection (k); Visser collection (l); and Bondarenko collection (m). Photo credit: Eugene Gryba (b, e–n); Royal Alberta Museum (a); Shayne Tolman (c); Alberta Culture and Community Spirit (d).

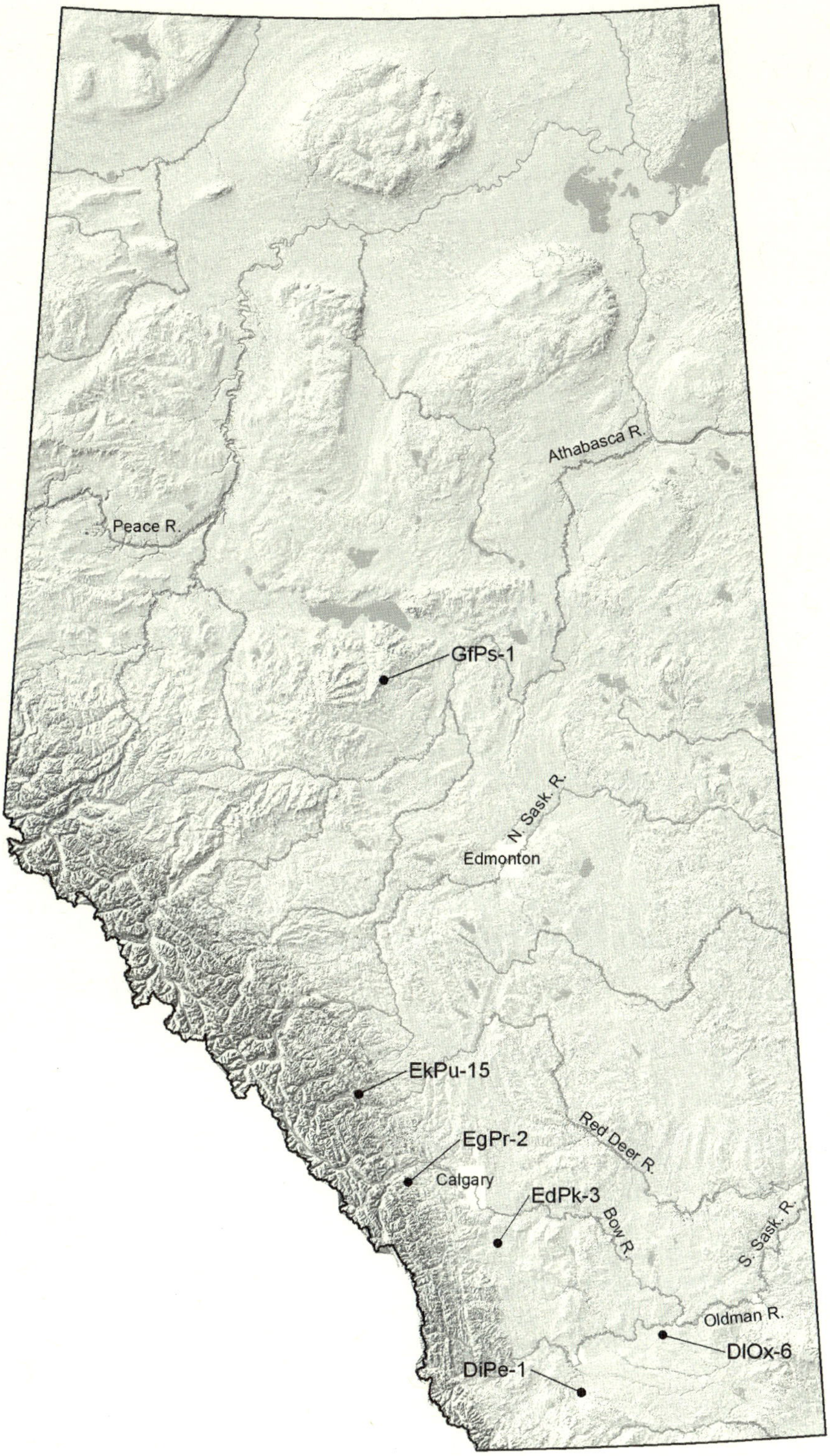

FIGURE 4
Folsom sites within Alberta

TABLE 2 Folsom points listed in Eugene Gryba, *An Inventory of Fluted Point Occurrences in Alberta* (1988)

Collection	Find Spot	Portion	Raw Material	Other
Don King	EdPk 3	base	chalcedony	
Don King	Frank Lake	missing ear	chert	
John Visser	Frank Lake	blade	jasper	
Lloyd Peterson	Frank Lake	blade	siltstone	
Lloyd Peterson	Frank Lake	lateral margin	chalcedony	
Lloyd Peterson	Frank Lake	blade	chalcedony	failed in fluting
Lloyd Peterson	Frank Lake	complete	chert	reworked
Lloyd Peterson	Frank Lake	missing tip, ear	chert	impact damage
Brian Gablehouse	Champion	blade	chalcedony	
Roger Baines	High River	blade	chert	
J.A. Spence	DiPe 1	tip	chalcedony	failed in fluting
Eldon Plant	Medicine Hat	blade	chert	
E.V. Johnson	Red Rock Coulee	blade	chert	
A.G. Payne	Sand Hills	base, missing ears	quartzite	
Konrad Bondarenko	Bruderheim	base	chalcedony	
P. Rentiers	Vilna	complete	n/a	
Guy Ireland	Peace River	base, missing ear	Peace River chert	

Purple Springs (DlOx 6). The Purple Springs site was first recorded as a result of the recovery of a complete Folsom point from an erosional area in rolling sand dunes. The specimen is made on yellow chert and was recovered about 4 km north of the Purple Springs townsite, south-central Alberta (Peck et al. 2006). Excavation at the site determined that the Folsom point had likely been deflated onto glacial clay. The lowest palaeosol yielded Oxbow material, supporting the interpretation of erosion or little to no deposition since glacial times (Peck et al. 2006).

Kelley (EkPu 15). The Kelley site is located in James Pass Meadow just inside the Front Range of the Rocky Mountains about 100 km northwest of Calgary. A small, triangular concave-base Folsom point was surface collected by the Kelley family on the treed shores of Eagle Lake. In 1991, test excavations by the Archaeological Survey failed to recover diagnostic material. As well, stratified sediments were not observed (Ronaghan 1993:89–90).

Braseth (GfPs 1). A large Folsom blade tip made on lustrous black chert (cf. Peace River) was recovered from the surface of a farm near Grovedale in the Grande Prairie area. The specimen is in the Braseth Collection (Dawe 1997). Dawe (1997:13) provided a strong argument that the specimen was produced using Folsom technology, not merely mimicking the classic point form.

Folsom: High Mobility with a Focus on Bison

The base of a Folsom point was excavated out of sediments that clearly relate to an Oxbow occupation (C. Ramsay 2005). Also, a single Midland base fragment has been recovered in the bottom layer of highly compressed stratigraphic sediments at the Sibbald Creek site. Based on the identical morphology between the Alberta Folsom specimen and ones found in the United States, there is no reason the former should not date to the same time period as the latter. Thus, the Folsom phase in Alberta is expected to date between ca. 10,900 and 10,200 BP. The geographic distribution of the Folsom phase covers much of the plains area during the Early Holocene. At this early time, the area of the plains expanded to include vast areas along the east side of the Rocky Mountains in Alberta and western portions of the eastern tall prairie and temperate forest in the mid-continent.

Recoveries in the United States suggest that Folsom points and Midland points are part of a single cultural entity, and it seems reasonable to expect the same relationship in Canada. In terms of other ancestral relationships, Folsom lithic organization has strong ties to the preceding Clovis phase (Bradley 1993:254). Concerning descendent populations, Frison (1991b:148) argued that Midland points or Folsom preforms (i.e., the unfluted portion of the Folsom point assemblage) exhibit similarities to Agate Basin points. "One can start with a large Folsom preform and instead of preparing it for fluting, simply continue a transmedial flaking process to produce the lenticular cross-section diagnostic of the Agate Basin point" (Frison 1991b:148). Frison (1991b:148) continued by noting that near-finished Agate Basin specimens from the Agate Basin component at the Hell Gap site look remarkably similar to pre-fluting stages of Folsom preforms. Bradley (1993), however, did not consider the relatively simple technology found in Agate Basin point manufacturing to have derived from Folsom technology.

Folsom mobility is discussed above in terms of the transportable nature of its technology with its heavy reliance on high-quality lithic raw material sources. Gryba (2001) found that surface finds of Alberta Folsom points were ones commonly manufactured on exotic materials (ca. 50%), suggesting movement of raw materials, and likely people as well, in and out of what is now the province. This is in stark contrast to the preceding Clovis phase where very few points were made on exotic materials (< ca. 10%). In fact, Northern Alberta quartzite (n = 6), other quartzite, (n = 16), siltstone (n = 11), and black chert (n = 6) dominate the assemblage of sixty-one Clovis specimens in Gryba's (2001) study. Furthermore, Gryba (2001:264) indicated that many of the exotic lithic raw materials in the Folsom surface finds were derived from the south or southeast. He suggested that sites such as Lake Minnewanka, Sibbald Creek, and Vermilion Lakes would have provided good winter base camps while summer was spent in camps around small Holocene Lakes such as Frank Lake, southwestern Alberta (Gryba 2001:263).

As mentioned above, Folsom material is known from the provinces and states adjacent to Alberta. A brief review of this data will help place Alberta's data into perspective. In British Columbia, for example, a possible Midland point from the Pink Mountain site (HhRr 1) near Fort St. John was recovered (I. Wilson 1987).

A number of Folsom points are known from Saskatchewan (C. Howard 1939; Kehoe 1966a; Storck 1973). Folsom finds in Saskatchewan are all surface finds; none are from excavated contexts. Howard (C., 1939) illustrated three Folsom specimens and noted a fourth from the area west of Regina. Kehoe (1966a:533–534) recorded an additional nine Folsom specimens from west of Estevan (n = 3), south of Woodrow, northeast of Mortlach, near Roseray, southeast of Regina, near McCord, and in the Great Sand Hills northeast of Maple Creek. Storck (1973:4) illustrated a single Folsom point from the McKillop collection recovered near Moose Jaw.

For Manitoba, Gryba (1966) documented a Midland point recovered near Benito. The specimen is manufactured on Swan River chert. Gryba (1966:238) suggested that the geomorphological evidence indicated a point of recovery located on former Glacial Lake Agassiz or a smaller ice-bound lake. In this vein, Boyd (2000:30) reviewed the location of other known Folsom surface finds in the province. He noted five Folsom sites and a possible sixth unconfirmed site. Boyd (2000:31) argued that part of the Folsom land-use pattern was the utilization of recently drained proglacial lake surfaces. These areas would have been treeless fens, predisposed for entrapment or mass-drive methods possibly employed by bison-hunting

Folsom people (Boyd 2000:31). Still, the low productivity and uneven distribution of resources within the lake margin area likely accounts for the relative paucity of early Palaeoindian material in southwestern Manitoba (Boyd et al. 2003).

Montana has also produced Folsom material (e.g., Davis 1988). The MacHaffie site in the foothills near Helena was an open campsite with three occupation levels (Forbis and Sperry 1952). The Folsom material was recovered from the bottom occupation and included two Folsom points as well as choppers, scrapers, knives and flake knives; faunal remains included bison, deer, wolf, and rabbit (Forbis and Sperry 1952). The excavators noted the bison were larger than modern species. The Indian Creek site is south of the MacHaffie site, in the foothills southeast of Helena. Occupation 1 of the Downstream Locality produced basal fragments from two Folsom points, one Clovis point, and seven channel flakes, amongst other tools (Davis and Greiser 1992). Initially dated at 10,980 +/- 110 BP (Davis and Greiser 1992), more dates (e.g., ca. 10,600 and 10,400) and further analysis suggested an upstream Folsom occupation and a downstream Clovis occupation (Davis and Baumler 2000).

To summarize, Folsom exhibits some traits that overlap or are found in the preceding Clovis phase, such as fluted lithic technology and an adaptation towards high mobility. At the same time, it is set apart in that the range of site types suggest a stronger familiarity with the landscape. In Alberta, local materials are more prevalently used in manufacturing Folsom points compared to Clovis points, again suggesting increased familiarity with the landscape. In terms of subsistence, the Folsom and Clovis phases are similar. Large mammals are still a focus but bison become prevalent on the menu during the Folsom phase, likely because of the changing environment.

SIBBALD PHASE (CA. 10,500 BP)

As early as the 1950s, fluted points that are short and stubby had been recognized from artifact collections in Alberta (Wormington and Forbis 1965:86, 88, fig. 27c). Not only were these specimens shorter in length than Clovis points, but they also often exhibited basal thinning rather than fluting. Specifically, *fluting* is a term generally reserved for cases where a single large flake has been detached up the middle of a point preform, while basal thinning refers to the removal of a series of smaller flakes of similar size, as many as three to five, that have been struck from the base of a point preform (Gryba 1988:10).

Gryba (1985:30) has observed that the small, stubby, multiple fluted point form has also been reported for Alaska and the Yukon (Clark 1984; Clark and Clark 1983), Charlie Lake Cave in northeastern British Columbia (Fladmark et al. 1988:376), and Saskatchewan, where they have been referred to as "atypical" fluted points (Kehoe 1966a, fig. 4). Gryba (1988:31) indicated a number of these small, basally thinned points have been reworked, thus creating their diminutive size. He proposed that since such reworked points were more common in the north than the south, it might have been the difficulty in procuring stone during winter months in the north that led to retooling of the fluted points (Gryba 1988:31). This model, however, fails to acknowledge that a number of these "stubby" points do not exhibit signs of resharpening but appear to have been shaped as stout forms. It also assumes contemporaneity with Clovis points, which is not likely given that a specimen from Charlie Lake Cave dates to about 10,500 BP.

As noted above, short Clovis points recovered in Alaska or the Yukon Territory are called Northern Fluted points (Clark 1984). Most of these have been found on the surface, making their age difficult to determine. Blood residue analysis has recovered evidence of mammoth on Northern Fluted point specimens, suggesting potential contemporaneity between Clovis and Northern Fluted points (Loy and Dixon 1998). Although no formal analysis has been conducted, it is possible that some of the shorter Clovis points in Alberta are related to the Northern Fluted point material.

The rubric of Northern Fluted points may not accommodate all the variability within the small fluted specimens. In 1983, a single short, basally thinned point was recovered from a deeply buried context at Charlie Lake Cave in northeastern British Columbia. Eight 1-×-1-m units were excavated around a sandstone bedrock ridge at the south end of Charlie Lake near Fort St. John (Fladmark et al. 1988). Eleven cultural components were defined. The lowest component produced a basally thinned or fluted point, a retouched flake, a keeled core, a perforated schist bead, and six flakes (Fladmark et al. 1988:376–377). The Charlie Lake Cave specimen was very short (ca. 4 cm) and triangular in shape. Radiocarbon dates for this component include: 10,450 +/- 150 BP (SFU 300); 10,380 +/- 160 BP (SFU 378); and 10,770 +/- 120 BP (SFU 454) (Fladmark et al. 1988:375). The basally thinned point was considered comparable to the two specimens recovered at the Sibbald Creek site (Fladmark et al. 1988:377).

The Sibbald Creek site (EgPr 2) provided the first in situ evidence of the time-depth of basally thinned triangular points in Alberta. The site represents a campsite on a low terrace, exhibiting a shallow and poorly stratified series of occupations overlooking Sibbald Flats in the foothills of the Rocky Mountains near Banff (Gryba 1983). In 1980, a block area of 159 m^2 was excavated. Based on projectile point form, it was determined that a record of at least 10,000 years was compressed into 50–55 cm (Gryba 1983:37). In the lower sediments, a Scottsbluff point, an Alberta point base, a Midland point, three Agate Basin points, two Mount Albion points, a drill, and a retouched flake were associated with two basally thinned triangular points (Gryba 1983:62–69). The radiocarbon date obtained from the lowest sediments with charcoal was 9,570 +/- 320 (GX-8808) (Gryba 1983:24, 122–123). However, the lab noted that it is possible that the date was too old owing to equipment failure (Gryba 1983:123). While this makes the date suspect, the sequence of burial supports the interpretation that basally thinned triangular points are old specimens in a long sequence of occupations.

The basally thinned specimen from Charlie Lake Cave exhibits fairly distinct morphology, even from other small fluted and basally thinned points including Clovis and Northern Fluted points. The Charlie Lake specimen is exceptionally stout and exhibits a triangular outline form with basal thinning, not fluting. As well, firm dates that indicate an age of ca. 10,500 BP also distinguish the point from other fluted material. The fluted points from the Sibbald Creek site are also quite stout with triangular outline forms. They, too, are basally thinned, not fluted. A firm date for this material could not be determined. Thus, it would appear that there may be Clovis points in the province, as well small Clovis-like points that are not unlike the Northern Fluted points found in Alaska and the Yukon, and even smaller basally thinned triangular points that apparently postdate both these point forms and also postdate Folsom points. Following previous usages, these small point forms will be referred to as basally thinned triangular points, or stubbies.

The Sites

There are two sites that have produced in situ material in the province. First, the Sibbald Creek site has been briefly discussed above; it lacks discrete stratigraphy and dates from good contexts. Second, the Twin Pines site (EkPu 8) produced a basally thinned point from well-defined stratigraphic context in the James Pass Meadow, southwest of Sundre. A third site, the oldest cultural materials from the Vermilion Lakes site, is the appropriate age but diagnostic material was not associated with the level so its affiliation is uncertain (see Plate 4 and Figure 5).

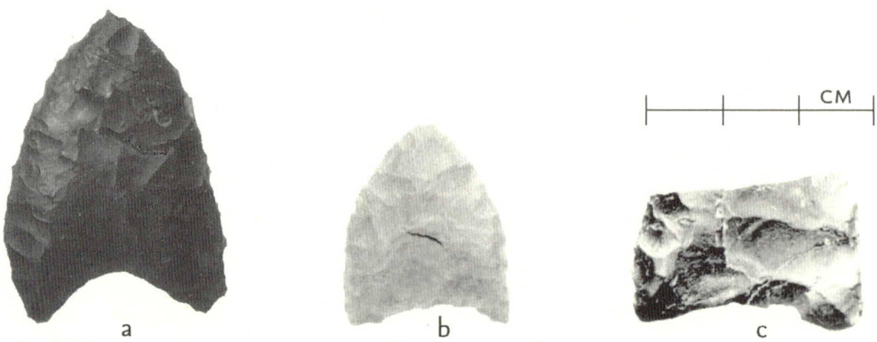

PLATE 4 Basally thinned points. Illustrated are points from Charlie Lake Cave in British Columbia (a) and Sibbald Creek (EgPr 2) (b and c). Photo credit: Jason Gillespie (a); Eugene Gryba (b and c).

Sibbald Creek (EgPr 2). The Sibbald Creek site is located in a large open meadow at the fringe of the foothills in Sibbald Flats, west of Calgary. The site provided evidence of a highly compressed sequence of cultural material in which Late Side-notched projectile points were recovered near the surface and basally thinned triangular points were recovered in the deepest sediments (Gryba 1983:37). The site was excavated in response to a highway construction project. In 1980, a major block area with outlying smaller blocks totalling 159 m^2 was excavated.

Two basally thinned triangular projectile points were recovered at the base of the excavations (Gryba 1983:66, fig. 30b, c). The points were recovered between 40 and 45 cm BS. One specimen is complete with a reworked tip, a single flute on one surface and multiple fluting on the other, and made on dull green crystalline siltstone (Gryba 1983:66). The other specimen is two co-joining pieces, triangular in shape, with a large flute on one surface and numerous flake scars on the other, and is made on fine-grained black siltstone or chert (Gryba 1983:68). A possible channel flake was present higher in the profile at 30–35 cm BS (Gryba 1983:69). Other lithic diagnostics recovered in close association with the basally thinned triangular points include the base of a Scottsbluff point, an Alberta point base, a Midland point, three Agate Basin points, and two Mount Albion points (Gryba 1983:62–69).

Twin Pines (EkPu 8). The Twin Pines site is a multicomponent campsite located in James Pass Meadow just inside the front range of the Rocky Mountains, about 100 km northwest of Calgary. Six occupation levels

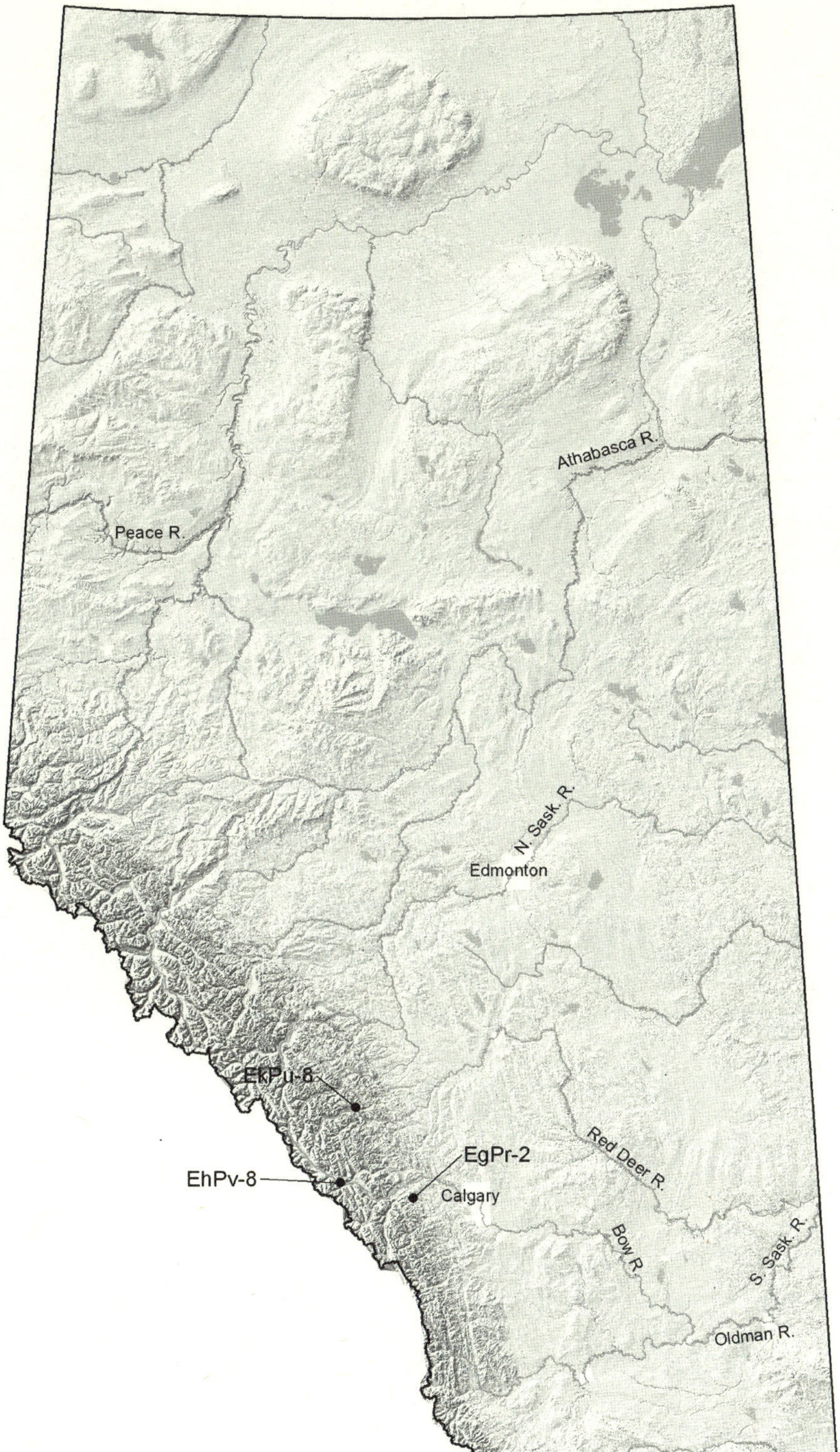

FIGURE 5
Sibbald sites within Alberta

were recorded at the site (Beaudoin et al. 1996:121; Ronaghan 1993). From oldest to youngest the cultural occupations include materials representing the Sibbald phase, the Agate Basin/Hell Gap complex, the Plains/Mountain (Lovell Constricted) complex, the Mummy Cave complex with Salmon River-like points, and two occupations with Besant-like specimens (Ronaghan 1993:88–89; Ronaghan and Dawe 1998).

A single basally thinned triangular point was recovered from the lowest occupation. Fifteen other lithic tools were recovered: a scraper/plane, three unifacially retouched end scrapers on expanding flakes, ten marginally retouched flakes, and a marginally retouched blade-like flake (Ronaghan and Dawe 1998). Local siltstone accounts for about 95 percent of the assemblage. Small amounts of fauna were recovered, with most occurring as calcine bone fragments (Ronaghan and Dawe 1998). The identifiable element in this cultural level was a bison tibia fragment. Four radiocarbon dates are available on bone from this occupation (see Table 3). The occupation was interpreted as a short-term campsite exploited by mobile hunters using a highly curated toolkit.

TABLE 3 Radiocarbon dates for Sibbald sites (calibrated by OxCal 3.10 [Ramsey 2005])

Site [LAB NO.]	Conventional ^{14}C Age	$^{13}C/^{12}C$ Ratio	Material	Calibration	Reference
EkPu 8 [TO-3000]	10120 +/- 80	?	collagen	10100–9400 B.C. (p = 0.954)	Ronaghan 1993:89; Beaudoin et al. 1996:122
EkPu 8 [CAMS-12913]	9930 +/- 60	-18.5‰	collagen	9670–9270 B.C. (p = 0.954)	Brian Ronaghan, personal communication 2009
EkPu 8 [CAMS-12914]	9990 +/- 60	-19.3‰	collagen	9770–9300 B.C. (p = 0.954)	Brian Ronaghan, personal communication 2009
EkPu 8 [CAMS-13192]	9990 +/- 80	-18.5‰	collagen	9900–9250 B.C. (p = 0.954)	Brian Ronaghan, personal communication 2009

Vermilion Lakes, Locality A (EhPv 8, 153R). The Vermilion Lakes site is located on a debris-flow fan on the north side of the Bow River Valley just west of Banff (Fedje 1986). The western excavation block, or Locality A, produced a stratified site with thirteen occupations, of which seven were well separated. The bottom occupation produced five hundred lithics, a few tools, and the bones of sheep, deer, an unidentified large ungulate, and a squirrel-sized rodent. Two small surface hearths and a hearth associated with post-moulds and lithic and faunal debris were also identified. The post-moulds coincided with the extent of the lithic and faunal detritus, suggesting a dwelling (Fedje 1986:36). Dates recovered from this occupation included 10,270 +/- 110 BP (RIDDL); 10,390 +/-140 BP (SFU 348); 10,570 +/- 150 BP (RIDDL 85); 10,410 +/- 400 BP (RIDDL 216); 10,660 +/- 650 BP (RIDDL 215); 10,900 +/- 270 (SFU 314); 11,000 +/- 480 BP (SFU 348); and 9,200 +/- 1300 (SFU 348) (Fedje 1986:36). The dated materials were derived from two separate blocks but produced similar mean dates of ca. 10,400 BP. Unfortunately, no diagnostic materials were recovered in this occupation within these excavations. Fedje (1986:38) suggested this occupation might be attributable to Folsom or Clovis. The lack of exotic lithics and the site's geographic location within the front range of the mountains likely indicates an association with the Sibbald phase. Landals (2008) argued that the calibration of the radiocarbon dates allows for the Vermilion Lakes site to be amongst the oldest sites in the New World, leaving a Folsom or Clovis affiliation a possibility.

Sibbald: The Beginning of Regionalization

Additional research will be required to clarify the relationship between reworked Clovis/Northern Fluted/basally thinned triangular points. The nature of Folsom material, on the other hand, is likely distinct enough in morphology and temporal span to avoid being reconsidered. Importantly, the fluted and basally thinned points in Alberta are expected to have been produced from ca. 11,050 BP to about 9,900 BP. This is a time span that, no doubt, includes Clovis material during the earliest times and stout basally thinned stubbies during more recent times. Regardless, a stronger understanding of the relationships between fluted and basally thinned points based on excavated sites is needed. Given the problem with the classification of the fluted and basally thinned projectile points, it is difficult to differentiate specimens without associated radiocarbon dates. There are no sites in Saskatchewan, Manitoba, or Montana with radiocarbon dates, but reworked Clovis/Northern Fluted/basally thinned triangular points are known from surface collections.

Alaska has produced a site with small triangular points with basal thinning. The Broken Mammoth site is located near the confluence of Shaw Creek and the Tanana River in east-central Alaska (Holmes 1996a:312). The middle palaeosol produced dates of 9,690 +/- 960 BP; 10,270 +/- 110 BP; 10,790 +/- 230 BP; and 10,290 +/- 70 BP (Holmes 1996a:314).

The fauna recovered included bison, elk, caribou, small rodents, ground squirrel, snowshoe hare, possible otter, swans, geese, ducks, other birds, and fish (Holmes 1996a:314). Two or possibly three hearth smears with associated hearth stones were recorded; lithics and fauna were recovered within and around these features (Holmes 1996a:317). Artifacts included a point base with slight basal thinning (Holmes 1996a, fig. 6-6n), and an almost complete triangular point (Holmes 1996a, fig. 6-6 m), possibly reworked, exhibiting basal edge grinding. Other lithics included numerous tiny flakes, retouched flakes, large biface fragments, hammers, and anvils. As well, a small, eyed, bone needle was recovered.

Similarly, Swan Point also produced small triangular points. It is located on the Shaw Creek Flats in the central Tanana Valley in central Alaska (Holmes 1996b:319). In a palaeosol encountered at a depth of 50–55 cm BS, cultural material associated with hearth charcoal was recorded. A date of 10,203 +/- 80 BP was obtained. Artifacts recovered included thin triangular points, small lanceolate points with convex to straight bases, gravers, and pebble choppers/hammerstones (Holmes 1996b).

Broken Mammoth and Swan Point exhibit a number of features that make it tempting to draw parallels with the Sibbald phase in Alberta. Most alluring are the form of the projectile points and the age of the deposits from which the points have been recovered. Furthermore, bifacial technology is dominant while microblade technology is absent. The lithic raw materials tend to be local in nature; exotic materials that require long-distance trade or movement are not present. These sites are also located in the front ranges of the mountains or large open valleys within mountain systems. Ronaghan and Dawe (1998) summarized the evidence as follows: "There appears to be an emerging pattern of Late Pleistocene/Early Holocene use of the postglacial landscapes of the so called Ice-free Corridor. All of the occupations identified to date are too late to have bearing on the initial peopling of the interior of North America, and in fact, most probably represent colonization from the south." Although tenuous, it is possible that the people of the Sibbald phase were adapted to a specific niche; this would be quite different from the preceding Clovis hunters who used landscape in a homogeneous fashion, but more similar to the Folsom bison hunters on the late Pleistocene/early Holocene plains.

AGATE BASIN/HELL GAP COMPLEX (CA. 10,200 TO 9,600 BP)

Agate Basin and Hell Gap represent two distinct point types, with the latter developing from the former (Frison 1991a:62). These two point types comprise the earliest point forms of the Plano tradition. Generally speaking, the term *Plano* has come to refer to any group of assemblages exhibiting lanceolate points with parallel flaking, starting with Agate Basin times and lasting into the early Hypsithermal (Arnold 1985). Differing usages of the term exist. Pettipas (1982) provided a developmental review of the various perspectives concerning the term *Plano*.

Agate Basin points were named for the Agate Basin site in eastern Wyoming. Significantly, Agate Basin material has always been found stratigraphically above Folsom material despite the possible temporal overlap suggested by radiocarbon dates (Frison 1991a:59). Roberts (1942) conducted the initial work at the site and was influenced in naming it by its location in the Agate Basin on a tributary of the Cheyenne River. Hell Gap points were named for the Hell Gap site in the Hell Gap Valley in southeastern Wyoming (e.g., Irwin-Williams et al. 1973). In this text, these cultural entities are lumped together in a single complex because of their close relationship and the general paucity of in situ recoveries in the study area. To the south in the United States, Agate Basin sites are usually found as discrete from Hell Gap sites. On occasion, however, Agate Basin projectile point assemblages, such as the relatively large assemblage of points at the Agate Basin site, include specimens that display the beginnings of the distinctive shouldering of the Hell Gap projectile point. The Agate Basin materials at the Hell Gap site are inferred to date between ca. 10,500 and 10,000 BP while Hell Gap materials at the site are inferred to date between 10,000 and 9,500 BP (Irwin-Williams et al. 1973:52).

Morphologically the Agate Basin projectile point is a long, narrow point with a relatively thick cross-section, likely designed for easy penetration (Frison 1993b:243). The related Hell Gap point is a modified Agate Basin point with slight shoulders; this change does not appear to have had a functional purpose (Frison 1993b:243). The beginnings of the distinctive shouldering of Hell Gap projectile points can be seen in the relatively large Agate Basin point assemblage from the Agate Basin site (Frison 1991b:148). Bradley (1993) suggested that the makers of Hell Gap points chose to terminate the point manufacturing process at an earlier stage than did the makes of Agate Basin points. Still, the basic sequence was the same, with percussion thinning and shaping giving way to pressure thinning and flaking (Bradley 1993:258). The degree of finishing was similar between Agate Basin and Hell Gap points. For Hell Gap points, specifically, finishing techniques included either pressure flaking the face of the tip and stem only, or pressure thinning/shaping the majority of the point surface (Bradley 1993:258). Frison (1991a) noted that the point style is easy to secure into either a notched or socketed haft.

As noted above for the Folsom phase, Frison (1991b:148) considered Midland points and/or Folsom preforms to exhibit strong similarities to Agate Basin points. In sharp contrast, Bradley (1993) argued that the relatively simple technology found in Agate Basin point construction could not have derived from Folsom technology. Yet, Shelley and Agogino (1983) provided further evidence of a technological link between Folsom and Agate Basin. The recovery of a serrated, point-sized artifact in the Agate Basin level of the Hell Gap site was reinterpreted from a cutting tool to a blank prepared with platform isolation (Shelley and Agogino 1983). The platform isolation technique used in thinning serrated Agate Basin points is very similar to platform isolation employed in preparation to flute Folsom points (Shelley and Agogino 1983:118). Shelley and Agogino (1983) suggested that this manufacturing change might have been the result of attempts to increase successful tool completion rates. Ultimately, the fate of Agate Basin and Hell Gap technology may be that it was ancestral or developmental to Alberta, Cody, and Eden point styles (Agogino and Galloway 1965:190).

Agate Basin and Hell Gap sites tend to focus on the procurement of bison. The Agate Basin component at the Agate Basin site attests to the bison-centered subsistence strategy (Frison 1991a:164–170). Frison (1991a:166) argued the Agate Basin bison kill at the Agate Basin site was the product of an arroyo trap in which about twenty animals in a nursery herd were driven into a steep-banked area and dispatched. Similarly, the Carter/Kerr-McGee site is an Agate Basin/Hell Gap bison kill/processing site (Frison 1984, 1991a:170). Bison kill sites associated with Hell Gap points include the Casper site (Frison 1974, 1991a:170–177), the Hell Gap component at the Agate Basin site (Frison and Stanford 1982), and the Jones-Miller site (Stanford 1978a; Frison 1991a:171–172).

In contrast, the Agate Basin component at the Mangus site in Montana produced only mule deer and cottontail (Husted 1969:34). Similarly, the Sister's Hill site in north-central Wyoming is a Hell Gap site that produced antelope, mule deer, porcupine, and small rodents (Agogino and Galloway

1965:192). The Allen site, an apparent Agate Basin site, produced antelope, deer, coyote, fox, prairie dog, rabbit, fish, freshwater mussel, a variety of birds, and, of course, bison (Bamforth 1991b). While bison was a significant aspect of both Agate Basin and Hell Gap subsistence, diets at this time were clearly flexible enough to exploit other species.

The focus on bison procurement during the Agate Basin/Hell Gap complex has left other aspects of this archaeological culture less well explored (O'Brien 1984). Lithic raw material utilization during this time, for example, has not been well studied. Still, it appears lithic procurement was more locally oriented for the Agate Basin/Hell Gap complex compared to earlier times. For example, surface collections in North Dakota have revealed Folsom finds that were dominated by Knife River flint while Agate Basin/Hell Gap finds included chert, porcellanite, and Swan River chert as well as Knife River flint (Ahler and McGonigal 2001:1). At the Tim Adrian site in western Kansas, O'Brien (1984) has data suggesting Hell Gap people extracted Niobrara jasper at a local outcrop to make tools. Similarly, Bamforth (1991b) found most of the lithics at the Allen site to be recoverable within a 75- to 100-mile (~120–160-km) radius.

Possible habitation structures were uncovered in the Agate Basin deposits at the Hell Gap site, Locality II. The possible structures were described as a circular arrangement of post-moulds about 2 m in diameter with a superimposed arc of roughly the same size post-moulds, and a short series of post-moulds running straight through both roughly north–south (Irwin-Williams et al. 1973:47, 51, fig. 10). There were no features within the proposed structures but there was correlation between the occupational debris and the post-mould distribution (Irwin-Williams et al. 1973:47).

The geographic distribution of Agate Basin and Hell Gap materials is limited to the Northern Plains. In Montana, the Indian Creek site produced a deeply buried Agate Basin/Hell Gap component (Davis 1986; Davis and Greiser 1992:266) and the Mangus site contained a possible Agate Basin component (Husted 1965). In North Dakota, the Beacon Island site near New Town has produced twenty-three complete or fragmentary Agate Basin points (Ahler and McGonigal 2001). There are a number of Agate Basin and Hell Gap sites in Wyoming. As previously noted, the Hell Gap site in southeastern Wyoming has both Agate Basin and Hell Gap occupations. The Agate Basin site in east-central Wyoming has an Agate Basin bison kill component. The Sister's Hill site is a Hell Gap site in north-central Wyoming. The Brewster site is an Agate Basin site in eastern Wyoming. Agate

Basin and Hell Gap occur together at the Carter/Kerr-McGee site in northeastern Wyoming. In Colorado, the Frazier site is an Agate Basin site and the Jones-Miller site is a Hell Gap kill site (Stanford 1978a). In western Nebraska, the Allen site appears to represent Agate Basin occupations (Bamforth 1991b). In western Kansas there is a Hell Gap quarry site (O'Brien 1984).

The Sites

As noted above, for the purposes of refining Alberta's culture-historical record, Agate Basin and Hell Gap material have been lumped together in a single complex. This is justified based on the overlap in form and their association during recovery at a few sites such as the Carter/Kerr-McGee site. As with the preceding Palaeoindian materials in Alberta, very few Agate Basin/Hell Gap occupation sites have been recorded in situ (see Plate 5 and Figure 6).

PLATE 5 Agate Basin / Hell Gap points. Illustrated are points from the Eclipse site (EhPv 14) (a–d); the Lindoe site (EaOp 9) (e); and DgPm 1 (f and g). Photo credit: Alberta Culture and Community Spirit.

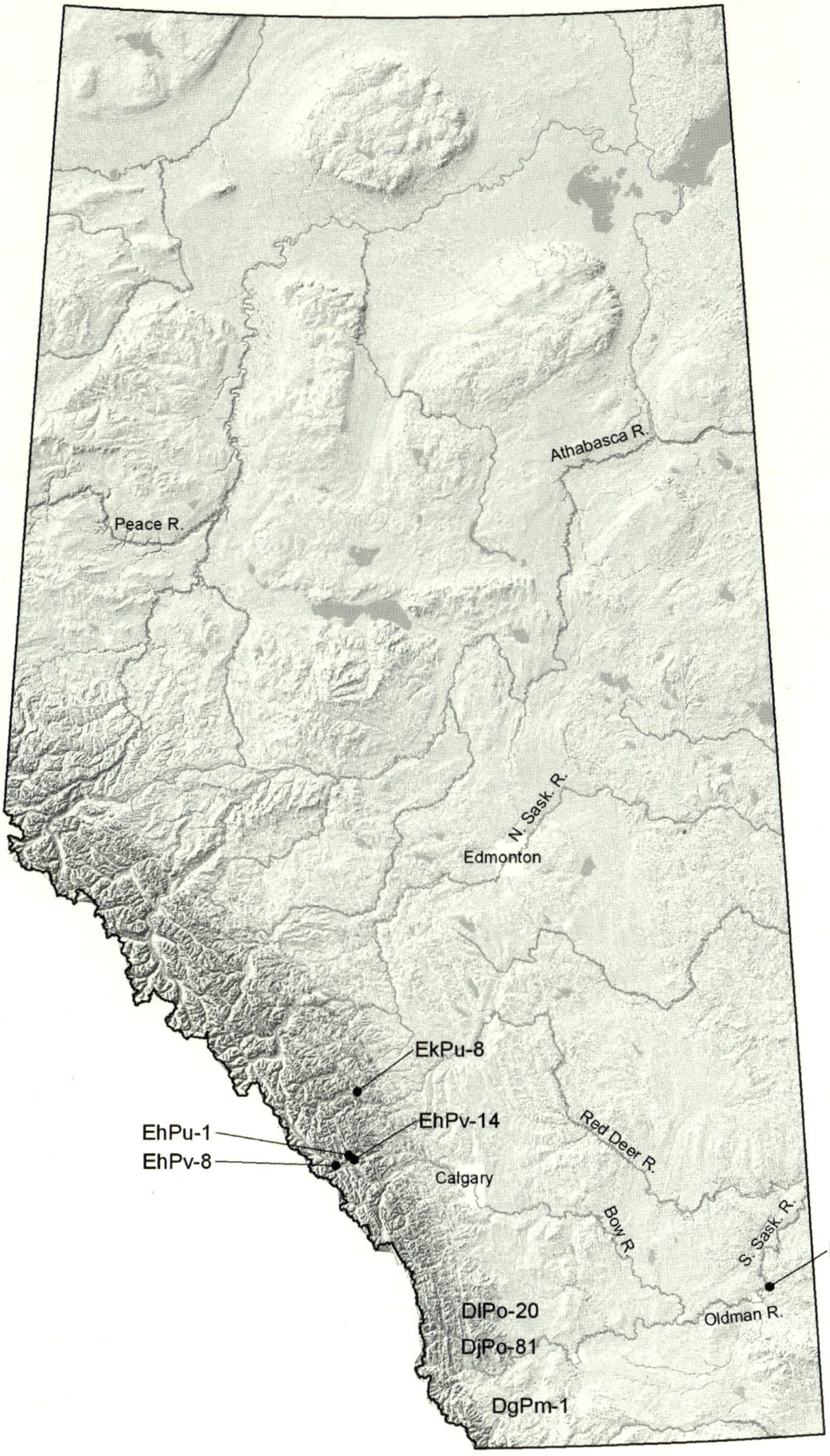

FIGURE 6
Agate Basin sites within Alberta

Vermilion Lakes, Locality A (EhPv 8, 153R). The Vermilion Lakes site, Locality A, is located on a debris-flow fan on the north side of the Bow River Valley west of Banff near Highway 1 (Fedje 1986:25). The site is discussed in the above section on the Sibbald phase. In Occupation 6a, a single reworked Agate Basin/Hell Gap point was recovered in association with two circular hearth features and surrounding activity areas (Fedje 1986:34). The only other formed tool recovered was a pointed biface preform. An additional 500 lithics were recovered from this level. The faunal assemblage included sheep and large ungulate. Table 4 presents the three accepted radiocarbon dates obtained for the site. Fedje (1986:34) calculated an average date of 9,650 BP.

Vermilion Lakes, Locality B (EhPv 8, 502R). The Vermilion Lakes site, Locality B, is located over a ridge in the next valley to the east of Locality A (Fedje 1986:26). It too was recovered in debris flows; however, only four occupations were differentiated at this locale (Fedje 1986:38). Again, historic material (Occupation 1) was recovered near the surface. This overlaid Middle Prehistoric material. Under the Middle Prehistoric material was a faunal assemblage that could not be conclusively identified as culturally created. Beneath the indeterminate material was an Agate Basin occupation. A single Agate Basin point was recovered in association with lithic and bone items scattered around a probable hearth (Fedje 1986:38). The material was retrieved from 1.4 m beneath the surface and was limited to about a 10-m^2 area (Fedje 1986:38). The point was constructed on an exotic sandy chert and was reworked on one side. Approximately 100 lithic and bone fragments were recovered. Table 4 presents three radiocarbon dates that were obtained from materials in this level. Fedje (1986:40) concluded that these dates, with an average of 9,910 +/- 95 BP, fit well with those expected for an Agate Basin occupation.

Eclipse (EhPv 14, 62R). The Eclipse site is a multicomponent campsite located on the north side of the Trans-Canada Highway just east of the Minnewanka Interchange (Fedje 1988:25). Two cultural layers were encountered. Late Prehistoric material was recovered in the A Horizon, overlying Hell Gap material about 0.5 m below the surface. A total of 6.5 m^2 were excavated at the site. The site was assessed in response to construction associated with the Trans-Canada Highway (Fedje 1988:1).

TABLE 4 Radiocarbon dates for Agate Basin / Hell Gap sites (calibrated by OxCal 3.10 [Ramsey 2005])

Site [LAB NO.]	Conventional ^{14}C age	$^{13}C/^{12}C$ Ratio	Material	Calibration	Reference
EhPu 1 [BETA 122723]	9990 +/- 50	?	collagen	9760–9710 B.C. (p = 0.041) 9700–9310 B.C. (p = 0.91)	Landals 2008:162
DjPo 81 [N/A-39]	9860 +/- 320	?	collagen	10700–8400 B.C. (p = 0.954)	Reeves 1975; Morlan n.d.
EhPv 8, A [RIDDL-83]	9700 +/- 130	?	collagen	9450–8650 B.C. (p = 0.954)	Fedje 1986:34; Morlan n.d.
EhPv 8, A [SFU-347]	8950 +/- 600	-25.0‰	charred wood	10100–6500 B.C. (p = 0.954)	Fedje 1986:34; Morlan n.d.
EhPv 8, A [RIDDL-75]	9570 +/- 150	?	charred wood	9300–8450 B.C. (p = 0.954)	Fedje 1986:34; Morlan n.d.
EhPv 8, B [RIDDL-77]	9840 +/- 200	?	collagen	10100–8700 B.C. (p = 0.954)	Fedje 1986:40; Morlan n.d.
EhPv 8, B [RIDDL-82]	10010 +/- 180	?	charred wood	10500–9100 B.C. (p = 0.954)	Fedje 1986:40; Morlan n.d.
EhPv 8, B [AECV-121C]	9880 +/- 140	-25.0‰	charred wood	10100–8800 B.C. (p = 0.954)	Fedje 1986:40; Morlan n.d.
DlPo 20 [GX-0956]	9600 +/- 240	-20.0‰	charred collagen	9800–8200 B.C. (p = 0.954)	Reeves and Dormaar 1972:333; Morlan n.d.
EhPv 14 [RIDDL-525]	10230 +/- 160	?	carbonized fat	10700–9300 B.C. (p = 0.953)	Fedje 1988:38
EhPv 14 [RIDDL-627]	9850 +/- 140	?	carbonized fat	9900–8800 B.C. (p = 0.954)	Fedje 1988:38
EhPv 14 [RIDDL-524]	9420 +/- 130	?	charred wood	9200–8300 B.C. (p = 0.954)	Fedje 1988:38
EhPv 14 [RIDDL-626]	9210 +/- 180	?	charred wood	9200–7900 B.C. (p= 0.954)	Fedje 1988:38
EaOp 9 [S-230]	9900 +/- 120	-25.0‰	organic sediment	10500–9100 B.C. (p= 0.954)	Bryan 2000:2, 1966:6
EaOp 9 [GAK-5097]	9710 +/- 190	-20.0‰	collagen	n/a	Bryan 2000:2
EkPu 8 [TO-2999]	9750 +/- 80	?	collagen	9400–8800 B.C. (p =0.954)	Ronaghan 1993:898

Six stemmed spear points were recovered from the site. Two were fairly complete examples of Hell Gap points while the remaining four were basal fragments fitting within the Hell Gap range of variability. Other recovered tools included a point preform, an ovate biface, biface fragments (n = 4), a side scraper, a spall chopper, a cobble chopper, a scraper on a spall, hammerstones (n = 2), retouched/utilized flakes (n = 13), burin spalls (n = 4), a unidirectional core, a discoidal core, core fragments (n = 14), and a groundstone soapstone pendant. Lithic debitage (n = 4,988) was dominated by local siltstone (52.3%), cherts (31%), and quartzite (16%), with the remainder (0.5%) being non-local cherts, chalcedony, and soapstone (Fedje 1988:32).

No faunal material was preserved in the main block at the site, likely because of soil conditions, but many stone tools for working organic materials were recovered (Fedje 1988:32). The lithics suggest core reduction and biface reduction for the purpose of rehafting tools. The burin spalls suggest use on moderately hard objects and were interpreted as the detritus from chisel-like tools for preparing wood or bone sockets for new points (Fedje 1988:34). Other general camp activities such as hide working were represented, as evidenced by the scrapers (Fedje 1988:35). A hearth provided a centre for much of the activity at the site. Three radiocarbon dates of ca. 9,800 BP were obtained from the hearth feature (Table 4).

Minnewanka (EhPu 1). The Minnewanka site is located on a bench on a valley wall overlooking the confluence of the Cascade River and Devils Creek near the former's confluence with the Bow River. A reservoir has raised water levels, periodically inundating the site. Landals (2008) excavated at a number of locations at the site between 1997 and 2001. An Agate Basin-like point was recovered from Operation 18, Occupation 2/3. It was associated with a flake tool, a scatter of lithics, and a few badly deteriorated bison bones. Much of the lithic assemblage was manufactured on local silicified sandstone and grey quartzite (Landals 2008:166). Landals (2008:165) noted the similarity of the point to specimens from the nearby Eclipse site. A single date of ca. 10,000 BP was obtained for the occupation (Table 4; Landals 2008:162).

Lindoe (EaOp 9). The Lindoe site is a bison kill site located on the north bank of the South Saskatchewan River about 16 km downstream from Medicine Hat (Bryan 2000:2). The site was named after its discoverer, Luke Lindoe, an avocational archaeologist (Bryan 2000:2). It contains at least two occupations: an upper occupation preserved in aeolian sand and a lower occupation consisting of a bison bone bed partially embedded in a peat bed. The site was excavated in the summer of 1966, including a west area (36 m^2), an east area (32 m^2), and a test unit (4 m^2). A bulldozer trench was cut between the two main excavation blocks to examine the stratigraphy.

A complete projectile point was found on the sand talus slope immediately below the peat containing the bone bed. The specimen is a brick-coloured siltstone not found in the overlying layers. It is leaf shaped with round shoulders gradually converging near the midsection to form a parallel-sided stem (i.e., a Hell Gap point) (Bryan 2000:6–7). A small retouched scraper of silicified wood may have also eroded out of the bone bed. Otherwise, all the flaked stone artifacts excavated from the site are inferred to have been recovered from the poorly developed soils and deflated basins within the later dune deposits that overly the bone bed.

The faunal assemblage suggested the animals were larger than modern bison, perhaps belonging to *Bison occidentalis*, but horn cores were not recovered to substantiate this inference (Bryan 2000:3). Evidence for human agency within the bone bed came from five broken ribs cut repeatedly by a knife, and a deep cut at the base of the head of a left humerus (Bryan 2000:5). As well, an intentionally fractured tibia was found, and the edges of the broken shaft may exhibit use wear (Bryan 2000:5).

A radiocarbon date on the peat layer produced an age of ca. 9,900 BP; bone found in the peat provided a date of ca. 9,700 BP (Table 4). The latter date was established at the Gakushuin Lab and is not considered valid (Blakeslee 1994). The peat dates from the peat layers are solid, and bone was found projecting into the peat. The correlation of the early date and the Hell Gap point suggest the site is a Palaeoindian kill.

Gap (DlPo 20). The Gap site is a poorly understood multicomponent campsite located along the Oldman River in the front range of the Rocky Mountains (i.e., the "Gap" of the Livingstone Range) (Reeves and Dormaar 1972:325). The site, recorded by Forbis (1966) during a survey for a proposed dam, had largely been destroyed by earlier road construction. In 1968, Reeves and Dormaar (1972) conducted salvage excavations at the site. A total of 64 m^2 was excavated (Reeves and Dormaar 1972:328–329). Four cultural levels were encountered. The upper two levels, the Third and Fourth Occupations, were above Mazama Ash but did not contain diagnostics. The Second Occupation contained a Bitterroot/Blackwater side-notched point. A broken lanceolate point, considered to be Agate Basin, was found on the surface at the site. The excavators suggested it derived from the earliest occupation. A radiocarbon date of 9,600 +/- 240 BP (GX-0956) from the earliest levels supports this interpretation (Reeves and Dormaar 1972:330; Morlan n.d.).

Red Rock Canyon (DgPm 1). The Red Rock Canyon site is a multicomponent campsite on the east side of Red Rock Canyon, about 8 m above the channel, in Waterton Lakes National Park (Reeves 1972:47). Four cultural levels were recognized. The lowest level contained two Agate Basin points as well as two Lusk, two Lerma, and two Scottsbluff points (Reeves 1972:332, table 6). These points were recovered with widely scattered lithic tools and debitage but very little bone or FBR. An excavated basin hearth was recorded, 0.30 m in diameter by 0.2 m deep, with three small post-moulds evenly spaced around about 0.2 m from the rim. A single radiocarbon date on charcoal from the hearth produced a date of 8,220 +/- 260 BP (GX-1435) (Reeves 1972:94). This date matches expectations for Lusk material, but is late for Agate Basin.

Twin Pines (EkPu 8). The Twin Pines site, as described above, is a multicomponent campsite located in James Pass Meadow just inside the front range of the Rocky Mountains, about 100 km northwest of Calgary. Possible Agate Basin/Hell Gap material occurred in the second lowest of six occupations (Ronaghan 1993:88–89; Ronaghan and Dawe 1998).

Three projectile point bases were recovered: a concave-based, basally thinned lanceolate point; a parallel-sided, slightly concave-based point stem; and a point tip (Ronaghan and Dawe 1998). All the specimens are extremely finely flaked, with the latter exhibiting collateral pressure flaking. Ronaghan and Dawe (1998) suggested the classification of the points was problematic: their square appearance suggested similarities to the Cody complex but shoulders are not present. The level was dated to about 9,750 BP (Table 4) (Ronaghan and Dawe 1998; Beaudoin, personal communication 2007). Ronaghan and Dawe (1998) concluded that the material seemed most similar to the stemmed points of the Agate Basin/Hell Gap complex. Other lithics recovered from the occupation included eleven bifacial knives, some end scrapers, some retouched flakes, some large "boat-shaped" cores, and four choppers.

Other sites. Four other assemblages deserve to be mentioned as Agate Basin/Hell Gap sites. First, the Bad Waters (DgOp 15) site is a surface collection of an Agate Basin assemblage from the north side of the Milk River (Graspointer 1980:87). Two Agate Basin points and at least twelve lithic items including bifaces and flakes were found together on the open plains (Graspointer 1980:87). Second, the Dancehall (DjPp 3) site is a multicomponent campsite located on the south bank of the Crowsnest River at its outlet from Crowsnest Lake. At least one Agate Basin point was recovered from the lowest component of the site (Loveseth 1980). Third, the Crowsnest Valley campsite (DjPp 8) is located on the north bank of the Crowsnest River directly across the river from the Dancehall site. Driver (1983:12) identified as many as five Agate Basin-like point bases from the six 2-×-2-m and one 1.5-×-1.5-m units that were excavated. Although the stratigraphy at the latter two sites was not conducive towards detailed analyses of discrete components, they appear to exhibit cultural deposition over the last 10,000 years (Driver 1983:98; Loveseth 1980). Fourth, the North Bellevue (DjPo 81) site is a possible Agate Basin site within the village of Bellevue in the Crowsnest Pass (Driver 1976). In 1974, during a survey in the townsite, Reeves (1976) recovered a bison skull along with campsite refuse at 250 cm below 3rd Street. It was dated to 9,860 +/- 320 BP (n/a-39) (Table 4; Reeves 1976; Morlan n.d.). The following year, Driver (1976) noted that a local collector had found an Agate Basin point under 2nd Street in what were inferred to be the same silts.

Agate Basin/Hell Gap: Continuity from Folsom to Scottsbluff?

There are very few dated Agate Basin/Hell Gap sites in the province. The well-dated components (i.e., Vermilion Lakes Localities A and B, Eclipse, and Twin Pines), as well as the sites with less secure dates (Lindoe, Gap, and North Bellevue), suggest an Agate Basin/Hell Gap occupation between 10,200 and 9,600 BP. All of the sites documented above, with the exception of the Lindoe and Bad Waters sites, are located in the foothills and mountain area. The large bison kill sites commonly reported for Agate Basin/Hell Gap sites to the south are almost absent from the Alberta record. With the possible exception of the Lindoe site, the sites in Alberta represent small campsites exhibiting domestic activities rather than the large bone beds associated with kill sites. Agate Basin/Hell Gap sites are equally uncommon in the known archaeological record of the provinces and states immediately surrounding Alberta.

In Saskatchewan, very few Agate Basin/Hell Gap sites are known. The Parkhill (EbNj 4) site near Moose Jaw is an Agate Basin surface find (Ebell 1980). Ebell (1980) reported the site produced over three hundred artifacts of which 137 are Agate Basin points. Chert and Knife River flint comprise the majority of the lithic raw materials. In the 1980s, Dyck (1983) reported that the Parkhill site was one of the few known Agate Basin sites in the province and that it had likely been destroyed. Dyck (1983:66) further noted that fifteen other Agate Basin/Hell Gap point surface finds were known in the province; all were located within the southwestern and south-central area.

The evidence of Agate Basin/Hell Gap peoples is even less common in Manitoba. Gryba (1968) found a large lanceolate point with parallel flaking in Swan Valley (FbMi 5). Both Agate Basin and Scottsbluff points had been recovered as surface finds near the site, but the actual affiliation of the specimen could not be determined. The Duck River site (ElMb 10) is an Agate Basin occupation site in Manitoba consisting solely of lithics. Haug (1981) argued that the assemblage provided evidence of butchering, hide working, and woodworking. Mapping of these activity areas indicated that a structure such as a windbreak might have been present at the site. Saylor (1975) excavated a possible Palaeoindian site (DhLb 1) on the Campbell Strandline of Glacial Lake Agassiz in southeastern Manitoba. The strandline was estimated to have formed about 10,000 to 9,500 BP. No diagnostics were recovered but two bifaces, a retouched flake, and six scrapers were found (Saylor 1975:246). For Saylor (1975), the geological age of the site suggested an Agate Basin or Hell Gap affiliation. In this vein, Pettipas (1996a:38) recognized both an early stemmed tradition (Agate Basin, Alberta, Scottsbluff) and a later stemmed tradition (Lusk) with the former existing only west of the Campbell strandline and the latter being found both east and west of the Campbell strandline.

Montana has produced the Indian Creek site. It is the first in situ Hell Gap component in the state (Davis 1986; Davis and Greiser 1992:266). The material is deeply buried, providing one possible reason for the general paucity of recoveries of such sites on the Northern Plains. The Mangus site has a possible Agate Basin component (Husted 1965). In contrast to the deeply buried Indian Creek material is information from surface finds that indicate Agate Basin and Hell Gap points are the most commonly surface-collected Palaeoindian point types in Montana (Davis 1986:28).

In summary, Agate Basin/Hell Gap sites in Alberta are coeval with their counterparts to the south. Yet, in Alberta, sites are largely restricted to small campsites while a wider range of sites including large bison kill sites are known to the south. A possible exception is the Lindoe site in southeastern Alberta, which consists of an extensive bison bone bed. Associations with cultural materials at this site, however, have yet to be demonstrated. As with all previous Palaeoindian sites in Alberta, archaeological visibility is likely one agent behind the differences in the numbers and range of sites between northern and southern areas of the plains.

ALBERTA PHASE (CA. 9,600 TO 9,000 BP)

The Alberta phase is characterized by the Alberta point. It is related to Scottsbluff material as part of the Cody tradition. Wormington (1957:134) first recognized the Alberta point, which she named, as a distinct style while examining a number of surface collections recovered in Alberta. She noted: "They resemble [Scottsbluff points] sufficiently that it seems probable there is some close relationship. They differ, however, in a number of respects. They are larger, the stem is longer, the base is slightly convex, and the tip is somewhat blunted. It is suggested that they be called Alberta points" (Wormington 1957:134).

The first Alberta points recovered in situ were excavated at the Hell Gap site. From 1959 through 1966, Harvard University and the University of Wyoming excavated at the various localities of the Hell Gap site in the Hell Gap Valley of southeastern Wyoming (Irwin-Williams et al. 1973). Locality I was interpreted as a multicomponent occupation site starting with a Goshen workshop, followed by a Folsom/Midland campsite, an Agate Basin workshop, a Hell Gap temporary camp, an Alberta living surface, a Cody occupation, and two Frederick components (Irwin-Williams et al. 1973:44–45). The Alberta component had a restricted distribution in the northern part of the locality. Irwin-Williams et al. (1973:48) suggested that the Alberta point reflected a trend from earlier Hell Gap times, exhibiting a constriction in the lower part of the point to delineate a stem. Although originally defined as Scottsbluff (Irwin and Wormington 1970), Irwin-Williams et al. (1973:48) later recognized the Alberta point with its stem about one third the length of the piece, its parallel-sided base, and abrupt shoulders. A radiocarbon date of ca. 8,600 BP in the level above the Alberta material led to the estimated age range of 9,500 to 9,000 BP for the Alberta complex at the Hell Gap site (Irwin-Williams et al. 1973:52). A re-evaluation of the Hell Gap site's stratigraphy questioned the traditional unilinear model of culture change in the Palaeoindian sequence, but did not specifically address the Alberta material, leaving the relationship of Hell Gap, Alberta, and Cody uncontested (Sellet 2001).

Shortly after the Hell Gap excavations, Forbis (1968a) excavated the Fletcher site, a bison kill site in southern Alberta. He recovered six points from a deeply buried bone bed, four of which he classified as Alberta points.

The remaining two fragmentary specimens could equally be considered Alberta points. Scottsbluff material was recovered, but only from the spoil pile of the dugout that initially exposed the site. Directly dating the bone bed initially proved problematic, leading to a limiting date based on seeds in the underlying clay layer (Vickers and Beaudoin 1989). A subsequent date on seeds from within the bone bed corroborated the limiting date, suggesting an age of about 9,500 BP (Beaudoin and Lemmen 2000). While this age suggests an Alberta occupation, Scottsbluff material was found at the site, complicating this interpretation. Still, in another investigation of the site, Quigg (1976:108) observed faunal remains in two closely spaced living floors (2–5 cm apart), allowing for speculation that an Alberta component was found in situ by Forbis, while the overlying Scottsbluff material was only recovered on the surface in the dugout spoil pile.

The Hudson-Meng site is the only well-dated, single-component Alberta site on the Northern Plains (Agenbroad 1978a). The site is an arroyo bison kill site in northwestern Nebraska that was excavated in the late 1960s and the 1970s (Agenbroad 1978a). Based on three radiocarbon dates, an age range of 9,820 to 8,990 BP was suggested (Agenbroad 1978a:116). A total of twenty Alberta projectile points and point fragments were recovered (Agenbroad 1978a:67–80). Agenbroad (1978a:80–85,122–124; 1978b) was prompted by the recovery of a Cody knife to reassess the relationship between the Alberta complex and the later Cody complex as the latter was usually associated with Cody knives. He suggested that this evidence provides justification for the inclusion of Alberta material under the Cody complex (Agenbroad 1978a:122–124, 1978b).

Frison (1991a:62) recognized the Alberta complex on the Northern Plains. He observed that it likely dates between 9,800 and 9,000 BP (Frison et al. 1996:13). He also recognized possible regional variants of the Alberta point: Alberta-Cody I and Alberta-Cody II points (see Bradley and Frison 1987:199–231). The only site from which these point styles have been recovered is the Horner site in northwestern Wyoming. These point styles exhibit subtle technological differences from the later Cody material that constituted the bulk of the Horner site material. Two radiocarbon dates thought to be associated with the Alberta-Cody points were close to ca. 10,000 BP. The potential age, coupled with Alberta-like point morphology, suggests this material may be a regional variant or transitional point of the Alberta complex, but a relationship with the Scottsbluff material or an as-yet undefined complex is also possible (Frison

1991a:63). Other than a refinement of lithic technology, represented by Eden and Scottsbluff points, little separates points of the Cody complex from those of the preceding Alberta, so they were called Alberta-Cody (Frison et al. 1996:15).

The Sites

In situ assemblages exhibiting Alberta points are rare on the Northern Plains. Fortunately, the province of Alberta has produced one of the more classic examples of such a site, the Fletcher site. As noted above, the interpretation of the Fletcher site is not without problems. Other sites in Alberta have yielded Alberta points. However, like Fletcher, they too have problematic interpretations or lack dates (see Plate 6 and Figure 7).

Fletcher (DjOw 1). The Fletcher site is a bison kill site in gently rolling terrain, just south of a crescent-shaped esker ridge. It is located a few kilometres north of Chin Coulee in southwestern Alberta (Forbis 1968a:1–2). The site was named for the leaseholder at the time of discovery, Frank Fletcher. It was found by Armin Dyck who observed numerous bones and Palaeoindian points around a recent dugout. He reported the find to the Glenbow Foundation. The bone bed is 200–250 cm BS in clay pond deposits resting above culturally sterile clay deposits and below aeolian sand deposits (Vickers and Beaudoin 1989). Forbis (1968a) did not mention the extent of his excavations at the site, but a subsequent visit by Quigg (1976) involved the excavation of five 2-×-2-m test pits, with Roderick Vickers conducting the most recent excavation (2 × 2 m) at the site (Vickers and Beaudoin 1989). Only Forbis' (1968a) excavations recovered diagnostic material.

Four Alberta points were found in situ within the bone bed (Forbis 1968a:4–5). Four Scottsbluff points were recovered as surface finds. Two fragmentary specimens that were found in situ were not classified, although these are strikingly like Alberta points (Dawe 2004; Forbis 1968a:3–4, fig. 1d, h). Two aberrant points are small and possibly reworked Palaeoindian points (Forbis 1968a:3). A possible corner-notched point exhibiting good craftsmanship appears to have been found in association with the bone bed. Four other small points from the surface, however, exhibited poor craftsmanship and inferior raw materials; they likely date to a later time (Forbis 1968a:5). Other tools recovered from the site included a Cody knife (Forbis 1968a:7, fig. 2h), gravers (n = 2), a spokeshave, a side scraper, end scrapers

PLATE 6 Alberta (phase) points. Illustrated are points from the Bayrock site (DkPb 2) (a); the Wally's Beach site (DhPg 8)(b–d); EhPv 43 (e and f); the Fletcher site (DjOw 1) (g and h); and GgQt 10 (i and j). Photo credit: Glenbow Museum (a); Shane Tolman (b–d); Alberta Culture and Community Spirit (e–j).

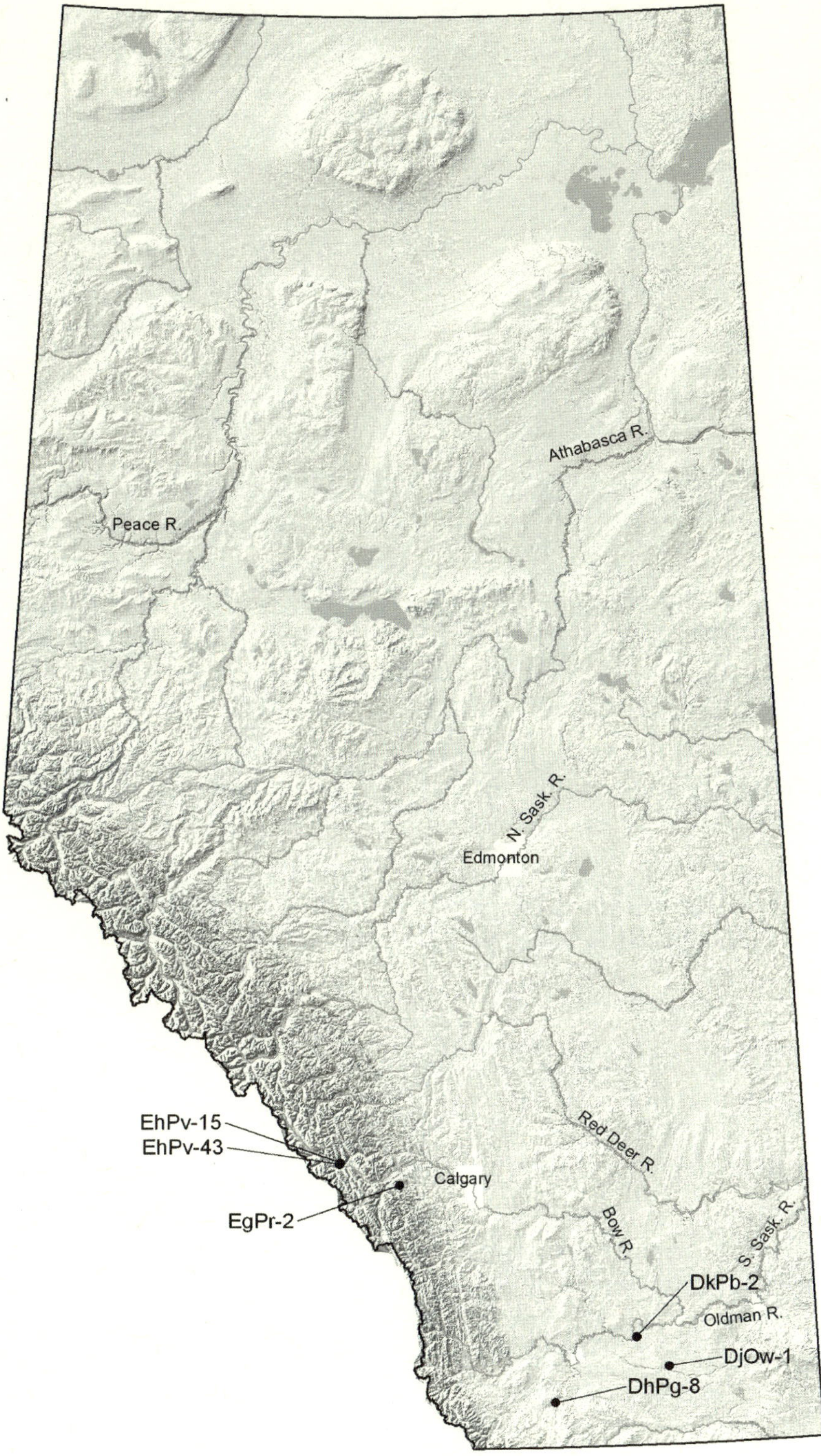

FIGURE 7
Alberta (phase) sites within Alberta

(n = 2), bifaces (n = 2), a reamer, a hammerstone/anvil, and a grooved maul (Forbis 1968a:8; Dawe 2004). The grooved maul is potentially a very early example of this tool form but, based on the lack of other mauls of comparable age, the Fletcher specimen has been regarded with some scepticism (Wormington and Forbis 1965:120; Forbis 1968a:7).

All the bone recovered during Forbis' (1968a) excavations was considered bison. As an aside, Quigg (1976:109) noted that his excavations at the site produced a bison bone bed, as Forbis had described, with the addition of a single deer phalanx. The bones were in particularly poor condition but some evidence of butchering was observed. The surface on which the bone bed rested dipped to the southeast but not sufficiently enough to conduct a jump. No evidence of posts for a corral was observed, nor was evidence for miring the animals in a marsh identified (Forbis 1968a:3). More recently, interpretation of biotic remains from the site suggested permanent water was present at the Fletcher site, lending support to a scenario in which bison that became mired in mud at the edge of a water body were ambushed (Beaudoin and Lemmen 2000:23).

Numerous attempts have been made to date the bone with unsatisfactory results owing to its condition (see Forbis 1968a:2; Quigg 1976; and Vickers and Beaudoin 1989). A sample of Cyperaceae (sedge family) seeds from clay deposits beneath the bone bed provided a lower limiting date of ca. 9,400 BP, and seeds recovered from the bone bed provided a date of ca. 9,500 BP (see Table 5). These dates are similar to dates for Alberta points recovered at Hudson-Meng (Agenbroad 1978a:115–117) and dates estimated for the Alberta component at the Hell Gap site (Irwin-Williams et al. 1973). While the association of the Alberta points and the Scottsbluff material at Fletcher is unclear, the recovery of the Alberta points in the bone bed and the dates available suggest an early Cody event represented by Alberta points.

Bayrock (DkPb 2). The Bayrock site is a bison kill site observed eroding from a highway cut north of Taber (Wormington and Forbis 1965:116). An extinct form of bison with a cobble chopper inside its skull was found eroding from the road cut, suggesting human involvement in its death. Further along the same formation, an Alberta point made on distinctive dull red material, lithic debitage, and fragmentary bison bone were collected. Excavations at the kill site recovered lithic debitage of the same dull red material, increasing the likelihood of an association with the point. Except for two spokeshaves, few tools were recovered during the excavation. The bone bed was six inches (~15 cm) thick in places and represented a large number of animals. A date on wood underlying the bone bed produced a maximum age estimate of between ca. 10,500 BP and 11,000 BP (Table 5). It is reasonable to infer that this is an early Cody bison kill that yielded an Alberta point.

TABLE 5
Radiocarbon dates for Alberta (phase) sites (calibrated by OxCal 3.10 [Ramsey 2005])

Site [LAB NO.]	Conventional ^{14}C Age	$^{13}C/^{12}C$ Ratio	Material	Calibration	Reference
DkPb 2 [GSC-3]	10500 +/- 200	-25.0‰	wood	11000–10150 B.C. (p = 0.954)	Morlan n.d.
DkPb 2 [S-68]	11000 +/- 250	-25.0‰	wood	11500–10200 B.C. (p = 0.954)	Wormington and Forbis 1965:117; Morlan n.d.
DjOw 1 [TO-1097]	9380 +/- 110	-25.0‰	seed	9150–8300 B.C. (p = 0.954)	Vickers and Beaudoin 1989:264
DjOw 1 [CAMS-42980]	9540 +/- 110	-25.0‰	seed	9250–8600 B.C. (p = 0.954)	Beaudoin and Lemmen 2000:22

Norquay (EhPv 15, 156R). The Norquay site is a camp-quarry site along the north and south side of the Trans-Canada Highway about 200 m east of the Norquay-Highway 1 Interchange in Banff National Park (Fedje 1988:5). The highway bisected the site in 1958. In 1983, an initial investigation excavated 18 m² on the north side and 27 m² on the south side of the highway (Fedje 1988:5). While the site was well stratified, the south side exhibited cryoturbation, making the recovery of an Alberta point in a palaeosol underlying a Mazama Ash layer difficult to interpret (Fedje 1985:4). In 1986, an additional 57 m² were excavated in three blocks (west, central, and east) when landscaping on the north side of the highway threatened 25 percent of the remaining site. Two cultural layers were observed. The single Alberta point recovered in a pre-Mazama Ash context during the 1983 assessment could not be positively related to the 1986 excavations (Fedje 1988:21). Still, Fedje (1988:210) noted that a distinctive red chert from this component was also found in Cody points recovered from the Minnewanka site (356R). The Bayrock site, mentioned above, also exhibits an Alberta point manufactured on a distinctive red material. Other tools recovered at the site include biface fragments (n = 3), a hafted biface, end scrapers (n = 3), choppers (n = 2), cores (n = 28), retouched lithics (n = 4), utilized lithics (n = 13) and a preform.

In general, lithic debitage and tools were concentrated in well-defined activity areas. Exotic or good-quality lithic materials dominated the tool assemblage and debitage, a hallmark of Palaeoindian technology.

The faunal assemblage (n = 2,092) was in poor condition. All preserved bone was charred, a condition likely required for preservation (Fedje 1988:11). No hearth or FBR features were recorded. Only bison and/or large ungulates were found. Lithic debitage and bone tended to concentrate around large boulders found at the site. Fedje (1988:11) interpreted the boulders as knapping locations and/or anvils for butchering.

As noted above, a single Alberta point was recovered in a pre-Mazama Ash context at the site in 1983, but could not be directly linked to the lowest component revealed in the 1986 excavations. Given that both years of excavation were conducted to depths below a layer of Mazama Ash and exhibit rare red chert found predominantly in Alberta phase sites, a tenuous link to the Alberta phase is inferred.

Wally's Beach (DhPg 8). The Wally's Beach site consists of lithic and faunal material deflated during drawdown on part of the bottom of the St. Mary Reservoir near Cardston, southwestern Alberta (Tolman 2001). Two Scottsbluff, four Eden, and thirty Alberta points were recovered from the surface (Tolman 2001; Dawe 2004). Tolman (2001:104) noted that Knife River flint was used continuously through time at the site, but peaked during the Cody tradition based on weight of diagnostic tools by raw material. A possible Alberta cache of twenty-two items within a 3-m radius included two Alberta points, four end scrapers (two spurred), three large broken flakes (possibly blanks), six small flakes of Knife River flint and two non-Knife River flint flakes (Tolman 2001:106).

Other sites. Numerous other sites exhibiting Alberta material are worth noting. The Timberline site (EhPv 43), overlooking Vermilions Lakes in Banff National Park, produced what appears to be an Alberta point base recovered in a 15–20-cm veneer of sediment on a moraine (Fedje 1985:4). Russell Johnston recovered Cody material at several locales near Cereal in east-central Alberta (Pettipas 1980; Wormington and Forbis 1965:56–97). Adams (1976:13) noted that the Russell Johnston Collection included six Alberta points, as well as seventy-three Scottsbluff, seventeen Eden, and five Cody knives. FfQh 26 produced the base of an Alberta point amongst other Palaeoindian material within compressed stratigraphy near Cadomin

(Meyer et al. 2007). As well, an unusual assemblage of material from a cultivated field at GgQt 10 near Beaverlodge may represent Alberta material (Fedirchuk et al. 1998:306–314). Numerous other sites in the province have yielded Alberta points from surface contexts. Dawe (2004) has conducted an invaluable study of Cody materials in the province. Sites with Alberta points from his comprehensive list also include materials from private collections.

Alberta: Earliest Point Style of the Cody Tradition

Alberta points are rarely recovered from excavated contexts within or outside Alberta. With the exception of the Hudson-Meng site (Nebraska) and potentially the Hell Gap site (Wyoming), excavated Alberta assemblages are often recovered from problematic contexts across the Northern Plains. Within Alberta, the Fletcher site produced Alberta points within a bone bed dating to 9,500 BP, but Scottsbluff points were also recovered from the spoil pile that revealed the site. At the Bayrock site, an Alberta point was indirectly associated with the bone bed, which in turn was indirectly dated by a limiting date of ca. 10,500 BP. The Norquay site is problematic in that the Alberta point was recovered in a pre-Mazama Ash context that could not be directly linked to the lowest component revealed in the subsequent excavations and a date was not obtained. At the same time, the possibility cannot be dismissed that unspoiled Alberta assemblages occur and date earlier than Scottsbluff assemblages.

Yet, the Alberta and Scottsbluff point forms exhibit such a striking resemblance. The Cody knife, so common to the Cody tradition, was found at the Hudson-Meng site and Fletcher site bone beds. The similarity of the morphology of the point forms and the continued use of the Cody knife provide overlap between the two phases. Arguably, the Alberta point and its associated materials represent a distinct, early variant of the Scottsbluff materials. As such, Alberta and Scottsbluff-Eden are the diagnostic points of the Cody tradition. The Alberta point variant of the Cody tradition dates from ca. 9,800 to 9,000 BP. The Alberta point is the sole diagnostic point of the Alberta phase, although Cody knives do occur but are a diagnostic of the tradition as a whole. Further research may attest to the validity of this relationship whether synchronic, diachronic, or otherwise.

British Columbia has produced a number of Alberta points, all in the northeast part of the province. Roberts (1984:15–16) reported that five localities produced Alberta points; these were observed in a collection procured in the area of Lone Prairie. At the Pink Mountain site (HhRr 1), a rather lanceolate Alberta point was recovered (Wilson 1987:217). In Saskatchewan, surface finds of lanceolate stemmed points are common south of the North Saskatchewan River (Dyck 1983:78). Dyck (1983:80, fig. 10.6b, d–g) illustrated a few surface collected Alberta points, including specimens from the Craik area, EcNk 1 in the Boharm area, and the Osage area. Phenix (1965, in Forbis 1968a:6) noted surface finds of Alberta points in west-central, south, and east-central parts of the province. For Manitoba, Pettipas (1996a:44) noted that several decades of archaeological fieldwork in the province had shown that, with few exceptions, artifacts of the early stemmed point tradition (i.e., Alberta and Scottsbluff) were restricted to the southwest corner of the province above the western Campbell strandline of Lake Agassiz.

For northeastern Montana, Jerde (1981) reported the surface recovery of an Alberta point at the Buried Fence Line site (24SH560) and the McKean Ridge site (24SH578). In the adjacent Rocky Mountains, Davis et al. (1989) have defined the Alder complex. The complex was identified at the Barton Gulch site near the Ruby Reservoir in southwestern Montana. Ten lanceolate points with parallel-oblique flaking, labelled Ruby Valley points, were recovered in an occupation dated to ca. 9,400 BP. The researchers noted that morphologically similar points are distributed throughout the Rocky Mountains, especially southwestern Montana, east-central Idaho, and northwestern Wyoming (Davis et al. 1989:8). Frison (1991a:77) remarked that this recovery pushes the age of parallel-oblique flaked assemblages back in time, coeval with earliest Cody tradition times.

At the Benz site at the Knife River flint quarries in North Dakota, Root (1998) excavated a Cody occupation. He recovered a resharpened Alberta point and two Scottsbluff point bases in a trench. The latter were associated with a palaeosol that did not extend to where the Alberta point was recovered, making their association indiscernible (Root 1998:62). Further, the Alberta point appeared to be in disturbed context. The excavation of 11 m^2 at the locale of the Scottsbluff material exposed numerous lithic concentrations at various levels, suggesting several occupations. A date on a hearth excavated beneath the Scottsbluff points produced an age of about 9,500 BP (Root 1998:63). Thus, the date from the hearth is earlier than other Cody occupations, and an association with the Alberta phase occupation is possible (Root 1998:63). In South Dakota, the Trail Draw site (39PN97) is a surface find of an Alberta point in the Black Hills just north of the Hudson-Meng site (Cassells 1986:40).

In north-central Wyoming, Frison (1992) excavated the deeply stratified rockshelter called the Medicine Lodge Creek site. At least twenty cultural layers of Palaeoindian material were recorded. Alberta points appear to have been recovered from a layer dated to ca. 9,600 BP. The Alberta material is separated from Scottsbluff material (ca. 8,830 BP) by layers containing other cultural material (Frison 1992:328, fig. 9.3m, n, r, s). In northeastern Wyoming, Frison (1991a:62) excavated the Carter/Kerr-McGee site, a multicomponent site with a mixed Alberta/Scottsbluff component. The site is a bison processing site from which Scottsbluff and Eden points were recovered among the bones, while Alberta points were recovered at the bottom of the bone bed. Dates for the site could not be obtained because of the lack of charcoal and the disintegrated nature of the bone (Frison 1984:292). Frison (1984:298) considered the Alberta material as a different complex not associated with the overlying Scottsbluff/Eden bison processing site. Further, in east-central Wyoming, Frison (1991a:62) reported a surface find of an Alberta point near the Agate Basin site, although there is no Alberta component within the Agate Basin site itself. In Yuma County of Colorado, Gebhard (1949:132, fig. 48b) illustrated a specimen identified as Scottsbluff, but which is more consistent with Alberta point morphology. Colorado appears to delimit the most southwestern extent of the Alberta point style. Forbis (1968a:6) refers to a possible specimen in Nebraska. Blackmar and Hofman (1997:10) noted the recovery of two Alberta points in Oklahoma. Similarly, Wyckoff (1992:47–48) illustrated a number of specimens he feels exhibit attributes of Alberta points. Oklahoma is likely the southeastern extent of the Alberta point.

In summary, with the exception of the Hudson-Meng site and the Hell Gap site, excavated Alberta assemblages are often recovered from problematic contexts across the Northern Plains. The province of Alberta has produced a number of Alberta phase sites that exhibit problematic contexts including Fletcher, Bayrock, and Norquay. Despite these issues, the Alberta phase appears to present a distinct projectile point that predates Scottsbluff-Eden material. The recovery of Cody knives at Hudson-Meng and Fletcher indicate continuity between Alberta and Scottsbluff-Eden phases. Furthermore, the point forms are morphologically similar, also arguing for continuity. It remains to be established whether there are cultural ties between Alberta material to earlier Agate Bain/Hell Gap material and to later Lusk material.

SCOTTSBLUFF-EDEN PHASE (CA. 9,000 TO 8,600 BP)

The Scottsbluff point derived its name from the town of Scottsbluff, Nebraska. It was near the Scottsbluff townsite in 1932 that the first point of this type was recovered in an excavated context (Barbour and Schultz 1932, cited in Wormington 1957:118): surface finds of this point type had been made prior to this time, but never in situ (Wormington 1957:118). Similarly, in 1940, an Eden point was first recovered from excavated context at the Finley site. The site is near the town of Eden in Wyoming, from which it derived its name (Wormington 1957:124). The difference between a Scottsbluff point and an Eden point is that the latter is much narrower in relation to its length, has a less strongly indented stem, and usually has collateral flaking that produces a diamond-shaped cross-section (Wormington 1957:124). During 1949–1950, excavations at the Horner site near the town of Cody, Wyoming, produced both Scottsbluff and Eden points in association with a diagnostic knife that had a transverse blade that was stemmed on one side: the Cody knife (Wormington 1957:128). This complex of archaeological materials was termed Cody, after the nearby town (Jepson 1953).

The story of the Scottsbluff-Eden phase has a connection to the province of Alberta. During the droughts of the 1930s, surface collections were made by Russell Johnston from blowouts near Cereal in east-central Alberta (Wormington and Forbis 1965:57). Following the suggestion of Marie Wormington, Johnston maintained careful records on the sequence in which artifacts were being uncovered at various blowout sites. By following this method, he was the first to recognize the association of Eden points, Scottsbluff points, and stemmed knives (Wormington and Forbis 1965:56). Johnston named this associated material "Little Gem," but prior publication had labelled it the Cody complex (Jepson 1953; Wormington and Forbis 1965:56). In Alberta, Reeves (1969:24) first proposed the Alberta-Cody complex, which he dated ca. 9,500 to 8,500 BP. At the time, Alberta archaeologists were only aware of the Bayrock and Fletcher sites. In his review of the literature, Vickers (1986:36–45) indicated little reason to accept or revise the model for the Cody complex in Alberta. For Saskatchewan, Dyck (1983:79–83) included Cody material within the Lanceolate Stemmed tradition, which he estimated lasted from ca. 10,150 to 8,600 BP.

In the United States, Frison (1991a:66) considered the Horner site to be the type site for the Cody (Scottsbluff-Eden) complex because of the occurrence of Scottsbluff and Eden points and the various forms of Cody knives. The site was dated to ca. 8,800 BP. The Cody material at the Hell Gap site was estimated to date between ca. 8,800 and 8,400 BP and contained Scottsbluff points, Eden points, and Cody knives (Irwin-Williams et al. 1973:52). Radiocarbon dates for the Finley site were ca. 9,000 BP (Frison 1991a:26, 66). The Scottsbluff material at Medicine Lodge Coulee was dated to ca. 8,800 BP (Frison 1991a:66, 1992:328). In general, Scottsbluff-Eden material is considered to date roughly 9,400–8,200 BP (Frison et al. 1996:15).

Challenges to the concept of the Cody complex have been presented. Not all materials from this time period have been classified as Cody complex despite their distinct appearance. At the Olsen-Chubbuck site in northeastern Colorado, Wheat (1967) originally classified the points from the bone bed in the arroyo kill site as variants of the Scottsbluff point. Subsequently, he reclassified this material as Firstview and San Jon points, based on subtle differences in form (Wheat 1972:140–155). The site was dated to ca. 8,500 BP (Wheat 1967). Similarly, Wheat (1979:72) proposed that the Cody-like material at the Jurgens site, north of Denver, be classified as the Kersey complex. The site also dates to ca. 8,500 BP (Wheat 1979). The Firstview and Kersey complexes exhibit assemblages very similar to the Cody complex. Frison (1991a:178–186) included Olsen-Chubbuck and Jurgens within his review of Cody sites.

Similarly, Pettipas (1980) noted that the Little Gem complex was often subsumed under the Cody complex. He and Russell Johnston, the man who named it, viewed it rather as a co-phase or a phase related by a common past or projectile points to the Cody complex. He suggested the Little Gem materials could be differentiated as they included different point styles (i.e., Sandia-like, Agate Basin-like, Lerma-like) , as well as microblades, microblade cores, corner-tanged pendants, and six classes of side scrapers, among other artifact types. The Cody complex, on the other hand, includes bifacial side scrapers, shaft smoothers, denticulates, and four classes of bifaces (Pettipas 1980:17). While the combinations found in the Little Gem complex are possible, the collection techniques used to establish the Little Gem complex could also have led to spurious correlations. There are now many sites on the Northern Plains that confirm the Scottsbluff-Eden pattern.

The Sites

Sites with in situ Scottsbluff assemblages are fairly common on the Northern Plains, but rare in Alberta. As with the earlier Alberta phase, the sites that have been excavated in Alberta tend to be problematic in terms of either stratigraphic separation or their dates. This leaves correlation with the sequence in the United States as a basis for much of our understanding (see Plate 7 and Figure 8).

J-Crossing (DjPm 16). The J-Crossing site is a small lithic workshop located on a 10-metre-high terrace on the south side of the Crowsnest River. In 1988, backhoe testing encountered deeply buried material below Mazama Ash. During 1988–1989 a total of 96 m^2 was excavated. Material was concentrated in two areas.

Component One produced a Palaeoindian point base and point blade (Van Dyke 1994:112). The shape and size of these specimens suggest they are Scottsbluff points. Other tools recovered include two bifacial knives, two cores, an elongate pebble, and a possible grinding stone (Van Dyke 1994:112). The lithic debitage (n = 839) was dominated by black and grey cherts and a few pieces of Knife River flint (n = 2). The faunal assemblage consisted of two pieces of freshwater shell, a probable deer phalanx, five bison bone fragments, and about eight hundred miscellaneous mammal bone fragments (Van Dyke 1994:112–113). Burned and calcine bone fragments were recovered within a 5-m^2 area, along with two unmodified cobbles. A single radiocarbon date of ca. 8,600 BP was obtained (see Table 6).

Component Two did not yield any diagnostic tools. It did contain two cores, a cobble-core hammer, a spokeshave, a side scraper, retouched flakes, and an end/side scraper. The latter tool appears to have been made on a reworked stemmed point. The faunal assemblage included a freshwater shell, two rabbit bones, a small/medium canid bone fragment, an ungulate limb bone, and numerous miscellaneous bone fragments (Van Dyke 1994:114). A concentration of burned and calcine bone fragments occurred in this locale as well. A single radiocarbon date was obtained of ca. 9,600 BP (Table 6).

The dates are contradictory as the older date is associated with the material in the western excavation block (Component 2), which stratigraphically is 50 cm above the other material (Component 1), so is inferred to be older. Van Dyke (1994:115) suggested the rejection of either would be premature given the knowledge of Scottsbluff at the time. Few Cody (Scottsbluff-Eden) sites predate 9,000 BP (Frison 1991a).

PLATE 7
Scottsbluff points. Illustrated are points from FlOt 2 (a); the J-Crossing site (DjPm 16) (b and c); the Stonepine site (EgPn 480), Component 1 (d); Head-Smashed-In Buffalo Jump (DkPj 1) (e and h); the Wally's Beach site (DhPg 8) (f and g); and EkPo 10 (i). Photo credit: Fedirchuk-McCullough and Associates (a); Bison Historical Services Limited (b–d); Royal Alberta Museum (e and h); Shane Tolman (f and g); Laurie Milne and John Brumley (i).

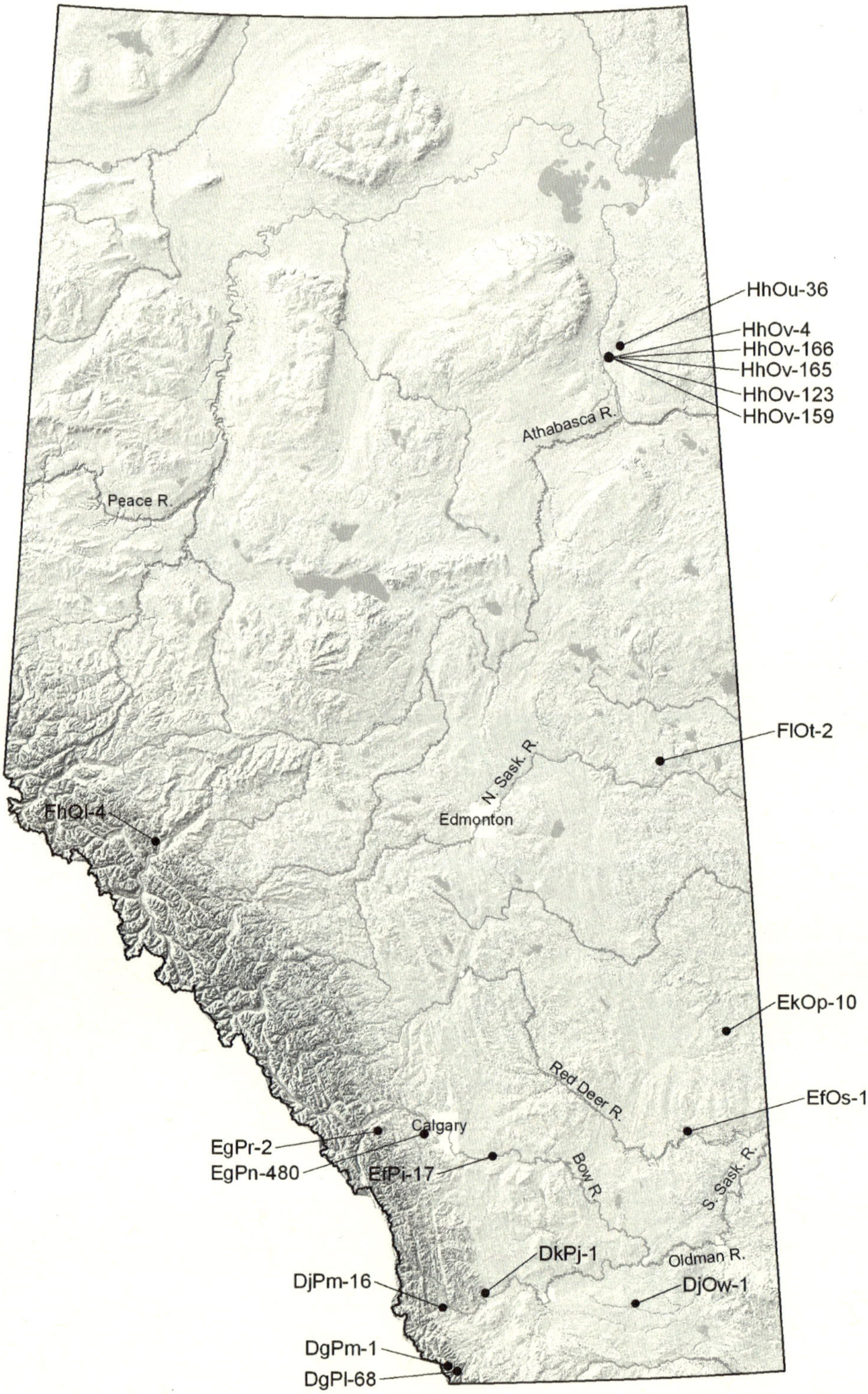

FIGURE 8 Scottsbluff-Eden sites within Alberta

Given the recovery of Scottsbluff points in association with a radiocarbon date of ca. 8,600 BP, it would seem reasonable to infer that the 9,600 BP date could be associated with Alberta material, or be reconsidered.

FhQl 4. FhQl 4 is a multicomponent site located on the west site of Brule Lake at Swan Landing, along the Athabasca River north of Jasper (Ball 1986b:133). At least three cultural occupations were observed in an eroding cut bank exposed during gravel and sand quarrying. The lowest occupation, Level 33, produced a reworked Cody point made on black siliceous siltstone (Ball 1986b). Dawe (2004) classified the point as an Alberta point, but the stem width is narrow, the shoulders have been very reworked, and the basal edge is not particularly convex. A few other lithic items were recovered but their proveniences have not been fully disclosed. Two dates on charcoal of about 8,600 BP were obtained for the level (Ball 1986b:147–150). These dates fit nicely within the range expected from the Scottsbluff-Eden phase (Table 6).

Fletcher (DjOw 1). A discussion of the Fletcher site has been presented above in the section on the Alberta phase. The site's relevance to the Cody-Eden phase rests in Quigg's (1976:108) observation of the two closely spaced living floors (2–5 cm apart) mentioned above. It leaves open the possibility that sediments with Scottsbluff material overlying Alberta material may be present at the site. Conversely, the materials may all be from the same stratigraphic level.

Site [LAB NO.]	Conventional ^{14}C Age	$^{13}C/^{12}C$ Ratio	Material	Calibration	Reference
DjPm 16 [AECV 1198C]	8580 +/- 160	-19.3‰	collagen	8300–7200 B.C. (p = 0.954)	Van Dyke 1994:110
DjPm 16 [AECV 746C]	9600 +/- 210	-15.5‰	collagen	rejected	Van Dyke 1994:110
FhQl 4 [AECV-10CX]	8630 +/- 100	-25.0‰	charcoal	8200–8100 B.C. (p = 0.011) 8000–7450 B.C. (p = 0.943)	Ball 1986:147–150; Morlan n.d.
FhQl 4 [S-2178]	8675 +/- 270	-25.0‰	charcoal	8500–7000 B.C. (p = 0.954)	Ball 1986:147–150; Morlan n.d.
DgPm 1 [GX-1435]	8220 +/- 260	-25.0‰	charcoal	7800–6400 B.C. (p = 954)	Reeves 1972:94, Morlan n.d.

TABLE 6 Radiocarbon dates for Scottsbluff-Eden sites (calibrated by OxCal 3.10 [Ramsey 2005])

Stonepine (EgPn 480), Component 1. The Stonepine site is a multicomponent campsite situated west of Calgary in a prominent basin that drains northwest into the Elbow River (de Mille and Head 2001:54). In 1998, 65 m² were excavated prior to the start of a residential development (de Mille and Head 2001:56). The site had four occupation levels. The lowest occupation, Component 1, exhibited Cody materials. Component 2 had Lovell Constricted material stratigraphically located beneath Mazama Ash. Component 3 exhibited Estevan material from above Mazama ash. The uppermost occupation, Component 4, was Old Women's material.

In Component 1, a single point base was recovered and tentatively classified as Scottsbluff (de Mille and Head 2001:65). Other tools recovered included bifaces and biface fragments (n = 4), a uniface, end scrapers (n = 2), a retouched lithic, and a multidirectional core (de Mille and Head 2001:65). Quartzite dominated the assemblage, followed by siltstone and sandstone. The faunal assemblage (n = 109) consisted mainly of unidentifiable mammalian fragments. Four unidentifiable bone fragments were burned. A single radiocarbon date was obtained from a small piece of bison bone: 5,850 +/- 40 BP (Beta-127236) (de Mille and Head 2001:70). Problems during processing led the researchers to reject this date. However, a radiocarbon date obtained from a small piece of bison bone in the overlying occupation, Component 2, produced a date of 9,540 +/- 70 BP (Beta-127235) (de Mille and Head 2001:85). The researchers suggested the date is likely associated with underlying Scottsbluff material in Component 1. Still, it appears to be a few hundred years earlier than what is expected for Scottsbluff material and over 1,000 years too early for the Lovell Constricted material recovered in Component 2 (de Mille and Head 2001:88).

EfPi 17. EfPi 17 is a multicomponent campsite located on the valley edge above the Bow River southeast of Carseland (Hanna 2002:51–65). The site has two occupations: a lower Scottsbluff component and an upper Pelican Lake component. Three excavation blocks were opened with Scottsbluff material recovered from the west block, where 28 m² were excavated (Hanna 2002:ii). Subsequent to mitigative action, the site was developed into a subdivision and golf course.

Six point fragments, including three Scottsbluff point base fragments, a point tip, a point midsection, and a notched point fragment (possibly Pelican Lake), were recovered from the lower component (Hanna 2002:70–73). Other tools recovered were bifaces (n = 2), scrapers (n = 2), a chopper, a hammerstone, unidirectional cores (n = 4), retouched flakes (n = 12), and a utilized flake. The tools were almost exclusively chalcedony and chert. Still, the vast majority of the assemblage was tools made on quartzite, with small amounts of quartz and miscellaneous cherts. Obsidian from the site was analyzed using X-ray fluorescence and identified as originating from the Bear Gulch quarries in eastern Oregon (Hanna 2002:75).

The faunal assemblage consisted of two pieces of weathered ungulate long bone, one of which was subsequently destroyed for a radiometric date. No features were identified but clusters of similar debitage suggested remnant activity areas (Hanna 2002:64). Fifty-one pieces of small, angular FBR were found scattered across the site. A single radiocarbon date of 3,120 +/- 40 BP (Beta-157613) was obtained from bone thought to be contextually associated with the lower Scottsbluff component. The date reflected an age expected for the overlying component and was interpreted to be intrusive (Hanna 2002:76–77). While mixing appears to have occurred at the site, most of the recovered materials seem to be consistent with a Scottsbluff-Eden occupation.

EkOp 10, Occupation 2. EkOp 10 is a campsite/workshop on a knoll in gently rolling terrain north of Oyen. The excavations were conducted to mitigate a highway program. A total of 16 m² was excavated at the site: 6 m² in Sub-area A and 10 m² in Sub-area B. Sub-area A produced a single occupation with most of the material coming from 0 to 10 cm BS. Sub-area B exhibited two occupation levels: an upper occupation at 5 to 15 cm BS and a lower occupation at 45 to 70 cm BS. No diagnostic material was found in the upper occupation, but a reworked Scottsbluff point was recovered in the lower occupation (Milne Brumley and Brumley 1977:42–43, 45).

The Scottsbluff point was manufactured from a non-local mottled pink and white chert that may have been heat treated, as suggested by its waxy feel and greasy lustre (Milne Brumley and Brumley 1977:45). Other tools recovered included end scrapers (n = 4), a biface, a retouched lithic, a multidirectional core, pebble cores and fragments (n = 44) and heavily chipped/pecked artifacts (n = 5). Black chert and chert pebbles dominated the lithic assemblage, although some exotic materials were found. No evidence of bone was recorded, no features were observed, and no radiocarbon dates were obtained for this occupation.

Nezu (HhOu 36). The Nezu site is located on a knoll above the Muskeg River northeast of Fort Mackay in northeastern Alberta. The site was named after ancient Lake Nezu, believed to have existed about 9,100 BP, as evidenced in sedimentological analyses (Saxberg and Reeves 2003:310). The site contained stemmed Scottsbluff points along with lanceolate Plano types and constricted, concave-base specimens similar to James Allen points (Saxberg and Reeves 2003:309). Other tools recovered include large bifaces, large bifacial cores, dorsally finished scrapers, and retouched flakes. Blood residue on the tools suggested that bison, moose, beaver, bear, canid, and miscellaneous cervids were hunted. A few bones were recovered but none had enough organic matter to date (Saxberg and Reeves 2003:300). At least seven other sites in this area share similar traits with the Nezu site, including Scottsbluff points, large triangular bifaces, a lithic reduction technology represented by large flakes produced from prepared cores, and a variety of scrapers, especially large dorsally finished end scrapers (Saxberg and Reeves 2003:300). To summarize, according to Saxberg and Reeves (2003), Scottsbluff points have also been recovered from HhOv 123; Eden points have been recovered from HhOv 4, 159, and 196; and HhOv 165, 166, and 198 did not produce diagnostic material but exhibited other materials similar to the Cody tradition. The researchers considered Frison's (1992) discussion of the breakdown of the separation between the subsistence organization on the open plains and the foothills and mountains during Cody tradition times. They further noted that Cody materials have been found over a large geographic range, including as far east as western Ontario, Michigan, Wisconsin, as far west as Colorado, and as far north as northeastern British Columbia and northeast Alberta (i.e., Nezu).

Sibbald Creek (EgPr 2). The Sibbald Creek site is described above for the Sibbald phase. The base of a Scottsbluff point (Gryba 1983:64, fig. 28, C) and an Alberta point base (Gryba 1983:64, fig. 28, D) were recovered in the lower part of the sediments in association with two basally thinned points, amongst others (Gryba 1983:62–69). Three radiocarbon dates were obtained but were not considered representative of the age of the associated points.

Little Gem Complex, Johnson Locality (EfOs 1). The Little Gem complex, as mentioned above, consists of a series of surface collections made by Russell Johnston near Cereal, east-central Alberta (Wormington and Forbis 1965:57). Adams (1976:13) noted that the Russell Johnston Collection included seventy-three Scottsbluff, seventeen Eden, and six Alberta points, and five Cody knives. Russell Johnston indicated that many of these points appear to have been made on exotic raw materials (Pettipas 1980:79).

Head-Smashed-In Buffalo Jump (DkPj 1). Head-Smashed-In Buffalo Jump is a large campsite/kill site located near Fort Macleod. Best known for its stratified sequence of bison kill site deposits, it was also the recovery locale for two Scottsbluff point bases. In 1949, Boyd Wettlaufer recovered the points as a result of the excavation of previous fill from a cattle dugout in a spring channel that bisected the kill deposits. The points are manufactured on obsidian from Burns, Oregon, and Knife River flint from North Dakota (Dawe 2004). The original spot from which the points were recovered has never been revisited by archaeologists.

Other sites. Three other sites merit mention. First, DgPl 68 is a multicomponent site in Waterton Lakes National Park (Reeves 1972:75). Although no Scottsbluff points were mentioned, Plate 18, no. 24, is clearly a Scottsbluff specimen, but labelled as Besant, from Occupation 1. Second, the Red Rock Canyon site (DgPm 1) in Waterton Lakes National Park contains two Scottsbluff points, amongst other Palaeoindian styles, near a hearth that produced a date of roughly 8,200 BP (Table 6). It could not be determined which points were associated with the hearth. Third, FlOt 2 produced a Scottsbluff point in a ploughed field with excavated materials clustered in five of twenty-six 1-×-1-m units (Haley et al. 1982:46–76). A total of 452 lithic artifacts were recovered with 94.2 percent consisting of fine-grained grey-white quartzite. Over half of the items were recovered from beneath the plough zone (Haley et al. 1982:48).

Early on, Wormington and Forbis (1965:185) noted the prevalence of Scottsbluff material in surface collections within the province. They stated that "the first intensive occupation of Alberta appears to have been by people with a lithic complex characterized by Scottsbluff and Eden points and Cody knives" (Wormington and Forbis 1965:185). As of 2005, Dawe (2004) tallied the known Scottsbluff and Eden points, as well as Cody knives that have been found in the province. Specifically, he reported that there are 330 Scottsbluff points, 103 Eden points, and 23 Cody knives, along with 122 Alberta points and 43 miscellaneous Cody complex-like points, known from the province. These materials provide strong evidence of a substantial occupation in Alberta during late Palaeoindian times.

Scottsbluff-Eden: The First Major Occupation?

Despite some arguments to the contrary (e.g., Pettipas 1980; Wheat 1967, 1979), the Scottsbluff-Eden material in Alberta, and abroad, consistently exhibits key diagnostics, including Scottsbluff points and/or Eden points and/or Cody knives. Scottsbluff points were recovered in good stratigraphic context at the J-Crossing site, FhQl 4, EgPn 480, EfPi 17, and EkOp 10, and under noteworthy conditions at the Fletcher site, Sibbald Creek, Head-Smashed-In Buffalo Jump, DgPm 1, and various sites around Fort MacKay. Scottsbluff points occur in all of these sites, while Eden points and Cody knives are less frequent. As Dawe's (2004) tabulations indicate, there are large numbers of Scottsbluff points relative to both Eden and Cody knives. The Scottsbluff-Eden material in the United States and that for the Alberta sites (Table 6) dates to between ca. 9,000 and 8,500 BP. As Meyer (1985:30) noted, Cody "dates range from 9,000 through to 8,500 years ago. Dates as much as 500 to 1,000 years younger have also been obtained but have generally been rejected by the researchers." Under the convention used in this text, this archaeological material entity is termed the Scottsbluff-Eden phase of the Cody tradition, rather than Cody complex.

Wormington (1957:136) described the Scottsbluff point as fairly wide relative to its length, with a parallel-sided or somewhat triangular blade that is lenticular in cross-section with horizontal flaking that is essentially parallel. Two types of Scottsbluff points are often recognized: Scottsbluff I (described above) and II (Wormington 1957:137). The latter subtype tends to exhibit a triangular blade with more pronounced shoulders and a flared base (Wormington 1957:137). The Eden point is much narrower than the Scottsbluff in relation to its length; it has a less strongly indented stemmed, and it usually has collateral flaking that produces a diamond-shaped cross-section (Wormington 1957:124). Importantly, our knowledge of the technology behind the manufacturing process has increased (e.g., Bradley and Stanford 1987).

Numerous tools have been identified with Scottsbluff-Eden assemblages, but only one single diagnostic non-projectile tool form, the Cody knife, has been identified. It is "a transverse blade and is usually stemmed on one side" (Wormington 1957:128). Other tools commonly associated with Cody assemblages include scrapers, bifaces, engraving tools, perforators, choppers, pounders, and rubbing stones (e.g., Forbis and Sperry 1952:128; Frison 1984; Irwin and Wormington 1970; Irwin-Williams et al. 1973; Wormington 1957:128).

Concerning lithic raw material use, Frison (1991a:66) noted small amounts of Knife River flint and Yellowstone Obsidian amongst more southern exotic materials recovered at the Horner site. In Alberta, the impression from surface collections is that exotic materials, especially Knife River flint, were common in tool manufacture. Dawe (2004) provided evidence to support this impression, noting that about a quarter of all Scottsbluff points, in the province are manufactured on Knife River flint. Still, quartzite accounts for about a fifth of the Scottsbluff points as do miscellaneous cherts (Dawe 2004). EgPn 480 and EfPi 17 produced reasonably large lithic assemblages. At the two sites, quartzite accounted for about 65 percent of the lithic assemblage, while more siliceous materials such as chalcedony (3.1%) and miscellaneous cherts (8.6%) were less common, and were usually employed to make tools.

Many Scottsbluff-Eden sites, including Horner, Finley, Carter/Kerr-McGee, Franca, and Jurgens, attest to the entrapment of bison as a major subsistence strategy (Frison 1991a:181). At the Horner site, in addition to bison, faunal material from deer, antelope, wolves, rabbits, turtles, and birds was recovered (Jepson 1953:20). As the distribution of the Cody tradition is expanded, a broader range of fauna is being considered under subsistence. At the Gorto site in Michigan, net sinkers, which suggest that fish were taken, were found in association with the Cody tradition (Buckmaster and Paquette 1988). In northern Alberta at the Nezu site, blood residue and faunal material suggest that bison, moose, caribou, beaver, and rabbit were taken. At the J-Crossing site in southwestern Alberta, faunal evidence for bison, deer, small canid, rabbit and freshwater shell was recovered. In Alberta, with the possible exception of the Fletcher site, large-scale bison procurement localities have yet to be located.

Features are rare in Scottsbluff-Eden sites. Besides the obvious concentrations of bones in bone beds, few other features are noted. For example, at Locality 1 of the Hell Gap site, no features were noted (Irwin-Williams et al. 1973). At the Horner site, burned areas were interpreted as hearths, and some possible pits were unearthed (Jepson 1953; Frison and Todd 1987). The Niska site, in Saskatchewan, provided evidence for a hearth in association with Scottsbluff material (Meyer 1985). For the Carter/Kerr-McGee site, Frison (1984) suggested that bone arrangements indicated that meat units were stacked and frozen for future use. For the sites in Alberta, some Cody occupations exhibited small amounts of burned bone but no obvious hearths, perhaps suggesting unprepared surface hearths that have eroded because of their exposed positions.

Scottsbluff-Eden sites occur over a fairly large area. The greatest number of sites occurs in the high plains. Sites also occur as far north as northeastern British Columbia, northern Alberta, and south-central Saskatchewan. Scottsbluff material has been found as far east as western Ontario and Michigan, and as far south as Texas. Because of the large number of Scottsbluff-Eden sites, especially in the high plains south of Montana, the following review is restricted to areas immediately adjacent to Alberta.

In south-central British Columbia, Carlson (1994:124) reported a Scottsbluff point in the Sewell Collection from the Vanderhoof locality in the central interior. In northeastern British Columbia, Roberts (1984:16) reported seven localities that produced Scottsbluff points from surface contexts. Raw materials of these finds include black obsidian (n = 3), tan chalcedony (n = 1), and various cherts (n = 4).

In southwestern Saskatchewan, Meyer (1985) excavated 24 m^2 in two blocks at the Niska site. The west block produced a hearth in association with a Scottsbluff stem fragment, as well as other tools. The eastern block produced two stem fragments associated with a variety of tools. Surface finds that initially drew attention to the site included two complete points, three stem fragments, five Cody knives, twelve end scrapers, a concave uniface, and a utilized flake. Most of the artifacts were manufactured on grey porcellanite or Knife River flint. Because of variation in the toolkit, Meyer (1985:31) did not infer that the Niska assemblage entirely conformed to the Cody tradition. The only accepted radiocarbon date for the Scottsbluff Component was 8,475 +/- 650 BP (S-2510) (Meyer and Liboiron 1990:299).

The Heron-Eden site is located near Prelate in southwestern Saskatchewan (Corbeil 1995; Linnamae and Johnson 1999). It is a Cody bison-processing site. Projectile points are mainly Scottsbluff points (Linnamae and Johnson 1999:21, fig. 4a–e, k), some points are Eden points (Linnamae and Johnson 1999:21, fig. 4f, l), and one is possibly an Alberta point (Linnamae and Johnson 1999:21, fig. 4j). Other lithic tools included end scrapers, unifaces, burins, bifacial choppers, and retouched flakes (Linnamae and Johnson 1999:22–26). The lithic assemblage emphasizes chalcedony, quartzite, miscellaneous chert, and jasper, with minor use of other materials. A minimum of thirty-seven bison was represented, with the majority of those identified as males, but also some as females and immature animals (Corbeil 1995; Linnamae and Johnson 1999:18). Two separate kills, a bull herd and a nursery herd, may be present. Five radiocarbon dates fall between ca. 10,200 and 9,000 BP, with a mean of 9,080 BP. There are probably two components, an earlier Alberta component and a later Scottsbluff-Eden Component.

For the McLeod site, Joyes (2000:47–48) reported eighty-five Scottsbluff-Eden points and five Cody knives possibly associated with other artifacts in a blowout near Radville in southeastern Saskatchewan. Two miniature points, similar to those described by Bonnichsen and Keyser (1982) for Montana, were recovered. At Quill Lakes in east-central Saskatchewan, Novecosky (2002b) reported twenty-three Scottsbluff points, four Eden points, a Cody knife, and a drill, amongst other artifacts in a cultivated field. The Dunn site (Ebell 1988) is a surface site in south-central Saskatchewan that contained a large number of points classified as Firstview and Kersey. Joyes (2000:49) considered the McLeod site to be a Cody kill/processing site closely related to the Dunn site 53 km to the northwest. Cody knives are also known in Saskatchewan. Ebell (1982) describes three Cody knife surface finds from southern Saskatchewan while Joyes (2000:48) notes the Saskatchewan total is twelve.

In Manitoba, few Scottsbluff-Eden and related types have been recovered. When they are recovered, they are almost invariably found on and above (west of) the western Campbell strandline of Lake Agassiz suggesting they were used when Glacial Lake Agassiz stood at the Campbell level at ca. 10,000–9,500 BP (Pettipas 1996b:86). Most Scottsbluff points are known from west of the strandline while a single Scottsbluff point, likely curated and later deposited, was found east of the strandline (Pettipas 1996b; Wowchuk 1990).

The MacHaffie site south of Helena, Montana, produced two Scottsbluff components overlying two Folsom components (Forbis and Sperry 1952; Davis et al. 1991). The open-air campsite also produced other tools including scrapers, knives, flake knives, choppers, and sandstone abraders in the Scottsbluff components. The fauna included bison, antelope, rabbit, and ground squirrel (Forbis and Sperry 1952). Radiocarbon dates of approximately 8,600 BP for Component 1 and about 8,200 BP for Component 2 were obtained for the Scottsbluff material (Davis et al. 1991:19). Helmick (1984) reports on surface finds of one Eden point and one Scottsbluff Type II point to the west of Helena at Canyon Ferry Lake. Bonnichsen and Keyser (1982) discuss three diminutive Scottsbluff points from various surface locations in Montana. Although their function is unknown, they illuminate the difficulty in defining the Cody tradition.

Excavations at deeply stratified Mammoth Meadow I produced two levels of Cody material. However, the upper Cody level was intermixed with Bitterroot points, while the lower level contained an unusual Cody lithic workshop that also produced a lanceolate corner-notched point (Bonnichsen et al. 1992). Jerde (1981) reported a number of Scottsbluff and Eden points from northeastern Montana. In southwestern Montana in the Upper Yellowstone Valley, Lahren (1976; Frison et al. 1996:15) recorded a Scottsbluff component at the Myers-Hindman site dated to ca. 8,900 BP that contained bison, deer, elk, mountain sheep, and canids. In south-central Montana, Mulloy (1958:31–33) recovered Eden Valley Yuma points, now called Scottsbluff, intermixed with basally thinned points, Lovell Constricted points, and Castle River points in the lowest level of Pictograph Cave. The Pryor Mountains, in south-central Montana, produced Scottsbluff material dated to ca. 7,700 BP at the Pretty Creek site (Loendorf et al. 1981, cited in Frison et al. 1996:15). The Sorenson site in the Bighorn Canyon area in south-central Montana also produced a possible Scottsbluff blade fragment in Occupation I associated with Agate Basin-like and Alberta-like base fragments (Husted 1969:11). The occupation produced a date of ca. 8,000 BP.

Another cultural phenomenon in Montana of the time was the Hardinger complex (Davis 1988, 1993). This complex is a set of material with distinctive, basally indented projectile points recovered from Barton Gulch site east of the Ruby Reservoir in southwestern Montana. The points — Metzal points — were recovered from two living floors dated to approximately 8,700 BP. This material appears to represent a manifestation of a Plains/Mountain cultural adaptation coeval with Scottsbluff material (Frison 1991a:77). This archaeological complex has not been recovered in Alberta.

Gregg (1986) provided a review of the Cody tradition in North Dakota. Much of the evidence is from surface finds. At the Benz site, however, Root (1998) identified a Cody occupation in a 1-×-14-m trench. Two Scottsbluff points were recovered in a palaeosol at one end of the trench and an Alberta point in disturbed context was noted at the other end of the trench. A total of 11 m² at the Scottsbluff occupation produced multiple occupations. The date from the surface of the palaeosol was ca. 8,590 BP while a hearth feature into the palaeosol dated to ca. 8,600 BP (Root 1998).

In summary, the Scottsbluff-Eden phase exhibits cultural continuity from the preceding Alberta phase. Projectile point morphology between the phases is strikingly similar and Cody knives provide overlap in a diagnostic tool form between the two phases. Scottsbluff-Eden campsites (i.e., J-Crossing, Stonepine, EfPi 17, EkOp 10) in Alberta appear to exceed the number of kill sites (i.e., Fletcher). To the south, kill sites for this phase are more commonly reported in the archaeological literature. Archaeological visibility could account for the lack of Scottsbluff-Eden sites but one would expect bone beds to be more visible than small campsites. Perhaps the sample of overall sites is simply too small to address this issue. The ultimate fate of the Cody tradition is not clear. The stemmed point tradition continues on the Plains in the Lusk complex, but little evidence is available to link these cultural entities.

3 *Early to Middle Prehistoric Period Transition*

CA. 8,600 TO 7,500 BP

Around 10,000 BP, a warming trend began, following the end of glaciation. Called the Hypsithermal interval, this period was the warmest postglacial episode. It reached a maximum between about 9,000 and 8,000 BP. The Hypsithermal interval may have ended as late as 4,000 BP.

PLAINS/MOUNTAIN COMPLEX (CA. 8,600 TO 7,700 BP)

During an archaeological survey prior to the construction of the upper Yellowtail Reservoir on the Bighorn River in south-central Montana and north-central Wyoming, Husted (1969) recovered numerous late Palaeoindian lanceolate points from a number of rockshelters. He named one of the point types Lovell Constricted after the nearby town of Lovell, Wyoming, and another point type of similar age Pryor Stemmed after nearby Pryor Mountain (Frison 1976:151). At both the Sorenson Rockshelter site and the Bottleneck Cave site, Lovell Constricted points were found stratigraphically below levels containing Pryor Stemmed points (Husted 1969). Lovell Constricted material dates to about 8,000 BP or slightly earlier, and is immediately postdated by Pryor Stemmed material (Husted 1969; Frison and Grey 1980).

Husted (1969:13) characterized Lovell Constricted points as medium to large lanceolate points with concave bases and a definite constriction of the lateral edges slightly distal to the base. The lateral edges above the constriction are smooth and convex while the basal edge varies from shallowly to moderately concave (Husted 1969:12–13). The cross-section is lenticular with parallel-oblique flaking (Husted 1969:13). Basal grinding covers the base and up to half the length of the point (Husted 1969:13). The Pryor Stemmed point is described as "a large point with convex, bevelled and serrated lateral edges and a stem with concave edges and base" (Husted 1969:14). The bevelling is alternate with uneven serration (Husted 1969:14). Shoulders are a product of an angle between the stem and lateral edges (Husted 1969:14). Husted (1969:83) coined these new point styles as they had not been observed in the better-known sites on the open plains to the east; they were restricted to the mountains and/or mountain-plains border region.

Although never construed as a cultural entity, Lovell Constricted points have been recovered in a number of sites in south-central Montana and north-central Wyoming. They have been recovered in Layer 14 at the Mummy Cave site and dated to ca. 8,000 BP (Husted and Edgar 2002). The lowest level in Pictograph Cave in south-central Montana produced two points very similar to the Sorenson and Bottleneck specimens (Mulloy 1958, figs. 6, 7, 8; Husted and Edgar 2002:98). These points are in the same layer as specimens that look like Pryor Stemmed points, as well as Castle River points (discussed below); however, no dates are available for the apparently palimpsestic occupation. Frison (1976:163) noted the recovery of Lovell Constricted points below Pryor Stemmed points at Medicine Lodge Coulee where they were dated to ca. 8,400 BP. The Lookingbill site produced four points of which two point bases (Frison 1983, fig. 4j, k) are similar to Lovell Constricted points, but dates are not available. The Lovell Constricted material at the Sorenson site dates to ca. 7,900 BP, while at the Bottleneck site it dates ca. 8,300 BP (Husted 1969:82). Generally, these points tend to be associated with chipped stone tools and fauna that include small amounts of bighorn sheep, mule deer, and bison. Grinding stones are also present, presumably used for processing seeds (Frison 1976:164).

The Pryor Stemmed horizon or bibevelled projectile point complex is largely restricted to the Big Horn Mountain area (Frison 1976:165; Frison and Grey 1980). At the Medicine Lodge Creek site, Pryor Stemmed points were dated to ca. 8,200 BP; they were stratigraphically above Lovell

Constricted points (Frison 1976:165; 1992:328). Frison (1976:165) also reported Pryor Stemmed points at Schiffer Cave on the north fork of the Powder River on the eastern slopes of the Big Horn Mountains dating ca. 8,500 BP, and at rock shelter 48JO303 in the southern Big Horn Mountains dating ca. 7,900 BP. The Pryor Stemmed material at the Sorenson site, Occupation III, dates to ca. 7,600 BP, while at the Bottleneck site, Occupation III dates ca. 8,100 BP (Husted 1969:82). An undated specimen similar to the Pryor Stemmed type may also occur at Birdshead Cave in the lower part of Level II (Bliss 1950:189, fig. 58, L II), in the Wind River Basin, Wyoming.

Initially, Husted (1969:81–97) suggested that a Mountain-Plains culture might exist coevally with the Cody tradition, or perhaps earlier. This echoed the findings at the Mummy Cave site where Cody materials were absent. In Alberta, Reeves (1969:28) agreed with this interpretation noting that DgPm 1 in Waterton Lakes National Park, like the Sorenson site in Husted's (1969) study, produced Cody points in association with lanceolate points. Later he considered the same assemblage to fit into Swanson's (1962:155) Mountain-Plains culture, which reflected the earliest people in the Rocky Mountains of southeast Idaho and western Montana (Reeves 1972:129). By 1973, Reeves (1973:1247) used the term *Plains/Mountain* to refer to late Early Prehistoric cultural complexes on the east flank of the Rocky Mountains from Wyoming to Alberta, in contrast to coeval northern Plains sites. Driver (1978:97–98) developed a classification system in which the Ptolemy subphase, ca. 9,000 to 7,500 BP, roughly coincided with the Reeves' Plains/Mountain culture. Driver's (1978:98) subphase relied on Agate Basin, Pryor Stemmed, Lovell Constricted, Lusk, and Cascade points as diagnostics. Although never formally defined, the archaeological material dating to about 8,500–7,500 BP from the east flank of the Rocky Mountains, at least in Alberta, has been labelled the Plains/Mountain complex.

The Sites

The lack of a clear definition for the Plains/Mountain complex in Alberta suggests an examination of assemblages immediately postdating the Scottsbluff-Eden phase might assist in delineating the range of cultural material for this period. Thus, in order to establish the nature of the Plains/Mountain complex, assemblages dating immediately after 8,500 BP with radiocarbon dates from good contexts will be outlined below. The following sites are used to formally establish criteria for the Plains/Mountain complex (see Plate 8 and Figure 9).

PLATE 8 Plains/Mountains points. Illustrated are DjPm 36, Welsch Locality, Component 1 (a and b); DjPm 36, Welsch Locality, Component 2 (c–h); DjPm 36, Welsch Locality, Component 3 (i, k–o); the Maple Leaf site (DjPo 47) (j); the Stonepine site (EgPn 480), Component 2 (p and r) and EhPv43 (q). Photo credit: Bison Historical Services Limited (a–i, k–p, r); Alison Landals (j), Alberta Culture and Community Spirit (q).

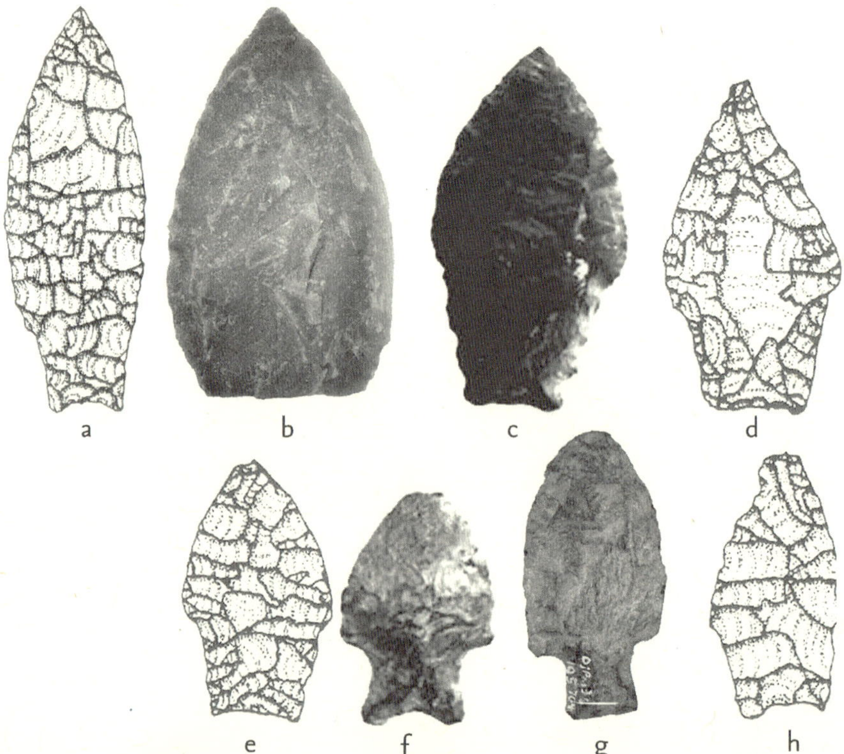

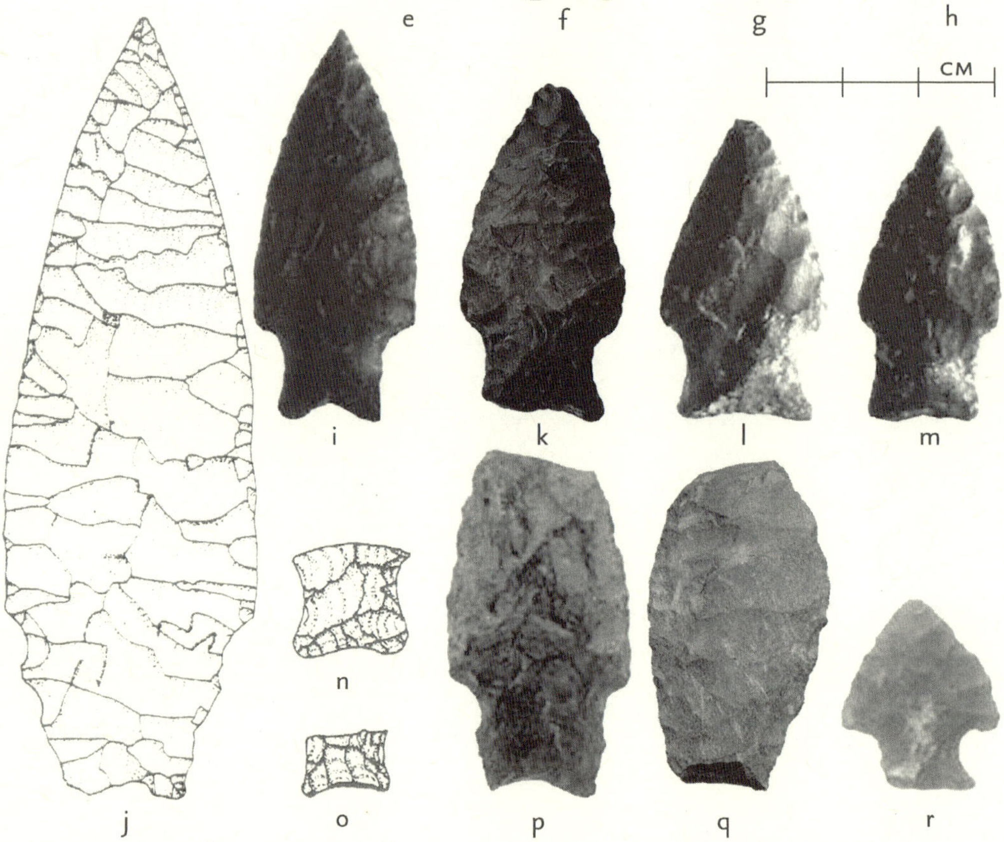

FIGURE 9
Plains / Mountain sites within Alberta

Maple Leaf (DjPo 47). The Maple Leaf site is a multicomponent site on a terrace immediately above the Crowsnest River, south of Bellevue in the Crowsnest Pass (Landals 1986:37; Driver 1982). The earliest component represented a bighorn sheep-processing site (Driver 1982) and a hunting stand or cache (Landals 1986:66). The component was recovered in clay that contained a bison kill dated to 7,200 +/- 230 BP (RL-876). The component overlay a layer of marl and underlay a layer of Mazama Ash. The site was found in 1973, tested in 1976, and excavated during 1977 and 1978 with 36 m^2 excavated (Landals 1986; Driver 1982). Driver (1982) presented material from the 1977 excavations in an analysis of the oldest component.

Two points were recovered in a backhoe trench beside the 1977 excavation. The points were recovered in the same basal clays as the sheep bones. One point was a Lovell Constricted point and the second was a non-diagnostic midsection (Reeves and Driver 1978; Driver 1982:270). In terms of the faunal assemblage (n = 526), the sheep bones were recovered in a small cluster, and were interpreted as *Ovis canadensis*. Some bone exhibits cut marks, ruling out natural death. At least three animals were present: two subadults and an adult. The absence of certain bones, such as phalanges, metapodials, vertebrae, and ribs, suggested discrete portions of the carcass were brought to this location from a kill site (Driver 1982:268–269). Butchering units likely included three forelimbs, two pairs of mandibles, a hindlimb, a distal hindlimb, and a small portion of a ribcage. A single fragment of a bison humerus shaft was recovered and was interpreted as an expedient meat-stripping tool (Driver 1982:269). Other faunal remains were scattered, sparse, and fragmentary; there was evidence of three bison and a canid (Landals 1986:56). No features or additional stone tools were noted in the main excavation areas. A single radiocarbon date was obtained for the site. Bison bone in the same stratigraphic context as the sheep bone produced a date of ca. 8,550 BP (see Table 7). This date fits well with those expected for Lovell Constricted material.

Stonepine (EgPn 480), Component 2. The Stonepine site is described above in the section on the Scottsbluff-Eden phase. Component 2 contained Lovell Constricted material below Mazama Ash (de Mille and Head 2001:56). Three points were recovered, including a Lovell Constricted point, a large corner-notched point, and a non-diagnostic corner-notched base. The corner-notched point is similar to contemporary Burmis barbed points (see Country Hills complex below). The remaining eighty-six tools included bifaces (n = 8), end scrapers (n = 2), side scrapers (n = 3), a possible spurred scraper, wedges (n = 3), choppers (n = 4), retouched lithics (n = 8), a utilized flake, a hammerstone, anvils (n = 2), bipolar cores (n = 2), multi-directional cores (n = 17) and a unidirectional core. The lithic assemblage was dominated by sandstone (34.3%), siltstone (30%), and quartzite (19.1%), with minor amounts of chert (8.5%), chalcedony (1.4%), and quartz (1.3%).

TABLE 7 Radiocarbon dates for Plains/Mountain sites (calibrated by OxCal 3.10 [Ramsey 2005])

Site [LAB NO.]	Conventional ^{14}C Age	$^{13}C/^{12}C$ Ratio	Material	Calibration	Reference
EgPn 480 [BETA-127235]	9540 +/- 70	?	collagen	8300–6500 B.C. (p = 0.954)	de Mille and Head 2001
DjPo 47 [RL-873]	8630 +/- 270	-20.0‰	collagen	8500–7000 B.C. (p = 0.954)	Driver 1982:267; Morlan n.d.
DjPm 36, C1 [AECV-1380C]	8390+/- 120	-18.6‰	collagen	7600–7050 B.C. (p = 0.954)	Van Dyke 1994:157
DjPm 36, C1 [AECV-1379C]	8180 +/- 110	-18.9‰	collagen	7550–6800 B.C. (p = 0.954)	Van Dyke 1994:157
DjPm 36, C1 [BETA-43906]	7170 +/- 80	-20.0‰	collagen	rejected	Van Dyke 1994:157
DjPm 36, C2 [BETA-43905]	8250 +/- 110	?	?	7540–7040 B.C. (p = 0.954)	Van Dyke 1994:148
DjPm 36, C2 [AECV-1369C]	8190 +/- 110	-17.4‰	collagen	7550–6800 B.C. (p = 0.954)	Van Dyke 1994:148; Morlan n.d.
DjPm 36, C2 [AECV-1374C]	8160 +/- 110	-17.6‰	collagen	7500–6800 B.C. (p = 0.954)	Van Dyke 1994:148; Morlan n.d.
DjPm 36, C2 [AECV-1370C]	8110 +/- 110	-15.6‰	collagen	7450–6650 B.C. (p = 0.954)	Van Dyke 1994:148; Morlan n.d.
DjPm 36, C2 [AECV-1372C]	8090 +/- 110	-18.4‰	collagen	7450–6650 B.C. (p = 0.954)	Van Dyke 1994:148; Morlan n.d.
DjPm 36, C2 [AECV-1373C]	7920 +/- 110	-17.2‰	collagen	7100–6500 B.C. (p = 0.954)	Van Dyke 1994:148; Morlan n.d.
DjPm 36, C2 [AECV-1371C]	7890 +/- 110	-17.9‰	collagen	7100–6500 B.C. (p = 0.954)	Van Dyke 1994:148; Morlan n.d.
DjPm 36, C2 [AEVC-1207C]	7830 +/- 160	-18.2‰	collagen	7150–6350 B.C. (p = 0.954)	Van Dyke 1994:148; Morlan n.d.
DjPm 36, C2 [BETA-38788]	7620 +/- 60	?	?	6600–6380 B.C. (p = 0.954)	Van Dyke 1994:148
DjPm 36, C2 [BETA-38787]	7070 +/- 80	?	?	rejected	Van Dyke 1994:148
DjPm 36, C3 [AECV-1378C]	8000 +/- 120	-18.4‰	collagen	7300–6600 B.C. (p = 0.954)	Van Dyke 1994:188
DjPm 36, C3 [AECV-762C]	7890 +/- 130	-22.4‰	collagen	7100–6450 B.C. (p = 0.954)	Van Dyke 1994:188
DjPm 36, C3 [AECV-742C]	7690 +/- 210	-20.2‰	collagen	7100–6050 B.C. (p = 0.954)	Van Dyke 1994:188
DjPm 36, C3 [AECV-1377C]	7450 +/- 100	-18.6‰	collagen	6470–6080 B.C. (p = 0.954)	Van Dyke 1994:188

The faunal assemblage (n = 1,219) included remains of at least two bison, a moose or elk, a deer, and a canid. The bison limb elements were most numerous and fragmented, suggesting meat sections were brought to the campsite and processed for marrow (de Mille and Head 2001:78). Burned and calcine bone was also observed. A dark reddish soil stain was interpreted as a hearth; it contained bits of charcoal and burned bone. As well, 3,405.4 grams of FBR were recovered from the site, most of which was interpreted to have resulted from immersing hot rocks in water for stone boiling (de Mille and Head 2001:63).

The researchers noted the similarity in the form of the Lovell Constricted point to others at the Welsch site (DjPm 36) and DjPo 47, which date between 8,500 and 8,000 BP (de Mille and Head 2001:87). A single radiocarbon date of about 9,500 BP was obtained (Table 7; de Mille and Head 2001:85). De Mille and Head (2001) suggested that the date is about 1,000 years earlier than expected and may possibly be associated with the underlying Scottsbluff material in Component 1 (de Mille and Head 2001:88).

DjPm 36, Welsch Locality, Components 1 to 3. DjPm 36, Welsch Locality, is located on a series of terraces at the confluence of the North Fork of the Oldman River and the Crowsnest River (Van Dyke 1994:116). The Welsch Locality was named after the landowner (Van Dyke 1994:117). Three components were identified with palaeosols at various depths across the various blocks. The site was originally recorded in 1965, tested in 1985–1986, and excavated in 1988–1990. Four excavation blocks (north, central, west, and south) yielded a total of 278 m^2 (Van Dyke 1994:116).

Component 1 was represented in both the north and west blocks. It produced a Lovell Constricted point and a large lanceolate point blade in association with a post-mould, a hearth, and a bone concentration (Van Dyke 1994:150). Other tools recovered included a biface, a pebble chert core, and a cobble core chopper. The lithic assemblage, although small, was dominated by siltstone, miscellaneous cherts, and quartzite (Van Dyke 1994:152, table 6). The faunal assemblage (n = 5,230) yielded an undifferentiated small ungulate, a small mammal, at least four bison, and a bivalve shell (Van Dyke 1994:150). A fair amount of the bone was burned or calcine. While bone was generally scattered across the occupation floor, one concentration consisted of a portion of an articulated adult animal (i.e., vertebrae and ribs). A hearth feature produced a scatter of burned and calcine bone, unmodified cobbles (n = 6), and FBR spalls (n = 3). A cultural origin for the post-mould seems likely but a firm interpretation of the feature was not provided (Van Dyke 1994:156). Three radiocarbon dates in the west block suggest an age of 8,200 BP (see Table 7; the youngest date was rejected) (Van Dyke 1994:157).

Component 2 was largely present in the south block of the excavation. Eleven projectile points were associated with a massive bone bed in an abandoned braided river channel system (Van Dyke 1994:157). The points included four Lovell Constricted/Cowley Stemmed points, one Castle River stemmed, a straight stemmed, and a lanceolate point. The remaining specimens were too fragmentary to be classified. Other tools included core tools (n=26), bifaces (n=9), retouched flakes (n=7), end scrapers (n=3), unifaces (n=3), and a hammerstone (Van Dyke 1994:157). The faunal assemblage (n=150,191) was mainly bison with evidence of deer, large and small canids, and bird. A minimum of 107 bison were represented in the excavated material (Van Dyke 1994:160). In addition, six identifiable and twenty-eight fragmented bison fetal bones were recovered. There were many butchering sections but a scarcity of direct evidence of butchering; only four bones exhibited cut marks, four bones exhibited impact scars, one bone had hack marks, and fifty-three bones exhibited green bone fracture. In addition, a radius had a projectile point tip stuck in it (Van Dyke 1994:166). Calcine and burned bone occurred in concentrations throughout the bone bed, in blackened soils. The size of the kill site and the lack of butchering led the researcher to question whether the mechanism of the kill was cultural or not. The site might represent a natural event that was scavenged. The researcher remained neutral on this issue (Van Dyke 1994:180). Ten radiocarbon dates were obtained for the bone bed. One date was an outlier (i.e., 7,070 +/- 70 BP, Beta-38787); averaging the remaining dates produced an age of ca. 8,006 BP (Table 7). If the bone deposits in the deepest part of the channel are considered a separate event from the bone bed, an average of five dates produces an age date of 8,126 BP; the overlying material, estimated on four dates would average 7,857 BP. This supports the possible inference of two separate episodes of occupation.

Component 3 occurred in the west, north, and south excavation blocks. Five points were recovered: three Castle River stemmed points and two smaller stem fragments. An additional Castle River stemmed point was recovered from the backhoe spoil pile, which consisted of material from just above the occupation. Other lithic items recovered from the site included bifaces (n=4), an end scraper, a uniface, a drill, cores (n=6), marginally retouched flakes (n = 5), a hammerstone, unmodified cobbles (n = 5), and FBR (n = 13). Silicified siltstone, quartzite, and argillite dominated the lithic assemblage. The faunal assemblage (n = 4,757) was dominated by bison bone fragments. Non-bison items included a large canid limb fragment, deer teeth, mandible and metapodial fragments, and a few small mammal fragments (Van Dyke 1994:184). A minimum of three bison was present, based on two left astragali and fetal bone. Well-defined features were absent but areas exhibiting surface burns or reddened soils were observed (Van Dyke 1994:185). In the west block a feature intersected during backhoe testing contained unmodified cobbles, FBR, stained soil, burned bone and flecks of charcoal; the distribution of debitage also centred on the feature (Van Dyke 1994:185). In the south block, a stone-lined hearth was identified with a scatter of bone and debitage. Four radiocarbon dates were obtained for this occupation. They suggested an age of about 7,700 BP (Table 7).

Narrows (DgPl 4). The Narrows site is located on a rocky spur that forms a constriction between the Upper and Lower Waterton Lakes in Waterton Lakes National Park (Milne Brumley 1971:75). The site received its name from this constriction. The site, with 64 m² excavated, is on a spit on the west side of the narrows. Discrete cultural components could not be defined because of disturbance and compressed stratigraphy (Milne Brumley 1971:78). A variety of point specimens was recovered, including one base of a lanceolate point interpreted as Lovell Constricted (Milne Brumley 1971:82–83).

Plains/Mountain: Transition from Spears to Darts in the Foothills/Mountains

A review of sites immediately postdating 8,500 BP illustrates that Alberta's cultural sequence is somewhat different from the sequence to the south developed by Husted (1969), Frison (1976, Frison and Grey 1980), and others. Still, lanceolate points comparable to Lovell Constricted defined in Montana and Wyoming occur in the eastern flanks of the Rocky Mountains in Alberta. They tend to date to ca. 8,500–8,000 BP. However, they exhibit a slightly different basal configuration not found in the south. By about 8,000 BP, these lanceolate points are found in contexts with Castle River stemmed points, with the latter becoming more common from shortly after 8,000 BP until about 7,500 BP. The Plains/Mountain complex is captured in this developmental sequence.

These lanceolate points do not appear to be true Lovell Constricted points as defined by Husted (1969). The specimen from DjPm 36, Component 1, most closely resembles Lovell Constricted (Van Dyke 1994:153). The other points from this period (i.e., Maple Leaf site, EgPn 480, the Narrows site, and Component 2 of DjPm 36) all exhibit a stem with subtle, multiple shoulders that lead into a gradually outwardly flaring stem. It might be best to think of these points as a northern variant of the Lovell Constricted point given their overall temporal, geographic, and morphological similarity. The subsequent Castle River stemmed points exhibit a fair amount of variability. The points have fairly pronounced shoulders with short, relatively straight stems that exhibit either a straight or concave base. In addition to the Castle River points, there were two small specimens (Van Dyke 1994:183, fig. 87d and e) that were very similar to a stem fragment recovered at the Hawkwood site in the foothills at Calgary (Van Dyke and Stewart 1985: plate 13, no. 1). Van Dyke (1994:188) noted that the Hawkwood stem fragment was associated with a Salmon River point and a Lusk point, and was dated to ca. 8,250 BP.

Another interpretation of this small data set would have the sequence from DjPm 36 providing a "study" of Lovell Constricted materials changing slowly to Castle River materials in situ. Recently, Hutching (1997) suggested that fracture rates in Palaeoindian lanceolate points indicated that they were propelled by atlatls rather than thrown by hand. Hughes (1998) examined four hunting systems — thrusting spear, throwing spear, atlatl/dart, and bow/arrow — using engineering principles. Like Hutchings (1997), Hughes found evidence that atlatls were used with lanceolate points. Interestingly, she argued that the change from large lanceolate points to smaller notched points reflected the appearance of fletching on the darts; the fletching was interpreted as helping accuracy, velocity, and lift of the dart (Hughes 1998:397). Based on the assemblage from Mummy Cave, she suggested that the transition and the appearance of fletching was about 7,600 BP. This coincides roughly with the Alberta sequence, so the Lovell Constricted and Castle River materials possibly indicate the initial steps towards the transition. Thus, the wide range of projectile point variability at this time period may partially be reflecting experimentation taking place in the flight characteristics of the dart and atlatl.

The limited sample of non-projectile point tools does not lend itself to further analysis. As mentioned, the recovery of the possible spurred scraper from EgPn 480 harkens back to a Palaeoindian past. In contrast, the hammerstone and two anvils from the same site may reflect changing times when increasingly thorough processing was required within subsistence strategies. Still, an analysis of the functions of these early possible grinding specimens has yet to occur. The apparent recovery of a corner-notched point associated with the Lovell Constricted-like specimen at EgPn 480 is also notable and may relate to the subsequent Country Hills complex. The association of stemmed and corner-notched points, if valid, makes EgPn 480 comparable to the Hawkwood site in terms of exhibiting transitional hunting technology at an early time.

Taken as a group, the lithic raw materials from EgPn 480 and DjPm 36 show a heavy reliance on local sources. Quartzite, silicified siltstone, and siltstone each constitute about 20 percent of the raw materials. Fine-grained materials such as argillite (4%), chalcedony (2%), Avon chert (2%) and miscellaneous cherts (7%) occur infrequently. The fauna reflects the foothills/mountains location of the sites in this complex. Bison continue to be the most commonly recovered animal. Importantly, DjPm 36, Component 2, may represent a large bison kill. However, some scepticism on its cultural origin was outlined. Canids are also relatively common. Mountain sheep were clearly a focus at the Maple Leaf site. Deer and other cervids, such as moose or elk, appear to have been taken. A single bird is also represented in the faunal material from the sites.

Few features were associated with the sites of this complex. Surface hearths were observed in Components 1 and 3 of DjPm 36. A stone-lined basin hearth was also recorded in Component 3 of DjPm 36. Very little FBR was recovered in these sites. DjPm 36 produced three pieces of FBR in Component 1 and eleven pieces in Component 3. The only site with any real amount of FBR was EgPn 480. The general lack of pit features for stone boiling suggests the FBR is being created as spall from associated hearth ring rocks.

Other sites from areas adjacent to the province may fit into the Plains/Mountain complex. Conforming to Reeves' (1973) original vision, these sites are located along the eastern flanks of the Rocky Mountains of Alberta with ties to similar sites in Montana and Wyoming. Some similar assemblages to the Plains/Mountain complex are known to the east in Manitoba. Pettipas (1985:50, fig. 4a, b) illustrated Manitoba points that resemble Lovell Constricted specimens. As well, Buchner (1981a:42, plate 7d–f) illustrated three specimens similar to Castle River stemmed points. Perhaps the Plains/Mountain complex represents more than people subsisting only in the western foothills: the presence of similar material in the plains periphery to the east might signal an early forest/forest-edge adaptation.

A single specimen from Medicine Lodge Creek site in north-central Wyoming exhibits striking similarity to the northern Lovell Constricted points (Frison 1992:328, fig. 9.3a). The point was dated to ca. 8,050 BP. It postdates some specimens considered to be Pryor Stemmed points, contrary to Husted's (1969) original classification. Otherwise, the above discussion of the southern Lovell Constricted points covers this poorly understood time period and point style.

Castle River stemmed points may have counterparts in the eastern slopes of the United States. Mulloy (1958:33, fig. 6, nos. 5, 6, 9–12) illustrated a series of points recovered in the oldest level of Pictograph Cave, Montana, in association with basally thinned and Scottsbluff points. They appear to exhibit the attributes of Castle River stemmed points.

The Paint Rock Canyon V (48BH349) site is a large rock shelter high in the wall of a deep canyon on the eastern slopes of the Big Horn Mountains, north-central Wyoming (Frison 1976:168, 1991a:40–41). Two occupations were observed with radiocarbon dates 8,140 +/- 150 BP (RL-391) and 8,340 +/- 160 BP (RL-160) (Frison 1976:168; Frison 1991a:27). Mountain sheep and mule deer were recovered from both levels. A distinct point and two similar bases were also recovered (Frison 1976:168, fig. 8.10e; Frison 1991a:73, fig. 2.38e–f). The Paint Rock Canyon V specimens are morphologically very similar to specimens of the same age from DjPm 36, Welsch Locality, Components 2 and 3. Frison (1976:168, fig. 8.10e) noted that a similar specimen and broken base were recovered at the Medicine Lodge Creek site. Frison (1976:168, 1991a:74) argued that these occur at the same time as the Pryor Stemmed complex but are significantly different, perhaps reflecting a variant of the form. The Lookingbill site in northwestern Wyoming also produced three basally indented points in association with a lanceolate point. They are quite similar to Castle River stemmed specimens and were estimated to date to about 8,000 BP (Frison 1983:9). Frison (1983:9) suggested this material may represent a transitional stage between terminal Palaeoindian lanceolate and Early Plains Archaic side-notched points.

At the Sawmill Canyon (10BT62) site in Birch Creek, eastern Idaho, a Pinto point was recovered during a series of tests (Swanson et al. 1964, fig. 36, jj). This specimen is strikingly similar to the Castle River specimens. It exhibits an indented base with parallel sides and soft shoulders that lead into a leaf-shaped blade. Swanson et al. (1964:72) labelled the specimen

Pinto, based on similarities it exhibited to Wormington's (1957:165–166) Pinto Basin points in Riverside County, California. The aforementioned correlations to Alberta materials provide a better fit both morphologically and geographically.

In summary, Lovell Constricted projectile points exhibit strong similarities to their counterparts to the south, but subtle morphological differences are present. The components at the Welsch site might represent the development of this northern Lovell Constricted material into Castle River stemmed materials. Although a comparable sequence is not known to the south, examples of similar point forms do occur. The presence of similar forms to the east in Manitoba entice speculation that a forest/forest-edge adaptation may be represented in the Lovell Constricted/Castle River materials. Pryor Stemmed materials do not appear to be present in Alberta.

LUSK COMPLEX (CA. 8,300 TO 7,500 BP)

The Lusk complex is a poorly understood set of material that dates ca. 7,700 BP. The Lusk assignment falls upon a group of lanceolate points that immediately follow the Cody tradition on the Plains. Some of these points include Frederick, Angostura, Allen, and Haskett points. For some researchers, Lusk would fall within the Late Plano complex (Arnold 1985). Others would classify all the various point styles that follow the Cody tradition under the rubric of the Parallel-Oblique Point complex (Bradley 1993:260). Still others call this material the Lanceolate Point tradition (Pettipas 1996a:44). A Lusk point is usually made on a flake with a triangular cross-section such that the projectile point tends to have a plano-convex cross-section. The base is usually concave compared to Frederick points and the flaking is more haphazard and less controlled (Irwin-Williams et al. 1973:51; Frison 1991a:69). Lusk points appear similar in form to the Angostura type (Irwin-Williams et al. 1973:51) or the Haskett type (Butler 1968).

Lusk material was originally identified at the Betty Greene site near Lusk, Wyoming (Irwin-Williams et al. 1973). Initially a date of ca. 7,900 was obtained for the site; however, it is now known to exhibit more than one component, bringing in to question the age of each component (Frison 1991a). Lusk material was also reported at Locality II of the Hell Gap site where it is believed to postdate the Frederick material at Locality I (Irwin-Williams et al. 1973:45). The age of the Lusk complex is estimated to be about 8,000 to 7,500 BP, based on the Hell Gap sequence (Irwin-Williams et al. 1973:52).

Frison (1991a:393–394) considered Lusk points to be technologically related to Frederick, Allen, and Angostura points. He argued that serial pressure thinning, which produced a parallel-oblique pattern, separates these points from Palaeoindian points. Holder and Wike (1949) have called this group of material the Frontier complex. Frison (1991a:394) argued that while Alberta and Cody technology developed on the plains, the Frontier complex developed in the high elevations of the interior mountain west. It is possible that Lusk materials bear some relationship to Plains/Mountain materials.

In Alberta, Reeves (1969:24) initially suggested that Lusk and Frederick complexes dated between 8,500 and 7,500 BP, based on surface collections similar to sequences known to the south. At the time, Reeves (1969:24) noted that both point forms were rarely encountered in surface collections, especially the Frederick point. In a subsequent report, Reeves (1972) listed sites in the Big Horn Canyon, the Mummy Cave site, and the Shoup Rockshelter as containing Lusk material. Recently, Vivian and Reeves (1999:24–26) provided a stronger argument for the Lusk complex in Alberta, citing Reeves' (1972:113) previous work as well as sites in the Crowsnest Pass, the Sibbald Creek site, Hawkwood, Tuscany, and more recently discovered EgPn 428. Despite these efforts, the Lusk complex remains poorly understood and rarely recognized in Alberta.

The Sites

Sites that exhibit Lusk points often have them as the sole diagnostic point in the component; however, they occasionally occur with notched point forms. The following reviews sites with Lusk points and associated materials that have been recovered from dated context within Alberta (see Plate 9 and Figure 10).

Hawkwood (EgPm 179). The Hawkwood site is a multicomponent campsite in two sediment basins on the south side of the lower slopes of Nose Hill in Calgary (Van Dyke and Stewart 1985). Six distinct components were recognized including, from oldest to youngest, Lusk, two unidentified, Mummy Cave, Oxbow, and an Old Women's component. The Lusk occupation, Component 1, was only observed in a palaeosol in the east basin. During 1979–1980, a total of 62 m^2 was excavated within the east basin. The excavations mitigated anticipated impacts of a housing development.

PLATE 9 Lusk points. Illustrated are points from the Boss Hill site (FdPe 4) (a–e); the Hawkwood site (EgPm 179) (f–i); the Scapa site (ElPa 1) (j); DgPl 1 (k and n); DgPm 1 (l and o); DjPo 78 (m); and the Tuscany site (EgPn 377) (p). Photo credit: Alberta Culture and Community Spirit (a–e, j, k–p); Royal Alberta Museum (f–i).

FIGURE 10
Lusk sites within Alberta.

In Component 1, a Lusk point, a "Salmon River" point, an atlatl point, two point midsections, a point tip, and a stemmed base were recovered (Van Dyke and Stewart 1985). Other tools included a symmetrical bipoint lanceolate biface, ovate bifaces, a split pebble end scraper, spall tools (n = 2), a bifacial chopper, unifacial choppers (n = 2), retouched flakes (n = 6), a possible grinder, and cores (n = 37) (Van Dyke and Stewart 1985:21–31). The large number of cores suggested primary core reduction was occurring at the site. Most of the debitage was quartzite (59.7%) with some siltstone (20.1%) and pebble cherts (15%). Two of the chert tools were inferred to have been heat-treated.

TABLE 8 Radiocarbon dates for Lusk sites (calibrated by OxCal 3.10 [Ramsey 2005])

Site [LAB NO.]	Conventional ^{14}C Age	$^{13}C/^{12}C$ Ratio	Material	Calibration	Reference
EgPm 179 [RL-1554]	8330 +/- 330	-20.0‰	collagen	8300–6500 B.C. (p = 0.954)	Van Dyke and Stewart 1985:39; Morlan n.d.
EgPn 428 [BETA-125408]	6840 +/- 70	n/a	?	rejected	Vivian and Reeves 1999
DjPo 78 [RL-512]	1600 +/- 100	-20.0‰	collagen	rejected (not associated with material)	Morlan n.d.
DjPm 1 [GX-1435]	8220 +/- 260	-25.0‰	charcoal	7800–6400 B.C. (p = 0.954)	Reeves 1972; Morlan n.d.
EgPn 377 [TO-9262]	9950 +/- 120	?	?	10050–9200 B.C. (p = 0.954)	Oetelaar 2004b:735; Siegfried 2002
EgPn 377 [TO-9263]	7840 +/- 100	?	?	7050–6450 B.C. (p = 0.954)	Oetelaar 2004b:735; Siegfried 2002
EgPn 377 [TO-9264]	7610 +/- 70	?	?	6610–6350 B.C. (p = 0.937) 6310–6260 B.C. (p = 0.017)	Oetelaar 2004b:735; Siegfried 2002
EgPn 377 [OXA-11622]	7475 +/- 45	?	?	6430–6240 B.C. (p = 0.954)	Oetelaar 2004b:735; Siegfried 2002
EgPn 377 [OXA-11583]	7310 +/- 45	?	?	6250–6060 B.C. (p = 0.954)	Oetelaar 2004b:735; Siegfried 2002
FdPe 4 [S-1251]	7875 +/-130	-20.0‰	bone	7100–6450 B.C. (p = 0.954)	Doll 1982:139; Morlan n.d.
FdPe 4 [S-1371]	7750 +/- 105	-25.0‰	charcoal	7050–6440 B.C. (p = 0.954)	Doll 1982:139; Morlan n.d.

A single adult bison was represented in the faunal assemblage. The highly fragmented assemblage was interpreted as indicative of marrow extraction (Van Dyke and Stewart 1985:36). Burned and calcine fragments were recovered, suggesting the use of bone as a fuel. Fragments of some of the meaty bones such as the humerus and femur suggested transportation of limb elements to the site for processing. Two hearths were present. One hearth (1.5 × 0.5 m) was represented by a soil stain associated with charcoal and small, unidentifiable fragments of burned and calcine bone (Van Dyke and Stewart 1985:38). The second hearth (0.4 × 0.2 m), a few metres to the southwest of the first, was also an elongate concentration of burned and unburned bone (Van Dyke and Stewart 1985:38). The two hearths were outside the areas suggested as shelters. Clusters of cobbles on the living floor have been interpreted as anchors for one or more shelters. A single radiocarbon date of about 8,330 BP was obtained (see Table 8). The excavators suggested that the inhabitants of the Hawkwood site stalked small herds of bison from this fairly open campsite during mild weather (Van Dyke and Stewart 1985:40–41).

Tuscany (EgPn 377). The Tuscany site is a multicomponent site in a depression near the edge of a terrace overlooking the Bow River Valley in northwest Calgary (Oetelaar 1998:2). Four cultural components were differentiated: the lowest was a Lusk component, followed by a Bitterroot component, then an Oxbow component, and lastly a Besant/Old Women's component. A total of 92 m² was excavated in the main excavation area prior to the beginning of a housing development.

A single Lusk point was recovered from the lowest component of the site. Blood residue analysis suggested contact with a canid (i.e., dog, wolf, or coyote). Other tools recovered included biface fragments (n = 2), hammerstones, and an edge-modified flake. The faunal assemblage included elements from bison, elk, mountain sheep, deer, antelope, black bear, mountain lion, hare, cottontail, muskrat, vole, lemming, grouse and duck. A small hearth, 0.25 m in diameter, had a shallow basin-shaped profile. The faunal material was concentrated east of the hearth while debitage was adjacent to the southeast part of the hearth. Some FBR was recovered from the site. Although the FBR pieces were interpreted as products of rapid heating and cooling, the researcher warned that such conditions can be created by stone boiling, sweat bathing, or oven roasting (Oetelaar 1997:8).

Four radiocarbon dates were obtained from this component and one from beneath it (Table 8). The most reliable date came from charred plant remains from the hearth, which produced the age estimate of 7,840 BP (Siegfried 2002). The Lusk point was associated with this feature. The date of the underlying material was ca. 10,000 BP. In addition, purified bone collagen from a bone near the hearth produced an age estimate of 7,610 BP. The two other dates are slightly more recent.

EgPn 428. EgPn 428 is a campsite on a large bench below the west end of the Paskapoo Slopes, overlooking the Bow River on the west side of Calgary (Vivian and Reeves 1999:1). A single cultural component was observed below Mazama Ash. A total of 120 m² was excavated between 1996 and 1998 (Vivian and Reeves 1999). The excavation was part of mitigative action undertaken prior to the development of a subdivision.

One Lusk point and one Lusk base fragment were recovered in association with two activity areas (Areas 1 and 2) and a refuse disposal area (Area 3). Other tools recovered included bifaces (n = 2), biface fragments (n = 6), spurred scrapers (n = 5), end scrapers (n = 8), a graver/awl, spokeshaves (n = 3), burinated/spurred tools (n = 5), a utilized core, and utilized/retouched flakes (n = 9). An antler tine was the only non-lithic tool recovered; the item was highly weathered and no use wear was visible on it (Vivian and Reeves 1999:18). Within the lithic assemblage (n = 1,790), the vast majority of the raw materials used were quartzite (n = 1,443) and Banff chert (n = 283), with a few fine-quality materials such as cherts (n = 23) and a piece of obsidian (Vivian and Reeves 1999:19). The obsidian of the Lusk point was sourced by trace elements to Obsidian Cliffs, Wyoming (Vivian and Reeves 1999:30). The researchers argued that this early site exhibits a high number of formed tools and less expedient tools, in contrast to later cultural assemblages, especially those associated with mass bison kill sites (Vivian and Reeves 1999:20). The blood residue analysis, which indicated bison, bear, deer, sheep, and rabbit, illustrated that the inhabitants returned to the site from a variety of local resource areas (Vivian and Reeves 1999:20).

The faunal assemblage (n = 527) was highly fragmented. Although heavily mineralized and stained, it appeared that a few fragments were calcine or burned (Vivian and Reeves 1999:21). A few identifiable adult bison bones were recovered, as was a fetal or immature bison rib. A number of canid mandible fragments were found in the same unit. A highly weathered bear proximal humerus was recovered. An antler tine from a deer or elk was also found. Areas 1 and 2 were roughly circular areas, about 8 × 8 m, exhibiting the same range of tools and debitage. The researchers interpreted these locales as utilized by discrete domestic groups that shared food resources but maintained their own toolkits (Vivian and Reeves 1999:22). Large fragments of animal bones were discarded in the slough to the south, Area 3. A single date of about 6,840 BP was obtained from a composite sample of bone (Table 8). The date was rejected based on the point style and stratigraphic position well beneath Mazama Ash. The site was interpreted as a warm-weather camp inhabited by two or more families on the northeast side of a slough between 7,750 and 9,000 BP.

Scapa Ribstone (ElPa 1), Basin 4, Component 1. The Scapa Ribstone site is a ribstone on a prominent knoll on the west side of Sullivan Lake with associated campsites (Hanna and Neal 1992). A pipeline passing near the site required mitigative excavations within a series of basins associated with the landform on which the ribstone was located. Basin 4 produced a stratigraphic sequence with a Lusk point in Component 1, a Burmis barbed point in Component 2, no diagnostics in Component 3, a layer of Mazama Ash, a Maple Leaf point in Component 4, Calderwood points in Components 5 and 6, and Pelican Lake material in Component 6. A total of 40 m^2 was excavated in Basin 4 but only 27 m^2 in Component 1.

A single large lanceolate Plano series point base was recovered in the lowest level. The concave base and size suggest it is a Lusk point. Other tools recovered include two cores, a core fragment, and four retouched flakes (Hanna and Neal 1992:96). Eighty-two pieces of debitage reflect mainly late-stage reduction. Petrified wood (48.8%), quartzite (34.1%), chert (8.5%), pebble chert (6.1%) and crystal quartz (2.4%) indicated that primarily local raw materials were used (Hanna and Neal 1992:96). One Montana chert flake and five Swan River chert flakes (7.3%) were considered exotic. The faunal assemblage consisted of three unidentifiable bone fragments (Hanna and Neal 1992:98). A small spalled rock was recovered as were thirteen unmodified cobbles, all randomly distributed. A radiocarbon date was not obtained for the component but it is stratigraphically below Mazama Ash.

Red Rock Canyon (DgPm 1). The Red Rock Canyon site is a multicomponent campsite on the east side of Red Rock Canyon, about 8 m above the channel, in Waterton Lakes National Park (Reeves 1972:47). Four cultural levels were recognized. The lowest level contained two Lusk, two Agate Basin, two Lerma, and two Scottsbluff points (Reeves 1972, table 6). Little bone or FBR was associated with these points but a range of lithic tools and debitage was present. An excavated basin hearth produced a date of about 8,220 BP (Reeves 1972:94). This age estimate falls well within the period expected for Lusk material rather than that of the other diagnostic materials, although an association between the hearth and any of the aforementioned diagnostics was not demonstrated.

Boss Hill (FdPe 4). The Boss Hill site, Locality 2, is located at the base of Boss Hill at the northeast corner of Buffalo Lake. The site produced a long sequence of occupations; the earliest occupation contained two Parkhill lanceolate points, five Boss Hill corner-notched points, and three unidentified point fragments. The remainder of the lithic assemblage consisted of nine bifaces, seven scrapers, a spokeshave, thirteen unifaces, seven cobble tools, four hammerstones, four anvils, and many other pieces of tool fragments and stone debitage (Doll 1982). The faunal assemblage consisted of elements representing five bison, three snowshoe hare, an elk, a black bear, a canid (possibly dog), a fox, a badger, a beaver, a muskrat, a jackrabbit, a few birds, a few fish, and a number of rodents (Doll 1982). All of this material was associated with two hearths, dated to about 7,800 BP (Table 8).

The Parkhill lanceolate points are Lusk-like in form but somewhat wider. In terms of the Boss Hill points, Peck (2006) argued that the two large Boss Hill specimens were fractured across the neck and that the small-bladed, complete specimens provide better examples for delineating a Boss Hill corner-notched type specimen. The redefined Boss Hill corner-notched points exhibit broad corner notching, and an expanding stem, a convex base, grinding on the notches and the base, and shoulders close to right angles but not square with the centreline of the point body. A specimen of similar age and form was noted at the Hawkwood site. As well, the large-bladed Boss Hill specimens that are missing their bases are not unlike the Salmon River specimen at Hawkwood, although all three points are fragmentary (Peck 2006).

Other sites. Four other sites merit mention with regards to the Lusk phase. DgPl 1 is multicomponent kill site and campsite located in the entrance to Pass Creek Valley in Waterton Lakes National Park (Reeves 1972:41). Two Lusk points were recovered from the lower of two levels along with Scottsbluff, Bitterroot, Salmon River, and McKean points. Reeves (1972:56) suggested that a series of closely spaced floors existed but presentation of the data indicates an inability to differentiate these occupations (see Reeves 1972, table 6).

The Mona Lisa (EgPm 3) site is located within the southwest side of downtown Calgary. It is situated on a large remnant terrace with three areas yielding archaeological materials: Localities A, B, and C. A bone bed found at Locality A and B that is overlaid by Mazama Ash was dated to 8,080 +/- 150 BP (GSC-1209) (Wilson 1980:6). At Locality C, the lower component underlying Mazama Ash produced a date of 8,545 +/- 280 BP

(GX-6397 A). While appearing to be cultural, neither of these occupations produced diagnostic materials.

In contrast, the base of a Lusk-like point was recovered in the earliest period of cairn use at Majorville Medicine Wheel (EdPc 1) (Calder 1977:74). The Lusk point was likely picked up as a curiosity during the earliest use of the cairn and included in the structure after its original use-life during Late Palaeoindian times. Otherwise there would be a gap of a few thousand years between the initial start of the cairn and subsequent use.

Lastly, FkOo 8 is a surface scatter at the prairie level above the North Saskatchewan River near its confluence with the Vermilion River (McCullough 1980). A single quartzite Lusk point was recovered in a ploughed field. The scatter also included a siltstone pebble spall and a hammerstone. The site had been ploughed except for an adjacent treed area. The pipeline project that instigated the survey was rerouted to avoid disturbing the treed area (McCullough 1980:35–36). The context of these finds make it difficult to be certain whether the specimens are Lusk points and what materials are associated with them.

Lusk: Transition from Spears to Darts on the Plains

An examination of sites containing lanceolate points with concave bases indicates that these often occur in single-component sites that date ca. 7,700 BP (EgPn 428, EgPn 377, and ElPa 1). These same point forms have also been recovered in association with other point forms, most notably corner-notched specimens (EgPm 179 and FdPe 4). Even in the subsequent archaeological culture, the Country Hills complex, the Everblue Springs site (EgPn 700) and EgPn 230 produced fragments of possible Lusk points within assemblages with barbed, triangular-bladed dart points. The range of point variation at this time mirrors that in the Plains/Mountain complex. It would appear that a transition from unfletched large darts (lanceolate) to fletched dart points may have occurred (Hughes 1998). Experimentation with various dart tips seems natural as the hunting system is being honed over time. This transition appears to have taken place largely during the Plains/Mountain complex and Lusk complex over roughly 1,000 years, from ca. 8,500 to 7,500 BP.

The Lusk toolkit includes bifaces, end scrapers, and retouched flakes; however, a few more pounding/grinding implements appear to be present. As well, a single exquisite bipointed biface from the Hawkwood sites stands out for its craftsmanship and form. The raw materials are largely local in origin. Quartzite and cherts were most prevalent, with petrified wood and siltstone common. Few exotics were recovered although a Lusk point was manufactured on a piece of obsidian from Obsidian Cliffs, Wyoming.

The fauna at Boss Hill and Tuscany were highly varied and included bison, elk, mountain sheep, deer, antelope, black bear, mountain lion, hare, cottontail, muskrat, vole, lemming, canid (possibly dog), fox, badger, beaver, jackrabbit, grouse, duck, and a few fish. In contrast, EgPn 428 and Hawkwood yielded mainly bison and some canid. The difference in these assemblages may represent seasonal strategies or unrecognized cultural diversity. In terms of features, many of the sites exhibit one or two small hearths (Hawkwood, Tuscany, Scapa, and Boss Hill). FBR appears to consist of spalls produced from hearth rocks. At EgPn 428, two activity areas were delimited and interpreted as work areas for domestic groups.

There are few comparable Lusk sites on the adjacent plains. In Saskatchewan, surface finds of Lusk-like points have been noted (Dyck 1983:82–83), but only a single in situ site producing a Late Plano point is known, dated to ca. 7,800 BP (Amundson and Meyer 2003). The St. Louis site is located in central Saskatchewan above the South Saskatchewan River. Within a thin palaeosol was a Late Plano point, a scatter of fauna, FBR and debitage associated with a small hearth (Amundson and Meyer 2003:1). A radiocarbon date of 7,810 +/- 70 BP (Beta-173609) was obtained (Amundson and Meyer 2003:1).

In Wyoming, at the Mummy Cave site, Layers 8 to 12 have numerous lanceolate points with concave bases that date between ca. 8,500 and 8,000 BP (Husted and Edgar 2002:178). This material may be considered Lusk because of the concave bases and lack of parallel oblique flaking (common on Frederick points). Material of similar form and age was also recovered at Medicine Lodge Creek (Frison 1992:328, fig. 9.3g–l). There, it dates to about 8,600 BP (Frison 1992:328). Husted (1969:31, figs. 13 and 14) also recovered Lusk-like points in the earliest occupation of the Mangus site in south-central Montana. This material dates to about 8,600 BP (Husted 1969:82).

In summary, the Lusk complex may represent the transition from spear or unfletched dart points to fletched dart points on the Plains. Apparently, point morphology was manipulated as a variable in utilizing this new technology. The subsistence base also exhibits change. Bison hunting is still prominent but a wide variety of faunal resources are being procured, at least at certain times, by the people who created the Lusk material. Evidence of pounding and grinding tools support an interpretation that resources are being used more thoroughly. These changes are likely in part a response to the Hypsithermal interval reaching its maximum around 9,000–8,000 BP.

Middle Prehistoric Period 4

CA. 7,500 TO 1,500 BP

Buried soils in river valleys indicate increased landscape stability by 8,500 BP. Some data suggest cooler, moister conditions at this time with worldwide glacial expansion, while others predict increasing aridity (Beaudoin and Oetelaar 2003:199–200). The difference is likely a discrepancy between local and broad-scale records, as most authorities infer a trend toward increased aridity beginning around 10,000 BP with a peak about 9,000 to 8,000 BP. The eruption of Mount Mazama in Oregon (now Crater Lake) occurred at roughly 6,730 +/- 40 BP, which produced a significant ash fall event in southern Alberta and much of North America (Zdanowicz et al. 1999). The ash is a very fine-grained, silty material like flour; it darkened the skies of Alberta for up to two days (Beaudoin and Oetelaar 2006). The weak archaeological record for immediately after the ash fall suggests conditions were not particularly good for some time. By 6,000 BP, conditions were still warmer and drier than today, with elevated treelines in the mountains and lower lakes on the plains (Vance et al. 1995). Reeves (1973) suggested that the low frequency of Early Middle Prehistoric period sites, in general, was a product of sampling and not a response to the increased aridity. Recent studies suggest that Hurt's (1966) refugee model best explains the absence of sites (Sheehan 1995). Under this model, Early Middle Prehistoric period sites are predicted to concentrate around reliable water sources such as major river basins. Vance (1991) suggested that by 4,000 BP a regime of climate that was cooler and moister than the preceding millennium may have aided people in establishing themselves in southern Alberta. By 3,000 BP, the Plains had receded southward to its modern distribution relative to the boreal forest. Between ca. 2,000 and 1,000 BP was an interval of infrequent drought, which likely produced abundant and dependable animal resources (Vance 1991:155).

COUNTRY HILLS COMPLEX (CA. 7,500 TO 7,300 BP)

In 1982, an excavation in two small in-filled basins overlooking a glacial outwash channel in northwest Calgary produced a stratified sequence of material that defied classification by the archaeological knowledge of the day (Wright 1983). Material from the Wimpey site (EgPn 146) was recovered both above and below a 15-cm-thick layer of Mazama Ash, ensuring that the recovered items were of some antiquity. The earliest level with cultural material in Area A contained a large triangular barbed point described by the researcher as "Pelican Lake-like" (Wright 1983:125). A second point in this level was originally interpreted as a Mummy Cave point (Wright 1983:125) but its form most resembles the resharpened Pelican Lake-like specimen with which it was associated. The poorly defined occupations lead to the conclusion that no clearly defined sequence of projectile points had been recovered and that early and late Mummy Cave occupations (respectively above and below the ash) may be represented based on the existing understanding of that time period (Wright 1983:155). Beyond this, the points were never named and the cultural components were not further defined.

In 1984, Ronaghan (1992:121–133) revisited the Jensen Spring site (DjPn 90) on a high outwash terrace above the Crowsnest River valley. During testing of the site, he recovered a large Pelican Lake style point below Mazama Ash (Ronaghan 1992:130). Similarities to specimens from Indian Creek, Montana, were noted, as were similarities to the specimens from the Wimpey site. Ronaghan (1992:131) reiterated that firm typological systematics for Early Middle Prehistoric points had not been established. He argued that the deeply corner-notched style of projectile point, bearing some resemblance to Pelican Lake points, may be diagnostic within recognizable Early Middle Prehistoric period components in the foothills area of Alberta (Ronaghan 1992:131).

Large, barbed projectile points were again uncovered in west Calgary in Component 1 of EgPn 230 (Vivian et al. 1998). Vivian, Bosch, and Reeves (1998:15) noted the similarity of some of the specimens from EgPn 230 to Ronaghan's Jensen Spring specimen. They did not commit, however, to any specific relationships between the points and any of the other point assemblages from the numerous sites in the transitional Early Middle Prehistoric period. Nor did they lump the material within the Mummy Cave complex. Rather, they noted that the transitional Early Middle Prehistoric period appeared to exhibit remarkable and rapid technological and/or cultural changes (Vivian et al. 1998:16–17).

The Sites

Although few in number, there are now enough assemblages with diagnostic projectile points and contemporary radiocarbon dates to support Ronaghan's (1992:131) suggestion that they are part of an Early Middle Prehistoric period cultural phenomenon. The broad, bladed points with very pronounced tangs, deep corner-notches, and a stemmed-like appearance have been radiocarbon or relatively dated to about 7,500 BP in a number of sites (see Plate 10 and Figure 11). Brian Ronaghan (personal communication 2006) offered the term *Burmis barbed point* for the diagnostic projectile point, based on the name of a nearby town to the Jensen Spring site. Collectively, the sites yielding Burmis barbed points have been labelled the Country Hills complex, owing to the recovery of the first known in situ Burmis barbed point at the Wimpey site, which is adjacent to Country Hills Boulevard in Calgary. These sites tend to fall within the foothills of the Rocky Mountains, making "Country Hills" a somewhat appropriate moniker. This synthesis of the Early Middle period follows Peck (2005).

Everblue Springs (EgPn 700), Component 1. The Everblue Springs site is a multicomponent bison kill site located in a wide shallow basin in Twelve Mile Coulee, southeast of its junction with Crowchild Trail, in northwest Calgary (Vivian 2007a). The site was named for the Everblue Tree Nursery once located at the spot. There were two components identified at the site. Above Mazama Ash, there was diffuse scatter of material culture. Below Mazama Ash was a large bone bed. In 2006, 104 m^2 were excavated at the site (Vivian 2007a). Archaeological mitigation was carried out at the site prior to the construction of a housing subdivision.

a
b
c
d
e
CM
f
g
h
i
j
k
l
m
n
o

PLATE 10 Burmis barbed points. Illustrated are points from EgPn 625 (a–j); EgPn 633 (k–m); Wimpey (EgPn 146) (n and o); the Everblue Springs site (EgPn 700) (p–t); the Jensen Spring site (DjPn 90), Component 1 (u); the Scapa site (ElPa 1) (v); and EgPn 230 (w–cc). Photo credit: Alberta Culture and Community Spirit (a–m, p–v); ARESCO (n and o); Lifeways of Canada Limited (w–cc).

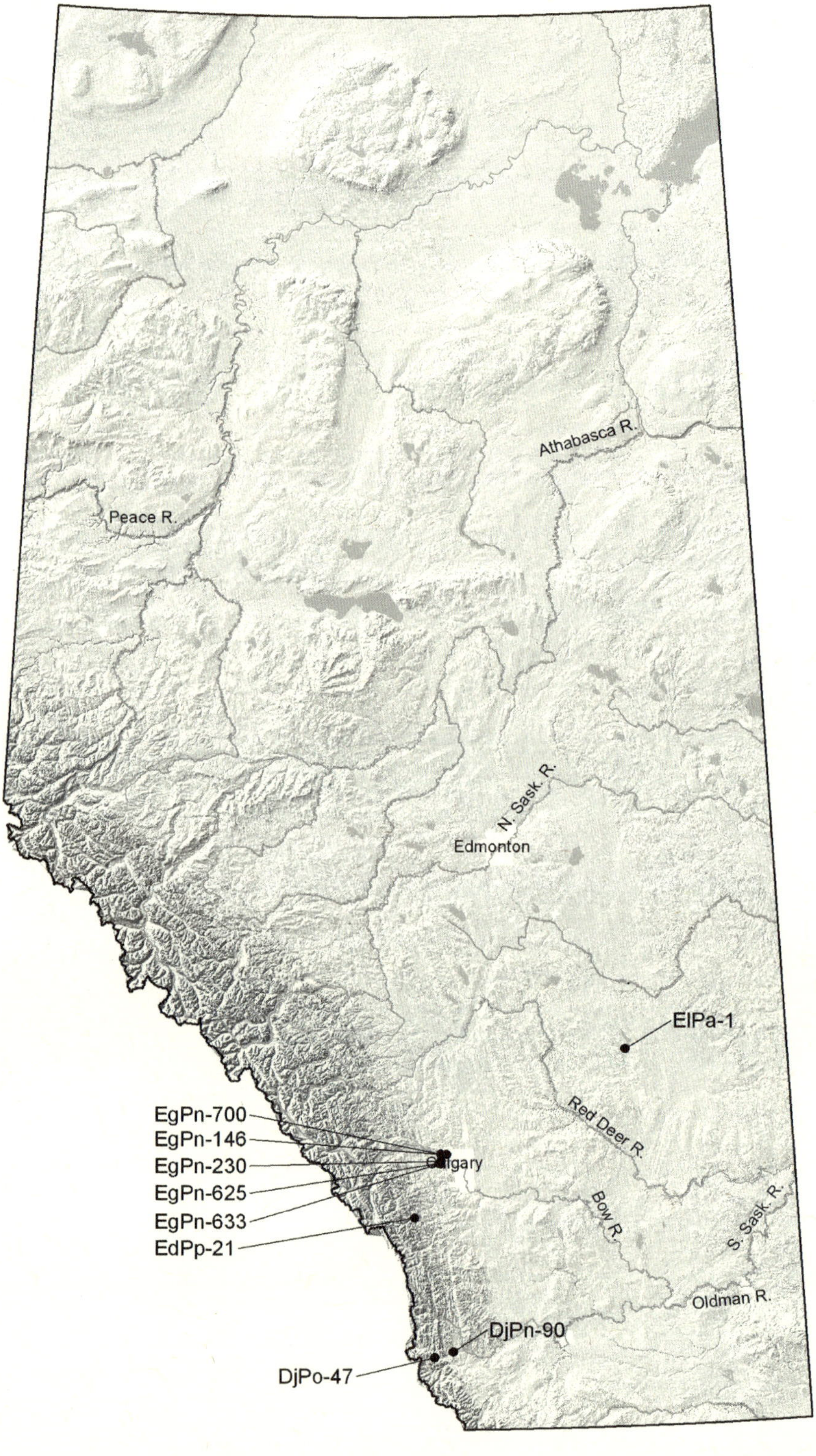

FIGURE 11 Country Hills sites within Alberta

Nine projectile points were recovered from the site: six barbed and corner-notched points, two lanceolate point blades (not unlike Lusk point blades), and a point tip. The lithic tool assemblage also included a biface, a retouched flake, and choppers (n = 6). The lithic assemblage (n = 126) contained dolomite (n = 25), quartzite (n = 21), Top-of-the-World chert (n = 20), black siltstone (n = 10), chert (n = 10), and basalt (n = 1). Thus, raw material sources are restricted to local or nearby mountain sources (Vivian 2007a:14).

The faunal assemblage (n = 78,356) was in variable states of preservation, suggesting multiple use events (Vivian 2007a:17). The assemblage was largely bison (99.6%). Analysis suggested that the materials represented a robust form of *Bison bison*, a late form of *B. antiquus*, or a transitional form. Deer and antelope (n = 112) were also recovered with an MNI of four adult antelope being positively identified in the assemblage. The lack of deer and antelope bone in the centre of the site suggested that the material may mark a separate event, or that all the material may be a single event in which the smaller deer and antelope carcasses were transported to the edge of the site for processing (Vivian 2007a:21). Canid (n = 3) bones likely represent a large dog or wolf (Vivian 2007a:21). Cottontail and hare (n = 41), beaver (n = 1), prairie chicken/grouse-sized bird (n = 6), and various intrusive rodents were also recovered. The recovery of mollusc shells in the water-saturated bone bed indicated the wet/dry environment had been present at the site for quite a while (Vivian 2007a:22). An analysis of the bison bone suggested a minimum of forty mature animals. Metric analysis of navicular cuboids (n = 29 rights) produced nineteen female and ten male animals; a similar conclusion was reached with metapodials (Vivian 2007a:25). Fetal bone (n = 8) was recovered at the site, suggesting a late fall to late winter occupation (Vivian 2007a:26–27). In terms of butchering, few cut marks were observed. Hump meat, ribs, upper forelimb muscle, and upper hind limb muscle were selectively removed with little processing of the remaining bone (Vivian 2007a:42).

Two radiocarbon dates of about 7,800 and 7,400 BP were obtained (see Table 9). These dates, while both considered valid, were statistically unlikely to be dating the same event (Vivian 2007a:6). The earliest component of the site likely represents a main kill and several other closely spaced kills between 7,800 and 7,400 BP (Vivian 2007a:43). A mixed herd of at least forty mature bison and two calves, likely *B. antiquus*, were ambushed at a spring-fed watering hole in late fall or early winter (Vivian 2007a:43). The consistency within the lithic raw material and projectile point assemblages supports the argument that the pre-Mazama Ash bone bed is a single cultural/depositional event (Vivian 2007a:6). Vivian (2007a:47–58) argued that the Everblue Springs site illustrates a movement toward a broader, more thorough utilization of the bison than is typical of earlier Palaeoindian kill sites such as Fletcher, Heron-Edon, Horner, Casper and Olsen-Chubbuck.

TABLE 9 Radiocarbon dates for Country Hills sites (calibrated by OxCal 3.10 [Ramsey 2005])

Site [LAB NO.]	Conventional ^{14}C Age	$^{13}C/^{12}C$ Ratio	Material	Calibration	Reference
EgPn 700 [BETA-226504]	7,820 +/- 50	-19.3‰	collagen	6760–6570 B.C. (p = 0.954)	Vivian 2007a:161–162
EgPn 700 [BETA 204365]	7430 +/- 70	-18.8‰	collagen	6440–6200 B.C. (p = 0.896) 6190–6100 B.C. (p = 0.059)	Vivian 2007a:159–160
DjPo 47 [RL-876]	7280 +/- 230	-20.0‰	collagen	6600–5700 B.C. (p = 0.954)	Landals 1986:70; Morlan n.d.
EgPn 230 [BETA-107315]	7030 +/- 70	?	collagen	6350–6310 B.C. (p = 0.025) 6270–6000 B.C. (p = 0.929)	Vivian et al. 1998:16
DjPn 90 [AECV 112C]	6120 +/- 450	-20.0‰	collagen	rejected	Ronaghan 1986:206, 1992:128; Morlan n.d.

Maple Leaf (DjPo 47), Component 2. The Maple Leaf site is a multicomponent site on a terrace immediately above the Crowsnest River south of the town of Bellevue and the Hillcrest Mines in the Crowsnest Pass (Landals 1986:37; Driver 1982). The site is described above in the section on the Plains/Mountain complex. In Component 2, lying just below Mazama Ash, an Elko Eared point was recovered. Evidence for the occupation just below Mazama Ash was found in both Areas One and Two of the site. Reeves and Driver (1978:12) initially reported the recovery of an Elko Eared point made of Knife River flint associated with Area B (i.e., Area Two), as well as a widely scattered bone bed on pond sediments underlying Mazama Ash in Area B (i.e., Area Two) and between Mazama Ash and marl in Area A (i.e., Area One). Reeves and Driver (1978:12) referred to the specimen as an Elko Eared point because of its similarity in form to specimens near the northern part of the Great Basin. While not identical, the specimen does exhibit strong morphological similarity to large, barbed corner-notched specimens proposed to exist locally in the foothills and mountains of Alberta. It seems most appropriate to classify this specimen with local specimens of similar age and morphology: a Burmis barbed point. In view of the faunal assemblage, they interpreted the widely scattered butchered bone as signs of butchering and processing (Reeves and Driver 1978:12). Other species recovered included deer, represented by a single shed antler, two paired, and butchered mandibles of wolf, and a butchered badger mandible (Reeves and Driver 1978:13).

Landals (1986:70–81) provided a comprehensive analysis of Component 2 material from Area One. She noted that no diagnostic lithic artifacts were found, but three lithic artifacts were recovered, including a small flake end scraper, a chert flake fragment, and a rounded and pitted pebble hammerstone (Landals 1986:71). A spherical stone that may be cultural was also recovered. The faunal assemblage was small (n = 1,150) and consisted of distinct clusters of articulating elements. The limbs of a single young adult male bison are represented in the assemblage. No sign of carnivore activity was apparent (Landals 1986:72). The two paired mandibles were considered to be "extra large" dogs, not wolves, but no signs of butchering were observed on them (Landals 1986:80). The deer antler was stratigraphically located between Component 1 and 2 and considered non-cultural (Landals 1986:80). The unusual faunal assemblage might not be cultural; however, attributing the finds to natural causes was also problematic. A single radiocarbon date of about 7,300 BP was obtained for the component (Table 9).

EgPn 230, Component 1. EgPn 230 is located on the south side of the Bow River, but north of Highway. 1, in the south end of a deep gully on the west side of Calgary (Vivian et al. 1998:2). Three components were observed at the site. The lowest component, in a palaeosol, contained Country Hills material below a layer of Mazama Ash. In 1997, 84 m^2 were excavated at the site as part of mitigative action prior to development of a golf course (Vivian 1998:2).

Eight projectile points were recovered, including five large corner-notched Burmis barbed points, a blade fragment of a possible Lusk point, and two blade tips (Vivian et al. 1998:6–9, 194). Other tools recovered include end scrapers (n = 2), retouched flakes (n = 3), cores (n = 5), and a wide side-struck flake exhibiting retouch and polish. Debitage (n = 377) was scattered randomly across the site and largely reflected tool finishing and maintenance. Three of the projectile points were observed to be burinated, apparently for reuse as another tool form. Raw materials emphasized local sources, dominated by quartzite and siltstone (Vivian et al. 1998:10–11, 102).

The faunal assemblage (n = 1,275) consisted of small fragments of bone representing at least two bison with a single possible deer element (Vivian et al. 1998:12). The researcher suggested that identifiable elements are larger than modern bison. Marrow extraction was suggested as an explanation for some of the bone fracturing. Burned bone was uncommon and FBR (n = 48) was almost absent from the component. A single radiocarbon date was obtained for the component (Table 9). Importantly, Vivian, Bosch, and Reeves (1998:15) noted the comparability of projectile points styles recovered at EgPn 230 and the specimen from the Jensen Spring site (Ronaghan 1992).

Jensen Spring (DjPn 90), Component 1. The Jensen Spring site is a multicomponent site located in a swale on a high bedrock ridge about 60 m above the outwash terraces of the Crowsnest River valley (Ronaghan 1992:121). The site was presumably named for the landowners at the time of the survey and the spring at the site's location. In 1984, four backhoe test pits and eight 1-×-1-m test pits were excavated, exposing places across the site's five natural sedimentary units (Ronaghan 1992:124). One of the natural layers was believed to be a Mazama Ash, which dates to ca. 6,800 BP. However, a radiocarbon date of about 6,000 BP (Table 9) from beneath the ash is problematic. Still, the error range for the radiocarbon date allows for overlap between the age of the apparent Mazama Ash and the radiocarbon date (Ronaghan 1992:128).

A single projectile point was recovered at 20 cm beneath the tephra near the springhead. It has a broad blade, very pronounced barbs, deep corner-notches, and a stemmed-like based. Stylistically the point fits well with other large, corner-notched Early Middle Prehistoric points. The point appears to have been recovered in situ beneath Mazama Ash. No other lithic artifacts were recovered at this depth. Faunal material was recovered at 10 cm beneath the tephra in this unit and two others. The faunal assemblage (n = 117) from beneath the ash layer was very sparse and only ten pieces could be identified as medium to large mammal, and three as bison or large ungulate (Ronaghan 1992:131). Like most other sites in this period, features are lacking, bone is highly fragmented and scarce, and it is hard to characterize the site.

Wimpey (EgPn 146), Level 7. The Wimpey site is a multicomponent campsite on a bench overlooking a glacial outwash channel in northwest Calgary. The site is named for the company for whom the mitigative excavation was being conducted. This mitigative action was taken prior to the development of a subdivision (Wright 1983:1). In 1982, two basins were excavated that produced material above and below Mazama Ash. The more productive of the two basins, Area 5, was investigated using thirteen 2-×-2-m units to depths between 40 and 90 cm BS (Wright 1983:8). Level 7 exhibited Burmis barbed points. Level 6 produced Blackwater side-notched material. Level 5 produced a base that fits relatively well with the Bitterroot material, but is too fragmentary to be certain. Level 4 contained Mazama Ash. Level 3 produced a large point that defies classification. Level 2 produced a single point that fits well with the Maple Leaf material. Level 1 did not produce a diagnostic projectile point (Wright 1983).

Regarding Level 7, the larger point is very similar to those at EgPn 700, while the small specimen is clearly resharpened but exhibits a similar base to those at EgPn 700 and EgPn 230. Other tools recovered in this excavation level included a bipolar wedge, utilized flakes (n = 2) and a biface (Wright 1983:54). The points were made of quartzite and siltstone, the wedge was made of mudstone, the utilized flakes of siltstone, and the biface was made of chalcedony. The level also contained sixty-three pieces of debitage, reflecting early stages of reduction (Wright 1983:133). The assemblage was heavily dominated by local materials, especially quartzite and siltstone (Wright 1983:134).

The faunal remains (n = 285) were highly fragmented and unidentifiable (Wright 1983:149). Most of the fragments are believed to be bison bone. FBR was not present (Wright 1983:145). The basin likely represents a refuse dump for bone, debitage, and broken tools, as it is too small to have held a dwelling of any size. Dates were not available for this material and the levels were differentiated arbitrarily, not by sedimentation. Still, the materials clearly predate the Mazama Ash fall (Level 4) by some time.

Scapa (ElPa 1), Basin 4. The Scapa site is described in the section on the Lusk complex. A possible Burmis barbed point was recovered in Component 2. Originally classified as an Alberta point (Hanna and Neal 1992:102), the specimen in Component 2 is more likely a Burmis barbed point. The point has slightly barbed shoulders and a slightly flared base. Other tools recovered included a biface and biface fragment, a scraper, a uniface, cores and core fragments (n = 24), bipolar cores (n = 4), and marginally retouched tools (n = 17). Seven tools were tested for blood residue. The point tested positive for antelope. The biface and a core with edge crushing were positive for bison. The biface fragment, the scraper, and two marginally retouched tools had no blood residue. The vast majority of the assemblage was quartzite and petrified wood with very small amounts of exotic material such as Knife River flint and porcellanite. The faunal assemblage included one unidentifiable bone fragment and an unspecified fossil fragment (Hanna and Neal 1992:106). Four FBR pieces were found along with sixty unmodified cobbles. Some of the cobbles may have been arranged into a linear feature; the feature entered the southern wall, making the nature of the feature indeterminate (Hanna and Neal 1992:106).

A date was not obtained for the occupation, but it overlies what appears to be a Lusk occupation and underlies Mazama Ash, making a Country Hills affiliation reasonable. The researchers suggested the occupation reflected a living floor where lithic tool manufacturing, food acquisition, and food processing took place in the Early Middle Prehistoric period (Hanna and Neal 1992:106).

Other sites. The Gooseberry kill site (EgPn 625) and the Snack site (EgPn 633) are recently discovered Country Hills sites on Paskapoo Slopes; they produced Burmis barbed points within bison bone beds (Vivian et al. 2009; Vivian and Blakey 2009). As a caveat, a large barbed point was recovered at EdPp 21 in a multicomponent site exhibiting compressed stratigraphy, west of Turner Valley (McCullough and Fedirchuk 1983, plate 9c). The recovery of large, barbed points in contexts that can be dated is crucial to their identification. Without the dated context these points are often mistaken for Pelican Lake points. The aforementioned specimen was classified as a Pelican Lake point despite its barbed-like shoulders, large size, and stemmed appearance.

Country Hills: Barbed Darts in the Front Range and Foothills

Country Hills assemblages appear to have gone unrecognized in Alberta and abroad. The Burmis barbed point is relatively distinct, yet only a few appear to have been encountered in situ within the archaeological record of Alberta. This may be due, in part, to the association of the complex with the foothills of Alberta. This area has not been thoroughly surveyed. Thus, three of the four sites attributed to the complex are located within the City of Calgary. The Calgary area is one of the few areas of the foothills that has been extensively surveyed for archaeological sites. The Crowsnest Pass has similarly been examined more than most foothills areas. A second factor affecting the visibility of these sites is that they tend to be buried fairly deeply. The Country Hills component at the Scapa site was buried under four other components. Still, while these sites are relatively deeply buried, they are not buried at prohibitive depths. As alluded to, it would seem that a superficial resemblance to Pelican Lake points may play a substantial role in misidentifying some specimens. Yet, the recovery of these points in situ at the aforementioned sites and the appreciation of their significance by the researchers has provided firm steps toward recognizing more of these Early Middle period sites.

The Burmis barbed point is diagnostic of the Country Hills complex. It is a fairly large point with deep corner-notches producing a strongly barbed appearance to the overall point. The blade tends to be fairly triangular in shape, often with slightly convex margins. The deep notching at the base can produce a stemmed-like appearance. Often the tip has a needle sharp point. Resharpening of this basic form appears to straighten the margins of the blade from its original slightly excurvate form. With time, these traits appear to become less well formed (e.g., EgPn 230). As well, Lusk points appear to have been recovered in both EgPn 230 and 700. At the Scapa site, however, the Country Hills complex apparently overlies Lusk material. It is unclear what the relationship is between these cultural entities.

In addition to the points, few other tools have been recovered in Country Hills assemblages. In terms of the raw materials, quartzite and siltstone are common at EgPn 230 and the Wimpey site while quartzite and petrified wood were common at the Scapa site. Projectile points made of Knife River flint were recovered at both the Maple Leaf site and the Scapa site; this suggests ties to the Plains to the south and east.

The fauna recovered from the Country Hills assemblages suggest a Plains adaptation. The Everblue Springs site is a large bison kill site at the edge of the foothills, indicating that these people were accomplished bison hunters. A fair amount of antelope bone was also recovered at this site. The Maple Leaf site in the Crowsnest Pass also indicates bison were procured, possibly along with some large dogs. EgPn 230 at the foothills in Calgary produced both bison and deer bone. Similarly, Jensen Springs in the Crowsnest Pass had a small assemblage that suggested both bison and small ungulate were procured. The Wimpey site in the foothills produced small amounts of bone thought to be bison while the Scapa site in the parkland periphery produced no identifiable bone, although blood residue on a projectile point was identified as antelope. Although limited, these faunal assemblages attest to a bison-oriented adaptation with supplementary subsistence from other animals resources. None of these sites are located on the Plains proper, but in the foothills and parkland on the Plains periphery.

Also in Alberta, a bison kill dated to 7,600 BP was identified below Mazama Ash at Locality C of the Mona Lisa site. No diagnostic material was recovered but it was suggested that a coulee was used to funnel animals to a pond "trap" (Wilson 1980). The date of this site and the method of entrapment are similar to the Country Hills complex such as the Everblue Springs site's entrapment of bison at a natural wetland/spring (Brian Vivian, personal communication 2007). The people living during the Country Hills complex apparently exploited unaltered landscapes as natural traps to capture numerous bison.

Other Country Hills sites exist outside of Alberta. The sharply barbed specimens do not appear to have been recovered in Saskatchewan or Manitoba. Still, more lanceolate barbed points from surface finds near Quill Lakes in Saskatchewan show some affinity to the Burmis barbed points and may be culturally and/or temporally related (Novecosky 2002a).

In Montana, the Mammoth Meadow site at the Mammoth Meadow I locality produced large, triangular, barbed points. These were referred to as Elko and Pelican Lake points despite being immediately overlying and/or in possible association with Scottsbluff material (Bonnichsen et al. 1992:309–310). The morphology and possible temporal position of these specimens suggest they are candidates for Burmis barbed points in Montana. The Cremer site (24SW264) is a multicomponent site in south central Montana (Nowatzyk 1983). Five cultural components were recognized. The second deepest layer, Layer IV, produce large barbed points in apparent association with side-notched points and fishtail points. The material in this layer could be interpreted as representing a palimpsest of Burmis barbed points (Nowatzyk 1983:76, fig. 13m and n), Mummy Cave points (Nowatzyk 1983:76, fig. 13d–h), and Maple Leaf fishtail points (Nowatzyk 1983, fig. 13a–c, i–l).

A more comparable site is the Mummy Cave site in northwestern Wyoming. The Mummy Cave site is a large rockshelter on the left bank of the North Fork of the Shoshone River about 55 km west of Cody, Wyoming (Husted and Edgar 2002:1). Thirty-eight cultural occupations were recognized. In Layer 16, an "expanding stem sharp shouldered" point and "expanding stem sharp shouldered indented base" point were recovered in association with a number of Blackwater side-notched points (Husted and Edgar 2002:45–46, plate 13g, h). The former points exhibit a striking resemblance to the more barbed specimens in Alberta. A radiocarbon date of 7,630 +/- 170 BP (I-1588) was obtained for the level (Husted and Edgar 2002:26). Given the contemporary dates, remarkable similarity between point morphology, and similar foothills environment, a direct relationship between the makers of the points in Alberta and northwestern Wyoming seems evident.

MUMMY CAVE COMPLEX (7,300 TO 6,700 BP)

The Mummy Cave complex was named after the Mummy Cave site in Wyoming after numerous points in the stratified sequence were observed to be similar to those found in surface collections in Alberta (Reeves 1969:30). Reeves (1969:30) characterized the complex as exhibiting side-notched atlatl points. At the time he defined the complex, he noted that no components of such sites had been excavated on the plains of Alberta, but excavations at the Gap site in the front range of the Rocky Mountains and a few sites in Waterton Lakes National Park in the Rocky Mountains had produced these points (Reeves 1969:31). The complex was considered intrusive into the plains with its ultimate origins in the East, but possibly with origins in the mountainous west (Reeves 1969:31). Reeves (1969:30) estimated the timing of this complex to have been roughly between 7,500 to 5,500 BP.

The material recovered in the salvage excavations at the Gap site (Reeves and Dormaar 1972:333) and in Waterton Lakes National Park (Reeves 1972:442) included side-notched points that had well-defined basal edges, relatively "square" notches, and sharp shoulders. Reeves and Dormaar (1972:333) labelled them Bitterroot points based on similarities they saw to a type originally defined in the Idaho area (Swanson et al. 1964). Soon after, in 1971, Gryba (1976) discovered side-notched points in a deeply buried layer at the Stampede site in the Cypress Hills. Gryba (1976:95–96) considered the six point fragments and single unfinished point to be Bitterroot points of the Mummy Cave complex, comparable to the material from the Gap site. In the early 1980s, Walker (1992:133) considered the points from the Stampede site to be more appropriately classified as Blackwater side-notched points because of the striking similarity of their "rocker-shaped" basal edges to specimens from Layer 16 of the Mummy Cave site (Husted and Edgar 2002:98–99).

Walker's (1992) statistical study of projectile point variability in the Early Middle Prehistoric period on the Northern Plains allowed him to argue that Blackwater side-notched points were the earliest point form, followed by Bitterroot side-notched (a.k.a. Northern, Pahaska, or Mummy Cave), then Hawken side-notched, Gowen side-notched, and most recently Mount Albion corner-notched points (Walker 1992:132–142). He considered Blackwater side-notched points to be found at a few sites such as the Stampede site in Alberta and the Mummy Cave site (i.e., Layer 16) in Wyoming (Walker 1992:137). Bitterroot side-notched points were considered widespread, occurring at sites such as the Gap in southwestern Alberta, and Mummy Cave (i.e., Layers 17 and 18) and Lookingbill in northwestern Wyoming (Walker 1992:137). Gowen side-notched points were noted at the Gowen 1 and 2 sites in south-central Saskatchewan, the Welsch site in southwestern Alberta, and the Sorenson site in Wyoming (Walker 1992:141). Hawken side-notched points, recovered in Wyoming, and Mount Albion corner-notched points, found in sites along the Colorado Front Range, have not been discovered in well-stratified contexts in Alberta.

More recently, Dyck (1983:92) reconsidered the use of the term *Mummy Cave complex* for all cultural materials across the Northern Plains that date from the Bitterroot side-notched sequence to the beginning of Oxbow side-notched points. He indicated that there was a strong possibility more than one complex may be represented in this lengthy time range. He preferred to substitute the term *Mummy Cave series*. His warning was well founded as the term *Mummy Cave / Bitterroot* has been used to label most cultural manifestations that occur between 7,500 and 4,500 BP on the Northern Plains. The standard criteria for the Bitterroot side-notched point (i.e., defined basal edges, relatively "square" notches, and sharp shoulders) have been very loosely applied to assemblages from this period. Subsequently, so-called Bitterroot side-notched points have been recovered from numerous sites, including Head-Smashed-In Buffalo Jump, Vermilion Lakes (Locality A), Hawkwood, Maple Leaf, EgPn 87, Sara, Michalsky, DjPo 9, Anderson and Boy Chief amongst others, while Mummy Cave points were reported at EgPn 480.

When Reeves and Dormaar's (1972:333) Bitterroot projectile point criteria are strictly applied to projectile point assemblages, only a handful of sites in the province can be considered Mummy Cave sites. Possibly related to Bitterroot side-notched points and slightly predating these assemblages are those with Blackwater side-notched points (Walker 1992:132–142). Blackwater side-notched points have relatively "square" notches, sharp shoulders, and their basal edges are well defined but often "rocker-shaped."

Assemblages with Blackwater side-notched points often exhibit straight-based, Bitterroot-like points as well. Blackwater side-notched assemblages at both the Stampede site (Gryba 1976:105, fig. 51a) and the Mummy Cave site (Husted and Edgar 2002:183, plate 13f) produced points that would be considered Bitterroot had they been found in the subsequent level.

The Sites

In order to assess the Mummy Cave complex as presented above, assemblages exhibiting projectile points with sharp shoulders, square notches, and well-defined basal edges and with reliable radiocarbon dates are outlined below. These sites are used in a critical evaluation of the current view of the Mummy Cave complex (see Plate 11 and Figure 12).

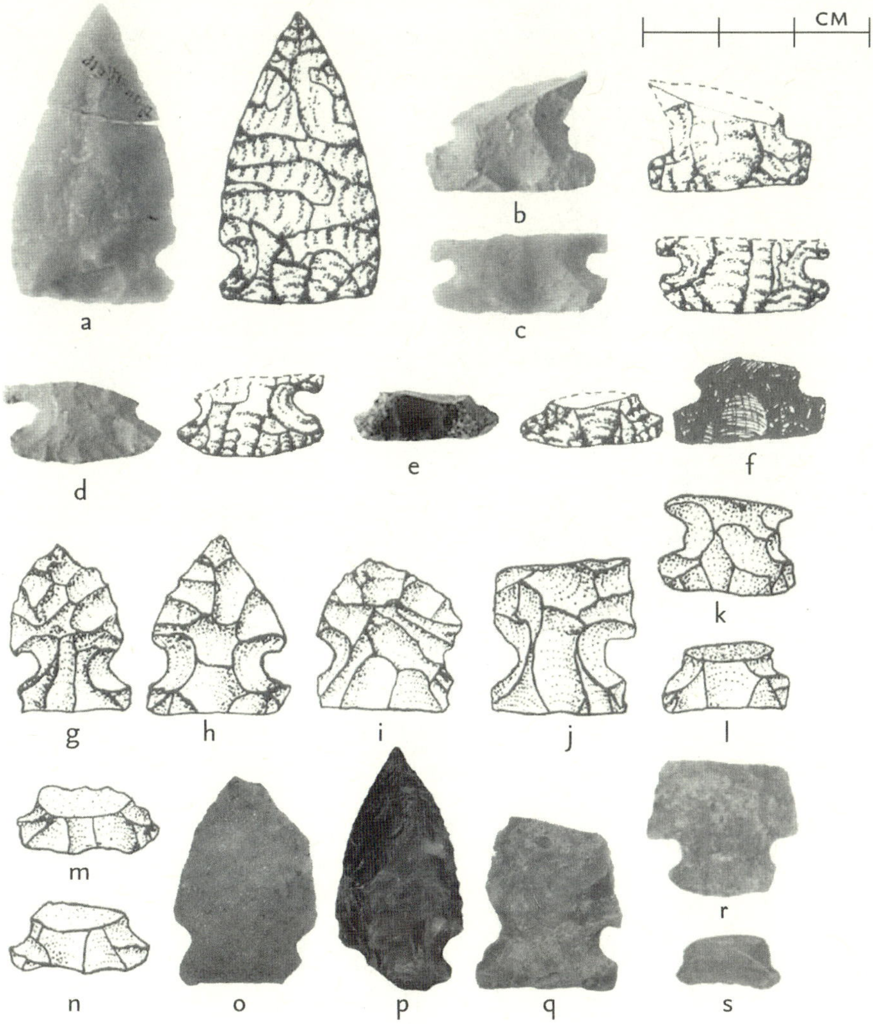

PLATE 11 Mummy Cave points. Illustrated are points from the Stampede site (DjOn 26) (a–e); the Gap site (DlPo 20) (f); the Vermilion Lakes site (EhPv 8), Locality A, Occupation 4 (g–n); the Hawkwood site (EgPm 179) (o and q); the Tuscany site (EgPn 377) (p); and the Wimpey site (EgPn 146) (r and s). Photo credit: Royal Alberta Museum (a–n); Alberta Culture and Community Spirit (o and q); Gerald Oetelaar (p); ARESCO (r and s).

FIGURE 12
Mummy Cave sites within Alberta

Stampede Site (DjOn 26). The Stampede site is a multicomponent campsite near Elkwater in the Cypress Hills. The site exhibits at least an 8,000-year record of occupation as witnessed in a minimum of fourteen culture-bearing layers. Many discrete palaeosols mark former land surfaces used by people in the past. Palaeosol 12A contains the Mummy Cave material. The site was excavated in 1971–1972. Approximately 7 m² of cultural layer 12A were excavated. Oetelaar (2004a) revisited the site in the late 1990s. The Archaeological Survey contracted additional research in 2007–2008.

From the initial excavations, a total of six points and point fragments was recovered in association with a basin-shaped hearth, a diversity of stone and bone tools, a large quantity of lithic debitage, and faunal remains (Gryba 1975:133). Gryba (1975:135) classified the points as similar to Bitterroot points, comparable to those at the Gap site, discussed below. In a synthetic review of points characteristic of this period, Walker (1992:137) suggested the Cultural Layer 12A points were most similar to Blackwater side-notched points found at Mummy Cave, Wyoming (Husted and Edgar 2002:98–99, 183). Other tools that were recovered included asymmetrical ovate bifaces (n=2), a drill tip, retouched flakes (n=9), bipolar cores (n=11), and other cores (n=2). A bone tool consisting of two refitting fragments of a bone needle was also recovered (Gryba 1975:143).

The faunal assemblage consisted of 965 bone fragments, of which twenty-five were identifiable. Bone from at least one bison, one elk, and one gopher were recovered. The remaining fauna were too fragmented to be identified. Seasonal information was not determined. The fauna tended to be associated with the hearth. Within and immediately around the hearth was charred bone. The hearth was a circular, basin-shaped, unlined, 0.60 m-wide, and 0.08 m-deep pit (Gryba 1975:145). No other features were observed.

In the original excavations, a single radiocarbon date was obtained for this material: 7,245 +/- 255 BP (NMC-571). Gryba (1975:145–146) interpreted the site as an Early Side-notched campsite where tools were fabricated and meals were consumed presumably in a warm season, owing to the lack of evidence for a shelter. More recently, Oetelaar (2004a) obtained a date of 7,115 +/- 50 BP (OxA-11614) for this level, complimenting the previous date.

Vermilion Lakes, Locality A (EhPv 8, 153R), Occupation 4. The Vermilion Lakes site, Locality A, is a multicomponent site in a debris-flow fan on the north side of the Bow River Valley, west of Banff. It contains ten cultural occupation layers dating from 10,500 BP to about historic times.

Occupation 4 contains Bitterroot side-notched points in a mixed layer containing Mazama Ash (Fedje 1986:29). In 1983 and 1984, excavations took place at the site in response to construction on the Trans-Canada Highway. The highway was redesigned to avoid impacting this important site (Fedje 1986:25). Nine points and point fragments were recovered from a layer containing Mazama Ash. Fedje (1986:29) classified the points as Bitterroot given the association of the side-notched points and the Mazama Ash.

Tuscany (EgPn 377). The Tuscany site is described in the section on the Lusk complex. In a palaeosol beneath a Mazama Ash layer a single fragmented dart point was recovered in association with a few pieces of debitage (Oetelaar 1998). Although fragmented, the point exhibited shoulder and base structure similar to Bitterroot points. A concentration of bison bones and some antelope constituted the faunal remains recovered. A number of the bones exhibited cut marks but were otherwise relatively complete. The large size of the bison led the research to suggest they may represent *Bison occidentalis*. The occupation was interpreted as a kill event consisting of several animals dating to ca. 6,900 BP (Table 10; Oetelaar 1998).

TABLE 10 Radiocarbon dates for Mummy Cave sites (calibrated by OxCal 3.10 [Ramsey 2005])

Site [LAB NO.]	Conventional ^{14}C Age	$^{13}C/^{12}C$ Ratio	Material	Calibration	Reference
DjOn 26 [NMC-571]	7245 +/- 255	-25.0‰	charred bone	6600–5600 B.C. (p = 0.954)	Gryba 1975:133
DjOn 26 [OXA-11614]	7115 +/- 50	?	collagen	6070–5890 B.C. (p = 0.954)	Oetelaar 2004a; Freeman 2006:465
EgPn 377 [TO-9261]	6940 +/- 70	?	?	5990–5700 B.C. (p = 0.954)	Oetelaar 2004b:735
EgPn 377 [OXA-11585]	6775 +/- 40	?	?	5370–5620 B.C. (p = 0.954)	Oetelaar 2004b:735
DlPo 20 [GSC-1298]	6720 +/- 170	-25.0‰	charcoal	6000–5300 B.C. (p = 0.954)	Reeves and Dormaar 1972; Morlan n.d.

Gap (DlPo 20), Occupation 2. The Gap site is described in the section on the Agate Basin/Hell Gap complex. Of interest is the second occupation, which lies directly beneath a layer of Mazama Ash. A single point base exhibiting a square base and deep notches was recovered. Reeves and Dormaar (1972:333) classified the specimen as Bitterroot. The point is made on fine-grained black chert. There are no other lithic materials described for this site. The faunal assemblage consists of a bison metatarsal, two tarsals, and a radius (Reeves and Dormaar 1972:332). A single radiocarbon date of about 6,700 BP is available for this assemblage (Table 10). This date is slightly late but fits with the known age for the Mazama Ash event (ca. 6,800 BP).

Hawkwood (EgPm 179). The Hawkwood site is described under the Lusk complex. Component 4 produced two side-notched projectile points. The researchers interpreted these as Bitterroot side-notched points (Van Dyke and Stewart 1985:69–71). Other tools recovered include asymmetrical bifaces (n=2), a scraper, wedges (n=3), retouched/utilized spall tools (n=7), and retouched flakes (n=7). Local materials make up most of the raw materials utilized, especially quartzite, siltstone, and pebble cherts. The debitage suggests that the full range of tool manufacturing was undertaken, from blank manufacture to retouching used tools.

The faunal assemblage represented a minimum of two bison and an elk. There were numerous bison bones whereas the elk was represented by a single phalanx (Van Dyke and Stewart 1985:80). The sample was so fragmented that it was not possible to determine seasonality or sexing. Very few burned or calcine specimens were recovered (Van Dyke and Stewart 1985:84). Cobbles scattered randomly across the living floor were noted but no mention of FBR was made (Van Dyke and Stewart 1985:82). No features or clear concentrations of material were noted. The occupation was immediately above a layer of Mazama Ash (ca. 6,800 BP). The researchers noted that the lithic assemblage was similar to Component 3, immediately above the ash layer, possibly indicating cultural continuity (Van Dyke and Stewart 1985:76, 83).

Other sites. EhPd 55, Component 1, is potentially a Mummy Cave occupation within a palaeosol in the Wintering Hills (Loveseth 1984). A single Bitterroot point and five point fragments were recovered beneath a McKean occupation. Radiocarbon dates were not obtained (Loveseth 1984:167, plate 17-1).

Mummy Cave: The Earliest Side-notched Point Assemblages

The Mummy Cave complex in Alberta was defined by Reeves (1969) based on sites in the foothills-mountain area (i.e., the Gap site and sites in Waterton Lakes National Park) knowing that surface collections on the Plains proper contained similar specimens. Despite the small samples sizes, a number of parallels exist between Alberta assemblages and comparably dated assemblages in Wyoming. For example, Layer 16 at the Mummy Cave site contained similar material and was dated to 7,630 +/- 170 BP (I-1588) (Husted and Edgar 2002:26). While this layer produced Burmis barbed points (discussed above), it also produced four Blackwater side-notched points. These points exhibit deep, broad notches often with a rocker-shaped base. Walker (1992:132–142) has effectively argued that assemblages exhibiting Blackwater side-notched points predate those exhibiting Bitterroot points. In fact, in the stratified Wyoming sequence, a single specimen was classified as a Pahaska (i.e., Bitterroot) side-notched point amongst the Blackwater side-notched points in Layer 16, while the two subsequent layers produced nineteen points, all Pahaska (i.e., Bitterroot) side-notched points (Husted and Edgar 2002, plates 13f, 14a–f, and 15a–m).

In the Alberta material, this sequence is reproduced through radiocarbon-dated assemblages rather than stratigraphic sequences. The Stampede site is the only site in the province that clearly exhibits Blackwater side-notched points (Gryba 1976). The Blackwater side-notched specimens predate all other side-notched point assemblages in the province. The components that exhibit Bitterroot side-notched points at the Gap, Vermilion Lakes, and Hawkwood sites are all occupations that occurred close in time to the Mazama Ash fall, ca. 6,800 BP. In fact, the Hawkwood site may provide evidence that people producing the Bitterroot side-notched point survived the Mazama eruption, with the previous occupation at the site hinting at continuation in land tenure (Van Dyke and Stewart 1985:76, 83). Bitterroot side-notched points continue to be characterized by well-defined basal edges that tend to be straight, relatively square notches and sharp shoulders that can be somewhat barbed (see also Reeves 1972; Reeves and Dormaar 1972:333).

Importantly, subtle morphological variation is apparent between the Alberta Bitterroot side-notched points, the Pahaska points from Mummy Cave (Husted and Edgar 2002:99) and Lookingbill (Frison 1983:10, fig. 7a–k) in Wyoming, and the original Bitterroot type specimens in Idaho (Swanson et al. 1964:67). Comparisons of well-dated point assemblages from these areas will likely illustrate that there is a range of regional micromorphological variation in the large side-notched points at this time. Blackwater side-notched points exhibit similar attributes to Bitterroot side-notched points; they have relatively square notches, but their sharp shoulders have few barbs and their well-defined basal edges tend to be rocker-shaped not straight. The small sample size that this point type has been based on, however, indicates that further research is required to solidify the nature of projectile point systematics for this poorly understood period.

In Saskatchewan, Bitterroot and Blackwater side-notched points do not appear to be present, at least not in an excavated context (e.g. Dyck 1983). Even within surface collections, these points or similar styles are not common. Likewise, Manitoba has not produced assemblages from dated contexts that are comparable to the Alberta material.

Just south of Manitoba, the Rustad site (32RI775) in southeastern North Dakota has produced numerous "Early Archaic projectile points" dating to about 7,400 BP. Michlovic and Sather (2005:143) equated the material with Logan Creek/Mummy Cave points. Using the strict definition for Alberta's Bitterroot points (i.e., well-defined basal edges, relatively square notches, and sharp shoulders) presented above, it is fair to differentiate Alberta's Mummy Cave material from the Rustad site material. The latter exhibits well-defined basal edges but lacks relatively square notches and sharp shoulders. However, Michlovic and Sather's (2005:143) comparison of the Rustad material to Gowen material deserves further attention. Also of interest is the focus of relatively local lithic raw materials at the Rustad site during the Early Archaic period (Michlovic and Sather 2005).

In Montana, the Barton Gulch site along the Madison River in the southeast is described as containing Bitterroot side-notched points post-dating the Mazama Ash fall (Aaberg et al. 1996:86). Illustrations of the point specimens, however, were not available for comparison. Similarly, the Mammoth Meadow site in southwestern Montana produced a sequence of early points, some of which were called Bitterroot points (Bonnichsen et al. 1992:310). Published images of the Bitterroot specimens (Bonnichsen et al. 1992:310), with their curved bases and deep notching, suggest stronger similarities to Pahaska points rather than Alberta's Bitterroot points. Smith (1981, fig. 7a–c) illustrated a number of points from west-central Montana, considered to be Middle Prehistoric period in age. Although recovered during a surface reconnaissance, these specimens exhibit square bases and subtle barbs, making them quite similar to the Bitterroot and Blackwater side-notched points described above for Alberta. Interestingly, they were recovered in the same geographic area from which Mammoth Meadows produced Pahaska-like points.

In Wyoming, the Eagle Shelter site (48BH657) produced a number of points in Levels 6–8 that are similar to Alberta's Mummy Cave points (Chomko 1990). The points have relatively rectangular bases with slightly concave basal edges. Level 8 has an associated date of 6,790 +/- 110 BP (Chomko 1990:56). In essence, they are most similar to the Pahaska points at Mummy Cave and elsewhere. Thus, besides the Blackwater side-notched material from the Mummy Cave site, little else exhibits a strong resemblance to the material from Alberta's Early Middle Prehistoric period. Materials to the south are properly labelled Pahaska points, such as those in Levels 17 and 18 of Mummy Cave (ca. 7,150–6,750 BP) and the Lookingbill site (ca. 7,000 BP) (Frison 1983:9–10, fig. 7a–k). The Pahaska points are a cohesive group of material; both formally and temporally, they are different from the Bitterroot points in Alberta.

MAPLE LEAF COMPLEX (CA. 6,300 TO 5,200 BP)

Traditionally, archaeologists have designated cultural materials that immediately postdate the Mazama Ash fall event either Mummy Cave complex or Mummy Cave series (e.g., Dyck 1983:92–95; Reeves 1969:30–31, 1990:177–180; Vickers 1986:58–63). Projectile points recovered in such components are typically labelled "Bitterroot side-notched" despite obvious deviation from the established criteria (see previous section).

In 1978, Wilson (1980:17) recovered three relatively complete points from two discrete bone beds above Mazama Ash at Locality C of the Mona Lisa site in Calgary. These bone beds were dated to roughly 5,500 BP. He likened the points to specimens from the Hawken site but classified them using the convention of the day: Bitterroot side-notched points of the Mummy Cave complex (Wilson 1980:17). The specimens lacked the defining criteria of Bitterroot side-notched points (Wilson 1980:54, plate 1).

Excavations in the mid-1970s at the Maple Leaf site in the Crowsnest Pass produced projectile points from above Mazama Ash that potentially dated to about 6,300 BP (Reeves and Driver 1978; Landals 1986). The points were initially classified as Bitterroot side-notched points of the Mummy Cave complex (Reeves and Driver 1978). Landals (1986) subsequently suggested the points be classified as Salmon River/Bitterroot side-notched attributable to the Early Middle Prehistoric period. The term *Salmon River side-notched* was meant to reflect similarities to specimens in Idaho (Swanson and Sneed 1966:24–26, fig. 18h–j). Swanson and Sneed's (1966:26) Salmon River points have shallow side notches close enough to the base to remove a small portion of the corner of the point. They also have flat bases. This description was similar but not identical to that for specimens recovered at the Maple Leaf site (Landals 1986:99–108).

In the mid-1980s, Ronaghan (1992) recovered five points in an Early Middle Prehistoric component. He considered two specimens to be Bitterroot side-notched points, one a possible Salmon River/Bitterroot side-notched point, while the remaining two points were considered unclassifiable (Ronaghan 1992:52). He assigned the material to the early Mummy Cave complex; in local terminology, this was Driver's (1978) Maple Leaf subphase (Ronaghan 1992:52). Importantly, Ronaghan (1992:52) noted his projectile point specimens did not closely resemble the classic type specimens. Echoing Dyck's (1983) concern about the range of variability in the Mummy Cave series, Ronaghan (1992:52) pointed out the need for clarification of the chronological placement and range of styles at this time period. Similarly, excavations in 1997 at EgPn 87 produced two diagnostic points in the lowest component, dated to about 5,800 BP. The smaller rounded-base point specimen was classified as a Bitterroot side-notched point while the larger broad, shallow notched point was classified as a Gowen side-notched point (Hanna and Head 2000:98–99).

The points from these sites exhibit obtuse shoulders, deep but open notches and slightly concave bases. None of these sites that postdate Mazama Ash produced points exhibiting the attributes of Bitterroot side-notched points. Bitterroot side-notched points were defined as exhibiting well-defined basal edges, relatively square notches, and sharp shoulders (Reeves 1972:442; Reeves and Dormaar 1972:333).

The Sites

The following presents well-dated sites with diagnostic materials that postdate the Mazama Ash fall event. There are no dated sites in Alberta with diagnostic materials that *immediately* postdate Mazama Ash (see Plate 12 and Figure 13).

Maple Leaf (DjPo 47). The Maple Leaf site is discussed in the section on the Plains/Mountain complex. The third component, of concern here, represents a bison kill site in a natural trap, representing at least two and possibly several small-scale events (Landals 1986). The thickness of the component varied between 5 and 50 cm and overlaid Mazama Ash. The site was examined in 1975, 1977, and 1978.

Ten projectile points were associated with a wetland feature, a hearth

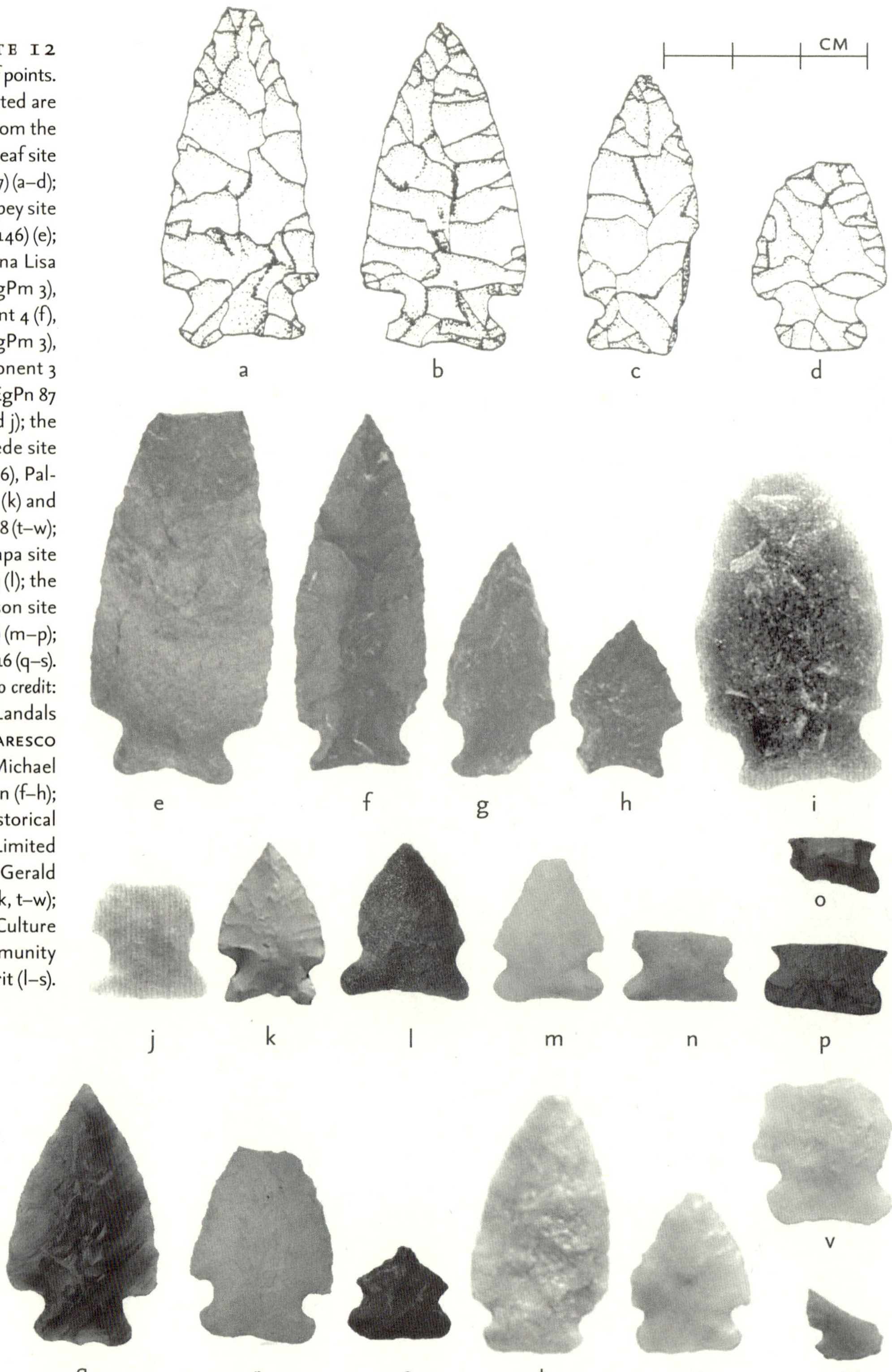

PLATE 12 Maple Leaf points. Illustrated are points from the Maple Leaf site (DjPo 47) (a–d); the Wimpey site (EgPn 146) (e); the Mona Lisa site (EgPm 3), Component 4 (f), and (EgPm 3), Component 3 (g and h); EgPn 87 (i and j); the Stampede site (DjOn26), Palaeosol 10 (k) and Palaeosol 8 (t–w); the Scapa site (ElPa 1) (l); the Anderson site (FdOt 1) (m–p); DjPn 16 (q–s). Photo credit: Alison Landals (a–d); ARESCO (e); Michael Wilson (f–h); Bison Historical Services Limited (i and j); Gerald Oetelaar (k, t–w); Alberta Culture and Community Spirit (l–s).

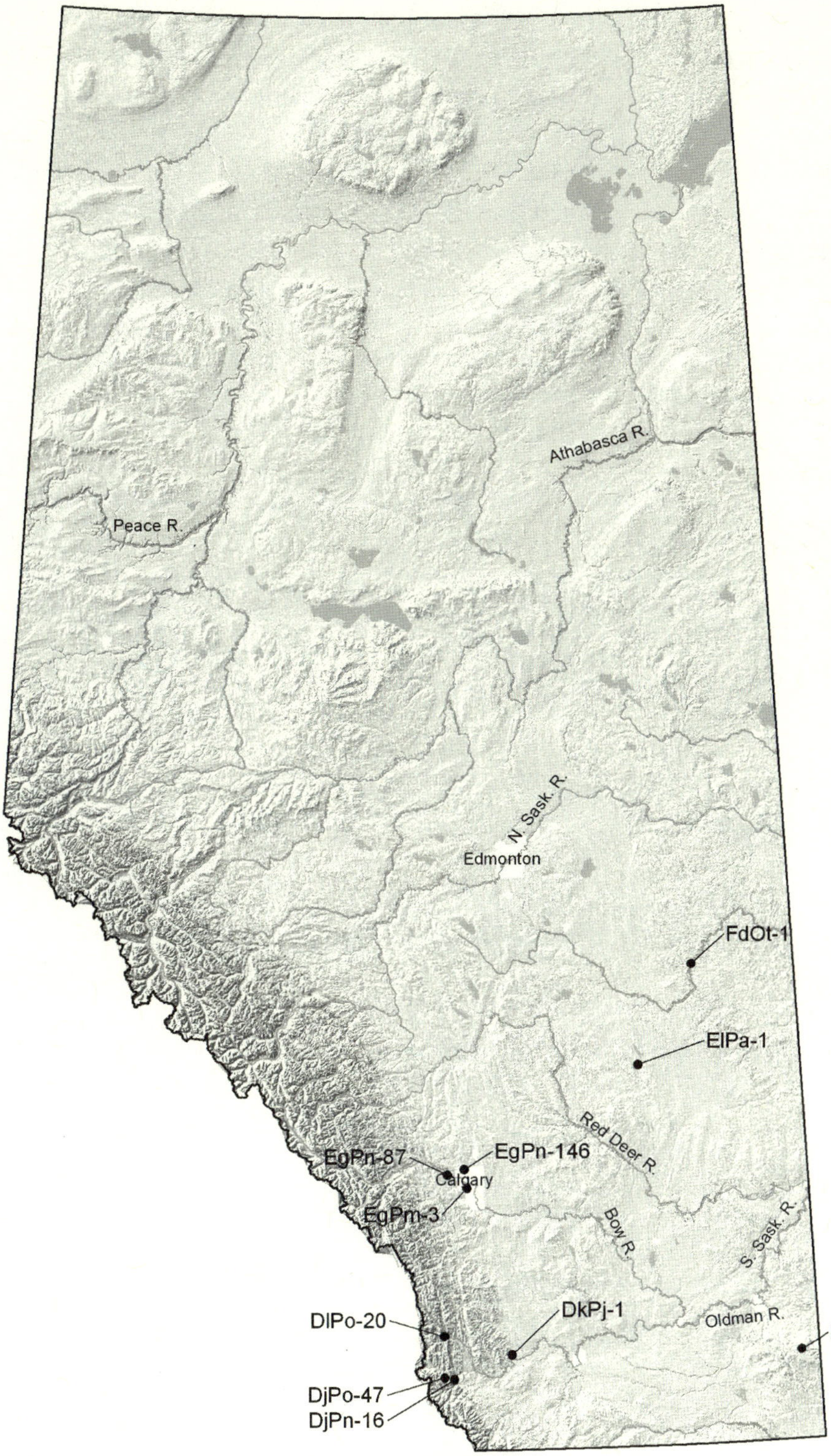

FIGURE 13
Maple Leaf sites within Alberta

feature, and two possible post-mould features. Landals (1986:99–109) identified two Oxbow points, seven Bitterroot/Salmon River side-notched points and one unclassifiable specimen. The remaining lithic tools support an interpretation of specific tasks relating to killing, butchering, tool sharpening/maintenance, and limited hide processing (Landals 1986:97). The assemblage indicated the use of local raw materials (Landals 1986:104). The faunal assemblage contained at least seventeen bison, four canids (two possible dogs), a badger, and a goose (Landals 1986:124–128). Three fetal bison bones were recovered, suggesting late winter to early spring use (Landals 1986:136). A single bone tool of unknown function was manufactured on a radius.

TABLE 11 Radiocarbon dates for Maple Leaf sites (calibrated by OxCal 3.10 [Ramsey 2005])

Site [LAB NO.]	Conventional ^{14}C Age	$^{13}C/^{12}C$ Ratio	Material	Calibration	Reference
DjPo 47 [RL-508]	6420 +/- 160	-20.0‰	bone	5650–5000 B.C. (p = 0.954)	Landals 1986; Morlan n.d.
DjOn 26 [OXA-11621]	6195 +/- 45	?	?	5300–5020 B.C. (p = 0.954)	Oetelaar 2004a
DlPo 20 [GSC-1255]	6060 +/- 140	-23.6‰	charcoal	5350–4600 B.C. (p = 0.954)	Reeves and Dormaar 1972:333; Morlan n.d
EgPn 87 [BETA-115161]	5800 +/- 80	-19.6‰	collagen	4840–4460 B.C. (p = 0.954)	Hanna and Head 2000:94, 108
EgPm 3 [GX-6395A]	5715 +/- 150	-10.0‰	apatite	4950–4250 B.C. (p = 0.954)	Wilson 1980:46; Morlan n.d.
EgPm 3 [GX-6394A]	5390 +/- 170	-10.0‰	apatite	4600–3750 B.C. (p = 0.954)	Wilson 1980:46; Morlan n.d.
DjPn 16 [AECV-214C]	4730 +/- 110	-20.0‰	collagen	3800–3100 B.C. (p = 0.954)	Ronaghan 1992:53; Beaudoin 1987; Morlan n.d.
DjPn 16 [AECV-215C]	5280 +/- 160	-20.0‰	collagen	4450–3700 B.C. (p = 0.954)	Ronaghan 1992:53; Beaudoin 1987; Morlan n.d.
DjPn 16 [AECV-216C]	4040 +/- 140	-20.0‰	collagen	rejected	Ronaghan 1992:53; Morlan n.d.
FdOt 1 [GX-6129-G]	4805 +/- 150	-20.0‰	collagen	4000–3100 B.C. (p = 0.954)	Quigg 1984:155-156; Morlan n.d.
FdOt 1 [GX-6130-G]	5540 +/- 160	-20.0‰	collagen	4750–3950 B.C. (p = 0.954)	Quigg 1984:155-156; Morlan n.d.

Three dates were obtained from the component: 6,400, 4,400 and 4,200 BP (see Table 11). Landals (1986:171) noted it was unlikely that a single event was evinced in the third component. The radiocarbon dates and the projectile points suggest that at least two time periods were represented in the formation of the assemblage. The earlier date reflected Bitterroot/Salmon River occupation(s) and is supported by the materials' stratigraphic position immediately above Mazama Ash. The latter dates reflected Oxbow occupation(s). Based on this and a thorough analysis of the faunal remains, Landals (1986) rejected an interpretation of a large-scale communal kill event in favour of a series of small-scale kills, likely occurring in late winter/early spring.

EgPn 87, Lower component. EgPn 87 is a multicomponent campsite in a large, flat-bottomed depression at the prairie level above the Bow River, just west of Calgary (Hanna and Head 2000:63). Three components were observed. The uppermost and middle components did not produce diagnostic materials but the lowermost component produced diagnostic cultural material. These lowest sediments exhibited a discontinuous layer of what is believed to be Mazama Ash overlying a thin but well-defined brown-red palaeosol; cultural materials were predominantly recovered from the palaeosol (Hanna and Head 2000:93).

Two points and a point tip were recovered from the site. The smaller specimen was classified as a Bitterroot point despite its rounded base, while the larger point was classified as Gowen in spite of its large size (Hanna and Head 2000:98–99). Other lithic tools include biface fragments (n = 3), end scrapers (n = 5), side scrapers (n = 4), a wedge, a retouched flake, utilized split pebbles (n = 2), a utilized flake, core fragments (n = 4), an anvil, and hammerstones (n = 2). Miscellaneous cherts predominated as the raw materials used in tool manufacture, but quartzite was also common. The reverse was true of the lithic debitage; the majority of the debitage is quartzite but miscellaneous cherts, siltstones, and basalts were relatively common.

The faunal assemblage (n = 1,579) was limited and fragmentary, of which only fifty-four fragments were identifiable to species. Only mature animal bone was recovered so neither seasonality nor herd composition could be reliably determined from the sample. No discrete features were observed at the site but the distribution of materials in the east block did suggest a circular pattern (Hanna and Head 2000:93). No FBR was recovered, an omission likely reflecting cultural practices not the scale of the work, given the area sampled (Hanna and Head 2000:94).

A single radiocarbon date, 5,800 BP, was obtained for the site (Table 11) (Hanna and Head 2000:94). The age estimate is too recent for a pre-Mazama Ash fall event. It is possible that the ash was redeposited at EgPn 87, but this was considered unlikely. Mixing of assemblages was also considered unlikely given the sparse nature of the materials. Stylistically, the points fit well with the radiocarbon date. Alternatively, some soil processes can superficially mimic ash layers, making the identification of ash incorrect.

Mona Lisa (EgPm 3), Component 3 and 4. The Mona Lisa site is a multicomponent kill site beneath the urban core of Calgary. The materials discussed here are from Locality C. The site is on a prominent terrace about 8 m above the Bow River, although the archaeological materials were recovered from an infill coulee in this terrace. Two cultural components were noted above and two cultural components were noted below Mazama Ash. The pre-Mazama Ash components (1 and 2) consisted of "two closely spaced sets of organic horizons, containing charcoal along with butchered and burnt bone." However, only a single flake was recovered from what appeared to be redeposited materials washed into the coulee from the slope and rim (Wilson 1980:11). The post-Mazama bone beds (Components 3 and 4) were devoid of charcoal but produced bone and stone tools in components 10 cm apart. Remnants of the site likely exist in areas where urban basements have not disturbed the ground (Wilson 1980:46, 1986:63).

Component 3 produced two projectile points and a point fragment (Wilson 1980:17). The researcher likened the points to specimens from the Hawken site but classified them as Bitterroot side-notched points and placed the site in the Mummy Cave complex (Wilson 1980:17). The points were made of basalt, quartzite, and lamprophyre while the unidentified tool was made on schist. The remaining lithics were all quartzite. The faunal assemblage had a minimum of seven bison, representing two fetal animals, two subadults, and three adult females. The faunal specimens were generally clustered; this was interpreted as a product of activity around specific animals (Wilson 1980:36). Variable butchering, from animal to animal, made generalizations unwarranted. The longitudinal splitting of bone using wedges, however, was noted as an unusual activity (Wilson 1980:43). A late winter/early spring use of the kill site, based on the recovery of fetal bone, was suggested (Wilson 1980:43). A single radiocarbon date of about 5,700 BP was obtained from this component (Wilson 1980; Brumley and Rushworth 1983:155).

Component 4 produced a single projectile point. It, too, was likened to Hawken points but classified as Bitterroot and considered part of the

Mummy Cave complex (Wilson 1980:17). Other tools include three cores/choppers, one flake, and a hammerstone. The point was made on basalt, one chopper was made of limestone, the flake was chert, and the remaining choppers and the hammerstone were quartzite. The faunal assemblage had a minimum of two bison, representing an adult male and an adult female. The bone was relatively scattered in this component. No material was recovered to suggest seasonality. A single radiocarbon date of about 5,400 BP was obtained (Wilson 1980; Brumley and Rushworth 1983:155).

Sara (DjPn 16), Component 3. The Sara site is multicomponent campsite on a low terrace on the south side of the Crowsnest River. The site was named for Dr. Sara, the landowner at the time of its discovery (Ronaghan 1992:36). Five post-Mazama Ash components were differentiated: Component 1 was culturally unidentified, Component 2 was tenuously linked to Mt. Albion, Component 3 contained Bitterroot material, Component 4 was a mix of Oxbow and McKean material, and Component 5 was agriculturally mixed with Component 4 and represented material over the last 4,500 years (Ronaghan 1992:63). The site was initially discovered and tested by the University of Calgary. Ronaghan (1992:39) re-evaluated the site with seventeen dispersed 1-×-1-m units.

Five projectile points were recovered from Component 3. Four of the points have rounded bases and open notches, with the remaining point simply a tip. The researcher considered these to be Bitterroot points (Ronaghan 1992:52), but the points lack rectangular bases and clear side-notches. Other tools recovered include a biface preform, side scrapers (n = 2), a perforator, retouched flakes (n = 10), utilized flakes (n = 8), and two split pebble cores. The lithic assemblage was largely local materials (72.6%), with exotic materials emphasizing sources in British Columbia (6.5%).

The faunal assemblage (n = 2,722) was highly pulverized (Ronaghan 1992:53); the majority of the bone (n = 2,378) could only be classified as mammal bone fragments. Recognized species include mule deer, moose, and bison. Only three green-bone fractures and one instance of butchering marks were observed. No clear features were recorded although FBR (n = 114) was recovered, some apparently arranged in a linear or clustered distribution (Ronaghan 1992:54). Three radiocarbon dates are available to assess this component: 3,960, 4,650, and 5,200 BP (Table 11). Although the researcher accepted the range of dates, the first date is late and well within the succeeding Oxbow time period, but the latter two dates overlap.

Anderson (FdOt 1). The Anderson site is a campsite near the Battle River on high ground overlooking Hardisty Lake (Quigg 1984). In 1978, a series of tests were conducted at the site. Test excavation Unit B, 2 × 4 m, encountered a cluster of artifacts at 48–63 cm BS and contained atlatl points, among other things. The excavation was part of a research program on archaeological sites in the parkland.

Seven side-notched points were recovered from the well-defined occupation layer. Quigg (1984:153) classified these as Bitterroot points after Reeves' (1969) definition. However, two basic forms are present: a large Oxbow-like point with a slightly concave base and wide, *v*-shaped notches (Quigg 1984:155, figs. 3, 5–7) and a smaller point with a rounded base with minimal basal convexity and wide, open notches (Quigg 1984:155, fig. 3, nos. 1–4). Other tools recovered include bifaces (n = 3), end scrapers (n = 8), unifaces (n = 3), retouched tools (n = 15), an anvil, and a hammerstone. There was little primary reduction detritus but secondary and sharpening/resharpening flakes were relatively common (Quigg 1984:153). Quartz and quartzite accounted for 80 percent of the raw material use, while pebble cherts and silicified wood account for most of the remaining lithic material (Quigg 1984:153). The faunal assemblage consisted of over one thousand bone fragments, of which fewer than one hundred were identifiable. All identifiable bone was bison. Every element was represented except those in the front quarter (i.e., humerus, radius, and ulna). A minimum of eight animals were present. No seasonal information was derived. Some burned bone (500 g) was also recovered. No features were observed and only eleven pieces of FBR were noted.

Two disparate radiocarbon dates were obtained for this occupation (Table 11). Given the vertical distribution of the material in the site (15 cm), the presence of two distinct projectile points, and two distinct dates, the site likely represents a palimpsest. The smaller, rounded-base points are most likely associated with the Maple Leaf phase and the earlier date while the larger more Oxbow-like points likely associate with the pre-Oxbow Estevan phase and the later date.

Other sites. A few other Alberta assemblages exhibit traits that might be considered representative of the Maple Leaf complex. At Head-Smashed-In Buffalo Jump, Reeves (1978) recovered Bitterroot, Salmon River, and Pelican Lake-like points in layers dated between 5,600 and 5,000 BP. Specimens that morphologically appear to correlate to the current use of Salmon River fishtail points occur in the Head-Smashed-In material (Reeves 1978:171, fig. 17.21, nos. 9, 10, and 13). The current model would suggest these points could occur in the earlier levels of what Reeves (1978) lumped together as the Mummy Cave complex. The Wimpey site (EgPn 146) in northwest Calgary is discussed in previous sections. This stratified sequence produced a Salmon River fishtail point about 10 cm above the Mazama Ash layer. It exhibits striking resemblance to the points from the Mona Lisa site. The lack of radiocarbon dates is not too significant given the strong sequence of material that can be typologically dated. Similarly, a single specimen from Scapa, Basin 4, Component 4, is very similar to the Wimpey and Mona Lisa points. The specimen is heavily resharpened and, although not radiometrically dated, it is stratigraphically located between Mazama Ash and a component of Calderwood material (Hanna and Neal 1992:112–118). The Stampede (DjOn 26) site in the Cypress Hills of southeastern Alberta also produced projectile points that exhibit some traits similar to Salmon River fishtail projectile points, in Palaeosols 8 and 10, dating to ca. 6,100 BP (Oetelaar 2004a).

Lastly, the third occupation at the Gap site (DlOp 20) overlies Mazama Ash and produced a point blade associated with some bison rib fragments, two navicular cuboids, one proximal metacarpal, four partially burned carpals, miscellaneous burned bone fragments, and an ash-fill pit (Reeves and Dormaar 1972:332). A date of about 6,000 BP was obtained (Table 11). This material fits temporally with the material discussed here.

Maple Leaf: Subsisting in the Foothills and Front Range

Driver (1978) used the term *Maple Leaf subphase* to label culture-historical events in the Early Middle Prehistoric period in the Crowsnest Pass dating between 7,500 to 3,000 BP. As well, the Maple Leaf site provided significant materials that date to this period. For these reasons, the term *Maple Leaf* is retained from its earlier use in this model of culture history and applied here as the Maple Leaf complex. The Maple Leaf complex is defined by the large and small varieties of Salmon River projectile points; this material dates between ca. 6,300 and 5,200 BP. The terminological alteration is meant to acknowledge the previous research, at the same time reflecting the refined temporal distribution of the material and the enlarged geographic spread of the similar assemblages well into the foothills and perhaps the Plains proper.

The Salmon River side-notched projectile point derives its origin from the misclassification of Alberta materials using the typology Swanson and Sneed (1966) developed for materials in Idaho. The Salmon River point as originally defined does not occur in Alberta, as they are strictly defined as a regional variant of Bitterroot side-notched points found only at the Shoup rockshelters site in Idaho and not common abroad (Swanson and Sneed 1966:24). The point was originally described as a flat-based, shallow, side-notched point with notching close enough to the base to remove a small portion of the corner of the point. Morphologically the point is not particularly similar to the material described for Alberta (see Swanson and Sneed 1966:36, fig. 18h–j). The Alberta material tends to be larger overall, with much more of the base being removed in notching, making a narrower base (i.e., fishtail appearance) that is straight to concave. Still, the term is somewhat ingrained, so for Alberta modifications of the original term are suggested here, in order to address these specimens. Thus, in Alberta, for the larger dart points that exhibit the narrow, concave base the term *Salmon River fishtail point* is suggested. For the smaller points that exhibit a narrow, flat to convex base, the term *Salmon River oval-base* is suggested. Compared to other periods and typological classifications, this material is more varied. At some point in the future it would not be surprising to find a number of cultural complexes/phases and projectile point types represented in what is defined here as the Maple Leaf complex.

The only reasonably sized assemblages recovered of Maple Leaf material came from EgPn 87 and at the Sara site. It is difficult to generalize about such limited samples. Still, raw material occurred in large enough numbers at EgPn 87 and the Sara site to be quantified. Quartzite, basalt, siltstone, and miscellaneous cherts predominate the two assemblages. Some Knife River flint, Avon chert, Montana chert, Etherington chert, obsidian, and Top-of-the-World chert also occur in small amounts in these assemblages.

The fauna from the sites is largely restricted to bison. EgPn 87, Mona Lisa, and Anderson produced bison bone. The Sara site produced bison bone along with evidence of moose and mule deer. The Maple Leaf site also contained bison, along with dog, badger and goose. The associations between the projectile points and the faunal assemblages was questionable at the Sara and Maple Leaf sites. Certainly, bison were a major subsistence focus at this time. The animals were being taken in small ambushes at natural traps such as the wetland at the Maple Leaf site or the coulees at the Mona Lisa site.

Features are not common in these sites. The absence of FBR was noted at EgPn 87. FBR was not reported at the Maple Leaf site, the Mona Lisa site or the Gap site. Eleven pieces were reported at the Anderson site. At the Sara site no clear features were recorded but clusters of FBR, totalling one hundred fourteen pieces, were present. The low occurrence of FBR in these assemblages suggests it was being produced by spalling around a campfire, rather than as a product of intensive stone boiling. The FBR patterning at the Sara site is difficult to interpret but it might reflect the use of cooking platforms.

The majority of the known sites in Alberta are located in the foothills (e.g., DjPo 47, EgPn 87, EgPm 3, DjPn 16, DlPo 16, and EgPn 146). Sites on the periphery of the Plains are known but are much less common (e.g., FdOt 1 and ElPa 1), while no sites are known from the Plains proper, with the exception of prairie "oases" such as the Cypress Hills (e.g., DjOn 26).

Looking further abroad, dated components of Maple Leaf material or sites dated to this period are not known from Saskatchewan. In Manitoba, the Atkinson (DiMe 27) site on the north bank of the Souris River dates to ca. 5,400 BP (Nicholson and Playford 2009). Beneath a McKean occupation, seven projectile points were recovered and classified as Gowen points (Nicholson and Playford 2009:31–33). The form of the Atkinson site Gowen points are not similar to Maple Leaf specimens, nor are they similar to Alberta's Gowen.

In Montana, there may be point styles similar to the Maple Leaf complex. The Cremer site (24SW264) is a multicomponent site in south-central Montana, exhibiting five cultural components (Nowatzyk 1983). The second deepest layer, IV, was interpreted as an Early Middle Prehistoric period occupation that produced large barbed points in apparent association with side-notched points and fishtail points (Nowatzyk 1983:88). The layer could be interpreted as representing a palimpsest of Burmis barbed points (Nowatzyk 1983:76, fig. 13m, n), Mummy Cave points (Nowatzyk 1983:76, fig. 13d–h), and Salmon River fishtail points (Nowatzyk 1983, fig. 13a–c, i–l). To the south, in North Dakota and Wyoming, there does not appear to be cultural material equivalent to the Maple Leaf complex. More data will assist in addressing this assessment. The Maple Leaf complex appears to be a geographically restricted cultural phenomenon exhibiting distinctive projectile points over a relatively brief period of time. Perhaps with a larger and better-dated sample this apparent "complex" of material may be recognized as something more culturally discrete.

CALDERWOOD COMPLEX (CA. 5,200 TO 4,700 BP)

In the late 1960s and early 1970s, Reeves (1978) recovered what he termed Mummy Cave materials in the deepest culture-bearing levels at Head-Smashed-In Buffalo Jump. In both the north and south excavation areas, materials were recovered that dated between 5,700 and 5,100 BP. The projectile points exhibited a wide range of variability, being classified as Bitterroot, Salmon River, and Pelican Lake-like (Reeves 1978:164, 171). A similar range of projectile point variability was recovered from EfPs 3 in the Kananaskis area (Reeves 1974). At EfPs 3, sixteen points were recovered from a context geologically dated to ca. 7,000 to 5,000 BP. Like the Head-Smashed-In Buffalo Jump material, the points were classified as Bitterroot, Salmon River, and Pelican Lake-like points. Again in the mid-1970s, Reeves (1976) excavated DjPo 9 near Bellevue in the Crowsnest Pass. A single point was recovered in the earliest occupation; it was classified as Bitterroot, despite its rounded base and fairly broad notches.

Other materials that date to this time period have been similarly classified as Bitterroot, Salmon River, or Pelican Lake-like. At the Michalsky site, Ronaghan (1992:117) recovered a single point from a dated context of ca. 5,000 BP. He classified it as a Bitterroot point despite its rounded ears and concave base. In Component 2 at the Vermilion Lakes site, Fedje (1986:38) recovered numerous points considered to "compare favourably to the Pelican Lake type." The component was not radiocarbon dated and the assemblage exhibited the range of morphological variability similar to the aforementioned assemblages (see Fedje 1986:39, fig. 11b–f).

The Sites

The following presents well-dated sites with diagnostic materials that post-date the Mazama Ash fall event but predate the highly recognizable Oxbow phase. As alluded to above, the assemblages from this period, ca. 5,000 BP, do not exhibit the classic Bitterroot criteria of well-defined basal edges, relatively square notches, and sharp shoulders, but rather a wide range of morphological variability (see Plate 13 and Figure 14).

Head-Smashed-In Buffalo Jump (DkPj 1). Head-Smashed-In Buffalo Jump consists of a kill site and an associated processing site located at the southeastern edge of the Porcupine Hills in southwestern Alberta. This kill site complex consists of a gathering basin and drive lanes located to the west of the Porcupine Hills, which lead to the jump at their eastern edge.

PLATE 13 Calderwood points. Illustrated are projectile points from Head-Smashed-In Buffalo Jump (DkPj 1) (a–f); the Stampede site (DjOn 26), Palaeosol 7b (g–i), Palaeosol 7 (j–o) and Palaeosol 6 (aa and bb); DjPo 9 (p); the Majorville Medicine Wheel (EdPc 1) (q–u); EfPs 3 (v); the Scapa site (ElPa 1) (w–y); and the Michalsky site (DjPn 66) (z). *Photo credit:* Royal Alberta Museum (a–f); Gerald Oetelaar (g–o, aa and bb); Alberta Culture and Community Spirit (p–z).

FIGURE 14
Calderwood sites within Alberta

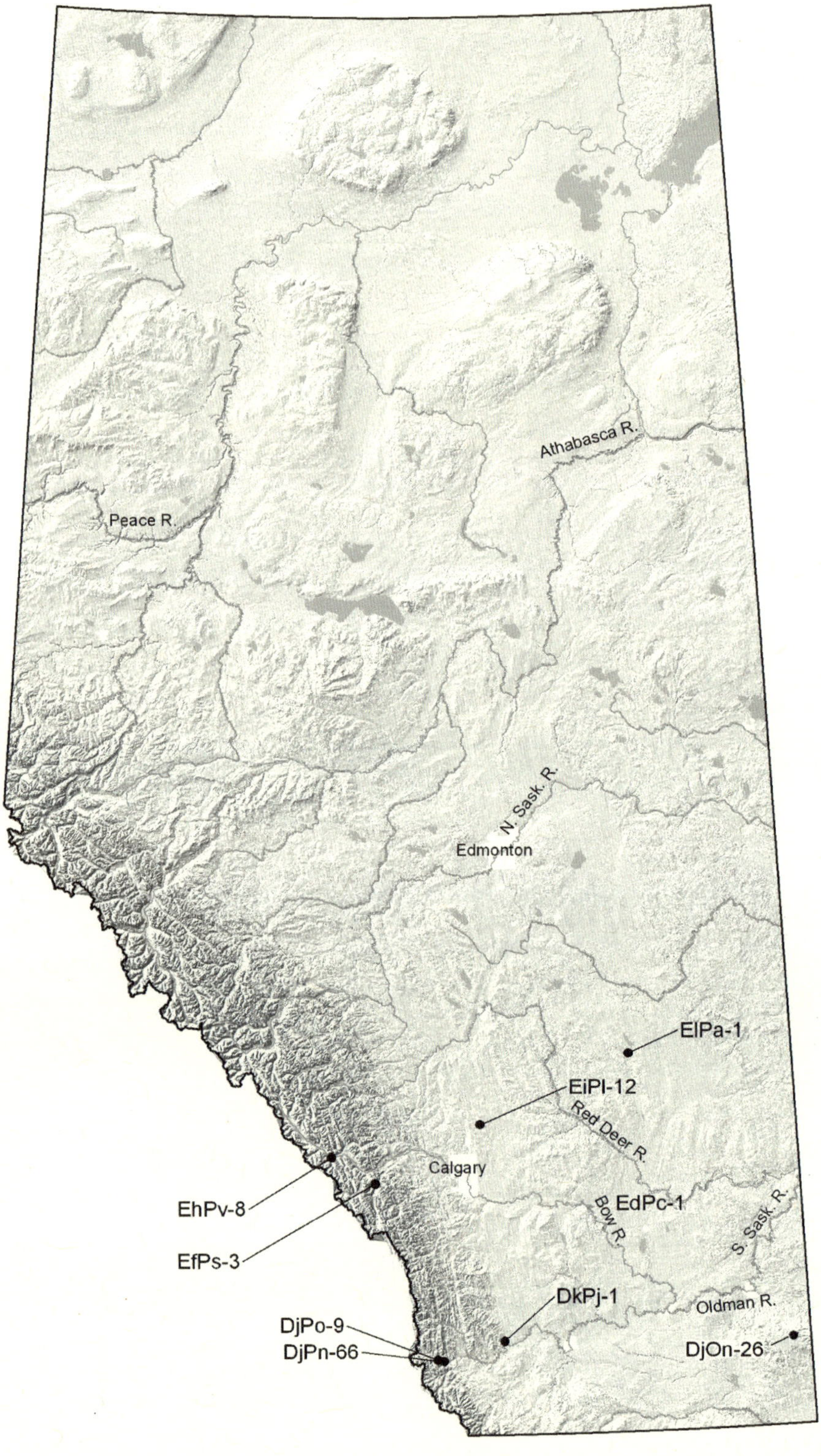

The jump consists of a sandstone outcrop running a lateral distance of 350 m with drops of approximately eleven to thirteen metres. At the base of the jump is a bison bone midden. The associated processing site is located below the jump, to the east, on flatter ground. In the late 1960s and early 1970s, Reeves (1978) excavated in the north and south areas of the kill site deposits.

Reeves (1978) defined the oldest culture-bearing levels as the Mummy Cave complex. The South Area produced three Mummy Cave levels while the North Area produced four levels; these levels dated to between ca. 5,700 and 5,100 BP. Fourteen points were recovered from the Mummy Cave levels. The points were classified as Bitterroot, Salmon River, and Pelican Lake-like (Reeves 1978:164, 171). Despite the lack of strict provenience, it was argued above that the Maple Leaf complex is represented by the Salmon River points (i.e., Reeves 1978:171, fig. 17.21, nos. 9, 10, 11, and 13); these were likely recovered from the earliest of Reeves' Mummy Cave levels. The remaining points, although morphologically varied, may fall into what is labelled here as the Calderwood complex.

Four dates were obtained from the Mummy Cave levels at Head-Smashed-In Buffalo Jump (see Table 12). The date from the Gakushuin lab (GAK) is known to be unacceptable (Blakeslee 1994). The remaining dates suggested an age for the material likely postdating ca. 5,500 BP.

Majorville Medicine Wheel (EdPc 1). The Majorville Medicine Wheel is a cairn made of cobbles approximately 9 m in diameter, from which twenty-six to twenty-eight spokes radiate out to a larger ring of stones that encircles the cairn. The stone circle has a radius of approximately 14 m. The site is located on the highest hilltop in the vicinity of Bassano (Calder 1977:4–5). Calder (1977) excavated the south half of the cairn and inferred it was likely created by the slow accumulation of successive layers of stone. The traditional interpretation is that a sequence of projectile points from the Oxbow phase through to the Old Women's phase was represented in the accretional layers, suggesting that there is chronological significance in the cairn's construction (Calder 1977:8–41). In this traditional assessment, Calderwood points were grouped with Oxbow (i.e., Calder 1977, fig. 33, nos. 24–28). The projectile points suggest the initiation of the cairn predates the Oxbow phase by a few hundred years with the actual commencement of use during the Calderwood phase.

TABLE 12 Radiocarbon dates for Calderwood sites (calibrated by OxCal 3.10 [Ramsey 2005])

Site [LAB NO.]	Conventional ^{14}C Age	$^{13}C/^{12}C$ Ratio	Material	Calibration	Reference
DkPj 1 [RL-333]	5160 +/- 120	-20.0‰	collagen	4350–3700 B.C. (p = 0.954)	Reeves 1978; Morlan n.d.
DkPj 1 [GAK-1476]	4050 +/- 100	—	—	rejected	Reeves 1978
DkPj 1 [RL-334]	5740 +/- 100	-20.0‰	collagen	4800–4360 B.C. (p = 0.954)	Reeves 1978; Morlan n.d.
DkPj 1 [GSC-803]	5490 +/- 300	-20.0‰	collagen	5000–3600 B.C. (p = 0.954)	Reeves 1978; Morlan n.d.
DjOn 26 [TO-10925]	6100 +/- 70	?	?	5220–4840 B.C. (p = 0.954)	Oetelaar 2004a
DjOn 26 [TO-10922]	5230 +/- 100	?	charred bone	4350–375 B.C. (p = 0.954)	Oetelaar 2004a
DjOn 26 [OXA-11579]	4660 +/- 38	?	?	3630–3600 B.C. (p = 0.032) 3530–3360 B.C. (p = 0.922)	Óetelaar 2004a
DjPn 66 [AECV-224C]	5120 +/- 200	-25.0‰	charcoal	4400–3500 B.C. (p = 0.954)	Ronaghan 1992:117; Morlan n.d.
DjPn 66 [AECV-225C]	4980 +/- 90	-25.0‰	charcoal	3970–3630 B.C. (p = 0.954)	Ronaghan 1992:117; Morlan n.d.
DjPn 66 [AECV-223C]	4930 +/- 100	-25.0‰	charcoal	3960–3520 B.C. (p = 0.954)	Ronaghan 1992:117; Morlan n.d.
DjPn 66 [AECV-222C]	3390 +/- 100	-25.0‰	charcoal	rejected	Ronaghan 1992:117; Morlan n.d.
DjPo 9 [RL-507]	4770 +/- 130	-20.0‰	bone	3950–3100 B.C. (p = 0.954)	Morlan n.d.

Michalsky (DjPn 66), Component 1. The Michalsky site is a multi-component campsite at the head of a spring that originates high above the valley of the Crowsnest River in the lower slopes of the Livingstone Range (Ronaghan 1992:110). The site was named for the landowner. The University of Calgary originally discovered the site in 1973. It was identified as a series of isolated finds and an historic homestead. In 1985, Ronaghan (1992:110) excavated a dispersed series of 1-×-1-m (5.575 m²) units at the site (Ronaghan 1992:110). Two components were differentiated: a lower Bitterroot component and a culturally unidentified component. The site was estimated to be 15,000 m².

A single point was recovered from the lower component. The researcher classified it as a Bitterroot point (Ronaghan 1992:117), but its rounded ears and concave base suggest this is not appropriate. A small assemblage of material was found associated with the point, including a perforator and some debitage (n = 16). The raw materials are all local, including siltstones, miscellaneous cherts, and basalts. The faunal assemblage (n = 94) was small, fragmented, and of little interpretive value (Ronaghan 1992:117)

Four radiocarbon dates are available for this component (Table 12). The youngest date can be rejected owing to its conflict with its stratigraphic position; the other dates are highly consistent (Ronaghan 1992:117). The site locale provides a good spot for short-term camping and game observation but the limited excavations conducted in the meadow were not enough to infer onsite activities, duration and season of occupation, or other subsistence settlement characteristics.

DjPo 9, Test 10, Occupation 1. DjPo 9 is a stratified campsite in a sheltered swale on an outwash terrace in the Bellevue/Maple Leaf area of the Crowsnest Pass (Reeves 1976:29). The 1975 investigations exhibited four occupation levels. The lowest level, Component 1, was considered late Mummy Cave. A single point was recovered. The researchers classified it as a Bitterroot side-notched point but the rounded ears and broad notches suggest this designation may not be appropriate. Other tools recovered included an end scraper, retouched flakes (n = 2), and large stone flake tools (n = 2). Twenty-two pieces of lithic debitage were also associated with this occupation. The small lithic assemblage was dominated by quartzite and local cherts. The faunal assemblage produced evidence of a single adult bison. The bone was highly fragmented and only a few skull and tooth fragments were recovered (Reeves 1976:49). For this occupation there was no mention of FBR or features, and a single date of about 4,800 BP was obtained (Table 12).

Vermilion Lakes, Locality B (EhPv 8, 502R). The Vermilion Lakes site is described in a previous section. Locality B, Occupation 2, contained side- and corner-notched points considered similar to Pelican Lake points (Fedje 1986:39, fig. 11b–f). A corner-notched specimen does exist, as does round based specimens with large notches. In addition to the points, a large lithic assemblage (n = 5,300) was recovered from a fairly small area. The bulk of the material was recovered from a 10-m^2 area (Fedje 1986:38). Morphologically this assemblage appears to exhibit much of the variability found within assemblages dating to ca. 5,000 BP. Radiocarbon dates, however, were not available for this level.

EfPs 3. EfPs 3 is a single-component campsite located in the Kananaskis Valley, southwest of Barrier Lake (Reeves 1974). The site is situated on a 7-m-high gravel terrace produced by glacial outwash, above the Kananaskis River (Reeves 1974). In 1973, a total of 104 m^2 was excavated at the site. The site area was estimated to be 1,510 m^2. It was excavated as a mitigation project prior to a highway alignment (Reeves 1974:1). The majority of the site was destroyed by the highway construction.

Sixteen projectile points were recovered from the site. The researcher suggested these included Bitterroot (n = 4), Salmon River (n = 3), Pelican Lake (n = 2), Lusk (n = 1), ground argillite (n = 1), and unclassifiable (n = 5) points. There is a wide range of variability within these points. This variability includes corner-notched points; round-based, broad-notched points; and side-notched points. Other tools recovered from the site included bifaces (n = 16), end scrapers (n = 22), retouched flakes (n = 71), perforators (n = 3), gravers/cutters (n = 210), a wedge, cores (n = 88), choppers (n = 8), hammerstones (n = 8), anvils (n = 3), a grinding slab, rubbing stones (n = 14), and ochre fragments (n = 8). Banff chert dominated the lithic assemblage, with smaller amounts of miscellaneous cherts, quartzite, and chalcedony (Reeves 1974:61).

The faunal assemblage was very sparse, likely having been reduced by the acidic podzol soil (Reeves 1974:49). Only twelve calcine long-bone fragments and five pieces of tooth enamel were recovered. The tooth fragments were identified as bison (Reeves 1974:50). FBR was also very rare at the site. A total of sixty-eight small fragments was recovered, all of local quartzite, sandstone, and conglomerate cobbles (Reeves 1974:49). No clear activity areas were delineated (Reeves 1974:49).

The site was not radiocarbon dated, but typological cross dating suggested an age between 7,500 and 5,000 BP. This date was arrived at by acknowledging that Oxbow and McKean points, which were known at the time to postdate 5,000 BP, did not occur in the assemblage (Reeves 1974:8). Geological dating also suggested an age estimate between 7,500 and 5,000 BP (Reeves 1974:9). The range of variability within the assemblage typologically compares to assemblages estimated to date about 5,000 BP.

Scapa Ribstone (ElPa 1). The Scapa Ribstone site is described above. Three projectile points were recovered in Components 5 and 6 that exhibit striking similarity to those describe as dating to ca. 5,000 BP. This includes two round-based, broad-notched points and a corner-notched specimen. The corner-notched specimen from Component 5 and the side-notched points from Component 6 were all classified as likely Besant (Hanna and Neal 1992:120, 129). This assignment is refuted by the stratigraphy, as Besant invariably overlies Pelican Lake (Component 4), not the reverse. Component 5 had a burned bone concentration and a random scatter of FBR. Component 6 exhibited a debitage concentration, a bone concentration and random scatter of FBR, and a possible stone circle with a central hearth. Although a radiometric date is not available for the components, their stratigraphic position relative to other point styles supports an age estimate of approximately 5,000 BP.

Stampede (DjOn 26). The Stampede site also contained components that produced projectile point assemblages exhibiting tremendous variability. Palaeosols 8, 7B, 7A, and 6 have morphologically diverse projectile point samples that date to ca. 6,000–5,000 BP (Oetelaar 2004a). Palaeosol 8 was dated to ca. 6,100 BP. Palaeosol 7A produced two dates: ca. 4,700 BP and 5,200 BP (Table 12). An initial evaluation of the sediments suggested the assemblage was not the result of deflation or mixing (Brian Vivian, personal communication 2007).

Other sites. In the Wintering Hills, EhPd 88 is a stratified site with five complete and four fragmentary points in a context immediately above Mazama Ash (Loveseth 1984:102). The point styles were interpreted as Late Plains, but under the current classification system they are considered Calderwood points (Loveseth 1984: plate 17, nos. 2, 3, 4, 10, 11, 17, and 19). No dates were obtained for the material. Another possible Calderwood site is EiPl 12, west of Beiseker. It consisted of a small campsite exhibiting "Salmon River" points (Loveseth 1981). The six relatively complete points (Loveseth 1981: plate 4, nos. 1–6) appear similar in their range of variation to the Calderwood projectile points.

Calderwood: Social and Material Culture Diversity Five Thousand Years Ago

The lack of a single iconic projectile point within the assemblages from this period in time provides problems for classification. Additionally, the assemblages that exhibit a diverse range of projectile point morphology were recovered from across southern Alberta, including the Crowsnest Pass area in the southwest (i.e., Michalsky, DjPo 9), the Kananaskis area in the west-central (i.e., EfPs 3), the Cypress Hills in the southeast (i.e., Stampede), and the parkland periphery in the south-central (i.e., Majorville, Scapa) parts of the province. None of the projectile points exhibit the morphological features of Bitterroot side-notched points. Yet, some commonalities occur across the assemblages. Whether this material is culturally cohesive remains to be demonstrated, but it is presented here as such. Collectively this material has been labelled Calderwood complex owing to the first excavated assemblage occurring at Head-Smashed-In Buffalo Jump on the Calderwood family's land (Reeves 1978). These assemblages date between 5,200 and 4,700 BP.

Perhaps four projectile point forms can be subjectively differentiated within the larger range of variation of Calderwood material. One form has an elongate outline with broad-round notches and a straight base. One complete specimen was recovered at DjPo 9, and another from Palaeosol 7A at the Stampede site, and a base was recovered from Palaeosol 7B at the Stampede site. Another form is stout with very sharp shoulders, almost barbed-like in appearance, small round notches, and a slightly concave base. Fairly complete specimens of this form were recovered at Michalsky, Palaeosol 7A at Stampede, Majorville, and Component 6 at Scapa. Yet another form is Oxbow-like in general outline, but with smaller ears, round open notches, and a concave base. This form was recovered at Majorville, in Palaeosols 7B and 7A at Stampede, and in Component 6 at Scapa. Lastly, a type of almost-corner-notched specimen with an irregular to straight base and very wide-open notches was recovered from Majorville, Component 5 at Scapa, and Palaeosol 7A at Stampede. To reiterate, the projectile point samples presented here are small and the range of diversity is quite wide. Further research may find that the point assemblages are palimpsests, truly associated, or culturally intertwined.

There is nothing exceptional about the non-projectile point tools associated with the Calderwood complex. Typical items such as bifaces, end scrapers, retouched flakes, choppers, and hammerstones have been recovered. The Calderwood lithic assemblage is based on local raw materials. Few if any exotics were recovered from these sites. Quartzite, siltstone, and Banff chert are amongst the more common toolstones. Bison are the primary animal identified in the faunal assemblages. The quantity of bone recovered is usually small and other species (e.g., fox and moose) were also recovered. Although there is some evidence for large bison kills at Head-Smashed-In Buffalo Jump, these major events appear to be rare. Most sites appear to be small habitation sites with minimal features and processing.

The likelihood of cairn building commencing at the Majorville Medicine Wheel adds a new level to social complexity that might be mirroring requirements for communal bison killing.

GOWEN COMPLEX (CA. 5,900 TO 5,200 BP)

In 1977, a site was uncovered by earth-moving equipment in terrace deposits along the South Saskatchewan River within the City of Saskatoon, Saskatchewan (Schroedl and Walker 1978; Walker 1992:1). The site was named Gowen 1 (FaNq 25) after its discoverer Charlie Gowen. Three years later, a second cultural deposit, Gowen 2 (FaNq 32), was discovered 70 m to the west (Walker 1992:1). Five radiocarbon dates were obtained for Gowen 1 and four dates for Gowen 2 (Walker 1992:24). An average date of about 5,900 BP was produced for the assemblages. The projectile point assemblages from the two sites were considered similar (Walker 1992:72). Lateral margins of the point blades were usually convex or straight, asymmetry was not uncommon, the maximum width of the blade was usually at the shoulders except in reworked points, most points were side-notched with shallow and wide notches low on the lateral margins, and the basal margin was usually straight to slightly concave (Walker 1992:44, 72). Walker (1992) called these "Gowen side-notched points." Other recovered lithic tools included hafted bifaces (possible spear tips), bifacial knives, end scrapers, side scrapers, unifaces, gouges, gravers, drills, spokeshaves, retouched lithics, anvils, and hammerstones (Walker 1992:45–66, 77–94). Bone tools included a possible bone tube, awls, and other miscellaneous altered bone fragments (Walker 1992:66–70, 94–95). Lithics used at the Gowen sites focused on locally available quartzite and chert, with chalcedonies and petrified wood used to a lesser extent (Walker 1992:65).

The Gowen sites' faunal assemblages are highly fragmented. The Gowen 1 site produced two wolf-sized canids, one antelope, and seven bison. The bison bone suggested transport of select body portions to the site for processing. The presence of two young animals indicated that the site was occupied in the summer (Walker 1992:101). A smudge pit produced Chenopodiaceae, likely utilized as a smudge material or possibly embedded in utilized dung (Walker 1992:103). A number of shallow basin pits and surface hearths were also recovered. The Gowen 2 site produced one muskrat, a variety of canid bone (possibly coyote, wolf, and/or dog), and fourteen bison (Walker 1992:103–107). Similar bone reduction patterns were observed. Hearths in this site seemed to have been excavated to be more basin-like (Walker 1992:115–119). Lastly, small quantities of bulky pieces of FBR were recovered from both sites (Walker 1992:94).

In 1988, during the excavation of the basement beneath his home in Saskatoon, Les Norby encountered archaeological remains. The Norby site (FbNp 56) is a Mummy Cave bison kill that produced two complete Gowen side-notched points and a stemmed point (Zurburg 1991). The lithic assemblage consisted of local materials (Zurburg 1991:65–66). Three radiocarbon dates were obtained for the site, suggesting an age of about 5,700 BP (Zurburg 1991:175). Interestingly, the kill was interpreted as a male bison herd of twenty-six individuals; not surprisingly, young animals were absent (Zurburg 1991:182).

The Below Forks (FhNg 25) also produced Early Side-notched projectile points reminiscent of Gowen side-notched forms (Kasstan 2004:159). The lower component produced four points: two side-notched Gowen-like points, a small stemmed point, and a non-diagnostic blade (Kasstan 2004:98–99). As with the Gowen sites and the Norby site, the lithic assemblage consisted of mainly local raw materials (Kasstan 2004:51). Three radiocarbon dates suggest an age about 5,900 BP (Kasstan 2004:44).

Gowen side-notched points have been demonstrated to exhibit a fairly consistent form, with some variability, during a relatively limited period of time in central Saskatchewan (Kasstan 2004; Walker 1992; Zurburg 1991). As Walker (1992:72) outlined, these points have convex to straight blades, often exhibit asymmetry, distal blade width is maximum, wide and shallow notches are low on the lateral margins, and the basal margin is usually straight. The Gowen 1, Gowen 2, Norby, and Below Forks sites have all been radiocarbon dated to about 5,900 to 5,700 BP. Still, researchers have not delimited an archaeological culture that would distinguish the Gowen sites from the Early Side-notched/Mummy Cave series.

The Sites

In Alberta, there are two sites that may exhibit diagnostic materials similar to the Gowen side-notched assemblages in Saskatchewan. These sites are the Snyder Farm Locality at DjPm 36 and the Spring Kill site (EgPs 51). These two sites have been distinguished from other sites of a similar age by the presence of projectile points exhibiting straight to convex blades, asymmetry, maximum width at the distal blade and shallow, wide notches low on the lateral margins. In short, they seem to exhibit projectile points reminiscent of the Gowen forms in Saskatchewan (see Plate 14 and Figure 15).

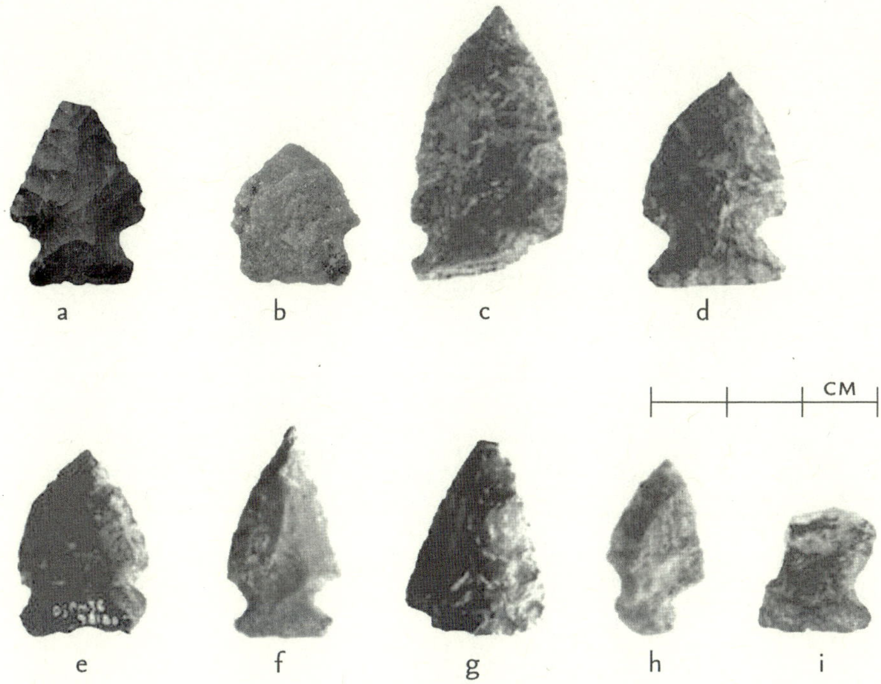

PLATE 14 Gowen points. Illustrated are projectile points from the Spring Kill site (EgPs 51) (a and b); and DjPm 36, Snyder Farm Locality, Component 1 (c–i). Photo credit: Alberta Culture and Community Spirit (a and b); Bison Historical Services Limited (c–i).

DjPm 36, Snyder Farm Locality, Component 1. DjPm 36, Snyder Farm locality, named after the tenant of the land, is located at the confluence of the North Fork of the Oldman River and the Crowsnest River (Van Dyke 1994:116). This part of the DjPm 36 site was excavated between 1988 and 1990. Evidence of Component 1 (the component exhibiting the Gowen side-notched material) was found in three excavation blocks. However, a large area was only opened up in one block. A total of 51 m^2 was excavated (Van Dyke 1994:122). The site was part of the mitigation program in response to the construction of the Oldman River Dam.

Twelve points or point fragments were recovered in association with a possible hearth and lithic and bone concentrations. Van Dyke (1994:128) acknowledged that the majority of the points are very comparable to the Gowen side-notched type. Other tools recovered included bifaces (n = 2), cores (n = 33), end scrapers (n = 12), retouched flakes (n = 12), a unifacial knife, a scraper/plane, a hammerstone, and an anvil (Van Dyke 1994:123). The lithic assemblage emphasized local quartzite and siltstones but also exhibited more exotic materials such as Knife River flint, Montana chert, and obsidian (Van Dyke 1994:246). The vast majority of the debitage is tertiary detritus. There are two concentrations of debitage within the excavation block: a retooling location by a possible hearth and a second location away

FIGURE 15
Gowen sites
within Alberta

from the hearth. Two pieces of worked bone were also recovered. The faunal assemblage (n = 4,608) had a minimum of four bison (two fetal), a deer, a bird, a large canid, and a medium to small canid (Van Dyke 1994:126). The differential development of the fetal bison bone suggested both early and late winter events, which might indicate prolonged use of the site. The bone, like the tools and the debitage, was distributed in two major clusters of material culture on the living floor. A few burned and calcine pieces of bone were recovered. FBR was rare (Van Dyke 1994:121).

A single radiocarbon date of about 5,900 BP was obtained for the site (Van Dyke 1994:126). The researchers interpreted the site as a possible household structure in which people who manufactured Gowen side-notched points produced two clusters of activities, including lithic workshop debitage and domestic detritus around a possible hearth (surface burns) during winter (Van Dyke 1994).

Spring Kill (EgPs 51). The Spring Kill site is located along the Bow River near Exshaw in the front range of the Rocky Mountains (Kooyman 2000a:1). The site derived its name from a nearby spring that had waterlogged the site sediments, thus eroding bison bone. Six general stratigraphic layers were identified with major bone deposits in Layers 3 and 4. Each general stratigraphic layer was further subdivided into more discrete depositional events. Only Layer 3 produced diagnostic material; two Gowen side-notched points were recovered (Kooyman 2000a:10–14). A total of 10 m^2 was excavated as part of a research program (Kooyman 2000a:3)

Two points and an apparent point tip were recovered in possible association with the bone beds (Kooyman 2000a:55–56). Kooyman (2000a:55–56) considered the points to be most similar to Gowen side-notched points. No other tools were recovered in Layer 3 but a few pieces of debitage (n = 12) were noted. Banff chert was the most exotic raw material used while quartzite and chert dominated the small assemblage (Kooyman 2000a:95–96). The faunal assemblage was largely bison but a single large canid bone was also recovered. The bison were larger than modern bison. The absence of the humerus and femur indicated the highest-utility bones were removed from the site (Kooyman 2000a:52). Marrow removal was not conducted, at least not on the entire skeleton. The butchering pattern and sediment deposition suggested that several episodes likely occurred at the site with individual animals being dispatched (Kooyman 2000a:50–51). No features were observed.

A total of five radiocarbon dates was obtained for Layer 3 (see Table 13). Layer 4, immediately beneath this layer, provided a date of 5,400 BP. However, Newton's (1991:121) initial discovery of the site provided a radiocarbon date for Layer 3 of approximately 6,000 BP. Kooyman (2000a:18) could not provide a reasonable explanation for the asynchronous dates.

TABLE 13 Radiocarbon dates for Gowen sites (calibrated by OxCal 3.10 [Ramsey 2005])

Site [LAB NO.]	Conventional ^{14}C Age	$^{13}C/^{12}C$ Ratio	Material	Calibration	Reference
DjPm 36 [AECV-1200C]	5920 +/- 170	-18.5‰	collagen	5250–4580 B.C. (p = 0.954)	Van Dyke 1994:126
EgPs 51 [AECV-2004C]	5190 +/- 70	n/a	charcoal	4240–4190 B.C. (p = 0.063) 4180–3890 B.C. (p = 0.765) 3880–3790 B.C. (p = 0.126)	Kooyman 2000a:126
EgPs 51 [AECV-1910C]	5330 +/- 90	n/a	charcoal	4340–3980 B.C. (p = 0.954)	Kooyman 2000a:126
EgPs 51 [AECV-2006C]	5370 +/- 90	n/a	charcoal	4360–3980 B.C. (p = 0.954)	Kooyman 2000a:126
EgPs 51 [AECV-2005C]	5010 +/- 90	n/a	charcoal	3970–3640 B.C. (p = 0.954)	Kooyman 2000a:126
EgPs 51 [AECV-2003C]	5000 +/- 80	?	collagen	3960–3650 B.C. (p = 0.954)	Kooyman 2000a:126

Gowen: A Distinct Cultural Entity?

The Snyder Farm Locality and EgPs 51 appear to yield Gowen side-notched points along with lithic assemblages that focus on local raw materials but exhibit some exotic material, small campsites, and small kill sites that date between 5,900 and 5,200 BP. For historical reasons, the Gowen side-notched points have consistently been interpreted as part of the Early Side-notched/Mummy Cave series of projectile points, and these points and their associated assemblages have been placed within the Early Middle Prehistoric period or Mummy Cave complex. In this review, the term *Mummy Cave complex* has been restricted to sites exhibiting Bitterroot side-notched points, an approach that applies a strict definition for Bitterroot points. Similarly, it is argued that the Gowen side-notched points and their associated assemblages are distinct and should be recognized as such. As defined, assemblages with apparent Gowen side-notched points appear to be rare in Alberta, if they exist at all. Notwithstanding, the original Gowen material in Saskatchewan exhibits a wide range of variability, so considerable research is still required to better understand the true nature of this phenomenon.

For purposes of this book, the Gowen side-notched point is considered to be diagnostic of the Gowen complex. As originally described by Walker (1992:44, 72) these points exhibit convex or straight blade margins, frequent asymmetry, maximum blade width at the shoulders, wide and shallow side-notches low on the lateral margins, and straight to slightly convex basal margins. Walker (1992:133) indicated that Gowen side-notched points may be synonymous with the Salmon River side-notched type (Swanson and Sneed 1966). Reeves (1973:1244) included both Swanson's (1962) Bitterroot and Salmon River side-notched points as diagnostics of the Mummy Cave complex. Although a statistical comparison of Walker's (1992) Gowen side-notched points and Swanson's (1962) Salmon River side-notched points has never been conducted, a visual examination suggests they are not particularly comparable. Partly for these reasons, the Salmon River side-notched point terminology has been retained in this book to describe projectile points associated with the Maple Leaf complex.

Given that only two sites in Alberta may contain Gowen material, little can be generalized about Gowen assemblages in the Province. There does not appear to be any unique tools associated with the Gowen complex, save the projectile points. The lithic raw material utilization appears to be focused on local raw materials such as quartzite and siltstone. In terms of subsistence, EgPs 51 appears to be a small ambush site, while the Snyder Farm Locality appears to be more domestic with a larger range of fauna reflected in the assemblage, including deer, a bird, and large and small-to-medium canids. A single feature was recorded at the Snyder Farm Locality; it was a small surface hearth with associated lithic and bone concentrations, suggesting domestic activities of a small group of people. Importantly, very little FBR was recovered, suggesting extensive processing had not been undertaken. Dates for the Gowen complex in Saskatchewan fall between 5,900 and 5,700 BP. For Alberta, the date for Snyder Farm Locality falls nicely within this range of dates but EgPs 51 is an outlier, dating to about 5,200 BP. The small number of possible sites and the range of dates mean there is work to be done, to increase our understanding of the Gowen complex.

ESTEVAN PHASE (CA. 4,900 TO 4,500 BP)

Reeves (1969:32) suggested that the co-occurrence of side-notched points with Oxbow points and McKean points provided evidence for a relationship between the Mummy Cave, the Oxbow, and the McKean complexes.

Reeves (1969:32) postulated that the Oxbow complex derived from the Mummy Cave complex and that the occasional McKean point in some assemblages was a product of cultural contact between two culturally distinct populations. A few years later, Reeves (1973) divided the Oxbow complex into Early and Late segments. He defined the Early Oxbow complex, ca. 5,000–4,500 BP, by the co-occurrence of Bitterroot and Oxbow points and the Late Oxbow complex, ca. 4,500–4,000 BP, by assemblages containing only Oxbow points. Reeves (1973:1240–1242) cited Long Creek Levels 8 and 9, Oxbow Dam, and Sorenson V as Early Oxbow sites.

Similarly, Dyck (1983:92–96) noted that both the Oxbow Dam site and Level 9 of the Long Creek site dated to the threshold of the Oxbow complex. Unlike Reeves (1973), who considered the material to be Early Oxbow with historical ties to the Mummy Cave complex, Dyck (1983) classified the material as Late Mummy Cave series assemblages. Materials from Levels 7 and 8 of the Long Creek site, on the other hand, he classified as Oxbow assemblages (Dyck 1983:96–100). This debate went beyond the Oxbow Dam and Long Creek sites. Large side-notched points recovered from the Anderson site in east-central Alberta were compared to the point assemblage recovered from Level 8 at Long Creek, amongst other sites (Quigg 1984). Despite calling the Anderson points Bitterroot side-notched points, the researcher considered the specimens to be comparable to the Oxbow specimens from Level 8 at Long Creek. Walker (1992:144) considered some similarities between Gowen side-notched points and the earliest Oxbow specimens from the Oxbow Dam and Long Creek sites. He noted that the comparisons were subjective and would require statistical confirmation. If correct, however, the Oxbow complex would be an in situ development from the preceding Gowen/Mummy Cave complex and not a cultural migration (Walker 1992:144). In his model there was no recognizable or discrete intermediate culture or diagnostic material culture, only similarity in point forms during a transition from Gowen to Oxbow.

The original Oxbow Dam site material was excavated in 1956. Green (2005) reviewed the interpretations surrounding the Oxbow Dam in a historical context. As well, he conducted additional excavations (18 m^2) at the site. His synthesis of this material is most illuminating. Oxbow dam is a multicomponent site, of which one level contained Oxbow material. The site was initially considered to be the type site for the Oxbow complex, but as more Oxbow sites were excavated it was gradually reinterpreted as an early transitional or proto-Oxbow site because of a radiocarbon date of ca.

5,200 BP (Green 2005:107). Green (2005:108) persuasively argued that material was mixed from both earlier and later levels, because of deformation of stratigraphic layers, into the level containing the Oxbow type assemblage. As well, the radiocarbon date was likely conducted on intrusive material from a lower level (Green 2005:4). Further complicating the picture was the inclusion of material from Levels 7 and 8 of the Long Creek site in the original assemblages used to define the Oxbow complex (Green 2005:3). Green's (2005:104–105) excavation at the Oxbow Dam site recovered a Late Oxbow assemblage dating to ca. 4,300 BP rather than the original 5,200 BP. Importantly, only "classic" Oxbow points (n = 5) were recovered, with no Mummy Cave material. This left Long Creek Level 8 appearing unusual, with its Oxbow-like points being associated with corner-notched specimens and a radiocarbon date of ca. 4,700 BP (earlier than "classic" Oxbow material). Regardless, Green (2005) considered Oxbow to derive from Gowen. The commonalities he saw between Gowen and Oxbow included small groups inhabiting sites for short periods of time, stalking lone animals or conducting small bison kills, with lithic technology such as split pebble technology, and tool assemblages including large hafted bifaces, ovoid bifaces, and flake perforators (Green 2005:102–103).

Bryant (2002, 2007) conducted an important reanalysis of the Long Creek site. Based on the original field notes for Level 8, she noted that as many as three occupations may be represented. A reconstruction of the provenience of specific artifacts, however, was not possible. Bryant (2002:185) classified all the points as Early Side-notched and/or Mummy Cave series points. A radiocarbon date of ca. 4,650 BP was originally obtained. Bryant (2002:204) got another radiocarbon date of ca. 4,960 BP, which supports the initial date. She interpreted these dates as placing the assemblage within the late Mummy Cave complex and early Oxbow complex, possibly representing a series of transitional levels (Bryant 2002:206). She emphasized that the points should not be confused with Bitterroot points but suggested there may be similarities to Gowen materials (Bryant 2002:223–224).

The Sites

A number of sites with radiocarbon dates in the period immediately predating the "classic" Oxbow material have been found in Alberta. These sites are presented in order to assess the various lines of thinking regarding archaeological assemblages immediately predating the Oxbow phase (see Plate 15 and Figure 16).

PLATE 15 Estevan points. Illustrated are projectile points from the Anderson site (FdOt 1) (a–c); EgPn 480, Component 3 (d and e); and the Boy Chief site (EeOv 68) (f). Photo credit: Alberta Culture and Community Spirit (a–c, f); Bison Historical Services Limited (d and e).

Anderson (FdOt 1). The Anderson site is a campsite near the Battle River on high ground overlooking Hardisty Lake (Quigg 1984). The site is discussed under the Maple Leaf complex. Testing encountered a concentration of artifacts at 48–63 cm BS containing, amongst other things, atlatl points exhibiting two distinct forms: a large block-eared, Oxbow-like point and a smaller round-based point. Similarly, two radiocarbon dates were obtained for this occupation: ca. 4,800 BP and 5,500 BP. Given the vertical distribution of the material in the site (15 cm), the presence of two distinct projectile points, and two distinct dates, it was previously suggested that the site is a palimpsest. The smaller, round-based points are most likely associated with the Maple Leaf complex and the earlier date. The larger, block-eared, more Oxbow-like points are likely associated with the pre-Oxbow date.

EgPn 480, Component 3. EgPn 480 is a multicomponent site in a prominent basin southeast of the Elbow River, west of Calgary (de Mille and Head 2001:54). The site is outlined in the section on the Scottsbluff-Eden phase. The second component exhibits both a corner-notched and side-notched projectile point. The two points were recovered in association with an FBR feature and a diffuse scatter of lithics and bone. The researchers indicated that the recovered points were most similar to Mummy Cave material. One specimen exhibited block ears similar to an Oxbow point while the second point was corner-notched, resembling a Pelican Lake point. Other tools recovered included bifaces (n = 2), end scrapers (n = 4), retouched tools (n = 12), side scrapers (n = 2), a utilized flake, choppers (n = 2), hammerstones (n = 2), a maul fragment, unidirectional cores (n = 4), multidirectional cores (n = 19), and miscellaneous cobbles (n = 31). The lithic assemblage was dominated by quartzite, siltstone, and sandstone (de Mille and Head 2001:97). In terms of the quartzite debitage, a high cortex to non-cortex ratio, heavy representation of larger-sized detritus, and large number of single-faceted

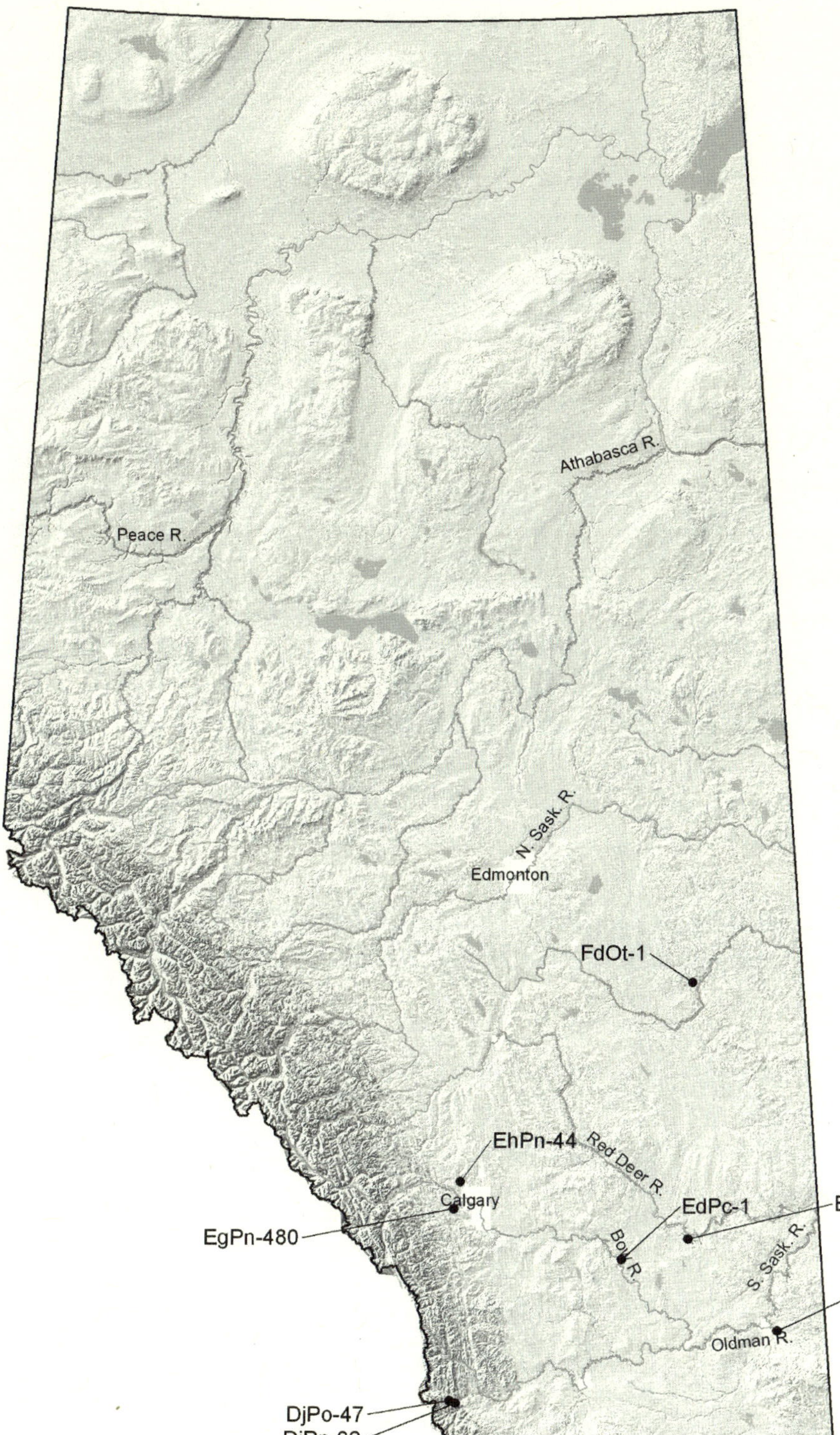

FIGURE 16
Estevan sites within Alberta

and cortex-covered platforms were interpreted as indicating early stages of core preparation and bifacial reduction. Few quartzite tools were recovered, suggesting their use elsewhere (de Mille and Head 2001:99). The siltstone debitage indicates a similar pattern.

The faunal assemblage (n = 222) consisted of bison, based on only thirty-eight identifiable fragments. A minimum of a single bison was observed in the sample. The highly fragmented material was interpreted as campsite consumption, marrow removal, and processing activities (de Mille and Head 2001:96). Only two burned and four calcine bones were reported, possibly indicating rodent transportation from lower levels where burning was more common (de Mille and Head 2001:96). A linear FBR feature consisting of a concentration of a single layer of five large and five small FBR were recorded but not interpreted. Across the site, researchers recorded 22,487.1 grams of water-fractured FBR within a total of 29,961.6 grams of general FBR (de Mille and Head 2001:94). No other artifacts were recovered in the area of FBR concentration.

A single radiocarbon data of ca. 4,700 BP was obtained for this occupation. The authors noted that the materials in this component were widely distributed and lacked concentrations in contrast to the underlying occupations and suggested the possibility of extensive bioturbation (de Mille and Head 2001:102).

Boy Chief (EeOv 68). The Boy Chief site is also known as Saahkómaapíina in honour of Boy Chief, a Siksika who travelled through the area as young man (Head et al. 2003:i). The site is a multicomponent site near the town of Princess and is located above an intermediate terrace on Little Sandhill Creek, a tributary of the Red Deer River. Block 3 exhibited six components with the earliest component underlying three Oxbow components, followed by a Hanna component and a Pelican Lake/Besant component. The site was excavated in 1990 and 1994, with a total of 97 m^2 excavated during the earlier excavation phase and an additional 166 m^2 excavated during the later phase (Head et al. 2003:v).

Occupation 1 produced one point in association with six hearths (Head et al. 2003:32–51). The researchers classify this point as a Bitterroot point (Head et al. 2002:51). Walker (1992), however, strongly suggested that points of this morphology and time period should be classified as Gowen points. Moreover, he argued that Gowen points are morphologically distinct from Bitterroot points, which occur much earlier in time (Walker 1992).

Although one ear is damaged, it has the overall look of a block-eared Oxbow point with a very shallowly indented base. Other tools included side scrapers (n = 2), retouched flakes (n = 5), and cores/choppers (n = 13). Most of these were recovered in the southwest corner of the excavation block (Head et al. 2003:47). The assemblage was dominated by quartzite, miscellaneous cherts, and massive quartz (Head et al. 2003:44).

The faunal assemblage includes at least three bison, a bird, and a canid (Head et al. 2002:37). Only 183 of the 2,085 bone fragments were identifiable. Faunal analysis suggested the presence of a juvenile animal while sexing indicated a female and two males were present (Head et al. 2003:38–39). An analysis of the assemblage suggested that a secondary processing locale was used to "pare down limbs removed from the main kill areas into more manageable portions" for subsequent processing (Head et al. 2003:43). FBR was largely clustered in the southeast corner of the excavation block where three hearths were present. Angular specimens were recovered, which suggests immersion in water for stone boiling (Head et al. 2003:44). All the features were small surface hearths. One hearth exhibited a bison mandible placed upright into the sand with unmodified rocks holding its anterior end (Head et al. 2003:50); the purpose of this feature could not be determined.

Five radiocarbon dates were obtained for this occupation (see Table 14). The average age for the occupation was 4,439 +/- 36 BP (Head et al. 2003:50). The researchers noted that this was late for a Mummy Cave/Bitterroot occupation (Head et al. 2003:50).

TABLE 14 Radiocarbon dates for Estevan sites (calibrated by OxCal 3.10 [Ramsey 2005])

Site [LAB NO.]	Conventional ^{14}C Age	$^{13}C/^{12}C$ Ratio	Material	Calibration	Reference
FdOt 1 [GX-6129-G]	4805 +/- 150	-20.0‰	collagen	4000–3100 B.C. (p = 0.954)	Quigg 1984:155-156; Morlan n.d.
FdOt 1 [GX-6130-G]	5540 +/- 160	-20.0‰	collagen	4750–3950 B.C. (p = 0.954)	Quigg 1984:155-156; Morlan n.d.
EgPn 480 [BETA-127234]	4690 +/- 70	-19.8‰	collagen	3640–3350 B.C. (p = 0.954)	de Mille and Head 2001:101, Morlan n.d.
EeOv 68 [AECV-2025C]	4360 +/- 80	-22.5‰	collagen	3340–2870 B.C. (p = 0.954)	Head et al. 2002:50
EeOv 68 [AECV-2027C]	4420 +/- 90	-23.8‰	collagen	3350–2900 B.C. (p = 0.954)	Head et al. 2002:50
EeOv 68 [AECV-2028C]	4530 +/- 80	-23.5‰	collagen	3500–2900 B.C. (p = 0.954)	Head et al. 2002:50
EeOv 68 [AECV-2029C]	4500 +/- 70	-24.1‰	collagen	3400–2900 B.C. (p = 0.954)	Head et al. 2002:50
EeOv 68 [BETA-43912]	4350 +/- 90	-21.8‰	collagen	3350–2700 B.C. (p = 0.954)	Head et al. 2002:50

Other sites. Other sites in Alberta exhibit block-eared Oxbow points but have not been radiocarbon dated. EhPn 44 is a small campsite in the gently rolling knob-and-kettle topography northwest of Calgary (Vivian and Dow 2006). A single point base was recovered from the site, exhibiting a striking similarity to the corner-notched specimen from Component 3 of EgPn 480 (de Mille and Head 2001). The specimen is quite fragmentary so this identification is tenuous. Two bifaces, two retouched flakes and forty-five pieces of debitage rounded out the rest of the lithic assemblage (Vivian and Dow 2006:5). Similarly, the S.S. Burmis site (DjPn 62), adjacent to the Crowsnest River near the town of Burmis, produced a point reminiscent of a block-eared Oxbow point (Quigg 1975b:17, plate 1, no. 28). Unfortunately, the specimen was considered to be out of context, as it appeared to be associated with two Hanna points (Quigg 1975b:5).

Estevan: Oxbow Beginnings on the Alberta Plains

A review of sites that immediately precede "classic" Oxbow material but do not exhibit Oxbow points illustrates a strong trend toward block-eared, Oxbow-like points associated with corner-notched points that date between 5,000 and 4,500 BP. The similarity of the block-eared Oxbow-like points to "classic" Oxbow points is striking, although no comparable material to the corner-notched points in the later assemblages is apparent. Reeves (1973:1240–1242) originally called this material Early Oxbow complex, dating to ca. 5,000–4,500 BP. He defined it based on the perceived co-occurrence of Bitterroot and Oxbow points and cited Long Creek Levels 8 and 9, Oxbow Dam, and Sorenson V as examples of this site type. Green (2005) has shown that the Oxbow Dam site is a mixed assemblage and is more accurately a "classic" Oxbow site. Originally, Reeves (1973) saw similarities and continuity between the Early Oxbow points and Bitterroot specimens. It is now known that Bitterroot points were produced about 7,000 BP (see the Mummy Cave complex). This means that two thousand years separate the two forms. While there may be some stylistic similarities between Bitterroot and the Early Oxbow points, there is likely little cultural continuity between these forms. Thus, it is suggested that the term Long Creek points be used to label these distinct block-eared specimens that immediately precede the "classic" Oxbow material. This terminology follows Taylor (2006:312–313), who recognized the distinctive nature of the points. Likewise, rather than Early Oxbow complex for the cultural entity, a more traditional name seems appropriate. "The

Estevan phase of the Oxbow tradition" better reflects the formative and emergent nature of the "Oxbow" phenomenon. *Estevan* has been used as the phase name, to commemorate the Oxbow Dam site's proximity to the local town of that name.

At least two diagnostic point forms are associated with the Estevan phase: Long Creek and Souris points. The Long Creek point tends to be short and broad with fairly shallow side notches and a slightly concave base. The Souris point exhibits shallow corner notches and a relatively straight base. The points are named after drainages near the Long Creek site.

In terms of the tool assemblage, the usual range of tools is present with side scrapers being more common than in later times. Also of interest is a maul fragment in EgPn 480. This is amongst the earliest evidence of mauls recovered in a well-preserved context. Three mauls were recovered at the Gray site (EcNx 1) in Saskatchewan, but they were not in direct association with the Oxbow burials (Millar 1978:305–309). Mauls are interpreted as indicators of increased processing. The lithic raw materials from Boy Chief and EgPn 480 are largely quartzite, quartz, siltstone, petrified wood, and miscellaneous cherts. Although some chalcedony was recovered, almost no exotic material was found in the assemblages from these sites. The faunal assemblages indicate that the subsistence of these people included bison, the most common species recovered at Boy Chief and EgPn 430, with bird and canid being additionally recovered at the Boy Chief site. The bison remains at the Boy Chief site suggested that individual or small kills occurred at remote locations, and that selective processing resulted in selected carcass segments being transported back to the campsite.

A possible technological innovation may make its first appearance at this time. Importantly, both the Boy Chief site and EgPn 480 provide evidence of angular, water-fractured FBR. Associated pit features, however, were not observed. The implication is that stone boiling may be appearing in the archaeological record at this early period, with the purpose of extracting grease from boiled bone. The presence of the maul may be related to this phenomenon, as it could be used for fragmenting bone in order to increase the surface area for grease extraction. At EgPn 480, the FBR was considered to be water fractured and was observed scattered across the site but not associated with any features (de Mille and Head 2001:94). At the Boy Chief site, FBR was largely recovered in the southeast corner of the excavation block around three surface hearths. The researcher noted that the angular specimens suggested water fracturing likely from stone boiling

(Head et al. 2003:44). This is the earliest that substantial quantities of FBR occur in Alberta's archaeological record.

Other sites that should be considered part of the Estevan phase of the Oxbow complex that are located outside of Alberta include the Long Creek and the Gray sites in Saskatchewan, and the Sorenson and Sun River sites in Montana. The Long Creek site is located on Long Creek just above its confluence with the Souris River in southeastern Saskatchewan (Bryant 2002, 2007; Wettlaufer and Mayer-Oakes 1960). In 1957, 193.5 m^2 were excavated in Level 8 of the site (Bryant 2002:185). Bryant (2002) has illustrated that as many as three occupations are present in Level 8. Although originally called Oxbow points (Wettlaufer and Mayer-Oakes 1960) and later called Early Side-notched points (Bryant 2002:185–188), the current research considers a total of ten Long Creek and two Souris points to have been recovered. These points were largely manufactured on fused shale and Knife River flint. Other recovered tools include preforms, numerous end scrapers, a few side scrapers, biface, a hammerstone, and retouched flakes. Bone tools include awl tips, a bone scraper, and some polished bone. Most of the fauna was bison (n = 4) but canid and squirrel were also recovered. A number of hearths were uncovered in association with lithic and bone scatters. Two radiocarbon dates were obtained for this level: 4,620 +/- 80 BP (S-52) and 4,650 +/- 150 BP (S-53) (Morlan n.d.). Bryant (2002:203–206) obtained a third date of 4,960 +/- 70 BP (Beta-168214).

The Gray site is located in southwestern Saskatchewan. It has been interpreted as a burial ground attributed largely to peoples of the Oxbow phase (Millar 1978). Projectile points recovered within the excavated burials tend to be "classic" Oxbow points; however, some un-notched Oxbow points or possibly McKean points were also recovered. Two large points, possibly spear tips, are Oxbow-like in form but more similar to the Long Creek points in outline morphology (see Millar 1978:263, fig. 117a, b). One of the specimens was recovered in two pieces from a grave dated to ca. 5,000 BP (Millar 1978:260–263, fig. 117a). As well, a few block-eared, Oxbow-like points were recovered at the site. One specimen was recovered within an undated burial (Millar 1978:267, fig. 118g), a second was recovered on an extinct soil surface (Millar 1978:267, fig. 118i), while a third was recovered in a burial dated to ca. 5,000 BP (Millar 1978:267, fig. 118b). All of these potential Long Creek points exhibit the block ears and very slight basal concavities. One point (Millar 1978:267, fig. 118a) has block ears but a deep basal concavity, differentiating it from Long Creek points. The point, however, was recovered from a burial dated to ca. 5,100 BP, suggesting it should be included within the Estevan phase. A large standard deviation for this date (Millar 1978:387) might place it with more morphologically similar "classic" Oxbow points. Also important, although circumstantial, is that dates for the site range between ca. 5,000 BP and 3,000 BP. This is roughly coincidental with the beginning of the Estevan phase and lends support to the idea that the two phases are sequential in time and possibly culturally related. The cultural relationship goes beyond being sequential in time to include exhibiting similar point morphology, the solitary stocking of game, coincidental use of burial/ceremonial sites, and the utilization of new technologies such as stone boiling. The continuity or overlap between Estevan block-eared Oxbow-like material (ca. 5,000–4,500) and "classic" Oxbow material (ca. 4,500–4,000; see next section) is the reason for placing the Estevan phase and the Oxbow phase within the Oxbow tradition.

Based on surface finds, Taylor (2006:313–315) suggested that Long Creek points might also be found in eastern Montana and western North Dakota. At the Sorenson site in south-central Montana, a single point resembling the Long Creek type was recovered in Occupation V (Husted and Edgar 2002, plate 11, no. l). The occupation was radiometrically dated to ca. 5,000 BP. At the Sun River site, Oxbow material dating before and after 4,500 BP was recovered (Greiser et al. 1985). These early dates suggest a closer examination of these materials might shed light on developments that led to the Oxbow phase. Perhaps an origin to the southwest has merit. To the south in Nebraska is a burial site (25SF17) on a hilltop on the south side of the North Platte River (Carlson et al. 1999:113–115). The burial was disturbed by land levelling. No information was obtained on burial type, sex, age, or number of individuals (Carlson et al. 1999:114). Associated with the burial were five large side-notched knives, four points, an unperforated bead possibly of amber, and possible fragmentary bird bone. The five side-notched knives (Carlson et al. 1999:115, fig. 7A–E) are strikingly similar in size and form to the large side-notched spear point recovered in the 5,000 BP burial at the Gray site (Millar 1978:263). Three of the four points were classified as Oxbow (Carlson 1999:114, 115, fig. 7F–H), but the suite of points is most similar to the Long Creek points defined above. They tend to exhibit block ears with fairly shallow basal concavities. An examination of Oxbow materials in the Nebraska area might prove fruitful in understanding the Oxbow tradition on the Northern Plains. Perhaps Wettlaufer and Mayer-Oakes (1960:116–118) and Wormington and Forbis

(1965:190) were close when they suggested long ago that the Oxbow complex was derived from an Archaic culture on the prairie-woodland border zone to the east of the Great Plains.

OXBOW PHASE (CA. 4,500 TO 4,100 BP)

In 1956, a cut in the Souris River bank, produced by spring flooding, exposed a site just below the dam near the town of Oxbow, Saskatchewan (Nero and McCorquodale 1958:82). Nero and McCorquodale (1958:82) noted that the upstream dam provided the site with an appropriate name: the Oxbow Dam site. Five points, four scrapers, two blade fragments, a flake knife, and part of a shell gorget were recovered (Nero and McCorquodale 1958:85–87). Comparisons of the Oxbow Dam site material to material from the lower levels of the Long Creek site were made (Nero and McCorquodale 1958:88). Building on this newly recovered material, Wettlaufer assigned Level 7 and 8 of the Long Creek site to the Oxbow culture (Wettlaufer and Mayer-Oakes 1960:52–67). In this same report, Mayer-Oakes suggested Wettlaufer consider the term *Long Creek Side-notched* instead of *Oxbow* for the recovered projectile points, given that the material was known best from the Long Creek site (Wettlaufer and Mayer-Oakes 1960:116). He did admit, however, the Long Creek material was strikingly similar to the Oxbow Dam site material (Wettlaufer and Mayer-Oakes 1960:116).

Such was the preamble that led up to the series of discussions concerning the nature and relationship of the Oxbow Dam site material and material from the Long Creek site Levels 7 and 8. Many of the developments are outlined in the preceding section on the Estevan phase. In summary, there have been numerous views concerning Oxbow and Oxbow-like projectile points and their associated assemblages (e.g., Dyck 1983; Quigg 1984; Reeves 1969, 1973; Walker 1992). Green's (2005) review of interpretations surrounding the Oxbow Dam site and Long Creek site placed the previous excavations into historical context. His additional excavations at the original location of the Oxbow Dam site indicated the earlier excavations had examined mixed assemblages (Green 2005:108). As well, the radiocarbon date had likely been derived from intrusive material from a lower level (Green 2005:4). Green's (2005:104–105) excavation at the Oxbow Dam site produced a "classic" Oxbow assemblage dating ca. 4,300 BP exhibiting no Mummy Cave material. While Green (2005) saw Oxbow materials as derived from the Gowen complex, the preceding section provides a reasonable argument that the Estevan phase, in essence, is a proto-Oxbow entity exhibiting all the hallmark features of the Oxbow phase. Thus, the Estevan phase is an ancestor to the Oxbow phase within the Oxbow tradition.

The Sites

Green's (2005) review of the literature exposed the Oxbow Dam site as an example of an Oxbow campsite that had originally been interpreted from mixed deposits. This data fits Reeves' (1973) criteria for "classic" Oxbow assemblage with no Mummy Cave material intermixed. Oxbow points exhibit shallow side-notches located relatively high on the lateral edges and a deep concave base, which combine to give the point a characteristic eared or lugged appearance (Green 2005:53). As well, the points tend to exhibit basal thinning flake scars projecting upward from the concave portion of the base (Green 2005:53). Using these criteria, the following reviews the Alberta archaeological record for well-dated sites with appropriate material (see Plate 16 and Figure 17)

Southridge (EaOq 17). The Southridge site is a processing site in Medicine Hat. The site was named for the subdivision in which it was found (Brumley 1981). The site is located at the prairie level just southeast of Seven Persons Creek valley (Brumley 1981:1). It was excavated in fall 1979 and fall 1980. Three sub-areas were defined with Sub-area B producing the Oxbow material; a total of 152 m^2 was excavated (Brumley 1981:40).

Seventeen Oxbow points and three preforms were associated with two hearths and two boiling pits (Brumley 1981:40–91). Other tools recovered included marginally retouched flakes (n = 69), utilized flakes (n = 4), end scrapers (n = 3), bifaces (n = 20), anvils/hammerstones (n = 3), a spokeshave, and a graver. All these items would be used in the processing of carcasses. Most of the raw materials were local with fine tools manufactured on the better toolstone (Brumley 1981:68). The bison faunal assemblage (n = 3,207) consisted almost entirely of fractured limb elements (Brumley 1981: 52–54). The assemblage was highly fractured. Brumley (1981:47) argued that each hearth was associated with a different boiling pit, suggesting two activity areas were present; the distribution of FBR and bone delimiting an area around these features supported his interpretation (Brumley 1981:47–48).

Three radiocarbon dates were obtained for this area of the site (see Table 15). The two earlier dates were from fill within a feature and were considered acceptable. The more recent date was derived from bone within several shallowly buried units and was possibly contaminated (Brumley 1981:89–90).

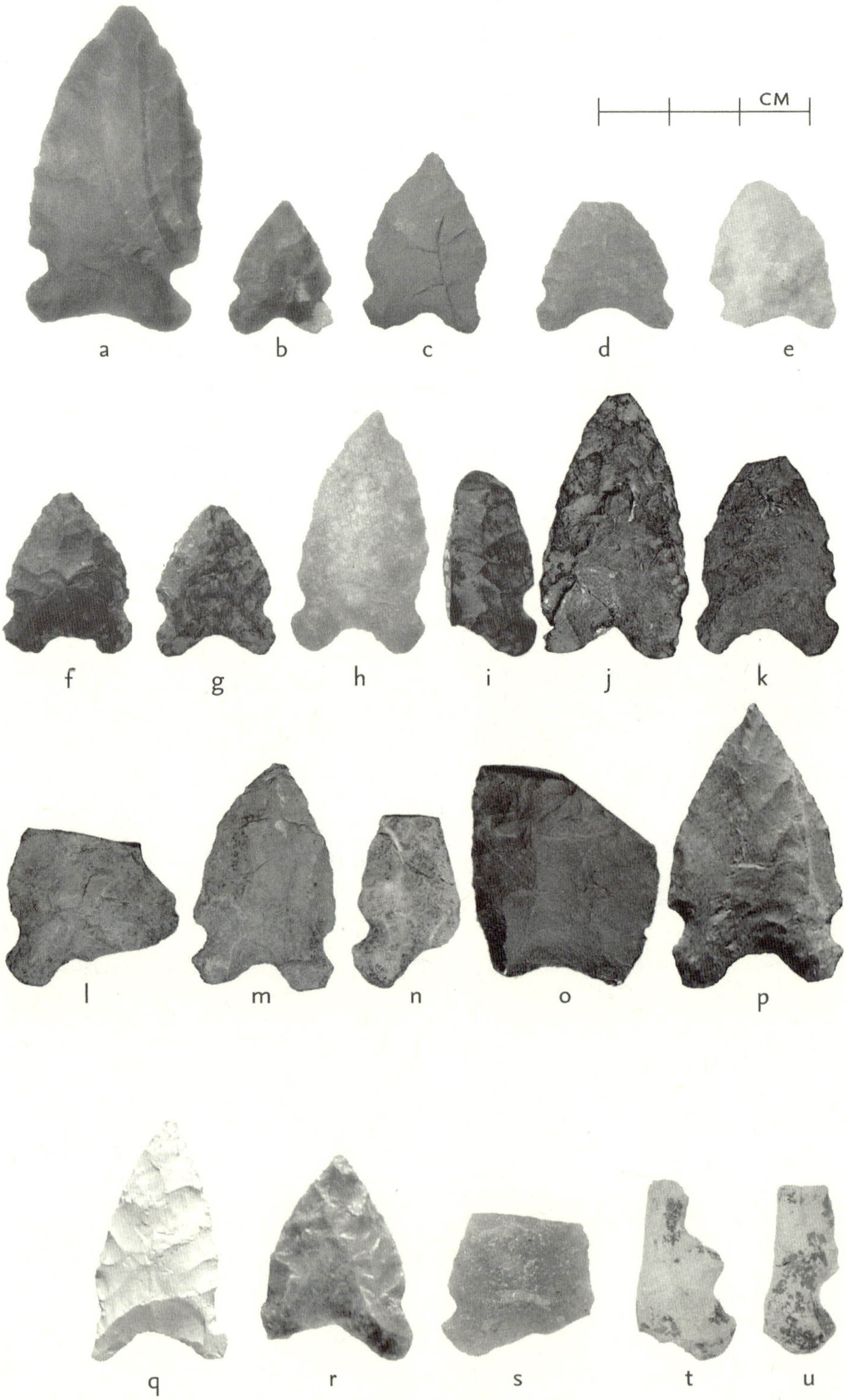

PLATE 16 Oxbow points. Illustrated are projectile points from the Ross Glen site (DlOp 2) (a and b); the Southridge site (EaOq 17) (c–e); the Boy Chief site (EeOv 68) (f–i); the Castor Creek site (FbOw 1) (j–o); the Stampede site (DjOn 26), Palaeosol 5b (p and q), and Palaeosol 5c (r); and EhPm 72 (s–u). Photo credit: Alberta Culture and Community Spirit.

FIGURE 17
Oxbow sites within Alberta

TABLE 15 Radiocarbon dates for Oxbow sites (calibrated by OxCal 3.10 [Ramsey 2005])

Site [LAB NO.]	Conventional ^{14}C Age	$^{13}C/^{12}C$ Ratio	Material	Calibration	Reference
EdPc 1 [S-854]	2170 +/- 210	-20.0‰	collagen	800 B.C.–A.D. 300 (p = 0.954)	Morlan n.d.
EdPc 1 [S-856]	3925 +/- 160	-20.0‰	collagen	2900–1950 B.C. (p = 0.954)	Morlan n.d.
FbOw 1 [N/A-47]	4475 +/- 1000	?	charcoal	5500–600 B.C. (p = 0.954)	Forbis 1970:17; Brumley and Rushworth 1983:155
DjPo 47 [RL-508]	6420 +/- 160	-20.0‰	collagen	not associated	Landals 1986:94; Morlan n.d.
DjPo 47 [RL-877]	4220 +/- 150	-20.0‰	collagen	3350–2450 B.C. (p = 0.954)	Landals 1986:94; Morlan n.d.
DjPo 47 [GX-6384 A]	4405 +/- 150	-10.0‰	apatite	3550–2600 B.C. (p = 0.954)	Landals 1986:94; Morlan n.d.
EaOq 17 [RL-1535]	4340 +/- 140	-20.0‰	collagen	3400–2550 B.C. (p = 0.954)	Brumley 1981:89; Morlan n.d.
EaOq 17 [RL-1534]	4240 +/- 150	-20.0‰	collagen	3350–2450 B.C. (p = 0.954)	Brumley 1981:89; Morlan n.d.
EaOq 17 [RL-1536]	3750 ± 130	-20.0‰	collagen	2600–1750 B.C. (p = 0.954)	Brumley 1981:89; Morlan n.d.
DlOp 2 [RL-1585]	4260 +/- 140	?	calcined bone	3350–2450 B,C. (p = 0.954)	Quigg 1986:124; Morlan n.d.
EeOv 68 [BETA-43910]	4350 +/- 80	-20.1‰	collagen	3350–2750 B.C. (p = 0.954)	Head et al. 2003:21; Morlan n.d.
EeOv 68 [AECV-2026C]	4350 +/- 90	-23.8‰	collagen	3350–2700 B.C. (p = 0.954)	Head et al. 2003:21; Morlan n.d.
EeOv 68 [BETA-38789]	4400 +/- 55	-20.0‰	collagen	3330–3210 B.C. (p = 0.17); 3190–3150 B.C. (p = 0.03); 3130–2900 B.C. (p = 0.754)	Head et al. 2003:21; Morlan n.d.
EeOv 68 [AECV-2030C]	4280 +/- 90	-24.1‰	collagen	3350–2550 B.C. (p = 0.954)	Head et al. (2003:21); Morlan n.d.
EeOv 68 [BETA-43911]	3220 +/- 150	-19.9‰	collagen	1900–1050 B.C. (p = 0.954)	Head et al. (2003:21); Morlan n.d.
EhPm 72 [BETA-223884]	4160 +/- 40	-20.1‰	collagen	2890–2629 B.C. (p = 0.954)	Vivian 2007b:3

Majorville Medicine Wheel (EdPc 1). The Majorville Medicine Wheel is described in the Calderwood section. As noted above, Oxbow is traditionally considered to represent the earliest use of the cairn (Calder 1977:30–48), however, Calderwood points in the cairn's assemblage provide an earlier commencement date. Firm stratigraphic associations could not be determined between items within the cairn because of its accretional formation. Still, Oxbow points (n = 26) were mainly recovered in Layers 14–16 at the center of the cairn (Calder 1977:36). Calder (1977:202) suggested that cairn making was introduced during the Oxbow phase, but he remained non-committal with respect to the origins of the practice or the people that carried it out. This excavation approach only attributes the cairn to the Oxbow phase, not the spokes or the large circle. Like the cairn itself, these may have been added with time. The ceremonial function of the medicine wheel seemed self-evident. Calder suggested that the presence of projectile points, utilitarian tools and the site's vantage point likely related to bison hunting ceremonialism.

Three radiocarbon dates were obtained from the medicine wheel; two of the dates were from Oxbow layers near the center of the cairn (Calder 1977:41–42). Bone recovered from near the center produced a date of ca. 2,000 BP; it was rejected because the date did not reflect the assumed age of the associated projectile points. The second date on bone produced a date of ca. 3,850 BP, supporting an Oxbow phase age (Table 15).

British Block Cairn (EdOp 1). The British Block Cairn is located on a high hill with a view of the South Saskatchewan River valley and the Cypress Hills (about 50 miles, or 80.5 km, away) to the southeast (Wormington and Forbis 1965:122). The site is within the Canadian Forces Base Suffield near Medicine Hat; this part of the base is known as the British Block for which the site was named. The site consists of a cairn approximately 2 m high and 9 m in diameter and a human (Napi) effigy, which are encircled by a ring about 24 m in diameter. Forbis excavated the British Block Cairn in the early 1960s. Like the Majorville Cairn, it produced a wide range of artifacts, including Oxbow points as the earliest diagnostic (Wormington and Forbis 1965:124). The cairn was not excavated accretionally (by peeling off layers like an onion) so the arbitrary layers crosscut the depositional layers. Thus, the stratigraphic relationships between the points and other artifacts were not evident in the recorded data (Wormington and Forbis 1965:124). No dates are available from the cairn.

See-Everywhere (EcOr 34). The See-Everywhere site is a cairn located on a prominent knoll at the highest point in the area, with a commanding view of the surrounding landscape for kilometres in all directions, on the Canadian Forces Base Suffield (Brumley 1972:27). The site consists of the hilltop cairn, about 2 m north–south, 1.5 east–west, and 0.5 m high, within an encompassing scatter of debitage over an area of 30 m in diameter. Also nearby are five stone circles (Brumley 1972:27). A 2-×-2-m unit was excavated into the cairn and five test units of varying sizes were conducted atop the prominent knoll. The mitigative excavations were undertaken to mitigate potential impacts by military activity (Brumley 1972:1).

Excavations revealed that the cairn extended 25 cm BS and contained large amounts of lithic debitage and tools, small amounts of prehistoric pottery, and some historic items. Rodents appeared to have disrupted any stratigraphic elements of the cairn. Items recovered within the cairn included Oxbow (n = 4), McKean (n = 1), Avonlea (n = 2), Cayley Series (Late Side-notched) points (n = 6), and unclassified (n = 1) points (Brumley 1972:28–29). Given the sequence of points at Majorville Cairn and apparently at British Block Cairn, it is tempting to suggest a similar sequence at the See-Everywhere site, starting with Oxbow. While it is possible the points reflect offerings left by passers-by, the items may be curated items or curiosities from other times and locations (Brumley 1972:95). A single radiocarbon date on a bison horn core from the base of See-Everywhere cairn produced an age of ca. 160 +/- 60 BP (S 1014), which does not reflect events as old as the Oxbow phase.

Boy Chief, Block 3 (EeOv-68), Occupation 2, 3, and 4. The Boy Chief site is discussed in the section on the Estevan phase. The earliest Oxbow component, Occupation 2, produced one reworked and three complete Oxbow points in association with four hearths. The other lithic tools included bifaces (n = 2), retouched flakes (n = 6), cores (n = 9), an end scraper, a side scraper, a wedge, a chopper, and a hammerstone. The lithic assemblage emphasized local raw materials, especially Swan River chert, quartzite, and petrified wood. The faunal assemblage suggested secondary processing took place at the site. A minimum of eleven bison, one canid, and one porcupine were represented in the sample. Four juvenile, one fetal and at least one neonatal (n = 24 fragments) bison were represented (Head et al. 2003:58–59). The presence of young animals and sexing analysis suggested that cow/calf herds were taken in late winter or early spring (Head et al. 2003:63). A structured pattern of discard was suggested by the distribution of the faunal assemblage: limbs and body portions were removed at the kill and secondary removal of extreme upper and lower limbs was conducted at the site (Head et al. 2003:62).

The four hearths were each associated with some bone and FBR.

A lithic reduction area appeared to be associated with one of the hearths. The concentration of lithics, 8 m wide, around one of the hearths suggested a possible structure, with the detritus possibly outlining the inside of a circular dwelling (Head et al. 2003:70). Substantial amounts of FBR were recovered, which exhibited angular fractures associated with stone boiling, but stone-boiling pits were not observed (Head et al. 2003:66). Three radiocarbon dates were obtained for this component (Table 15). A late date does not correlate with previous Oxbow dates and is inconsistent with dates from other levels of the site (Head et al. 2003:70–71). On these grounds it was rejected while the other two dates were accepted (Head et al. 2003:70). In summary, Occupation 2 at the Boy Chief site is an Oxbow campsite/processing site with an average date of 4,300 BP (Head et al. 2003:70–71).

The next component, Occupation 3, also produced Oxbow material. Three Oxbow points were recovered in association with two hearths in the southwest part of the excavation. Other tools recovered included bifaces (n = 2), end scrapers (n = 10), side scrapers (n = 2), wedges (n = 6), retouched tools (n = 1), bipolar cores (n = 15), multidirectional cores (n = 7), and unidirectional cores (n = 2) (Head et al. 2003:80–83). Most of the tools and debitage were associated with the hearths. A minimum of three adult bison and one canid was recovered in the faunal assemblage; four juvenile and one fetal bison were also represented (Head at al. 2003:72–75). Sexing of the sample could only differentiate one female. This assessment, along with the juvenile and fetal bison, suggested procurement from cow/calf herds in late winter/early spring. The faunal material was concentrated in association with a hearth. As in the earlier level, axial elements were rare and a secondary processing area was represented (Head et al. 2003:76–77). FBR was recovered in substantial amounts and was concentrated in the southwest part of the excavation with the hearths. The sample largely exhibited angular fractures associated with stones immersed in water for stone boiling, but no pits were recovered (Head et al. 2003:77). A single radiocarbon date of ca. 4,350 BP was obtained for this occupation (Head et al. 2003:84).

The next component at the site, Occupation 4, produced two basal fragments of Oxbow points in association with three hearths (Head et al. 2003:91). Other tools recovered included bifaces (n = 10), end scrapers (n = 12), side scrapers (n = 8), wedges (n = 2), retouched lithics (n = 15), bipolar cores (n = 33), multidirectional cores (n = 8), and unidirectional cores (n = 3) (Head et al. 2003:88–93). The lithic assemblage was dominated by quartzite, miscellaneous cherts, and petrified wood. The lithics did not exhibit any patterned distribution. The reduction strategy appeared to focus on bifacial reduction with a "strong pebble chert industry" (Head et al. 2003:91). The faunal assemblage consisted of at least one bison and one canid. The sample was small but upper forelimbs and hindlimbs were emphasized, suggesting tertiary butchering with meat stripping, marrow extraction, and possibly grease extraction (Head et al. 2003:88). Substantial FBR was recovered; it was spread throughout the excavation and not clustered around any of the three hearths (Head et al. 2003:88). The nature of the FBR suggested stone boiling although pits were not observed (Head et al. 2003:92). The hearths were shallow surface hearths generally exhibiting flecks of charcoal and maybe charred bone. No radiocarbon dates were obtained for this occupation. Its stratigraphic position above two dated Oxbow occupations suggested an age around 4,350 BP (Head et al. 2003:92). Based on evidence of tertiary butchering, the site was interpreted as a camp involved with the final stripping of meat (Head et al. 2003:92).

Castor Creek (FbOw 1). The Castor Creek site is located in a hanging valley about 11 m above Castor Creek near Castor, southeastern Alberta. In 1961, Forbis investigated the site after a copper crescent reminiscent of the Old Copper culture of the Great Lakes area was recovered downstream (Wormington and Forbis 1965:115). No materials attributable to the Old Copper culture were recovered from the excavations. However, six Oxbow points and a McKean point were recovered from a deeply buried palaeosol. To explain the co-occurrence of Oxbow and McKean, Forbis (1992:49) considered the assemblage might indicate contemporaneity or the "McKean" point may simply be an Oxbow preform. All other material recovered from the site appears to have been lithic (Wormington and Forbis 1965:116). A single radiocarbon date of ca. 4,500 BP was obtained (Table 15).

Maple Leaf (DjPo 47), Component 3. The Maple Leaf site is described above in the section on the Plains/Mountain complex. Ten projectile points were associated with a wetland, a hearth, and two possible post-mould features. Landals (1986:99–109) identified two Oxbow points, seven Salmon River fishtail points, and one unclassifiable specimen. The remaining lithic tools support an interpretation of specific tasks relating to killing, butchering, sharpening/maintenance, and limited hide processing (Landals 1986:97). The composition of the assemblage indicated the use of local raw materials; however, the Oxbow points were made on non-local chalcedonies (Landals 1986:104).

The faunal assemblage suggested at least seventeen bison, four canids (two possible dogs), a badger, and a goose were present (Landals 1986:124–128). Three fetal bison bones were recovered at widely separated locations, suggesting late winter to early spring use (Landals 1986:136). The majority of the bone was associated with the wetland feature (Landals 1986:150). A single bone tool of unknown function was manufactured on a radius. Three dates were obtained from the third component, ca. 6,400 BP, 4,200 BP, and 4,400 BP (Table 15). As stated above, the radiocarbon dates and the projectile points suggest at least two periods are represented in the formation of the assemblage: the earlier date reflecting the Maple Leaf occupation (6,400 BP) and the later dates reflecting an Oxbow occupation (4,200 BP and 4,400 BP).

EhPm 72. EhPm 72 is a buried processing site at the base of a sandstone sill on the western side of Nose Creek and Symons Valley (Vivian 2007b:3–15). The site consists of continuous cultural deposits with two levels exhibiting distinct concentrations of material: Levels 6–7 and Levels 11–12 (Vivian 2007a:5). These concentrations were interpreted as two cultural occupations although each produced the same cultural diagnostics. In 2006, a total of 26 m² was excavated at the site (Vivian 2007b:3–4). The site was excavated as mitigation prior to subdivision development.

Three Oxbow base fragments were recovered from the site: two in the upper occupation and one in the lower occupation (Vivian 2007b:5–6). Other lithic tools recovered included a biface fragment, a wedge, a teardrop-shaped scraper, cores (n=4), a hammerstone, and retouched flakes (n=2). The lithic raw materials were largely local quartzites and siltstones with only a few exotic cherts and chalcedonies (Vivian 2007b:10). The assemblage had a surprisingly high tool-to-debitage ratio.

The faunal assemblage (n=2,936) was small and fragmented with only a few items identifiable to element (n=80). All the identifiable bone was bison. The material from both occupations was mainly axial elements of little economic value that had been discarded at a processing site (Vivian 2007b:14). A single burned bone was recovered, and no associated processing features were recognized. (Vivian 2007b:14). Reworking of the site was ruled out because of the recovery of an intact vertebral articulation and the observation of a core in association with some of its own debitage.

A radiocarbon date of ca. 4,160 BP (Table 15) was obtained from bone recovered in the lower component, an appropriate age for the Oxbow phase.

Other sites. A number of other sites contain Oxbow material but have not been fully reported in the literature. The Bill White site (DjPo 25), named after the landowner, is a multicomponent campsite located just north of the town of Bellevue in the Crowsnest Pass (Reeves and Kennedy 1980). In 1975, two intersecting backhoe trenches and nine 2-×-2-m units were excavated adjacent to the main trench, and revealed a complex geological history. At least ten buried soil horizons were observed with three possibly producing Oxbow material. The Stampede (DjOn 26) site is a well-stratified campsite in the Cypress Hills. A least a couple of levels have been attributed to the Oxbow phase (Gryba 1976, Oetelaar 2004a). Oetelaar (2004a) obtained a very late date of 3,000 +/- 70 BP (TO-10926) for the uppermost Oxbow level (5B) (Freeman 2006:454). The Tuscany (EgPn-377) site is a multicomponent site that produced an Oxbow component. A date of 3,680 +/- 40 BP (Beta-222821) was obtained for bone associated with several large unmodified cobbles that appear to outline a rough circle, possibly representing a stone circle (Oetelaar 1998). Again, this is a late date for an Oxbow site.

Another possible Oxbow-age stone circle was suggested at EfOp 53, a large stone circle site on a series of terraces along Alkali Creek (Adams 1978:51). In 1976, two stone circles were excavated, yielding 160 m^2. The excavations uncovered a buried ring with the second level producing a possible Oxbow point (Adams 1978:59–60, plate 14b). Adams (1978:60) acknowledged that the recovered point was a poor specimen and that stratigraphy within stone circles lent themselves to mixing. It is unlikely this stone circle dates to the Oxbow phase.

Ross Glen (DlOp 2) is a stone circle site on the prairie level above Bullshead Creek in Medicine Hat (Quigg 1986). The main occupation was by Besant people but evidence of Oxbow and Hanna peoples was also recovered. Two Oxbow points were recovered at the site. In Stone Circle 13, an unusual Oxbow-like point was recovered that exhibited a shallow basal concavity and slightly upturned ears This point was initially classified as Bitterroot (Quigg 1986:60), but would now be consider to be a Long Creek point. A point tip and a Hanna-like point base were also recovered under the stone circle. Importantly, no Besant points were recovered in this part of an otherwise Besant-dominated site. A "classic" Oxbow point was found less than 20 m to the north of Stone Circle 13 near two ancillary features. Lastly, an ancillary feature consisting of a basin-shaped pit full of burned faunal material about 15 m northeast of Stone Circle 13 produced a radiocarbon date of 4,260 +/-140 BP (RL-1585), a date that fits well with known Oxbow dates. While there appears to be an Oxbow occupation at the site, there is little evidence for an Oxbow association with any of the stone circles. The Oxbow phase at the site most likely relates to a scatter of material in the area underlying the more recent stone circle.

Oxbow points have been recovered north of the Plains in Alberta as well. For example, Gruhn (1981:88) noted the similarity of a number of specimens recovered at sites GhPh 102, 103, and 106 to Oxbow points. While superficially similar to "classic" Oxbow points, the Calling Lake specimens are slightly aberrant; these specimens may represent something quite different. Without secure dating and more thorough comparisons any conclusions are very tenuous.

Oxbow: Cemeteries, Boiling Pits, and More

The Oxbow phase designation has had a long and tumultuous history (Green 2005). In Alberta, numerous sites speak to a discrete material culture that exists during a delimited period of time. The Oxbow phase thrived on the Alberta plains between 4,500 and 4,100 BP. Oxbow's ties to Estevan make it part of a tradition rather than part of a complex. Most of the radiocarbon dates for the phase fall within this period with a few dates as late as 3,500–3,000 BP (e.g., Stampede, Tuscany). It is currently unclear whether these late dates exhibit aberrant dates or represent a late expression of the Oxbow phase (see below). The diagnostic artifact of the Oxbow phase is the Oxbow point, described above. The points are almost invariably bifacial, never flake points.

A number of cultural innovations occurred during the Oxbow phase. The process of stone boiling to extract bone grease may have been introduced as early as the Estevan phase. The presence of boiling pits, however, during the Oxbow phase confirms this innovation. The Southridge site provides evidence of Oxbow people using stone-boiling pits. The extraction of grease from bone is important in preserving meat from kills where surplus has been created. Thus, stores of food can be created, allowing for a whole new range of mobility and behaviours not possible for people tethered to procuring fresh meat.

The toolkit of the Oxbow phase was largely produced on local materials.

Few exotic materials are found in the assemblages. Oxbow assemblages near the mountains utilized materials from the mountains such as Etherington chert. Quartzite and miscellaneous cherts account for most lithic raw materials during the phase. As for the tools themselves, end scrapers are slightly more common than side scrapers. Bifaces occur in ovate and triangular form but other configurations occur. Hammerstones are relatively more common in Oxbow assemblages, likely owing to the need to crush bones for the grease extraction process. Cores of all sorts are recovered including multidirectional and bipolar cores. Retouched flakes are quite common in Oxbow sites.

The fauna reflect a strategy of bison procurement via stalking. Bison kills tend to be small with only a few animals being taken at any time. Repeatedly using the same strategy at one location can produce misleading faunal assemblages (e.g., DjPo 47) in which large assemblages are really products of repeated smaller kills. Often, only some elements of the bison make it back to the campsites (e.g., EeOv 68) with much being left at the kill site (e.g., EhPm 72, DjPo 47). The people of the Oxbow phase apparently did not conduct large-scale kills. Despite a focus on bison, other animals were taken, including canid (possibly dog), badger, porcupine, and goose as part of a subsistence strategy.

The Oxbow phase exhibits an increase in features within sites compared to previous periods. Surface and basin hearths occur in a number of sites. FBR and charred-bone concentrations also increase in number. Most of the Oxbow sites produced FBR in contrast to previous archaeological cultures, which produced very little, if any. Boiling pits, as already mentioned, provide archaeological evidence for stone boiling and grease extraction not previously represented in the archaeological record.

It now seems apparent that the people of the Oxbow phase were not the first to establish cairns, which later became "medicine wheels," on high points of land. This honour falls to the Calderwood complex. Still, items that likely represent offerings, such as projectile points, geodes, and bone fragments, were placed inside cairns in prominent locations at this time. The spectacular viewscapes almost certainly played a role in the location and function of these features. It is not known when the radiating spokes and larger circles were associated with the cairns; it is possible that initially only a small cairn marked the top of prominent hills and subsequent visitors elaborated on the design for millennia.

Importantly, the Oxbow phase is found well beyond Alberta's borders.

Saskatchewan has produced a number of well-dated Oxbow sites. The Oxbow Dam site is discussed. It produced Oxbow points with an associated radiocarbon date of ca. 4,300 BP (Green 2005). Also, the Long Creek site, Level 7, produced a diffuse campsite that contained two Oxbow points and two preforms (Wettlaufer and Mayer-Oakes 1960:53–55). A radiocarbon date of ca. 4,600 was obtained for the level (Wettlaufer and Mayer-Oakes 1960:136; Morlan n.d.).

The Gray site (EcNx 1) is located northwest of Swift Current, Saskatchewan. The site was named after the family who owned the land in 1963, when human skeletal material first came to light (Millar 1978:65). The site consists of multiple interments on a south-facing hillside covered in windblown sands (Millar 1978). From the initial discovery of the site until 1973, approximately ninety-eight burials were examined in whole or in part, not including non-professional investigations (Millar 1978:70). An estimated 40 percent of the northern part of the site (EcNx 1a) remained unexcavated after the work in 1973, while work at the southern area (EcNx 1b) was restricted to very limited testing (Millar 1978:72). Almost all the points from the burials are Long Creek or Oxbow points. A couple, recovered from a single grave, were basally indented, lanceolate-shaped specimens that superficially appear to be McKean points but were interpreted as preforms owing to the coincidental recovery of an Oxbow point and a basally indented leaf-shaped form in a common burial unit (Millar 1978:275). Nine radiocarbon dates from nine burials were obtained from the site (Millar 1978:386–389). Millar suggested the dates may represent random points on a continuum, or five groups with four hiatuses (ca. 5,500–4,800 BP; 4,600–4,100 BP; 3,930–3,600 BP; 3,850–3,300 BP; and 3,000–2850 BP). As noted above, Estevan material may represent the initiation of this site. Oxbow material occurs in many of the burials, and most of the dates fall within the accepted Oxbow period. A few dates are particularly late to be Oxbow phase; Burial B70 is dated to 3,015 +/- 85 BP (S-1449). It is important too, that four of the five most recent dates were derived from insoluble collagen extraction, which can produce aberrantly young dates (Morlan 1994:19). As discussed below, it is also possible that the Oxbow phase lingered in southern Alberta and north-central Montana Plains as late as ca. 3,500 BP.

The Greenwater Lake site (FcMv 1) is an incomplete, single, primary extended interment that eroded from a steep backslope of a municipal road (Walker 1981). Red ochre or powdered hematite was observed on the surface of the bone and in nodular form (Walker 1981:8). A single Oxbow point manufactured on Swan River chert was recovered from the thoracic region of the burial (Walker 1981:8). The skeleton represents an adult male in his early twenties (Walker 1981:11). A radiocarbon date of 4,490 +/- 105 BP was obtained for the site (Morlan et al. 2002; Walker 1981:8). Similarly, the St. Brieux site (FdNf 2) is a burial radiocarbon dated at 5,085 +/- 80 BP (S-520) (Morlan et al. 2002:51; Walker 1981:11). An adult male was identified lying face down in a sandy kame on a lacustrine plain near St. Brieux, north of Lenore Lake (Morlan et al. 2002:51). The burial was associated with ochre but no diagnostic artifacts (Morlan et al. 2002:51). It would appear to be an Oxbow interment.

As an aside to the preceding discussion on burials, of considerable interest is the possible association of Oxbow materials with native copper. The Castor Creek site provided evidence that suggested an association between Oxbow and a copper crescent, but an actual association could not be demonstrated. Green (2005:98) provided similar examples of Oxbow materials and native copper items found together in unconvincing contexts in Saskatchewan. Importantly, native copper has been recovered archaeologically from three interments at the Gray site, suggesting contact with the east (Green 2005:99). Recoveries such as these strengthen suggestions that the people of the Oxbow phase had relationships to people in the east, and especially to the Old Copper culture (see Green 2005:98–100).

The Harder site (FbNs 1) is a campsite in the Dunfermline Sand Hills in the parkland west of Saskatoon (Dyck 1977). Dyck (1977) recovered many Oxbow points and preforms in 129.5 m^2 of excavation. Bison were the primary species represented. A reanalysis of the bison remains at the site suggested that they represent an attritional assemblage, indicating numerous solitary kills and possibly some communal events (Morlan 1994:770). Features recovered included general disposal areas, hearths, and bone spill piles. Dyck (1977:184) argued the bone fragments were evidence of bone breaking for marrow and pulverizing for grease. Despite unearthing four pits with amounts of coarse stone toward the edge, boiling for grease was not clearly demonstrated. Six to eight roughly circular detritus areas were interpreted as large features reflecting social activity, specifically dwelling floors (Dyck 1977). Originally dated to ca. 3,400 BP (Dyck 1977), more recent efforts suggest an age between ca. 4,400 and 4,100 BP is more appropriate (Morlan 1994:760–761). Morlan (1994:760) had noted during his compilation of radiocarbon dates that all the youngest Oxbow dates in Saskatchewan were obtained prior to instilling the protocol of extraction of soluble collagen to reduce contaminants. Redating of the site produced a more acceptable age.

The Moon Lake site (FaNq 5) is a small, temporary occupation overlooking a former channel of the South Saskatchewan River, southwest of Saskatoon (Dyck 1970). A number of Oxbow points and unnotched points were found within a palaeosol (Dyck 1970; Morlan et al. 2002:40). A number of activities took place at the site, including bison procurement and processing, flintknapping, and possibly the hunting of birds (Dyck 1970:16–17). An interesting feature at the site consisted of a series of post-moulds in a southwest–northeast line extending for 6 ft (~2 m) and ending in a hearth. A radiocarbon date of 4,180 +/- 90 BP (S-403) was obtained.

Carruthers (FbNs 3) is a single-component Oxbow site in the Dunfermline Sand Hills west of Saskatoon (Morlan et al. 2002:50). Two complete and one broken Oxbow point were recovered along with a few faunal remains. A single radiocarbon date of 3,130 +/- 80 BP (S-742) was obtained by combining charred and comminuted bone from nine of the profiles to form a composite sample based on insoluble extraction (Morlan et al. 2002:50). As noted above for the Harder site, the Carruthers sample falls within these early radiocarbon dates that are not reliable.

East Pasture (EcNx 4) is a multicomponent campsite. The third level contains Oxbow material, including a point missing an ear and an ear of a (different) point (Millar et al. 1971:27–29). A radiocarbon date of 4,315 +/- 60 BP (S-637) from Level 3 was recovered from a test pit several metres from the test unit where the more complete Oxbow point was recovered (Morlan et al. 2002:29).

The Amisk site (FbNp 17) is a multicomponent site with Oxbow campsite material in Levels 4 and 5 (Amundson 1986). In Level 4, seven Oxbow points were recovered. Most of the lithics were local, with the exception of chalcedony and welded volcanic tuff. The vast majority of the faunal remains were bison (MNI = 4), with smaller amounts of clam and beaver (Amundson 1986:134). A hearth and small amounts of FBR were also recorded. A date of 4,015 +/- 195 BP (S-2336) was obtained. In Level 5, a single Oxbow point fragment was recovered. Lithic use mirrored Level 4 with the addition of obsidian to the exotics. Bison dominated the faunal assemblage (MNI = 6), with a wolf-sized animal and clam. A hearth, FBR, and a bone-filled pit were also uncovered at the site, but no reddening was observed in the pit (Amundson 1986:155). The level was dated to 4,120 +/- 190 BP (S-2535) (Amundson 1986:193). The underlying level, Level 6, may be Oxbow but no diagnostics were recovered and an aberrant radiocarbon was obtained.

Manitoba has also produced a number of Oxbow sites. The Cherry Point site is on the north shore of Oak Lake in southwestern Manitoba. Syms' (1974) survey of a campground formally recorded the site, in which numerous archaeological cultures from Palaeoindian to Late Woodland time periods were represented. Subsequent excavation at the site produced, among other things, Oxbow points, which were also known from local collections obtained from the site (Haug 1975).

Buchner (1979) excavated Oxbow material near Caribou Lake in east-central Manitoba. The site consisted of eight Oxbow points in association with broken bifaces (n = 3), scrapers (n = 2), unifacial knives (n = 2), a graver/burin, and charred bone (n = 89) (Buchner 1979:31–32). Nearby is the Whitemouth Falls site (EaLa 1) along the Winnipeg River in southeastern Manitoba. It produced Oxbow material from buried context and a radiocarbon date of 4,625 +/- 150 BP (GX-4416) (Buchner 1979:80–81). This component overlaid a primary flexed interment associated with a bison skull and a shell paint dish (Buchner 1979:80). The Gakushuin lab dates obtained for the interment were rejected (Blakeslee 1994), but it seems reasonable to suggest a possible link between burial and the overlying Oxbow occupation.

The Hacault site (DkLm 1) is an Oxbow occupation site located southeast of Brandon in southwestern Manitoba (Nero 1997). Surface reconnaissance and excavation produced sixty projectile points with as many as twenty-two classifiable as Oxbow. Triangular points and/or preforms were also numerous. A large side-notched point was recovered in several pieces that emulate the smaller Oxbow points (Nero 1997, fig. 3v). Similar specimens have been recovered from the Harder site and Connell Creek site. Two radiocarbon dates of 3,150 +/- 550 BP (BGS-1717) and 2,915 +/- 125 BP (BGS-1953) were obtained for the site (Nero 1997; Morlan n.d.).

Montana has produced a number of dated Oxbow components. The Sun River site (24CA74) is a stratified site with three Oxbow components (Greiser et al. 1985). The site is located on a floodplain of the Sun River just above its confluence with the Missouri River. Cultural Level IV was an Oxbow living floor that produced a date of 3,450 +/- 350 BP (Greiser et al. 1985:855–856). A sand-filled, basin-shaped hearth was associated with the living floor. Lithics were all derived from local sources. Fauna included bison (MNI = 3), rodent, rabbit, fish, and amphibian. Cultural Level V was an Oxbow occupation dated by three radiocarbon dates to about 4,500 BP (Greiser et al. 1985:860). Most, if not all, of the lithics were obtained from local sources. Fauna included bison (MNI = 6), pronghorn, wapiti, deer, and bird. Cultural Level VI was an occupation dated by three radiocarbon dates to about 5,200 BP. Seven Oxbow points are associated with a bone-processing area and an excavated hearth. The lithics were all derived from local sources. The fauna included pronghorn (MNI = 4), bird, deer, rodent, bison, jackrabbit, and wolf. Cultural Level VI was amongst the earliest dated Oxbow levels on the plains. Frison (1991a:88) illustrated some of the Oxbow points from the Sun River site. Although they are not labelled by stratigraphic level, some specimens exhibit the block-eared form but lack the shallow indented base (Frison 1991a:88, fig. 2.48d and e) of the Long Creek points of the Estevan phase, which date to ca. 5,000+ BP. Examining the Sun River site point assemblage in light of its stratigraphy and age might be instructive on Oxbow continuity and change.

The King site (24PH3886) is a multicomponent site on the Fort Belknap Indian Reservation on the eastern margin of the Little Rocky Mountains in north-central Montana (Brumley and Rennie 1999). The site is located in the Bear Gulch drainage. In XU-6 (excavation unit 6) a single occupation consisted of a concentration of bone and lithic debitage in association with three Oxbow points and a preform (Brumley and Rennie 1999:60–61). The fauna produced a minimum of a single bison. A radiocarbon date of 3,590 +/- 80 BP (Beta-60244) was obtained. Brumley and Rennie (2005:16) noted that Oxbow points, although only recovered from a few dated contexts in northern Montana, are "a common occurrence in surface collections . . . from throughout northern Montana."

Cree Crossing (24PH3396) is an Oxbow winter campsite adjacent to a ford of the Milk River in north-central Montana (Aaberg et al. 2003). Six Oxbow points and four point fragments were recovered along with five preforms. Other tools recovered included bifaces, end scrapers, side scrapers, flake tools, cores, and hammerstones (Aaberg et al. 2003:66). The faunal assemblage reflects large artiodactyls. An immunological analysis of the tools did confirm sheep and deer residues but also indicated the butchering of rabbit and dog (Aaberg at al. 2003:46–54). Three features were recorded at the site. Two deep features produced the majority of the burned bone along with slight concentrations of FBR. Still, FBR was scattered across the site (Aaberg et al. 2003:43–44). A third shallow feature produced only an organic stain and charcoal flecks. The former produced dates of ca. 3,570

BP and 3,410 BP while the latter produced a surprisingly recent date of ca. 2,100 BP (Aaberg et al. 2003:42).

Site 24BL1176 is located in the Bears Paw Mountains in north-central Montana (Brumley and Rennie 2005:15). The site is a small campsite with an Oxbow component that was dated to 3,910 +/- 80 BP (Beta-32009) (Brumley and Rennie 2005:15).

In North Dakota, very few Oxbow sites have been reported. Gregg (1986:105–108) noted two surface finds of Oxbow points: the Moe site and the Cinnamon Creek Ridge site. Similarly, South Dakota has produced a few Oxbow points, but not from excavated contexts. McNerney (1970) recovered numerous projectile points during a surface survey along Blue Dog Lake in northeast South Dakota. Of these he identified two Oxbow points from a 35-m stretch of beach labelled site 39DA201 (McNerney 1970:292).

In Nebraska, the Sidney Burial has been proposed as an Oxbow site (Carlson et al. 1999). The burial was located on a low hill along Lodgepole Creek. Two individuals (a young man in a flexed position and very fragmentary remains of an infant) were recovered from what appears to be a burial pit (Carlson et al. 1999:107). A notched biface, five small worked amazonite pendants, a fragmented turtle carapace, several bird bones, other vertebrate remains, and some freshwater shell fragments were also recovered (Carlson et al. 1999:108). The point/notched biface is not Oxbow in form. A radiocarbon date of 3,910 +/- 60 BP (Beta-66571/CAMS-9886) was obtained. The Sidney burial, however, exhibits many common traits to Oxbow burial phenomena, including the locale, the nature of the surroundings, red ochre, points and/or knives, pendants, shell, bird bone, rock clusters marking the burial, and exotic materials (Carlson et al. 1999:116). Still, no diagnostic artifacts were recovered and Oxbow material has rarely, if ever, been found south of the northern part of South Dakota. Even there, Oxbow is only known in surface finds. A stronger explanation of their similarity is that they share a recent common origin. The Oxbow phase derives from the Estevan phase, which may have had its origins in the periphery of the Eastern Woods, perhaps even in Nebraska (see Estevan phase above).

In northwestern Wyoming, the Mummy Cave deposits dating to the Oxbow phase exhibit Oxbow-like points. In Level 28, very square-eared, Oxbow-like points were recovered with corner-notched material dating to ca. 4,600 BP (Husted and Edgar 2002). It is overlaid by Level 30, which contained Oxbow-like points that have their ears "pointing down-shaft" and very elongate McKean points dating to ca. 4,100 BP (Husted and

Edgar 2002). The similarity in form between these materials and the Oxbow materials is no doubt a product of common historical past but their temporal congruity suggests it is not a product of intense cultural contact or the similarity would likely be stronger. Thus, northern Montana would appear to be the southern boundary of the Oxbow phase.

In terms of the fate of the Oxbow phase, Reeves (1969:34) postulated that the Oxbow phase might be ancestral to Besant in the Napikwan tradition. Syms (1970:125–127) placed the Oxbow and McKean phases as mostly contemporaneous on much of the Plains. A number of archaeologists have noted that there are Oxbow and Oxbow-like points in sites within the boreal forest. Moreover, these sites often date relatively late compared to the majority of Oxbow sites. To account for the presence of Oxbow in the boreal forest, Buchner (1981b) proposed the "Anomalous Winter Hypothesis." Buchner noted the reliance on bison, which is evident in the faunal assemblages of Oxbow sites, and reckoned that the Oxbow people must have had a close relationship with the seasonal movements of this animal. He suggested that as the Hypsithermal period ended, changes in winter weather severity altered the ability of bison to arrive at their wintering grounds. The Oxbow people, already at the bison's wintering grounds in the parkland, gradually became increasingly more dependent on forest resources (Buchner 1981b:142). Other archaeologists have also noted the presence of Oxbow and/or Oxbow-like points in the parkland and boreal forest (Gibson 1981; Pollock 1981; Spurling and Ball 1981). Some have suggested a movement of people from the plains into the boreal forest (Gibson 1981; Spurling and Ball 1981) while others have suggested that the apparent spread of Oxbow may relate to a technological tradition rather than an archaeological culture or cultures (Pollock 1981). This text suggests the Oxbow phase was displaced off the Northern Plains at ca. 4,100 BP by the McKean complex. A pocket of Oxbow people persisted on the Plains in north-central Montana. This is witnessed in the late-dated sites in southern Alberta and northern Montana such as Tuscany, Stampede, Sun River, King, Cree Crossing, and 24BL1176. Perhaps other people of the Oxbow phase were displaced into the northern and eastern parkland periphery as a result of the McKean influx.

MCKEAN COMPLEX (CA. 4,200 TO 3,500 BP)

The McKean Lanceolate projectile point was first described by Wheeler (1952) after its recovery in the lower of two levels at the McKean site in northeastern Wyoming. Mulloy (1954) described the assemblage associated with the McKean Lanceolate points and elaborated on its possible relationship to similar assemblages on the plains. Mulloy (1954:445) recognized that the term *McKean Lanceolate* addressed only a small part of the projectile point assemblage recovered from the McKean level at the site. Subsequently, Wheeler (1954) elaborated upon his typology, confirming that *McKean Lanceolate* referred to basally notched lanceolate points. He added the term *Duncan* to refer to stemmed McKean points that had, thus far, been labelled *McKean Stemmed*, to avoid confusion with *McKean Lanceolate*. The Duncan point is characterized by a straight converging or bilaterally convex blade, insloping and non-barbed shoulders, straight parallel-sided stem, and a notched base (Wheeler 1954:7–8). As well, he used the term *Hanna*, instead of the previous suggestion of *Perry*, for points with straight converging and incurving blades, straight or sloping and slightly barbed shoulders, an expanding stem, and a shallow notch on the base (Wheeler 1954:8–9). Similar points and assemblages were noted at Pictograph Cave, Signal Butte, Ash Hollow, Dead Man Cave, Promontory Caves, Black Rock Cave, Billings Bison Trap, and Birdshead Cave (Mulloy 1954:453–454).

On the Northern Plains, McKean sites are not particularly common, leading to relatively little literature on the subject (Webster 2004). Initially, Wormington and Forbis (1965:191) dated the McKean occupation in Alberta to between ca. 4,500 and 3,300 BP based on work at the type site, among others. They contended that a subsistence based on bison was present, rather than foraging, despite acknowledging that the McKean material may represent a migration of people (Wormington and Forbis 1965:190–192). Reeves (1969:33) suggested a similar date for the McKean phase (4,500–3,500 BP) signified by McKean points, and acknowledged a Hanna phase (3,500–3,000 BP) signified by Hanna points. Like Wormington and Forbis (1965:190–192), he noted that these point styles quite often co-occurred in sites. Syms (1970:125), working in Manitoba, noted an increasing degree of "stemness" through time from McKean, with no stem, to Duncan and Hanna, with substantial stemness. He argued the typological boundary between McKean and Duncan, as well as Duncan and Hanna, was arbitrary based on the measure of stemness (Syms 1970:125). Most recently, Webster (2004:106–122) examined stratified and radiocarbon dated McKean/Duncan/Hanna sites to suggest McKean sites predate Duncan/Hanna material. His review produced evidence that McKean sites date mainly from 4,400 to 3,900 BP on the Canadian Plains, while Duncan and Hanna sites largely postdate this time period. Co-occurrence of the points could not be entirely ruled out, however, and he suggested that the three points be conceived as a "series" (Webster 2004:121).

Perhaps the most influential McKean site in the development of an understanding of the McKean complex on the Northern Plains has been the Cactus Flower site (EbOp 16). Brumley (1975) excavated this well-stratified site, which is located on the Canadian Forces Base Suffield, north of Medicine Hat. Ten occupation floors were recognized. The oldest occupation, X, did not contain diagnostic material. A single McKean point was recovered in the overlying occupation, IX. The next occupation, VIII, produced two McKean points, five Duncan points, and two Hanna points. Occupation floors VII to III each produced at least one Duncan or one Hanna point, and a single McKean point was recovered in occupation VI. Two flake points occurred in Occupation II while two Pelican Lake points were recovered in Occupation I (Brumley 1975). Features at the site included hearths, ash concentrations, and earth pits (Brumley 1975:19). Cobble-lined hearths are common in McKean sites to the south but were not observed at the Cactus Flower site. Similarly, grinding slabs often recovered at McKean sites in southern Montana and Wyoming were not recovered. The Cactus Flower site was interpreted as a campsite positioned for ambushing prey at a river crossing used by bison (Brumley 1975, 1978).

Numerous perspectives have been expressed regarding the origin of McKean material. Mulloy's (1954:440) impression of the materials from the McKean site lead him to make comparisons with historically known people in the Great Basin living in small groups and subsisting on wild vegetable products and small game. In the 1950s and 60s, years of cave site excavations on the Plains periphery had produced long cultural sequences while open sites dating to the Middle Prehistoric period on the Plains proper were rare. This fuelled the debate concerning the abandonment of the Plains during the Middle Prehistoric period Hypsithermal interval, supporting proposals of a McKean migration in response to climate amelioration (see Reeves 1973:1221–1222 for a summary; Webster 2004:82). Importantly, a Great Basin origin has been soundly rejected, based on technological comparisons and increasing similarities to materials in the foothills and mountains of the northwestern United States (Green 1975, cited in Webster 2004:83). Husted (1969) rejected a Great Basin origin for McKean, suggesting a mountain origin within the Western macrotradition in Idaho, Oregon, and Wyoming with continuity back to the Agate Basin complex. Black (1991) argued that there is little evidence to relate mountain-adapted people back to the Agate Basin complex, given the widespread Mountain tradition.

In Canada, Syms (1970:131) followed prominent American researchers (e.g., Husted) in suggesting that the McKean complex represented people that moved down from the foothills of the Rockies as the Hypsithermal developed. He used radiocarbon dates to illustrate that the earliest McKean sites were generally located around the Big Horn Basin of northwestern Wyoming (Syms 1970:131). Reeves (1969) initially presented three possible scenarios for McKean origins: (1) McKean might have had antecedents in the Oxbow phase, (2) McKean might represent an intrusive population from the mountains, or (3) McKean might be an indigenous culture that became highly enculturated by its neighbours. Subsequently, Reeves (1973) suggested that an Oxbow/McKean complex exhibited both point types, followed by a McKean complex featuring only McKean points; the origin of McKean, however, is not overtly stated. Reeves later classified the cultural historical sequence as Oxbow/Late Mummy Cave followed by McKean as the two distinctive cultural traditions in the Early Middle Prehistoric (i.e., 2,800–1,000 B.C.) (Reeves 1990:180).

Keyser and Davis (1984) suggested that McKean materials might represent the diffusion of a techno-complex through existing populations. Similarly, Tratebas (1998) also argued for diffusion based on analyses indicating long-term cultural continuity in the Black Hills. Ramsay (1993:337–348) updated Syms' site chrono-distribution data, which increased the age of some of the outlying areas but maintained the earliest dates in the Bighorn Basin and surrounding areas.

Despite the various lines of argument, migration models appear to be a prominent theoretical position among many Canadian researchers (Brumley 1975; Pettipas 1996a; Ramsay 1993; Reeves 1983a; Syms 1970). Webster (2004:89–105) recently summarized archaeological knowledge concerning McKean migration. Importantly, he states confidently that Canadian McKean material is the same, more or less, as American McKean material (Webster 2004:91). He did point out, however, that Canadian McKean points tend to be shorter and wider than their American counterparts (Webster 2004:91). Webster (2004:91–92) suggested that the best evidence for cultural continuity between northern and southern McKean can be found in human interments including the McKean site (Haspel and Wedel 1985; Mulloy 1954), the Dead Indian Creek site (Gill 1984), the Crown site (Walker 1986), the Graham site (Walker 1984a), and possibly two interments from the Gray site (Millar 1978). With the exception of the Graham cremation and the two possible McKean interments at the Gray site, all the burials were shallow pits in primary living floors that generally lacked grave goods, and were not associated with red ochre (Webster 2004:93). This practice is in stark contrast to the Oxbow phase, in which there are isolated interments away from campsites (or interments in the Gray site), consistent use of red ochre, and a tendency towards primary extended burials (Webster 2004:94). Webster (2004:95–99) used a revised version of Syms' chrono-distribution of McKean data to, once again, determine that the oldest sites occur in the headwaters of the Yellowstone River and the mountains of the Bighorn Basin. He suggested an origin of ca. 4,900 BP with expansion to the Black Hills by 4,700–4,500 BP (Webster 2004:96). By ca. 4,400 BP, McKean was in southern Saskatchewan and by ca. 4,200 BP in southern Alberta. The impetus for a migration is likely multicausal and will be difficult to determine. It is possible McKean developed at the end of the Hypsithermal in the Bighorn Basin area and expanded when conditions were favourable (Webster 2004:100). Linked to this may be population increases and the need to exploit new land.

The Sites

The following presents well-dated sites with diagnostic materials that can be considered part of the McKean complex (i.e., McKean/Duncan/Hanna). As Webster (2004) suggested, McKean Lanceolate points are the earliest McKean point, followed by Duncan and Hanna points. It has not been equivocally determined if McKean precedes both Duncan and Hanna or whether the McKean-Duncan-Hanna series of points co-occur in McKean sites. Webster (2004) suggested leaving the projectile points as a series of temporally overlapping styles until more data is accumulated (see Plate 17 and Figure 18).

Cactus Flower (EbOp 16). The Cactus Flower site is a multicomponent campsite located above the South Saskatchewan River within the boundaries of the Canadian Forces Base Suffield. The site was named for the cactuses that were flowering when the site was excavated (John Brumley, personal communication 2007). Ten occupations were defined. The site was found in 1969 by Archie Stalker of the Geological Survey of Canada, but excavation did not take place until 1974. Brumley (1975, 1978) excavated six areas at the site, totalling 364 m^2 as part of a program to minimize the impact of the military presence on the base.

PLATE 17 McKean points. Illustrated are projectile points from DgPl 1 (a–c); the Austech site (EhPo 55) (d–f); the Boy Chief site (EeOv 68) (g and h); and EhPm 113 (i and j). Photo credit: Alberta Culture and Community Spirit (a–h); Stantec (i and j).

As noted, Occupation X, the earliest occupation, did not produce a diagnostic point. It did contain one retouched flake, one core, a hammerstone, and three heavy chipped tools. Faunal remains indicated a single bison was present. A hearth and a possible earth pit were also recorded. The occupation was radiocarbon dated to ca. 3,700 BP (see Table 16), a date out of sequence with dates in the other occupations, so was rejected.

Occupation IX produced a McKean Lanceolate point, bifaces (n = 14), retouched flakes (n = 32), end scrapers (n = 5), a graver, pebble cores (n = 8), heavy chipped tools (n = 4), hammerstones (n = 5), a shell bead, and shell fragments. The fauna included a minimum of six bison, an antelope, a cottontail rabbit, and a freshwater clam. Two basin hearths were also recorded. A radiocarbon date of ca. 2,100 BP was considered to be in error (Brumley 1975).

Occupation VIII produced two McKean Lanceolate, five Duncan, two Hanna and four fragmentary points. Other lithics recovered include bifaces (n = 34), marginally retouched tools (n = 54), end scrapers (n = 9), spokeshaves (n = 2), a tit graver, pebble cores (n = 35), heavy chipped tools (n = 14), hammerstones (n = 2), and anvil stones (n = 2). Part of a ground-stone pipe and

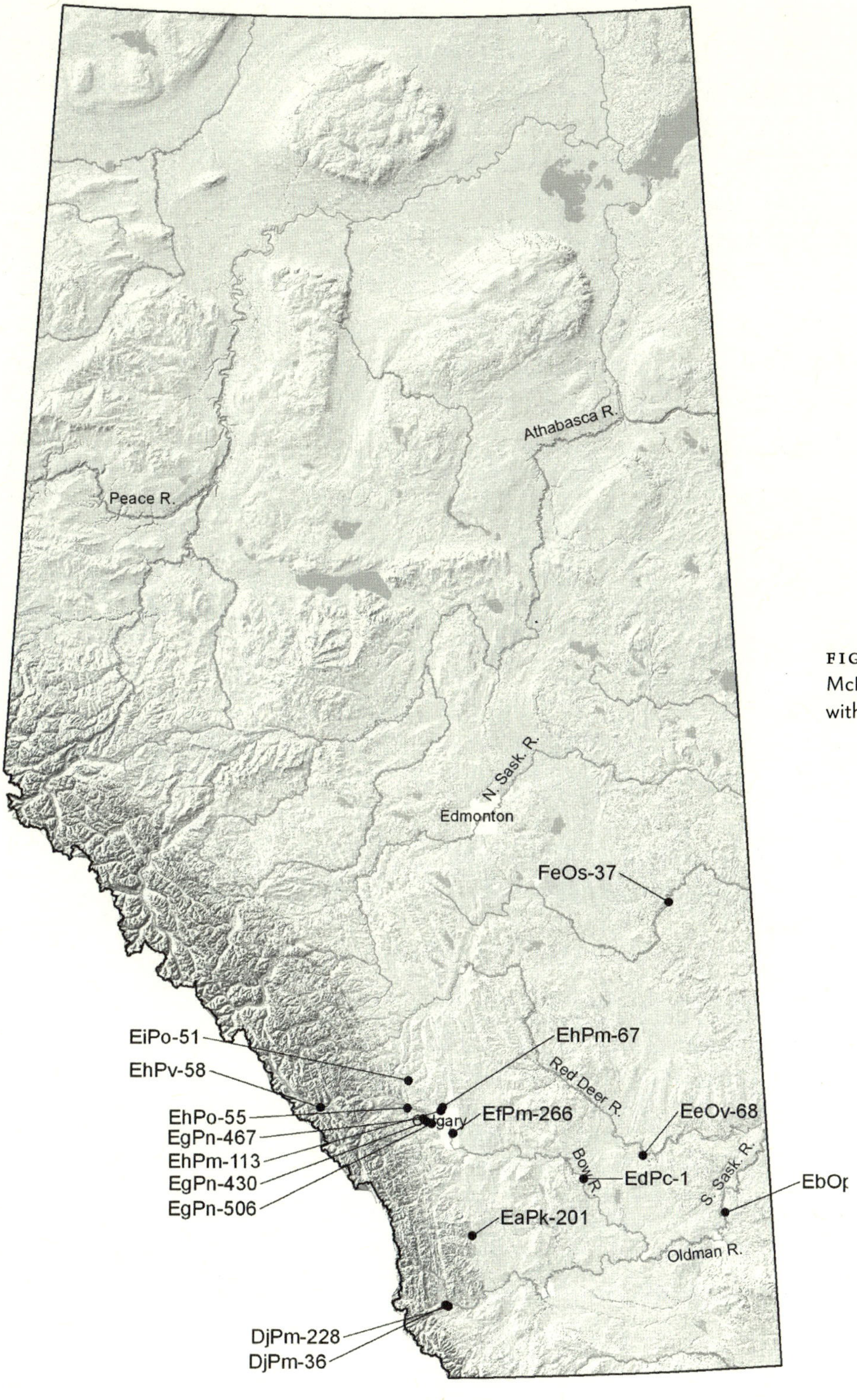

FIGURE 18
McKean sites within Alberta

an ammonite septum were also recovered. Bone tools include three awls, two beads, and other polished fragments. Fauna recovered from the site include a minimum of twenty bison, an antelope, three dogs, a kit fox, a cottontail rabbit, a jackrabbit, a bird, and a fish. A total of four basin hearths, an earth pit, and a circular distribution of material interpreted as a former structure were also recorded. Two radiocarbon dates were obtained: ca. 4,130 BP and 4,220 BP (Table 16).

TABLE 16 Radiocarbon dates for McKean sites (calibrated by OxCal 3.10 [Ramsey 2005])

Site [LAB NO.]	Conventional ^{14}C Age	$^{13}C/^{12}C$ Ratio	Material	Calibration	Reference
EbOp 16, LIIIV [S-1210]	4220 +/- 130	-25.0‰	charcoal	3350–2450 B.C. (p = 0.954)	Brumley 1975; Morlan n.d.
EbOp 16, LIIIV [S-782]	4130 +/- 85	-25.0‰	charcoal	2900–2480 B.C. (p = 0.954)	Brumley 1975; Morlan n.d.
DgPl 1 [GX-1460]	3890 +/- 215	-10.0‰	apatite	3000–1700 B.C. (p = 0.954)	Brumley 1975; Morlan n.d.
EaPk 201 [S-3985]	3860 +/- 320	?	collagen	3400–1400 B.C. (p = 0.954)	Brumley 1975; Morlan n.d.
EaPk 201 [S-3984]	3720 +/- 260	?	collagen	2900–1500 B.C. (p = 0.954)	Brumley 1975; Morlan n.d.
EbOp 16, L X [S-821]	3725 +/- 95	-25.0‰	charcoal	rejected	Brumley 1975; Morlan n.d.
EbOp 16, L VI [S-820]	3970 +/- 160	-20.0‰	collagen	2900–2000 B.C. (p = 0.954)	Brumley 1975; Morlan n.d.
EbOp 16, L VI [S-823]	3615 +/- 95	-25.0‰	charcoal	2300–1650 B.C. (p = 0.954)	Brumley 1975; Morlan n.d.
EbOp 16, L IV [S-784]	3705 +/- 80	-20.0‰	collagen	2400–1850 B.C. (p = 0.954)	Brumley 1975; Morlan n.d.
EbOp 16, L IV [S-822]	3620 +/- 95	-25.0‰	charcoal	2300–1650 B.C. (p = 0.954)	Brumley 1975; Morlan n.d.
EbOp 16, L III [S-1013]	3930 +/- 110	-25.0‰	charcoal	2900–2050 B.C. (p = 0.954)	Brumley 1975; Morlan n.d.
DjPm 36 [AECV-1190C]	3670 +/- 130	-18.3‰	collagen	2500–1700 B.C. (p = 0.954)	Van Dyke 1994:128
EgPn 430, Area 2 [BETA-126647]	3580 +/- 70	-20.0‰	collagen	2140–1740 B.C. (p = 0.954)	Vivian et al. 2005, Vol. 1:6
EhPv 58 [S-2778]	3560 +/- 135	?	charcoal	2300–1500 B.C. (p =0.954)	Fedje 1986:52
EhPv 58 [S-2754]	2540 +/- 120	?	bone	rejected	Fedje 1986:52, 54
EhPo 55 [AECV-1354C]	3540 +/- 60	-18.9‰	collagen	2040–1730 B.C. (p = 0.941); 1720–1690 B.C. (p = 0.013)	Van Dyke 1993

EhPo 55 [AECV-1355C]	3400 +/- 60	-18.8‰	collagen	1880–1530 B.C. (p = 0.954)	Van Dyke 1993
EgPn 467 [BETA-115161]	3330 +/- 90	-19.5‰	collagen	1880–1840 B.C. (p = 0.032) 1830–1420 B.C. (p = 0.922)	Hanna and Head 2000:174
EiPo 51 [BETA-1672]	3680 +/- 75	-20.0‰	collagen	2300–1870 B.C. (p = 0.954)	Wilson 1983:104; Morlan n.d.
EeOv 68 [AECV-2024C]	3360 +/- 80	-21.9‰	collagen	1750–1530 B.C. (p = 0.943) 1480–1460 B.C. (p = 0.011)	Head et al. 2003:21
EeOv 68 [AECV-2053C]	3400 +/- 90	-20.2‰	collagen	1940–1490 B.C. (p = 0.954)	Head et al. 2003:21
EhPm 113 [BETA-236168]	2880 +/- 40	-19.0‰	collagen	1210–920 B.C. (p = 0.954)	Malasiuk 2007, Appendix F

Occupation VII produced two Duncan points, bifaces (n =12), marginally retouched flakes (n=18), end scrapers (n=4), a graver, pebble cores (n=6), and heavy chipped tools (n=8). Bone tools include a blunt end tool. The fauna included a minimum of three bison, a cottontail rabbit, two birds, and a freshwater clam. Features were numerous, including four basin hearths, three surface hearths, five ash concentrations, and an earth pit. Occupation VII was not dated.

Occupation VI contained one Duncan, three Hanna, and three fragmentary points. Other lithics include bifaces (n=6), marginally retouched tools (n=25), end scrapers (n=5), pebble cores (n=4), heavy chipped tools (n=23), and an anvil. A ground-stone disk was also recovered. Bone tools include four awls, two blunt end tools, and antler tine fragments. A shell disk was also recovered. Fauna included a minimum of four bison, three antelope, a mule deer, a dog, and a freshwater clam. Features recorded included two basin hearths and two surface hearths. Two radiocarbon dates were obtained for this level: ca. 3,600 BP and 3,900 BP.

Occupation V contained a Duncan point along with a biface, marginally retouched tools (n=6), end scrapers (n=4), and heavy chipped tools (n=2). A circular, polished stone and a bone awl were also recovered. A minimum of one bison and one bird were represented in the faunal assemblage. A single surface hearth was recorded in this occupation. No radiocarbon dates were obtained for this level.

Occupation IV produced one McKean Lanceolate, one Duncan, two Hanna, and two fragmentary points. Other lithics include bifaces (n=6), marginally retouched flakes (n=37), end scrapers (n=7), spokeshaves (n=2), pebble cores (n = 5), and heavy chipped tools (n = 12). Bone tools include four awls and a bone bead. A shell bead was also recovered. The faunal assemblage suggests a minimum of two bison, an antelope, a dog, and a freshwater clam at the site. Two radiocarbon dates were obtained for this occupation, both of which date to approximately ca. 3,600 BP.

Occupation III contained one Duncan point, two Hanna points, and one fragmentary point. The lithic assemblage also included a marginally retouched flake and four heavy chipped tools. A minimum of one bison was recovered. The features recorded included a basin hearth, eight earth pits, and five surface hearths. A radiocarbon date of ca. 3,900 BP was obtained for the occupation. This date is out of sequence with the other occupations so was rejected.

Brumley (1975, 1978) considered the Cactus Flower site to be a campsite that was repeatedly used over time by a series of single families or a small number of family groups. Brumley argued that the site is well-situated for ambushing animals that water themselves along the South Saskatchewan River. The area is ideal for ambushes owing to the steep banks, which offer few access points. Brumley (1975, 1978) argued the stratified deposits represent a sequence documenting the cultural changes from the McKean complex to the Pelican Lake phase (part of Reeves' Tunaxa tradition), with the abandonment of the site during the later Pelican Lake phase, illustrating the move to communal kills and away from ambush kills (Brumley 1978).

Pass Creek Cabin (DgPl 1). The Pass Creek Cabin site is a kill site and campsite located on the south side of the Pass Creek Valley entrance north of the Waterton town site in Waterton Lakes National Park (Reeves 1972:41). The site consists of "a series of closely, vertically superimposed living floors which vary horizontally" (Reeves 1972:55). The lowest occupation, 1A, produced a Lusk point, 1B produced Bitterroot and Salmon River points, 1C produced McKean Lanceolate points, and the level above 1C, which was considered disturbed, produced Late Side-notched material. The site was excavated in 1968 and 1969 as part of a systematic study and inventory of archaeological materials for the National Parks Service.

Four McKean Lanceolate points were recovered from Level 1C in association with a surface hearth, a stone platform hearth, and a possible cairn (Reeves 1972:56–57). Side-notched points were recovered within this level but were considered intrusive from overlying levels because of rodent disturbance (Reeves 1972:55). Few pieces of FBR were recorded in the closely spaced McKean complex floors. A radiocarbon date of ca. 3,890 BP was obtained for the material (Reeves 1972:56).

EaPk 201. EaPk 201 is a multicomponent site on a large flood plain terrace on the east bank of Willow Creek a few kilometres upstream from its confluence with Pine Creek (Hjermstad 1998:76). The site consisted of three components that were investigated mainly using three excavation blocks: west, central, and east. A total of 122 m^2 was excavated at the site to mitigate the construction of a dam.

The west block (25 m^2) produced a possible Hanna point in the second-lowest cultural unit (CU-2) and a classic Hanna point in the underlying level, CU-3 (Hjermstad 1998:88). CU-2 also contained two features: a basin hearth and a cobble platform associated with one *t*-butt drill and two end scrapers. A total of 173 pieces of debitage was recovered with most being secondary flakes. Quartz (40%), chert (27%), and quartzite (15%) dominated the assemblage (Hjermstad 1998:104). Four pieces of obsidian were recovered from the level and were sourced to the Bear Gulch quarry in the Centennial Mountains of eastern Idaho. FBR (n=171) was small in size. The faunal assemblage (n=2,300+) was relatively large. A minimum of nine bison was inferred from this sample. As well, six canid bones and the bones of a large bird were recovered. A radiometric date of ca. 3,700 BP was obtained for the occupation (Hjermstad 1998:99). The level was interpreted as a secondary butchering locale.

In CU-3, in addition to the classic Hanna point recovered, lithic tools included two end scrapers and a utilized flake. Thirty-five lithics were recovered, most of which were quartzite (51%). Quartz (13%), siltstone (8%), petrified wood (8%), shale (3%), chert (10%), obsidian (5%), and chalcedony (3%) were also present. The faunal assemblage (n=445) produced a minimum of six bison (Hjermstad 1998:118). Deer, dog, and wolf were also present. FBR (n=47) were small in size (Hjermstad 1998:118). A radiometric date of 3,860 BP was obtained for the occupation (Hjermstad 1998:116). The occupation was interpreted as an early-winter campsite and bison processing area. The other block excavations failed to produce diagnostics or even large assemblages.

DjPm 36, Snyder Farm Locality, Component 2. DjPm 36, Snyder Farm Locality, is discussed in the section on the Gowen complex. The lowest level at the site provided evidence of Gowen side-notched material that was overlain by a sparse Hanna occupation. This occupation, in turn, was overlain by a Pelican Lake occupation. Most of the Hanna material was recovered within a single block between 100 and 120 cm BS.

A single Hanna projectile point was recovered. Other lithic tools included cores (n = 2), a biface, an elongate pebble, and retouched flakes (n = 3) (Van Dyke 1994:128), as well as pieces of debitage (n = 10) and FBR (n = 93). The faunal assemblage (n = 45) was fragmentary. No features were recorded. A radiometric date of ca. 3,670 BP was obtained for the overlying level in a nearby block providing a *terminus ante quem* (Van Dyke 1994:128).

EgPn 430, Area Two. EgPn 430 is large multicomponent bison kill/processing campsite on the northwest slope of the West Paskapoo Escarpment in west Calgary (Vivian et al. 2005, vol. 1:1). Six areas were defined for this site. The main occupation was associated with the McKean complex (Vivian et al. 2005, vol. 1:4). Some mixing of subsequent occupations occurred, with items being sorted by mass and weight (Vivian et al. 2005, vol.1:5–6). In Area 2, a total of 27 m^2 in a block excavation and thirteen 1-×-1-m scatter units were excavated prior to the development of a subdivision at the site (Vivian et al. 2005, vol. 1:2).

Twelve McKean Lanceolate and two Hanna points or point fragments were recovered along with two Late Side-notched points, three Pelican Lake points, and four non-diagnostic points associated with the processing area (Vivian et al. 2005, vol. 1:6–15). Numerous other tools were recovered in the processing area, including bifaces, end scrapers, wedges, retouched flakes, utilized flakes, cores, a drill, a graver, and a chopper (Vivian et al. 2005:15–24). Bone tools recovered included a bone hammer and three bone awls (Vivian et al. 2005, vol. 1:24–25). Four fossilized shell fragments were also recovered (Vivian et al. 2005, vol. 1:25). Lastly, a kaolin pipe stem fragment from the Proto-historic period was also recovered (Vivian 2005:25). The lithic suite was considered comparable to the Austech site (see below) but possible mixing makes this comparison problematic (Vivian et al. 2005, vol. 1:26).

The faunal assemblage included mainly bison (MNI = 14), with wolf, fox, wapiti, rabbit, and bivalves (Vivian et al. 2005, vol. 1:30). Two fetal bones likely representing one fetal animal and a mandible of a two- to three-month-old calf were recovered, suggesting a spring kill (Vivian et al. 2005, vol. 1:33–34). No discrete features were observed, and FBR was scattered across the site (Vivian et al. 2005:45). A radiocarbon date of ca. 3,580 BP supports a McKean affiliation for at least some of the bone in the site. The researchers argued that the site is a McKean processing area with other materials incidentally mixed into it. They suggested the site shows many similarities to the Austech site (see below). Both are considered to be processing sites without features, both sites produced primarily McKean points, and their dates are McKean complex in age (Vivian et al. 2005, vol. 1:46–47).

Second Lake (EhPv 58, 162R). The Second Lake site is a multicomponent campsite within Banff National Park. It consists of nine separate occupations on an alluvial fan on the northwestern edge of Second Lake (Fedje 1986:48). In 1985, a total of 19 m^2 was excavated at the site (Fedje 1986:48). An overlying roadway protects the deposits. In Occupation 6, two Hanna-like points were recovered along with 650 pieces of lithic debitage and a faunal assemblage including bison, deer, and beaver (Fedje 1986:54). Two dates were obtained for this level: ca. 3,560 BP and 2,450 BP. The later date was rejected as intrusive (Fedje 1986:54).

Austech (EhPo 55). The Austech site is a butchering area at the base of the fourth and highest terrace along the Bow River, near its confluence with Jumpingpound Creek (Van Dyke 1993). The site was discovered in 1982 although mitigative excavations did not take place until 1993. A North block (10 m^2) and a South block (32 m^2) were excavated (Van Dyke 1993:38–40). In both blocks, cultural material occurred in the ploughzone, at 30–60 cm BS and at 100 cm BS. The layer of interest occurred between 30 and 60 cm BS.

The south block contained one McKean and one Hanna point in association with a discrete horizon of bone (Van Dyke 1993). The lithic assemblage also included a marginally retouched flake and four heavy chipped tools. Debitage (n = 189) most commonly recovered was siltstone, miscellaneous chert, and quartzite.

The faunal assemblage had an MNI of twelve bison, as well as a neonatal bone and a fetal bone (Van Dyke 1993:52–53). A few fragments were burned or calcine and many exhibited impact marks (n = 26) and cut marks (n = 3). The low incidence of axial elements, other than ribs, suggested the main focus of activity was butchering and processing of animals killed nearby (Van Dyke 1993:61). No features were observed although FBR, both spalled and water-fractured, were generally clustered in the east-central area of the excavation (Van Dyke 1993:53).

The North block produced five tools and twenty-two pieces of debitage. The tools included an unclassifiable point base, a core, a chopper, a retouched tool and a retouched flake (Van Dyke 1993:46). The faunal assemblage produced an MNI of three bison. FBR, spalled and water fractured, was common in the southeast part of the block (Van Dyke 1993:47). Two radiocarbon dates were obtained from the South block: ca. 3,540 BP and 3,400 BP (Table 16). These dates, taken with the context of the excavated material, were interpreted as a single event: a McKean butchering site where bison were dispatched in late winter/early spring about 3,500 years ago (Van Dyke 1993:62).

EgPn 467. EgPn 467 is a multicomponent campsite located in hummocky terrain above the Bow River southwest of the Bearspaw Reservoir, just west of Calgary (Hanna and Head 2000). The site consisted of an upper and lower component, both of which were attributed to the McKean complex based on the presence of Hanna points. A total of 50 m^2 was excavated as part of a mitigative program for a subdivision.

The Lower Component produced a single Hanna base (Hanna and Head 2000:181). Other lithic materials recovered include a biface, a side scraper, four retouched flakes, a utilized flake, a core, and two hammerstones. Debitage consisted of flakes (n = 37), flake fragments (n = 18), and shatter (n = 21) (Hanna and Head 2000:181). Most of the raw materials were quartzite (56.7%) or chert (23.3%), but obsidian (3.3%), chalcedony (6.6%), and quartz (1.1%) were also found. The faunal assemblage (n = 683) was highly fragmented with only seventy-three pieces assigned as bison. Neither seasonality nor herd composition could be determined. FBR (n = 857) was considered relatively rare at the site; it was largely crenulated not spalled. A radiometric date was not available for this component. The site was interpreted as a late-winter base camp that had been repeatedly occupied (Hanna and Head 2000:199).

The Upper Component produced seven Hanna points, a Duncan point, a possible McKean Lanceolate point, an Oxbow point and a point tip (Hanna and Head 2000:154). Other lithics included bifaces, scrapers (n = 4), flake tools (n = 19), cores (n = 4), and hammer stones (n = 3). Debitage (n = 239) was also common. Raw materials were dominated by chert (44.9 %), quartzite (32.6%), chalcedony (9.1%), and siltstone (7.6%), with some obsidian (2.9%), basalt (2.5%), and petrified wood (0.4%) (Hanna and Head 2000:155). The faunal assemblage (n = 1,499) was highly fragmented. Only 235 bison bones were identifiable to species. This included two neonatal pelvis fragments, suggesting a late winter/early spring occupation. FBR (n = 3,437) was relatively common. Small crenulated specimens were dominant, with few spalled pieces suggesting repeated use in stone boiling. A radiometric date of ca. 3,330 BP was obtained (Table 16). Like the Lower Component, this occupation was interpreted as a late-winter base camp. The site is considered to represent serial occupations over relatively long periods of time by what appears to be a single cultural group (Hanna and Head 2000:155).

Hitching Post Ranch (EiPo 51). The Hitching Post Ranch site is a bison assemblage near Bottrel in the foothills northwest of Calgary (Wilson 1983:110). In 1980, the site was discovered on the Hitching Post Ranch (the site's namesake) during backhoe excavations at a spring (Wilson 1983:100).

The faunal assemblage was very diverse. Bones from eleven species were present, including a goose-sized bird, a medium-sized duck, a large sandpiper, snowshoe hare, a mouse-sized rodent, ground squirrel, wolf or wolf-like dog, white-tailed deer, wapiti, moose, and a large number of bison. An estimated 130 bison were recovered. The large number of young and adult male animals in the age distribution suggested a catastrophic die-off rather than selective hunting and processing. This interpretation was supported by the lack of mid-shaft breakages and cut marks, and high frequencies of tooth scoring from scavengers (Wilson 1983).

Cultural material was also recovered. One complete and two fragmentary Hanna points were recovered in apparent association with the bone bed (Wilson 1983:127). Also recovered were five flakes, an antler hammer, an antler punch, an antler wedge, and a *Dentalium* bead. The flakes did not exhibit retouch or use wear. Except for the points, this is not an assemblage useful for bison procurement or processing (Wilson 1983:128). Wilson (1983:128) speculated that the association of the tools with the catastrophic die-off may have resulted from scavenging of animal carcasses after a prairie fire. A single radiocarbon date of ca. 3,680 BP was obtained (Table 16) (Wilson 1983:104).

Boy Chief (EeOv 68), Block 4, Occupation 3. The Boy Chief site is described in the section on the Estevan phase. Block 4, Occupation 3 is the dated McKean component. It produced two Hanna points and an unidentifiable point associated with a small surface hearth (Head et al. 2003:135–142). Other tools in the assemblage include two edge modified flakes, an end scraper, and a bipolar core (Head et al. 2003:138–140). The lithic assemblage is dominated by quartzite and miscellaneous chert (Head et al. 2003:139).

The faunal assemblage was suggestive of a small secondary processing camp focusing on the forelimbs (Head et al. 2003:137). A total of 525 bone fragments was recovered. A minimum number of two bison is represented in the sample. Neither fetal bones nor elements for differentiating sex were recovered (Head et al. 2003:137). There was a concentration of unidentifiable limb elements and bone fragments in the southeast corner of the excavation. Three bone fragments have ochre on them, while a few (n=45) were charred. The FBR assemblage (n=161) was widely scattered. Angular fractures suggested stone boiling (Head et al. 2003:138). FBR appeared to be clustered to the north and west of the hearth (Head et al. 2003:141). Artifacts were distributed in a semicircular fashion around the hearth potentially outline a structure (Head et al. 2003:141). Two radiocarbon dates were obtained: ca. 3,400 BP and 3,360 BP (Table 16). The dates yield an average age of 3,376+/- 55 BP and support a Hanna-age cultural affiliation (Head et al. 2003:141).

EhPm 113. EhPm 113 is a multicomponent kill/processing site located on a small upper valley bench above Beddington Creek in north-central Calgary (Malasiuk 2007:6). A total of 4 m² was excavated in two blocks of 1-×-2-m units. Three cultural horizons were established based on the sediments and their cultural contents. The upper horizon, Horizon 1, did not produce diagnostic material. Horizon 2 produced the base of a Hanna point. The bottom horizon, Horizon 3, produced a complete Hanna point.

Horizon 2 correlates with the palaeosol that produced the base of an atypical Hanna point (Malasiuk 2007:53). The point has a relatively straight stem, pointed basal corners, and less defined shoulders than other Hanna points. A radiocarbon date of 2,880 BP was obtained (Table 16). Horizon 3 produced another complete Hanna point, exhibiting the slightly unusual style mentioned above (Malasiuk 2007:55). The late date for a Hanna occupation, the unusual point morphology, the lack of clear stratigraphy, and an expressed concern for disturbance by rodents indicate that EhPm 113 needs to be studied further.

Other sites. Surface finds of projectile points from this time period are fairly common south of the North Saskatchewan River in Alberta (Wormington and Forbis 1965:188). Two sites with points exhibiting deeply notched bases are FeOs 37 on the Canadian Forces Base Wainwright and EhPm 67 in Barn Coulee in north Calgary (Vivian and Reeves 2002:16–17, 84; McCullough and Landals 1995:133). The deep basal concavity may reflect an earlier form of McKean point than the less-indented form that is much more common. EfPm 266 is a buried partial stone circle associated with hearths and a basal portion of a stemmed point (Vivian 2006a). A date of ca. 3,600 BP was established for the occupation. This is amongst the oldest dated stone circles in Alberta.

Two sites that produced good McKean assemblages but lack radiometric dating and/or exhibit some mixing are DjPm 228 and EgPn 506. DjPm 228 is a multicomponent site on a relict landform near Horseshoe Canyon in the Oldman River Dam area (Van Dyke 1994:259–264). Four areas, based on the level of testing and excavation, were assigned to the site. In Block B, from 30 to 40 cm BS, a Hanna point, end scrapers (n = 2), a core, retouched flakes (n = 3), debitage (n = 40), and two bone fragments were recovered in 6 m^2 (Van Dyke 1994:262). Immediately overlying this occupation is a Bracken occupation with two radiocarbon dates of ca. 2,500 BP. EgPn 506 is a multicomponent processing site on a high bench on the Paskapoo Slopes, about 12 m below the escarpment in west Calgary (Vivian et al. 2003a). A McKean occupation represented by twenty-one complete or broken Hanna points, as well as Avonlea and Old Women's occupations, was present at the site (Vivian et al. 2003a:89). The cultural complexes, however, were not stratigraphically discrete (Vivian et al. 200a3:89). There were many features at the site, especially along the terrace edge. The features may be grouped in associated clusters of stone-boiling pits, hearths, and dump piles; the lack of stratigraphic control makes temporal interpretations difficult. Overall, the site appears to be a series of mid-winter to early spring campsites that focused on domestic activity (Vivian et al. 2003a).

Another possible McKean site is located in west-central Alberta is FfQh 32 (Kulle and Neal 1998:36). The site is an artifact scatter on a mid-level terrace above the McLeod River. A total of 8 m^2 produced a McKean Lanceolate point, two bifaces, seven expedient tools, and 385 pieces of debitage. Most of the raw materials were silicified siltstone or quartzite (Kulle and Neal 1998:41–42). A scatter of FBR was also noted with some calcine bone. The site was interpreted as a small campsite centred on a hearth (Kulle and Neal 1998:50). The site was not radiometrically dated.

McKean: Migrants from the Big Horn Basin/Black Hills Area

The McKean complex in Alberta dates roughly between 4,200 and 3,500 BP. In general, McKean Lanceolate points occur during the earliest part of this period, followed by Duncan points occurring over the middle of the period, and Hanna points occurring over the last part of the period. Thus, it is possible to get sites with only a single McKean diagnostic or all three diagnostics. Importantly, McKean Lanceolate points and Duncan points generally conform to Wheeler's (1954) defined types. The earliest McKean points may have deep basal concavities and be slightly more lanceolate compared to later specimens. Similarly, Hanna points tend to become atypical toward the end of the McKean complex. Specimens at the Hitching Post Ranch site and EhPm 113 exhibit fairly straight and parallel stems with very slightly indented basal edges. Also, the two specimens from the Boy Chief site Occupation 3, Level 4, are almost corner-notched, appearing to be transitional between Hanna and Pelican Lake forms.

In terms of stone tools, McKean tool kits emphasize end scrapers over the nearly absent side scrapers. Utilized flakes and retouched flakes are common. Lithic raw materials are mainly locally procured; very few exotics have been recovered in these sites. Bone and antler tools appear to be more common in the McKean complex than earlier archaeological cultures. Interestingly, shell beads occur frequently in McKean sites. As well, the oldest known stone pipe in Alberta dates to this time period. It is tubular in form and was recovered at the Cactus Flower site.

Subsistence during the McKean complex in Alberta is diverse but still focused on bison. The main strategy for procuring bison appears to be stalking of solitary animals or perhaps ambushing prey at watering holes. Thus, bison are the most common animal recovered in McKean sites. However, bison are only being taken in small numbers. Other animals recovered include antelope, wolf, dog, kit fox, cottontail rabbit, jack rabbit, birds, and fish.

Many features are known from this period. Hearths are common with both surface and basin hearths being present. Earth pits were reported but mostly from the Cactus Flower site. Ash concentrations and plenty of FBR suggest stone boiling operations were conducted. The cobble platform at EaPk 1 is unique for the McKean complex; it is associated with a basin hearth and may represent a roasting platform. As well, at the Cactus Flower site a circular distribution of debris was noted around a small hearth. This was interpreted as reflecting material kept inside a shelter. Similar circular debris distributions have been noted during the Oxbow phase and these seem likely to be indicative of shelters. Whether these interesting distributions of materials reflect locations of actual tipis or other kinds of shelters is difficult to assess, as tipi pegs or stones and the all-important central tie-down stake, a hallmark of a true tipi, have not been recovered. Still, EfPm 266 produced a partial stone circle potentially culturally associated with the twilight of the complex.

Having defined the McKean complex in Alberta, it is appropriate to look further abroad. In Saskatchewan, there are a number of McKean sites. EgNo 23 is a multicomponent site just north of the Douglas Park Sandhills (Webster 2004:6). Seven occupations were observed, of which three were McKean occupations (Occupations 2a, 2b, and 3) (Webster 2004:10). Level 2a centred on a spill pit for a nearby but unexcavated stone-boiling pit; the level produced a Hanna point, a Duncan point, and a date of 3,427 +/- 50 BP (BGS 2363). Level 2b was a temporary camp likely related to Level 2 materials; it did not produce diagnostics but dated to 3,520 +/- 40 BP (Beta-167310). Level 2, combining Levels 2a and 2b where stratigraphic separation was not evident, focused around a boiling pit and FBR, yielding a Hanna point, a Pelican Lake-like point, and a date of 3,537 +/- 55 BP (BGS 2364). Level 3, the lowest level, produced a single McKean Lanceolate point and a small side-notched point in a bison kill (MNI = 3) or processing site that was dated to 4,240 +/- 60 (Beta-183521) (Webster 2004:10–18).

The Redtail (FbNp 10) site is located in Wanuskewin Park near Saskatoon. The site is a multicomponent site with about twenty-six cultural occupations, in a small basin above the South Saskatchewan River. Seven levels produced McKean material. Occupation 8 exhibited a possible pit house. Occupation 11 produced a Hanna point and a date of 3,580 +/- 80 BP (S-3372) (Ramsay 1993:88–91). Planview artifact distribution patterns show a circular patterning, which suggests a possible structure (Ramsay 1993:288). Occupations 12(1) and 12(2) produced six Hanna points and two radiocarbon dates: 3,570 +/- 80 BP (S-3373) and 3,740 +/- 75 BP (S-3008) (Ramsay 1993:88–91). An oval distribution of material around a hearth was suggestive of a structure (Ramsay 1993:289). Occupation 13(1) did not produce diagnostics or radiocarbon dates. Occupation 13(2) produced the base of a McKean Lanceolate point, the base of a Duncan point, and a possible grinding tool in association with materials that provided two radiocarbon dates: 3,965 +/-70 BP (S-3374) and 3,980 +/- 70 BP (S-3375) (Ramsay 1993:88–91). Occupation 13(3) did not produce diagnostics or radiocarbon dates. The oldest McKean occupation that exhibited diagnostics was Occupation 13(4). Two McKean Lanceolate points with deep basal notches were recovered. A date of 4,280 +/- 80 BP was obtained (Ramsay 1993:88–91).

The Thundercloud (FbNp 25) site is located on the floodplain of the Opimihaw Valley about 1 km from the South Saskatchewan River. About eleven cultural occupations were recorded. Level 4 had Pelican Lake material, Level 5 contained three McKean occupations, and Level 6 contained two Oxbow levels (Webster 2004:34). Level 5c produced three McKean points and a date of 4,145 +/- 90 BP (S-3645) (Webster 2004:35). The intermediate level between 5c and 5b produced two Duncan points. Level 5b produced a third Duncan point and two radiocarbon dates: 3,375 +/- 50 BP (BGS-2367) and 3,382 +/- 55 BP (NZA-15749) (Webster 2004:35–36). Level 5a produced two possible Hanna points and a radiocarbon date of 3,172 +/- 50 BP (BGS-2369) (Webster 2004:35–36). One of these points exhibited a broken stem while the second was a base fragment with broad notches and a straight base. Given the age of these specimens and their fragmented form, they could also fall within the range of barbed Pelican Lake points.

The Cut Arm site (FbNp 22) is located in Wanuskewin Park near Saskatoon. This multicomponent site is located in a basin above the confluence of the South Saskatchewan River and the Opimihaw Creek. Of the twelve occupations at the site, Level 8 produced at least one McKean component. The upper component in Level 8 contained a McKean Lanceolate point and produced a radiocarbon date of 3,441 +/- 50 BP (SBGS-2383) (Webster 2004:41; Morlan n.d.). The lower component of Level 8 did not produce a diagnostic but was dated to 3,520 +/- 60 BP (BGS-2384).

The Crown site (FhNa 86) was found during a cultural resource management study conducted prior to the construction of the Nipawin Reservoir. The site is located at the southern edge of the boreal forest on a small terrace above an unnamed tributary of the Saskatchewan River. Three components were recognized, with the middle component containing Hanna material and the lower component containing McKean material. The Hanna level produced a burial.

The Sjovold site (EiNs 4) is a multicomponent site on the South Saskatchewan River near Outlook. Twenty-one occupations were observed, with Layer XXI considered a Hanna occupation (Dyck and Morlan 1995). The site was interpreted as a camp periphery. A single Hanna point was recovered and the level produced a radiocarbon date of 3,610 +/- 115 BP (S-2062) (Dyck and Morlan 1995; Morlan n.d.).

The Billet site (EkNv 36) is located near the town of Harris. Many artifacts have been recovered from the surface of this cultivated sand dune. Limited testing, however, produced five points in the vicinity of two hearths. Four of the points were Hanna points. The hearths produced three dates: 1,560 +/- 160 BP (S-2053), 3,180 +/- 65 BP (S-2054), and 3,470 +/- 120 BP (S-2063) (Dyck 1983:90; Webster 2004:50–51, Morlan n.d.).

The Graham site (FaNq 30) is a cremation burial within a habitation floor located about 3.5 km south of Saskatoon (Walker 1984a). A single Duncan point, a large hafted biface, ten other bifaces, a core fragment, twenty-one pieces of debitage, a cut deer antler burr, an antler segment possibly representing a hammer, and a split rib awl were recovered from a rough circular stained area (Walker 1984a:140–142). A radiocarbon date of 3,350 +/- 55 BP (S-1574) was obtained from comminuted human bone (Walker 1984a:142).

The Mortlach site (EcNl 1) is located in the Besant Valley south of the town of Mortlach. It produced four Hanna/Duncan points in its earliest level (Zone 8). Originally, the material was labelled "Thunder Creek culture" and compared to Duncan and McKean points to the south (Wettlaufer 1955:71). Currently, the material is considered part of the McKean complex (Dyck 1980:101). A radiocarbon date of 3,480 +/- 200 BP (S-2) was obtained for the level (Wettlaufer 1955:81, Morlan n.d.).

The Long Creek site (DgMr 1) is a multicomponent site near Estevan. Nine occupation levels were recorded with Level 5 producing a Hanna point (Wettlaufer and Mayer-Oakes 1960:47–50, 109). The level produced a radiocarbon date of 3,370 +/- 145 BP (S-63a) (Wettlaufer and Mayer-Oakes 1960:109; Morlan n.d.). Bryant's (2002:155, 2007) reanalysis of the site produced a radiocarbon date of 3,865 +/- 55 BP (BGS-2362).

Other Saskatchewan sites that are of interest but lack radiocarbon dates include: the Meewasin site (FbNp 9), which contained nine occupations with at least one McKean occupation; the Sullivan site (EjNr 1). which contained Duncan points in a palaeosol overlying Oxbow points; the Lubyk site (FhNh 138), which was a surface site that produced mainly Hanna points; and the Big Kill site (EbNj 2), which was a surface collection that contained seven McKean Lanceolate points (Webster 2004).

In Manitoba, McKean is concentrated in the southwestern part of the province (Syms 1970:127). The Pas Reserve site (FkMh 5) is located on the Saskatchewan River in west-central Manitoba (Webster 2004:62). Hanna and Duncan points were recovered from the lowest level of the four occupations at the site. A radiocarbon date of 3,190 +/- 60 BP (A-1369) was obtained (Webster 2004:62). Other McKean sites in Manitoba include the Trailrace Bay site that produced some McKean points, as well as a possible Duncan point. Similarly, the Cemetery Point (EaKv 1) site produced McKean points and a reworked Duncan point. Both sites exhibit mixed assemblages (Syms 1970:129; Webster 2004:62–63). The Larter site produced McKean Lanceolate points and a possible Hanna point in disturbed context along the Red River (Syms 1970:129). Boyd (2000:35) has recently argued that the distribution of McKean sites in Manitoba is broadly associated with modern lowlands, rivers, wetlands, and lakes with less emphasis on high areas of the Manitoba Escarpment.

In North Dakota, a few McKean sites are known from the western half of the state. The Red Fox site (32BO213) is located on Spring Creek in the southwest corner of the state (Keyser 1982:32). Within the McKean component, which produced at least four occupations, there were at least nine Duncan points in association with a storage pit, sixteen hearths, and possible a pit house. Fire pits tend to be circular and shallow but a conical pit with a rock bottom was present. A radiocarbon date of 3,770 +/- 90 BP was obtained from Level 4 (Keyser 1982:32).

In northwestern South Dakota, the Lightning Spring site (39HN204) is a deeply buried multicomponent site in the North Cave Hills, less than 30 km from the Red Fox site in North Dakota (see above) (Keyser 1982:31). Eleven occupations were recorded with Levels 8–11 attributed to the McKean complex. Level 8 dated to 3,430 +/- 270 BP (Tx-4084), Level 9 dated to 4,190 +/- 110 BP (Tx-4083), and Level 10 produced two dates of 3,870 +/- 210 BP (Tx-4082) and 3,850 +/- 150 BP (Tx-4081) (Keyser 1982:32). Hearths at the site tend to be shallow and round, but conical rock-filled hearths occur (Keyser 1982:36).

In Montana, only a limited number of McKean sites with radiocarbon dates are known. All are within the southern portion of the state. At the Sorenson site (24CB202), a possible McKean Lanceolate point was recovered in Level VI (dating ca. 1,300 BP) in association with bowl-shaped pits (Husted 1969:21–22, 82, 116: plate 11k). There appears to be a dating problem here. The Pictograph Cave site in south-central Montana also appears to have McKean material in its lowest level, Level I (Mulloy 1958:31–32, fig. 6). The Dodge site (24RB1225) is a McKean cache in the Tongue River Valley in southeastern Montana (Davis 1976). Although the four recovered points were called McKean stemmed at the time (Davis 1976:39), the specimens would be called Duncan today (i.e., Wheeler 1954). Also recovered were large, notched bifaces (n = 5), symmetrical ovate bifaces (n = 14), asymmetrical bifaces (n = 2), a symmetrical uniface, ovoid unifaces (n = 3), and flakes (n = 2). The points are quite large and well formed compared to Alberta specimens. The Cremer site (24SW264) in south-central Montana produced an assemblage of Duncan material from a buried context. At least six Duncan points were recovered from Cultural Layer II, immediately overlying what was interpreted as Early Prehistoric period material (Nowatzyk 1983:72, fig. 11j–o). No radiometric dates were acquired for the level.

In northern Wyoming, there are numerous sites that appear to contain McKean components. The Bottleneck Cave site (48BH206) contained McKean Lanceolate points and a Duncan point in Occupation IV and dated to ca. 3,800 BP; the material was recovered in association with both basin-shaped fire pits and deep rock-filled pits (Husted 1969:56–57, 82, plate 30a, c, and d). At the Wedding of the Waters Cave (48HO301) in north-central Wyoming, McKean and Hanna points were recovered in the lowest level (Frison 1962:248, fig. 1a–b). At Dead Indian Creek in northwestern Wyoming, so-called McKean projectile point variants were recovered and dated to ca. 4,400, 4,200, and 3,800 BP (Frison 1991a:99). The serrated artifacts, however, distantly resemble McKean material on the Northern Plains. The Scoggin site in south-central Wyoming has elongate McKean Lanceolate points with deep basal notches in association with large side-notched Mallory points (Lobdell 1974). Both the shape of the McKean points and the association with Mallory points are foreign to the Northern Plains assemblages. A single date on charcoal from a food processing area was obtained for the site: 4,540 +/- 110 BP (RL-174). Similarly, the Mummy Cave site produced a number of elongate McKean points in Layer 30, ca. 4,400–4,000 BP (Husted and Edgar 2002).

In summary, the distribution of lanceolate points that have been called McKean is quite wide-ranging, from the Great Basin to the forest edge of the Canadian Plains. The review above, however, illustrates that a variety of point morphologies and lifeways occurs within this vast geographic area. Brumley and Rennie (2005) have proposed that culturally meaningful divisions are observable within the broadly defined McKean complex. They suggest that the southern McKean assemblages — those in southern Montana, Wyoming, northeast Colorado, western South Dakota, and western Nebraska — are distinguishable owing to the use of grinding slabs, cobble-lined hearths, and edge-ground cobbles in the foothills/mountain assemblages (Brumley and Rennie 2005). The sites exhibiting these features would include, but not be limited to, DesRosier (Brumley 1974), Dodge (Davis 1976), Myers-Hindman (Lahren 1976), Lightning Spring (Keyser 1982), Red Fox (Keyser 1982), Scoggin (Lobdell 1974), Dead Indian Creek (Frison 1991a), Mummy Cave (Husted and Edgar 2002), McKean (Mulloy 1954), Fourth of July Valley (Benedict and Olson 1973), and Signal Butte (Strong 1935). The limited presence of Mallory points in association with McKean points is also restricted to southern McKean sites (Brumley and Rennie 2005:23–24). Mallory points have been found in southeastern Montana, central Wyoming, northeastern Colorado, and western Nebraska (Brumley and Rennie 2005:23; Frison 1991a:91).

Brumley and Rennie (2005:24) indicated that this distinctive set of traits within the southern McKean complex does not occur in McKean sites north of Helena, Montana. The northern McKean sites are those in northeastern Montana, southern Alberta, southern Saskatchewan, and southern Manitoba. Sites appear earliest in southern Saskatchewan, ca. 4,400 BP, and then occurred in Alberta by about 4,200 BP, and later into Manitoba. Interestingly, at the earliest Saskatchewan sites, the diagnostic McKean Lanceolate points are similar to the southern McKean Lanceolate point style; they exhibit a relatively deeper basal indentation and are relatively long. As Webster (2004) observed, the northern specimens tend to be smaller than the southern specimens in overall size.

A number of lines of evidence link the northern and southern McKean complexes. There can be little doubt that the projectile points are very similar despite the variation in size. These artifacts are common throughout the McKean complex. At the Redtail site in Saskatchewan a possible grinding stone was recovered in Level 13(2). However, the item in question is quite unlike grinding stones to the south in terms of form, and its function was not unequivocally determined: the flat surface of the gneiss cobble in question had not been used extensively (Ramsay 1993:143–146). This artifact does not provide good evidence of grinding stones in the northern McKean sites. Similarly, in Level 8 of the Redtail site a possible pit house was revealed, but, no evidence of construction or a structure was presented.

The evidence for the origin of the McKean complex appears to lie in the south. A number of sites at the headwaters of the Yellowstone River and the Bighorn Basin are dated to about 4,900 BP. By 4,700 to 4,500 BP the McKean complex had expanded to the Black Hills (Webster 2004:96).

Likely following river systems, the McKean complex was in southern Saskatchewan and in southern Alberta by ca. 4,200 BP.

The split between northern and southern McKean might simply be a result of geography and/or resource base. In the northern McKean sites, there is ample evidence of bison procurement by solitary stalking or ambush of small herds. Bison occur in small numbers in most northern McKean sites. Larger kills by McKean complex were possible, of course. Webster (2004:144–158) argued that EgNo 23 represented a McKean bison kill site that dates to ca. 3,550 BP. No projectile points were recovered in firm association with the bone bed. The Austech site provides another possible bison kill site. The Scoggin site in the southern McKean complex exhibited a bison corral and processing area. Still, bison kill sites of this nature appear rarely in the southern McKean complex. In the southern McKean tradition a wide range of fauna was exploited, with a focus on bison. The common recovery of milling stone technology at southern sites suggests that plant materials were also important elements in people's diets. Still, only a few sites have exhibited direct evidence of plant exploitation (e.g., Haberman 1986; Keyser 1986). The archaeologically visible diet breadth of the northern McKean complex was focused on hunting game, predominantly of bison, but also included antelope, wolf, dog, kit fox, cottontail rabbit, jackrabbit, birds, and fish.

In terms of lithic resource utilization, northern McKean materials are mainly locally derived. Similarly, at least at some of the southern McKean sites, lithic procurement is locally oriented. For example, the Lightning Spring site in North Dakota yielded a group of bifaces manufactured on Tongue River silicified sediment, which is locally available (Keyser and Fagan 1993). Similarly, the Dodge cache consisted of porcellanite and chert, both locally available in southern Montana (Davis 1976).

Features associated with food processing are frequent in the northern McKean complex. Surface and basin hearths are both common. EaPk 1 produced an unusual cobble platform possibly associated with roasting. Earth pits were repeatedly observed at the Cactus Flower site but not elsewhere. Evidence of stone boiling was indicated by the recovery of substantial amounts of FBR at most sites. Circular distributions of debris were noticed at the Cactus Flower site and the Redtail site; in both cases these were interpreted as delimiting the former locations of a structure. Centre stakes or tie-down pegs were not found with these debris distributions, making it difficult to determine whether they represented tipis or another form of circular structure. The possible identification of a pit house was also noted at the Redtail site. The available data did not substantiate this claim.

There will likely be much debate about whether the McKean complex's rapid appearance across the Northern Plains can be attributed to the spread of technology, people, or both. Certainly, it was replaced by the Pelican Lake complex, which exhibits a large corner-notched dart point. Some researchers perceive the change from the McKean complex's Hanna point to the Pelican Lake corner-notched point as a shift in a continuum of style and technology (Reeves 1983a; Webster 2004). The view taken in this text is that this dramatic shift likely represents a change in the people using the technology and not just the introduction of technology to an extant population.

PELICAN LAKE COMPLEX (CA. 3,600 TO 2,800 BP)

The "Pelican Lake culture" was first defined based on materials recovered in Occupations 5A, 5B, 6 and 7 of the Mortlach site, south-central Saskatchewan (Wettlaufer 1955:54–57). Wettlaufer (1955:55) described the points as corner-notched, with oval cross-sections, bevelled to the edges and toward the base, widest just above the notches, with the base narrower than the blade and tapered to a long symmetrical point. The Pelican Lake point and culture likely received its name from Pelican Lake, a body of water several kilometres north of Mortlach, Saskatchewan (Kehoe 1974:109).

Subsequently, Reeves (1983a) provided a more thorough description of Pelican Lake material culture as a 'phase' by focusing on its spatial and temporal distribution. Reeves (1983a:94) accepted the description of the Pelican Lake atlatl point provided by Wettlaufer (1955:55). In addition, he noted that flake points were infrequent but that Hanna points were present in some early components (Reeves 1983a:82–83). Ceramics were found in only one site, the Mule Creek Rock Shelter, making the Pelican Lake phase largely aceramic (Reeves 1983a:85). Reeves (1983a:76) subdivided the geographic distribution of the Pelican Lake phase into eight regional subphases based on varying degrees of distinctive environments and specific areas of archaeological activity. For this review there are four relevant subphases including Blue Slate Canyon in the Rocky Mountains of northern Montana and southern Alberta (Duke 1985), Keaster in the upper Missouri Basin, Mortlach across the Canadian Plains as far north as the parkland, and Larter in southwestern Manitoba (Reeves 1983a:2–4, 78–79). Reeves (1983a:5, 80–81) considered the initial appearance of Pelican Lake on the Northern Plains to be about 3,400 BP, with it lasting until about 1,800 BP.

Focusing on the Northern Plains, Kehoe (1974:109–111) proposed a Pelican Lake point type with five varieties exhibiting temporal and/or morphological significance, based on materials recovered from the Walter Felt site. The varieties included both a large and a small Classic Pelican Lake barbed point that appear earliest. The Hudson Barbed, convex-based variety follows and is similar to the large Classic Pelican Lake barbed variety but with a convex base. The most recent varieties include the Danker shouldered, straight-base point and Bracken Shouldered, convex-based variety. The Sandy Creek material separated the Classic Pelican Lake point varieties from the later Danker Variety of Pelican Lake points at Walter Felt, the site upon which the typology was developed. More recently, Dyck (1983:105) proposed a similar but simpler classification, in which two varieties of Pelican Lake points existed. One variety had straight sides, a straight base, and corner notches that usually created sharp tangs on the shoulders; toward the end of Pelican Lake times, this variety developed a wider base to almost the full width of the shoulders, and the notches were narrow. Dyck credited Pendree (1981) with first recognizing this in materials from the Harris Sand Hills. The other variety appeared about midway through the sequence with straight sides and corner notches but a convex instead of a straight base. Brumley and Dau (1988:33–34) concurred with Dyck's assessment of Pelican Lake on the Northern Plains. Regarding the distributional and lithic utilization patterns among Pelican Lake points, however, they suggested that straight-based Pelican Lake points are most common in southeastern and south-central Alberta and rare in central and northern Montana. The points were commonly manufactured on local lithics. When an exotic material was used, it was often Knife River flint. Convex-based Pelican Lake points were most common in southwestern Alberta and northern and central Montana (Brumley and Dau 1988:34). These were commonly made on Avon chert, Madison Formation chert, and porcellanite. Echoing Dyck's (1983:107) remarks about frequent small Pelican Lake points, Brumley and Dau (1988:33) suggested their possible employment as arrow tips used with bows.

Currently, Wettlaufer's (1955) original definition of Pelican Lake corner-notched point is utilized without any subdivisions or varieties being noted (e.g., Vickers 1986). Similarly, the geographic distribution of the Pelican Lake sites does not retain its subphases with their geographic variability. None of Reeves' (1983a) Pelican Lake subphases are systematically used. Dyck (1983:107) recognized that points with tangs and corner-notches are widespread throughout North America at this time, making questions about Pelican Lake origins, distribution, and fate difficult to address. Still, he did note that the three prairie provinces of Canada have produced similar Pelican Lake assemblages of comparable age (Dyck 1983:105). Vickers (1986:76) glosses over the issue of distribution by noting that Pelican Lake appears coevally from the Saskatchewan plains to the Wyoming Basin. Presumably, this statement refers to a formally similar point type and not a single archaeological culture. Temporally, Reeves (1983a:5, 80–81), Dyck (1983:105), and Vickers (1986:76) concur that the Pelican Lake phase begins about 3,300–3,500 BP roughly coeval with the end of the McKean complex. Similarly, Reeves (1983a:5, 80–81) and Dyck (1983:105) suggest a terminal age of 1,900–1,800 BP.

The origin of the Pelican Lake phase is not agreed upon. Reeves' (1983a) model of culture history provides the most commonly cited framework. He included the Pelican Lake phase within his Tunaxa tradition, which includes McKean, Duncan, Hanna, Pelican Lake, and Avonlea (Reeves 1983a:7, 80). He cited basic technological continuity in tool types and technology between Hanna and Pelican Lake material as evidence of this cultural link (Reeves 1983a:7), and used the stratigraphic sequence at the Cactus Flower site to illustrate this argument. Still, he recommended more thorough analyses of these assemblages be undertaken to assess the model (Reeves 1983a:7). In contrast, Brumley (1975:73) noted that the small Pelican Lake assemblage from Cactus Flower was all chipped stone, while the McKean assemblages exhibited pecked, ground, and miscellaneous stone, as well as shell tools and antler. He suggested the difference between the layers may either be a result of sampling or actual cultural differences (Brumley 1975:73). Dyck (1983:105–107) proposed that, in view of the widespread nature of tanged and corner-notched points during this time period, a large study would be required establish the origins of Pelican Lake.

The demise of the Pelican Lake phase, like its origin, is unclear. Reeves' (1983a:17) Tunaxa tradition linked Pelican Lake to Avonlea. He suggested that the mountain subphases of the Pelican Lake phase were forbearers to the Avonlea phase. He cited similarities of early corner-notched Avonlea arrows to Pelican Lake points, and comparable lithic use patterns between the two phases as evidence of this pedigree (Reeves 1983a:17). Vickers (1986:80) aptly pointed out that Reeves' own data suggested the Pelican Lake phase shares more in common with the Besant phase than with the Avonlea phase in terms of artifact types. As with the origins of Pelican Lake, Dyck (1983:107) expected that the commonness of the point form would require a broad investigation to address its fate.

The Sites

To assess the various lines of thinking presented above, Pelican Lake assemblages from Alberta with reliable radiocarbon dates are outlined below. These sites will be used to critically evaluate the current view of the Pelican Lake complex (see Plate 18 and Figure 19).

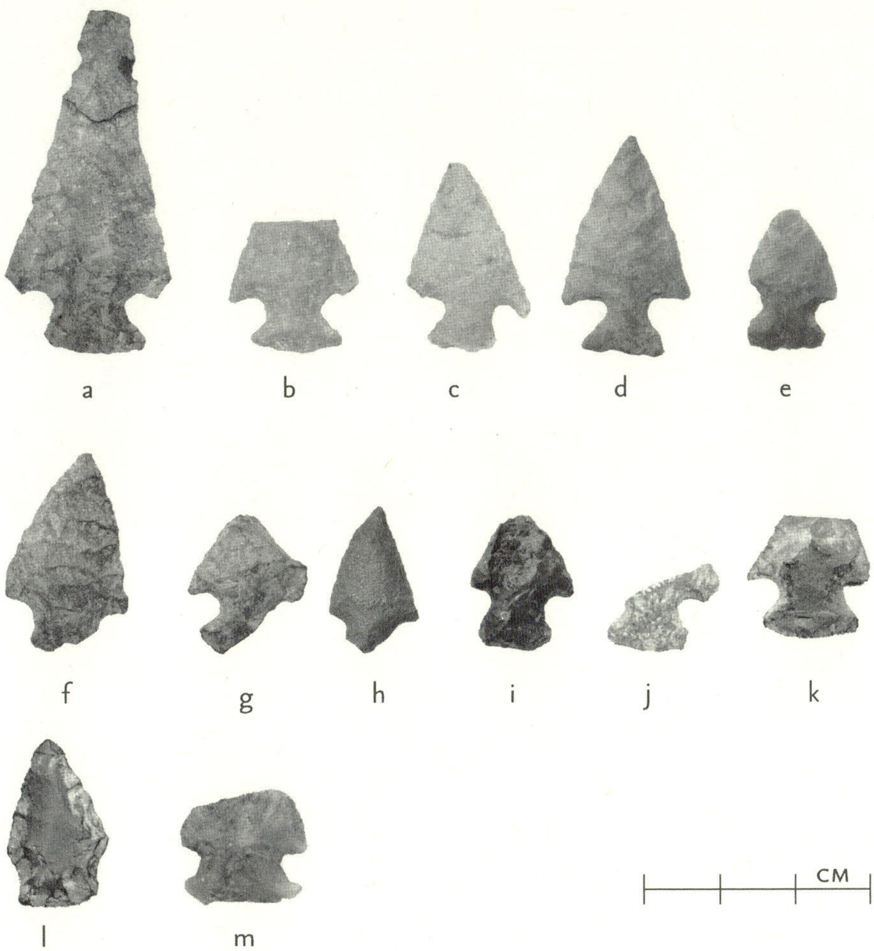

PLATE 18 Pelican Lake points. Illustrated are projectile points from DjPm 44 (a–c); the Boy Chief site (EeOv 68) (d–g); the Scapa site (ElPa 1) (h and i); and the Second Lake site (EhPy 58) (j–m). Photo credit: Alberta Culture and Community Spirit.

FIGURE 19
Pelican Lake sites within Alberta

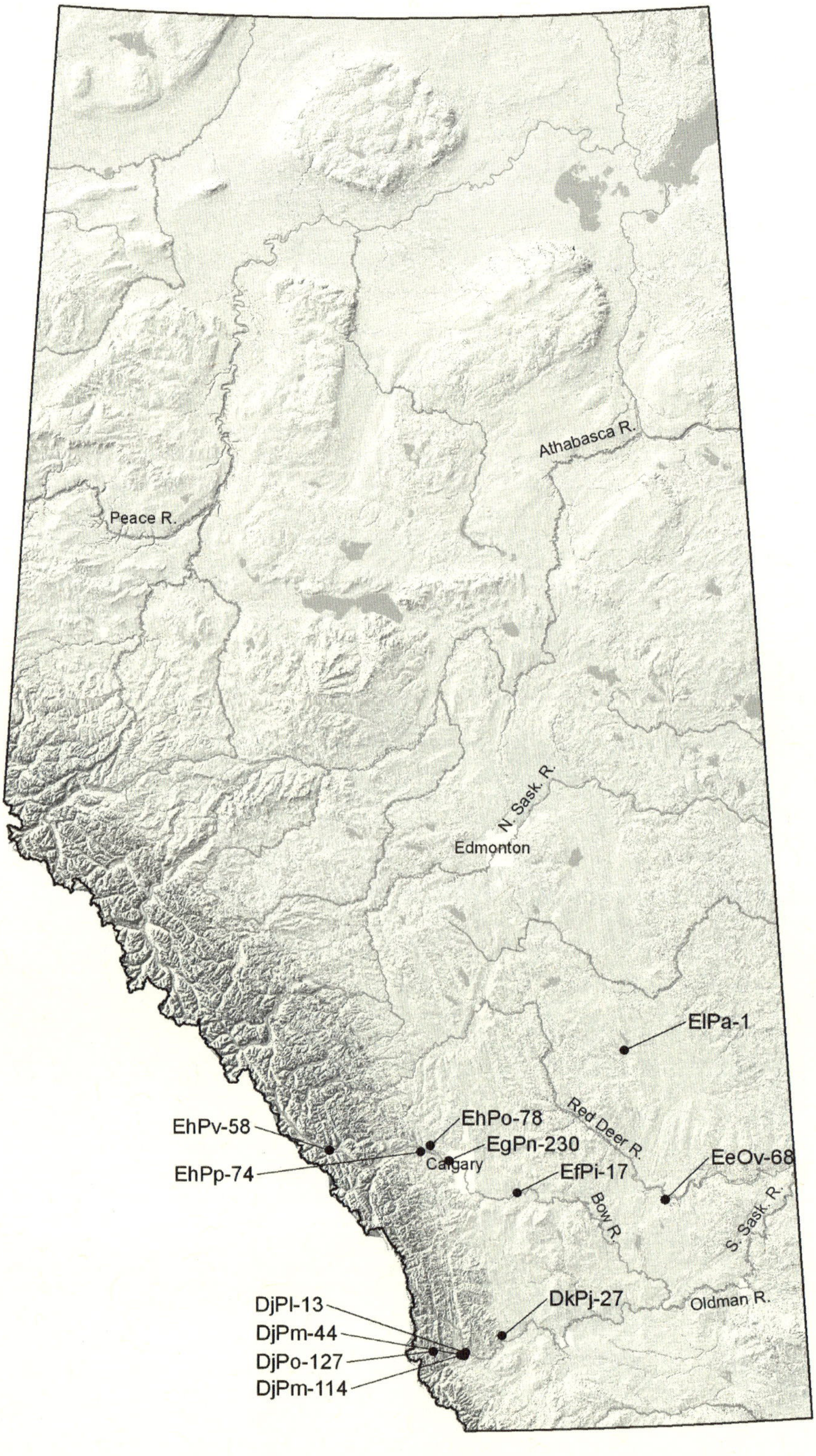

Boy Chief (EeOv 68), Block 4, Occupations 4 and 5. The Boy Chief site is discussed in the above section on the Estevan phase. In Occupation 4, three barbed Pelican Lake points and a triangular unnotched point were found in association with two hearths and a scatter of ash (Head et al. 2003:142–148). Because of the early date for the occupation and the fragmentary points, the original researchers suggested this site might represent transitional material between Hanna and Pelican Lake materials (Head et al. 2003:148). While this is possible, the illustrated specimens exhibit the classic features of Pelican Lake points, including straight sides, narrow necks, and large corner-notches that create barbed shoulders. Other tools recovered in this occupation include three retouched flakes, two end scrapers, a biface, a side scraper, and a bipolar core (Head et al. 2003:146–147). The lithic assemblage is dominated by quartzite, petrified wood, and massive quartz (Head et al. 2003:145). Concentrations of the various debitage types occur within the site, suggesting individual reduction sites or workshops (Head et al. 2003:146).

The faunal assemblage represented at least one bison. Its age and sex could not be determined. Only fourteen of the 415 bone fragments were identifiable, as the assemblage is very fragmented. Processing seemed to focus on removal and discard of elements at the tarsal-metatarsal joints (Head et al. 2003:144). FBR, consisting largely of quartzite, was widely scattered across the site. Much of the FBR exhibited crenulated fractures, suggesting stone boiling; these specimens are more associated with the hearth. The hearth is a circular surface hearth about 50 cm in diameter and 2 cm deep. Thirty-five pieces of FBR with bedding plane fractures are associated with the small hearth and ash scatter.

A single radiocarbon date of ca. 3,350 BP was obtained (se Table 17). This date is from a combined sample of bone from numerous units, but is consistent with dates from overlying occupations. The occupation is interpreted as a campsite living floor where minimal processing occurred.

Occupation 5 produced two barbed Pelican Lake points and two possible Pelican Lake points in association with a hearth and a lithic concentration. Other lithic tools recovered include bipolar cores (n = 65), multidirectional cores, (n = 11), retouched flakes (n = 17), end scrapers (n = 4), side scrapers (n = 3), bifaces (n = 2), unifaces (n = 2), wedges (n = 2), choppers (n = 2), and a graver. Some of the tools appear to have a patterned distribution; for example, bipolar cores are largely found in the north and east while retouched flakes were found in two clusters in the northeast and southeast part of the excavation block (Head et al. 2003:154). The lithic assemblage is dominated by quartzite, miscellaneous chert, and massive quartz (Head et al. 2003 151). The different percentages of cortex on various raw materials suggest different reduction strategies (Head et al. 2003:152). The spatial distribution of the various lithic raw materials also suggests patterned activity around the hearth.

TABLE 17 Radiocarbon dates for Pelican Lake sites (calibrated by OxCal 3.10 [Ramsey 2005])

Site [LAB NO.]	Conventional ^{14}C Age	$^{13}C/^{12}C$ Ratio	Material	Calibration	Reference
EeOv 68 [AECV-2051C]	3350 +/- 90	-19.4‰	collagen	1880–1440 B.C. (p = 0.954)	Head et al. 2003:21
EeOv 68 [AEVC-2052C]	3270 +/- 90	-18.7‰	collagen	1770–1370 B.C. (p = 0.954)	Head et al. 2003:21
DjPm 44 [AEVC-773C]	2770 +/- 120	-19.4‰	collagen	1350–750 B.C. (p = 0.939) 700–550 B.C. (p = 0.015)	Van Dyke 1994:196
DjPm 44 [AEVC-759C]	2690 +/- 140	-26.6‰	collagen	1250–400 B.C. (p = 0.954)	Van Dyke 1994:196
DjPm 44 [AEVC-740C]	3600 +/- 100	-19.0‰	collagen	2300–1650 B.C. (p = 0.954)	Van Dyke 1994:196
DjPm 44 [AEVC-764C]	3520 +/- 210	-20.1‰	collagen	2500–1400 B.C. (p = 0.954)	Van Dyke 1994:196
DjPm 44 [AEVC-1195C]	3110 +/- 90	-19.3‰	bone	1610–1120 B.C. (p = 0.954)	Van Dyke 1994:196
DjPm 44 [AEVC-1196C]	3160 +/- 100	-18.5‰	bone	1520–1370 B.C. (p = 0.923) 1340–1310 B.C. (p = 0.031)	Van Dyke 1994:196
EfPi 17 [BETA-157613]	3120 +/- 40	-18.1‰	collagen	1500–1290 B.C. (p = 0.954)	Hanna 2002:76–77
EhPv 58 [S 2755]	3100 +/- 125	-20.2‰	charcoal	1700–1000 B.C. (p = 0.954)	Fedje 1986:52
EhPp 74 [BETA-226858]	3020 +/- 40	-17.4‰	collagen	1400–1120 B.C. (p = 0.954)	Goldsmith 2007a
EhPp 74 [BETA-226860]	2990 +/- 40	-18.2‰	collagen	1390–1110 B.C. (p = 0.944) 1100–1080 B.C. (p = 0.01)	Goldsmith 2007a
EhPv 58 [S 2779]	2760 +/- 95	-10.0‰	bone	1210–770 B.C. (p = 0.954)	Fedje 1986:52
EbOp 16 [S-1011]	2770 +/- 95	-20.0‰	collagen	1300–810 B.C. (p = 0.954)	Morlan n.d.

The faunal assemblage included a minimum of two bison from a very fragmented assemblage of bone. Age and sex could not be determined. The identifiable elements are among the first to be discarded within a butchering sequence (Head et al. 2003:150). The FBR was widely scattered and dominated by quartzite. Angular fractures suggested fracturing during stone boiling; these pieces are generally west and north of the hearth (Head et al. 2003:151). Spalled FBR (n = 5) was associated with the hearth (Head et al. 2003:151). The hearth was roughly circular, about 55 cm in diameter and 2 cm thick (Head et al. 2003:156). A single radiocarbon date of ca. 3,270 BP was obtained (Table 17). The site was interpreted as a campsite with a very fragmentary faunal assemblage, FBR, and a substantial lithic assemblage associated with a hearth. The researchers suggest the range and frequency of tools represent an occupation during a cooler season when people were confined around the hearth within a structure (Head et al. 2003:157).

EfPi 17, Upper Component. The Upper Component of EfPi 17 is a diffuse and indistinct campsite (Hanna 2002:51–65). The site is discussed in the section on the Scottsbluff-Eden phase. Two barbed Pelican Lake points were recovered in the diffuse scatter of lithics, FBR, and bone. Unfortunately, the stratigraphy at the site produced indistinct separation from the lower Scottsbluff component. Raw materials and technology aided in differentiating these materials, but nothing could be established with certainty. Other tools recovered included a hammerstone, a biface, end scrapers (n = 2), retouched flakes (n = 13), and a utilized flake. The lithic assemblage was dominated by quartzite, miscellaneous cherts, and massive quartz (Hanna 2002:58). A single piece of obsidian was likely associated with the optically identical obsidian in the lower component, suggesting mixing (Hanna 2002:64).

The faunal assemblage consisted of very small weathered fragments (n = 159), with only a few identifiable as bison. Recovered FBR (n = 289) was mostly angular and highly fractured suggesting repeated use in stone boiling (Hanna 2002:62). A single radiocarbon date of 3,120 BP was obtained from bone thought to be contextually associated with the lower Scottsbluff component (Table 17). The researcher noted that the date reflected an age expected for the Upper Component, especially given the high potential for mixing (Hanna 2002:76–77). While problematic, this diffuse campsite exhibited many classic characteristics of a Pelican Lake site: narrow-necked, barbed points, use of local lithics especially massive quartz, and a date around 3,100 BP.

DjPm 44. DjPm 44 is a multicomponent campsite with surface deposits dating to the Protohistoric Period and subsurface deposits dating to the Pelican Lake complex. The site is located on a 10-metre-high terrace along the Castle River at the south end of Horseshoe Canyon (Van Dyke 1994:191). A total of 196 m^2 was excavated at the site in six excavation blocks (i.e., A–F) in 1988 and 1990 (Van Dyke 1994:191). Subsequently, waters behind the Oldman River Dam have inundated the site.

Seven barbed Pelican Lake points, three unidentifiable points, a midsection, and two tips were recovered in association with unmodified cobbles that might represent stone circles in blocks E and F. Other tools recovered from the multiple occupations included a biface, end scrapers (n = 12), retouched flakes (n = 55), cobble cores (n = 11), and pebble cores (n = 3). The faunal assemblage included bison, canid, beaver, and a small ungulate (probably deer). A minimum of six bison was present. Six radiocarbon dates were obtained (Table 17). The researcher noted the dates form three clusters with averages of 2,730 BP, 3,135 BP, and 3,560 BP (Van Dyke 1994:201).

EhPp 74. EhPp 74 is a buried stone circle site on a terrace above Jumpingpound Creek near Cochrane (Goldsmith 2007a, 2007b). The site consisted of two buried stone circles in close proximity (ca. 5 m apart) and of similar river cobble and sandstone slab construction (Goldsmith 2007a). A total of 82 m^2 exposed the two circles. A subdivision necessitated the mitigation.

Two small reworked Pelican Lake points, a base of a similar form, and a large Duncan-like point were associated with the stone circles. Non-projectile tools included a chopper, bifacially reworked tools (n = 2), and marginally retouched flakes (n = 6). The lithic debitage assemblage (n = 85) from the two circles was small and included flakes (n = 27), broken flakes (n = 22), and pieces of shatter (n = 36). Quartzite (n = 71) was dominant but massive quartz, siltstone, chert, sandstone, chalcedony, and obsidian were also recovered. Fauna included only bison, most of which was recovered from a bone-filled pit stratigraphically below the occupation floor and thus dated to an earlier period. Only eighty-seven bones were recovered in association with the two Pelican Lake stone circles. FBR (n = 985) appeared to be cracked by rapid water-cooling. FBR was mainly quartzite, but sandstone and granite were also used. Distribution of FBR suggested little horizontal or vertical disturbance at the site (Goldsmith 2007a).

Two radiocarbon dates of ca. 2,900 BP for Stone Circles 1 and 2, respectively, and 4,650 +/- 50 BP for the bone pit beneath Stone Circle 2 were obtained (Goldsmith 2007a). The dates, their proximity to each other, and the artifacts suggest that the two stone circles were likely contemporaneous to Pelican Lake times. The pit is stratigraphically earlier than the stone circle, an inference supported by the radiocarbon dates, and possibly is associated with the Duncan-like point.

Second Lake (EhPv 58, 162R). The Second Lake site is described in the section on the McKean complex. In Occupation 5, two barbed Pelican Lake points and a point preform were associated with a hearth and a scatter of lithics and bone (Fedje 1986:53). The lithic assemblage contained 350 items. The faunal assemblage included bison, deer, dog/wolf, mallard, and trout. Two dates were obtained for the site: ca. 3,100 BP and 2,760 BP (Table 17). The researcher suggested that temporally distinct activities may be represented, but the dates are not significantly different; a mean date of 2,885 +/- 75 BP was determined (Fedje 1986:53–54).

Cactus Flower (EbOp 16). The Cactus Flower site is discussed in the section on the McKean complex. Occupation 1 capped seven McKean occupations and an anomalous occupation. It produced two barbed Pelican Lake points and four point fragments associated with a basin hearth. Approximately 182.77 m^2 of Occupation 1 was excavated (Brumley 1975:110). Other recovered tools included a crude biface, retouched flakes (n = 21), end scrapers (n = 4), spokeshaves (n = 2), bipolar cores (n = 3), and some miscellaneous heavy chipped stone tools (n = 4) (Brumley 1975:123–125). The faunal assemblage produced a minimum of one bison, based solely on skull fragments (Brumley 1975:129–130). A single radiocarbon date of ca. 2,770 BP was obtained (Table 17).

St. Pierre (DjPo 127). The St. Pierre site is a large campsite on the east side of the Livingstone Mountain Range north and west of Lundbreck. Cayley Series (i.e., Old Women's) (n = 25), Pelican Lake (n = 5), Oxbow (n = 1), and non-diagnostic (n = 3) points were recovered. The cultural material was concentrated in the second excavation level, although the researchers made a reasonable argument that Old Women's material was located in the north and was largely horizontally separated from Pelican Lake material in the south (Head and Kennedy 1994). Four radiocarbon dates supported this argument. Three recent dates were associated with the Old Women's occupation and an earlier date of ca. 3,000 BP (Table 17) was associated with the Pelican Lake occupation (Head and Kennedy 1994:88). Still, the potential for mixing of material into this assemblage makes it suspect for archaeologically defining the Pelican Lake complex.

DjPl 13, Block D-1. DjPl 13 is a multicomponent site excavated during the Oldman River Dam project. Four major and four minor block excavations of various sizes, labelled A through H, were opened at the site. The earliest occupation in Block D appeared to contain Pelican Lake and Hanna material. Five points were recovered in association with a stone-ringed hearth and a possible boiling pit (Van Dyke and Unfreed 1992:78). Three of the points are fairly barbed, narrow-necked specimens not unlike the Pelican Lake material. One point specimen is a base fragment that is suggestive of Hanna; in fact, the researchers considered the component to be a mixed occupation of Pelican Lake and Hanna (Van Dyke and Unfreed 1992:82). The remaining point specimen was a non-diagnostic tip fragment. Further analysis might clarify whether this site represents a palimpsest of material, a transitional site, an aggregation locale, or something else.

Scapa Ribstone (ElPa 1). This site is described above under the Lusk complex. Three Pelican Lake points were recovered in Components 6 and 7. While one is broken at the neck, the remaining two points exhibit large, open corner notches, barbed shoulders, and narrow necks. Although a radiometric date is not available for the components, their stratigraphic positions relative to other point styles support a Pelican Lake assignment.

Other sites. Numerous other Pelican Lake sites that lack radiocarbon dates or good context exist in Alberta. In west Calgary, Component 2 of EgPn 230 produced two barbed Pelican Lake points associated with three other less-barbed specimens in a bison kill site. No date was available for this component but it was stratigraphically above a Country Hills component and beneath an Old Women's component. The Calderwood Buffalo Jump (DkPj 27) produced three barbed, narrow-necked Pelican Lake points in Layer 6 (Brink et al. 1987:72, fig. 24, three points in bottom row, centre; Marshall 1988). Layer 5, the overlying level, was radiocarbon dated to about 2,000 BP while the underlying Layer 8 was dated between 2,900 and 2,300 BP (Marshall 1988:60). DjPm 114, at the Oldman Reservoir, produced a barbed and narrow-necked specimen not unlike Pelican Lake points. It was apparently associated with a Bracken point and two other fragmentary point specimens and dated to about 2,000 BP. It is possible the barbed point was mixed into the assemblage although Landals (1993) suggested it most resembles interior British Columbia specimens such as Columbia Valley corner-notched. Lastly, of interest is EhPo 78 at the Cochrane Ranch in Cochrane. This site is located within a terrace above Big Hills Springs Creek. At a depth of 70 cm BS, three barbed Pelican Lake points were recovered in association with a maul (de Guzman 2008). Mauls have been found in good context as early as the Estevan phase (ca. 5,000 BP). Regardless, the recovery of a maul in situ is rare at any age.

Pelican Lake: The Twilight Days of Bison Stalking

Wettlaufer (1955:55) originally defined the Pelican Lake corner-notched point based on barbed, narrow-necked specimens from zone 5A at the Mortlach site. A review of Pelican Lake sites in Alberta illustrates an overwhelming trend toward barbed, narrow-necked points dating between 3,600 and 2,800 BP. More broadly corner-notched, wide-necked specimens postdate these barbed points. While these have commonly been included within the Pelican Lake complex, they are differentiated here owing to distinct chronostratigraphic placement and associated behavioural differences inferred from the assemblages exhibiting these points. For the purposes of this review, the latter have been labelled Bracken points (see the Bracken section below).

Two main competing models of Pelican Lake point forms have been mentioned. Dyck (1983) suggested that barbed points with straight, narrow bases occur earliest but gradually change to exhibit wider bases with narrow notches. Midway through this sequence a convex-based point emerges and co-occurs through the remainder of the Pelican Lake sequence. Kehoe's (1974) typology, based on material from the Walter Felt site in south-central Saskatchewan, presented more of a temporal dichotomy. The early Pelican Lake points, called Small and Large Classic Pelican Lake, have straight sides, are barbed, and have narrow necks and bases. When these points have convex bases they are labelled "Hudson barbed (convex-based variety)" (Kehoe 1974:110). Stratigraphically, the more recent Pelican Lake point, the Danker Shouldered (straight-based variety), postdates 2,500 BP and exhibits a broader neck and notching with a straight base. Similarly, the Bracken Shouldered, convex-based variety of the Pelican Lake point, not found in the Walter Felt sequence, is very similar to the Danker variety, with a convex rather than straight base. Both point varieties are considered transitional from Pelican Lake to Besant. These two varieties would appear to be most similar to the second of Dyck's forms. Kehoe's (1974) point varieties have discrete distributions in time, rather than Dyck's (1983) evolving forms, and mirror the situation in Alberta. Between 3,600 and 2,800 BP, the Pelican Lake complex exhibits a corner-notched, barbed, narrow-necked, straight-based, narrow-based, straight-sided projectile point. No obvious evolution into subsequent forms is apparent. As Kehoe (1974) described, at ca. 2,800 BP a corner-notched, shouldered, wide-necked, straight-to-slightly convex-based, wide-based, excurvate-sided projectile point appears to quickly replace the barbed form in the archaeological record.

Thus, for the purposes of this text, Pelican Lake complex refers to the cultural materials recovered that date to between ca. 3,600 and 2,800 BP, and includes barbed, corner-notched points. In terms of the tool assemblage of the Pelican Lake complex, bifaces, end scrapers, and retouched flakes are common, while side scrapers and utilized flakes occur infrequently. Flake points have not been recovered. No bone tools have been noted. The lithic raw materials show a clear dependence on quartzite, miscellaneous cherts, chalcedony (much of which may be Knife River flint), and massive quartz. DjPm 44 shows clear attachments to the mountains (i.e., Etherington chert, Banff chert, Top-of-the-World chert) and Montana (i.e., Avon chert and obsidian) not reflected in the other sites. The different lithic procurement patterns might simply reflect geography. DjPm 44 is in the Oldman Dam area near the mountains. EeOv 68 and EfPi 17 (for example) are much further onto the plains and lack the same suite of mountain-oriented raw materials.

Recovered faunal assemblages suggest a subsistence relying on bison. The limited number of sites makes further inference difficult. The sites all appear to be campsites with little evidence of large scale bison procurement. The faunal assemblage from almost every site exhibits a few bison with only certain elements represented. This strongly suggests stalking of solitary animals away from the campsite; hunters would return with specific meat units after butchering carcasses for easy transport. A variety of other animals are also known, including deer, dog/wolf, beaver, mallard, and trout.

Only a handful of features were observed at these sites. Surface hearths were noted at a few. As well, a stone-ringed hearth and a possible boiling pit were observed at DjPl 13. In fact, FBR was recovered in such quantities at most of the sites that it suggested that stone boiling for grease extraction from bone was being conducted. Perhaps most importantly is the secure dating of two buried stone circles. These almost certainly represent living structures. Evidence for a central tie-down stake was not recovered, but stone circles are commonly interpreted as representing tipis (see Kehoe 1960).

Pelican Lake materials are also known from Saskatchewan. The Walter Felt (EcNm 8) site is a multicomponent campsite near Mortlach (Kehoe 1974:103). From the perspective of this text, the sequence consists of Mortlach Group points (Layers 1–5), Early Cayley Series points (Layers 6 and 7), Avonlea and Sonota points (Layer 10), Besant points (Layer 13), Bracken points (Layer 15a), Sandy Creek points (Layer 15b), and Pelican Lake points (Layer 15d) from top to bottom in a stratified sequence (Kehoe 1974). The Pelican Lake point in Layer 15d exhibits the classic barbed shoulders and straight base that is absent in later points. A radiocarbon date from the overlying Sandy Creek layer (15b) produced an appropriate age of 2,430 +/- 90 BP (S-279) (Kehoe 1973:164; Morlan n.d.). The underlying Pelican Lake material is slightly older, of course. The Mortlach (EcNl 1) site is a multicomponent campsite in the Besant Valley near Mortlach (Wettlaufer 1955). Pelican Lake points (n = 6) were recovered in Zone 5A with point blades recovered from Zones 5B, 6, and 7 (Wettlaufer 1955:56–58). Zone 4E contained Sandy Creek material that immediately overlaid the Pelican Lake material. A radiocarbon date from organic sediment in Zone 4E produced a date of 2,400 +/- 173 BP (S-28) (Wettlaufer 1955:81; Morlan n.d.). Pelican Lake material is expected to be somewhat older.

The Long Creek (DgMr 1) site is a multicomponent campsite located on a terrace of Long Creek near Estevan (Wettlaufer and Mayer-Oakes 1960). The sequence of cultural occupations from top to bottom included Mortlach phase (Level 1), Avonlea phase (Level 2), Sonota phase (Level 3), Pelican Lake phase (Level 4), Hanna phase (Level 5A), Oxbow (Level 7), and Estevan phase (Level 8), with no diagnostics in Levels 6 or 9 (Wettlaufer and Mayer-Oakes 1960; see also Bryant 2002). The Pelican Lake points are typical barbed points. Bryant (2002:150) classified all the projectile points as Dyck's first variety, the straight-based, earlier Pelican Lake form. The debitage emphasized Knife River flint and fused shale (Bryant 2002:147). Also found in this level was a feature consisting of a bison skull placed on its occipitals, horn tips down, with a rock under the foramen magnum (Bryant 2002:252). Two dates were available for this level. The upper part of the level produced a date of 2,230 +/- 100 BP (S-49a) while the lower part of this level, possibly intrusive from the level below, produced a date of 3,710 +/- 70 BP (S-49b) (Bryant 2002:140–141; Morlan n.d.). Pelican Lake material is expected to date between these dates.

The Sjovold site (EiNs 4) is a highly stratified site at the confluence of the South Saskatchewan River and Sjovold Creek (Dyck and Morlan 1995). Layers XIX and XX produced four barbed, narrow-necked points that fit well with the Pelican Lake form. Layer XIX revealed two hearths surrounded by FBR, an abundance of bison bone, and other fauna, including dog or coyote, marten, rabbit, and a few bird bones. Other lithic tools included bifaces (n = 3), an end scraper, large scrapers (n = 2), and a retouched flake. The layer was interpreted as a Pelican Lake summer camp and produced a date of 3,355 +/- 160 BP (S-1769). The underlying layer, XX, was interpreted as sparse Pelican Lake occupation. It produced a date of 3,675 +/- 150 BP (S-2061).

EdNh 35 produced a Pelican Lake component on the second terrace of the Moose Jaw River just above its confluence with the Qu'Appelle River, in south-central Saskatchewan. The component underlay a co-occupation by people of the Sonota and Avonlea phases. The site produced two barbed, narrow necked projectile points associated with the Pelican Lake complex (Cloutier 2004:117, fig. 6.9). A date of 3,678 +/- 80 BP was obtained from a composite bone sample from the component (Cloutier 2004:96).

The Crane site (DiMv 93) is a multicomponent site along the Souris River near the town of Estevan. The lowest cultural component contained Pelican Lake material, including three points (Gibson and McKeand 1992:80). One is very barbed with deep notching while another is mildly barbed with a narrow neck (Gibson and McKeand 1992:81–82). An early radiocarbon date on bone of 3,330 +/- 95 BP (S-2969) reinforced that they are Pelican Lake points (Morlan n.d.).

In Manitoba, the barbed Pelican Lake point has also been called the Larter tanged point. Reeves (1983a) considered the Manitoba assemblages to represent the Larter subphase of the Pelican Lake phase, based on recovered items from the Larter and Lockport sites. Subsequently, charcoal from the Lockport (EaLf 1) site provided an age estimate for the Larter assemblage of ca. 3,300 BP (Buchner 1988; Morlan n.d.). Other sites that fit in this phase include the Paddon (DlPg 1) site, which produced Larter points dating to 3,075 +/- 105 BP (Morlan n.d.), and the Bjorklund (EaLa 3) site, Component 3, which produced Larter points from context dated to ca. 3,000 BP (Morlan n.d.). Interestingly, immediately north of the Pelican Lake/Larter occupation in southwestern Manitoba, the Eriksdale (EfLl ? [*sic*]) site produced a burial containing a Larter point embedded in a femur shaft dated to 3,460 +/- 100 BP (Rutherford et al. 1981:95).

In Montana, Pelican Lake material appears to be rare. At the King site in the Little Rocky Mountains in north-central Montana a single barbed specimen was found in the same layer as a Sandy Creek point (Brumley and Rennie 1999:69, fig. 18, nos. 2 and 3). The Keaster site, a multicomponent kill site in north-central Montana, may contain some Bracken points but few if any Pelican Lake points (see Davis and Stallcop 1965). Although the site report is brief and the recovery techniques complicated, the site may have Pelican Lake points in its earliest level. Level IV produced points that appear to have narrow necks and barbed shoulders (i.e., Davis and Stallcop 1965:11, plate 3, nos. 102 and 103; plate 5, no. 104). Better illustrations or firsthand comparisons would be necessary to confirm this suggestion. Surface finds of Pelican Lake points appear to have been recovered near Fort Benton (Shumate 1984:20, fig. 3i–r). The rarity of Pelican Lake material in Montana may be due to the presence of the Yonkee complex (ca. 2,900–2,100 BP), which has been found as far north as the Bears Paw Mountains. Kooyman (2000b:122) suggested the Yonkee cultural manifestation was an in situ development from McKean in the Powder River Basin. As suggested previously, the relatively unique Yonkee point style possibly deriving from the late Oxbow phase that appears to linger in southern Alberta and central Montana until ca. 3,500 to 3,000 BP (see Oxbow, above).

In summary, the Pelican Lake complex has a strong presence on the plains of Alberta, Saskatchewan, and Manitoba. As early as 3,600 BP the complex is found across the plains of the Prairie Provinces and likely into northern Montana. Based on the stratigraphic sequence at the Cactus Flower site, Reeves (1983a:7) argued that there were basic technological continuities within tool types and technology between McKean and Pelican Lake material, suggesting a cultural link. In contrast, Brumley (1975:73) noted that the Pelican Lake assemblage at Cactus Flower was largely chipped stone tools while the McKean-Duncan-Hanna assemblages exhibited pecked, ground, miscellaneous stone, antler, and shell tools. Both Reeves and Brumley were cautious in their assessments. Reeves (1983a:7) recommended further assessment of the data before accepting the Hanna-Pelican Lake cultural link. Similarly, Brumley (1975:73) indicated that the perceived differences between Hanna and Pelican Lake at the Cactus Flower site might be a result of sampling rather than actual cultural differences.

The current evidence would suggest McKean and Pelican Lake are unrelated cultural phenomenon. The range of features found in McKean sites is not apparent in Pelican Lake sites. The presence of ground stone and bone technology in McKean sites is absent in Pelican Lake sites. Ambush bison hunting practices used by McKean people are not found for the Pelican Lake complex; the latter utilizes stalking as the predominate form of bison procurement. The Pelican Lake point is technologically divergent from the Hanna form. It appears to be functionally designed to penetrate animal hides and, once imbedded, the barbs are designed to keep it inside the target. Thus, the prey's own movements agitate the imbedded point to continue to cut the animal apart, causing increased bleeding. This design would be implemented among hunters stalking solitary prey that was prone to flight once wounded. Such barbed points would not be required by people operating a pound, as these animals are contained and would not require tracking once injured. McKean-Duncan-Hanna points are all lanceolate points designed more for piercing. Such points are expected for hunters using blinds and ambushes where prey has less opportunity to escape at natural traps. The craftsmanship of the Pelican Lake point further suggests something different was happening: Pelican Lake points are relatively well crafted with good flaking, while the same cannot be said for most McKean points. Thus, technologically the barbed Pelican Lake points appear to reflect a different level of manufacture as well as hunting strategy.

The suite of lithic tools between McKean and Pelican Lake are relatively similar. Raw material use does tend to be more far-ranging for the Pelican Lake complex compared to the McKean-Duncan-Hanna complex. Pelican Lake assemblages exhibit Knife River flint and Rocky Mountain sources whereas the McKean-Duncan-Hanna does not. In addition, the Pelican Lake complex exhibits a stone circle camp while the McKean complex produced circular debris distributions, but nothing that was clearly indicative of a shelter. Of course, this difference might be attributed to season, a modest technological innovation, or archaeological sampling.

The craftsmanship and technological changes suggest the Pelican Lake complex is intrusive. As Dyck (1983:107) points out, however, the commonness of corner-notched points at this time makes pinpointing an origin for the Pelican Lake complex difficult. Still, the improved craftsmanship and the apparent trend toward solitary stalking of prey suggest an origin to the east where these practices were previously in place.

With regard to the fate of the people of the Pelican Lake complex, there are many lines of evidence to suggest they continued to culturally evolve, with innovations into the Bracken phase. Much of the tool kit remains the same, as do lithic raw material use patterns. Importantly, the corner-notched point loses its barbed shoulders in the Bracken phase. At the same time, jumping and impounding of bison begins to be significant. From this time forward, this technique is used continuously. Previous use of jumps occurred in earlier time periods but their use was episodic (i.e., Maple Leaf, Calderwood complex). The lack of barbed shoulders in the Bracken points likely reflects the increasing obsolescence of stalking of solitary prey. In contrast, bison that are impounded have limited chances of escape. Any dart piercing internal organs will eventually produce the animal's demise within the pound. Barbed points that continue to cut at the animal, slowing it down and leaving a trail of blood to follow, would not be needed by a society that impounded bison such as that of the Bracken phase. Aside from the innovation of bison jumps and impounding, the Pelican Lake complex and the Bracken phase appear to be culturally similar.

OUTLOOK COMPLEX (CA. 2,500 BP)

While working within the highly stratified deposits at Head-Smashed-In Buffalo Jump, Reeves (1978:164, 172, fig. 17.22; Reeves 1983a:98) noted Besant points within the productive Pelican Lake (i.e., Bracken) bone layers. Based on other dated layers within the bone bed, he estimated the age of the layers with the Besant points to be ca. 2,500 BP (Reeves 1978:172, fig. 17.22). These points had notches low on the lateral margins and straight-to-slightly indented bases, all manufactured on Knife River flint. By designating these early points as Besant, he was clearly suggesting cultural continuity with the Besant phase that traditionally begins much later at ca. 2,000 BP. Reeves (1983a:14) has, however, labelled the Sandy Creek complex as a likely progenitor of the Besant phase. It could not be discerned whether Reeves considered the Head-Smashed-In Buffalo Jump Besant points (ca. 2,500 BP) to be Sandy Creek points.

At the Sjovold site along the South Saskatchewan River in southern Saskatchewan, relatively lanceolate-shaped points with shallow side-notched and straight-to-slightly concave bases were recovered in Layer XIV. The materials from the layer produced a radiocarbon date of 2,580 +/- 85 BP (S-2060) (Dyck 1983:207–108; Dyck and Morlan 1995:446). Noting the similarity to Reeves' (1978) Besant points at Head-Smashed-In Buffalo Jump, Dyck

(1983:107–108) labelled the group of materials the Un-named complex (Dyck 1983:107–108). He suggested the material might represent an expanding population of Early Woodland people from Minnesota, Illinois, and/or Ohio, whose population base increased in size at about 2,500 BP (Dyck 1983:108).

Subsequently, the Sjovold projectile points from Layer XIV have been labelled Outlook side-notched points after the nearby Saskatchewan town of the same name (Dyck and Morlan 1995:425). Dyck and Morlan (1995:425) maintained that the point style is an early manifestation of the Besant point, exhibiting a relatively straight base and side notches; they also consider Outlook side-notched points to be arrow tips, not dart tips. They argued that the Outlook material represents an influence from the eastern and central edges of the plains, despite its lack of ceramics (Dyck and Morlan 1995:446).

Elongate points made of Knife River flint have also been recovered at the Fincastle (DlOx 5) site in south-central Alberta (Bubel 2007; Varsakis and Peck 2005). These points were recovered in a bone bed and date to roughly 2,500 BP. Varsakis and Peck (2005) argued that the Fincastle assemblage strongly resembled assemblages from Sjovold (XIV), Head-Smashed-In Buffalo Jump, and the Happy Valley site. Subsequently, a comparison of the Fincastle site materials to a broader range of sites led Varsakis (2006) to note that, during this period, there were long points manufactured from Knife River flint (i.e., Fincastle, Muhlbach, Smith-Swainson), and shorter side-notched points often co-occurring with Pelican Lake points (i.e., EbPi 63, EgPn 111, Kenney). Following Joyes (1984) and Duke (1991), Varsakis (2006) proposed that the Besant phase be divided minimally into three subphases: Sonota subphase, Kenney subphase, and Fincastle subphase. Importantly, the Fincastle subphase may represent an early manifestation of the Sonota subphase. She argued that the Fincastle subphase came from the Dakotas on to the Northern Plains for trading purposes with the people of the Kenney subphase. Later, this trade continued but with the Sonota subphase. In Varsakis' (2006) model the term Outlook was not used to represent any of this material.

The Sites

In order to assess the various lines of thinking presented above, Outlook assemblages from Alberta with solid radiocarbon dates are outlined below. These sites are used to critically evaluate the current view of the Outlook complex (see Plate 19 and Figure 20).

PLATE 19 Outlook points. Illustrated are projectile points from the Fincastle Kill site (DlOx 5) (a–o); Head-Smashed-In Buffalo Jump (DkPj 1) (p and q); and EgPn 290 (r–w). Photo credit: Alberta Culture and Community Spirit (a–o, r–w); Royal Alberta Museum (p and q).

FIGURE 20
Outlook sites within Alberta

Fincastle Kill site (DlOx 5). The Fincastle site is a single-component bison kill site in a stable dune complex a few kilometres north of Purple Springs and south of the Oldman River (Bubel 2007). The site was named for the nearby town of the same name. In 2004, 2006, and 2007 the University of Lethbridge conducted field schools at the site, while a total of 76 m² has been excavated. The field school project was initiated, in part, as a response to vandalism at the site.

Seventy-two complete and/or fragmentary points were recovered in association with five features in a bison bone bed (Varsakis 2006). Other lithics included several end scrapers and debitage. The vast majority of the lithic raw material was Knife River flint, although some Swan River chert was recovered (Varsakis 2006:99). The features included a small hearth and four bone uprights made of bison bone (Varsakis 2006:100–106). Scattered FBR was recovered throughout the bone bed (Varsakis 2006:100). The faunal assemblage consisted of large amounts of bison and some canid bone. Two radiometric dates of roughly 2,500 BP were obtained for the site (see Table 18).

TABLE 18 Radiocarbon dates for Outlook sites (calibrated by OxCal 3.10 [Ramsey 2005])

Site [LAB NO.]	Conventional ^{14}C Age	$^{13}C/^{12}C$ Ratio	Material	Calibration	Reference
DlOx 5 [BETA-201909]	2540 +/- 50	?	collagen	810–500 B.C. (p = 0.954)	Varasakis 2006:110–111
DlOx 5 [BETA 201910]	2490 +/- 60	?	collagen	790–410 B.C. (p = 0.954)	Varasakis 2006:110–111
EgPn 290 [RL-1657]	2440 +/- 120	-20.0‰	collagen	850–350 B.C. (p = 0.915) 300–200 B.C. (p = 0.039)	Shortt 1993:41–43; Morlan n.d.
EgPn 290 [BETA-51285]	2350 +/- 80	-20.0‰	collagen	800–200 B.C. (p = 0.954)	Shortt 1993:41–43; Morlan n.d.
EgPn 290 [RL-1658]	2450 +/- 120	-20.0‰	collagen	850–350 B.C. (p = 0.926) 300–200 B.C. (p = 0.028)	Shortt 1993:41–43; Morlan n.d.

Happy Valley (EgPn 290). The Happy Valley site is a single-component bison kill site on the south side of the Bow River below Canada Olympic Park (Shortt 1993). The site appears to be named for the Happy Valley Trailer Park, which formerly occupied the location. A total of 39.25 m² was excavated at the site (Shortt 1993:13–15), which was mitigated prior to the development of a golf/residential complex.

Thirteen projectile points and point fragments were recovered from the bone bed, including Besant side-notched (n = 3), Pinched Creek side-notched (n = 2), Pelican Lake corner-notched (n = 1), and unidentifiable fragments (n = 7). These specimens fall within the range of variation described above for Outlook side-notched points and for those recovered at the Fincastle site. Other tools recovered included bifaces (n = 3), retouched flakes (n = 11), choppers (n = 2), flake choppers (n = 4), cobble spalls (n = 5), and a hammerstone (Shortt 1993:43–57). Quartzite (46%) was the most common raw material, followed by chert (16%), Knife River flint (16%), siltstone (11%), obsidian (5%), and others (5%) (Shortt 1993:44). A number of bone tools for heavier carcass segmentation and processing were recovered. Distal humeri (n = 4), posterior humeri (n = 2), a distal radii, proximal radius (n = 2), and distal tibia (n = 2) had shafts shaped for cleaving meat, but little polish was discernable (Shortt 1993:59–60).

The faunal assemblage (n = 38,826) was mostly bison, but non-bison (n = 43) elements, including small and large canid, that exhibited signs of butchering were identified (Shortt 1993:63–64). An MNI of thirty-one bison was established based on the calcaneum. No fetal bone was recovered (Shortt 1993:192). Three radiocarbon dates were obtained from the bone bed, suggesting an age of ca. 2,400 BP (Shortt 1993:41–43). The site represents an Outlook bison kill and processing site.

Head-Smashed-In Buffalo Jump (DkPj 1). As mentioned above, Reeves (1983a:98) noted Besant-like projectile points within Pelican Lake (i.e., Bracken) layers in his excavations at Head-Smashed-In Buffalo Jump. "The three Besant Side Notched points from the Pelican Lake phase components . . . have wider notches, longer stems and broader necks than is usual. They probably predate Besant occupation of southwestern Alberta by 500 years" (Reeves 1983a:98). Although only three specimens were recovered, they exhibit a lanceolate form, slightly concave base, and wide-shallow side notch. It is also important to note that all three specimens were manufactured on Knife River flint (Reeves 1978:172, fig. 17.22). These points are Outlook points in both age and morphology.

Other sites. Few other sites exhibit Outlook-like point specimens in Alberta. One possible exception is the Stampede (DjOn 26) site in the Cypress Hills. It produced a single brown chalcedony projectile point in Cultural Level 2. The specimen was classified as a large Samantha variety of Besant point but radiocarbon dates were not obtained (Gryba 1975:92–93). Little material was associated with this cultural level. The recovered point could be an Outlook point or a Sonota point (see Sonota phase below).

Outlook: The First Wave of Middle Missouri Invaders

Large dart points made on Knife River flint dating to approximately 2,500 BP have been repeatedly interpreted as antecedents to Besant (Dyck and Morlan 1995; Reeves 1983a; Shortt 1993; Varsakis 2006). Yet no known assemblage or assemblages bridge the temporal gap between the Knife River flint darts at 2,500 BP and the Besant phase at ca. 2,000 BP. It seems more reasonable for the material to stand on its own until more data can be brought to bear on the origin and demise of the Outlook complex. Dyck and Morlan (1995) provided the first name, other than Besant, for this material. The term *Outlook* is retained to refer to both the distinctive large Knife River flint dart points and to the related archaeological complex.

The Outlook point exhibits a range of variability but tends to be slightly elongate, wide-necked, straight- to concave-based points made on Knife River flint with side-notches low on the lateral margins (Reeves 1983a:31–33, fig. 17.22; Shortt 1993:48–49, fig. 13; Varsakis 2006). Few other tools have been recovered at sites of this type in Alberta. Varsakis (2006) noted some end scrapers while Reeves (1983a) only noted points. Shortt (1993), on the other hand, noted bifaces, retouched flakes, choppers, flake choppers, cobble spalls, a hammerstone, and some bone segmentation tools for chopping carcasses. The lithic raw material at these sites contains a large amount of Knife River flint. Although it is not always the dominant raw material, it occurs in unusual amounts relative to other periods in Alberta's past.

In terms of features, a small hearth and four bone uprights were uncovered at the Fincastle site. No other features were noted at the other sites. Importantly, the Outlook components at the Fincastle site, the Happy Valley site, and Head-Smashed-In Buffalo Jump are all bison kill sites. The processing of the bison appears to have been geared toward drying meat and obtaining hides, since little FBR, few hearths, and no pits have been recovered at these sites. Still, given the small sample size of sites, this observation might simply mean that such an aspect of Outlook processing has not been exposed yet. The apparent emphasis on bison kill sites might also be a product of visibility and sampling.

As noted above, an Outlook site is also known from Saskatchewan. The Sjovold site (EiNs 4) is a highly stratified site on the South Saskatchewan

River near the town of Outlook. Layer XIV produced two hearths surrounded by bone and chipped stone. Nine projectile points were recovered. These points are elongate specimens with straight-to-slightly concave bases and notches low on the lateral margins. Dyck and Morlan (1995:436) presented metric measurements to suggest the points are arrows rather than darts. The neck widths range from 11 to 13 mm. Neck widths greater than 10 mm tend to be interpreted as dart points rather than arrow points; these points are interpreted here as falling within the range of atlatl and dart technology rather than bow and arrow technology. Dyck and Morlan (1995:437) argued that the prevalent use of Knife River flint in the projectile points and tools suggested a tie to the Besant phase. More appropriately, the abnormal occurrence of Knife River flint demarks ties to North Dakota and begs explanations of quarrying expeditions by Outlook peoples to North Dakota, exchange networks between Outlook peoples and those in North Dakota, or an origin of Outlook people in North Dakota.

In North Dakota, there are few known sites from this period. The Naze site (32SN246) is a multicomponent site with an Early Plains Woodland component underlying a Sonota Component (i.e., Middle Plains Woodland) and a Plains Village/Protohistoric Component (Gregg 1987). Five radiocarbon dates were obtained for the Early Plains Woodland level: 2,472 +/- 45 BP (SMU-1759); 2,448 +/- 44 BP (SMU-1760); 2,388 +/- 44 BP (SMU 1761); 2,440 +/- 70 BP (Beta-14746); and 2,780 +/- 80 BP (Beta-14745) (Gregg 1987:74). The Early Plains Woodland component produced forty-four tools of which five were projectile points. Four of the points were corner notched while the fifth had low side notches, a relatively wide neck, and a straight base (Gregg 1987:258, fig. 8.2a–e). The latter is not unlike the Outlook points found in the study area. The researcher considered the recovered points to be Besant and Pelican Lake points (Gregg 1987:442). Eighteen of the tools were manufactured on Knife River flint, with Swan River chert and basalt also common (Gregg 1987:255). A structure with footing trenches and central supports stood at the location. Four cord-roughened ceramic sherds exhibiting punctates were also recovered at the site (Gregg 1987:441). The fauna was dominated by bison, but elk, coyote or dog, beaver, and possibly wolf were present (Gregg 1987:443). The material was not assigned to any specifically named archaeological culture other than the Early Plains Woodland period (Gregg 1987:443). Importantly, Gregg (1987:443) considered the Sonota phase an in situ development out of this earlier yet-to-be named phenomenon.

The Outlook material in Alberta and Saskatchewan likely has links to this cultural phenomenon. They are coeval and some of the point forms are similar. The use of Knife River flint is prevalent in the archaeological assemblages from both areas. Within the Alberta and Saskatchewan sites, the predominance of bison kill sites and Knife River flint in the toolstone may suggest an intrusive group entering into the Northern Plains with a specific procurement pattern. For example, Early Plains Woodland people exhibiting a semi-sedentary lifestyle in North Dakota could have been frequenting the Northern Plains with the purpose of procuring bison for trade to neighbours further east. This would explain the large number of Outlook kill sites, a paucity of campsites, and the reliance on Knife River flint. Also important is that the Outlook material appears to have been deposited during the tenure of the Bracken phase. These Early Plains Woodland peoples may be invited guests or intruders on the Northern Plains.

The Outlook complex is dated to ca. 2,500 BP. It seems to be a very brief utilization of the Northern Plains. All the dates for the various sites in Alberta and Saskatchewan fall within a few decades of ca. 2,500 BP. By ca. 2,000 BP, the Sonota phase frequented the Northern Plains in a very similar fashion as the Outlook complex had 500 years earlier. The Sonota phase is characterized by large lanceolate points that are often found in bison kill sites. Currently, it is difficult to differentiate these specimens without an associated radiocarbon date. This difficulty is likely due to a common cultural background within North Dakota that bridges the 500 years over which the two cultures are absent from the Northern Plains.

The sudden appearance and then disappearance of the Outlook complex is difficult to explain. Development and growth of cultures in the east appears to have been constant. A decline in trade does not seem to be a reasonable answer. One possibility is the more firm protection of the Northern Plains by the occupying Bracken phase. At roughly this period, the Bracken phase commenced bison jumping and pounding, a hunting technique that had not been systematically applied until then. Associated with this subsistence shift is the first evidence of large social groups cohabitating. Until this time period, campsites had been small, suggesting no more than a few families together. The Bracken phase exhibits stone circle camps, suggesting tipi camps of as many as fifteen to eighteen families (or more than a hundred people). Such larger communities are in a better position to defend themselves from unwanted intruders.

SANDY CREEK COMPLEX (CA. 2,500 BP)

The Sandy Creek culture was defined based on materials recovered at the Mortlach site (Wettlaufer 1955:50–53). The distinctive Sandy Creek projectile point is described as "having shallow side notches and an indented base forming 'lugs' or 'ears'" (Wettlaufer 1955:49). Further, these specimens are "short, thick, rather misshapen points ... characterised by shallow notches and slightly indented bases" (Wettlaufer 1955:52). Additional artifacts of the Sandy Creek culture include plano-convex scrapers and several bone tools (i.e., polished perforator/awl, bladed tanning tool) including evidence of bone tool manufacture by flaking bone (Wettlaufer 1955:50–51). The Sandy Creek culture at the Mortlach site stratigraphically underlies two Besant occupations (4A and 4B), and a Bracken occupation (4C), and overlies several Pelican Lake occupations (5B, 6 and 7) and a Hanna occupation (8). Level 4E, the level labelled by Wettlaufer as containing the Sandy Creek culture, produced a radiocarbon date of 2,400 +/- 173 BP (S-28) while the younger Sandy Creek level (4D) was not dated.

Dyck (1983:108–109) resurrected the Sandy Creek projectile point type to account for materials that resembled Oxbow projectile points that were recovered from sites dating hundreds of years too recent. In the Sandy Creek complex he included Levels 4D and E of the Morltach site, Level 15b of the Walter Felt site dated to 2,430 +/- 90 BP (S-297), Level XII of the Sjovold site with a date of 2,435 +/- 105 BP (S-2059), the Heron site with dates of 2,280 +/- 65 BP and 2,330 +/- 70 BP, and Level 2 of the East Pasture site with no diagnostics but a date of 2,405 +/- 80 BP (S-639). For Manitoba, he included Component B of the Cherry Point site dated to 1,850 +/- 100 BP and 2,060 +/- 130 BP, and for British Columbia he suggested HaRk 1, a late Oxbow site dated to ca. 2,485 BP, was likely Sandy Creek (Dyck 1983:109).

Reeves (1983a:14) noted that Sandy Creek materials are interfingered between Pelican Lake materials at the Mortlach, Walter Felt, and Sjovold sites. He considered Sandy Creek projectile point technology to be transitional between late Oxbow and Besant side-notched owing to their squat form, low side notches, shallow offset *v*-shaped bases, and emphasis on local lithic raw materials (Reeves 1983a:14). Thus, the Sandy Creek complex emerged from the parkland, having developed out of the Oxbow phase, at the end of the Bracken phase, to become the Besant phase (Reeves 1983a:14).

More recently, Dyck has reversed his position on the Sandy Creek complex

(Dyck and Morlan 1995:405). He indicated that "as the evidence from the Sjovold site unfolds we are beginning to question ever more strongly the idea that an archaeological complex, much less the looser series grouping, can be defined by a single point type" (Dyck and Morlan 1995:405). Thus, he no longer advocated classifying the projectile point from Level XII of the Sjovold site as Sandy Creek. Dyck and Morlan (1995:405) recommended classifying the point as Sandy Creek, a point type common within the Besant series or related materials through time.

Based on the recovery of in situ Sandy Creek material at the Aldon Plant site (EaOq 43) within Medicine Hat, Brumley (1995:17–18) argued for a slightly earlier appearance of the Sandy Creek complex. He obtained dates of 3,000 +/- 80 BP (AECV 1569C) and 2,730 +/- 90 BP (AECV 1570C) on material from the small bison jump or pound site (Brumley 1995:17). He suggested the Sandy Creek complex may begin as early as ca. 2,800 BP and terminate at ca. 1,950 BP (see also Dyck 1983:108–109). Another subtle observation was that Sandy Creek points are not so much Oxbow points "out-of-time" but are more similar to Besant in morphology. Brumley and Rennie (2005:18) included the Sandy Creek complex as intermediate between Oxbow and Besant within their Mondak tradition.

The Sites

In order to assess the various lines of thinking presented above, Sandy Creek assemblages from Alberta with reliable radiocarbon dates are outlined below. These sites are used to critically evaluate the current view of the Sandy Creek complex (see Plate 20 and Figure 21).

PLATE 20 Sandy Creek points. Illustrated are three projectile points from EgPn 666. Photo credit: Alberta Culture and Community Spirit.

Aldon Plant Bison Kill (EaOq 43). The Aldon Plant site is a small bison kill located in a coulee bottom that joins to the South Saskatchewan, in the City of Medicine Hat. The site was test excavated in 1988. The site was determined to be 20–30 m wide and 100 m long. Modern cultivation

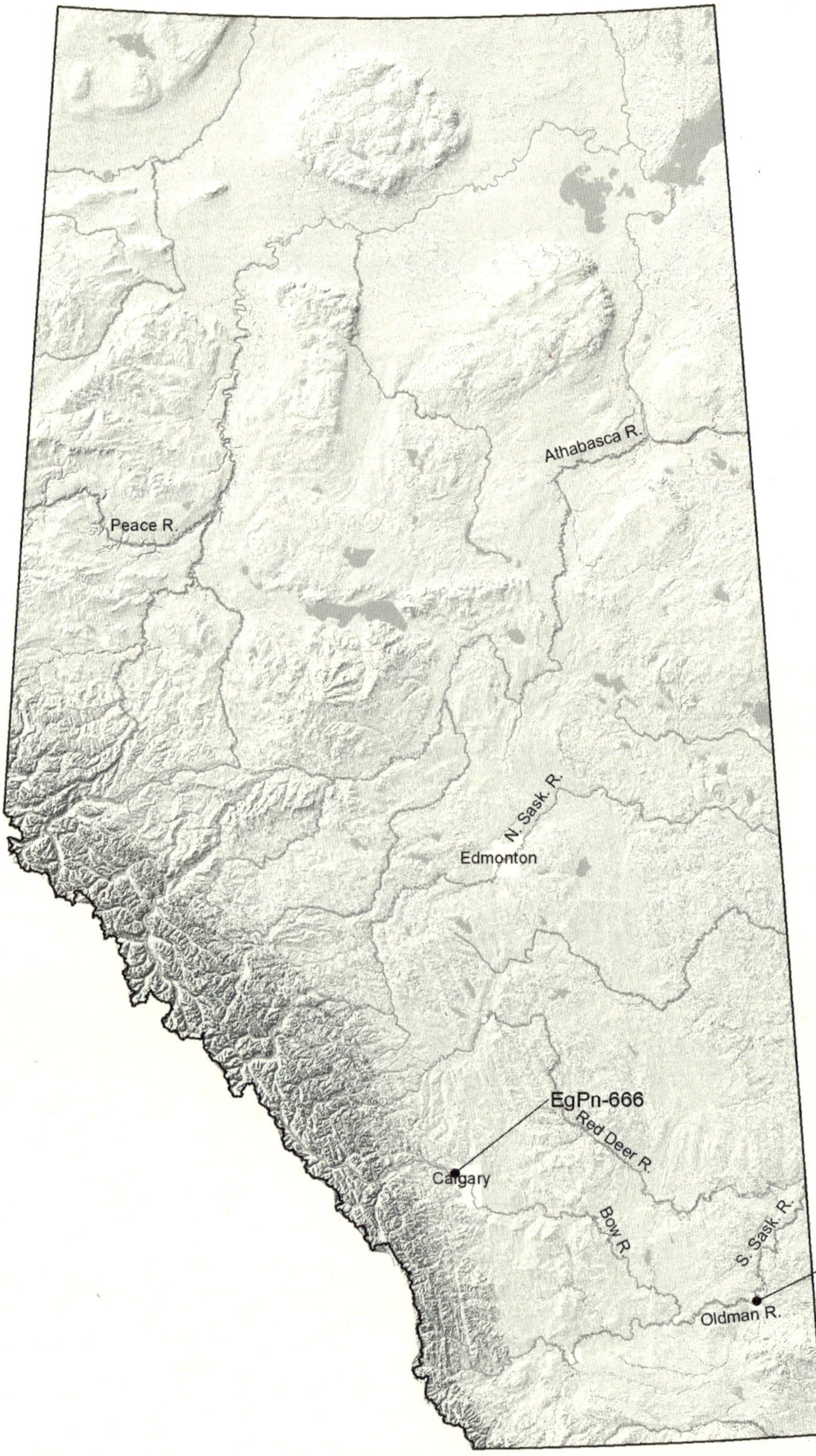

FIGURE 21
Sandy Creek sites within Alberta

had severely impacted the site. A series of Besant projectile points and a single Pelican Lake point were recovered from what appeared to be a single event kill. Brumley (1995:17) classified the Besant points as Sandy Creek points. Two radiocarbon dates of ca. 3,000 BP and 2,700 BP were obtained (Brumley 1995:17).

EgPn 666. EgPn 666 is a small temporary campsite on a terrace at the mouth of a main coulee that leads north to the Bow River (Vivian et al. 2003b:66). In 2002, 23 m^2 were excavated at the site, which was mitigated prior to a housing development.

Three projectile points were recovered from EgPn 666, including a Sandy Creek side-notched point and two unidentifiable point blades (Vivian et al. 2003b:68–69). Other tools recovered included a biface fragment, an end scraper, a wedge, a spokeshave, retouched flakes (n = 2), and a unidirectional core (Vivian et al. 2003b:69–71). The large number of tools and the late stage exhibited in the reduction of the debitage suggested winter retooling activity (Vivian et al. 2003b:72). An examination of the raw materials indicated that quartzite (44%) was most commonly used, followed by Knife River flint (14%), silicified siltstone (10%), white chalcedony (8%), Montana chert (8%), silicified sandstone (6%), Swan River chert (4%), Bowman chert (4%), and basalt (2%) (Vivian et al. 2003b:72, 115).

TABLE 19 Radiocarbon dates for Sandy Creek sites (calibrated by OxCal 3.10 [Ramsey 2005])

Site [LAB NO.]	Conventional ^{14}C Age	$^{13}C/^{12}C$ Ratio	Material	Calibration	Reference
EaOq 43 [AECV-1569C]	3000 +/- 80	-18.3‰	collagen	1430–1010 B.C. (p = 0.954)	Brumley 1995:17; Morlan n.d.
EaOq 43 [AECV-1570C]	2730 +/- 90	-17.9‰	collagen	1200–750 B.C. (p = 0.954)	Brumley 1995:17; Morlan n.d.
EgPn 666 [BETA-172900]	2420 +/- 40	-19.0‰	collagen	760– 680 B.C. (p = 0.178) 670–610 B.C. (p = 0.068) 600–390 B.C. (p = 0.708)	Vivian et al. 2003b
DjPl 1 [AECV-0422C]	2810 +/- 90	-18.6‰	collagen	1260–1230 B.C. (p = 0.011) 1220–800 B.C. (p = 0.943)	Ball 1987; Morlan n.d.
DjPl 1 [AECV-0418C]	3000 +/- 90	-18.2‰	collagen	1440–970 B.C. (p = 0.954)	Ball 1987; Morlan n.d.

The faunal assemblage (n=798) was very fragmentary and often burned. An MNI of two bison was established from a very small number of identifiable elements (Vivian et al. 2003b:72–73). The fauna exhibited a scatter of highly fragmented elements of low economic value. Two small oval open hearths and a boiling pit were also observed. The researchers suggested that the site represents a single household where bison were intensively butchered during a period of winter scarcity. A second household may also have been present, represented around the second hearth 12 m from the first hearth-pit processing area. A radiocarbon date of ca. 2,400 BP was obtained (see Table 19). This date falls within the range for the Sandy Creek complex. The morphology of the single complete projectile point from the site is not unlike points defined as Sandy Creek. The researchers classify it as such (Vivian et al. 2003b:68–69).

Other sites. Projectile points classifiable as Sandy Creek are very rare in Alberta. One site possibly exhibiting such a point is the Pincher Creek Buffalo Jump (DjPl 1) located north of Pincher Creek, just south of the Oldman River (Ball 1987:31). Excavations to determine the temporal extent of the site produced late side notched points in the upper bone beds. Interestingly, a lower bone bed in Test Unit 1 produced two dates of 2,810 +/- 90 BP (AECV-0422c) and 3,000 +/- 90 BP (AECV-0418c). At the same time, test pits in stone circles adjacent to the jump produced a Sandy Creek-like point specimen (Ball 1987:22, fig. 22b). The large dart point exhibits the classic characteristics of Sandy Creek points, including a slightly concave base, ears, and shallow notches. It is also much larger than the other Late Prehistoric arrow points recovered at the site, as it has a neck width much greater than 10 mm.

Sandy Creek: Besant Beginnings?

The Sandy Creek complex is poorly known in Alberta and adjacent areas. The projectile points are relatively distinct, and are described as short, thick, and rather misshapen, with shallow side notches and indented bases forming lugs or ears. The consistency in point style and age is common enough to beg questions concerning the nature of this material. As noted above, Sandy Creek material has also been recovered outside of Alberta.

In Saskatchewan, the Mortlach site (EcNl 1) produced two levels with Sandy Creek points. Levels 4D and 4E both exhibit points with shallow side notches and indented bases forming lugs. These specimens are in stark contrast to the overlying Besant material (4A–C) and the underlying Pelican Lake material (5A). Level 4E produced a date of ca. 2,400 BP while the overlying Sandy Creek level (4D) was not dated.

The Sjovold site (EiNs 4) produced a single Sandy Creek point and a tip fragment in Layer XII (Dyck and Morlan 1995:397, fig. 16.4e). The points were associated with hearths. Utilized lithic raw material showed a partiality for Knife River flint. While the point was acknowledged as Sandy Creek, the researchers explained they considered it just one in a range of point forms found in the Besant series, dating roughly from 2,500 to 1,500 BP. A radiocarbon date obtained from this level was 2,435 +/- 105 BP (S-2059).

The Walter Felt site (EcMn 8) in south-central Saskatchewan produced two Sandy Creek points in layer 15b (Kehoe 1974:107, fig. 4h, i). One specimen was missing an ear while the second specimen was simply a blade. Below this material were barbed Pelican Lake points in Layer 15d and above was Bracken material in Layer 15a. A radiocarbon date of 2,430 +/- 90 BP (S-279) was obtained for Layer 15b (Kehoe 1974:111). Kehoe (1974:104) considered Sandy Creek to be a variety of the Pelican Lake point that immediately predates Besant. Dyck (1983; see also Morlan et al. 2002:29) also suggested the Heron site (EcNx 2) be considered a possible Sandy Creek site, owing to the presence of Oxbow-like points and radiocarbon dates of ca. 2,300 BP.

In Montana, at the King site in the Little Rocky Mountains in north-central Montana, a possible Sandy Creek point was found in the same level as Pelican Lake material (Brumley and Rennie 1999:69; fig. 18, no. 3.2). Brumley and Rennie (2005:18) stated that Sandy Creek points have not been found in excavated context in northern Montana, but are well represented in surface finds.

The Sandy Creek phenomenon is not well defined or understood. Initially defined as a discrete cultural phenomenon (Wettlaufer 1955), more recent investigators consider it the first point type in a series that make up the Besant series (Dyck and Morlan 1995). For the purpose of this review, the Sandy Creek point form and associated material seems too poorly understood to confidently associate it with another archaeological culture. Having stated that, the Sandy Creek material provides enough variability in form that it may fall within the dramatic range of variability exhibited by Bracken projectile points. Thus, there would be no justification for treating it as a separate unit. Clearly, further evidence needs to be brought to bear on the issue.

BRACKEN PHASE (CA. 2,800 TO 2,100 BP)

As noted earlier, the term Pelican Lake culture was applied by Wettlaufer (1955:54–57) to material at the Mortlach site. Level 5A produced corner-notched points with oval cross-sections and fine parallel or diagonal flaking that was widest just above the notches, with straight sides that taper to a point. Currently, the term *Pelican Lake* has become synonymous with corner-notched dart points (e.g., Gregg 1987:261). The important micro-stylistic variation captured in Wettlaufer's (1955) description has been ignored. In this review, Wettlaufer's original Pelican Lake material, dating to 3,500–2,800 BP and associated with points with barbed shoulders and narrow necks, is presented as culturally distinct from the corner-notched points and associated materials commonly referred to as Pelican Lake, which roughly date to between 2,800 and 2,000 BP. The former points exhibit less discrete shoulders and more convex bases than true Pelican Lake points. These subsequent less-descript corner-notched points are labelled Bracken points and are diagnostic of the Bracken phase.

Kehoe (1974) provided the term *Bracken* to be used with the Pelican Lake points in his system of large corner-notched points. He described the "Bracken shouldered, convex base variety" as having wide corner notches and straight shoulders, and a convex base that was ground like a Besant base (Kehoe 1974:111). Kehoe considered his Bracken Pelican Lake point to be a transitional form from Pelican Lake to Besant. He named it for the point style recovered from the Bracken Cairn site (see E. Walker 1982). The distinction between the Pelican Lake material and the Bracken material, however, goes beyond subtle projectile point morphological changes over time. There are major changes in cultural phenomenon that suggest that the two phases may be culturally unrelated.

Wettlaufer's (1955) Pelican Lake culture at the Mortlach site was not radiometrically dated, but it stratigraphically underlay a Sandy Creek component dated to ca. 2,500 BP. Wettlaufer and Mayer-Oakes (1960) later applied the term to Level 4 of the Long Creek site, dated to ca. 2,300 BP. The main difference noted between the specimens from Mortlach and Long Creek was that the former had convex bases and the latter had straighter bases (Wettlaufer and Mayer-Oakes 1960:108). Despite the relatively late date for the Long Creek material, these two sites are examples of true Pelican Lake sites. Perhaps the apparently aberrant late date is part of the reason for the failure to recognize the distinction between barbed Pelican Lake points and later corner-notched points in the literature.

In 1965, Wormington and Forbis (1965:192) acknowledged the presence of Pelican Lake material on a large part of the Northern Plains. They realized that sites such as Keaster indicated large bison pounds were being used, although large Pelican Lake jumps were yet to be discovered. They attributed bison jumps to Besant (Wormington and Forbis 1965:192).

In 1969, Reeves (1969, 1983a) proposed the name Pelican Lake phase, based on Wettlaufer's (1955) Pelican Lake culture at the Mortlach site. The diagnostic point type was named *Pelican Lake corner-notched*. He divided the area with known Pelican Lake corner-notched points into eight regional subphases (see Pelican Lake complex above). Unfortunately, the micro-stylistic variability within the projectile points that helped distinguish the subphases in Reeves' (1969, 1983a) classification of Pelican Lake has rarely been applied in practice. Dyck (1983:105) recognized two basic varieties of Pelican Lake points but lumped them under the Pelican Lake complex, which he dated to ca. 3,300–1,850 BP. Following Reeves (1969, 1983a), Vickers (1986:76–81) considered Pelican Lake to appear on the plains about 3,300 BP and last until about 2,000 BP. As noted earlier, while Reeves (1983a) suggested Pelican Lake was the antecedent to Avonlea, Vickers (1986:80) used Reeves' own data to suggest Pelican Lake lithic assemblages exhibit more in common with Besant lithic assemblages than they do with Avonlea lithic assemblages

The Sites

In order to assess the various lines of thinking presented above, Pelican Lake assemblages from Alberta with reliable radiocarbon dates are outlined below. The barbed Pelican Lake material, dated to between ca. 3,600 and 2,800, will be left out of this discussion despite having been lumped together in most previous models of Pelican Lake materials. Only Pelican Lake sites exhibiting corner-notched points with obtuse shoulders and wide necks from contexts dated between ca. 2,800 and 2,100 BP are examined (see Plate 21 and Figure 22).

Highwood River (EePk 272). The Highwood River site is a secondary interment on the prairie level of the highest local crest overlooking the Highwood River valley (Brink and Baldwin 1988). The site is located southeast of Calgary about 4 km above the Highwood River's confluence with the Bow River. Ploughing, erosion, and collecting had disturbed the site, but a tightly grouped surface exposure of human bone and associated

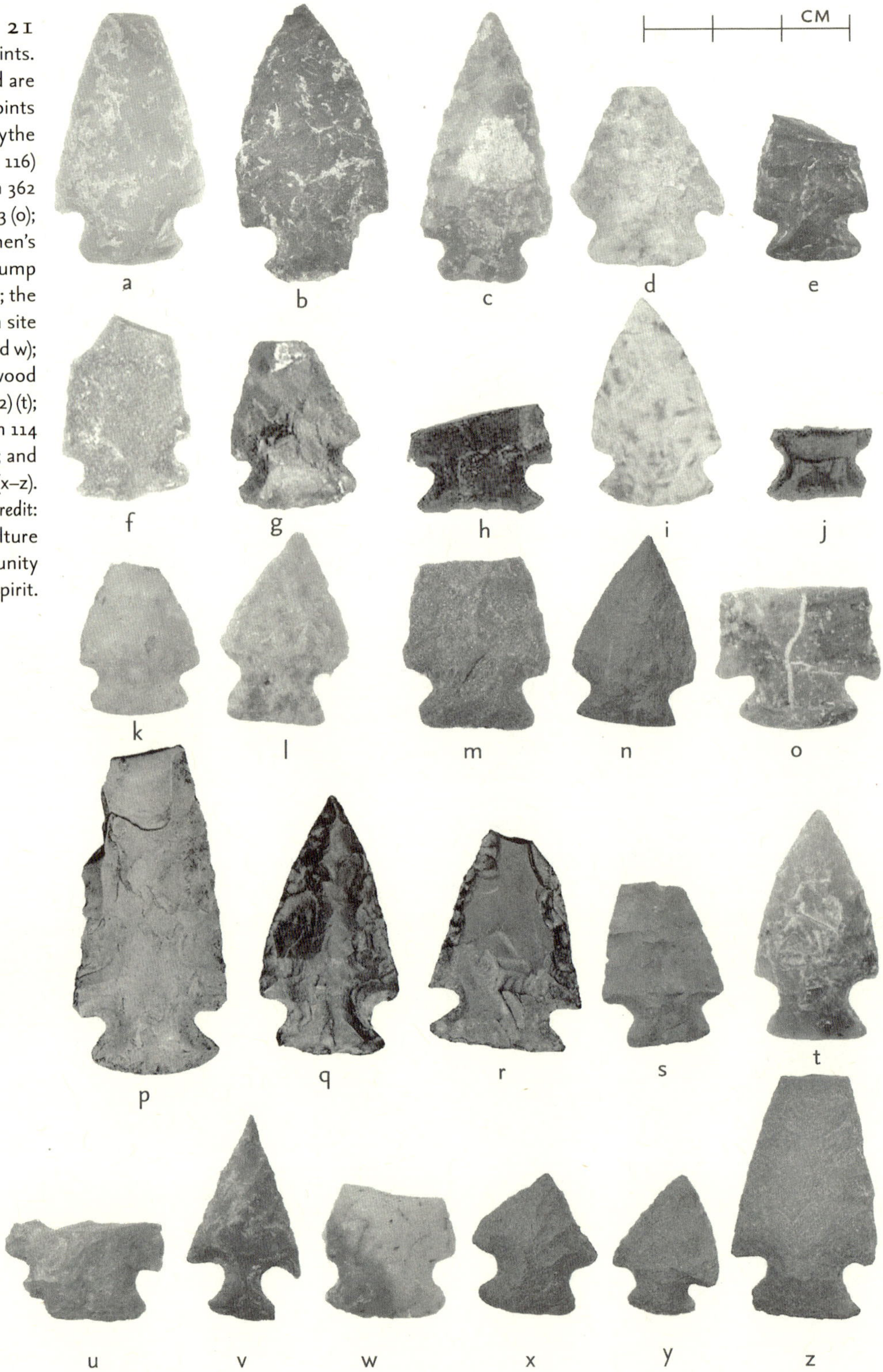

PLATE 21 Bracken points. Illustrated are projectile points from the Smythe site (DjPm 116) (a–j); EgPn 362 (k–n); DjPf 83 (o); (Old) Women's Buffalo Jump (EcPl 1) (p–r); the Cattle Baron site (EcPn 2) (s and w); the Highwood site (EePk 272) (t); DjPm 114 (u and v); and EgPn 598 (x–z). Photo credit: Alberta Culture and Community Spirit.

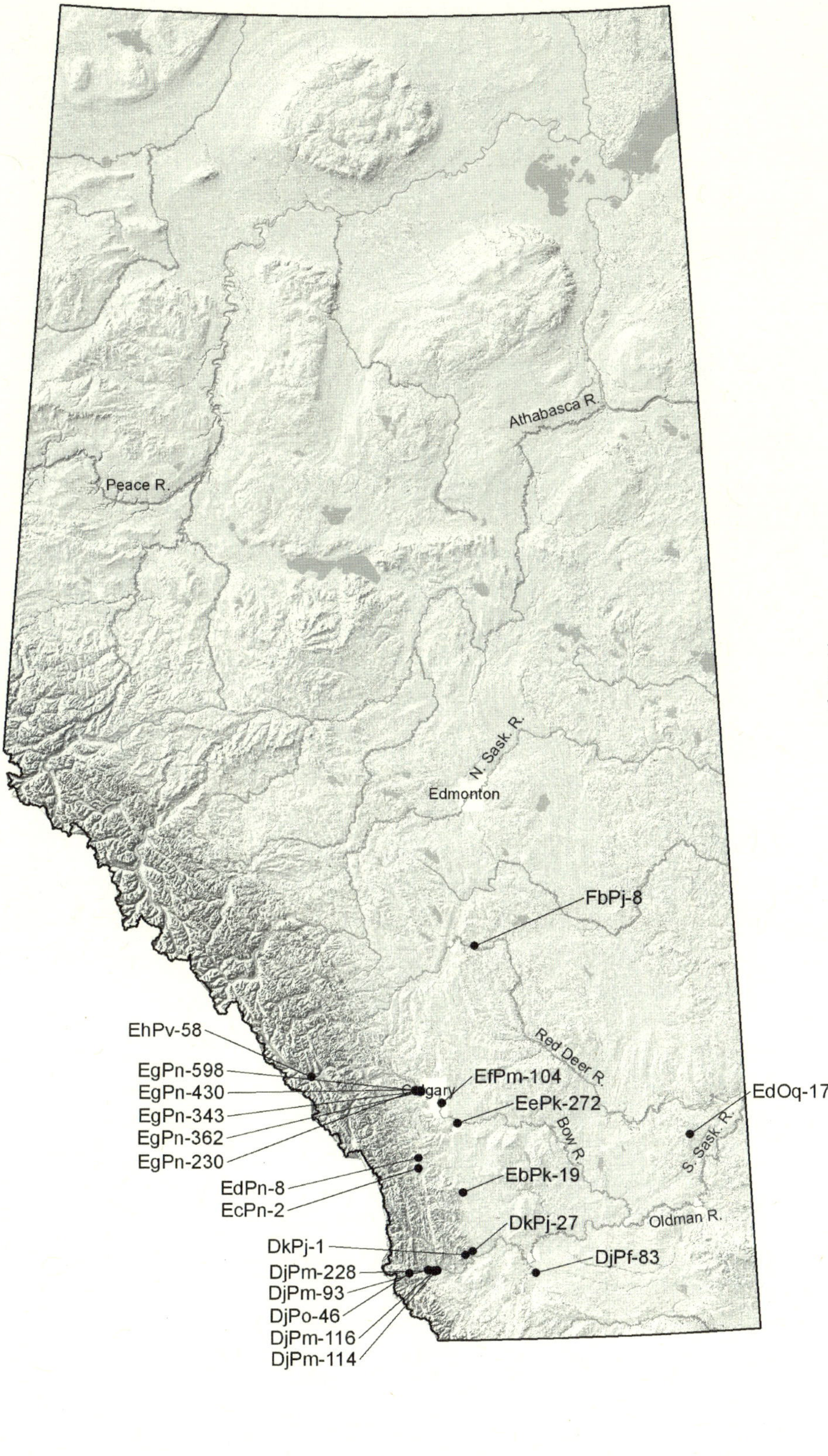

FIGURE 22
Bracken sites
within Alberta

grave goods were observed (Brink and Baldwin 1988:112). The surface sand and artifacts were stained a deep red colour and this stain continued to a depth of 35 cm BS (Brink and Baldwin 1988:112). The original burial pit appeared to have been an oval, red ochre stained area about 1.5 m long east–west and 0.8 m north–south. The original depth of the burial or whether it was capped with rock could not be determined (Brink and Baldwin 1988:113). About 15 percent of the artifacts were recovered in situ.

The recovered skeletal material suggested that two individuals were present (Brink and Baldwin 1988:114). These appear to have been children, one perhaps ten years of age, whose bodies were defleshed in open air, perhaps on a scaffold. It is unclear if elements of one individual, represented by only a few bones, were inadvertently or intentionally included in the interment (Brink and Baldwin 1988:114–119). Items confidently recovered in association with the burial include three lithics (i.e., a Pelican Lake point, a retouched flake, and a chert core), one piece of native copper, perforated shell beads (n = 4), a gastropod shell bead, *Dentialium* shell beads (n = 2), pieces of unworked bivalve shell (n = 3), perforated grizzly bear claws (n = 11), and drilled bison incisors and canines (n = 66). A primary quartzite flake, a piece of shatter, and an FBR fragment were observed in close proximity to the burial but could not be confidently associated with the burial (Brink and Baldwin 1988:119). A single radiocarbon date of ca. 2,800 BP (see Table 20) was obtained for the interment (Brink and Baldwin 1988:125; Morlan n.d.).

Head-Smashed-In Buffalo Jump (DjPk 1). Head-Smashed-In Buffalo Jump is discussed in the previous section on the Calderwood complex. Bracken material was recovered by Reeves (1978) from numerous levels in both his north and south kill excavations (Reeves originally called all this material Pelican Lake). The Bracken points exhibit the slightly convex base, the obtuse to very mildly barbed shoulders, and the open corner notches (Reeves 1978:172, fig. 17.22, nos. 8–30). Two dates were obtained from the initial layers of the Pelican Lake (i.e., Bracken) layers: 3,100 BP and 2,770 BP (Table 20). The former date was analyzed from a laboratory that is not considered reliable (Blakeslee 1994). The remaining date suggests that Bracken phase bison jumping at Head-Smashed-In Buffalo Jump began about 2,800 BP. A terminal Bracken phase date of ca. 2000 BP was obtained near the top of the Pelican Lake (i.e., Bracken) deposits (Table 20).

TABLE 20 Radiocarbon dates for Bracken sites (calibrated by OxCal 3.10 [Ramsey 2005])

Site [LAB NO.]	Conventional ^{14}C Age	$^{13}C/^{12}C$ Ratio	Material	Calibration	Reference
EePk 272 [S-1962]	2825 +/- 95	-19.0‰	collagen	1260–800 B.C. (p = 0.954)	Brink and Baldwin 1988:125; Morlan n.d.
DkPj 1 [RL-332]	2770 +/- 90	-20.0‰	collagen	1210–790 B.C. (p = 0.954)	Reeves 1990:162; Morlan n.d.
DkPj 1 [GAK-1474]	3040 +/- 120	?	collagen	rejected	Reeves 1990:162; Morlan n.d.
DkPj 1 [GX-1253]	2005 +/- 80	-20.0‰	collagen	250 B.C.–A.D. 250 (p = 0.954)	Reeves 1978:162; Morlan n.d.
EbPk 19 [AECV-1922C]	2630 +/- 80	21.5‰	bone	980–510 B.C. (p = 0.954)	Brewer et al. 1995:171
EbPk 19 [AECV-1923C]	2530 +/- 70	21.4‰	bone	810–480 B.C. (p = 0.888) 470–410 B.C. (p = 0.066)	Brewer et al. 1995:171
EhPv 58 [S-2757]	2520 +/- 210	?	charcoal	1200–100 B.C. (p = 0.954)	Fedje 1986:52
EhPv 58 [S-2756]	2805 +/- 130	?	charcoal	1400–750 B.C. (p = 0.954)	Fedje 1986:52
EcPn 2 [RL-797]	2520 +/- 110	-20.0‰	collagen	900–350 B.C. (p = 0.954)	Morlan n.d.
EdPn 8 [RL-799]	2440 +/- 170	-25.0‰	collagen	950–100 B.C. (p = 0.954)	Morlan n.d.
EfPm 104 [RL-1417]	2530 +/- 120	-25.0‰	charcoal	950– 350 B.C. (p = 0.954)	Van Dyke 1982:230; Morlan n.d.
EfPm 104 [RL-1623]	2640 +/- 260	-25.0‰	charcoal	1500–100 B.C. (p = 0.954)	Ronaghan and Landals 1983:54
EfPm 104 [RL-1700]	2330 +/- 150	-25.0‰	charcoal	800–50 B.C. (p = 0.954)	Ronaghan and Landals 1983:63
EfPm 104 [RL-1528]	2290 +/-120	-25.0‰	charcoal	800–50 B.C. (p = 0.954)	Van Dyke 1982:230; Morlan n.d.
EfPm 104 [RL-1688]	690 +/- 110	-25.0‰	charcoal	rejected	Ronaghan and Landals 1983:59
EgPn 362 [BETA-145205]	2360 +/- 60	-18.9‰	collagen	800–350 B.C. (p = 0.911) 300–200 B.C. (p = 0.043)	Vivian et al. 2003:30
EgPn 598 [BETA-145209]	2290 +/- 70	-19.2‰	collagen	750–650 B.C. (p = 0.014) 550–150 B.C. (p = 0.94)	Vivian et al. 2003:233
DkPj 27 [AECV-367C]	2170 +/- 90	-17.5‰	collagen	400 B.C.–A.D. 1 (p = 0.954)	Marshall 1988:60; Morlan n.d.
DkPj 27 [AECV-369C]	1910 +/- 90	-24.3‰	collagen	160–130 B.C. (p = 0.01) 120 B.C.–A.D. 340 (p = 0.944)	Marshall 1988:6); Morlan n.d.

TABLE 20 (continued)

DjPf 83 [RL-1408]	2220 +/- 100	-20.0‰	collagen	550 B.C.–A.D. 50 (p = 0.954)	Brumley and Rushworth 1983:149; Morlan n.d.
DjPm 114 [AECV-697C]	2090 +/- 260	-18.7‰	collagen	800 B.C.–A.D.500 (p = 0.954)	Landals 1993:21
FbPj 8 [RL-856]	1230 +/- 130	-20.0‰	collagen	rejected	Smith and Reeves 1978:13
DjPm 116 [AECV-345C]	2980 +/- 90	-25.0‰	wood	1430–970 B.C. (p = 0.954)	Morlan n.d.
DjPm 116 [AECV-1233C]	2880 +/- 100	-18.5‰	collagen	1400–800 B.C. (p = 0.954)	Landals 1993:181; Morlan n.d.
DjPm 116 [AECV-1232C]	2770 +/- 100	-17.1‰	collagen	1260–1230 B.C. (p = 0.01) 1220–780 B.C. (p = 0.944)	Landals 1993:181; Morlan n.d.
DjPm 116 [AECV-1228C]	2750 +/- 160	-18.5‰	collagen	1400–500 B.C. (p = 0.954)	Landals 1993:154; Morlan n.d.
DjPm 116 [AECV-869C]	2720 +/- 110	-18.5‰	collagen	1250–500 B.C. (p = 0.954)	Landals 1991b; Morlan n.d.
DjPm 116 [AECV-868C]	2650 +/- 140	-22.2‰	collagen	1200–400 B.C. (p = 0.954)	Landals 1993:217; Morlan n.d.
DjPm 116 [AECV-1229C]	2630 +/- 120	-18.3‰	collagen	1050–400 B.C. (p – 0.954)	Landals 1993:123; Morlan n.d.
DjPm 116 [AECV-1230C]	2590 +/- 90	-17.4‰	collagen	910–480 B.C. (p = 0.909) 470–410 B.C. (p = 0.045)	Landals 1993:181; Morlan n.d.
DjPm 116 [AECV-1236C]	2560 +/- 110	-18.7‰	collagen	910–400 B.C. (p = 0.954)	Landals 1993:164; Morlan n.d.
DjPm 116 [AECV-1234C]	2540 +/- 100	-18.3‰	collagen	850–400 B.C. (p = 0.954)	Landals 1993:181; Morlan n.d.
DjPm 116 [AECV-1231C]	2510 +/- 90	-18.4‰	collagen	810–400 B.C. (p = 0.954)	Landals 1993:217; Morlan n.d.
DjPm 116 [AECV-1237C]	2460 +/- 110	-18.1‰	collagen	850–350 B.C. (p = 0.954)	Landals 1993:164; Morlan n.d.
DjPm 116 [AECV-1235C]	2370 +/- 90	-16.3‰	collagen	800–200 B.C. (p = 0.954)	Landals 1993:181; Morlan n.d.
DjPm 116 [AECV-867C]	2290+/- 100	-17.9‰	collagen	800–50 B.C. (p = 0.954)	Landals 1993:217; Morlan n.d.
DjPm 116 [AECV-344C]	2300 +/- 110	-20.0‰	collagen	800–50 B.C. (p = 0.954)	Morlan n.d.
DjPm 116 [AECV-343C]	2020 +/- 160	-20.0‰	collagen	400 B.C.–A.D. 350 (p = 0.954)	Morlan n.d.
DjPm 116 [AECV-347C]	1980 +/- 180	-20.0‰	collagen	400 B.C.–A.D. 450 (p = 0.954)	Morlan n.d.
DjPm 116 [AECV-342C]	Modern			rejected	Morlan n.d.

Smythe (DjPm 116). The Smythe site is multicomponent bison jump site in the Oldman River Dam area. Named after the landowners, the site was formerly on a low terrace on the south side of the Crowsnest River, just upstream from its confluence with the North Fork of the Oldman River (Landals 1993:69). A bone bed, processing area, and campsite were identified. Campsite remains were in the west on a mid-level terrace, while kill deposits and processing area were located in the east at the toe of the slope (Landals 1993:69). The site was excavated between 1988 and 1990. A total of 276 m^2, in thirteen different blocks (labelled A through M), was excavated (Landals 1993:75). Discrete events were not discernable.

One hundred forty Bracken points were recovered in association with numerous kill, processing, and campsite deposits (Landals 1993:75). Although some of the points exhibited morphological affinities to Besant or Sandy Creek, Landals (1993:221) noted that they were recovered immediately adjacent to unmistakable corner-notched points. Other tools recovered included bifaces (n=29), end scrapers (n=35), marginally retouched tools (n=35), and cores (n=11). Lithic debitage (n=1,072) was also recovered. Many lithic raw materials came from the west, including Kootenay argillite, Top-of-the-World chert, and Etherington chert. The faunal assemblage consisted of numerous bones or bone fragments (n=227,157). The minimum number of bison killed at the jump was estimated at 1,200 to 1,600 animals (Landals 1993:219). An analysis of sex indicated comparable numbers of male and female bison. The researchers suggested that a late summer event during the rut was likely (Landals 1993:215).

Nineteen radiocarbon dates suggested the major period of use of the site was between 2,800 and 2,200 BP. The earliest date is ca. 3,000 BP (AECV-345C) and the most recent is ca. 2,000 BP (AECV-347C). One sample (AECV-342C) produced a date that was modern, while a second sample failed to produce a date; these samples were rejected.

Calderwood Buffalo Jump (DkPj 27). The Calderwood Buffalo Jump is a bison jump and kill site located on the southeastern edge of the Porcupine Hills about 20 km west of Fort Macleod (Marshall 1988). Head-Smashed-In Buffalo Jump is about 1 km south of the site, sharing the same sandstone outcrop of the Porcupine Hills (Brink et al. 1987:60; Marshall 1988). The Calderwood site was named after the landowners (Marshall 1988:42). Preliminary tests of two 1-m^2 units were conducted in 1985. In 1986, six 1-m^2 units were placed along a north–south baseline to determine the placement of fifteen contiguous 1-m² units (Brink et al. 1987:63; Marshall 1988:43–48). Deposits at the base of the jump consisted of four bone layers; the lower three were heavily burned, and separated by layers of sandy silt (Brink et al. 1987:66). Examples of Bracken points were recovered in Levels VI (n=3) and V (n=7). Level VI was interpreted as a sterile level, but Level V was a bone bed with dates of ca. 1,900 BP and 2,200 BP (Table 20). Initial analysis suggested that the site was used at least four times as a bison jump (Brink et al. 1987:75). In contrast, soil chemical tests suggested that the site may reflect a more continuous rather than episodic use (Dormaar and Beaudoin 1991).

Second Lake (EhPv 58). The Second Lake site was briefly described above in the section on the McKean complex. Occupation 4 was a campsite assemblage. Four Bracken projectile points were associated with a hearth and a small cultural assemblage of about one hundred artifacts (Fedje 1986:51). The faunal assemblage included bison, goat, and sheep (Fedje 1986:51). A slab-lined hearth produced charcoal. Two dates of ca. 2,800 BP and 2,500 BP were obtained for the site (Table 20). The mean date was 2,735 +/- 110 BP (Fedje 1986:53). The disparate dates may be explained by independent occupations on a stable land surface.

Cattle Baron (EcPn 2). The Cattle Baron site is a campsite on a terrace above Pekisko Creek, located a few kilometres south of Longview (Wilson 1977:32). The site name is stated to reflect, "the pride of southern Albertans in their ranching heritage, and the rich history of large-scale ranching in the foothills west of High River" (Wilson 1977:32). A total of 21 m² was excavated in 1975. The site was excavated to mitigate road construction (Wilson 1977:1–3).

Eight Bracken points/point fragments were recovered. Importantly, a careful analysis led the excavator to horizontally differentiate a Pelican Lake (i.e., Bracken) component from an Old Women's component (Wilson 1977:62–90). The Bracken points appeared to be associated with five FBR concentrations; three FBR concentrations are associated with shallow basins and two are associated with post-moulds (Wilson 1977:90–93). A single radiocarbon date of ca. 2,500 BP was obtained for bone associated with the Bracken material supporting the interpretation (Brumley and Rushworth 1983).

Boyd (EdPn 8). The Boyd site is a stone circle site located on a very high terrace on the north edge of the Highwood River valley just south of Longview (Wilson 1977:250). The site was named for the landowners (Wilson 1977:250). In 1975, 30 m² of excavation were conducted (Wilson 1977:252). The site was mitigated for highway construction.

Stone Circle 1 contained a slightly off-center concentration of FBR and a subtle soil stain, suggesting a small hearth. A second FBR concentration along the southwest wall appears to have been a dump. A single point body fragment of Knife River flint was recovered from the FBR dump pile. A rib fragment was also recovered. Stone Circle 2 had a central FBR cluster with slight staining, suggesting a hearth. A second FBR cluster just outside the circle to the north suggested a second hearth while two remaining FBR clusters were associated with the stone circle walls. A single fragmentary Bracken point was recovered (Wilson 1977:269). Stone Circle 3 contained a scatter of FBR but no concentrations suggesting any features (Wilson 1977:270).

The researcher suggested the spacing of the stone circles, lack of "ring rock cannibalism," and the light scattering of artifacts support a single occupation (Wilson 1977:275). A single radiocarbon date of ca. 2,400 BP (Table 20) supports a Bracken occupation (Brumley and Rushworth 1983).

EbPk 19. EbPk 19 is a stratified campsite next to a spring-fed stream in a tributary coulee on the west side of Pine Coulee (Brewer et al. 1995:142). A total of 21 m² of test excavation units were placed at the site. Ultimately, the site was not impacted by the Pine Coulee Reservoir and work beyond the testing phase was not conducted. In Test Unit 8, six cultural occupations were observed. Occupation 4 (120–150 cm BS) produced 980 artifacts within a 1-×-2-m area. A corner-notched point base was recovered along with two cores and twenty-three pieces of lithic debitage. As well, 954 bone fragments were recovered from this occupation. Most of the faunal assemblage was recovered from a small, irregularly shaped hearth feature. The hearth was about 25 cm north–south by 20 cm east–west. It contained FBR (n = 10), concentrations of burned and calcine bone, some lithic debitage, and the point base. The identifiable faunal material was bison, and an MNI of two was determined using metatarsals. Two radiocarbon dates were obtained from this site, ca. 2,600 BP and 2,500 BP (Table 20). The excavators concluded the corner-notched point was likely Pelican Lake (i.e., Bracken) based on the radiocarbon dates (Brewer et al. 1995:171).

Bow Bottom (EfPm 104). The Bow Bottom site is a stone circle campsite on a 7-metre-high terrace of the Bow River, in Calgary (Van Dyke 1982; Ronaghan and Landals 1983). In 1980, the site excavation included excavation of 200 m^2 at twelve of fourteen stone circles (Van Dyke 1982:ii). In 1981/82, an additional 113 m^2 were excavated at four stone circles and six external features (Ronaghan and Landals 1983). Between the two projects, sixteen stone circles were completely or partially excavated. All but one stone circle (Ring 10) had internal, ringed hearths and were associated with the same buried soil at a depth of about 40 cm BS. The earlier study found most of the rings aligned in a row with the north bank of the Bow River, while the subsequent study found additional rings following the same pattern immediately to the southeast. Following mitigation, the site was used for a transportation utility corridor and a subdivision.

During the initial mitigative excavations in 1980, thirty-nine points were recovered in association with twelve rings and two midden features. The researchers considered most of the points to be Pelican Lake (n = 16) but recognized a few Besant points (n = 4), some flake points (n = 6), a Samantha point, a preform, and a number of non-diagnostic points (n = 11). Other tools recovered included bifaces (n = 16), oval end scrapers (n = 25), a rectangular end scraper, side scrapers (n = 17), retouched flakes (n = 229), cores (n = 89), choppers (n = 13), and hammerstones (n = 2). The lithic assemblage was largely local with split pebble chert flakes representing 37.2 percent of the tool assemblage (Ronaghan and Landals 1983:iv). No fauna was reported within the rings. Fauna was only mentioned in passing concerning inter-ring midden Features 3 and 4. However, a winter occupation was inferred from the central hearths and the lack of fauna within the rings. Ring 1 had a ringed hearth that was slab-lined. Large amounts of FBR were recovered within the rings but it is not clear whether these are spalled hearth stones or rocks cracked from immersion in water. No boiling pits were observed. Two radiocarbon dates were obtained from these excavations ca. 2,500 BP and 2,300 BP. With the exception of overlain Ring 10, the researchers noted, "the evidence strongly suggests that the site represents a distinctive seasonal/functional variant of the Pelican Lake [Bracken] phase occupied sometime between 2,300 and 2,500 years ago" (Van Dyke 1982:x).

Mitigative excavations in 1981/82 produced similar material from four stone circles and six external features. Fourteen points were recovered, including Pelican Lake (n = 3), Kootenay side-notched (n = 3), triangular (n = 1), flake point (n = 2), small trianguloid (n = 1), preform (n = 1) and point fragments (n = 4). Other tools recovered include bifaces (n = 7), end scrapers (n = 7), side scrapers (n = 2), scraper fragments (n = 3), unifacial cutting tools (n = 3), wedges (n = 6), retouched/utilized flakes (n = 94), choppers (n = 2), large flake/cobble spall tools (n = 16), split pebble cores (n = 17), cores (n = 50), and enigmatic elongate pebbles (n = 21). The lithic assemblage was much like that recovered from the earlier excavations; it emphasised local materials and split pebble technology. The faunal assemblage was weathered although a bison and a deer were recovered. The researchers suggested that the lack of burned or calcine bone indicated that bone boiling and degreasing activities were not practiced (Ronaghan and Landals 1983:169–170). Regarding the stone circles, Ring 15 exhibited a bone upright consisting of a humerus, stood on end in an excavated pit and interpreted as an anvil. As well, a post-mould northeast of the hearth may represent a tie-down stake of the tipi (Ronaghan and Landals 1983:54, 206, fig. 30). Ring 17 exhibited a central hearth as well as an additional hearth along the northwest wall of the ring. This hearth was atypical in that it was dug down 29 cm into the floor and lined with large, flat, slab-like rocks. A piece of wood was recovered from this feature and dated (Ronaghan and Landals 1983:59). Six features were recorded external to the stone circles. These were concentrations of FBR and charcoal interpreted as hearths (Ronaghan and Landals 1983:62). Three radiocarbon dates were obtained from these excavations: 2,600 BP from the hearth in Ring 15; 690 BP on unburned wood from a secondary hearth in Ring 17; and 2,300 BP on charcoal from external hearth Feature 9 (Ronaghan and Landals 1983). The recent date from Ring 17 was rejected because it did not reflect the associated material (Ronaghan and Landals 1983:59). Ronaghan and Landals (1983:87) concluded that the site is a winter occupation that "appears to represent a distinctive variant of Pelican Lake with influence from the mountains." In a postscript, the authors considered that the assemblage might represent Sandy Creek material (transitional between Pelican Lake and Besant) (Ronaghan and Landals 1983:91–92). This text considers the Bow Bottom site to represent a Bracken campsite.

EgPn 362. EgPn 362 is a bison kill and processing site located on a north-facing, moderately sloping surface on the Paskapoo Slopes in Calgary (Vivian et al. 2003a). In 2000, a single cultural deposit (30–65 cm BS) was excavated (155 m^2), concentrating in three areas: the main bone bed, an unusual pit feature, and a processing area. The excavations mitigated a sewer right-of-way; portions of the site still remain intact.

Thirty-seven points or point fragments were recovered, including thirty Pelican Lake (i.e., Bracken) points and seven points too fragmentary to be classified. The researchers argued that there were two subgroups of points within the sample, based on raw material and manufacturing technique. They suggested that nine of the points made on siliceous siltstone were made using one manufacturing sequence, while six points made on heat-treated Swan River chert were manufactured using a different sequence. They also suggested that family and social ties explain both the similarities and differences between the points (Vivian et al. 2003a:50). Other lithic tools recovered at EgPn 362 included bifaces (n = 2), end scrapers (n = 7), side scrapers (n = 2), and a retouched flake (n = 1). The entire lithic assemblage consisted of only sixty-seven items with the majority made of siliceous siltstone (n = 23) and quartzite (n = 21) (Vivian et al. 2003a:48). The predominance of formed tools suggested little tool manufacturing or maintenance was conducted at the kill site (Vivian et al. 2003a:49). All but one end scraper was from the processing area. Chopping tools and bifacial knives were notably rare or absent, although large rocks in the kill area may have served as anvils (Vivian et al. 2003a:49, 60). A single bone tool may be represented by a split long bone with a well-rounded and polished tip, likely used in skinning or hide removal (Vivian et al. 2003a:48). In addition, a shell fragment of fossil freshwater clam was also recovered in the processing area adjacent to the primary kill; the researchers noted similar fossils used in beads found at sites in the area (Vivian et al. 2003a:48).

The faunal assemblage (n = 72,884) consisted almost entirely of bison. A minimum of 145 bison was killed at the site. Other species recovered included wolf, mule deer, muskrat, rabbit and a few species of bird, possibly crane and grouse (Vivian et al. 2003a:53–54). An analysis of sex suggested females (n = 50) were slightly more prevalent than males (n = 39). Fetal remains were absent from the site, although these may have been selectively removed from the kill area or differentially preserved (Vivian et al. 2003a:58). Still, the co-occurrence of males and females and the absence of fetal bone suggested a late summer/early fall kill during the rut. The bone elements in the kill itself do not appear to have been sorted, suggesting "an aggressive selective strategy was pursued; one focused on procuring skulls, hides, and muscle mass — a selective gourmet strategy" (Vivian et al. 2003:74). A single radiocarbon date of roughly 2,400 BP was obtained (Vivian et al. 2003a:30). This date supports a Bracken phase affiliation.

Two distinct activity areas were revealed in the excavations. The main excavation block exposed the bone bed of a primary kill event. Animals appeared to have been butchered around the perimeter of a pound enclosure with a refuse pile in the middle. Although no post-moulds were found, a pit feature at the base of a steep slope and just uphill from the bone bed was interpreted as a gate or trap entrance to a pound (Vivian et al. 2003a:75). The bone distribution suggested an oval area of 16 × 21 m for the pound, consistent with the size of known historical pound structures (Vivian et al. 2003a:76). Presumably brush interwoven into standing trees was used to create the pound structure. A second activity area contained highly fragmented bone and quantities of FBR. Spiral fractures on the bone were interpreted as evidence of marrow procurement. Also, large numbers of scrapers and the absence of points were interpreted as evidence for hide working. In sum, the site is a Bracken pound and kill site with a hide-working activity area on the site's eastern margin. Based on point similarity and age it may have cultural links to EgPn 598, just down slope (see below).

EgPn 598. EgPn 598 is a campsite/bison processing area on a wide bench about halfway down the Paskapoo Slopes in Calgary (Vivian et al. 2003a:232). A single cultural horizon was observed at the base of the Ah Horizon (Vivian et al. 2003a:233). In 2000, a 60-m² block was excavated to mitigate a sewer right-of-way. The site is large, ca. 40 × 40 m, with substantial portions remaining intact.

Eight points were recovered, including six Pelican Lake (i.e., Bracken) points and two indeterminate base fragments (Vivian et al. 2003a:234–237). The points were found in association with a hearth, an FBR concentration, and a scatter of bone. Other lithic tools recovered include bifaces (n = 4), end scrapers (n = 6), side scrapers (n = 15), drills (n = 2), spokeshaves (n = 4), wedges (n = 4), retouched flakes (n = 24), utilized flakes (n = 15), a unifacial tool (n = 1), a core (n = 1), an abrader (n = 1), hammerstones (n = 2), and an anvil (n = 1). A single bone bead made on fetal or neonatal bone was also recovered (Vivian et al. 2003a:258). The assemblage largely consisted of quartzite with a strong representation of basalt. As well, exotic materials appeared more common in this site than other sites in the area (Vivian et al. 2003a:259). Late-stage tool manufacturing and rejuvenation are mainly represented in the debitage.

The faunal assemblage (n = 3,692) consisted mainly of bison. A minimum of three bison was present, based on left distal humeri and left distal metacarpals. Numerous fetal bones (i.e., humeri, scapulae, and long bones) were recovered, suggesting a late winter/early spring event (Vivian et al. 2003a:262). Four canid bones were also recovered. Based on size, they likely represent mature wolf. The frequency of elements at the site suggested that it is a secondary processing locale to which specific items were brought from a nearby kill. Spiral fractures on bison long bones indicate marrow extraction (Vivian et al. 2003a:264). A concentration of FBR (n = 44) and a reddened soil were interpreted as a hearth; it was associated with burned fragments of bone (n = 97). A second concentration of FBR (n = 134) and bone (n = 198) did not exhibit any evidence of burning; the concentration was interpreted as a refuse pit (Vivian et al. 2003a:265)

A single radiocarbon date of ca. 2,300 BP was obtained for the site (Table 20). When the site was initially discovered, the amount of FBR and bone suggested that it was a processing camp. However, the range and diversity of tools suggest a camp used over a period of time. In summary, the researchers argued that this was a Pelican Lake (i.e., Bracken) campsite/processing site in which the spatial organization of activities was evident in the distribution of the stone tools. Projectile points, bifaces, scrapers, and drills were concentrated around a hearth and refuse pile for retooling. Scrapers, spokeshaves, and retouched and utilized flakes were common on the east side of the excavation and were strongly tied to secondary processing activities such as hide, wood, and bone working. In short, knapping activities were kept separate from intensive processing activities (Vivian et al. 2003a:266). As noted above, a Pelican Lake (i.e., Bracken) kill site of the same age, EgPn 362, was located just upslope from this site; the degree to which the sites are related cannot be determined, but they are roughly contemporary and complementary (Vivian et al. 2003a:266–267).

DjPm 114. DjPm 114 is a small multicomponent campsite on a 10-metre-high bench on the south side of the Crowsnest River, near its confluence with the North Fork of the Oldman River. Eastern (25 m^2) and western (23 m^2) excavation blocks were opened. In the western block, below a Late Prehistoric period component at 40–60 cm BS, was a Bracken component. The excavations were part of mitigative action associated with the Oldman Dam Reservoir project.

Four projectile points were recovered in association with a scatter of bone and FBR (Landals 1993:21). A barbed Pelican Lake point, a typical Bracken point, a blade fragment, and a tip were recovered. Other recovered tools include bifaces (n = 2), an end scraper, retouched tools (n = 3), and cores (n = 2). Etherington chert and quartzite dominated the small debitage assemblage while tools were largely manufactured on more fine-grained materials such as cherts. The faunal assemblage was mainly bison, with two fragments from small ungulates, a phalanx identifiable as small mammal, and a fox scapula (Landals 1993:139). A minimum of two bison was represented. Burned and calcine bone was rare; no hearth was recorded.

A single date was obtained of roughly 2,000 BP (Table 20). Landals (1993:137) suggested that the barbed point indicated links to the mountains and interior British Columbia, but considered the remaining points more typical of Pelican Lake (i.e., Bracken) points. The site was considered a Bracken campsite of limited size (Landals 1993:139). Alternatively, the barbed point conforms to the barbed Pelican Lake material, and site mixing or formation may have obscured its slightly older age.

DjPf 83. DjPf 83 is a buried campsite located on a terrace 60 m above the St. Mary River, north of Magrath (Ronaghan and Reeves 1980:10). The site is buried beneath about 1.5 m of sediment and is laterally continuous for 160 m. In 1980, 16 m^2 were excavated to mitigate placement of transmission line poles. A single Pelican Lake (i.e., Bracken) point was found in association with a hearth, differentially distributed artifacts, FBR, and macerated bison bone, representing activity areas. Other lithic tools recovered included bifaces (n = 2), end scrapers (n = 3), pièce esquillées (n = 1), retouched flakes (n = 25), and cores/choppers (n = 5). The tools were made on fine materials such as Avon chert, Knife River flint, green argillite pebbles, and miscellaneous cherts while the debitage was largely reduced from local quartzite and argillite cobbles (Ronaghan and Reeves 1980:14–15).

The faunal assemblage was mainly identified as bison (MNI = 3), with fetal long bones suggesting a late winter/early spring occupation (Ronaghan and Reeves 1980:11). Bison elements were heavily processed for marrow but lacked cut marks. Other fauna included a rib of an upland game bird, long bone fragments of a small unidentifiable ungulate (likely deer or antelope), and a mandible from a fish. The hearth was 100 cm in diameter and contained a surface cluster of FBR, charcoal and burned bone. A single radiocarbon date of ca. 2,100 BP was obtained for the site (Table 20), which has all the characteristics of a large winter campsite of the Bracken phase (Ronaghan and Reeves 1980:16–17).

Joffre (FbPj 8). The Joffre site is a stone circle campsite on an 8-metre-high terrace of the Red Deer River, about 12 km lower than the city of Red Deer (Smith and Reeves 1978). Based on a surface survey, sixteen 2-×-2-m test units were excavated across the terrace (Smith and Reeves (1978:9). A single cultural bearing Ah black soil was observed at 25–50 cm BS. The recovery of a Pelican Lake (i.e., Bracken) point led to four additional 2-×-2-m units. The productive nature of these tests led to an additional thirty-three 2-×-2-m test units, excavated in a block. The site was impacted by a water intake settling pond and related features (Smith and Reeves 1978).

Five corner-notched points/point fragments and an unidentifiable tip were recovered in association with a living floor, a stone circle and hearth, and a hearth/FBR concentration (Smith and Reeves 1978:14–16). A possible Sandy Creek point was also recovered with this material but was interpreted as a knife (Smith and Reeves 1978:23). Other tools included asymmetrical ovate bifaces (n = 7), end scrapers (n = 2), side scrapers (n = 2), gravers (n = 3), pièce esquillée (n = 3), retouched flakes and/or utilized flakes (n = 15), choppers (n = 10), spalls (n = 6), utilized cobbles (n = 4), hammerstones (n = 3), pecked or ground tools (n = 8), and a sandstone abrading tool (Smith and Reeves 1978:23–32). The lithic assemblage consisted mainly of two local sources: quartzite and Paskapoo chert (silicified limestone). Three bone tools were recovered: a pelvic gouging tool, a long bone compressor, and a rib shaft straightener (Smith and Reeves 1978:32–33).

The faunal assemblage was limited and poorly preserved. A minimum of four bison and two deer was represented. As expected from a faunal assemblage associated with a campsite, heavy, non-meaty bones are largely absent (Smith and Reeves 1978:20). A single weathered ungulate fetal bone suggested a winter occupation (Smith and Reeves 1978:17).

A single stone circle was uncovered. The stone circle consisted of sandstone slabs in a single row with rocks more tightly spaced in the south and west, presumably to protect from westerly winds (Smith and Reeves 1978:14). In the centre of the circle was an FBR scatter about 60 cm in diameter, presumably the remains of a hearth. A second hearth/FBR scatter was 7 m east of the circle. Neither hearth contained ash or charcoal (Smith and Reeves 1978:14). All the projectile points were recovered from the nine 2-×-2-m units around the stone circle (Smith and Reeves 1978:15). A single radiocarbon date of ca. 1,200 BP (Table 20) was obtained from a composite bone sample (Smith and Reeves 1978:13). The researchers rejected this date as it contradicted the age suggested by the recovered diagnostic point (Smith and Reeves 1978:13). The site appears to be a large Bracken winter campsite along the Red Deer River.

EgPn 430, Area Three. EgPn 430 is large multicomponent bison kill site, processing site, and campsite on the northwest slope of the Paskapoo Escarpment in west Calgary (Vivian et al. 2005, vol. 1:1). Six areas were defined in this site with Area Three representing a Bracken kill site. Some mixing of subsequent occupations occurred, with items being sorted by mass and weight (Vivian et al. 2005, vol. 1:5–6). A block excavation of 44 m^2 was conducted prior to subdivision development (Vivian et al. 2005, vol. 1:49).

Fourteen "Pelican Lake" points were recovered in association with the bone bed, along with a McKean Lanceolate point, four Late Side-notched points, and five non-diagnostic point fragments (Vivian et al. 2005, vol. 1:50–58). Other tools recovered included bifaces, a bifacial knife, an end scraper, a side scraper, a wedge, retouch flakes, a utilized spall, and two cores (Vivian et al. 2005, vol. 1:58–63). Bone tools recovered included awls, a scraper, and a wedge (Vivian et al. 2005, vol. 1:63–64). The lithic assemblage was mainly composed of local lithics, with some exotics. It was considered comparable to other Pelican Lake (i.e., Bracken) assemblages (Vivian et al. 2005, vol. 1:64).

The faunal assemblage consisted mainly of bison (MNI = 45) but also included wolf, coyote, mule deer, rabbit, and grouse (Vivian et al. 2005, vol. 1:68–69). A single immature bison was recovered although no evidence for fetal animals was observed (Vivian et al. 2005, vol. 1:70). Primarily low-utility elements were recovered. The excavators suggested a summer or early fall kill based on the lack of young bison and a fairly even male/female herd composition (Vivian et al. 2005, vol. 1:71). A radiocarbon date was obtained from the bone bed of ca. 2,600 BP (Table 20).

The excavators argued that EgPn 430, Area Three, represented a single-component kill site (Vivian et al. 2005, vol. 1:89). The recovery of many Pelican Lake (i.e., Bracken) points and an appropriate radiocarbon date testified to the integrity of the deposits, while the recovery of a few other diagnostic points was considered to illustrate only minor mixing (Vivian et al. 2005, vol. 1:93).

Other sites. There are other sites in Alberta that have produced Bracken material but lack dates or good context. For example, DjPo 46 is a multicomponent site within the town of Bellevue in the Crowsnest Valley (Reeves 1977a). Occupations 2 and 3 were interpreted as Pelican Lake (i.e., Bracken) occupations. These levels were overlaid by a Besant occupation and underlain by an occupation lacking diagnostic material. Both Occupations 2 and 3 produced Pelican Lake (i.e. Bracken) points, with Occupation 2 also producing a buried stone circle (Reeves 1977a:24). Unfortunately, stratigraphic separation of specific cultural entities did not appear to be discrete at this site.

Somewhat surprisingly, the Majorville Medicine Wheel may not exhibit any Bracken points (Calder 1977:249, fig. 32). The barbed Pelican Lake points are present in very low numbers (Calder 1977, fig. 32, nos. 7 and 8), and it is difficult to determine if any of the remaining points are Bracken points, especially without good context. It is possible that the people who produced the Bracken phase did not use the cairn (Calder 1977:202–203). Although a thorough analysis of British Block Cairn (EdOp 1) has never been conducted, Forbis (1970:30–31, Wormington and Forbis 1965:122) mention Oxbow, McKean, and Late points being recovered from the excavations, but not "Pelican Lake" points. It is possible that during the Bracken phase, a shift in spirituality, as witnessed in the apparent increase in subsurface interments, allowed the major cairns to fall into disuse for a period of time.

EdOq 17 is a large cairn on a prominent hilltop in the central part of the Canadian Forces Base Suffield (Brumley 1972:36). of which the west half was excavated, producing a number of tools and debitage as well as a Pelican Lake (i.e., Bracken) projectile point (Brumley 1972:36).

EgPn 343 is a small Pelican Lake winter campsite located adjacent to a large ravine on the Paskapoo Slopes in Calgary (Vivian et al. 2003a). A total of 14 m^2 was excavated at the site, resulting in the recovery of 286 stone artifacts, including two Pelican Lake (i.e., Bracken) dart points, a broken biface knife, scrapers, wedges, and a spokeshave. Interestingly, obsidian and other toolstones from the Montana Rockies were present. Highly fragmented bison bone (n = 1,075), including a fetal bison metapodial that suggests a winter occupation, was recovered (Vivian et al. 2003a). A hearth was identified with FBR, and all of the formed tools were in close proximity to the hearth. The excavators interpreted the material as representing a single lodge.

Component 2 at EgPn 230 produced seven Pelican Lake (i.e., Bracken) points (Vivian et al. 1998). Dyck and Morlan (1995:379) call this particular morphological expression Bratton, but the specimens fall within a continuum of degrading Pelican Lake forms that slowly deviate from the original corner-notched form. EgPn 230 appears to be a kill/processing site (Vivian et al. 1998:26).

DjPm 228 is an exposed site located on the high, relict landform of Horseshoe Canyon, now inundated behind the Oldman River Dam (Van Dyke 1994:259–268). A Pelican Lake (i.e., Bracken) occupation was uncovered yielding Pelican Lake (i.e., Bracken) projectile point specimens (n=6), bifaces (n=15), end scrapers (n=11), unifaces (n=7), a spokeshave, a drill, core tools (n=36), a hammerstone, elongate pebbles (n=2), and retouched flakes (n=60). Substantial amounts of bone and FBR were also recovered. However, one Duncan, one Samantha, and four Late Side-notched points were also recovered in the same deposits. Two radiocarbon dates supported the Bracken phase assignment: 2,480 +/- 100 BP (AECV-772C) and 2,530 +/- 90 BP (AECV-768C) (Van Dyke 1994:267).

Lastly, DjPm 93 is a buried multicomponent campsite along the Crowsnest River at Warriner's Coulee (Van Dyke et al. 1990:360–380). In Cultural Level 4, two Pelican Lake (i.e., Bracken) points were recovered in association with part of a stone circle and two radiocarbon dates: 2,510 +/- 90 BP (AECV-755C) and 2,520 +/- 110 BP (AECV-766C) (Van Dyke et al. 1990:379). A second Pelican Lake (i.e., Bracken) occupation overlies the aforementioned occupation.

Bracken: Industrializing Bison Procurement and Mobilizing a Workforce

The Bracken phase can be identified by its diagnostic point: the Bracken point. This phase is similar to Reeves' (1983a) Mortlach subphase of the Pelican Lake phase, although he included barbed Pelican Lake material in his definition. The Bracken point, a merger of Kehoe's (1974) Bracken and Danker points, can be identified by a straight to usually convex basal edge, open notches that tend to be up-sloping such that there is little barbedness in the shoulders, and a broad body and neck. Based on the radiocarbon dates presented above, the Bracken phase begins as early as 2,800 BP and lasts until as late as 2,100 BP. Subjectively, the Bracken points, during their approximately 700-year existence, initially exhibit a very rough similarity to barbed Pelican Lake points but through time look increasingly like Besant points (see also Kehoe 1974:111).

In terms of the tool assemblage, bifaces, end scrapers, side scrapers, and retouched flakes are common, while utilized flakes occur infrequently. Pentagonal drills are noted. Flake points are rare. With regards to bone tools, a possible shaft wrench was recovered and a bone bead was noted. Likely owing to the commencement of mass bison kills, choppers and hammerstones occur more frequently in the lithic assemblages. The lithic raw materials show a clear dependence on quartzite, basalt, siltstone, pebble chert, and miscellaneous cherts. Exotic materials such as Knife River flint, Avon chert, Montana chert, and obsidian are not common, but definitely present. Material from the mountains was not as prevalent as one would expect. As well, very little petrified wood was used. Some makeshift bone tools, including round-ended ribs, have been recovered and were likely used for removing hides and similar processing activities.

The subsistence pattern continues to reflect a reliance on bison; however, the repeated use of major kill sites appears to begin in earnest during this phase. Head-Smashed-In Buffalo Jump, the (Old) Women's Buffalo Jump, the Smythe site, and various sites on the Paskapoo Slopes exhibit repeated bison drives during this time. This bison utilization pattern is in stark contrast to the previous Pelican Lake complex. The Pelican Lake complex consisted of small campsites, with little evidence of large-scale bison procurement. Both Dyck (1983:107) and Wormington and Forbis (1965) partially grappled with Pelican Lake as potent communal hunters. This text strongly supports the notion that in Alberta, Bracken hunters provide the earliest evidence for the repeated use of key locations of mass bison pounds and jumps. In fact, the deterioration of Pelican Lake craftsmanship and form from the barbed Pelican Lake form through to the end of the Bracken phase (assuming continuity) might reflect the ease of mass kills versus the skill of stalking and killing individual prey. The former only required the hunter to pierce the hide and impact a key organ in the already impounded bison, while the latter required a deadly, accurate shot with a projectile that would pierce and bleed the prey, cutting apart the bison from the inside during the beast's attempt at flight. Besides bison, deer were the next most frequently taken animal by Bracken hunters.

Numerous features were recovered from the Bracken sites. Surface hearths were common although a couple sites exhibited slab-lined hearths. FBR, suggesting processing of some kind, was recovered in quantities at most of the sites listed. The associated pits for stone boiling have not been excavated.

An apparent innovation of the Bracken phase is the development of the tipi. Previous cultural periods have yielded stone circles but the Bracken phase produced evidence for internal hearths associated with tie-down stakes. The tie-down stake is crucial as an anchor for providing stability to the tipi. The three or four main support poles for a tipi are knotted together and then staked securely to the ground within the tipi. In this manner it anchors the main structure of the tipi against the elements. Moreover, the Bracken phase also exhibits the earliest evidence of large campsites. Bow Bottom represents the encampment of a large number of people together over the winter months. Similarly, DjPf 83 and Joffre will likely provide evidence of similar encampments upon further excavation. The ability to keep a large number of people together for lengths of time on the Plains is important. Large encampments are required to conduct large bison kills, but they also provide time for development of social activities, societies, and courtship. As well, large social groups are in a better position to protect a population and its territory from neighbours in an ever increasingly populated Northern Plains (see also Walde 2006b).

The Bracken phase is not restricted to Alberta. It can be found in southern Saskatchewan (but not southern Manitoba) and northern Montana. In Saskatchewan, the Walter Felt (EcNm 8) site provided the current name for the phase and point form: Bracken (Kehoe 1974:111). As alluded to above, Kehoe's (1974) Danker Shouldered (straight-based) variety of Pelican Lake point only differs from the Bracken Shouldered (convex-base) variety by having a straight rather than a convex base. Kehoe's (1974:111) Bracken points were not recovered at the Walter Felt site but Danker points were, in Level 15a. In this text, Bracken and Danker, despite their different basal edges, are considered Bracken points. Level 15a overlies Sandy Creek material dated to ca. 2,500 BP and underlies Sonota material dated to ca. 1,600 BP (see Kehoe 1974).

Newo Asiniak (FbNp 16) is a multicomponent site in Wanuskewin Park, just north of Saskatoon. Level 4 produced a Bracken point, although the researcher labelled it a Besant series point. The layer was associated with a date of 3,025 +/- 250 BP (S-2764) (Kelly 1986:156–170). This date is early for Bracken material. Interestingly, a barbed Pelican Lake point was found in the overlying layer (Kelly 1986, fig. 21, upper right). It is seems possible that some disturbance may have occurred at the site.

The Sjovold site (EiNs 4) produced a few levels attributable to the Bracken phase. Layer X produced thirty-nine tools and twelve features (Dyck and

Morlan 1995:333–362). Dyck and Morlan (1995:351) suggested that the side-notched specimens were likely Besant while the corner-notched points were Pelican Lake, making the assemblage a mixture of archaeological cultures. For this text, the specimens are all considered to fall within the range of variation for Bracken points. Layer X also produced three radiocarbon dates: 2,170 +/- 165 BP (S-1767); 2,340 +/- 120 BP (S-3367); and 2,190 +/- 140 BP (S-3366). Layer XI produced two points morphologically identical to side-notched specimens in Layer X (Dyck and Morlan 1995, fig. 15.6a and c compared to fig. 14.8a and e). The researchers called the points Bratton points, but for this review the material falls within the range of variation of the Bracken point type. (For a complete discussion of the Bratton point see Dyck and Morlan 1995:378–379.) The layer was radiocarbon dated to 2,585 +/- 90 BP (S-2058).

The Bracken Cairn (DhOb 3) derives its name from the nearby town of Bracken in southwestern Saskatchewan. The site is a burial in hill country overlooking the Frenchman River valley (E. Walker 1982:8). The burial consists of a least five individuals within a pit: three mature and two immature individuals. The pit was then covered with earth and the surface stained with red ochre. The entire burial was overlaid with boulders to form a rough 3-m diameter cairn (E. Walker 1982). The skeletons had red ochre on them. A radiocarbon date of 2,465 +/- 85 BP (S-912) was obtained. A single Bracken point was recovered along with a drill, end scrapers (n = 2), large ovate bifaces (n = 7), retouched flakes (n = 6), and a ground-stone pestle. As well, numerous mammalian bones were noted. Some of the bones were drilled for decorative purposes, and others were worked into pseudo-elk teeth (E. Walker 1982:25). A small rolled copper fragment was also recovered. The site was interpreted as the burial of a nuclear family or, more likely, individuals that were bundled and interred at the same time (E. Walker 1982:32). The Bradwell (EkNm 1) site near Bradwell is another possible Bracken burial in which a flexed skeleton, possibly associated with several eagle talons and a scraper, was recovered (Edmunds et al. 1938).

In Montana, Level 3 of the King site produced two Bracken points and the stem fragment of a possible third Bracken point (Brumley and Rennie 1999:48–49, fig. 9, nos. 6, 7, and 8). An associated radiocarbon date of 1,950 +/- 80 BP (Beta-60248) was obtained (Brumley and Rennie 1999:50).

The Keaster (24PH401) site is a multicomponent bison kill site located just south of Fort Belknap Indian Reservation in north-central Montana

(Davis and Stallcop 1965). Four bone layers were observed but few projectile points were found in situ. Most of the points are relatively large, broad points, with straight bases, and relatively deep corner-notches that create rounded barbs. This point style was the diagnostic point for Reeves' (1983a) Keaster subphase of the Pelican Lake phase. Placed side-by-side with Bracken points, a striking difference is noticeable. The Keaster site points have straight basal edges, relatively deep corner notches, slightly barbed shoulders, and relatively broad blades. Level I produced a radiocarbon date of 2,270+/- 95 BP (GX-1194); Level III produced a radiocarbon date of 1,945 +/- 250 BP (W-1366) (Reeves 1983a:259; Morlan n.d.). Despite the chronometric reversal, these dates are roughly coeval at one sigma. To complicate the interpretation, the earliest bone layer, IV, may represent barbed Pelican Lake material, as the points from this level appear to have narrow necks and barbed shoulders (i.e., Davis and Stallcop 1965:11, 102–104, plates 3, 5). Firsthand comparisons would be necessary to confirm this interpretation.

A number of other sites in Montana have produced point assemblages like the Keaster site. Pictograph Cave, Levels I and II, produced Projectile Point Type 5 (Mulloy 1958:33). Reeves (1983a:316) considered the Pictograph Cave material to fall within his Keaster subphase. The Ayers-Frazier (24PE30) bison trap is located in the Lower Yellowstone River drainage in southeastern Montana (Clarke and Wilson 1981). Seven points were recovered. They are similar to the Keaster style of point, exhibiting straight basal edges, relatively deep corner-notches, slightly barbed shoulders, and relatively broad blades. The researchers noted the similarity of their material to the points of Wettlaufer's (1955) Pelican Lake material. They also noted that this term has been applied to most corner-notched material in the general study area (Clarke and Wilson 1981:32; see also Gregg 1986:112). They placed the Ayers-Frazier assemblage in with Reeves' (1983a) Upper Mile subphase, based on the high frequency of porcellanite in the tool assemblage (Clarke and Wilson 1981:34). Based on point morphology, the Keaster and Upper Mile subphases are indistinguishable and could be combined. The Ayers-Frasier site produced a date of 2,180 +/-150 BP (TX-3170). Similarly, the Seline (24DW250) site, a bison kill located near Glendive, east-central Montana, produced Keaster style points (Roll et al. 1994); it was radiocarbon dated to 1,920 +/- 50 BP (Beta-24726) and 2,160 +/- 90 BP (Beta-24725) (Morlan n.d.).

In Wyoming, Pelican Lake-like material of Reeves' (1983a) Spring Creek subphase occurs at Mummy Cave, Layer 30 (Husted and Edgar 2002:202, plate 32a–j), the Kobold site (Frison 1970:10, fig. 9a–e), Daugherty Cave Level 1 (Frison 1968:261, fig. 3a–o) and Wedding of the Waters Cave Level 2 (Frison 1962:248–254, fig. 1c–j). These sites have points with very deep and narrow corner notches, relatively straight basal edges, and straight to excurvate lateral margins, and are somewhat diminutive compared to points of the Keaster subphase immediately to the north (see Reeves 1983a:81–82, fig. 12). In short, they are quite distinct from the Bracken and Keaster points.

The use of the term *Pelican Lake* needs to be reconsidered. Wettlaufer (1955) used it to describe a specific culture and projectile point recovered at the Mortlach site and then the Long Creek site. Reeves (1983a) used the term to define the Pelican Lake phase and Pelican Lake corner-notched point for which he defined several subphases. The corner-notched point was clearly used a horizon marker. Subsequently, few have recognized the micro-stylistic variation within the Pelican Lake corner-notched point horizon. Most researchers have opted to apply the term to any and all corner-notched dart points in the Northwestern Plains (e.g., Clarke and Wilson 1981:32; Gregg 1986:112). The various corner-notched dart forms from geographically distinct parts of the Northwestern Plains could likely trace their origin to a common source in their distant pasts; the notion does not necessarily link them as a single culture. Consequently, continuing to refer to all these archaeological materials under the rubric of "Pelican Lake" is problematic. It is suggested that Reeves' Pelican Lake subphases should be retained as phase names to reflect the differences between the peoples of the corner-notched horizon. Thus, the Keaster subphase would be the Keaster phase, and so forth. The barbed Pelican Lake material, exhibiting possible ties to the Bracken phase, should remain the Pelican Lake phase until more firm relationships between the two archaeological cultures are determined. The term *complex* can be inserted for *phase* when relationships to other cultural materials cannot be determined.

In summary, the Bracken phase occurs between 2,800 and 2,100 BP in southern Alberta, southern Saskatchewan, and northern Montana. The key diagnostic of the phase is the Bracken point. Traditionally, this material, exhibiting corner-notched points, has been lumped in with Pelican Lake materials; however, there are a number of attributes that separate these cultural units. First, the Pelican Lake complex (3,600–2,800 BP) predates the Bracken phase (2,800–2,100 BP). Second, the diagnostic dart points are distinguishable from each other. The Pelican Lake point is barbed and narrow-necked while the Bracken point is broadly corner-notched, wide-necked, and has obtuse shoulders. Third, the people of the Pelican Lake complex stalked bison while Bracken people repeatedly jumped and impounded bison in large numbers. Fourth, Pelican Lake peoples appear to have used tipis, although evidence of tie-down stakes has not been found. Still, small camps of stone circles are known. The Bracken phase exhibits the earliest evidence of tie-down stakes within stone circles strongly suggesting the tipi was being utilized. Perhaps more importantly, tipi camps of fifteen to eighteen contemporaneous lodges are known to exist, indicating large populations were gathering and staying together for lengths of time. This is likely due to the ability to drive bison in large numbers and feed more people at one locale. The issue of cause and affect begs the question of which came first: the need for more people to be together or the need for more food to be produced. Fifth, a Pelican Lake burial system is not known. In contrast, the Bracken phase has produced a small sample of burials that tentatively suggest that (1) burials are often placed in high, prominent spots, usually with a commanding view, often overlooking water, or found on side slopes of small hills and knobs; (2) interment is in small and usually shallow subsurface pits; (3) rock cairns are sometimes placed over the in-filled pits; (4) burials are typically secondary bundle burials but may be primary and, if so, are flexed; (5) often more than one individual is present in a burial pit; (6) red ochre or similar pigment is present, usually both in the pit fill and on the human remains and grave goods; and (7) diverse grave goods are common and typically include a variety of lithic tools, including Pelican Lake (i.e., Bracken) type projectile points, biface, end and side scrapers, and retouched flakes, native copper, freshwater clam shell, shell beads and gorgets, perforated and imperforated bison and elk teeth, bear claws, eagle talons, exotic marine shells (especially *Olivella* and *Dentalium*), faunal remains from a variety of animals (especially large- and medium-sized mammals, frequently modified into beads), awls, and other bone tools and pieces of antler (Brink and Baldwin 1988:131).

The morphology of the Bracken point is not static throughout the Bracken phase. In the earliest part of the phase, it vaguely resembles the Pelican Lake point with mildly barbed shoulders. Towards the end of the Bracken phase, it becomes increasingly varied in appearance, exhibiting growing similarity to Besant points.

BESANT PHASE (CA. 2,100 TO 1,500 BP)

In Alberta, the Besant phase has been considered the last phase in the Middle Prehistoric period before the transition to the Late Prehistoric period (Reeves 1983a:36; Peck and Hudecek-Cuffe 2003:73; Vickers 1986). Dyck (1983) included the Besant complex in the Late Plains Indians period, based on the recovery of pottery and side-notched arrow points. The term *Besant* was first applied by Wettlaufer (1955:39–43) to a sequence of four levels, Occupations 4A through D, at the Mortlach site, south-central Saskatchewan. He described the Besant point as "short and broad with shallow side notches and a slightly concave base" (Wettlaufer 1955:44). The term *Besant* apparently derives from the Besant Valley in which the site is situated.

Subsequently, Reeves (1983a) provided a more thorough description of Besant material culture and its spatial and temporal distribution. Reeves (1983a:94) accepted the description of the Besant atlatl point provided by Wettlaufer (1955). He added a later derivative of the Besant atlatl point, the Samantha side-notched arrow point, to the phase (Kehoe and Kehoe 1968; see also Kehoe 1974). He considered the Besant phase to exhibit pottery with vertically or horizontally corded surface impressions and bosses or punctates on conoidal vessels. He did note, however, that the use of pottery during the Besant phase was largely restricted to the Middle Missouri area (Reeves 1983a:96). With regard to lithic utilization, Knife River flint and Avon chert were considered common, while the use of obsidian was rare (Reeves 1983a:96). An unusual feature of the Besant phase was the practice of secondary interments within log-covered pits sunken into the ground surface beneath mounds. These burials were often associated with grave goods, including, among other items, bison remains. Such interments were only known from the Middle Missouri area (Reeves 1983a:97). Reeves (1983a) considered the Besant phase to be relatively widespread across the Northwestern Plains, with assemblages recovered from eastern Wyoming, eastern Montana, North Dakota, northern South Dakota, southern Alberta, southern Saskatchewan, and southwestern Manitoba. For the Saskatchewan River Basin, he suggested the phase began approximately 1,800–1,700 BP and was replaced by the Old Women's phase about 1,200 BP (Reeves 1983a:93–94).

Neuman (1975) and Syms (1977) suggested that much of the material in North Dakota, South Dakota, and southwestern Manitoba represented a separate phenomenon from the Besant phase: the Sonota complex. Neuman (1975) defined the Sonota complex based on the high frequency of Knife

River flint in tool manufacture, points resembling Besant and Samantha points, a distinctive conoidal pottery with vertical cord-roughened surface and punctates and bosses for decoration, low-domed burial mounds, bone uprights within campsites and kill sites, and an emphasis on bison for subsistence (Neuman 1975). Syms (1977:88–90) concurred with this assessment and added that Sonota sites have been found on the Alberta (i.e., Muhlbach) and Saskatchewan (i.e., Walter Felt) plains as well. Neuman (1975) dated the Sonota complex to between 1,950 and 1,350 BP while Syms (1977:90) suggested ca. 1,950 to 1,150 BP.

Most researchers have essentially sided with Reeves' (1983a) assessment of the Besant phase. Dyck (1983:113) acknowledged a distribution of Besant material across the Northwestern Plains between 2,000 and 1,150 BP. With the exception of the burial mounds and small differences in point styles, he found no justification for differentiating Besant and Sonota (Dyck 1983:114–115). Similarly, Vickers (1986:81–87, 1994:9–14) followed Reeves' distribution for Besant and suggested an age range of about 2,100 to 1,200 BP. Vickers (1986:85) did acknowledge the high frequencies of Knife River flint and the variation in point styles by considering the Sonota complex a regional subphase of the Besant phase. Walde et al. (1995) also mirrored Reeves' Besant phase distribution but indicated an age of 2,150 to 1,250 BP. Morlan (1988:305), using radiocarbon dates from sites assigned to the Besant phase, suggested an age range of between 2,350 to 2,150 BP and 1,250 BP.

The Besant side-notched atlatl point continues to be the diagnostic artifact of the phase. Wettlaufer's (1955) definition of a "short and broad" point continues to be adequate. Dyck (1983:115) noted that the notches are twice as high as they are deep while Reeves (1983a:55) noted that notches are often placed low on the point. Further, the point exhibits crude to well-controlled flaking, with the base often thinned or ground (Reeves 1983a:54–57). Kehoe (1974) provided a typology of large corner-notched points in which he outlined three varieties of Besant atlatl point and two varieties of Samantha arrow points. While the terms *Besant* and *Samantha* are commonly applied, Kehoe's varieties are rarely used (Vickers 1994:9). Importantly, Kehoe's (1974) typology was based on materials recovered at the Walter Felt site, a site Syms (1977) attributes to the Sonota complex. Samantha arrow points are morphologically similar to Besant atlatl points but smaller (Reeves 1983a:63). Reeves (1983a:63) further noted the similarity to early specimens of Late Side-notched points of the Old Women's phase, a similarity noted by Kehoe (1974:109) in his typology for large corner-notched points, and also by Duke (1988:268) and others.

Another important diagnostic artifact of the Besant phase is pottery. Reeves (1983a:9, 96) contended that Besant sites exhibit "vertically or horizontally corded, bossed, or punctated conoidal pottery vessels," although most pottery-bearing sites are in the Middle Missouri area. Byrne (1973:446–447) conducted the most detailed analysis of pottery in the province and concluded that the Besant phase was aceramic. At the time, he noted that sites in Saskatchewan with apparent associations between Besant material and ceramics, such as the Walter Felt and Long Creek sites, exhibited numerous stratigraphic problems that could account for the recovery of the controversial items in Besant levels (Byrne 1973:447). More recently in Alberta, the Ross Glen site, EhPc 105 and the One-Eleven site are believed to be pottery-bearing Besant sites. The pottery at the Ross Glen site consists of thirty-seven small potsherds recovered from inside and outside Stone Circle 14 (Quigg 1986:119). Only body sherds were recovered. The interiors of the sherds were smooth while the exterior surface was fabric- or cord-impressed (Quigg 1986:121). A single Besant point was recovered within the stone circle. Sixteen stone circles at the site have been attributed to the Besant phase. This is an unusual situation made more confusing given the surface stripping and shallow deposition within the stone circles. EhPc 105 produced thirty-four small potsherds associated with a shallowly buried surface hearth; Besant points were recovered deeper in an adjoining test unit (Loveseth 1983). The pottery was classified as Saskatchewan Basin ceramics although its actual relationship to the Besant points was not well established. In Alberta, the best case for Besant pottery can be found at the One-Eleven site (EgPn 111). The One-Eleven site is described as a single-component Besant kill site that produced eighteen potsherds from two areas within a 176-m^2 excavation block (Head et al. 2002:164). The potsherds exhibited fabric-impressed surfaces considered similar to other Besant-Sonota pottery commonly found to the southeast (Head et al. 2002:164).

Regarding lithic raw materials, Besant sites emphasize either local sources or exotic porcellanite and Knife River flint sources in North Dakota. In Alberta, the S.S. Burmis site, the Dersch site, EfOw 26, and the Wells site are all Besant sites that utilized local lithic raw materials. In contrast, the One-Eleven site, the Muhlbach site, the Pigeon Mountain site, and the Fewkes and Smith-Swainson surface collections predominantly utilized Knife River flint. Some have argued that the high percentages of Knife

River flint might reflect groups that had recently travelled to North Dakota and actually represent the physical movement of people between the Alberta/Saskatchewan Plains and the North Dakota quarry sites (Vickers 1994:13; Walde et al. 1995:19).

The origin of the Besant phase has been the focus of considerable debate in the archaeological literature. Reeves' (1983a) models of culture history are probably the most influential and commonly cited. Reeves (1983a) proposed two cultural traditions in southern Alberta for the last 4,000 years: the Tunaxa and Napikwan. In a more recent version of the model, the Tunaxa tradition culturally links the McKean, Pelican Lake, and Avonlea phases, while the Napikwan tradition links Besant and Old Women's phases (Reeves 1983a). Reeves (1983a) suggested that the Besant phase was resident on the northeastern periphery of the Plains as early as 2,450 BP. An expansion of the Besant phase on to the Northwestern Plains displaced the resident Tunaxa population further west. To account for the Napikwan expansion, Reeves (1983a) suggested that Besant people were involved in the Hopewell Interaction Sphere, allowing them better and stronger lines of communication, and trade and transportation of goods. Reeves (1983a) speculated that the involvement of Besant in the Hopewellian system resulted from the desire of high-status groups further east to control access to resources. In the case of Besant people, access to Knife River flint, obsidian, grizzly bear teeth, bison hides, and dried meat as trade items is suggested. Meanwhile, the people of the Tunaxa tradition had not been entirely displaced off the plains and coexisted as the Avonlea phase for a time with the people of the Besant phase, until around 1,250 BP (Reeves 1983a).

Some have argued that the evidence does not support this model (Byrne 1973:466; Vickers 1986:86–87, 1994:14). Byrne (1973:465) failed to see Hopewellian influence in Early Variant of the Saskatchewan Basin Ceramics. Rather, he concurred with a notion that Reeves (1983a) had rejected, which was that the Besant phase had a northern origin, represented in the emergence of aceramic people out of the boreal forest, likely on to the prairie of Manitoba. The development of mounds and the restricted use of pottery would be a local development rather than Hopewellian stimulation of the Napikwan tradition into the west (Byrne 1973:466). Vickers (1986:86–87, 1994:14) noted that Knife River flint is rare in Hopewellian sites, while obsidian is rare in both Hopewellian and Besant sites. Further, the unranked group interments in the mounds do not reflect the high status/ranked burials that Reeves expected to be associated with the Hopewell Interaction Sphere (Vickers 1986:86; 1994:14). More recently, Reeves (1983a:13–14) has suggested that the ultimate origin of the Napikwan tradition lies deep in time. The Oxbow complex is considered culturally related to the Besant phase, with the Sandy Creek complex as temporally and technologically transitional between the two cultural entities (Reeves 1983a:13–14).

The fate of the Besant phase has been debated as much as its origins. Morlan (1988) has illustrated, using a comprehensive set of radiocarbon dates, that the Besant phase was present on the Northwestern Plains before the Avonlea phase, but that there is considerable overlap between the two. Walde et al. (1995:19) argue that the radiocarbon dataset incorporates a great deal of noise. Besant components always stratigraphically underlie Avonlea components, never the reverse, suggesting that the former preceded the latter; there is no strong reason to expect temporal overlap (see Cloutier 2004). Still, most archaeologists have noted that whatever the fate of the Besant phase, it was closely connected to developments within the Avonlea and Old Women's phases (Peck and Hudecek-Cuffe 2003:77).

The Sites

In order to assess the various lines of thinking presented above, Besant assemblages from Alberta with reliable radiocarbon dates are outlined below. These sites are used to critically evaluate the current view of the Besant phase (see Plate 22 and Figure 23).

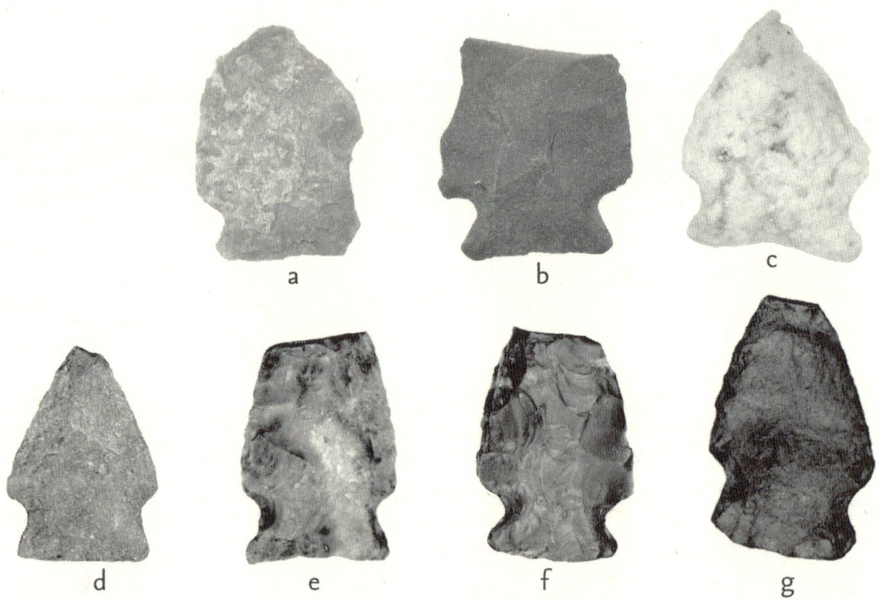

PLATE 22
Besant points. Illustrated are projectile points from the Ross Glen site (DlOp 2) (a–c); (Old) Women's Buffalo Jump (EcPl 1) (d–g); DjPl 13 (h–k); EgPn 220 (l–o); EfOw 26 (p–t); S.S. Burmis site (DjPn 62) (u–y); the Dersch site (DkPj 35), south knoll (z–bb) and Area 1 (cc); and EfOw 27 (dd). *Photo credit:* Alberta Culture and Community Spirit (a–t); Micheal Quigg (u–y); Fedirchuk-McCullough and Associates (z–bb); Alberta Culture and Community Spirit (cc and dd).

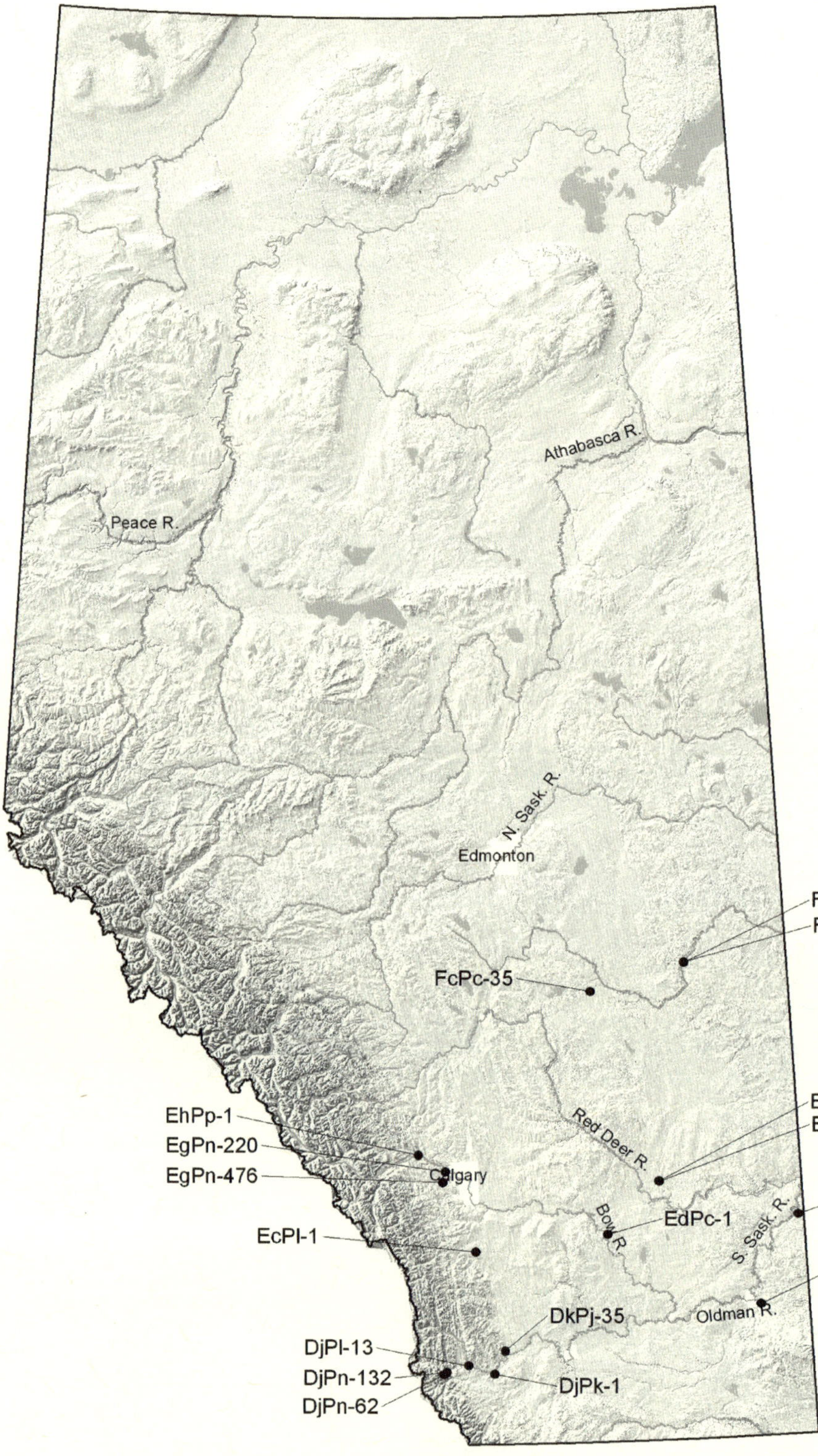

FIGURE 23
Besant sites within Alberta

(Old) Women's Buffalo Jump (EcPl 1). The Women's Buffalo Jump is located about 3 km northwest of Cayley on the south bank of Squaw Coulee (Forbis 1962:57). The site consists of low sandstone cliffs creating a six- to seven-metre drop to the slope deposits and bone bed that extend to the bottom of the valley (Forbis 1962:57). Forbis applied the adjective *old* in reference to the jump, as the site near Cayley was considered to be the oldest of the two possible locations for the Blackfoot's Akee'-piskun, or Women's Buffalo Jump. The name refers to a time when men and women lived separately and marks the location of the first marriages (Peck and Ives 2001:189). During the summer of 1957 through 1959, Forbis (1962) excavated an Upper and Lower pit at the site. The Upper Pit produced the best stratigraphy. Forbis (1962:74) divided the profile into an Upper Member consisting of Levels 1 to 14 and a Lower Member consisting of Levels 15 to 30. The Upper Member produced a long sequence of arrow points most recently called the Cayley Series (see Old Women's section below). The Lower Member produced a series of layers exhibiting dart points, mainly Bracken and Besant.

Forbis (1962:107, figs. A–E) recovered classic examples of Besant points in Levels 15–21. Forbis (1962:170, fig. 14f, g) classified some material as Besant that might represent late Bracken material; these point styles were recovered in Levels 17–22. Regardless, Forbis' (1962:107, figs. H, I) point type LM1 is a clear example of a Bracken point; it occurs in Levels 17–19. There appears to be stratigraphic co-occurrence of Besant and late Bracken at the Women's Buffalo Jump. Forbis (1962:107, fig. 14j–k, l–m) classified a number of other Bracken points under terms such as LM2 and LM3. These were recovered from as deep as Level 28.

A single radiocarbon date is available for this important stratigraphic sequence. Level 25 was minimally dated to 2,000 BP (see Table 21). This makes a certain amount of sense stratigraphically, as Bracken overlaps with Besant in Level 17, while pristine Besant phase occurs in Levels 16 and 15. The transition from the Bracken phase to the Besant phase, whether it is outright replacement or gradual change, is expected to occur about 2,100 BP, based on other dated sites. Thus, Level 17 could date about 2,000 BP given that Level 25 is minimally dated to ca. 2000 BP as noted above.

DjPl 13, Component B-2. DjPl 13 is a multicomponent campsite/processing site on a 12-metre-high terrace on the north bank of the Oldman River, just above its confluence with the Castle River (Van Dyke 1994:38). During 1988–1990, after substantial testing, four major excavation blocks were opened at the site: A (23 m²), B (50 m²), C (50 m²), and D (44 m²). Block B, Component 2, produced a stratigraphically isolated Besant assemblage.

Eight projectile points and point fragments were recovered in association with two FBR concentrations, two hearths, and an area of soil reddening (Van Dyke 1994:77). Three of the points were complete enough to classify as Besant with the remainder too fragmentary (Van Dyke 1994:78). Other tools recovered included bifaces (n=6), cores (n=2), end scrapers (n=7), a side scraper, retouched flakes (n=16), drills (n=2), elongate pebbles (n=2), and unifaces (n=2). A bone spatulate tool was also recovered. The lithic assemblage exhibited a strong use of quartzite, black chert, Avon chert, miscellaneous chert, Etherington chert, and siltstone. The lithic debitage is primarily concentrated near the hearths in the eastern half of the excavation area.

The faunal assemblage (n=1,225) was mainly bison (MNI=1) but included four freshwater shell fragments. Only thirty-three bones exhibited evidence of burning, although most of the bone was associated with the hearths, soil reddening, and FBR concentrations in the eastern half of the excavation (Van Dyke 1994:79). FBR (n=550) was lightly scattered across the western half of the excavation, with a concentration in the centre and around each feature. Two radiocarbon dates were obtained from this component of the site: ca. 2,150 BP and 2,060 BP (Table 21).

TABLE 21 Radiocarbon dates for Besant sites (calibrated by OxCal 3.10 [Ramsey 2005])

Site [LAB NO.]	Conventional ^{14}C Age	$^{13}C/^{12}C$ Ratio	Material	Calibration	Reference
EcPl 1 [S-91]	1,920 +/- 75	-20.0‰	collagen	100 B.C.–A.D. 260	Forbis 1962
DjPl 13, C, B-2 [AECV-1360C]	2150 +/- 120	-18.2‰	collagen	500 B.C.–A.D. 150 (p = 0.954)	Van Dyke 1994:79
DjPl 13, C, B-2 [AECV-753C]	2060 +/- 120	-17.8‰	collagen	400 B.C.– A.D. 250 (p = 0.954)	Van Dyke 1994:79
DjPn 62 [RL-434]	2020 +/- 110	-20.0‰	collagen	400 B.C.– A.D. 250 (p = 0.954)	Brumley and Rushworth 1983:149; Morlan n.d.
EfOw 26, C5 [BETA-188555]	1890 +/- 40	-19.4‰	collagen	A.D. 20–230 (p =0.954)	Goldsmith 2005:388
EfOw 26, C5 [BETA-190391]	1770 +/- 40	-18.6‰	collagen	A.D. 130–380 (p = 0.954)	Goldsmith 2005:385
EfOw 26, C4 [BETA-188554]	1870 +/- 80	-19.1‰	collagen	50 B.C.–A.D. 340 (p = 0.954)	Goldsmith 2005:390
EfOw 27, C6 [BETA-188557]	1800 +/- 60	-18.8‰	collagen	A.D. 80–390 (p = 0.954)	Goldsmith 2005:390

DkPj 35, Area 1 [AECV-1763C]	1930 +/- 80	?	collagen	160–130 B.C. (p = 0.014); 120 B.C.–A.D. 260 (p = 0.94)	Damkjar 1995:135
DkPj 35, Area 1 [AECV-1604C]	1860 +/- 80	?	collagen	40 B.C.–A.D. 350 (p = 0.954)	Damkjar 1995:135
DkPj 35, Area 1 [AECV-1764C]	1800 +/- 70	?	collagen	A.D. 70–400 (p = 0.954)	Damkjar 1995:135
EeOm 15 [SFU-NO#4]	1760 +/- 100	-20.0‰	collagen	A.D. 50–540 (p = 0.954)	Apland 1981:35; Morlan n.d.
EeOm 15 [SFU-NO#3]	1700 +/- 80	-20.0‰	collagen	A.D. 130–540 (p = 0.954)	Apland 1981:35; Morlan n.d.
FcPc 35 [BETA 225730]	1740 +/- 40	-20.0‰	collagen	A.D. 170–200 (p = 0.013) A.D. 210–410 (p = 0.941)	Spicer 2007a, 2007b
FcPc 35 [BETA 225729]	1700 +/- 40	-19.7‰	collagen	A.D. 240–420 (p = 0.954)	Spicer 2007a, 2007b
DkPj 35, s. knoll [AECV-1177C]	1550 +/- 90	-18.3‰	collagen	A.D. 260–280 (p = 0.011) A.D. 320–660 (p = 0.943)	Fedirchuk 1991; Morlan n.d.
DjPn 132 [BETA-106906]	1790 +/- 70		collagen	A.D. 10–300 (p = 0.954)	Van Dyke 1997: 39-40
DkPj 35, s. knoll [AECV-1178C]	1540 +/- 90	-18.9‰	collagen	A.D. 330–660 (p = 0.954)	Fedirchuk 1991; Morlan n.d.
DjPl 13, B-3 [AECV-758C]	1610 +/- 90	-19.0‰	collagen	A.D. 240–630 (p = 0.954)	Van Dyke 1994:83
DjPl 13, B-3 [AECV-1357C]	1010 +/- 90	-18.9‰	collagen	rejected	Van Dyke 1994:83
DjPl 13, C-4 [AECV-1361C]	1590 +/- 80	-18.3‰	collagen	A.D. 250–300 (p = 0.038) A.D. 320–640 (p = 0.916)	Van Dyke 1994:83
FdOt 9, Level 4 [BETA-23700]	1620 +/- 65	-20.0‰	collagen	A.D. 250–580 (p = 0.954)	Stuart 1988:88; Morlan n.d.
DlOp 2 [GX-5892-G]	1330 +/- 160	?	collagen	A.D. 350–1050 (p = 0.954)	Quigg 1986:124; Morlan n.d.
DlOp 2 [GX 5892-A]	1485 +/- 165	?	apatite	A.D. 100–950 (p = 0.954)	Quigg 1986:124; Morlan n.d.

S.S. Burmis (DjPn 62). The S.S. Burmis site is a multicomponent campsite/processing site on the first terrace on the north side of the Crowsnest River, south of the town of Burmis (Quigg 1975b:77–78). Three components were observed at the site, with Oxbow and Hanna material in the lowest component, Besant material in the second component, and Old Women's material in the most recent component (Quigg 1975b). In 1974, twenty-six 2-×-2-m units (104 m²) were excavated at the site. The excavations were conducted as part of the University of Calgary archaeological field school (Quigg 1975b:77).

Fifteen projectile points were recovered from this level. Originally considered similar to Pelican Lake specimens and labelled as "unknown" (Quigg 1975b:82–83, 92), they exhibit similarities to Besant points. These points were associated with a hearth surrounded by vertically positioned bison bone elements, FBR piles, bone scrap pits, fire-reddened stains, and a seed pit (Quigg 1975b:91). The use of local and non-local lithic raw materials was noted but not elaborated. Patterns in the lithic concentrations were noted with bifaces and end scrapers occurring in association with the main bone bed in the south area of the excavation and points, side scrapers, gravers, and retouched flakes associated with FBR in the north area of the excavation (Quigg 1975b:82).

The faunal assemblage was mainly bison but also included deer, beaver, elk, and coyote or dog (Quigg 1975b:82). Butchered bison remains and smashed bone in association with hearths and boiling pits indicated grease extraction from bones, presumably to produce pemmican (Quigg 1975b:82). For reasons not stated, the site was considered to be a winter/spring occupation (Quigg 1975b:91).

A single radiocarbon date of ca. 2,000 BP was obtained from Component 2 (Table 21). This date is among the earlier dates for Besant material. Some of the points have unusually sharp shoulders and Quigg (1975b) suggested that they might represent a transitional form of Pelican Lake (i.e., Bracken) points. In summary, the S.S. Burmis site is a rich Besant campsite/processing site with an array of unusual features.

Dersch, Area 1 (DkPj 35). The Dersch site is a southern extension of Head-Smashed-In Buffalo Jump, though distinctive from it both spatially and materially (Damkjar 1995:5). The site consists of three knolls and portions of the adjacent gullies. Area 1 is the northernmost of these knolls (Damkjar 1995:20). In 1991–1992, a block excavation of 24 m² was conducted with an additional two outlying 1-m² units at Area 1. A single occupation consisting of Besant material was revealed in the upper 20 cm of the excavation (Damkjar 1995:132). The mitigative excavations were conducted to assess the effects of planned road upgrading.

Twenty-one point fragments were recovered. The researcher classified twenty specimens as Besant, although five of these may be Samantha points, based on neck width, with one point considered to be an Oxbow specimen (Damkjar 1995:134). These points were recovered in association with FBR, lithic debitage, two hearths, three pit features, and a set of bone uprights. Other recovered tools included bifaces (n=6), cores (n=2), end scrapers (n=7), a side scraper, retouched flakes (n=16), drills (n=2), elongate pebbles (n=2), and unifaces (n=2). A bone spatulate tool was also recovered. The majority of the lithics were miscellaneous cherts (65%), with silicified siltstone (12%), quartzite (8%), Swan River chert (8%), and argillite (3%) also fairly common. Avon chert, a lithic raw material commonly used during the Besant phase according to Reeves (1983a:96), was observed in the lithic sample but was not quantified (Damkjar 1995:153).

The faunal assemblage (n=234) was small and mainly associated with the features. The taxa present included three bison, two canids, a coyote, a fox, and twelve freshwater mussel shell fragments (Damkjar 1995:156). Fetal bison bone (MNI=3, n=24) was common, suggesting a late winter/early spring occupation (Damkjar 1995:156). Large amounts of FBR (n=4,476) were recovered at the site. An FBR concentration associated with a hearth was in the east half of the block, with smaller FBR concentrations in the southeast and east-central part of the excavation (Damkjar 1995:136). The larger surface hearth exhibited a lot of FBR, a Besant point, and three fired clay objects (two balls and a piece with three finger impressions on one face and cord markings on the other face) (Damkjar 1995:144). The clay "doodling" suggested ceramic production although no evidence of ceramic vessels was found. The second surface hearth was smaller but similar. Three small pits with limited amounts of bone and FBR were also excavated at the site. Multiple bone uprights, consisting of a femur shaft, two pieces of a radius shaft, a vertebral spine section, and two scapular fragments had been hammered into the ground (Damkjar 1995:149).

Three radiocarbon dates were obtained from this site: ca. 1,800 BP; 1,860 BP; and 1,930 BP (Table 21). These dates are internally consistent with the expected range for a Besant occupation. The focus of these Besant people appears to have been meat roasting for immediate consumption, since boiling pits were not found (Damkjar 1995:156).

EfOw 26, South Block, Component 5. EfOw 26 is a multicomponent campsite located on a coulee-bottom terrace along Deadfish Creek (now at the eastern toe of Deadfish Dam) north of Brooks (Goldsmith 2005:42). Five components were observed with Besant assemblages in the lowest two components. These were overlain by an Old Women's component, which was overlain by two mixed components. A total of 43 m^2 was excavated at the site. Excavations focused on a north block (17 m^2) and a south block (15 m^2), while a series of other units were scattered across the terrace. Stratigraphic complexity across the site made strong correlations between the different excavation areas difficult (Goldsmith 2005:44–47). Excavations were undertaken as part of a mitigation program in response to the rehabilitation of the Deadfish Dam; unexcavated portions of the site lie outside the development footprint (Goldsmith 2005:1–6).

In Component 5, the lowest component, five points or point fragments were recovered in association with a possible buried stone circle and a hearth. Two of the points were Besant points, while two others are blade fragments that were similar in form but lacked bases. The fifth point was a McKean Lanceolate point. Other tools included biface fragments (n = 2), scrapers (n = 5), wedges (n = 2), a chopper, a bifacially retouched stone tool, unifacially retouched tools (n = 5), marginally modified flakes (n = 11), utilized flakes (n = 4), bipolar cores (n = 3), and multidirectional cores (n = 7). The lithic assemblage emphasized quartzite, massive quartz, and miscellaneous cherts (Goldsmith 2005:89). Lithic tools and debitage appeared to concentrate around a hearth feature.

The faunal assemblage (n = 893) was highly fragmented and consisted primarily of bison (n = 150) (Goldsmith 2005:126). A minimum of two bison were recovered. The materials contained little calcine or burned bone and few purposefully impacted pieces of bone. Still, the author argued the assemblage was consistent with campsite activities such as the processing of smaller meat portions and breaking of long bones for marrow (Goldsmith 2005:141). A basin hearth feature contained FBR, large amounts of bone, and some debitage. FBR (n = 1,062), while focused around the hearth, was common across the excavation area; it exhibited water fracture, was small (< 5 cm) and was made of quartzite. A second feature was an arc of unmodified cobbles interpreted as a stone circle.

Two radiocarbon dates were obtained for the component: ca. 1,900 BP and 1,800 BP (Table 21). The researcher suggested that the dates, along with four of the points, support a Besant-age occupation; the McKean point was considered intrusive. This interpretation fits with the stratigraphic position of the component beneath a second Besant component.

In Component 4, six projectile points or point fragments associated with four hearths and a micro-debitage cluster were recovered (Goldsmith

2005:196–200). Five of the points were Besant while the sixth point was an Avonlea side-notched point (Goldsmith 2005:82–85). Other tools included a T-butt drill, a wedge, a scraper, choppers (n = 2), bifacially retouched stone tools (n = 2), unifacially retouched stone tools (n = 7), marginally retouched flakes (n = 7), utilized flakes (n = 5), bipolar cores (n = 4), and multidirectional cores (n = 2) (Goldsmith 2005:81). The lithic assemblage emphasized quartzite, chalcedony, and miscellaneous cherts (Goldsmith 2005:81–82). Quantities of chalcedony, Knife River flint, and porcellanite were also recovered (Goldsmith 2005:81–82).

The faunal assemblage (n = 1,392) consisted of bison (MNI = 3), based on numerous identified fragments (n = 343). Remaining fragments were unidentifiable beyond mammal or ungulate (Goldsmith 2005:126, 136–139). The fragmentary nature of the assemblage suggested campsite activities and marrow extraction, with the primary kill and/or processing activities occurring elsewhere. Five basin-shaped hearths were recorded in this component. A large amount of FBR (n = 2,228) was recovered, roughly correlating with the five hearth features. Most of the FBR was small quartzite cobble fragments (< 5 cm) exhibiting a water-fractured pattern (Goldsmith 2005:150). There was also a concentration of Knife River flint micro-debitage in association with one of the hearths (Goldsmith 2005:198–199).

A single date of ca. 1,900 BP was obtained for the component (Table 21). This date corroborates the Besant affiliation of the majority of the projectile points, although an Avonlea point was also recovered. The researcher suggested that the close proximity of the numerous hearths indicate multiple occupations, rather than a single occupation; at least two palaeosols were incorporated in this component (Goldsmith 2005:200). These complexities suggest more refined excavations are required at the site before the relationships between these materials can be fully understood.

EfOw 27, Component 6. EfOw 27 is a multicomponent campsite in an alluvial terrace adjacent to Deadfish Creek at the toe of Deadfish Dam (Goldsmith 2005:208). Six components were observed, including, from bottom to top, Besant, non-diagnostic, Avonlea, non-diagnostic, non-diagnostic, and Old Women's components. A total of 40 m^2 was excavated at the site, with a focus in a western block (24 m^2). A smaller block was excavated in the east (2 × 2 m), as well as a scatter of individual units (12 m^2). The researcher suspected that two separate depositional events might have been present in Component 6 but the second layer could not be differentiated in the field or the subsequent analysis (Goldsmith 2005:308). The site was excavated as part of mitigative action in association with the rehabilitation of Deadfish Dam.

In Component 6, a Besant point and two point fragments were recovered in association with dense clusters of faunal material and a lithic scatter/activity area (Goldsmith 2005:231–232, 306–308). Other tools included a hammerstone and multidirectional cores (n = 2). Raw materials represented in the lithic assemblage were mainly quartzite (84%) and chert (8%) with the remainder being siltstone, granite, or sandstone. A concentration of twenty-four white or light brown quartzite flakes and shatter consisted of typical late-stage stone tool manufacturing debitage. The only bone tools included four bone beads manufactured on bird long bone shaft segments.

The faunal assemblage (n = 10,280) included bison (MNI = 14), dog or wolf (MNI = 1), bird, deer, fox, and four shell fragments (Goldsmith 2005:261–262). The west block contained the vast majority of the faunal deposits, with four clusters of material (Goldsmith 2005:306). The numerous skull fragments, taken with numerous axis and atlas fragments, suggested that primary skeletal segmentation occurred at a nearby kill site prior to being transported to this locale (Goldsmith 2005:265). Forelimbs and hind limbs were well represented in the assemblage. These carcass segments were brought to the site, stripped of meat, and further butchered for marrow. Sexing suggested both males (n = 5) and females (n = 8) were present, but seasonality was not assessed (Goldsmith 2005:269). FBR (n = 172) consisted of small water-fractured quartzite cobbles and was common across the west block, suggesting stone boiling activities (Goldsmith 2005:271).

A single radiocarbon date of ca. 1,800 BP was obtained for the Component 6 (Table 21). This date supports the Besant affiliation of the projectile point and point fragments. The site is a Besant secondary butchering and processing site near an as-yet unidentified kill site.

DjPn 132. DjPn 132 is a single-component campsite/processing site in a basin-like feature south of the Crowsnest River, east of Burmis (Van Dyke 1997:2–3). A total of 25 m^2 was excavated in a block. Generally, cultural materials were recovered between 5 and 35 cm BS (Van Dyke 1997:17). The excavations were conducted to mitigate impacts from a subdivision development.

Four Besant points were recovered in association with a scatter of lithics and bone. The researchers suggested that the points were Samantha points or Besant arrow points (Van Dyke 1997:23). The overall size of the points is small, with the neck widths on the points approaching 1.2 cm. Other tools recovered included biface fragments (n = 5), end scrapers (n = 2), and cores (n = 2). The lithic assemblage had a number of exotic lithics (i.e., Montana cherts, obsidian, and chalcedony) and a debitage-to-tool ratio that suggested high discard rates and low conservation (Van Dyke 1997:28).

The faunal assemblage (n = 699) consisted entirely of bison. An MNI of three adult bison was determined. A calf skull was also recovered. Seasonality was not determined, as fetal bone was not recovered and dentition was too fragmentary. Horizontal patterning in the sediments was absent, perhaps because of rodent activity. No features were observed and FBR was scattered across the site fairly evenly (Van Dyke 1997:33).

A single radiocarbon date of ca. 1,800 BP was obtained for this site (Table 21). The date supports the interpretation that this is a small Besant/Samantha campsite/processing site where tool maintenance and small-scale hunting took place, perhaps repeatedly over time (Van Dyke 1997:39–40).

EeOm 15. EeOm 15 is a stone circle site consisting of fifteen stone circles on the east side of the South Saskatchewan River, just west of the Alberta-Saskatchewan border (Apland 1981:22). In 1980, subsequent to a testing program, two rings were entirely excavated.

Stone Circle 9 was 7 m in diameter and consisted of 161 cobbles (Apland 1981:24). A hearth was observed in the centre of the circle with artifacts (FBR, unburned and burned bone, and lithic debitage) clustering around the feature (Apland 1981:26). The feature was thin, consisting of a 0.5–1.0-cm thick reddish brown soil, suggesting a surface hearth.

Stone Circle 15 was 5 m in diameter and consisted of ninety-two cobbles (Apland 1981:28). Two hearths were observed, one towards the center and the second northeast of centre (Apland 1981:28). The central hearth consisted of a reddish stain 3–6 cm thick while the small hearth was thinner; both appear to be surface hearths. Lithic debitage was associated with the hearths and perhaps deposited next to the northeast wall (Apland 1981:28–30). Two point fragments were recovered from Stone Circle 15. The researcher ascribed the more complete point as Irvine (i.e., Cayley Series), but its large size challenges this identification. Although fragmentary, it most closely resembles Besant/Samantha point morphology. Other tools recovered included scrapers (n = 5), retouched flakes (n = 10), bifaces (n = 2), spall tools (n = 7), a core tool, split pebble cores (n = 7), and cores (n = 15). Debitage (n = 1,915) was plentiful. Quartzite (58%), local chert (10.6%), and Avon chert (28.1%) were among the most common lithic raw materials while Knife River flint (9.7%), siltstone (1.1%), and petrified wood (0.2%) occurred in smaller amounts (Apland 1981:32).

A single radiocarbon date was obtained from material associated with each stone circle. Material from Stone Circle 9 produced a date of ca. 1,700 BP while material from Stone Circle 15 produced a date of ca. 1,760 BP (Table 21). The researcher struggled with these dates and the identification of the point as Irvine. Interpreting the point as Besant/Samantha accommodates the dates and the recovery of amounts of Avon chert (Reeves 1983a:96).

Henry James (FcPc 35). The Henry James site is a two-component bison processing site and campsite in the Red Willow Creek valley east of Red Deer. The lower component is Besant and the upper component is Old Women's. Three Besant points, an intrusive McKean point, and an unidentifiable body fragment were recovered in association with hearth features, scatters of FBR, and butchered bone. Two radiocarbon dates were obtained for the lower component: ca. 1,700 BP and 1,740 BP (Spicer 2007a, 2007b). Despite the intrusive McKean point, the lower component produced two Besant-age dates to accompany the Besant points, suggesting a fairly intensive Besant occupation.

EgPn 220, Area One. EgPn 220, Area One, is multi-use habitation site on a 10-metre-high terrace above the Bow River in west Calgary (Vivian 2002:1). In 1991, a 40-m^2 block excavation was conducted in this area. The site was mitigated relative to the construction of a golf course (Vivian 2002:1).

Eleven projectile points and point fragments were recovered from the site. These were classified as Besant (n = 2), Pelican Lake (n = 2), flake (n = 2), and non-diagnostic fragments (n = 5) (Vivian 2002:6–9). If reworking sequences and the exotic nature of the raw material are taken into account, these specimens are all strikingly similar to Besant points. Other tools recovered include biface fragments (n = 4), scrapers (n = 7), a drill, wedges (n = 5), gravers (n = 10), retouched and utilized flakes (n = 21), core tools (n = 6), and a hammerstone. A single bone tool (an awl shaft fragment) was recovered (Vivian 2002:15). Two bone beads were also recovered (Vivian 2002:119). The debitage (n = 361) consisted almost entirely of small retouching and resharpening flakes associated with retooling and curation (Vivian 2002:15–16). Quartzite (47%) was the most common raw material, with the remaining assemblage composed of local pebble cherts (9%), siltstones (7%), more exotic Montana cherts (22%), Bowman (i.e., Avon) chert (3%), chalcedony (7%), Knife River flint (2%), and obsidian (1%) (Vivian 2002:16).

The faunal assemblage (n = 10,281) was highly fragmented. Species present included bison (MNI = 2), at least one canid, a mountain sheep, a kit fox, and a deer (Vivian 2002:18). No fetal bone was recovered, although a juvenile bison mandible suggested a fall event (Vivian 2002:20). The excavator suggested a "gourmet" strategy was applied, as the highest utility elements were brought from the kill site/primary butchering location to be processed. Three features consisting of FBR concentrations with debitage and bone were observed. The northernmost pile was very large and interpreted as intentional disposal of exhausted FBR (Vivian 2002:27). The two other pits to the south were interpreted as boiling pits, although associated hearths were not observed (Vivian 2002:28). A single radiocarbon date of about 1,700 BP (Table 21) was obtained for the site.

DjPl 13, Components B-3 & C-4. DjPl 13 is a multicomponent campsite/processing site on the north side of the Oldman River (see above). Block B, Component 3 overlies Component 2, which also contains Besant material (discussed above). Based on stratigraphy, radiocarbon dates, and cultural similarities Block B, Component 3, is considered contemporaneous with Block C, Component 4 (Van Dyke 1994:81).

In Block B, Component 3, six projectile points were recovered. The researcher suggested that two Besant, two Samantha, one preform, and one unclassifiable fragment were present in association with a large FBR concentration, two smaller FBR concentrations, and four hearths (Van Dyke 1994:81). The lithic assemblage emphasized black chert, chalcedony, and quartzite, with substantial amounts of Avon and Etherington chert. The faunal assemblage (n = 878) consisted mainly of bison bone (MNI = 1) although a possible deer fragment and two pieces of freshwater shell were also recovered. The fauna was distributed fairly evenly throughout the block. Two radiocarbon dates are available for the component: ca. 1,600 BP and 1,000 BP (Table 21). The former date was accepted since it dates bone in the vicinity of a hearth (Van Dyke 1994:83). The latter date was rejected as too recent.

In Block C, Component 4, six projectile points or point fragments were recovered. Of these, two were classified as Besant while the remaining specimens classified as triangular preforms (one possibly an Avonlea preform) (Van Dyke 1994:84). The points were found in association with three hearths, a boiling pit, and an FBR concentration (Van Dyke 1994:83). The lithic assemblage emphasized chalcedony, Etherington chert, siltstone, and quartzite. The faunal assemblage (n = 863) was mainly bison (MNI = 1) but included four freshwater shell fragments and two fish bones. The fish are most easily caught during early fall spawning, but are available all year long (Van Dyke 1994:85). A single radiocarbon date of ca. 1,600 BP (Table 21) was obtained for the component.

Dersch, South Knoll (DkPj 35). The Dersch site, as mentioned above, is a southern extension of Head-Smashed-In Buffalo Jump (Fedirchuk 1991; Damkjar 1995). This part of the site is located on a knoll overlooking a coulee that shelters a springhead (Fedirchuk 1991:1). In 1989, a block of 33 m^2 and eleven isolated 1-×-1-m units were excavated at the site. The site was mitigated relative to road construction (Fedirchuk 1991:1).

Eighteen projectile points and point fragments were recovered. Of these, twelve are classified as Besant, with the remaining points too fragmentary to classify (Fedirchuk 1991:19). Other tools recovered included bifaces (n = 14), scrapers (n = 15), lateral unifaces (n = 13), retouched flakes (n = 24), tool edge fragments (n = 16), a chopper, a scraper plane, hammerstones (n = 4), and cores (n = 8). Two bone tools were recovered: a long bone shaft with a rounded spatulate end and a rib that was thinned and rounded at the distal end (Fedirchuk 1991:30). Debitage (n = 4,030) was equally composed of flakes and flake fragments/shatter. The raw materials present in the assemblage were mainly cherts (55%), although chalcedony (16%) and quartzite (13.5%) were also common. Exotic raw materials also occur in small amounts, including Avon chert, Helena chert, Knife River flint, and Top-of-the-World chert (Fedirchuk 1991:34). Two small episodes of tool resharpening were noted: one represented by a concentration of Knife River flint flakes near Feature 1 and another represented by a separate concentration of chert flakes near Feature 3 (Fedirchuk 1991:97).

The faunal assemblage (n = 13,341) was mainly bison (MNI = 9), although canid and a possible bird bone fragment may also be represented. A piece of *Dentalium* shell and two other unidentifiable pieces of shell were also recovered (Fedirchuk 1991:37). A small amount of fetal bone was recovered and believed to be bison. FBR (n = 23,878) was plentiful and highly fragmented. Four features were identified. Feature 1 consisted of an FBR and bone cluster in an excavated pit (approximately 1 × 0.75 m) covered with sandstone slabs in association with two hearths (Fedirchuk 1991:59). Feature 2 was a discard area for FBR. Feature 3 was an FBR concentration with an associated hearth. Feature 4 was a pit (approximately 1 × 0.35 m) with a sandstone slab base, filled with a bison cranium on its side and some long bone fragments. It was lined and/or covered by sandstone slabs (Fedirchuk 1991:85–89). At least one bone upright was also recorded. Besant points were associated with Features 1 and 4, and near Features 2 and 3.

Two radiocarbon dates were obtained for the site, both ca. 1,550 BP (Table 21). In summary, this site is a Besant bone-processing area most likely associated with a late winter/early spring bison kill at the southern end of Head-Smashed-In Buffalo Jump (Fedirchuk 1991:99).

Wells (FdOt 9), Component 1. The Wells site is a multicomponent campsite located southwest of Hardisty (Stuart 1988:1). In 1987, a total of 46 m^2 was excavated in four small block excavations (Stuart 1988:15–16). Two components were identified: a Besant/Samantha component underlying an Avonlea component. The site was mitigated prior to the construction of a proposed pipeline.

Three points were recovered in the lower component. These were classified as Samantha points and were associated with a hearth, a concentration of FBR and articulated bone, and an FBR feature. Other tools recovered in this component included a biface, scrapers (n = 5), retouched flakes (n = 7), utilized flakes (n = 8), cores (n = 3), a hammerstone, and split pebbles (n = 4). The lithic raw material assemblage was almost limited to quartzite (85.8%) with some miscellaneous cherts (10.5%) and trace amounts of exotics such as Knife River flint (1%) (Stuart 1988:29). It was suggested that the raw material selection likely reflected availability rather than preference (Stuart 1988:86).

The faunal assemblage (n = 345) was very fragmentary. One fragment was identified as bison while a second was identified as large ungulate (Stuart 1988:74–75). FBR (n = 652) was highly fragmented with most pieces smaller than 5 cm (Stuart 1988:69–70). Some FBR was associated with the hearth. Other pieces overlaid an articulated metacarpal-carpal bone feature. Still other pieces formed a separate FBR concentration presumably created from by-products of processing, and directly associated with a Samantha point. The bone feature was radiocarbon dated to ca. 1,500 BP (Table 21). In summary, the site is a small Samantha-Besant campsite on the northern periphery of the Plains, where meat was roasted and some stone boiling may have occurred.

Ross Glen (DlOp 2). Ross Glen is a stone circle site on the prairie level above Bullshead Creek in Medicine Hat (Quigg 1986:2–7). The site was named for the subdivision being developed at the time. It consisted of eighteen largely buried stone circles, forty-two ancillary features, and a large artifact scatter, all covering 180 × 210 m. The main occupation was by Besant people (but see Oxbow phase above). In 1978 and 1981, a total of 754 m² was excavated: 301.9 m² inside the stone circles and 452.1 m² outside the stone circles (Quigg 1986:130). As alluded to above, impacts to the site were mitigated prior to a housing development.

Eleven projectile points from the primary occupation of the site were classified as Besant (Quigg 1986:124). They were found within six stone circles but were argued to be associated with seventeen stone circles and thirty-six ancillary features (Quigg 1986:124, 132). Four stone circles had post-moulds towards the center of the circle that were interpreted as tie-down stakes (Quigg 1986:132). A number of scrapers represented the domestic activities at the site; many of these items were made with Knife River flint and Montana cherts, suggesting trade and exchange. A small assemblage of potsherds (n=24) was recovered in apparent association with the Besant material. The small size of the sherds limited description of them as "smooth with isolated occurrences of shallow striations" (Quigg 1986:121).

A patterned arrangement was seen in the distribution of the stone circles at the site. Quigg (1986:133) suggested that two groups or bands simultaneously met, with the ancillary features between the two groups providing common ground. Individual and/or family relationships would have determined the size of stone circles and their placement in relation to other circles within each group (Quigg 1986).

Three radiocarbon dates were obtained for the site although one clearly relates to earlier times (see Oxbow phase). The dates that reflect the Besant occupation are roughly 1,500 BP (GX-5892-A, on bone apatite) and 1,300 BP (GX-5892-G, on gelatin) (Table 21). Geochron Laboratory suggested the best date would be an average, ca. 1,458 +/- 156 BP (Quigg 1986:124). This is a late date for a Besant occupation, however, at two standard deviations, the site falls well within the usual parameters for Besant. Importantly,

Samantha points were not noted in this material, suggesting that the site may immediately predate the end of the Besant phase.

Other sites. There are numerous other Besant sites in Alberta that lack good context or radiocarbon dates or both. Others have not been fully reported upon. For example, the Coal Creek stone circle site (EhPp 1), west of Calgary, consisted of up to forty stone circles over three terraces (McIntyre 1978:19). Seven stone circles were fully or partially excavated. Four Besant points were recovered (McIntyre 1978:169, plate 17, nos. 1–4), all apparently associated with Level 2. Deposition in shallow sites, however, always leaves questions of stratigraphic integrity. The recovery of a stemmed atlatl point and a plains triangular preform in the same level supports the likelihood of mixed components (McIntyre 1978:56).

The Kenney site (DjPk 1) is a multicomponent campsite in southwestern Alberta (Reeves 1983b). The major occupational layers are a historic assemblage (Layers 1–3), Old Women's material (Layer 4), and Besant material (Layers 6 and 8) (Reeves 1983b:23–26). Two Avonlea points occurred in Layer 6 while a Pelican Lake-like point occurred in Layer 8 (Reeves 1983b:59). A radiocarbon date was available for each layer (GAK-1354 was rejected, Blakeslee 1994). Charcoal from a hearth in Layer 6 produced a date of 700 +/- 60 BP (S-271). But this date seems late for this material. Charcoal for another hearth in Layer 8 produced a more appropriate date of 1,600 +/- 115 BP (S-272) (Reeves 1983b).

Lastly, EgPn 476 is a short-term campsite adjacent to the Elbow River valley, west of Calgary (de Mille and Head 2001:35–45). A Besant point was recovered in both the south and north parts of the site. Unfortunately, not enough bone was recovered to obtain a radiocarbon date (de Mille and Head 2001:45).

Besant: A Renewed Perspective

This review of Besant sites in Alberta illustrates an overwhelming trend toward short, broad points made of local lithic raw materials in assemblages that date between 2,100 and 1,500 BP. As well, the next section shows that lanceolate points or flake points of Knife River flint customarily included in the Besant phase invariably date to between 1,500 and 1,350 BP. The multi-faceted nature of Besant point morphology and lithology is temporally separated in Alberta, providing strong evidence for inferring separate cultural units — a Besant phase and subsequent Sonota phase. Thus, the notion of a Besant-Sonota complex is no longer tenable. The following outlines the Besant phase, based on the materials reviewed above.

The Besant side-notched point is the diagnostic point of the Besant phase. As originally defined by Wettlaufer (1955:39–43), it tends to be "short and broad with shallow side notches and a slightly concave base." Dyck (1983:115) noted that the notches are twice as high as they are deep and Reeves (1983a:55) noted that notches are often placed low on the point. The flaking is crude compared to Sonota points. The Samantha arrow point appears late in the Besant phase. As Reeves (1983a:63) noted, the arrow points are morphologically similar to Besant atlatl points but are smaller. As well, there is a superficial similarity to early Cayley Series points of the Old Women's phase (Reeves 1983a:63; Kehoe 1974:109; Duke 1988:268). Importantly, Kehoe's (1974) Samantha points at the Walter Felt site were also classified as transitional between Avonlea and Besant (Kehoe 1973:164). It is argued in the next section, in fact, that Level 10 of the Walter Felt site represents Avonlea and Sonota materials co-existing at a site, rather than Samantha-Besant.

In terms of the tool assemblage, side scrapers are quite rare relative to end scrapers. Retouched and utilized flakes are common. Flake points appeared to be rare. One unusual type of artifact was recovered from a few sites in the Oldman River area: net sinkers. These would presumably be used for fishing, but only Level C-13 at DjPl 13 produced fish bone. Bone tools are rare in Besant sites. DkPj 35, South Knoll, produced two spatulate tools while DjPl 13, Level B-3, produced a single specimen. A *Dentalium* fragment was recovered at the South Knoll of DkPj 35 and freshwater mussel shell was recovered at EfOw 27, Area 1 of DkPj 35, and Levels B-2, B-3, and C-4 of DjPl 13. Presumably the recovered shell was used mainly for adornment.

The lithic raw materials used at various sites during the Besant phase show a heavy dependence on local sources. Based on the sites reviewed above, quartzite comprises about 22 percent of the lithic raw material in the sites discussed above, siltstones about 5.5 percent, Knife River flint about 5 percent, chalcedony about 7.6 percent, black chert about 5.6 percent, and miscellaneous cherts about 39.7 percent. Montana cherts account for 0.1 percent while porcellanite constitutes 0.4 percent of the raw materials. These numbers need to be taken with caution, however, owing to the disparate reports from which the data was gleaned.

Pottery appears to be almost entirely absent from the newly defined Besant phase in Alberta. Three sites have been considered Besant-Sonota sites that exhibit pottery: Ross Glen, EhPc 105 and One-Eleven. The pottery at Ross Glen was recovered from within and outside a shallowly buried stone circle. Associations between artifacts within shallow sites such as stone circle sites are notoriously difficult to establish because of the ease with which subsequent materials can infiltrate the site. At EhPc 105, the pottery was associated with a hearth but the diagnostic points were recovered in an adjacent unit at greater depth. This association is not particularly sound. The One-Eleven site provides firm evidence of pottery within a Besant-Sonota kill site. The large number of lanceolate and flake points made on Knife River flint, however, indicate this site is a Sonota site, not a Besant site. Of course, Sonota burial mound sites in the Middle Missouri area fairly frequently exhibit pottery, so pottery at the One-Eleven site is not out of the ordinary. Somewhat perplexing is the pottery recovered at DkPj 35, Area 1. Damkjar (1995:144) recovered three fired clay objects (two balls and a piece with three finger impressions on one face and cord markings on the other face), but evidence of vessel production was not found. This part of the site was dated to early in the Besant phase. This recovery begs the question of its significance, given an apparent lack of ceramic vessels at Besant sites.

The subsistence as reflected in the fauna suggests a heavy reliance on bison. As with the previous Bracken phase, bison procurement through jumping bison and large encampments continue into the Besant phase. Wolf and/or dog was found in a number of the sites, as was coyote, while only one site appears to have produced fox. When one considers that a single deer and a single fish were the only other faunal remains recovered at the sites, making the heavy reliance on bison is even more evident. Of course, this is only a small sample of Besant sites and many more sites should be looked at before firm conclusions regarding Besant subsistence can be drawn. The features observed in the reviewed Besant sites include stone circles, surface hearths, basin hearths, FBR concentrations, earth pits, a possible boiling pit, and a set of bone uprights.

The description of the Besant phase presented above can be found in assemblages outside of Alberta. In Saskatchewan there are a number of Besant sites that roughly correlate in time and space with the aforementioned Alberta sites. The Mortlach (EcNl 1) site, in south-central Saskatchewan, produced Besant material in Occupations 4A and 4B (Wettlaufer 1955:96–97, plate 6, nos. 2–4; 98–99, plate 7, nos. 1–3). Short Besant points and an absence of pottery support the Besant phase association. Wettlaufer's

(1955) assignment of Occupations 4C and 4D to the Besant phase is not supported by the diagnostics within the recovered assemblages. A review of the point forms suggest that Occupations 4A and 4B exhibit short, broad points with shallow notches and slightly concave bases. A Pelican Lake point appears to have been mixed into the assemblage in Occupation 4A (Wettalufer 1955:44). Wettlaufer (1955:80) noted that while chalcedony was recovered in fairly large amounts in Occupations 4A and 4B, petrified wood, quartzite, and crystalline cherts were recovered in very large amounts. This would be expected in Besant assemblages that invariably reflect local sources. Occupation 4B was radiocarbon dated to 1,660 +/- 159 BP (S-22).

The Elma Thompson (EiOj 1) site is a buried stone circle site near Flaxcombe (Finnigan and Johnson 1984:27). Three Besant points were recovered in association with a hearth and rock-filled pit. Lithic materials included Swan River chert, chalcedony, and quartzite, among others, but no Knife River flint (Finnigan and Johnson 1984:30–32). The site is dated to 1,755 +/- 145 BP (S-2202) (Morlan et al. 2002:39).

The Newo Asiniak (FbNp 16) site is a multicomponent site immediately north of Saskatoon (Kelly 1986). Level 3 produced seven Besant points and an anomalous Pelican Lake point (Kelly 1986:144). Most of the assemblage was quartzite although Knife River flint, jasper, and petrified wood were each used to make points (Kelly 1986:147). A date of 2,235 +/- 70 BP (S-2530) was obtained for the level (Kelly 1986:155).

In Montana, Herdegen's Birdtail Butte (24BL1152) is a multicomponent bison kill site and campsite on the southeast margin of the Bear Paw Mountains (Brumley 1990). Sixteen layers were revealed with Avonlea present in all but one of the upper twelve layers (see Avonlea section). Layer 13 did not produce diagnostic material. Layer 14 to 15 produced Besant points while the base of the excavation was reached in Layer 16, a culturally sterile layer (Brumley 1990:36–46). The Besant points were all appropriately stout forms (Brumley 1990:44, fig. 17; 45, fig. 18). The lithic assemblages exhibit a fair amount of Knife River flint and porcellanite (Brumley 1990:85, tables 9 and 11), but this is not unexpected so close to the quarries. Pottery was not recovered. Unburned bone from Layer 13 produced a date of 1,690 +/- 80 BP (Beta-31793) and unburned bone from Layer 15 produced a date of 1,960 +/- 80 BP (Beta-31794) (Brumley 1990:41).

The Fresno (24HL103) site is a multicomponent site on the south shore of the Fresno Reservoir. The lower cultural level produced two Besant points, and two were found eroded onto the beach. A boiling pit, a prepared basin-hearth, and two bone uprights were recovered within this level (Keyser 1979:64). A Gakushuin date (GAK-6266) was rejected (see Blakeslee 1994).

The Donovan (24HL91) site is a multicomponent site along the south shore of the Fresno Reservoir at the mouth of a coulee in north-central Montana (Keyser 1979:48–55). The lower of two components are a Besant bison kill and processing occupations. A complete Besant point and a specimen lodged in an ischium were manufactured on brown chert and white agate, respectively (Keyser 1979:51). A biface of Knife River flint was recovered but only chert flakes were mentioned amongst the debitage. A Gakushuin date (GAK-6272) was rejected (see Blakeslee 1994).

The Boarding School Bison Drive (24GL302) in north-central Montana produced a single, large corner-notched point in Level 31 below numerous levels containing Late Side-notched points (Kehoe 1967:46). Kehoe (1967:46) considered it similar to Middle Woodland forms but morphologically it seems most similar to points of the Besant phase (Kehoe 1967:135, plate 11). Another site that may have produced Besant points is Canyon Ferry Reservoir Localities VI (Greiser 1986, fig. 114m–s) and VII (Greiser 1986, fig. 125f–i). These points were surface collected over a period of nineteen years around the Canyon Ferry Reservoir (Greiser 1986). The lack of context for these points is unfortunate, as it precludes accurate dating and identification. Other possible Besant sites in Montana include 24PH601 (Hoy 1973:17) and the King site (24PH2886) (Brumley and Rennie 1999). In Manitoba, North Dakota, and South Dakota there are no Besant sites as defined here, only Sonota sites.

In summary, the Besant phase dates from ca. 2,100 to 1,500 BP. Besant material is found across southern Alberta, southwestern Saskatchewan, and north-central Montana. The Besant point is the diagnostic of the Besant phase. The Besant point is short and broad with shallow side-notches and a slightly concave base. Besant lithic assemblages almost invariably focus on local lithics. The use of jumps continued from the previous period and eventual excavation of Besant pounds may be expected. Stone circles exhibiting characteristics of tipis continue, as do large campsites that likely reflect winter encampments. The abrupt termination of the Besant phase occurs because of the spread of the Sonota phase from the Middle Missouri and southeastern Saskatchewan into southern Alberta at ca. 1,500 BP.

Middle to Late Prehistoric Period Transition 5

CA. 1,500 TO 1,350 BP

By about 1,500 BP, the Plains had been relatively stable in its modern distribution of vegetation for some time. The interval between ca. 2,000 and 1,000 BP was a period of infrequent drought that likely produced abundant and dependable animal resources (Vance 1991:155).

SONOTA PHASE (CA. 1,500 TO 1,350 BP)

Early ceramic assemblages associated with burial mounds in the Middle Missouri and adjacent areas have long been classified as a subset under the Besant phase in Alberta's culture-historical classification systems (e.g., Reeves 1983a). The inclusion of Sonota material under the Besant rubric is an idea that continues to be maintained by many practitioners on the Northwestern Plains (i.e., Dyck 1983:114–115; Scribe 1997; Vickers 1986:85; Walde et al. 1995). Still, other researchers have suggested there is a cultural distinction between Sonota and Besant materials (i.e., Neuman 1975:82; Syms 1977:88–90). The previous section on the Besant phase outlines the position taken here, that two different cultural traditions and sets of material culture are represented.

Neuman (1975) provided the first definition of Sonota as a separate entity distinct from the Besant phase. He defined the Sonota complex on the basis of materials excavated at Stelzer, Swift Bird, Grover Hand, Arpan, and Boundary Mound sites with additional data from the Baldhill, Schmidt, and Alkire sites, the Porcupine Creek Component at site 32SI6, and House 2 at the La Roche site (Neuman 1975). The sites were largely associated with the valley of the Missouri River in North and South Dakota. The name Sonota itself was derived from the proximity of these key sites to the South Dakota-North Dakota state line (SO for *South*, NO for *North*, and TA for *Dakota*) (Toom and Jackson 2001:14.2).

Basing his interpretation on eleven radiocarbon dates from six of the sites, Neuman (1975:88) suggested that the Sonota complex lasted between ca. 1,950 BP and 1,350 BP. Neuman (1975) indicated that the Sonota complex exhibited both campsites and burial mounds. Materials from campsites were not unlike other contemporaneous campsites, save the culturally diagnostic artifacts (especially pottery) and the presence of bone uprights. Sonota mounds, on the other hand, were unusual. On average, the mounds tended to be about 22 m in diameter by 1 m high with a pit in the center excavated about 0.5 m into the original ground surface. The pit usually contained numerous secondary burials of human remains along with offerings. Offerings included bison carcass segments as well as adornments such as pendants and beads made from bear, beaver, canids, shell (i.e., *Olivella* from the West coast, *Dentalium* from the northwest coast, and freshwater mussels found locally), fossils and copper (although rare). Other offerings included conoidal pottery, pottery pipe bowls, and pottery beads. Pottery vessels tended to have cord-marked or plain surface finishes and exhibited a row of punctates or possibly a series of arced, diagonally oriented, dentate stamps beneath a row of punctates (Neuman 1975:93). Bone tools such as flakers, fleshers, awls, and a squash knife have been recovered in the mounds but could also be found in the campsites. Chipped lithic tools were knapped almost exclusively from Knife River flint, although obsidian, chalcedonies, quartz, jasper, chert, and petrified wood were all utilized (Neuman 1975:91). Projectile point styles range from Besant-like points to long, slender, straight-based points with low, broad side notches. Other lithic tools typically recovered include a suite of knives, end scrapers, gravers, and utilized flakes. Importantly, among the ground stone tools recovered tend to be atlatl weights, suggesting that the projectile points were used with atlatl-and-dart technology. Evidence of shelters has only been recovered at the La Roche site in House 2, where post-mould patterns suggested a lightly framed ovoid structure about 20 ft long (~6.1 m) with a central fire pit (Neuman 1975:90). With regard to culture contact and trade, Neuman (1975:94) suggested trade and/or contact between Sonota and other cultures was evident in: (1) exotic shell, obsidian, and catlinite recovered from the mound burials, (2) the mounds with centrally located pits and human interments reminiscent of Hopewellian sites, and (3) speculative evidence that Knife River flint and obsidian have been recovered to the east in Hopewellian sites.

Neuman (1975:81) acknowledged the presence of the Besant phase in the recovery of Besant side-notched points at campsites and kill sites on the plains of Montana, Saskatchewan, and Alberta. Archaeological sites that he considered Besant sites included levels at Mortlach, (Old) Women's Buffalo Jump, Walter Felt, and Muhlbach. In his evaluation, he noted that a large number of points from Sonota sites closely resembled specimens labelled Besant points (Neuman 1975:82). Similarly, he observed that pottery recovered in Besant levels at the Walter Felt site resembles "Sonota complex and Plains Woodland ceramics" owing to their cord-marked exterior and profiles, indicative of a shoulderless vessel (Neuman 1975:82). Still, he remained firm that the Sonota complex was closely linked to Besant with the burial mounds of the former offsetting it from the latter owing to numerous exotic items indicative of contact with cultures further east (Neuman 1975:93).

Syms (1977:88) reiterated many of Neuman's distinguishing traits of the Sonota complex, including utilization of bison, emphasis on Knife River flint, production of bone uprights, and burial mounds containing multiple burials. He more explicitly stated, however, that the projectile points are "a distinctive variation of corner-notched projectile points that subsume Besant and Samantha side-notched types" (Syms 1977:88). Syms (1977:89) excluded the La Roche site material from his Sonota complex, based on the barbed points and limited Knife River flint. He added to the "complex" a number of sites from south-central Manitoba, including the Richards kill site, Richards Village site, and Zeb-Montroy site, and a number of surface collections known from the area. The Richards Village site, for example, is a surface collection from a multicomponent site that was described as "Sonota material, almost all of Knife River flint points, one obsidian projectile point, pottery that appears similar to Sonota materials, atlatl weights, large bifaces, trade blocks and nodules of Knife River flint, large awls similar to forms found at Stelzer, and small grooved mauls like the Sonota specimens." A burial mound appears to be associated with the site. On the western Canadian plains, Syms (1977:90) considered the Besant and Samantha material at the Walter Felt site and the Muhlbach site to be more properly classified as Sonota, based on the recovery of the characteristic point forms, numerous flake points, heavy utilization of Knife River flint, and the presence of bone uprights. Syms (1977:90) suggested an age for the Sonota complex between ca. 1,950 BP and 1,150 BP. He noted that dates in the western Sonota sites are slightly later possibly suggesting a westward shift. Regarding trade with more eastern cultures, Syms (1977:90) pointed out that no large caches of socio-religious items from Hopewellian sites had been recovered although some form of contact was apparent in the smaller-scale exchange of shell, obsidian, and catlinite.

The Sites

To assess the various lines of thinking presented above, Sonota assemblages from Alberta with reliable radiocarbon dates are outlined below. These sites are used to critically evaluate the current view of the Sonota phase as it has been differentiated from the Besant phase (see Plate 23 and Figure 24).

One-Eleven (EgPn 111). EgPn 111 is a bison kill site that has been informally named the One-Eleven site (Thomas Head, personal communication 2005). The site is located on the west side of Calgary on a small hill above the Elbow River (Head et al. 2002). It was excavated between 1998 and 2000. A total of 176 m² was excavated to mitigate potential impacts from a proposed subdivision.

Thirty-four projectile point fragments were associated with the bison bone bed (Head at al. 2002). The researchers suggested that both Besant-Samantha (n=25) and Pelican Lake (n=8) points were recovered; one specimen was considered unclassifiable (Head et al. 2002:128–144, 195–200). A number of the points exhibited work only on their margins. This review considers the material to be Sonota, as flake points and corner-notched points commonly occur in Sonota sites. Other tools at the site included bifaces (n=21), wedges (n=5), retouched tools (n=72), end scrapers (n=20), side scrapers (n=13), utilized debitage (n=6) choppers (n=7), hammerstones/manuports (n=7), mauls (n=1), and cores (n=4). The lithic assemblage was dominated by chert, quartzite, and siltstone while the tool assemblage was dominated by chert, Knife River flint, siltstone, and quartzite. The ceramic assemblage (n=18 potsherds) was interpreted as consisting of potsherds from two vessels. Vessel 1 exhibited evidence of a truncated fabric-impressed surface finish

PLATE 23 Sonota points. Illustrated are projectile points from the One-Eleven site (EgPn 111) (a–f); the Pigeon Mountain site (EgPt 28) (g–j); the Muhlbach site (FbPf 1) (k–o); Head-Smashed-In Buffalo Jump (DkPj1) (p–r); the Echo Creek site (EhPv 78) (s–v); and EeOm 51 (w–bb). *Photo credit:* Alberta Culture and Community Spirit (a–o, s–bb); Royal Alberta Museum (p–r).

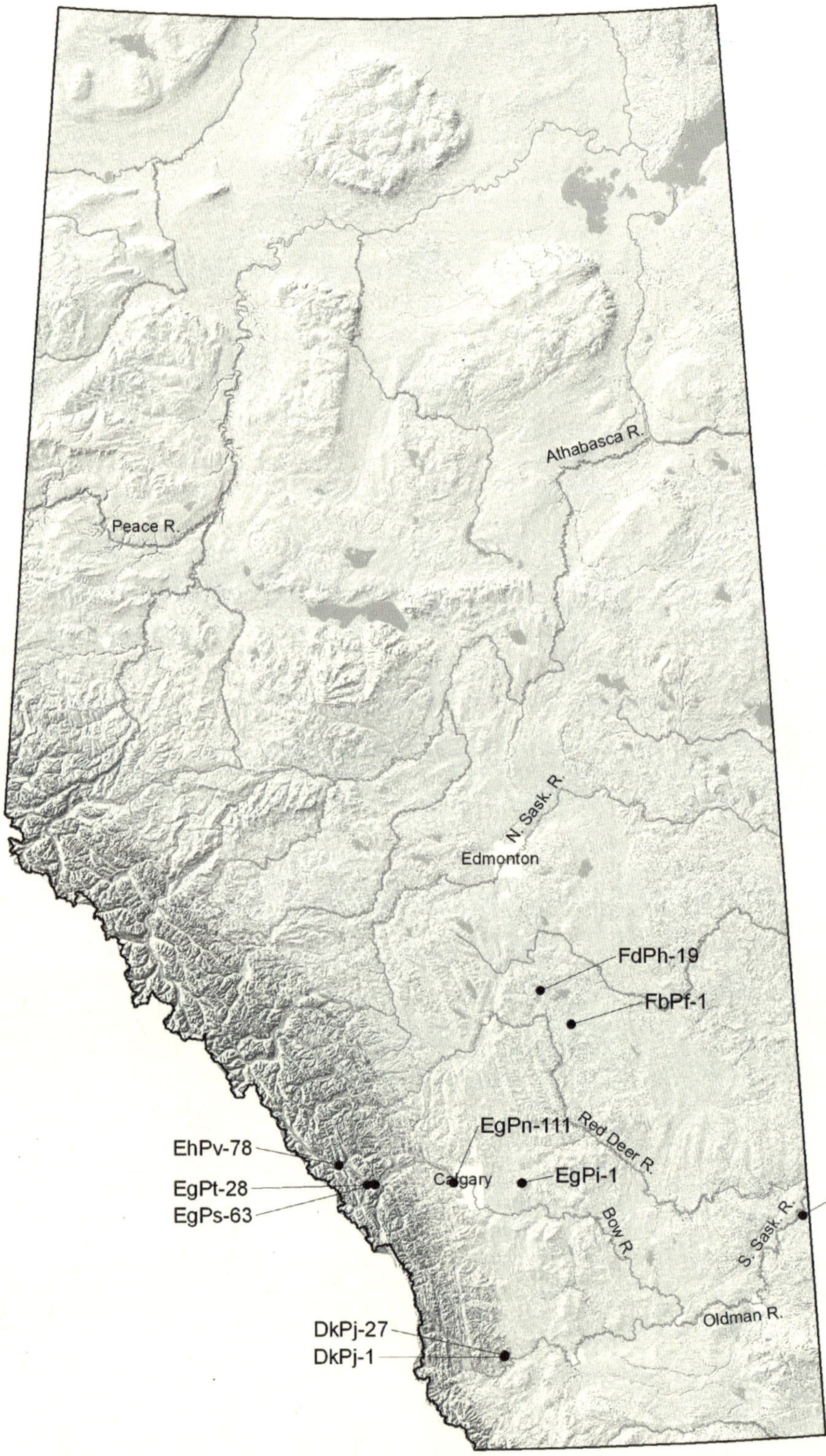

FIGURE 24
Sonota sites within Alberta

while Vessel 2 had a smooth surface finish (Head et al. 2002:164–168).

The faunal assemblage had a minimum of forty-eight bison represented. The sample included both male and female animals. Generalized patterning in the distribution of elements suggested hide removal and segmentation of the carcass into manageable units (Head et al. 2002:94–102, 169). A single fetal bone was recovered. Given the preservation of other fragile bones, it would be expected that more fetal bones would be recovered if they were present (Head et al. 2002:86). Tooth eruption and wear and thin sectioning analysis, along with the lack of fetal bone, suggested a late fall/early winter occupation (Head et al. 2002:80). The authors suggested a loosely combined male/female herd that had moved on to its winter range (Head et al. 2002:91). Little evidence of burned bone was recovered from the site, suggesting it was not prevalent (Head et al. 2002:93). The FBR assemblage was considered to be almost entirely fracture by stone boiling activities (Head et al. 2002:107). Three radiocarbon dates were obtained — ca. 1,500 BP; 1,400 BP; and 1,370 BP (see Table 22) — suggesting a single kill event (Head et al. 2002:209).

EgPs 63. EgPs 63 is a campsite on a Bow River meander scar southeast of Lac des Arcs, located on the south side of the TransCanada Highway (Clarke et al. 1998:234). The site was excavated during the summer of 1995. A total of 40 m² was excavated. A pipeline project impacted the site.

Two projectile point fragments were associated with a small debitage, bone, and FBR scatter (Clarke et al. 1998). Of the points, only the fragment of a base and a blade were recovered. The base falls within the range of Sonota points, but is made of quartzite. Other lithic tools include two relatively square scrapers, a side scraper, a core, a retouched flake, and two utilized flakes. The assemblage had a few pieces of Knife River flint (6.5%) with other locally available material much more common (Clarke et al. 1998:238–240).

The faunal assemblage was heavily weathered and consisted of 2,071 fragments. All 136 identifiable fragments were bison (MNI = 1) (Clarke et al. 1998:241). About 16 percent of the faunal assemblage was burned. The appendicular elements and concentrations of FBR suggested marrow and grease processing (Clarke et al. 1998:248). The quantities of bone suggested that processing was not a major activity and no hearths were unearthed to clarify the nature of the FBR (Clarke et al. 1998:257). No ceramics were recovered. A single radiocarbon date of 1,400 BP (Table 22) was obtained.

TABLE 22 Radiocarbon dates for Sonota sites (calibrated by OxCal 3.10 [Ramsey 2005])

Site [LAB NO.]	Conventional ^{14}C Age	$^{13}C/^{12}C$ Ratio	Material	Calibration	Reference
EgPn 111 [BETA-127231]	1480 +/- 70	-19.3‰	collagen	A.D. 420–670 (p=0.954)	Head et al. 2002:40
EgPn 111 [BETA-127232]	1410 +/- 60	-21.0‰	collagen	A.D. 530–730 (p=0.923); A.D. 740–770 (p=0.031)	Head et al. 2002:40
EgPn 111 [BETA-127233]	1370 +/- 60	-20.9‰	collagen	A.D. 560–780 (p=0.954)	Head et al. 2002:40
EgPs 63 [BETA-90057]	1410 +/- 60	-20.1‰	collagen	A.D. 530–730 (p =0.923); A.D. 740–770 (p=0.031)	Clarke et al. 1998:237
DkPj 1 [RL-331]	1410 +/-100	-20.0‰	collagen	A.D. 420–830 (p=0.941) A.D. 840–870 (p=0.013)	Reeves 1978; Morlan n.d.
DkPj 1 [GX-1220]	1540 +/- 90	-20.0‰	collagen	A.D. 330–660 (p=0.954)	Reeves 1978; Morlan n.d.
EhPv 78 [BSG 1013]	1540 +/- 100	?	charcoal	A.D. 250–300 (p=0.025) A.D. 320–670 (p=0.929)	Fedje 1986:57
EhPv 78 [BSG 1012]	1325 +/- 125	?	charcoal	A.D. 400–1000 (p=0.954)	Fedje 1986:57
FbPf 1 [GSC-696]	1350 +/- 150	-20.0‰	charred bone	A.D. 400–1050 (p=0.954)	Gruhn 1969:144; Morlan n.d.
EeOm 51 [BETA-222820]	1290 +/- 40	-25.7‰	charcoal	A.D. 650–820 (p=0.943) A.D. 840–860 (p=0.011)	Beaudoin, personal communication 2008

Muhlbach (FbPf 1). The Muhlbach site is a bison pound southwest of Stettler (Gruhn 1969). The researcher suggested the kill occurred under "marshy" conditions; however, at present, the site is located in an area of low grass-covered sand dunes near poplar and willow patches at the Parkland-Plains interface (Gruhn 1969:130–135). The site was excavated in the summer of 1965. A total of 128 m² was excavated, of an estimated potential 1,200 m² for the entire site (Gruhn 1969:129–132).

Sixty-one projectile points were associated with a bison bone bed (Gruhn 1969:140). Both bifacial (n=36) and flake points (n=25) were recovered. Although originally classified as Besant projectile points (Gruhn 1969:143; Reeves 1983a), this review considers these projectile points to be distinct from Besant specimens as described above. Other lithic tools included bifacial knives (one diamond shaped and one elongate), end scrapers (two square end scrapers), a possible perforator, five retouched flakes, two utilized flakes, and a polished pebble. The assemblage was dominated by Knife River flint, with a few artifacts made of black chert, silicified siltstone, and quartzite.

The bone bed was interpreted as a single component consisting entirely of bison bone. Few cranial bones were recovered. Most long bones had been fractured. Cobbles scattered throughout the bone bed were interpreted as hammers. Few bones were found in articulation. Mandibles were common and often appeared to have been stacked (Gruhn 1969:138). An MNI of at least one hundred animals was estimated. Eleven bone uprights occurred at the site; seven appeared to form parallel lines about 2 m apart. No ceramics were recovered. A single date of ca. 1,350 BP (Table 22) was obtained for the site (Gruhn 1969:144).

Echo Creek (EhPv 78, 515R). The Echo Creek site is a well-stratified site at the east end of Vermilion Lakes, northeast of Banff (Fedje 1986:55). Five occupations were observed. The lowest occupation was considered Besant and was overlaid by a possible Avonlea occupation, an Old Women's occupation, an unassigned Late Prehistoric occupation, and a post-1890s historic occupation (Fedje 1986:55–56). The Besant occupation yielded four large side-notched atlatl points. Three of the specimens are elongate. The points are manufactured on local Banff chert, Norquay chert, and an unsourced blue-grey chert (Greaves 1994:15). Some retouch detritus also occurred. The faunal assemblage included bison and a small ungulate that could not be identified to species. Limited amounts of FBR and two hearths were recorded. Two charcoal radiocarbon dates obtained from the occupation were ca. 1,300 BP and 1,500 BP (Table 22). These projectile points and retouched artifacts mirror items from Sonota sites and the dates place the assemblage in the appropriate time period. Still, the trademark lithic raw material Knife River flint was not recovered.

Pigeon Mountain (EgPt 28). The Pigeon Mountain site is a campsite on the south side of the Bow River at the base of Pigeon Mountain (Clarke et al. 1998:2). The site is located on level ground crosscut by a seasonal drainage tributary of the Bow River. Two distinct components were observed. The upper component contained Old Women's material. The lower component, however, contained Sonota material. The site was excavated during the summer of 1995. A total of 229 m² was excavated in the lower component (Clarke et al. 1998:8). A pipeline project impacted the site.

Thirty-two points (13 complete, 15 bases, 2 tips, and 2 refits) were recovered in association with fifty-five other tools, eleven hearths, nine FBR concentrations, lithic debitage (n = 5,531) and bone fragments (2,340) (Clarke et al. 1998). The illustrations indicated that many of the tools were marginally retouched flakes. Originally classified as Besant (Clarke et al. 1998:107–108), this review argues they should be classified as Sonota despite the range of variation exhibited by the sample. Other tools in the assemblage included bifaces (n = 3), scrapers (n = 17), multidirectional cores (n = 2), and utilized lithics (n = 33). Knife River flint and obsidian dominate the raw material used in tool manufacture and in the debitage. The preponderance of retouch and resharpening flakes in the debitage suggested tool-use and maintenance at the site.

The faunal assemblage was mainly bison (MNI = 16) although evidence of large and medium canid, elk, black bear, beaver, skunk, and two mollusc shells were recovered. A single bone awl was also present. The faunal assemblage had been heavily processed for marrow and grease. About 80 percent of the bone was concentrated around paired hearths and FBR features that presumably represent cooking and grease extraction (Clarke et al. 1998:193–206). No boiling pits, however, were identified at the site. Thirty-two fetal bison bones from at least two individuals suggested a late winter/early spring occupation (Clarke et al. 1998:154–160). No ceramics were recovered. No dates were available for the occupation.

EeOm 51. EeOm 51 is a Sonota-Avonlea campsite on an intermediate-level South Saskatchewan River terrace near McNeill on the Alberta-Saskatchewan border (Kozakavich 2001). Three distinct cultural components were observed. The uppermost and lowermost components were small scatters, while the middle component yielded the Sonota and Avonlea material. The site was tested by Green (2000) and excavated by Kozakavich (2001). A total of 31 m² was excavated (Kozakavich 2001:32). The site is in a pipeline right-of-way although it was avoided using directional drilling (Kozakavich 2001:74).

Three dart points, two arrow points, and five point preforms were associated with three hearths and a scatter of debitage and bone. Although the dart points were classified as Besant (Kozakavich 2001:54–55), this review reclassifies them as Sonota, based on the use of Knife River flint and the elongate form of the dart points. The remaining points are Avonlea and Avonlea preforms. Importantly, one of the Avonlea points was made of Knife River flint, a lithic resource within the distribution of the Sonota phase. The campsite appears to have been co-occupied by people producing both Sonota and Avonlea points. The stratigraphic placement of the material, the spacing of hearths, and the use of Knife River flint in both point styles support an interpretation of co-occupation.

The tool assemblage also included a single ovate asymmetrical knife, numerous biface fragments, multidirectional cores (n = 6), unidirectional cores (n = 7), retouched flakes (n = 15), and a utilized flake. A wide range of lithic raw materials were used at the site dominated by quartzite, quartz, Swan River chert, and petrified wood. The predominance of middle stage debitage suggested the manufacture of expedient tools rather than retooling (Kozakavich 2001:73).

The faunal assemblage yielded few identifiable bone fragments among the numerous fragments recovered (n = 10,450). Eight shell fragments were also recovered. All the bone fragments are expected to be bison (MNI = 1) with the exception of a single canid mandible fragment (MNI = 1). Bone fragments less than 5 cm were commonly associated with hearths and the cultural occupation level. These bone fragments together with FBR suggested food preparation and processing. No pottery was recovered. A date of ca. 1,300 BP (Table 22) was obtained. This date is at the end of the Sonota phase in Alberta and the beginning of the Avonlea phase.

Other sites. A number of other sites exhibit traits similar to the aforementioned sites, but lack rigorous presentation in the literature. They are reviewed here as reasonable candidates for inclusion within the Sonota phase of Alberta.

Reeves' (1978:158–159) excavations at the kill site of Head-Smashed-In Buffalo Jump produced Besant points from the youngest Middle Prehistoric period levels in both the South and North kill sites. Of the seven illustrated Besant points, five are made on Knife River flint (Reeves 1978:172). Unfortunately, the exact provenience of the specimens is not stated. The Besant material in the South Kill occurs immediately below an Avonlea level dated to 1,415 +/- 95 BP (GX-1399) (the associated GAK-1475 date is rejected, Blakeslee 1994) and above a Bracken level dated 2,005 +/- 80 BP (GX-1253). The Besant material in the North Kill occurs immediately below an Avonlea layer dated to 1,840 +/- 90 BP (RL-330) and 1,645 +/- 130 (GX-1252). It is within a layer that is possibly intermixed with Bracken material, dated to 1,330 +/- 100 (RL-331) and 1,460 +/- 90 BP (GX-1220). Reeves' (1978) geological cross-comparisons between the two excavations suggested that the two dates from the Avonlea layer in the North Kill are in error as the other three dates roughly correlate geologically and temporally. The two Avonlea dates in the North Kill are too early. Also, in the next section, strong evidence will be presented that Avonlea does not predate 1,350 BP in Alberta. It is not unreasonable to suggest the "Besant" (i.e., Sonota) material at Head-Smashed-In Buffalo Jump dates between 1,500 and 1,350 BP as expected for a Sonota assemblage. Still, a more rigorous evaluation of the points, their context, and dates at Head-Smashed-In Buffalo Jump is warranted.

At the Calderwood Buffalo Jump (DkPj 27), Level 4 produced a single elongate, straight-based point (Marshall 1988; Brink et al. 1987:72, fig. 2, lower left). Morphologically it is not unlike some of the larger Sonota specimens. Dawe (personal communication 2005) has indicated that it is made of miscellaneous hydrated chert. The culturally unassigned level overlying Level 4 produced four dates ranging between 1,300 and 1,530 BP, while a Bracken level below dated to between 1,900 and 2,200 BP.

Hartell Creek (EgPi 1) site is a multicomponent site west of Strathmore. Area A, on the east side of Hartell Creek, possesses eight occupation levels. The first occupation was considered Besant, the second and third occupations Besant and Avonlea, the fourth, fifth, and sixth occupations Old Women's with some intrusive Middle period points, and the seventh occupation was considered Old Women's. The eighth occupation lacks diagnostics but should date to the very Late Prehistoric/Early Protohistoric period. Unfortunately the site was not radiocarbon dated. The Besant specimens illustrated for Area A more closely resemble Sonota points (Murray et al. 1976:234, plate 11, nos. 3 and 4). With this perspective, their co-occurrence with Avonlea in the second and third occupations would be expected and does not require an explanation for the mixed assemblages.

Some surface collections also exhibit Sonota points. The Smith-Swainson collection is a large surface collection of projectile points made on brown chalcedony that strongly resembles Sonota materials. The find site was near Stettler. Similarly, Project Past recorded the Fewkes collection (FdPh 19). This surface collection consists of numerous elongate projectile points made of brown chalcedony; again, very similar in form to Sonota materials. The find site was located near Alix, east of Red Deer (George Chalut, personal communication 2008).

Sonota: Reviving the Neuman-Syms Perspective

The Sonota phase in Alberta can be distinguished from the earlier Besant phase by the presence of numerous elongate projectile points and flake points, intense utilization of Knife River flint, and post-Besant dates between 1,500 and 1,350 BP. As Syms (1977:90) alluded, Sonota sites date more recently in Alberta than most of those in the Middle Missouri, possibly indicating a population shift. As well, Sonota material in Alberta is represented by processing and kill sites, and an absence of campsites or burial mounds.

The projectile points associated with the Sonota phase have rarely been evaluated beyond likening them to Besant forms. Neuman (1975:17–18) provided the most detailed study of the points and outlined eleven groups (with one group being miscellaneous). Following Neuman's (1975:17–18) classification, most of the specimens are broad, triangular, convex-sided points with low, broad side-notches exhibiting a slightly convex, straight, or slightly concave bases. Some of the straight-based forms can have fairly straight-sided blades and be rather long and slender. Syms (1977:90) noted the high frequency of points made on trimmed flakes. These flake points are common at the Muhlbach, One-Eleven, and Pigeon Mountain sites. Syms (1977:90) considered the Besant and Samantha materials at Walter Felt to be Sonota based on point form, use of Knife River flint, and numerous flake points. Recall that Kehoe (1974) classified Layer 13 as containing Samantha and Besant points. The large Samantha points (Kehoe 1974:106, fig. 3A, B) fall within the Sonota range, while the Coteau and McLean Besant points (Kehoe 1974:106, fig. 3E–J) reflect Besant as defined in this text. Large Samantha points also occur in the subsequent level, Layer 10. Kehoe (1973, 1974) has produced somewhat conflicting interpretations of this material. In one instance he considered the material Samantha, a transitional Besant-to-Avonlea layer (Kehoe 1973:164), while in the second instance he suggested that it is a mixed assemblage of Prairie side-notched and Samantha points (Kehoe 1974:105). For the purposes of this review, the large Samantha points made on Knife River flint are considered to fall easily within the Sonota point form as defined above. As for the remaining points, Avonlea specimens are difficult to misidentify. The assemblage represents a co-occupation by people who made Sonota and Avonlea points.

The non-projectile part of the lithic tool assemblage might also provide some possible avenues to differentiate Sonota from Besant. Relatively large ovoid bifaces/knives appear to be fairly common in both the Sonota sites in Alberta and those in the Dakotas. Side scrapers are relatively common in the Alberta sites but were not noted in the Middle Missouri Sonota sites. Square-ended end scrapers were common across Sonota sites. Only a single bipolar core was noted in the Alberta sites, suggesting that such reduction techniques were not commonly utilized owing to abundant quarry materials. Retouched and utilized flakes appear to be very common across Sonota sites.

The lithic raw materials used at various Sonota sites show a heavy reliance on exotic sources. Based on this review, for the Sonota sites from Alberta discussed above, Knife River flint accounts for roughly 25.8 percent of all the raw material, followed by obsidian (20.1%,) miscellaneous cherts (17.7%), quartzite (11.5%), Swan River chert (7.4%), petrified wood (3.9%), and minor amounts of other materials. It should be noted that the high frequency of obsidian is somewhat misleading, as the majority of the flakes came from a single site and consisted largely of retouch flakes.

Pottery was only recovered from a single Sonota site in Alberta, EgPn 111. The small assemblage appeared to represent two vessels, based on rim sherds, conjoinable pieces, general similarities, and provenience (Head et al. 2002:164). The first vessel produced some sherds with exterior surfaces that exhibit smoothed fabric impressions, while the interior surface exhibits fabric impressions that have not been smoothed. A single potsherd that has a smooth exterior surface represents the second vessel (Head et al. 2002:167).

Canid remains, most likely wolf or dog, were recovered at almost every site. Individual specimens of fox, elk, deer, bear, beaver, skunk, and mountain sheep were also recovered. Most of this diversity came from the Pigeon Mountain site in the front range of the mountains. Regardless, just like sites in the Middle Missouri, there is an overwhelming reliance on bison for food. Wendy Unfreed (personal communication 2009) suggested there is a lack of intensive processing at the kill sites in Alberta, which might indicate that immediate retrieval of meat was the objective of the kills.

Features were relatively common at the reviewed sites. Hearths were primarily surface hearths although a few basin hearths were noted. Concentrations of bone and FBR were noted. Large amounts of FBR were reported for every site reviewed except Muhlbach, and this is likely because it was an excavation within the pound rather than a peripheral processing area. Only a single site possibly contained a boiling pit. The Muhlbach site was the only excavation to produce bone uprights. This is somewhat surprising given how common bone uprights are in Sonota sites in the Middle Missouri area.

Sonota material has been mistakenly attributed to the Besant phase in areas adjacent to Alberta. In Saskatchewan, Sonota sites are very similar in nature to those in Alberta. Campsites, processing sites, and kill sites have been excavated. Burial mounds have only been noted in Manitoba. In terms of dating, there is a tendency for Sonota sites in Alberta to date relatively late compared to the known range of the Sonota phase. This, however, is not true across Saskatchewan. Sites in the southeast corner of the province can date as early as any Sonota sites in the Middle Missouri.

At the Mortlach (EcNl 1) site, Sonota material was recovered from Zone 3 (Wettlaufer 1955:36). Wettlaufer (1955:36) called this assemblage the Caron culture. It consisted of two relatively elongate points made on Knife River flint, an ovoid biface, a partial blade of Knife River flint, a number of scrapers, retouched flakes, and a hammerstone. Wettlaufer (1955:39) noted the predominance of brown chalcedony as the lithic raw material and the absence of pottery at the site. This material overlaid four successive Besant levels, Occupations 4A–D. Occupation 4B produced a radiocarbon date of 1,660 +/-159 BP (S-22). The distinct point form, presence of Knife River flint, and the date all strongly support the inclusion of this assemblage within the Sonota phase.

The Long Creek (DgMr 1) site produced a Sonota assemblage in Level 3 (Wettlauffer and Mayer-Oakes 1960:40–43). Wettlaufer and Mayer-Oakes (1960:41) considered this assemblage to be Besant, although two of the four points are very elongate forms (reminiscent of Sonota points) and an ovoid biface. Brown chalcedony was mentioned, but a review of artifact material type was lacking. Two small pieces of pottery were noted but considered intrusive (Wettlaufer and Mayer-Oakes 1960:43). The level overlaid a Pelican Lake assemblage and was overlain by an Avonlea assemblage. A date was not obtained for this material. Bryant's (2002:126–139) reanalysis noted five points, all of Knife River flint, an ovoid biface, and four retouched flakes of Knife River flint. The true provenience of the pottery from this level was never clearly stated although a variety of lines of evidence suggested it is associated with the level (Bryant 2002:127).

EdOh 23, in the Great Sand Hills, was discovered in a dune blowout (Johnson 1983). The area produced two complete points, point fragments (n=5), a large ovoid biface, retouched flakes (n=14), and end scrapers (n=11). Of these, all are made on Knife River flint, except two retouched flakes of green jasper, and a white chalcedony biface (Johnson 1983:42). Pottery was not noted at the site (Johnson 1983:44). A radiocarbon date of 1,755

+/- 115 BP (S-2348) was obtained (Johnson 1983:43). Although the date is somewhat early for Sonota in western Saskatchewan, the point forms and presence of Knife River flint otherwise match the profile.

The Fitzgerald site (ElNp 8) is a single-component bison pound site in the Moose Woods Sand Hills about 15 km southeast of Saskatoon (Hjermstad 1996). Although classified as Besant, the point assemblage falls within Sonota as it is defined here, with 122 bifacial and twenty-one flake points or point fragments. Knife River flint dominated the lithic assemblage for points and debitage (Hjermstad 1996:76–81). Three pottery sherds and a rolled ball of dried clay were recovered but are not diagnostic (Hjermstad 1996:81). Bone uprights were also observed at the site (Hjermstad 1996:90). Four radiocarbon dates were obtained for the site: 1,240 +/- 170 BP (S-3547); 1,350 +/- 140 BP (S-3546); 1,420 +/- 65 BP (Beta-69004); and 1,570 +/- 90 BP (Beta-69005) (Hjermstad 1996:25–28).

The Melhagen (EgNn 1) site is a bison kill site about 6 km south of Elbow, south-central Saskatchewan. The projectile point assemblage consisted of elongate and flake points made mainly on Knife River flint (Ramsay 1991:95–125). Trampling in the once muddy bone bed obscured the stratigraphy at the site (Ramsay 1991:15). Radiocarbon dates have been interpreted as representing more than one occupation (Ramsay 1991:148–153). If a very recent date is rejected (i.e., 890 +/- 205 BP, S-2857), two clusters of dates occur, with the older dates coming from the south and central parts of the site and the more recent dates from the north and western parts of the site. Respectively, the older and younger groups of dates are: (1) 1,985 +/- 110 BP (S-2855); 1,990 +/- 75 BP (S-1640); 2,040 +/- 90 BP (S-491); and (2) 1,655 +/- 115 BP (S-2856) and 1,790 +/- 55 BP (S-1641). At two standard deviations, however, the dates overlap (Ramsay 1991:150).

The Walter Felt (EcNm 8) site is a multicomponent site on a wooded terrace about 10 km south of Mortlach (Kehoe 1964:51; 1973:164; 1974:103). Level 13 is dated at 1,610 +/- 70 BP (S-200) and contained both Besant and Sonota materials, including seventeen pottery sherds. Kehoe (1974) noted two large Samantha points of brown chalcedony (i.e., Sonota points) amongst the eight Besant points, four of petrified wood and one each of chalcedony, jasper, argillite, and quartzite. The layer immediately above contains both Sonota and Avonlea materials with dates of 1,535 +/- 80 BP (S-201) and 1,535 +/- 90 BP (S-260). Some of this material was made on brown chalcedony (Kehoe 1965, 1974).

The Garratt site (EcNj 7) is a multicomponent site on the alluvial flood plain on the west side of Moose Jaw Creek in Moose Jaw (Morgan 1979). Level 8 produced three points considered Besant-Samantha points (Morgan 1979:366–367). The points included one large specimen, a smaller flake point, and a base, of which two were made of Knife River flint and one of chert (Morgan 1979:366–370). The lithic assemblage as a whole consisted of 18.4 percent (n = 34) Knife River flint (Morgan 1979:370). A test pit about 50 m south recovered five pottery sherds exhibiting cord impressions and smoothing; the material was stratigraphically correlated to Level 8 of the main excavation described above (Morgan 1979:76, 90). While Morgan (1979:219) and Dyck (1983:120) have accepted the pottery as Besant, Syms (1977:92) suggested the pottery most resembles Sonota material. Morgan (1979:219) further acknowledged that the high frequency of Knife River flint in the lithic assemblage is diagnostic of the Sonota complex. Level 8 is dated to 1,990 +/- 75 BP (S-409) (Morgan 1979:246). Interestingly, the subsequent occupation is an Avonlea component that produced nineteen Avonlea points and a single Sonota-like point (Morgan 1979:322; plate 25, S). Three dates were obtained for this level: 1,450 +/- 70 BP (S-406); 1,280 +/- 60 BP (S-408); and rejected date 6,100 +/- 100 BP (S-407) (Morgan 1979:246). Level 8 of Garratt would appear to have more in common with Sonota than Besant.

The Crane site (DiMv 93) is a multicomponent campsite located on the Souris River northwest of Estevan (Gibson and McKeand 1992). Occupations VII–IX produced pottery and Sonota points, sometimes in association with bone uprights. The oldest Sonota occupation, Occupation IX, immediately overlaid an occupation dated to 2,050 +/- 75 BP (S-3212). The subsequent Sonota occupation, VIII, produced a date of 1,740 +/- 65 BP (S-3211), while the most recent Sonota occupation, VII, produced a date of 1,680 +/- 75 BP (S-3213) (Morlan n.d.). The significance of this sequence is that it illustrates a strong presence of the Sonota phase in southeastern Saskatchewan at an early date, prior to its expansion northwest.

EdNh 35 is a campsite/processing site on the second terrace of the deeply incised valley of Moose Jaw River, about 3.4 km upstream from its confluence with the Qu'Appelle River (Cloutier 2004:90–91). A total of 54 m^2 was excavated at the site, which produced a Besant/Avonlea component overlying a Pelican Lake Component. Radiocarbon dates from two features believed to be associated with the Besant/Avonlea component were 1,378 +/- 45 BP (BGS-2340) and 1,283 +/- 60 BP (BGS-2341), produced from a hearth and a bone upright, respectively. The features (n = 23) in the component included twelve hearths and eleven bone uprights. The Besant points were elongate, with five of six manufactured on Knife River flint. Knife River flint (n = 136) is the fourth most common raw material behind Swan River chert (n = 1,039), silicified peat (n = 407), and unidentified cherts (n = 203) (Cloutier 2004:115). Ceramics (n = 143) had fabric impressions (n = 42) and net impression (n = 2) and were classified as Rock Lake Net/Fabric-Impressed exteriors, an Avonlea pottery type. Some sherds (n = 16) were smooth and some (n = 5) had cord-roughened exteriors not unlike Sonota pottery. Most of the fauna was considered to be bison (Cloutier 2004:118). Cloutier (2004:121–130) argued that the Besant/Avonlea occupation is a result of component admixture rather than the simultaneous occupation of the site by Besant and Avonlea. Given the revision of the Sonota and Besant phases outlined above, it is here suggested that this is a co-occupation of Sonota and Avonlea at campsite/processing site at about 1,400 BP.

Based on the recovery of Besant points in apparent association with pottery, other sites in Saskatchewan might fit into the Sonota phase. Sites to reconsider include Bennett (DjMw 27), Ratigan (DhMs 10), and Biggar Bone (FaNx 3) (Scribe 1997:106 113). Similarly, the recovery of numerous long, side-notched Besant points often made on brown chalcedony at the Bakken-Wright (DiOa 1) site, along the Frenchman River, may indicate another Sonota site in Saskatchewan (Adams 1975:152, 195, plate IX, row 1).

In Manitoba, the Partridge Hill (DiLw 2) site is southeast of Brandon. It produced four potsherds with cord-roughened surfaces in association with fifty-five lithics of Knife River flint and Swan River chert (Scribe 1997:69–72; Scribe and Nicholson 1994). The material was considered a Sonota assemblage (Scribe 1997:72).

The 'Elk Love It' (DiLw 12) site is southeast of Brandon. One hundred sixty-seven potsherds were recovered, including tool-impressed body sherds, sherds with incised decorations, smooth sherds, and cord-roughened sherds (Scribe 1997:73–81; Scribe and Nicholson 1994). A point was associated with this material but not described. Still, the lithic assemblage was mainly Knife River flint, followed by Swan River chert. Interestingly, Tongue River silicified sediment from South Dakota was fairly common (Scribe 1997:74–75). A date of 1,220 +/- 75 BP (Beta-59415) was recovered from the upper levels of the Sonota component while a date of 1,660 +/- 75 BP (Beta-59414) was recovered from the lower part of the same component (Scribe 1997:81; Morlan n.d.).

The 'A Place Where Things Are Put Away' (DiLt 17) site is located adjacent to the McLaren Earthworks in southwestern Manitoba. The site is a multicomponent site that produced everything from Pelican Lake points to Late Side-notched points. Eight Plains Woodland potsherds were recovered in the same vicinity as Sonota/Besant and Avonlea points (Scribe 1997:83; Playford 1996:70). A co-occupation of the site by Sonota and Avonlea could not be demonstrated (Playford 1996:70).

The Richards site (DhLw 1) was assigned to the Sonota phase by Syms (1977) based on its similarity to Neuman's (1975) material in North and South Dakota (see above). An analysis of the surface collected projectile points from the Richards site noted extensive use of Knife River flint and elongate projectile points (Paulson 1980:10). Illustrated specimens are identical to elongate, low-notched Sonota points (Paulson 1980, plate 2-4). Following Syms (1977:92), other diagnostic items recovered included long awls on blade-like flakes, small grooved mauls, atlatl weights, and large spokeshaves (Paulson 1980:10).

At the Avery site (DhLs 2) in south-central Manitoba, Joyes (1970:210) described a Besant assemblage made largely of Knife River flint in association with cord-roughened pottery. This site might be a candidate to be reclassified as Sonota. Other sites in southwestern Manitoba that likely fall within the Sonota phase include United Church, Kain (Nicholson 1985, 1994), Mullet (Nicholson 1985; Scribe 1997:94), Calf Mountain (Joyes 1970:214), Vera (Nicholson and Hamilton 1997), and the Oak Lake Localities (Fardoe 1977).

In North and South Dakota, Neuman (1975) originally defined the Sonota complex using materials at the Stelzer (39DW242), Swift Bird (39DW233), Grover Hand (39DW240), Arpan (39DW252), and Boundary (32SL1) mound sites, with additional data from the Baldhill Mounds (32BA1), Schmidt (32MO20), and Alkire Mound (32SI200) sites, the Porcupine Creek Component at site 32SI6, and House 2 at the La Roche site. In addition to these sites are the following Sonota sites.

The High Butte (32ME13) site is a butte top occupation site and associated "turf cut turtle effigy "in the Missouri Valley, near the Garrison Dam in central North Dakota (Wood and Johnson 1973). Fourteen points were recovered; they tend to be elongate with low notches and manufactured on Knife River flint (Wood and Johnson 1973:45, 51, 52, fig. 4a–f). Twenty-five body sherds and five rim sherds were recovered, representing four vessels. Both a grooved paddle creating simple stamp impressions and cord-wrapped paddle whose impressions were smoothed were observed on the surface of the sherds. Decorations include bosses near the rim and tool impressions on the lip (Wood and Johnson 1973:42–44, 60, fig. 7). Charcoal from a hearth produced a date of 1,600 +/- 145 BP (N-1428) (Wood and Johnson 1973:70; Morlan n.d.)

Site 32OL270 is a stone circle site located on the southern edge of the Missouri River trench in central North Dakota (Fredlund et al. 1985:116). Fifty-two points were recovered, which were generally elongate with notches low on the lateral edges (Fredlund et al. 1985:134, fig. 6). Knife River flint accounts for a large part of the lithic material recovered at the site (Fredlund et al. 1985:135). Cord-roughed Plains Woodland pottery sherds were recovered but not described (Fredlund 1985:132). As well, seven bone uprights were noted (Fredlund et al. 1985:128). Fourteen radiocarbon dates suggested two periods were represented, an early occupation of about 1,550 BP and a later occupation of about 1,050 BP (Fredlund et al. 1985:137–138). Despite problems with associations this appears to be, at least in part, a Sonota campsite.

The Doaks Butte site (32BO222) is a large base camp on a high promontory (Doaks Butte) between the Little Missouri River and Box Elder Creek (Toom 2001). A wide range of points were recovered from the site but most fall within the range expected for the Sonota phase (Root et al. 2001:9.47, fig. 9-8). Knife River flint dominated the lithic and tool assemblage. Pottery recovered at the site is conical with cord-roughed exterior surfaces (Toom 2001:8.1). Ten dates suggest an age of about 1,750 BP (Toom 2001:5.61).

Naze (32SN246) is a multicomponent site that produced an early Sonota component with radiocarbon dates of ca. 2,003 +/- 43 BP (SMU-1758); 1,918 +/- 36 BP (SMU-1778); and 2,035 +/- 70 BP (UGA-1398) (Gregg and Swenson 1987:74). Twelve points were recovered. They were originally classified as nine Besant points, a Samantha point, and two Pelican Lake points (Gregg 1987:444). The generally elongate forms mixed with more corner-notched specimens fall within the range of variation expected for Sonota points. Large amounts of Knife River flint as well as obsidian from Obsidian Cliffs in Yellowstone, Rainy Buttes silicified wood, and porcellanite were all recovered (Gregg 1987:445). Some unsourced copper in the form of beads and an awl was also recovered. Potsherds were relatively common, often exhibiting exterior or interior bosses and mainly cord-roughened surfaces but sometimes smooth or fabric impressed (Gregg 1987:444).

Other sites in North and South Dakota that deserve consideration as Sonota sites include Highway 8, Nightstalkers Butte, Buffalo Lodge Lake, Beeber, Martain, Jamestown Mounds, Wounded Knee, Indian Hill and Natchke.

In Montana, the Whiskey Hill (24DW1001) site near Lambert in extreme eastern Montana is a surface-collected occupation site (Johnson 1977). Five points and nine pieces of pottery were recovered. The projectile points are elongate with low notches manufactured on Knife River flint (n=1) and porcellanite (n=4). The pottery is cord-wrapped impressed with smoothing on the inside and outside, with some sherds exhibiting a single row of bosses. A charcoal dated of 1,550+/- 60 BP (Wis. 914) was obtained from an exposed hearth (Johnson 1977:35).

Antonsen (24GA660) is a multicomponent bison kill site located west of Bozeman in southwestern Montana (Davis and Zeier 1978; Zeier 1983). Two hundred eighty points were recovered. Most of the points exhibit an elongate form with notches low on the base (Davis and Zeier 1978:229, fig. 21.6; Zeier 1983, figs. 14–16, 19). Only a few specimens were made of Knife River flint, with the majority manufactured on basalt, obsidian, and a mix of cherts, chalcedony, and jasper (Davis and Zeier 1978:230). A single radiocarbon date was obtained: 1,605 +/- 90 BP (I-7027) (Zeier 1983:5). Interestingly, Davis and Zeier (1978:230) suggested that the Besant assemblage represented newcomers to the area, based on their apparent lack of familiarity with local rock types.

Wahkpa Chu'gn (24HL101) is a bison kill site near Havre in north-central Montana (Davis and Stallcop 1966). Excavations in Area B of the site produced a single occupation, consisting of a bone bed and large side- to corner-notched points (Davis and Stallcop 1966). These points were classified as Besant, with 40 percent of the specimens manufactured on milky to brown chalcedony (Davis and Stallcop 1966). In Davis and Stallcop's (1966:41, plate 3) illustrations, some specimens are strikingly similar to the Sonota materials. A radiocarbon date for this material was not available.

The Mini-Moon site (24DW85) is a multicomponent site, with the upper component described as a Besant campsite, in the upper badlands of eastern Montana (Hughes 1991). Ten points were recovered but were neither described nor illustrated. Raw materials in the assemblage included porcellanite, Yellowstone River cobbles, silicified wood, and Knife River flint (Hughes 1991:28). There was no mention of pottery. A charcoal date of 1,520 +/- 70 BP (Beta-10044) was obtained (Hughes 1991:28). Given the previous review, it can be predicted that further research should find that the Mini-Moon site produced elongate, side-notched points comparable to Sonota material.

The Kobold site (24BH406) is a multicomponent bison kill site that may contain comparable material to the Sonota phase. The site is located at the head of Rosebud Creek in southern Montana (Frison 1970:1). Level III produced seventy points and point fragments (37 metamorphosed shale, 20 chert, 11 quartzite, and 2 obsidian) that are not unlike Sonota materials (Frison 1970:16–17, fig. 12). The level is estimated to date to the Late Middle period (Frison 1970:33)

Other sites in Montana that appear to exhibit traits of the Sonota phase include the Dago Hill (24CA72) and Stelling (24CA73) bison pound sites located west of Great Falls in west-central Montana. Both sites have been destroyed, but collections of artifacts from each exist. Illustrations of points from the Dago Hill site (Shumate 1976, figs. 4 and 5) and Stelling site (Shumate 1976, figs. 8 and 9) exhibit the elongate point form with low notches. At both sites the points are largely made of brown jasper and chert, but Knife River flint specimens were noted (Shumate 1976:15, 25). A radiocarbon date, GAK-1506, was not accepted (Shumate 1976:26; Reeves 1983a; Blakeslee 1994). As well, a survey on the Canyon Ferry Reservoir, west-central Montana, may have produced a number of Sonota points at Locality VIII (Greiser 1986:159, fig. 147f–n).

In Wyoming, the Ruby site (48CA302) is a single-component bison pound in the Power River Basin, in the northeast part of the state (Frison 1971). The illustrated points tend to be fairly elongate with low notches on the sides or possibly corners of the specimens (Frison 1971, fig. 4). The site has two dates: 1,670 +/- 135 BP (GX-1157) and 1,800 +/- 140 BP (M-2348) (Frison 1991a:34, 1971:77). The points are morphologically quite similar to the Sonota assemblages to the east, and the radiocarbon dates place the material as a contemporary.

The Butler-Rissler site (48NA100) is a single-component campsite that is located on a terrace of the North Platte River in central Wyoming (Miller and Waitkus 1989:1). Twelve elongate, side-notched points were recovered and classified as Besant or Samantha (Miller and Waitkus 1989:11–12). The lithic assemblage was in excess of 90 percent cherts most likely from Mississippian-age Madison limestone outcrops (Millar and Waitkus 1989:10). Many pottery sherds (n = 3,419) were recovered. At least two vessels are represented, based on rim and lip morphology and both have exterior cord-roughened surfaces. One vessel was decorated with a row of punctates below the rim while the other did not show decorative elements (Miller and Waitkus 1989:18; Miller et al. 1987). Two dates were produced for the site: 1,660 +/- 90 BP (Beta-17830) and 1,800 +/- 100 BP (Beta-25271; Eth-3782) (Miller and Waitkus 1989:23–24).

Other sites in Wyoming that could be included in the Sonota phase include the Muddy Creek site (48CR324) in south-central Wyoming (Hughes 1981; Frison 1991a:34), the Cedar Gap site (48NA83) (Frison 1991a:34; Meyer 1992), the Willow Springs site (48AB130) (Bupp 1981), and the Grayrocks site (48PL65) (Tibesar 1980).

To summarize, the Sonota phase began ca. 2,000 BP in North Dakota, South Dakota, and southeastern Saskatchewan. By ca. 1,800 BP, an expansion into Wyoming was underway but did not last longer than ca. 1,600 BP. By ca. 1,500 BP, Sonota had expanded into Montana and southern Alberta. For Alberta, this intrusion terminated the Besant phase. The abruptness of the event in time and the clear replacement of all aspects of Besant material culture by Sonota material culture suggest a movement of people out of the Middle Missouri, replacing the Besant people occupying southern Alberta.

Sites in the Middle Missouri consist of large tipi encampments, campsites, kill sites, and burial mounds. Similarly, sites in southeastern Saskatchewan tend to be tipi campsites and kill sites. As one moves to Alberta and Wyoming, areas occupied during the late Sonota phase, the sites tend to be mainly large kill sites. The preponderance of kill sites in Alberta and Wyoming is interesting. Wendy Unfreed (personal communication 2009) has suggested that a different subsistence pattern, with a focus on meat extraction at the expense of more extensive processing was being pursued. Perhaps Alberta, Wyoming, and Montana for that matter, were being exploited for bison resources as a hinterland, with people returning to the homeland in North Dakota, South Dakota, and southeast Saskatchewan. Alternatively, the pattern in Alberta may suggest winter exploitation of bison at the periphery of the Plains. Further, the sites may represent an abandonment of the Middle Missouri due to population pressures or economic issues relating to the Hopewell Interaction sphere.

Another perplexing aspect of the Sonota phase is its relationship with the Avonlea phase. There are a number of sites at which people of the Sonota phase and the Avonlea phase appear to have cohabited. The Miniota site in western Manitoba is one of the earliest Avonlea sites. It is a residential occupation exhibiting fifty-six Avonlea points, thirty-eight unnotched points/preforms, and a single possible Sonota point (Landals et al. 2004:78–86). Knife River flint dominates the lithic assemblage (Landals et al. 2004:102). The site dates to ca. 1,550 BP. The Walter Felt site is located in south-central Saskatchewan. Layer 12 produced Sonota and Avonlea materials and dates of 1,535 +/- 80 BP (S-201) and 1,535 +/- 90 BP (S-260). Some of this material was made on brown chalcedony (Kehoe 1965, 1974). The Garratt site near Moose Jaw in south-central Saskatchewan produced nineteen Avonlea points, twenty-nine Avonlea preforms, and a Sonota point in Level 6. Three dates were obtained for the level: 1,450 +/- 70 BP (S-406); 1,280 +/- 60 BP (S-408); and rejected date 6,100 +/- 100 BP (S-407) (Morgan 1979:246). EdNh 35 is a campsite/processing site on the Moose Jaw River just upstream from its confluence with the Qu'Appelle River (Cloutier 2004:90–91). Five of six Sonota points recovered were manufactured on Knife River flint while four of eight Avonlea points were on Knife River flint. Knife River Flint accounts for about 12 percent of the lithic raw material at the site. Radiocarbon dates for the occupation were 1,378 +/ 45 BP (BGS-2340) and 1,283 +/- 60 BP (BGS-2341). Lastly, EeOm 51 is a campsite in southeastern Alberta that produced three Sonota points, two Avonlea points, and five Avonlea preforms. A date of 1,290 +/- 40 BP (Beta-222820) was obtained for the occupation.

Since exotic lithics such as Knife River flint are rare in Avonlea sites (Vickers 1994:15), it is possible that the people of the Sonota phase to the south provided a source for this desirable lithic resource. Added to this is the time gradient from east to west for the timing of the cohabited sites. Sonota and Avonlea occur together earliest in the east (i.e., Miniota) and continue to meet farther west later in time. Thus, the most recent site to exhibit Sonota-Avonlea cohabitation is EeOm 51 in Alberta. It is possible that Avonlea was replacing Sonota from east to west. The people of the Sonota phase appear to be openly meeting and cooperating with people of the Avonlea phase during this movement west, as witnessed in the cohabited sites. The movement west by Avonlea at the apparent expense of Sonota is not surprising from a technological perspective, as the Sonota phase utilizes dart technology while the Avonlea phase is the first archaeological culture on the Northern Plains to exclusively use bow technology (e.g., Vickers 1994:14).

After the last cohabitation of Sonota and Avonlea at EeOm 51 in eastern Alberta, Sonota sites no longer occur. The movement of Sonota out of the Middle Missouri and the parallel movement of Avonlea from northern Minnesota ceases with Avonlea occupying southeastern Saskatchewan and southern Alberta. One final intriguing observation about Sonota and Avonlea concerns their apparently disparate weapons technology. The Sonota dart, when viewed without a scale, appears quite similar to the Avonlea arrow point in morphology (Barry Newton, personal communication 2008).

Late Prehistoric Period

6

CA. 1,350 TO 250 BP

Infrequent drought between ca. 2,000 and 1,000 BP likely produced a period of unprecedented abundance and dependability of plant and animal resources (Vance 1991:155). Roughly 1,060 BP demarks the onset of increased drought associated with the Medieval Warm period. Periods of high moisture interspersed with periods of low moisture created some uncertainty in the productivity of the environment. About 700 BP the period of increased drought ended, followed by a relatively modern regime. An exception to the modern regime was a wetter, cooler period from ca. 500 to 100 BP called the Little Ice Age.

AVONLEA PHASE (CA. 1,350 TO 1,100 BP)

In Alberta, the Avonlea phase ushers in the Late Prehistoric period, traditionally beginning around 1,700–1,400 BP and continuing until approximately 1,100–900 BP (Reeves 1983a). For Saskatchewan, Dyck (1983:113) placed the Besant phase as the first cultural unit of the Late Prehistoric period, on the inference that it was associated with ceramics. The Avonlea phase is widely distributed across Alberta, with most archaeological materials recovered from the Plains, but Avonlea materials have been found beyond the plains region in the parkland, foothills, and mountain front of Alberta (Reeves 1983a; Vickers 1986:92; Peck and Hudecek-Cuffe 2003). Similarly, Avonlea has been recovered on the plains of Saskatchewan and to a lesser extent in the parklands (Smith and Walker 1988) and forest edge (Meyer et al. 1988). As well, Avonlea points have been found in eastern Montana (Fraley 1988), South Dakota (Hannus and Nowak 1988), south of the Missouri (Brumley and Dau 1988:41), and in Manitoba (Joyes 1988) although they are scarce in these areas.

Forbis (1960) and Wettlaufer and Mayer-Oakes (1960) almost simultaneously began interpreting Avonlea material. Forbis (1960) described the Avonlea point based on excavations at the Upper Kill site in southern Alberta. Although he recognized the uniqueness of these points, Forbis (1960:123, 130) labelled them the "Upper Kill type." Wettlaufer and Mayer-Oakes (1960: 37–41, 107) coined the term *Avonlea* to describe the small, triangular, thin, side-notched projectile point observed at the Avonlea site. The term Avonlea was derived from a mid-1950s excavation of a single-component site near the town of Avonlea. The town had received its name from the most popular novel of the day, *Anne of Avonlea* (Morlan 1988:291). The first published reference to the Avonlea phase, however, is in the Long Creek report (Wettlaufer and Mayer-Oakes 1960:37–41, 107). Kehoe and McCorquodale (1961) described the point type as readily distinguishable and a horizon marker for archaeologists on the Plains. Basing his interpretations on his work at the Gull Lake site and the Boarding School Bison Drive site, Kehoe (1966:830) provided a synthesis of the Avonlea point and its place in the Small Side-notched point system of the Northern Plains. His review suggested the co-occurrence of three varieties of Avonlea points: Gull Lake Classic variety, Carmichael wide-eared variety, and the Timber Ridge sharp-eared variety.

In 1970, Reeves (1983a:161–162) produced an assessment of the characteristics of the Avonlea phase. The most striking artifacts of Avonlea assemblages are finely made, extremely thin, triangular points with side notches and slightly concave bases. All Avonlea points are believed to be arrow tips, as the Avonlea phase is regarded as the first phase on the Northwestern Plains that exclusively used bow technology (Vickers 1994:14). Based on his excavations at Head-Smashed-In Buffalo Jump, Reeves (1983a:61) distinguished two types of Avonlea points: Head-Smashed-In corner-notched and Timber Ridge side-notched. He differentiated the points by shoulder shapes. Head-Smashed-In corner-notched points are earlier and have acute or barbed shoulders, while Timber Ridge side-notched points are later and characterized by obtuse shoulders. Reeves' (1983a) use of the Timber Ridge side-notched point encompasses Kehoe's (1966) three varieties while the term *Head-Smashed-In Corner-notched* (Reeves 1983a) is recognized as an earlier variant of the Avonlea side-notched points (e.g., at Head-Smashed-In Buffalo Jump). Small, unnotched, triangular points commonly found in association with Avonlea assemblages are often interpreted as preforms, possibly manufactured for trade (Dawe 1987).

While the Avonlea side-notched point type is very similar throughout its entire distributional range, pottery associated with the Avonlea assemblage may exhibit regional variation (Walde et al. 1995:21). Kehoe (1966) originally described the Avonlea phase as being aceramic, but there is now overwhelming evidence that Avonlea assemblages are associated with pottery. Byrne (1973) provided evidence of this for Alberta with his definition of Saskatchewan Basin complex: Early Variant. Byrne (1973) characterized Avonlea pottery as exhibiting a plain-fabric/net-impressed exterior. The morphology was a simple globular or coconut form. The lips were flat or ridged with little or no trace of thickening. Decoration was largely restricted to one or more bands of punctates below the lip. Byrne (1973) suggested Alberta's pottery was related to Avonlea pottery in south-central Saskatchewan, with its ultimate origins in Laurel pottery from Manitoba.

As discussed in Peck and Hudecek-Cuffe (2003:80), differences in surface treatment and the distribution of parallel-grooved and net-impressed pottery possibly suggest separate origins, influences, interactions, and contact (Johnson 1988:141). Parallel-grooved pottery was identified in Avonlea components at the Morkin site (Byrne 1973) in Alberta (Walde et al. 1995:22), the Avonlea (Klimko and Hanna 1988) and Sjovold sites (Dyck 1983) in Saskatchewan, and at the Henry Smith (Quigg 1988a) and the Fantasy sites (Tratebas and Johnson 1988) in Montana. Johnson (1988:141) noted that the parallel-grooved type of Avonlea pottery was less common on the Canadian Plains than the net-impressed pottery. She suggested that parallel-grooved pottery may have an antecedent in previous pottery in the Northern Plains but possibly it derived from outside influences or a novelty within Avonlea populations (Johnson 1988:140). Quigg (1988a:148) supported this interpretation of pottery distribution by noting that net-impressed pottery is the predominant type recovered south of the Parkland during the Avonlea phase. Some sites have yielded both net-impressed and parallel-grooved ceramics (e.g., the Garratt site in Saskatchewan; Morgan 1979), indicating geographical overlap in the two kinds of pottery (Walde et al. 1995:22).

Quigg (1988b) identified a third Avonlea pottery type from northern Montana and the extreme southern portion of Alberta. This pottery is characterized by shouldered vessels with slightly constricted necks that have out-curving rims. Quigg (1988b) recovered it at the Corey Ranch site in Montana and noted its occurrence at the Morkin (Byrne 1973) and Upper Kill sites (Wormington and Forbis 1965) in southern Alberta (see also Walde et al. 1995:22). Walde, Meyer, and Unfreed (1995:22–23) have argued that the frequent occurrence of similar pottery to this Avonlea type in subsequent Old Women's assemblages suggests continuity between Avonlea and Old Women's in northern Montana and southern Alberta. This seems reasonable, as Quigg (1988b:151) demonstrated that shouldered vessels date up to the time of the Old Women's phase while parallel-grooved pottery does not appear to date this late.

Many other artifact types are associated with Avonlea assemblages, however, that are not regarded as diagnostic (Vickers 1994:15). Following Peck and Hudecek-Cuffe (2003), many Avonlea assemblages exhibit strong reliance on locally available lithics such as cherts, quartzites, and chalcedonies. Exotic lithics such as Madison Formation cherts from central and southern Montana, Knife River flint from North Dakota quarries, obsidian from the Yellowstone Park area in northwestern Wyoming, and porcellanite from various quarries in Montana and Wyoming are relatively rare in Avonlea assemblages (Brumley and Dau 1988:42). As Vickers (1994:15) points out, however, some Avonlea assemblages have relatively high percentages of exotic lithics, such as the components at the Garratt site (Morgan 1979) and the Gull Lake site (Kehoe 1966b) in Saskatchewan, and the Lost Terrace site (Greiser 1988) in Montana. The possible influence of the Sonota phase at such sites is discussed above.

A variety of Avonlea site types have been identified in Alberta. These include bison jump sites such as Head-Smashed-In Buffalo Jump (Reeves 1978; Brink et al. 1986; Brink and Dawe 1989) and bison pounds such as Ramillies (Brumley 1976). Other sites types included campsites such as Morkin (Byrne 1973), Manyfingers (Quigg 1988a), and H.M.S. Balzac (Head 1985, 1986), as well as processing sites such as Larson (Milne 1988), and tipi ring sites such as Empress (Hudecek 1989). Ceremonial sites include sites such as the Majorville Medicine Wheel and Cairn (Calder 1977) and the Manyberries Medicine Wheel (Brumley 1988:7–24).

The initial evidence suggested Avonlea people were semi-nomadic hunters using the bow and arrow at jumps and pounds to focus almost exclusively on the hunting of bison. Additional archaeological evidence has indicated that Avonlea peoples practiced diverse subsistence strategies. "These strategies included the exploitation of fish, waterfowl, and small mammals in the Saskatchewan parklands (Smith and Walker 1988); the use of elk, moose, bison, and beaver along the Saskatchewan forest edge (Meyer et al. 1988); and the hunting of pronghorn in Montana (Davis and Fisher 1988)" (Peck and Hudecek-Cuffe 2003). This range of procurement strategies were in addition and/or complementary to the exploitation of bison on the plains (Kehoe et al. 1988; Klimko and Hanna 1988; Milne 1988; Quigg 1988b; Ruebelmann 1988). Avonlea settlement patterns are not well understood. Avonlea sites are located in areas that suggest they moved in anticipation of where the bison would be next (Peck 2004). The Avonlea assemblages at the Ramillies site indicate spring to summer hunting on the open plains, whereas Avonlea assemblages at sites such as Head-Smashed-In Buffalo Jump likely reflect fall to winter harvesting of herds that were moving or had moved to their wintering grounds.

The origin of the Avonlea phase is a much-discussed issue. Kehoe (1966:839, Kehoe and Kehoe 1968:28–30) originally proposed that Athapaskans skilled in caribou driving moved from the northern forest onto the Plains, displacing the people of the Besant phase. Little data has been brought forth to support this hypothesis. First, there is substantial evidence to suggest that large communal bison kills predate Avonlea on the Plains (e.g., excavations at Head-Smashed-In Buffalo Jump indicate that human groups on the Plains were repeatedly driving bison since ca. 2,800 BP). As well, a technological precursor for Avonlea material in the boreal forest has not been found (Vickers 1994:17).

According to Reeves (1983a:166), the Avonlea phase developed out of the Pelican Lake phase as a result of diffusion of the bow and arrow from interior British Columbia and ceramics from the east. He based his proposal on evidence that arrowheads appeared first in the mountain areas of British Columbia while pottery technology arrived from the east (Reeves 1983a:163). Byrne (1973:456), based on data from the Morkin site, suggested there was little support for Kehoe's northern migration theory. Instead, he favoured Reeves' hypothesis of in situ development of the Avonlea phase from the Pelican Lake phase. The in situ model of Avonlea development has also been supported by other researchers (e.g., Adams 1977:139–140).

Focusing on pottery recovered from the Garratt site in Saskatchewan,

Morgan (1979:220) suggested the Avonlea phase represented displaced people that moved from the Upper Mississippi Valley into the Canadian Plains during 1,800 BP to 1,750 BP. Klimko (1985:70) also indicated that the distribution of Avonlea sites through time and across space suggested a northward and westward movement from the east or southeastern as hypothesized by Morgan (1979).

Brumley and Dau (1988:44) felt Reeves' model disregarded the evidence in the lithic utilization patterns. They argued that Avon chert, Madison Formation cherts, Fort Union Formation porcellanite, and obsidian were used extensively in sites with convex-based Pelican Lake points within southern Alberta, southern Saskatchewan, and northern Montana. During the Avonlea phase, however, these lithics were absent. The technological shift from dart to arrow suggested by Reeves would predict continuity in lithic utilization patterns. To explain the difference, Brumley and Dau (1988) suggested that convex-based and straight-based Pelican Lake points reflect significant cultural differences. In this model, straight-based Pelican Lake points developed into Avonlea points in a core area of southeastern Alberta, south-central Saskatchewan, and northern Montana around 2,000 BP–1,800 BP. Convex-based Pelican Lake points were located to the south and west of this area. According to Brumley and Dau (1988:44–45), they were displaced by the Avonlea phase to the south as far as the Missouri.

Brumley and Dau (1988:46) further extended their model by suggesting that the lower frequency of Avonlea sites, observed by Dyck (1983) and Vickers (1986), indicated a different social structure within the Avonlea phase, which was reflected in their subsistence and settlement pattern. They argued that Avonlea populations may have been of similar size to other cultural groups, but with different settlement patterns. Such a settlement system would have been characterized by less extensive and less frequent movement, resulting in larger but less numerous sites (Brumley and Dau 1988:46).

In addition, Brumley and Dau (1988:47–48) suggested that Avonlea peoples attempted to hide their bow and arrow technology from neighbours, delaying its acquisition by other groups and allowing Avonlea to maintain a technological, competitive advantage. Brumley and Dau (1988) suggested that the bow and arrow was integrated into Avonlea spiritual and shamanistic practices and, thus, it was socially regulated. By mid to late Avonlea times, neighbouring groups began to acquire bow and arrow technology resulting in the social regulation surrounding the technology, becoming less necessary. The lower quality of craftsmanship and variation in styles seen within later or "degenerate" Avonlea assemblages perhaps reflects this change (Brumley and Dau 1988:48). Although difficult to prove archaeologically, Vickers (1994:19) noted that before dismissing the hypothesis, the complexity involved in producing sinew-backed bow and arrows with good flight characteristics should be considered. He argued that it might be possible to limit or slow the diffusion of technology, especially if the knowledge was in the hands of craft specialists (Vickers 1994:19).

The Sites

In order to assess the various lines of thinking presented above, Avonlea assemblages from Alberta with reliable radiocarbon dates are outlined below. These sites are used to critically evaluate the current view of the Avonlea phase (see Plate 24 and Figure 25).

EfOw 27. EfOw 27 is a multicomponent campsite/processing site located along Deadfish Creek just upstream from its confluence with the Berry Creek (Goldsmith 2005:4–5). The site is described above in the section on the Besant phase. A single Avonlea point was recovered in the eastern block, in association with an utilized flake and twenty pieces of debitage. The small assemblage consisted of chert (n = 7), quartzite (n = 17), chalcedony (n = 1), and petrified wood (n = 1). The faunal assemblage (n = 5,416) consisted of bison (MNI = 6), a dog, a rabbit, and a fox (Goldsmith 2005:248). The lack of heavy elements such as the vertebral column and sacrum, with few scapulae and pelvi suggested that the site was some distance from the primary kill. Long bones were relatively well represented, with fewer carpals, tarsals, and phalanges, suggesting limbs were brought in as articulated units after trimming. Long bones were clearly fragmented during marrow extraction (Goldsmith 2005:254). A single radiocarbon date of ca. 1,550 BP was acquired for the site (see Table 23). This is a relatively early date for Avonlea in the province.

Head-Smashed-In Buffalo Jump (DkPj 1). Head-Smashed-In Buffalo Jump has been described above. In terms of the Avonlea phase, numerous Timber Ridge side-notched points, some Head-Smashed-In corner-notched points, and Avonlea triangular points were recovered in the thick bone beds between 3 and 4.5 m below surface in the South Kill and 0.5–1 m

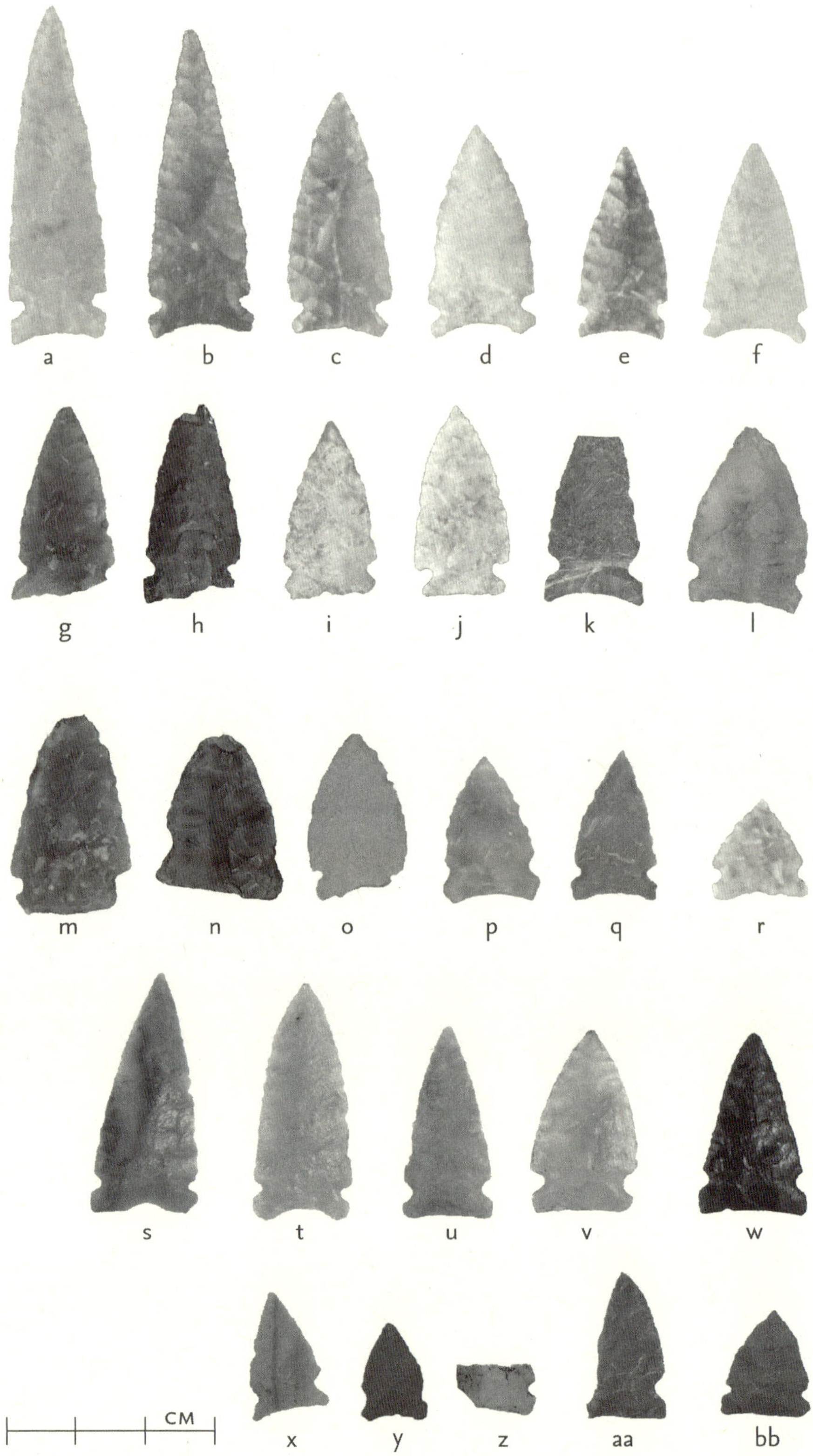

PLATE 24 Avonlea points. Illustrated are projectile points from Head-Smashed-In Buffalo Jump (DkPj 1) (a–r); the Ramillies site (EcOr 35) (s–w); EhPc 108 (x–z); EfOw 27 (aa); and the Wells site (FdOt 9) (bb). Photo credit: Royal Alberta Museum (a–f, r–w); Alberta Culture and Community Spirit (g–q, x–bb).

FIGURE 25
Avonlea sites
within Alberta

below surface in the North Kill. A number of radiocarbon dates were obtained from the Avonlea bone bed. In the South Kill, two dates were obtained for the initiation of Avonlea: 1,860 +/-120 BP (GAK-1475) and 1,335 +/- 96 BP (GX-1399). In the North Kill, two dates were obtained for the initiation of Avonlea: 1,645 +/- 130 BP (GX-1252) and 1,840 +/- 90 BP (RL-330). Three dates were obtained for terminal Avonlea in the South Kill: 1,010 +/- 140 BP (GSC-983); 1,000 +/- 110 BP (RL-256); and 1,330 +/- 85 BP (GX-1251). The early date in the South Kill from the Gakushuin lab can be rejected (see Blakeslee 1994). In the North Kill, the Sonota material underlies the Avonlea material and has been repeatedly dated in Alberta between 1,500–1,350 BP. The dates on the Sonota levels at the North Kill at Head-Smashed-In Buffalo Jump are between ca. 1,450 and 1,350 BP. Since Sonota underlies Avonlea, the earlier dates for Avonlea are questionable. In fact, compared to the rest of Avonlea dates in the province, an initial date prior to ca. 1,500–1,350 BP would require substantial explanation. The initiation date of ca. 1,645 BP has a great standard deviation that would place it with other Avonlea dates, even at one sigma. However, the ca. 1,840 BP date stands out as anomalous and it's likely in error. The terminal Avonlea dates are less problematic. All three dates overlap at two sigma. Thus, Head-Smashed-In Buffalo Jump exhibits Avonlea material dating to ca. 1,350–1,000 BP.

Tools recovered included well-formed bifaces (asymmetrical ovate and diamond ovate), end scrapers, pièces esquillées, retouched flakes, cobble choppers, anvils, and hammerstones. The lithic raw materials were dominated by cherts from Montana and the Canadian Rockies (Reeves 1978:165). Importantly, Reeves (1978:172) noted that the Women's Buffalo Jump, excavated in the late 1950s by Forbis (1962), contained few, if any, Avonlea points in its sequence (i.e., Pelican Lake, Besant, Old Women's).

Head-Smashed-In Buffalo Jump, Area 2b (DkPj 1). Area 2b at Head-Smashed-In Buffalo Jump consisted of level ground between the two parking lots on the flats below the kill site (Damkjar 1995). The focus of excavations in this area was a large pit feature excavated with a 9-m^2 block excavation. The pit was roughly oval in plan shape (70 × 100 cm long), narrowing as it descended to a depth of 120 cm below the surface.

Two Avonlea points and two point fragments displaying Avonlea qualities were recovered within the pit feature (Damkjar 1995:63). Lithic debitage (n = 284) was within the pit. The inclusion of this material was seen as incidental fill (Damkjar 1995:67). Similarly, FBR (n = 536) was recovered within the pit but seen as incidentally included. A number of pottery sherds (n = 19), largely representing one vessel (n = 15), were recovered. The remaining sherds appeared to be from other vessels (Damkjar 1995:64). Reconstruction of the vessel produced a conical vessel. The surface treatment was truncated fabric-impressed. The rim exhibited four rows of small finger pinches with a row of widely spaced punctuates below (Damkjar 1995:65). The pot was classified as Avonlea pottery (Damkjar 1995:65).

A number of unusual artifacts were recovered within the pit feature. Two bison bones (a proximal phalanx and a tibia shaft) exhibited stripes and patches of red ochre. In each of two right mandibles, the ramus was worked into a rounded spatulate at one end while the other end had the incisors removed to create a sharp point (Damkjar 1995:66). These artifacts were interpreted as digging tools. Other faunal material (n = 1,021) within the pit included portions of fifteen bison skulls and seventeen articulated limbs sections. Nine dog bones were also recovered. Twelve radiocarbon dates were obtained for the pit feature (Table 23). The author rejected two old dates and noted the remaining ten dates fell within an estimate of 1,250 +/- 50 BP. The points, pottery, and dates all suggest an unusual Avonlea pit feature (Damkjar 1995:80–83).

H.M.S. *Balzac (EhPm 34).* The H.M.S. Balzac site is a multicomponent campsite on an oxbow of Nose Creek just north of Calgary. The site was discovered in 1978. Five areas of occupation, labelled A–E, were outlined. In 1981, two blocks totalling 64 m^2 (Block 1, 24 m^2; Block 2, 40 m^2) were excavated. This excavation revealed a highly stratified Late Prehistoric site with up to six Old Women's occupations overlying up to six Avonlea occupations (Head 1985, 1986).

Avonlea points were recovered from sediment Levels 9 through 12 in Block 1, and Levels 8 through 13 in Block 2. The stratigraphic relationships between the two blocks were never established (Head 1986:13). Radiocarbon dates from the site are problematic. While the charcoal dates provide a sequence corroborated by the stratigraphy, the bone dates do not. Given that the site is a floodplain and that bone dates can be affected by groundwater (Head 1986:13–14), the latter are rejected as contaminated. Thus, for Block 2, Level 11 was radiocarbon dated to ca. 1,300 BP and Level 13 was dated to ca. 1,500 BP. The latter is one of the earliest Avonlea dates in the province.

TABLE 23 Radiocarbon dates for Avonlea sites (calibrated by OxCal 3.10 [Ramsey 2005])

Site [LAB NO.]	Conventional ^{14}C Age	$^{13}C/^{12}C$ Ratio	Material	Calibration	Reference
DkPj 1 [RL-256]	1000+/-110	-20.0‰	collagen	A.D. 680–1170 (p = 0.954)	Reeves 1978; Morlan n.d.
DkPj 1 [GSC-983]	1010+/-140	-22.9‰	collagen	A.D. 650–1300 (p = 0.954)	Reeves 1978; Morlan n.d.
DkPj 1 [GX-1251]	1330+/-85	-20.0‰	collagen	A.D. 420–780 (p = 0.954)	Reeves 1978; Morlan n.d.
DkPj 1 [GX-1399]	1335 +/- 95	-20.0‰	collagen	A.D. 410–810 (p = 0.954)	Reeves 1978; Morlan n.d.
DkPj 1 [GAK-1475]	1860 +/-120	-20.0‰	collagen	rejected	Reeves 1978; Morlan n.d.
DkPj 1 [GX-1252]	1645 +/- 130	-20.0‰	collagen	A.D. 1–600 (p = 0.954)	Reeves 1978; Morlan n.d.
DkPj 1 [RL-330]	1840 +/- 90	-20.0‰	collagen	170–130 B.C. (p = 0.018) 120 B.C.–A.D. 270 (p = 0.907) A.D. 280–330 (p = 0.029)	Reeves 1978; Morlan n.d.
DkPj 1, 2b [AECV-1765C]	1290 +/- 80	-19.5‰	bone	A.D. 600–900 (p = 0.938); A.D. 920–950 (p = 0.016)	Damkjar 1995
DkPj 1, 2b [AECV-1766C]	1200 +/- 80	-19.4‰	bone	A.D. 660–990 (p = 0.954)	Damkjar 1995
DkPj 1, 2b [AECV-1774C]	1320 +/- 80	-19.5‰	bone	A.D. 570–890 (p = 0.954)	Damkjar 1995
DkPj 1, 2b [AECV-1767C]	1190 +/- 70	-19.2‰	bone	A.D. 680–990 (p = 0.954)	Damkjar 1995
DkPj 1, 2b [AECV-1706C]	1450 +/- 80	-19.2‰	bone	A.D. 420–710 (p = 0.94); A.D. 740–770 (p = 0.014)	Damkjar 1995
DkPj 1, 2b [AECV-1768C]	1120 +/- 80	-19.3‰	bone	A.D. 680–1040 (p = 0.954)	Damkjar 1995
DkPj 1, 2b [AECV-1769C]	1260 +/- 80	-19.8‰	bone	A.D. 640–970 (p = 0.954)	Damkjar 1995
DkPj 1, 2b [AECV-1705C]	1540 +/- 70	-19.5‰	bone	A.D. 380–650 (p = 0.954)	Damkjar 1995
DkPj 1, 2b [AECV-1770C]	1360 +/ 80	-19.6‰	bone	A.D. 540–870 (p = 0.954)	Damkjar 1995
DkPj 1, 2b [AECV-1771C]	1260 +/- 80	-19.7‰	bone	A.D. 640–970 (p = 0.954)	Damkjar 1995
DkPj 1, 2b [AECV-1773C]	1210 +/- 70	-19.6‰	bone	A.D. 670–980 (p = 0.954)	Damkjar 1995
DkPj 1, 2b [AECV-1772C]	1290 +/- 80	-19.5‰	bone	A.D. 600–900 (p = 0.938); A.D. 920–950 (p = 0.016)	Damkjar 1995

EhPm 34, 14 [B-6441]	1280 +/- 50	?	charcoal	A.D. 650–870 (p = 0.954)	Head 1985:12
EhPm 34, 21 [B-13036]	1340 +/- 130	?	charcoal	A.D. 400–1000 (p = 0.954)	Head 1985:12
EhPm 34, 16 [B-13037]	930+/-130	?	collagen	A.D. 400–1000 (p = 0.954)	Head 1985:12
EhPm 34, 18 [B-6443]	1540 +/- 50	?	charcoal	A.D. 410–620 (p = 0.954)	Head 1985:12
EhPm 34, 18b [B-13035]	1110 +/- 60	?	collagen	A.D. 770–1030 (p = 0.954)	Head 1985:12
EhPm 34, 25 [B-6444]	1010 +/- 50	?	collagen	A.D. 890–920 (p = 0.045); A.D. 940–1160 (p = 0.909)	Head 1985:12
DhPj 31 [S-865]	1180 +/- 85	-20.0‰	collagen	A.D. 690–750 (p = 0.106); A.D. 760–980 (p = 0.848)	Quigg 1988a
DhPj 31 [S-866]	1155 +/- 90	-20.0‰	collagen	A.D. 670–1030 (p = 0.954)	Quigg 1988a
DlOn 3 [AECV-300C]	1140 +/- 90	?	charcoal	A.D. 670–1040 (p = 0.954)	Milne 1988
DlOn 3 [GX-9396 G]	1165 +/- 125	-18.5‰	collagen	A.D. 600–1200 (p = 0.954)	Milne 1988
DlOn 3 [AECV-299C]	1210 +/- 80	?	charcoal	A.D. 660–980 (p = 0.954)	Milne 1988
DlOn 3 [AECV 298C]	1190 +/- 80	-18.5‰	bone	A.D. 670–990 (p = 0.954)	Milne 1988
DlOn 3 [GX-9395 A]	1420 +/- 150	-9.1‰	bone apatite	A.D. 250–1000 (p = 0.954)	Milne 1988
DlOn 2 [GSC-1296]	1180 +/- 140	-23.3‰	charcoal	A.D. 600–1200 (p = 0.954)	Milne 1988
FdOt 9 [BETA-23701]	1220 +/- 80	-20.0‰	collagen	A.D. 660–980 (p = 0.954)	Stuart 1988
FdOt 9 [AECV-471C]	1030 +/- 150	-20.6‰	collagen	A.D. 650–1300 (p = 0.954)	Stuart 1988
EcOs 41 [RL-1125]	1020 +/- 110	-20.0‰	collagen	A.D. 770–1260 (p = 0.954)	Brumley and Dau 1988:43
EcOs 41 [RL-1126]	610 +/- 100	-20.0‰	collagen	A,D, 1210–1480 (p = 0.954)	Brumley and Dau 1988:43
EdOn 7 [S-1017]	1470 +/- 90	-20.0‰	collagen	A.D. 390–710 (p = 0.942); A.D. 740–770 (p = 0.012)	Brumley and Willis 1977
EfOw 27 [BETA-188556]	1560 +/- 60	-18.4‰	collagen	A.D. 380–640 (p = 0.954)	Goldsmith 2005

The site does not exhibit evidence of a level with both Avonlea and Old Women's material (Head 1986:16). A cursory review of the artifacts recovered from the site indicates bifaces, wedges, retouched flakes, end scrapers, side scrapers, drills, spokeshaves, cores, choppers, and pottery were associated with most levels of the site (Head 1986:16). Head's (1986:31, 36) thorough faunal analysis noted fetal elements within most levels of the site, indicating late winter/early spring occupations. Some degree of continuity between Avonlea and Old Women's was noted (Head 1986).

Shaw (EdOn 7). The Shaw site is a burial of a single individual in the sand hills west of Hilda, southeastern Alberta (Milne 1988:65). Excavated in 1974, the burial was a secondary interment, apparently situated about 45 cm BS beneath a small stone cairn. Most of the skeleton was present, and there were three stone tools and a few bison bone fragments. No culturally diagnostic material was recovered. A single radiocarbon date of ca. 1,500 BP was obtained (Table 23). The site was excavated prior to a pipeline development. Besides the indicative dates, it is not known if this site represents an Avonlea burial.

Larson (DlOn 3). The Larson site is a processing site and/or campsite located on a terrace along the Ross Creek Valley, approximately 3 km south of Irvine (Milne 1988). During an inspection near the Irvine Kill site (DlOn 2), butchered bone, FBR, and numerous flakes were observed eroding from a cutbank along an extinct oxbow channel of Ross Creek. Two cultural levels were recorded; the upper level represented a series of closely deposited Avonlea occupations while the lower level consisted of redeposited bone (Milne 1988:48–49). The site was named after the landowner, the Larson Cattle Company (Milne 1988). It was excavated by the Medicine Hat College in the summers of 1982 and 1986. Auger testing suggested that the site is at least as extensive as the terrace on which it is located (Milne 1988:48). In 1982, 6 m^2 were excavated; an additional 12 m^2 were excavated in 1986.

The 1982 excavations produced six Avonlea points, eleven Avonlea triangular preforms, and five indeterminate point fragments. The points were found in association with a stone-boiling pit adjacent to an unprepared hearth, a possible second boiling pit, two roasting pits, and assorted FBR, faunal material, and lithic debitage. Other tools included end scrapers (n = 5), biface fragments (n = 3), perforators (n = 4), pièces esquillées (n = 10), retouched flakes (n = 30), cobble choppers (n = 2), a graver, a core, and a scraping plane (Milne 1988). The lithic assemblage emphasized local raw materials, although Knife River flint and Hand Hills agate were present in small amounts. Production methods appeared to be material specific: direct percussion for quartzites, bipolar flaking for pebble cherts, and pressure flaking for siliceous materials (Milne 1988:63). Craftsmanship was poor by Avonlea standards, possibly reflecting the available raw materials (Milne 1988:63). Evidence of two ceramic vessels recovered from spatially separated features exhibited smoothed interior and exterior surfaces (Milne 1988:61).

The faunal assemblage was weathered but the fragmentation still supported the interpretation of food processing. A minimum of five bison and one fetal bison were represented in the assemblage, which was too fragmentary to address sex. Other species present in the sample were fox, mink, antelope, and duck. The presence of fetal bison and the duck suggest a late winter/early spring occupation. A few dog elements were also present. Two canid articulating lumbar vertebrae exhibit ankylosing spondylitis, which indicated the use of the dog for transport of travois (Milne 1988:56). A dog metapodial was fashioned into an awl. Other bone tools recovered included a second awl, a punch, and a flaked bone artifact (Milne 1988:61–62). A large amount of FBR (57,703.78 grams) was recovered at the site. Both heat-spall and water-fracture patterns were noted, supporting the interpretation of the features (Milne 1988:54).

Five radiocarbon dates were obtained (Table 23). The dates support the researcher's suggestion that the site represents a series of reoccupations between 1,300 BP and 900 BP (Milne 1988:63). One date (GX-9395 A) was rejected; the split nature of the sample may have contributed to contamination. The single date from the Irvine Kill site (DlOn 2) corresponds with the Larson site dates, reinforcing the possibility that the kill was contemporaneous with the campsite.

Irvine/Ross Creek Kill site (DlOn 2). The Irvine Kill site is a bone bed with an associated feature eroding out of the east bank of the Ross Creek. Alan Bryan originally reported the site in 1965 (Milne 1988). Avonlea points have been found in association with the eroding bone bed. A radiocarbon date of ca. 1,200 BP (Table 23) from an eroding hearth suggested a contemporaneous date with the nearby Larson site (Milne 1988). Vandalism and erosion from the creek threaten the site (Milne 1988:43).

Manyfingers (DhPj 31). The Manyfingers site is a processing site on the east side of the Belly River. It lies on the western border of the Blood Indian Reserve, about 30 km southeast of Pincher Creek (Quigg 1974a, 1974b). The site was excavated during the summers of 1972 and 1973 in response to erosion resulting from water management activities (Quigg 1988a:67). Material from stratified sediments came from three terraces; excavations focused on the second terrace, where 73 m^2 were excavated. Two levels containing Old Women's material overlaid the level with the Avonlea material; the researcher indicated there was little possibility of mixing (Quigg 1988a:67).

Five Avonlea points were associated with two features, bone, FBR, lithic debitage, and ceramics (Quigg 1988a). Other tools included cobble choppers (n = 22), bifaces (n = 3), end scrapers (n = 2), a side scraper, a uniface, and retouched flakes (n = 9). The debitage reflected the use of local lithics, especially argillite, quartzite, local cherts, and local chalcedonies, with little obsidian, Knife River flint, or Avon chert (Quigg 1988a:70–71). The pottery assemblage consisted of thirteen sherds from a single vessel (Quigg 1988a:74). The surface treatment was deep-knotted cord impressions that had been smoothed. Vessel form could not be determined although two sherds exhibited tapering exterior punctuates. Quigg (1988a:77) attributed the vessel to Byrne's (1973:77) Early Variant of the South Saskatchewan Basin complex.

The faunal assemblage was consistent with a processing site. A minimum of thirty-three heavily butchered bison were present. Fourteen bone tools were also recovered, including retouched bone, intentionally smoothed bone, bone exhibiting use wear, and a scraper handle (Quigg 1988a:73, 75). Sexing of the bison specimens was not conducted. Although two fetal bones were identified, they may be intrusive from overlying deposits. The researcher suggested that the paucity of fetal bone indicated a summer or fall occupation (Quigg 1988a:70, 78). The two features were a bone concentration (42 cm in diameter and 10 cm thick), which may have resulted from site cleanup by the occupants, and a bone-lined depression in gravel (70 cm in diameter, and excavated 20 cm deep), possibly used as a cooking pit (Quigg 1988a:70). The FBR assemblage was quite large and evenly scattered over the site; the stones' hackled edges suggested use in stone boiling (Quigg 1988a:70). Two radiocarbon dates were obtained, of ca. 1,150 BP and 1,200 BP (Table 23). A single occupation was suggested (Quigg 1988a).

Wells (FdOt 9), Component 2. The Wells site is discussed in the section on the Besant phase. In the Avonlea component, a single point was recovered. Originally, it was classified as a Late Plains side-notched point (Stuart 1988:21). Its short base height, slightly concave base, and very shallow notches, however, indicate that it is an Avonlea point. Other tools included cobble choppers (n = 22), bifaces (n = 3), end scrapers (n = 2), a side scraper, a uniface, and retouched flakes (n = 9). Raw materials focused on quartzite and pebble cherts. Six non-diagnostic pottery sherds were also recovered. A possible bone tool was identified in use wear on one end of a large ungulate long bone (Stuart 1988:71). The faunal assemblage (n = 1,442) was highly fragmented and only a few pieces were identifiable as bison (Stuart 1988:74). No features were noted although FBR (n = 1,480) was common and highly fragmented (Stuart 1988:70). Two radiocarbon dates were obtained from this material, of ca. 1,150 BP and 1,000 BP (Table 23). The dates and materials indicate a single occupation towards the end of the Avonlea phase.

EcOs 41. EcOs 41 is a buried processing site and/or campsite on Canadian Forces Base Suffield in southeastern Alberta. It is located on the edge of a coulee in an area of strongly rolling, hummocky moraine with a spring-fed pond that flows into the coulee below. The site was found during excavations for mud pits associated with a well site. Salvage excavations were undertaken in the summer of 1978. A total of 18 m^2 was excavated. The vast majority of the material was recovered from 5–15 cm BS, suggesting a single occupation (Brumley et al. 1983:6).

A single Avonlea point was recovered in addition to six point fragments. They were found in the same sediments as numerous stone tools, faunal remains, ceramics, and a large hearth (Brumley et al. 1983:2–24). Other tools recovered included retouched flakes (n = 15), end scrapers (n = 2), unifaces (n = 2), and small cores (n = 3). The assemblage was dominated by local cherts, quartzite, and petrified wood, with tools made on more siliceous raw materials such as Swan River chert, Montana chert, Avon chert, and Knife River flint (Brumley et al. 1983).

A number of small, badly fragmented pottery sherds (n = 310) were recovered. The sample was recovered from two separate areas and considered to represent at least two vessels. The majority of the sherds have smooth interior and exterior surfaces, although largely obliterated cord or fabric impressions appear on a few exterior ceramics and on two rim sherds. Despite the small sample, the assemblage was considered to exhibit similarities to the Saskatchewan Basin pottery (Brumley et al. 1983:22; Byrne 1973).

The site has a fairly large saucer-shaped excavated pit (110 cm wide and 12–18 cm deep) that contained considerable quantities of burned bone, unburned bone, and ash (Brumley et al. 1983:6). Although most of the faunal assemblage was burned hearth fill, the researchers determined that at least two adult bison were represented (Brumley et al. 1983:7). No clear concentrations of FBR were observed but a fairly substantial quantity (3,830.3grams) was recovered. The authors suggested it was a hearth or backfilled boiling pit (Brumley et al. 1983:6). Two radiocarbon dates were obtained. One sample from the hearth feature yielded a date of ca. 1,000 BP (Table 23), which is late for an Avonlea date (Brumley and Dau 1988:43). The second sample consisted of burned and unburned bone from several pits and produced a date of ca. 600 BP; this date is considerably late for Avonlea and was rejected (Brumley and Dau 1988:43).

EhPc 108. EhPc 108 is a campsite on a terrace above the Red Deer River in the Wintering Hills, south central Alberta (Loveseth 1983). The site was excavated in the summer of 1981 and consisted of shallow deposits in a small depression. A total of 57 m^2 was excavated (Loveseth 1983:23). The site was mitigated prior to a pipeline construction (Loveseth 1983:69, 94).

Four Avonlea points, two Avonlea preforms, and a tip were recovered in association with two hearths and an FBR concentration (Loveseth 1983). Other tools recovered included end scrapers (n=5), biface fragments (n=6), gravers (n=4), retouched flakes (n=79), utilized flakes (n=7), choppers (n=8), cores (n=107), a side scraper, and a uniface (Loveseth 1983:84). The debitage emphasized petrified wood and quartzite. Most of the petrified wood artifacts exhibited a greasy lustre and were associated with a rock-covered hearth. The researcher suggested that the material was being heat treated to improve its knapping qualities. This would explain the high incidence of petrified wood in an area usually dominated by quartzite. Many delicate tools at the site were made on petrified wood while tools requiring strength were made on quartzite (Loveseth 1983:84). A single pottery body sherd was recovered (Loveseth 1983:63).

The faunal assemblage was small (n=66) and suggested processing activities with lower limbs being brought to the site. Other elements were poorly represented, suggesting that they were left at an indeterminate kill site (Loveseth 1983:64). Most of the bone was found outside the features. The features include a rock-covered hearth (55 cm wide by 16 cm deep), an FBR concentration (75 cm wide), and a basin hearth (75 cm wide by 19 cm deep). A single radiocarbon date of ca. 900 BP was obtained for the site (Table 23). This is a very late date for Avonlea.

Ramillies (EcOr 35). The Ramillies site is a bison kill site and campsite located north of Medicine Hat, in the central part of the Canadian Forces Base Suffield, southeastern Alberta (Brumley 1976:1–2). The site's name comes from the term used by the military in referring to the portion of the base that the site is on within the reserve (Brumley 1976:2). The site was excavated during the summers of 1972 through 1974. A total of 133 m^2 was excavated (Brumley 1976:8–14).

Thirty-two Avonlea points and numerous Cayley Series points were recovered from the site. Brumley (1976:1–2) divided the site into three parts: Areas A, B, and C. Area C (88 m^2) consisted of stone cairn alignments that led to an enhanced oval depression with a rock-capped wall approximately 20 m long by 12 m wide by 2 m deep. These features were interpreted as drive lanes and a pound (Brumley 1976:1–2, 11–14). Three basic stratigraphic units were recorded for the oval depression with rock-capped walls (Brumley 1976:12). The bottom consisted of basal gravels, the layer above consisted of evidence of wall construction, and the top layer consisted of bison bones, projectile points, bone tools, and debitage. Area B is a midden along the coulee wall, directly adjacent to the pound that exhibited bison bone. The midden is attributed to the dumping of bison remains from the pound down the adjacent slope, to prepare the pound for subsequent pounding events (Brumley 1976:1–2, 9–11). For Area B, no stratigraphy was discernible (Brumley 1976:10). In Areas B and C, the cleaning process within the pound made it impossible to differentiate periods of use. Area A is a relatively flat area a few hundred metres north of the other Areas. At this location, the unearthing of hearths, pits, FBR, butchered faunal remains, lithic debitage, and ceramics was interpreted as indicative of campsite/processing activities (Brumley 1976:1–2, 9). In Area A, Brumley (1976:8) defined three cultural units in the stratigraphy, I, II, and III. Level I was the Avonlea phase, Level II was mixed, and Level III was the Old Women's phase. Still, the shallow deposition was not conducive to stratigraphic separation.

Based on fetal remains and bison tooth eruption and wear analysis, the site was considered to have been used in the spring, summer, and fall (Brumley 1976:20, 23). More recently, dental cementum increment analysis has refined this to suggest that kill events occurred between late March and late October (Peck 2004).

An Avonlea occupation is known from the campsite area, Level I, but radiocarbon dates are not available for this occupation. Level II, however, where mixed materials suggest a possible transitional assemblage, a radiocarbon date of ca. 1,050 BP (Table 23) was obtained. The overlying Old Women's occupation, Level III, produced a radiocarbon date of ca. 750 BP (Table 23). The site is unique in its construction on the Northern Plains. When the structure was operating it was quite small and could likely only contain a few animals. Still, it appears to have been used repeatedly during the Avonlea and the Old Women's phases, and possibly during a transitional phase between the two. Unfortunately, the poor stratigraphic separation at the site has made it difficult to assign the cultural material to any one time period.

Other sites. There are a number of other Avonlea sites in Alberta that lack reliable radiometric dating or context. For example, EfPi 17 is a campsite located on two long slump blocks on the north side of the Bow River, about 20 km southeast of Calgary. An Avonlea occupation predates the rotational slump and, thus, the site has been interpreted as a single occupation of a high bluff-edge camp (Hanna 2002:50). Four projectile points (two Avonlea, one body fragment, one basal fragment) were recovered in association with a hearth and a scatter of lithics, with a few bones and non-diagnostic pottery. Hanna (2002:37) noted that, based on the distribution of artifacts around the hearth, a buried tipi floor was possible although a stone circle was not found. The exposed location suggests a summer occupation but the author noted that the assemblage is not inconsistent with a winter occupation (Hanna 2002:50).

EbPi 93 is a campsite with Avonlea material underlying Old Women's material. The site is located on an intermediate terrace on the west side of the Little Bow River. A total of 36 m^2 was excavated. A radiocarbon date of 1,270 +/- 110 BP supports the Avonlea designation (Charles Ramsay, personal communication 2005). The Hartell Creek (EgPi 1) site west of Strathmore produced a number of Avonlea points in what appears to be mixed context although the Avonlea material may be associated with Sonota material (Murray et al. 1976).

In the Majorville Medicine Wheel, Calder (1977:87) identified twenty-two Avonlea points from the cairn. Only eight of twenty-eight pottery sherds were classifiable as Saskatchewan Basin complex: Early Variant pottery (Byrne 1973). DjOu 81 is a campsite that produced an Avonlea point and a radiocarbon date of 1,450 +/- 90 BP (Beta-19807) (Brumley and Dau 1988:245). An association between the point and dated material was fairly firmly established. EeOq 81 is a tipi ring site on a bench overlooking a slough north of the Canadian Forces Base Suffield but south of the town of Buffalo. A shovel test in one of the two rings recovered an Avonlea point. The site was avoided so further excavations were not required (Himour 2002). Likewise, EaOt 20 is a single tipi ring site on a small knoll, just above the floodplain of the South Saskatchewan River north of Bow Island. Shovel tests in the ring recovered a single Avonlea point, a retouched flake and some FBR. The pipeline development avoided the site making further work unnecessary (Brady 2004).

Evidence of Avonlea sites is not limited to the Plains. In Waterton Lakes National Park, Reeves (1972) noted Avonlea points from a number of sites (DgPl 42, 47, 68, 76, 85, 86, and 148). A discrete Avonlea component was found at DgPl 68, which is a site on a terrace above Pass Creek in the Pass Creek Valley. The Avonlea material is a campsite, underlying Old Women's material, in a well-defined level beneath the Ah horizon. Three Avonlea points and two Avonlea preforms were recovered along with an asymmetrical ovate biface, biface fragments (n = 2), triangular end scrapers (n = 4), oval end scrapers (n = 2), utilized flakes (n = 23), cobble choppers (n = 4), and core fragments (n = 4) (Reeves 1972:77, table 6). The material was recovered in association with a concentration (60 cm wide) of FBR and calcine bone that was interpreted as a hearth. Eight 4-m^2 units were excavated (Reeves 1972:75, 391). A number of sites with Avonlea points are known from the Crowsnest Pass: both DjPq 1 and DjPq 2 have produced Avonlea points.

Avonlea: Migrant Archers from the East

The Avonlea phase is very distinctive on the Alberta plains. It may start as early as 1,550 BP in Alberta although the vast majority of dates are considerably later. An initial occurrence of the Avonlea phase in Alberta likely occurs as late as 1,350 BP, given the proposed revision of dates at Head-Smashed-In Buffalo Jump, the numerous dates on the Head-Smashed-In Buffalo Jump pit (Area 2b), and the dates at the H.M.S. Balzac site.

The diagnostic projectile points of the Avonlea phase are the Avonlea side-notched point and the Head-Smashed-In corner-notched point. The Avonlea side-notched point is a thin, delicate, side-notched point that exhibits notches low on the margins and a straight to slightly concave basal edge. The neck width tends to be about 1.2 to 1.0 cm, which indicates an arrow point. The craftsmanship in the manufacture of these points is exquisite. Similarly, the Head-Smashed-In corner-notched point is, more or less, a corner-notched version of the point described above, but with more rounded shoulders and basal edges, given the relationship between Sonota and Avonlea, and the recovery of Head-Smashed-In corner-notched points in only the earliest "Avonlea" deposits, it seems possible that it represents a Sonota arrow point. This would be based on the premise that the people of the Sonota phase and Avonlea phase merged populations and/or ideas.

The non-projectile part of the Avonlea lithic assemblage is not particularly diagnostic. Reeves (1983a:103) suggested that a diamond-shaped biface occurs in early Avonlea assemblages, but this has not been confirmed. Frequently, asymmetrical lanceolate knives or blades are attributed to late Avonlea assemblages (e.g. Reeves 1983a:346–7, fig. 20, nos. 8–10). These "finger" bifaces are about the length and width of a finger and rounded at both ends.

The lithic raw material used at various Avonlea sites tends to come from local sources. In fact, Reeves (1983a:104) indicated that Knife River flint was absent from the Avonlea phase. As pointed out above, however, there are sites to the south and east, such as Garratt, Gull Lake, and Lost Terrace (discussed below), that do yield some exotic raw materials. Sites that demonstrate Avonlea cohabiting with Sonota exhibit substantial amounts of Knife River flint (see Sonota phase above).

Pottery was recovered from a number of the Avonlea sites. The pottery was initially identified as the Saskatchewan Basin complex: Early Variant pottery. Parallel-grooved, fabric/net-impressed, and plain surface finishes are known within the province. One or more rows of punctates below the rim have been found as decorative motifs. The lips tend to be flat or ridged, and are usually not thickened. The form was difficult to determine in many instances, but there is no reason to doubt the vessels are simple globular or coconut form (Byrne 1973).

Subsistence during the Avonlea phase in Alberta was focused on bison. All of the sites discussed above were related to bison jumping or pounding and/or processing, with the exception of the possible burial. It can be argued that bison procurement reached a pinnacle during the Avonlea phase. Most Avonlea sites show repeated use. This may, in part, provide a reason for the apparent limited number of Avonlea sites on the Plains (Brumley and Dau 1988:46; Dyck 1983); these people may have relied on a highly repetitive use of the landscape compared to earlier peoples, such as Besant phase. As well, the redating of the Avonlea phase to 1,350–1,100 BP dramatically shortens the potential time over which Avonlea sites could have been created, which would also have an affect on the number of sites that can be considered Avonlea.

There are a range of features that have been observed in Alberta's Avonlea sites including basin hearths, surface hearths, rock-lined hearths, roasting pits, and stone circles. A ceremonial pit feature from Head-Smashed-In Buffalo Jump defies obvious functional interpretation. Also, a possible burial may be indicated in a secondary interment under a cairn.

Avonlea sites are well known from across the Northern Plains. Southern Saskatchewan, southwestern Manitoba, eastern Montana, and northwestern North Dakota have yielded Avonlea sites. Areas on the periphery of this core, however, often attribute sites to the Avonlea phase when, in fact, they exhibit Avonlea-like traits and do not comply with the phase as described above. A review of some of the sites in these aforementioned geographic areas is appropriate to provide some clarity.

In Saskatchewan, the Avonlea site (EaNg 1) is a single-component bison drive and kill site located near the town of Avonlea in southeastern Saskatchewan. A radiocarbon date of 1,500 +/- 100 BP (S-45) was submitted from McCorquodale and Swanson's 1956 excavation (Kehoe 1988:7). Subsequently, Klimko and Hanna (1988) submitted two samples to be dated. Bone associated with Avonlea points produced a date of 1,565 +/- 205 BP (S2623) (Morlan et al. 2002) while bone from a hearth produced a date of 3,605 +/- 305 BP (S-2777) (Morlan et al. 2002:25). The dates on materials associated with Avonlea artifacts suggest a date ca. 1,500 BP.

The Sjovold site (EiNs 4) on the South Saskatchewan River produced parallel-grooved pottery and a single Avonlea point (Dyck and Morlan 1995:253–284). A radiocarbon date of 1,380 +/- 200 BP (S-1762) was obtained (Dyck and Morlan 1995:280, Morlan n.d.).

The Gull Lake site (EaOd 1) is a highly stratified bison kill southwest of Gull Lake. The site consists of Avonlea material underlying Old Women's material (Kehoe 1973; Peck 1996). Two radiocarbon dates were derived from the Avonlea layers at the site. The earliest Avonlea layer produced a date of 1,740 +/- 60 BP (S-255). The most recent Avonlea layer produced a date of 1,290 +/- 60 BP (S-254) (Kehoe 1973:43, Morlan n.d.).

The Garratt site (EcNj 7) is a multicomponent campsite along Moose Jaw Creek (Morgan 1979:74). The Avonlea level, Level 6, produced nineteen Avonlea points, twenty-nine Avonlea preforms, and a Sonota point. The lithic raw material contained high frequencies of Knife River flint compared to typical Avonlea assemblages. Pottery recovered in the level included net-impressed, plain, incised, and punctate surface treatments (Morgan 1979:348–350). Three dates were obtained for Level 6: 1,450 +/- 70 BP (S-406); 1,280 +/- 60 BP (S-408); and rejected date 6,100 +/- 100 BP (S-407) (Morgan 1979:246).

The Newo Asiniak site (FbNp 16) is a multicomponent site in Wanuskewin Heritage Park. It produced an Avonlea point and five Avonlea preforms (Kelly 1986:124). A grooved maul was also excavated from this level (Kelly 1986:131). Net-impressed and fabric finger-woven (sprang) impressed pottery was recovered. Kelly (1986:133–134) noted that the former is commonly recovered with Avonlea points while the latter is often associated with early Old Women's phase (i.e., Prairie side-notched) materials. A radiocarbon date of 915 +/- 70 BP (S-2533) was obtained (Kelly 1986:139; Morlan n.d.). The researcher interpreted the assemblage as transitional between Avonlea and Old Women's rather than considering the component mixed (Kelly 1986:134).

The Bethune site (EeNg 6) is an Avonlea burial located on a knoll northeast of the town of Bethune, south-central Saskatchewan (Dawson and Walker 1988). A cairn may have once covered the site although cultivation left only scattered cobbles. At least seven individuals, ranging from children to adult, were buried in flexed/semi-flexed/bundle interments (Dawson and Walker 1988:4–11). The associated material culture consisted of five chipped stone items, including an Avonlea point, a collection of turtle carapace fragments, a deer metapodial stained with red ochre, and an assortment of bison bone fragments (Dawson and Walker 1988:11–12). A radiocarbon date of 1,390 +/- 40 BP (S-1575) was obtained for the material (Dawson and Walker 1988:4). The Carroll site (EkNv 2) near Swanson on the west side of the South Saskatchewan River in south-central Saskatchewan is another possible Avonlea burial (Walker 1984b). A single burial of an adult female, approximately fifty years old, was placed in an elliptical pit in rolling sand dunes along the South Saskatchewan River (Walker 1984b). Associated with the burial was a fetal bison metacarpal. Nodules of red ochre were mixed within the sand matrix (Walker 1984b:37). A radiocarbon date of 1,570 +/- 100 BP (S-2226) was obtained for the site (Walker 1984b:37)

The Rousell site (FbNs 2) was found during testing in the Dunfermline Sand Hills, west of Saskatoon. In Test Pit 4, two Avonlea points were recovered with bone that was dated to 1,265 +/- 75 BP (S-670) (Morlan et al. 2002:50). Similarly, Goosen Pasture (FbNs 15) is located in the Dunfermline Sand Hills and produced a ceramic Avonlea component with an associated date of 1,095 +/- 100 BP (S-2690) (Morlan et al. 2002:50).

The Peg site (DiMv 61) is a stratified multicomponent campsite located on the north bank of the Souris River, about 56 km upstream from Estevan (Morlan et al. 2002:18). A number of levels produced Avonlea materials. Level 18 produced a radiocarbon date of 1,225 +/- 85 BP (S-2968) (Morlan et al. 2002:18).

The Yellowsky site (FjOd 2) is located in the east side of Turtle Lake in west-central Saskatchewan (Wilson-Meyer and Carlson 1985). Substantial amounts of Avonlea pottery were recovered (n = 1,339) with evidence of coiling manufacture, net-impressed surface finish, and rows of punctuates below the lip. The fauna included mammals and fish (Wilson-Meyer and Carlson 1985:30). Two radiocarbon dates were obtained for the site: 720 +/- 135 (S-2299) and 340 +/- 140 (S-2300) (Wilson-Meyer and Carlson 1985:28, Morlan n.d.). These are very late dates for an Avonlea occupation.

The Lebret site (EeMw 26) is a stratified multicomponent habitation site in the Qu'Appelle Valley in southeastern Saskatchewan (Smith and Walker 1988). Seven Avonlea points were recovered. The pottery assemblage included at least two vessels, one net-impressed and the other parallel-grooved. The faunal assemblage was mainly bison, but also included deer, beaver, river otter, hare, waterfowl, and fish (especially pike, white sucker, white fish, and possibly perch) (Smith and Walker 1988:85–86). In terms of radiocarbon dates, Area A, Level 3, produced Avonlea points and a date of 1,260 +/- 115 BP (S-2691). Area B, Level 3, produced three Avonlea triangular points and a date of 1,635 +/- 105 BP (S-2797). Area S, Level 4, produced net-impressed pottery and a date of 1,520 +/- 105 BP (S-2799).

In Manitoba, Avonlea finds are not especially common. Surface finds are much more numerous than excavated sites and both are almost invariably west of the Red River, apparently focused on more open grassland areas (Joyes 1988). The Avery site (DhLs 1) is a stratified multicomponent campsite in south-central Manitoba that produced numerous Avonlea points and

Avonlea preforms, as well as asymmetrical lanceolate bifaces often manufactured on Knife River flint. The pottery includes parallel-grooved and fabric-impressed sherds (Joyes 1988:230).

The Stott site (DlMa 1) is a large campsite and processing site along the north slope of the Assiniboine River Valley (Joyes 1988:230). The site has produced mainly Blackduck material, although Avonlea material has been recovered from Zones G and F but not in any particular context (Joyes 1988:231). The site may indicate Avonlea-Blackduck contact.

The Pas Reserve site (FlMh 2) is located on the north bank of the Saskatchewan River at the Pas (Joyes 1988:231). This site has an Avonlea component and is located fairly far north in the boreal forest. The Avonlea level produced two dates: 1,330 +/- 100 BP (A-1294) and 980 +/- 150 BP (A-1349) (Joyes 1988:232, Morlan n.d.). Joyes (1988:232) expressed concern that this material was not Avonlea but more likely related to Blackduck.

The Broadview site (EbMp 6) is a multicomponent occupation located at the south end of Ekapo Lake in southeastern Saskatchewan. The upper level was disturbed, while the lower level produced Avonlea points, net-impressed pottery with punctuates, and smooth pottery vessels (Landals 1995). A date was not obtained for this occupation.

The Miniota site (EaMg 12) is a single-component Avonlea residential occupation in the Assiniboine River Valley, near Miniota in southwestern Manitoba (Landals et al. 2004). In addition to trenching and test units, three blocks were opened: a main block (46 m^2), a north block (4 m^2), and a south block (6 m^2) (Landals et al. 2004:43–63). Fifty-six Avonlea points, thirty-eight unnotched points/preforms, and a single possible Sonota point were recovered (Landals et al. 2004:78–86). The lithic raw materials were dominated by Knife River flint (Landals et al. 2004:102). The Miniota pottery assemblage represented a minimum of four vessels. The most thoroughly reconstructed vessel exhibited net impression with square-headed punctates while the others have round hollow punctates, keyhole punctates, or round pointed punctates (Landals et al. 2004:107–110). Most of the fauna was bison, including fetal bison, although a few deer, canid, beaver, fox, rabbit, muskrat, and bird were also recovered. As well, a fair number of fish bones were recovered (Landals et al. 2004:137). Several dates were obtained, including a date on charcoal from the hearth that produced a date of 1,340 +/- 90 BP (Beta-58908), and a date on midden bone that was 870 +/- 90 BP (Beta-58907). The two dates do not overlap at two standard deviations despite the archaeological evidence for a single occupation (Landals et al.

2004:57). Intuitively, the older date seems more acceptable but this was difficult to justify. Thus, more dates were ultimately obtained. The new dates were 1,540 +/- 70 BP (BGS 1791) and 1,560 +/- 70 BP (BGS 1792); these dates supported each other but do not overlap with the previous dates, so the latter are rejected (Landals et al. 2004:58).

In Montana, Timber Ridge (24BL101) is a classic Avonlea bison pound site that is located between Bearspaw and the Little Rocky Mountains (Davis 1966). A radiocarbon date of 980 +/- 110 BP (GX-1195) was obtained for the material.

The Fantasy site (24PH1324) is a bison pound just south of the Milk River in northeastern Montana (Tratebas and Johnson 1988). Avonlea points and parallel-grooved pottery were recovered from the site (Tratebas and Johnson 1988:90–96). A radiocarbon date was obtained from a hearth in an adjacent processing area: 1,040 +/- 100 BP (RL-1717) (Tratebas and Johnson 1988:91, Morlan n.d.). Similar sites nearby include Beaver Bend (24PH1206) and TRJ (24PH569) (Tratebas and Johnson 1988:91–94).

The Lost Terrace site (24CH68) is an intensive pronghorn utilization locale on the north side of the Missouri River between Bearspaw and Highwood Mountains (Davis and Fischer 1988). Numerous Avonlea points were recovered and the material of the lithic assemblage in general suggested use of exotic raw materials from the east, southeast, and southwest of the site (Greiser 1988). Numerous radiocarbon dates were obtained for the site (Morlan n.d.). Subsequently, Davis et al. (2000:55–56) argued that the most recent date was processed poorly and the three oldest dates were well outside the known Avonlea age range, leaving the remaining seven dates to produce a mean age of ca. 1,200 +/- 25 BP.

The Goheen site (24WX30) is a single-component Avonlea campsite in a sheltered swale, about 150 m north of a spring that drains to Hodges Creek (Frayley and Johnson 1981). A partial Avonlea point and a preform were recovered with parallel-grooved pottery (Fraley and Johnson 1981:7–15; Johnson 1988). Four radiocarbon dates were obtained: 1,080 +/- 80 BP (WSU-2382); 1,240 +/- 60 BP (Beta-8971); 1,270 +/- 60 BP (WSU-2381 B); and 1,510 +/- 90 BP (WSU-2381) (Fraley and Johnson 1981:7; Morlan n.d.). The youngest date was suspect because of a high alpha count and was rejected (Fraley and Johnson 1981:7).

The Corey Ranch site (24TT83) is a stone circle camp on the north side of the Teton River (Quigg 1988b). Thirteen of more than twenty stone circles were tested and produced an Avonlea point and some pottery sherds (n=269) (Quigg 1988b:145). The pottery is plain with a cord-wrapped impression on the lip (Quigg 1988b:146). Three radiocarbon dates were obtained on associated bison bone: 890 +/-120 BP (Beta-14803); 1,110 +/- 80 BP (Beta-14805); and 1,080 +/- 80 BP (Beta-14804) (Quigg 1988b:145; Morlan n.d.).

The Herdegen's Birdtail Butte site (24BL1152) is a highly stratified, multicomponent bison kill site and campsite located on the southeast margin of the Bears Paw Mountains in north-central Montana. Levels 1 to 11 produced diagnostic Avonlea points, with Level 12 being indeterminate (Brumley 1990:36–41). Level 2 produced a radiocarbon date of 980 +/- 60 BP (Beta-31791) (Brumley 1990:36). Level 12 produced a radiocarbon date of 1,260 +/- 80 BP (Beta-31792) (Brumley 1990:41).

The Vestal site (24FR760) is a multicomponent processing site located near Denton, central Montana (Payette et al. 2006). Five block excavations comprising 473 m² were excavated (Payette et al. 2006:8). At least six occupations were represented. Many Avonlea points were recovered but they are somewhat irregular compared to classic examples of Avonlea points. As well, despite the processing nature of the site, pottery was not recovered (Payette et al. 2006:16). Seventeen radiocarbon dates were obtained, eleven from cultural features. Two were rejected (Payette et al. 2006:14–15). The dates range between ca. 1,130 to 1,260 BP, with outlying dates at ca. 1,400 and 1,680 BP (Payette et al. 2006:15).

In North Dakota, the Evans site (32MN301) is a multicomponent campsite located north of New Town in the northwest part of the state. Component 1 may be mixed but produced Avonlea points (Schneider and Kinney 1978, fig. 5f–g, l–m), Avonlea preforms (Schneider and Kinney 1978, fig. 5n), and an intrusive Pelican Lake or potentially contemporaneous Sonota point (Schneider and Kinney 1978, fig. 5e), along with smooth, unthickened, flattened lip pottery (Schneider and Kinney 1978:6–10). The lithics were mainly manufactured on Knife River flint. The fauna was largely bison although deer, bird, moose, swift fox, and dog or coyote were also recovered. Two radiocarbon dates were obtained for the component: 1,360 +/- 85 BP (I-7566) and 1,200 +/- 85 BP (I-7565) (Schneider and Kinney 1978:6; Morlan n.d.).

In summary, there is cohesiveness within the Avonlea phase. The Avonlea point is quite distinctive, although temporal variation is exhibited in a slow degradation from exquisite forms to less finely worked forms through time. Avonlea pottery is also distinctive whether it is parallel grooved, net impressed, or shouldered plain ware. The morphology and distribution of these diagnostic materials exhibit consistency through southern Alberta, southern Saskatchewan, southwestern Manitoba, northwestern Montana, and northwestern North Dakota.

The origin of Avonlea has been discussed repeatedly by Kehoe and Kehoe (1968) who advocated that Avonlea represented the migration of Athapascan speaking people moving to the south (see also Wilcox 1988; Frison 1988; Greiser 1994; and Schlesier 1994). Others have suggested different ethnic affiliations for Avonlea (e.g., Reeves 1983a; Morgan 1979). Landals (1995, Landals et al. 2004) provided a review of this issue and its intricacies. Based on excavations at the Miniota site, Landals, Kulle, and Cockle (2004:11–28) suggested that Avonlea pottery is related to Brainerd Ware in northern Minnesota. Morgan (1979; see also Landals et al. 2004:13) originally proposed this argument based on pottery from the Garratt site. The Garratt site and Brainerd Ware both exhibit net-impressed pottery with roughly the same vessel shape. A problem for the hypothesis was the lack of sites with Brainerd Ware in dated components. The dating of residue on Brainerd Ware demonstrates that it is as old as 2,800–2,700 BP, which shows it could be a potential Avonlea ancestor (Landals et al. 2004:14). The excavation of the Miniota site provided a very early Avonlea site just west of the Brainerd Ware heartland (Landals et al. 2004). Avonlea sites are increasingly younger as they are found further west. This led Landals (1995, Landals et al. 2004:15–17) to review a variety of theoretical issues regarding migration.

Key for any migration is push and pull factors. Push factors include population increase, resource stress, increased information about a destination, or technological innovation (Landals et al. 2004:17). Of these, population increase and resources stress seem like possible push factors, given the proximity to the Hopewell Interaction Sphere and its associated dynamics. With regards to pull factors, the strong association between Sonota and Avonlea might have played a role. A Sonota point was found at the Miniota site. The site also produced an unusual amount of Knife River flint. As mentioned earlier, this is not the only site at which this occurs. The Walter Felt site produced Sonota and Avonlea points manufactured on Knife River flint. The Garratt site contained many Avonlea points and a Sonota point along with an unusual amount of Knife River flint, as did EdNh 35 and EeOm 51. Avonlea's relationship with Sonota may have drawn it out onto the plains.

The Sonota phase was already present in southeastern Saskatchewan by ca. 1,800 BP. Avonlea may have entered the province by skirting the Plains/parkland periphery, north of Sonota, expanding west behind Sonota. This advancement was in the shadow of Sonota's success. In fact, the elimination of Besant at ca. 1,500 BP on the southwestern Saskatchewan and Alberta plains made way for Avonlea. Ultimately, by ca. 1,350 BP Sonota disappears and Avonlea is the only phase present on the southern Alberta and southwestern Saskatchewan Plains. The repeated co-occurrence of Sonota and Avonlea in sites, and the increased amounts of Knife River flint in the assemblages of those sites, suggests a sharing relationship in which Avonlea obviously benefited by gaining access to superior stone, but it is unclear what Sonota would have received in exchange. In Manitoba and Saskatchewan, Avonlea appears as early as ca. 1,550 BP. By ca. 1,350 BP it spreads to the plains of Alberta, although by ca. 1,300 BP it appears to be absent from Manitoba and southeastern Saskatchewan. This distribution illustrates the continued migration west as some force, possibly population pressure, drives Avonlea from its homeland.

At the periphery of this area are Avonlea-like materials. In Montana, there is a dramatic drop in the number of Avonlea sites south across the Missouri River (Fraley 1988). In fact, the Goheen site in east-central Montana is one of the few excavated Avonlea sites recorded that far south (Fraley and Johnson 1981). South of this is the Benson's Butte-Beehive complex (ca. 1,550–800 BP) (Fredlund 1988). The points are Avonlea-like, but they are not morphologically Avonlea. They are associated with rockshelters and circular rock wall dwellings (Fredlund 1988). Avonlea is more than a point style, rather it is a complex of technological (points and pottery), social (high redundancy in land use), and ceremonial (interment of individuals in pit burials under cairns) traits. Similarly, in Wyoming, sites from this period are often considered Avonlea sites (Frison 1988:155). Sites such as the Wardell site, Wortham Shelter, the Visborg site, the Leath Burial, and the Billy Creek Burial are not Avonlea sites. The resemblance in form between the points in the aforementioned sites and Avonlea points is considerable, but associated lifeways and features suggest substantially different cultural patterns. While social interaction may ultimately explain the similarity, the morphology of the points alone is well outside that required to be considered Avonlea. The transmontane west of southern British Columbia and northern Montana has also produced Avonlea-like points (Roll 1988, fig. 6a–k) but the vast majority do not fit the mould. The recovery of material associated with the montane Avonlea points should provide important information in assessing the relationship of these points to those on the plains.

The nature of Avonlea pottery has also produced lively debate. Three surface treatments have been recognized: net-impressed, parallel-grooved, and plain (Byrne 1973, Johnson 1988, Quigg 1988b). Net-impressed pottery appears most widespread, having been recovered in Alberta at EcOs 41 (Brumley et al. 1983), Morkin (Byrne 1973), Trout Creek (Byrne 1973), H.M.S. Balzac (Walde 2006a), Manyfingers (Quigg 1988a), and the Empress site (Clarke 2000:127–128), in Saskatchewan at Long Creek (Wettlaufer and Mayer-Oakes 1960), Garratt (Morgan 1979), Broadview (Landals 1995), Lebret (Smith and Walker 1988), Gravel Pit (Klimko 1985; Meyer et al. 1988; Walde 2006a), Wallington Flat (Meyer et al. 1988; Walde 2006a), Mineral Creek (Meyer et al. 1988; Walde 2006a), Yellowsky (Wilson-Meyer and Carlson 1985), Birch Hills (Walde 2006a), Harris Sand Hills (Walde 2006a), and Sjovold (Dyck and Morlan 1995), and in Manitoba at Miniota (Landals et al. 2004).

Parallel-grooved or spiral-channelled pottery has been noted in Montana at the Goheen site (Fraley and Johnson 1981), the Fantasy site (Tratebas and Johnson 1988), and the Henry Smith site (Quigg 1988b); in Alberta at the Morkin site (Byrne 1973) and the Empress site (Clarke 2000:127–128); in Saskatchewan at the Garratt site (Morgan 1979), the Sjovold site (Dyck and Morlan 1995), the Avonlea site (Klimko and Hanna 1988; Hanna 1986), and the Kerrobert surface find (Walde et al. 1995); and in Manitoba at the DlLg 33 (Speidel 1996).

Plain surface finish has been noted in Alberta at Morkin (Byrne 1973), Larson (Milne 1988), and EfPi 17 (Hanna 2002:49), and in Saskatchewan at Garratt (Morgan 1979), and in Montana at Henry Smith (Ruebelmann 1988) and Corey Ranch (Quigg 1988b).

Johnson (1988) was among the first to suggest that the variety of surface treatments in Avonlea pottery may have some bearing on interactions within the Avonlea culture. More recently, Walde (2006a) has taken this view a step further. He proposed a series of phases that exhibit Avonlea points in association with one of the three types of pottery. Small differences in decoration to the net-impressed pottery and subtle shifts in lithic resources are said to account for the Morkin phase (i.e., Avonlea points and net-impressed pottery in southern Alberta) and the Lebret phase (i.e., Avonlea points and net-impressed pottery in central and southeastern

Saskatchewan). Similarly, the Sjovold phase consists of parallel-grooved pottery and Avonlea points in southwestern Saskatchewan. The Upper Kill phase contains Avonlea points and relatively plain pottery in southern Alberta and northern Montana. Ultimately, the Upper Kill phase is considered ancestral to the Old Women's phase. As Landals (1995, Landals et al. 2004:23) has observed, approaches to Avonlea focusing on regional variation (especially in pottery) downplay the co-occurrence of different surface finishes in a single site. As well, the time-transgressive nature of Avonlea, with its occurrence across the plains almost instantaneously and then the disappearance of sites from Manitoba and then eastern Saskatchewan, has not been taken into account by regional models. Ceramics do not appear to exhibit patterning. Avonlea is a cohesive phase.

Ceremonial aspects of the Avonlea phase are poorly known. Avonlea offerings of points and pottery are known at the Majorville Medicine Wheel and Cairn and at Manyberries Medicine Wheel. The large pit at Head-Smashed-In Buffalo Jump clearly speaks to ceremonial practice. The interment of people during the Avonlea phase is also poorly understood. The Bethune site is an unequivocal burial of at least seven people of the Avonlea phase in a pit, possibly beneath a cairn. The Carroll site, dating roughly to the Avonlea phase, is an interment of an individual in a pit, although the presence or absence of a cairn could not be confirmed. The Shaw burial is another pit interment beneath a cairn that roughly dates to the Avonlea phase. Diagnostic materials were not found to confirm the archaeological cultural affiliation of the last two burials. The practice of pit interments beneath cairns seems reasonable to propose as the funerary practice used during the Avonlea phase.

Regarding the fate of the Avonlea phase, at roughly 1,100 BP it disappears from southern Alberta, southwestern Saskatchewan, and northern Montana. Most scholars would agree that the fate of Avonlea is deeply related to the rise of the Old Women's phase.

AVONLEA–OLD WOMEN'S TRANSITION (CA. 1,100 BP)

Forbis (1960:130) was the first to allude to a possible transitional period between the two main phases of the Late Prehistoric period. While excavating the Upper Kill site, he designated the vast majority of the points as the "Upper Kill type" with the remainder classified under a scheme designed for a later time period. Currently, the Upper Kill type is called the Avonlea point of the Avonlea phase and the "later" points found in association with them in the Upper Kill site are called Cayley Series points of the Old Women's phase.

Reeves (1983a) suggested that Besant gave rise to the Old Women's phase, based on similarities between Samantha points (Besant arrowheads) and Prairie side-notched (early Cayley Series) points. At the time, a problem with this scenario was that both Besant and Avonlea dates overlapped with those of the Old Women's phase (Brumley and Rushworth 1983; Morlan 1988; Vickers 1986, 1994:21).

Byrne (1973:468–469) inferred continuity in both pottery and projectile points between the Avonlea phase and the Old Women's phase. Hence, he placed the pottery associated with these phases under a single ceramic tradition: the Saskatchewan Basin complex. Still, he acknowledged the possibility that Avonlea and Besant may have merged to produce the Old Women's phase (Byrne 1973:470). He considered the Besant phase, however, to be aceramic.

By the 1980s, Reeves (1983a:19–20) concurred that an amalgamation of Avonlea and Besant might explain the origin of Old Women's. In a model very much like Reeves' (1983a:19–20), Duke (1988:99–100) also proposed an amalgamation of Avonlea and Besant to explain the origins of the Old Women's phase. He considered the earliest points associated with Old Women's to be most comparable to Besant points, while he viewed the pottery and later lithics as most comparable to Avonlea material (Duke 1988:99).

Based on excavations at the Estuary site (EfOk 16), Adams (1977:141–146) argued that the Avonlea phase outlasted or assimilated Besant people, giving rise to the Old Women's phase. Level 11, the lower level, produced Avonlea and Old Women's material dated to ca. 1,190 +/- 170 BP (S-641). The overlying Level 1, the upper level, consisted solely of Old Women's material and dated to 1,070 +/- 70 BP (S-640) (Adams 1977:142; Morlan n.d.). Adams (1977:143) suggested the term *Leader subphase* to capture this transitional component. He also listed numerous other sites, including Level 24 of the Gull Lake site, as further examples of co-occupations with Avonlea and Old Women's materials (Adams 1977:143)

Brumley and Dau (1988:51) saw the Old Women's phase as developing out of a regional variant of Avonlea in southern Alberta. Elsewhere, other regional variants of Avonlea and Besant developed into as-yet undefined complexes. Interestingly enough, this scenario takes on new meaning with

Walde, Meyer, and Unfreed's (1995) description of possible regional variation in Avonlea.

Hudecek-Cuffe (1989:216; 1992:327–329) provided evidence for continuity in lithic use and technology, ceramics, lithic tool types, and radiocarbon dates to support a model indicating connections between the Avonlea and the Old Women's phases. This work was based on excavations at the Empress (EfOo 130) site near Empress, Alberta, which represents a possible cohabitation of Avonlea and Old Women's peoples.

Clarke (1995) confidently identified the Hartley site (FaNp 19) as an Avonlea–Old Women's transitional site. His faunal assessment identified a single long-term winter occupation consisting of bone elements from twenty-two species of vertebrates, with bison being the most numerous. Fetal bison bone exhibited a wide developmental range, indicating that the animals were being taken repeatedly in small numbers. At the Empress (EfOo 130) site, Clarke (2000) re-examined the stone circle camp that provided the basis of Hudecek-Cuffe's (1989, 1992) model of continuity between Avonlea and Old Women's. His excavations reaffirmed Hudecek-Cuffe's (1989:216; 1992:327–329) findings that the Empress site contained both Avonlea and Old Women's material in association with one another (Clarke 2000:160).

The Sites

In order to assess the various lines of thinking presented above, sites with apparent co-occupations of the Avonlea phase and the Old Women's phase from Alberta that have been reliably dated are outlined below. These sites are used to critically evaluate the current view of the Avonlea–Old Women's transition (see Plate 25 and Figure 26).

Upper Kill (DlPd 1). The Upper Kill site is a bison kill site at the head of a draw on the Oldman River's south bank, 5 km above its confluence with the Little Bow River. Based on testing, an associated campsite may also be present on the prairie level (Forbis 1960:121). The Upper Kill received its name by being the uppermost of two kill sites in the draw. The other kill site 70 m down the draw is called the Lower Kill site, and consisted entirely of Old Women's material (Forbis 1960:121). Forbis excavated the site in 1957. The site was not interpreted as a jump, but was identified as rather an ambush in a draw, which may have had a corral (Forbis 1960:121; Wormington and Forbis 1965:142).

A total of 170 projectile points and point fragments were recovered from the Upper Kill site (see Nance [1972] for a statistical analysis of this point assemblage). Of the classifiable points, the majority of the points (90%, n=86) were labelled Upper Kill types (Forbis 1960:138–139), and are now referred to as Avonlea points (Wormington and Forbis 1965:142). An Avonlea triangular specimen was also recognised (Forbis 1960:40, plate 1). The remaining 10 percent of the points conformed to Cayley Series points of the Old Women's phase. Forbis (1960:130) firmly stated that these latter points were found "scattered throughout the cultural deposit of the Upper Kill." Forbis (1960:140) referred to a point knife in the assemblage "identical in outline to the majority of the points," which is likely a large version of the Avonlea specimen. Other tools recovered include biface fragments (n=7), retouched flakes (n=13), a push-plane, and an elongate cobble. Flakes were noted but not described (Wormington and Forbis (1965:142).

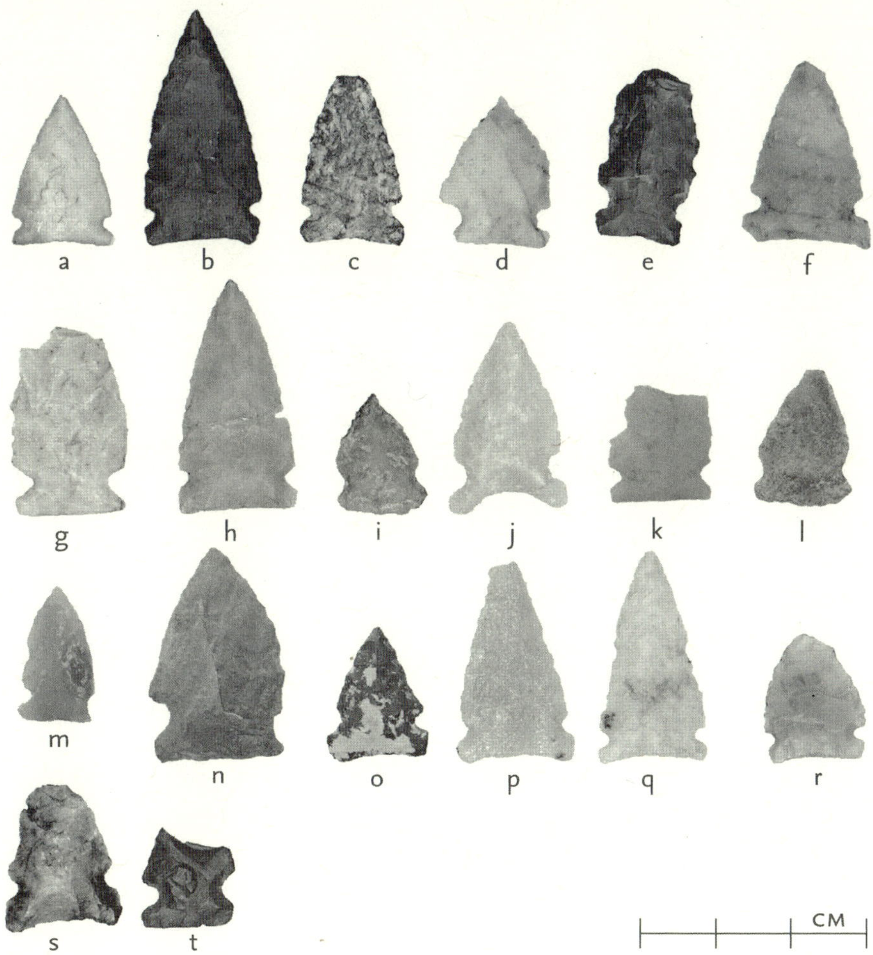

PLATE 25 Avonlea–Cayley Series transition points. Illustrated are projectile points from the Upper Kill site (DlPd 3) (a–j); and the Empress site (EfOo-130) (k–t). Photo credit: Alberta Culture and Community Spirit.

FIGURE 26
Avonlea–Old Women's transition sites within Alberta

The site also produced three fragments of pottery (Wormington and Forbis 1965:142). The fragments included portions of the neck and shoulder of a vessel. Walde and Meyer (2003:142) identify this pottery as Ethridge Ware. The recovery of two antler flakers from the bone bed was also reported (Forbis 1960:156). A single radiocarbon date of ca. 935 BP was obtained for the site (see Table 24). This is a late date for Avonlea, but might reflect the possible co-occupation of the site with Old Women's people (Morlan 1988:302).

Site [LAB NO.]	Conventional ^{14}C Age	$^{13}C/^{12}C$ Ratio	Material	Calibration	Reference
EcOr 35 [S-1015]	1045 +/- 70	-20.0‰	S-1015	AD 810–1160 (p = 0.954)	Brumley 1976; Morlan n.d.
DlPd 1 [GX-2295]	935 +/- 90	-20.0‰	charred bone	AD 890–920 (p = 0.015); AD 960–1270 (p = 0.939)	Byrne 1973:630
EfOo 130 [BETA-141284]	1190 +/- 40	-26.6‰	charred	AD 690–750 (p = 0.078); AD 760–970 (p = 0.876)	Clarke 2000
EfOo 130 [BETA-141285]	1160 +/- 40	-25.4‰	charred	AD 770–980 (p = 0.954)	Clarke 2000
EfOo 130 [BETA-141286]	1350 +/- 120	-24.6‰	charred	AD 400–1000 (p = 0.954)	Clarke 2000
EfOo 130 [BETA-141287]	1040 +/- 70	-19.2‰	collagen	AD 810–1170 (p = 0.954)	Clarke 2000

TABLE 24 Radiocarbon dates for Avonlea–Old Women's transition sites (calibrated by OxCal 3.10 [Ramsey 2005])

Empress (EfOo 130). The Empress site is a tipi ring camp on a small terrace on the south side of the Red Deer River, west of Empress. In 1976, mitigative excavations were undertaken at seven stone circles prior to the construction of a pipeline (Reeves 1977b, Hudecek 1989, Hudecek-Cuffe 1992). A total of 146 m² was excavated. No radiocarbon dates were obtained. In 1999, the site was threatened by another pipeline, and the mitigative excavation of two stone circles, examined in the previous excavations, was conducted (Clarke 2000:80). A total of 75 m² was excavated (Clarke 2000:80).

The original excavations recovered both Avonlea and Old Women's points and the researchers contended they were contemporaneous (Reeves 1977b, Hudecek 1989, Hudecek-Cuffe 1992). The subsequent mitigative excavations were designed to determine if co-occupation was indeed the case

(Clarke 2000). Twenty-seven points were recovered including Avonlea (n = 6), Cayley Series (n = 3), and unclassifiable fragments (n = 18). In addition, fifteen preforms were recovered. Other tools included bifaces (n = 12), end scrapers (n = 21), retouched flakes (n = 17), side scrapers (n = 5), unifaces (n = 2), pièces esquillées (n = 9), and a hammerstone. Miscellaneous chert and Swan River chert were the main raw materials used in tool manufacture. Information on the raw materials within the debitage was not available (Clarke 2000:108).

The pottery assemblage consisted of twenty-five sherds. Three different surface treatments were delineated. Most sherds exhibited fabric impression although a sherd exhibiting cord-wrapped paddle impression and a sherd with horizontal fluting (parallel grooving) were present (Clarke 2000:127–128). The two former surface treatments are common within Old Women's material while the latter is an Avonlea ceramic trait.

The faunal assemblage was varied, consisting of three adult bison, a coyote/small dog, a wolf/dog, a rabbit, fish, and a bird. The presence of three fetal bison bones suggested a late winter/early spring occupation. The seasonality is not in conflict with the presence of fish and bird bones, or freshwater molluscs from the nearby river, as these would have been available in spring (Clarke 2000:122–123). Seeds were recovered from seven features, using fine screens.

Four radiocarbon dates were obtained for the site (Table 24). The researcher suggested the dates indicated a single occupation around A.D. 760–810. Clarke (2000:160) was confident the Empress site was a further example of a growing number of sites with co-occurrence of Avonlea phase and Old Women's phase materials. Further, Clarke (2000:160) recognized that a number of late Avonlea sites exhibited Old Women's material traits, such as Corey Ranch and its Old Women's-like pottery.

Head-Smashed-In Buffalo Jump. Head-Smashed-In Buffalo Jump is described above. Reeves (1978:166) documented the recovery of Avonlea points (Timber Ridge side-notched) along with early Cayley Series points (Prairie side-notched) in the lower Old Women's levels. A clear transition between the two was not noted: the points were mixed in the kill deposits.

Ramillies. The Ramillies kill site and associated campsite is described in the section on the Avonlea phase. The kill site deposits contained both Avonlea and Cayley Series projectile points although the stratigraphic relationships have been destroyed by "prehistoric housekeeping" in the pound.

In the related campsite, however, three stratigraphic levels were recorded. In the lowest occupation, Occupation III, an Avonlea occupation was recognized but not radiocarbon dated. Occupation II produced both Avonlea and Old Women's phases materials together, suggesting a possible transitional assemblage. The radiocarbon date from this level was ca. 1,050 BP (Table 24). Occupation I, the overlying Old Women's occupation, produced a radiocarbon date of 740 +/- 115 BP (S-1016) (Brumley 1976; Morlan n.d.).

Avonlea–Old Women's Transition: End of Avonlea Within the Beginnings of Old Women's

The Avonlea–Old Women's transitional phase in Alberta received attention only at the end of the twentieth century (Clarke 2000; Hudecek 1989; Hudecek-Cuffe 1992). Previously, many theories concerning terminal Avonlea and/or Old Women's origins did not consider continuity between the two phases. Substantial data now exists to acknowledge the co-occurrence of Avonlea and Old Women's phase materials as part of a transition from the former to the latter. Adams (1977:143) suggested the term *Leader* to label this transition, based on the proximity of the Estuary site to the town of Leader, Saskatchewan. For this text it is considered inappropriate to label a transitional phase between two known phases by a totally different term, so a combination of the two phase names has been used.

The Avonlea–Old Women's transition consists of sites that exhibit Avonlea material culture such as Avonlea points and/or Avonlea pottery (net-impressed, parallel-grooved, plain) in direct association with Old Women's material culture such as Cayley Series points and Saskatchewan Basin complex: Late Variant pottery (Byrne 1973) or Ethridge Ware (Walde at al. 1995). The lithic raw material suite recovered at these sites tends to reflect local sources. There is strong continuity between subsistence strategies. Interestingly, evidence of fish occurs at EfOo 130. This is a rarity in later Old Women's sites but common in earlier Avonlea sites. In terms of the age of this putative transition, the sites date to about 1,100 BP.

Only a handful of sites outside Alberta exhibit characteristics of an Avonlea and Old Women's co-occupation. In Saskatchewan, the Estuary site (EfOk 16) is a bison kill site at the head of a coulee that produced numerous Avonlea and Cayley Series (Prairie side-notched) points in a single occupation. Associated with this level were two small sherds of pottery that were not particularly diagnostic (Adams 1977:84). This level was overlaid by an Old Women's component containing Cayley Series (Prairie side-notched) points. The lower level was radiocarbon dated to 1,190 +/- 170 BP (S-641) while the upper level was dated to 1,070 +/- 70 BP (S-640) (Adams 1977:142; Morlan n.d.).

The Hartley site (FaNp 19) is a multicomponent habitation site located southeast of Saskatoon (Clarke 1995). The site's stratigraphy, faunal assemblage, and distribution of diagnostics confirm that the Avonlea and Old Women's materials recovered are concurrent (Clarke 1995:205). The occupation was radiocarbon dated to 1,120 +/- 60 BP (S-3382).

The Newo Asiniak site (FbNp 16) is a multicomponent site in the Wanuskewin Heritage Park. It produced an Avonlea point and five Avonlea preforms (Kelly 1986:124). Net-impressed and fabric-impressed pottery was recovered. Kelly (1986:133–134) noted that the former is commonly recovered with Avonlea points, while the latter is often associated with early Old Women's (Prairie side-notched) materials. A radiocarbon date of 915 +/- 70 BP (S-2533) was obtained (Kelly 1986:139; Morlan n.d.). The researcher preferred to interpret the assemblage as transitional between Avonlea and Old Women's rather than mixed (Kelly 1986:134).

In Montana, the Henry Smith site (24PH794) is a multicomponent bison kill site on the Milk River in north-central Montana (Ruebelmann 1988). Six discrete bone layers were encountered in a 2-×-4-m unit block in the south part of the site. Every bone layer yielded both Avonlea and Prairie side-notched points, with a relative increase in Prairie side-notched points moving up through the levels. Layer 6, the oldest level, produced a radiocarbon date of 1,200 +/- 100 BP (RL-1597). Bone Layer 4 produced a date of 1,070 +/- 100 BP (RL-1513). Bone Layer 3 produced a radiocarbon date of 1,040 +/- 100 BP (RL-1514). Layer 1 produced a radiocarbon date of 940 +/- 90 BP (RL-1596) (Ruebelmann 1988:197–198). Excavations in another nearby block, 2 × 2 m, produced a similar sequence. Ruebelmann (1988:199) cautioned against considering the assemblage as a transitional Avonlea/Old Women's site. By way of explanation, however, he simply questioned the homogeneity of Avonlea sites and questioned the reality of a pure Avonlea site. This text suggests the site provides numerous excavated levels documenting the co-occurrence of Avonlea and Old Women's material.

The Meissner Ranch site (24HL188) consists of fifty-six stone circles and two cairns on the north side of the Marias River in north-central Montana (Brumley 1991). Cairn 2 (4 m in diameter) was on a bedrock knob forming part of the river valley wall well above the stone circles. An interment was found in the center of the cairn at the base of the stones (Brumley 1991:48).

Associated with the burial were four *Olivella* shell beads, an antler tool, a large canid molar, yellow iron oxide presumably used for pigment, and a projectile point pendant (Brumley 1991:49). A radiocarbon date of 1,100 +/- 70 BP (Beta-25343) was obtained for the interment. The point exhibits attributes of both late Avonlea and early Cayley Series points. The cairn-style burial is similar to Avonlea burials, but in this case it exhibits copious grave goods.

Clarke (2000:148–158) suggested that the Gull Lake (EaOd 1) site's Level 24, the Sheep Camp site (EeOc 3), the Bakken-Wright site (DiOa 1), and the Long Creek site (DgMr 1) in Saskatchewan, and the Morkin site (DlPk 2) in Alberta may represent transitional Avonlea–Old Women's sites as well.

In short, the transition from the Avonlea material culture to that of the Old Women's phase took place at about 1,100 BP. Avonlea artifacts have been repeatedly found in direct association with Old Women's artifacts. Furthermore, some late Avonlea sites such as Corey Ranch or Amisk show signs of changes in their material culture that foreshadow this transition. Hudecek-Cuffe's (1989, 1992) studies in continuity provide evidence of a connection between the two phases in terms of lithic use and technology, pottery, and lithic tool types. In fact, Byrne (1973) provided strong evidence for continuity and overlap between the pottery traditions of these two phases years ago. Geographically, the sites that exhibit transitional Avonlea/Old Women's components are limited to southern Alberta, southwestern Saskatchewan, and north-central Montana. Besant played little role in this transition, as it disappeared from the archaeological record approximately five hundred years earlier.

OLD WOMEN'S PHASE (CA. 1,100 TO 250 BP)

Traditionally, the Old Women's phase commences as early as 1,400 BP (Reeves 1978; Morlan 1988) with its earliest radiocarbon dates thought to overlap with both terminal Avonlea and Besant dates (Brumley and Rushworth 1983; Morlan 1988; Vickers 1986). The Old Women's phase was first recognized in the 1960s when Forbis (1962) developed a classification system for projectile points he excavated at the (Old) Women's Buffalo Jump near Cayley, Alberta. Reeves (1970) conceived of Old Women's as an archaeological phase shortly after this. In terms of the phase, Reeves (1970) did not elaborate on the specifics of the phase, but noted that it contained characteristic projectile points and pottery. Byrne (1973:356) refined the definition of the Old Women's phase by describing the pottery technology associated with it (i.e., Saskatchewan Basin complex: Late Variant pottery).

It was not until the early 1980s that Reeves (1983a:19) provided a relatively concise description of the Old Women's phase, stating, "Old Woman's [*sic*] phase is characterized by ceramics, emphasizes local Plains or Montana lithics to large measure, and has a technology characterized by the extensive use of split pebble techniques to produce blanks for end scrapers, points, pièce esquillées and burin-like spalls. There is also extensive use of petrified wood. Projectile point styles are microstylistically descrete [*sic*], particularly those representative of the close of Prehistoric time" (Reeves 1983a:19).

In a summary of the archaeological knowledge for the Alberta plains, Vickers (1986:95) acknowledged Byrne's (1973) inclusion of Saskatchewan Basin complex: Late Variant pottery within the Old Women's phase. Further, he noted that projectile points recovered from Old Women's sites were generally being classified as Prairie (ca. 1,100 BP-600 BP) and Plains (ca. 600 BP to the Protohistoric period) side-notched, using Kehoe's (1966b) classification rather than Forbis' (1962) seminal classification (Vickers 1986:95). It was in this vein that Brumley and Dau (1988:50–51) defined the Old Women's phase as containing Prairie and Plains side-notched projectile points (as defined by Kehoe 1966b:830–834) in association with Saskatchewan Basin complex: Late Variant pottery (as defined by Byrne 1973:331–356). Additionally, they considered aceramic finds of Plains and Prairie side-notched points to constitute a different phase, which they named the Saddle Butte phase (Brumley and Dau 1988:56).

In terms of geographic distribution, Meyer (1988) argued that the Old Women's phase reached beyond southern Alberta. He recognized Saskatchewan Basin complex: Late Variant pottery from sites in southern Saskatchewan and suggested that the Old Women's phase occurred on both the Saskatchewan and Alberta plains between 1,100 and 600 BP (Meyer 1988). After 600 BP, however, the Old Women's phase was replaced on the Saskatchewan plains by the Mortlach phase but continued on the Alberta plains (Meyer 1988).

Peck (1996; Peck and Ives 2001), argued that classification of Prairie and Plains side-notched point typology (Kehoe 1966b) masked the continuity in projectile points through time, and suggested that some of these points be reclassified as Cayley Series projectile points to more properly reflect the gradual change in projectile point form through time and across space. Cayley Series projectile points are side-notched, although corner notches are sometimes present, especially in specimens from the early part of the series. Basal edge shapes are usually straight but can be convex or concave, notch forms are largely rounded or *v*-shaped, and overall base outline shapes are largely fishtail, flattened hexagonal, or rectangular. The term *Cayley* was used since the first thorough attempt to classify these projectile points was by Forbis (1962) at the (Old) Women's Buffalo Jump near Cayley, Alberta. In contrast to the fluid form of the Cayley Series were the Mortlach Group points of the Mortlach phase in southern Saskatchewan, which consistently have deep, narrow notches, straight basal edges, and rectangular bases (Peck 1996; Peck and Ives 2001).

Cayley Series projectile points (Peck 1996; Peck and Ives 2001) are consistently recovered with Saskatchewan Basin complex: Late Variant pottery (as defined by Byrne 1973). This combination is considered to define the Old Women's phase (Peck 1996; Peck and Ives 2001). As Meyer's (1988) delimited, the geographic distribution of the Old Women's phase has an early expression (ca. 1,100–600 BP) across south-central and southwestern Saskatchewan, southern Alberta, and possibly northern Montana, and a later expression (ca. 600 BP to the Protohistoric period) in southwestern Saskatchewan, southern Alberta, and north-central Montana (Peck 1996; Peck and Ives 2001).

Saskatchewan Basin complex: Late Variant pottery vessels have relatively thick walls and are generally coconut or globular in shape but occasionally exhibit flattened bases (Meyer 1988:56). "Shoulders are quite common and pronounced frequently reflecting internal or external thickening in the vicinity of the ridge, and necks, when present, are generally shallow and short" (Byrne 1973:334). Most vessels exhibit some form of surface treatment (e.g., vertical cord impression or fabric impression, often smoothed) while the minority of the vessels exhibit completely smooth or plain surfaces. Similarly, most vessels exhibit some form of decoration. Meyer (1988:56) noted that surface treatments are produced by impressions from coarse, cord-wrapped tools while common decorations such as punctates and incisions were produced with pointed tools. Decorative elements are often incorporated into a variety of motifs and placed on the lip, just below the lip exterior, on the neck or along the shoulder (Byrne 1973:334–335).

The manufacturing process of Saskatchewan Basin Complex: Late Variant pottery is not clear. Based on ethnographic accounts and experimental archaeology, Simon (1979:39–57) suggested pottery was manufactured using in-ground moulds. She noted the occurrence of decorative motifs only on or above the shoulder of vessels (i.e., the part exposed when in a ground mould) and the occurrence of *u*-shaped pits at pottery-bearing sites to support this notion (Simon 1979), which has been looked upon with scepticism (e.g., Byrne 1973:509–510). Coiling and hand building are usually recognised as the likely modes of manufacture.

In terms of lithics, Old Women's assemblages exhibit an emphasis on locally available material such as cherts, pebble cherts, quartzites, petrified wood, and chalcedonies. Lithic materials from Montana (e.g., Madison Formation and Avon cherts) are fairly common (Brumley and Dau 1988:52) while more exotic materials such as Knife River flint from North Dakota and obsidian from Yellowstone Park in northwestern Wyoming and British Columbia are less common but far from absent.

Regarding subsistence, the single most commonly recovered animal species in archaeological sites of the Old Women's phase is bison. Owing to their reliance on bison, the people of the Old Women's phase were likely inclined to anticipate the movements of herds, in order to sustain themselves (Peck 2004). Thus, archaeologists have studied bison migration behaviour for its possible influence on human settlement strategies (e.g., Chisholm et al. 1986; Epp 1988; Morgan 1980; Peck 2004). To complement this indirect measurement of settlement strategy, Peck (2004) conducted research involving thin sections of archaeological bison teeth from Old Women's sites, to determine the season of death. The dental cementum increments from archaeological bison jaws suggested a tendency for winter sites to be found around the periphery of the plains and in large river valleys, while summer sites were much less common and located on the open plains.

Evidence of spiritual life during the Old Women's phase is limited. A number of medicine wheels have been excavated, including the Majorville Medicine Wheel (Calder 1977), British Block Cairn (Wormington and Forbis 1965), Manyberries Medicine Wheel (Brumley 1988), and the Grassy Lake Cairn (Forbis 1960). While some medicine wheels are known to have considerable antiquity, all of the aforementioned medicine wheels contain Cayley Series projectile points and/or Saskatchewan Basin Complex: Late Variant pottery.

The actual use of medicine wheels is poorly understood and the term itself likely represents a misnomer of sorts. There is strong evidence that these boulder arrangements represent a highly variable group of structures that have been lumped under the title "medicine wheel." In fact, some of these structures are known to be functionally unrelated phenomena. For example, one type of "medicine wheel," consisting of a tipi ring with cobble spokes, is analogous to "burial" wheels constructed by the Blood people in this century (Brumley 1985; Dempsey 1956; Peck and Hudecek-Cuffe 2003:89). One such medicine wheel is the Ellis Medicine Wheel. Excavation of the Ellis Medicine Wheel (EcOp 4) uncovered a partial human skeleton, some butchered bison bone, four points, numerous stone tools, and a painted wooden stake radiocarbon dated to about A.D. 1200–1500 (Brumley 1985). Taken with the historic evidence concerning Blackfoot medicine wheels, these cultural remains, which were assignable to the Old Women's phase, suggested that the Ellis Medicine Wheel was a burial lodge and memorial for a prominent person.

Small ammonite fossils exhibiting a bison-like appearance have been found at Old Women's sites, including the Majorville Medicine Wheel, the Ross site, the Grassy Lake Cairn, the Col Darse Cave site, the Saamis site, and EaOq 8 in southern Alberta, and the Wahkpa Chu'gn site in north-central Montana (Peck 2002). These fossils are called Iniskim by the Blackfoot. They are used as powerful objects for enticing bison to jumps and pounds, as personal charms, in curing bundles, and in ceremonial bundles (Peck 2002; Reeves 1993). Most recently, an ammonite has been recognized at the Bridgewater (EfPl 34) site (Karen Geiring, personal communication 2008); as expected, the site appears to be an Old Women's site.

Rock art provides another element of the spiritual life of the people of the Old Women's phase. Rock art in the form of petroglyphs and pictographs is fairly common in Alberta (see Klassen 2003). Magne and Klassen (1991) argued that a large number of these images, such as shield-bearing warriors, classic *v*-necked figures, and hourglass figures, date to the Late Prehistoric period and continue to be represented into the Protohistoric period. With regards to these images, Klassen (1995) argued that the rock art transmits iconic information for contacting the spiritual world and narrative information describing actual events as they took place. Barry (1991), using a perspective from religious studies, provided insights from outside traditional archaeological interpretation.

The Sites

In order to assess the various lines of thinking presented above, Old Women's sites with reliable radiocarbon dates are outlined below. These sites are used to critically evaluate the current view of the Old Women's phase. Because of their lateness in time, there are substantially more reliably dated Old Women's sites than can be discussed here, nor can the topic be thoroughly assessed in this space (see Plate 26 and Figure 27).

PLATE 26 Cayley Series points. Illustrated are projectile points from Head Smashed-In Buffalo Jump (DkPj 1) (a–m); and EhPm 34 (n–hh). Photo credit: Royal Alberta Museum (a–e); Alberta Culture and Community Spirit (f–hh).

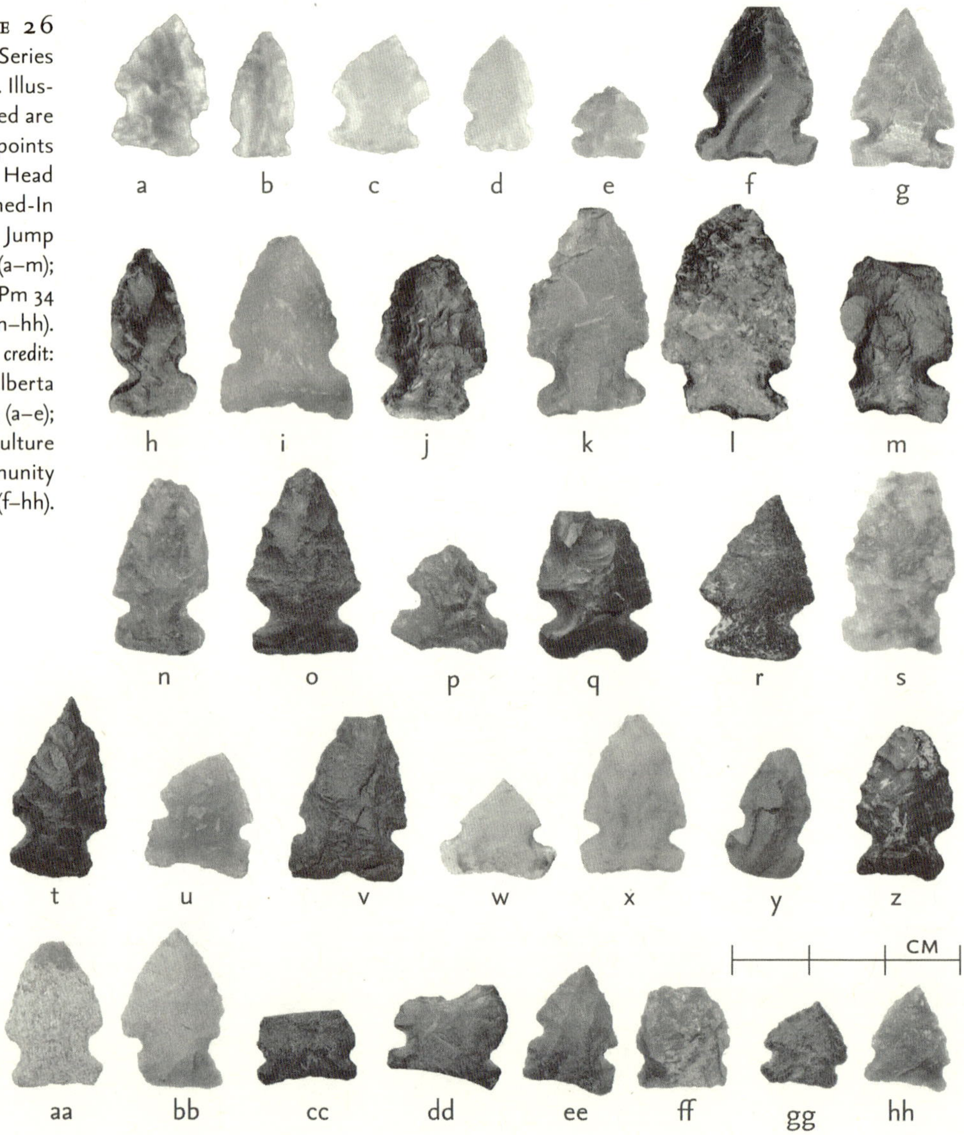

EgPn 440. EgPn 440 is a bison pound located on the western edge of Calgary in a flat-bottomed coulee on the south side of the Bow River. The site consists of five components. The lowest component, 5, was a bone bed associated with Cayley Series projectile points, Components 2 through 4 yielded small bone scatters with no diagnostics, while Component 1 was mixed prehistoric and historic material (Tischer 2000:15–18). In 1997, a total of 71 m² was excavated in a block. The site was mitigated prior to the construction of a wastewater pipeline.

FIGURE 27
Old Women's sites within Alberta

Seventy-seven projectile points and point fragments were found in association with a large bone bed, a possible hearth feature, and a few post-hole features that may represent corral posts (Tischer 2000:15–16). Other tools included bifaces (n = 12), end scrapers (n = 21), retouched flakes (n = 17), side scrapers (n = 5), unifaces (n = 2), pièces esquillées (n = 9), and a hammerstone. An analysis of the points suggested they were most similar to early Cayley Series points. The lithic tool assemblage was dominated by Montana chert (38.1%), black chert (16.7%), and petrified wood (15.5%) with low representation of Knife River flint, obsidian, Top-of-the-World Chert, Swan River Chert, and basalt, among others. Twenty-six possible bone tools were interpreted as scraping or chopping implements, based on polish and rounded ends (Tischer 2000:97).

The faunal assemblage (n = 68,478) was mainly bison (MNI = 67) but also included wolf, fox, elk, mule deer, snowshoe hare, Canada goose, red-tail hawk, and fish (Tischer 2000:48). The analysis suggested that the processing of the bison focused on back, chest, and upper limbs (Tischer 2000:94). Based on the analysis of cut marks, the hump meat, ribs, upper limbs, and tongue were selectively processed. Less emphasis was on the hind limb (Tischer 2000:95). Evidence of marrow extraction was not common. Sexing of the sample indicated a large number of males. Females and young are usually the focus of communal hunts. Two radiocarbon dates of roughly 1,250 BP were obtained for the site (see Table 25). These dates are very early dates for an Old Women's component.

DhPh 13. DhPh 13 is a campsite on the east side of the St. Mary River, in southwestern Alberta (Quigg 1975a:53). A single component was recovered within a buried Ah soil horizon. In 1973, blocks of four 4-m² units were excavated at the site. The site was found as part of a salvage program conducted along the St. Mary River valley. A crude Cayley Series point was found in association with a single piece of pottery, an FBR pile, and a circular rock-ringed hearth (Quigg 1975a:54). Other tools recovered included cores, a scraper, bifaces, an anvil, and a chopper. The lithic debitage did not suggest tool production was a major activity. The pottery fragment was not described other than assigning it to the Old Women's phase. The fauna was highly fragmented but included bison, dog, kit fox, and deer (Quigg 1975a:66). An anvil and a chopper were associated with bone splinters, suggesting marrow extraction. A single date of ca. 1,150 BP was obtained for the component. It is among the earliest dates for an Old Women's component (Quigg 1975a:61).

TABLE 25 Radiocarbon dates for Old Women's sites (calibrated by OxCal 3.10 [Ramsey 2005])

Site [LAB NO.]	Conventional ^{14}C Age	$^{13}C/^{12}C$ Ratio	Material	Calibration	Reference
EgPn 440 [BETA-141209]	1280 +/- 50	?	collagen	A.D. 650–870 (p = 0.954)	Tischer 2000
EgPn 440 [BETA-141211]	1240 +/- 50	?	collagen	A.D. 660–890 (p = 0.954)	Tischer 2000
DkPj 27 [AECV-320C]	1390 +/- 110	-20.0‰	collagen	A.D. 420–890 (p = 0.954)	Marshall 1988:60; Morlan n.d.
DkPj 27 [AECV-321C]	970 +/- 110	-20.0‰	collagen	A.D. 860–1280 (p = 0.954)	Marshall 1988:60; Morlan n.d.
DkPj 27 [AECV-319C]	470 +/- 100	-20.0‰	collagen	A.D. 1290–1650 (p = 0.954)	Marshall 1988:60; Morlan n.d.
DhPh 13 [S-829]	1150 +/- 120	-25.0‰	charcoal	A.D. 650–1060 (p = 0.91); A.D. 1080–1160 (p = 0.044)	Quigg 1975a:61; Morlan n.d.
DkPj 1, L7b [RL-257]	1270 +/- 90	-20.0‰	charred bone	A.D. 610–970 (p = 0.954)	Reeves 1978:162; Morlan n.d.
DkPj 1, L5 [GSC-992]	700 +/- 170	-23.8‰	charred bone	A.D. 950-1650 (p = 0.954)	Reeves 1978:162; Morlan n.d.
EcPl 1, L13 [S-87]	1100 +/- 80	-25.0‰	charcoal	A.D. 700–750 (p = 0.025) A.D. 760–1050 (p = 0.891) A.D. 1080–1160 (p = 0.035)	Forbis 1962:81; Morlan n.d.
EcPl 1, L13 [S-89]	1020 +/- 80	-20.0‰	charred bison	A.D. 860–1220 (p = 0.954)	Forbis 1962:81; Morlan n.d.
EcPl 1, L13 [AECV-1896C]	1120 +/- 70	-22.6‰	wood	A.D. 710–750 (p = 0.029) A.D. 760–1030 (p = 0.925)	Peck 1996:244
EcPl 1, L13 [AECV-1894C]	910 +/- 70	?	horn sheath	A.D. 1010–1260 (p = 0.954)	Peck 1996:244
EcPl 1, L7 [AECV-1897C]	320 +/- 70	-20.7‰	bone	A.D. 1400–1700 (p = 0.913) A.D. 1750–1800 (p = 0.031) A.D. 1900–2000 (p = 0.001)	Peck 1996:244
EcPl 1, L3a [AECV-1898C]	270 +/- 70	-22.0‰	hair	A.D. 1400–2000 (p = 0.954)	Peck 1996:244
EcPl 1, L3 [AECV-1899C]	180 +/- 70	-21.9‰	hair	A.D. 1520–1560 (p = 0.017) A.D. 1630–1960 (p = 0.937)	Peck 1996:244
EePi 1 [S-2095]	1110 +/- 85	-20.0‰	collagen	A.D. 680–1300 (p = 0.954)	Brumley and Rushworth 1983:154; Morlan n.d.

TABLE 25 (continued)

EaPh 4, L2 [AECV-155C]	1020 +/- 160	-20.0‰	collagen	A.D. 650–1300 (p = 0.954)	Beaudoin 1987:209; Morlan n.d.
EaPk 4, L2 [AECV-154C]	530 +/- 75	-20.0‰	collagen	A.D. 1280–1500 (p = 0.954)	Fedirchuk 1986:111–114; Morlan n.d.
EaPh 4, L1 [AECV-153C]	700 +/- 230	-20.0‰	collagen	A.D. 700–1800 (p = 0.954)	Fedirchuk 1986:111–114; Morlan n.d.
EhPm 34, L6 [BETA-6441]	320 +/- 50	?	charcoal	A.D. 1450–1660 (p = 0.954)	Head 1985
EhPm 34, L4 [BETA-6443]	modern	?	charcoal	n/a	Head 1985
DjPm 100 [AECV-734C]	930 +/- 130	-25.3‰	charcoal	A.D. 750–1300 (p = 0.954)	Van Dyke 1994:245
EhPv 78 L3 [BSG-1011]	710 +/- 100	-25.0‰	charcoal	A.D. 1050–1090 (p = 0.025) A.D. 1150–1430 (p = 0.929)	Fedje 1986:57; Morlan n.d.
EhPv 78 L3 [BSG-1014]	770 +/- 100	-25.0‰	charcoal	A.D. 1030–1330 (p = 0.852) A.D. 1340–1400 (p = 0.102)	Fedje 1986:57; Morlan n.d.
EhPv 78 L3 [BSG-1015]	650 +/- 100	-25.0‰	charcoal	A.D. 1180–1450 (p = 0.954)	Fedje 1986:57; Morlan n.d.
EhPv 78 L3 [BSG-1018]	620 +/- 100	-20.0‰	collagen	A.D. 1200–1470 (p = 0.954)	Fedje 1986:57; Morlan n.d.
DgOv 12 [S-2092]	785 +/- 65	-19.0‰	collagen	A.D. 1040–1100 (p = 0.055) A.D. 1120–1310 (p = 0.879) A.D. 1360–1390 (p = 0.019)	Brumley and Rushworth 1983:148; Morlan n.d.
DjPm 126 [AECV 859C]	460 +/- 80	-12.5‰	collagen	A.D. 1300–1360 (p = 0.095) A.D. 1380–1640 (p = 0.859)	Landals 1993:236
DjPm 126 [AECV 1239C]	710 +/- 130	-19.4‰	collagen	A.D. 1030–1440 (p = 0.954)	Landals 1993:236
DhPj 31 [S-864]	720 +/- 105	-20.0‰	collagen	A.D. 1040–1100 (p = 0.046) A.D. 1110–1430 (p = 0.908)	Brumley and Rushworth 1983:148; Morlan n.d.
DhPj 31 [S-947]	465 +/- 70	-25.0‰	charcoal	A.D. 1300–1360 (p = 0.094) A.D. 1380–1530 (p = 0.695) A.D. 1540–1640 (p = 0.166)	Brumley and Rushworth 1983:148; Morlan n.d.
DlPd 3 [S-2039]	615 +/- 120	-25.0‰	charcoal	A.D. 1150–1530 (p = 0.938) A.D. 1570–1630 (p = 0.016)	Morlan n.d.

DlPd 3 [S-2038]	540 +/- 135	-25.0‰	charcoal	A.D. 1210–1660 (p = 0.954)	Morlan n.d.
DlPd 3 [S-2040]	modern	-25.0‰	charcoal	n/a	Morlan n.d.
DjPm 84 [AECV-796C]	530 +/- 80	-19.4‰	collagen	A.D. 1280–1520 (p = 0.940) A.D. 1600–1620 (p = 0.014)	Van Dyke 1994:224
DjPl 13, C-5 [AECV-747C]	500 +/- 110	-21.8‰	collagen	A.D. 1280–1640 (p = 0.954)	Van Dyke 1994:92
DjPl 13, C-5 [AECV-748C]	470 +/- 80	-19.6‰	collagen	A.D. 1330–1370 (p = 0.134) A.D. 1380–1640 (p = 0.820)	Van Dyke 1994:92
EcOp 4 [BETA-8948]	450 +/- 160	?	wood	A.D. 1250–2000 (p = 0.954)	Brumley 1985:204
DgPl 68 [GX-2051]	330 +/- 95	-20.0‰	bone	A.D. 1400–1850 (p = 0.925) A.D. 1900–2000 (p = 0.029)	Reeves 1972; Morlan n.d.
DjPk 1 [S-270]	355 +/- 60	-25.0‰	charcoal	A.D. 1440–1650 (p = 0.954)	Reeves 1983b:24; Morlan n.d.
EfOw 26 [BETA-188553]	260 +/- 60	-19.0‰	collagen	A.D. 1460–1700 (p = 0.70) A.D. 1720–1820 (p = 0.19) A.D. 1910–1960 (p = 0.063)	Goldsmith 2005:390
EgPn 230 [BETA-109225]	440 +/- 50	?	collagen	A.D. 1400–1530 (p = 0.791) A.D. 1550–1640 (p = 0.163)	Vivian et al. 1998:52
EhPn 56 [BETA-176505]	310 +/- 70	-21.0‰	collagen	A.D. 1400–1850 (p = 0.939) A.D. 1900–2000 (p = 0.015)	Murphy 2003:85
DgPl 55 [GX-2053]	modern	?	collagen	n/a	Reeves 1972:108; Morlan n.d.
DgPl 1 [GX-2016]	220 +/- 90	-25.0‰	wood	A.D. 1480–1960 (p = 0.954)	Reeves 1972:59; Morlan n.d.
EgPt 28 [BETA-90062]	140 +/- 130	?		A.D. 1490–1960 (p = 0.954)	Clarke et al. 1998:265
EgPt 28 [BETA-90061]	modern	?		n/a	Clarke et al. 1998:265

NOTE: Radiocarbon dates for the past two hundred years are not reliable.

Head-Smashed-In Buffalo Jump (DkPj 1). In the South Kill of Head-Smashed-In Buffalo Jump, Cayley Series points primarily occurred in Levels 1 to 7B while Avonlea points underlay these, primarily in Levels 8 to 10. Trade items and metal points were recovered in the most recent component. Two radiocarbon dates are available from the South Kill excavations. Level 7B, the oldest Old Women's level, produced a date of 1,270 +/- 90 BP (RL-257). Level 5 produced a date of 700 +/- 170 BP (GSC-992).

(Old) Women's Buffalo Jump (EcPl 1). The Women's Buffalo Jump is described in the section on the Besant phase. Forbis' (1962) work has been the only systematic investigation of the site. The excavation consisted of an Upper Pit excavation block in the "heart of the bone bed," and a Lower Pit excavation block about 10 m downhill from the Upper Pit (Forbis 1962:71–74). Forbis (1962:74) divided the deposits in the Upper Pit into an Upper Member and a Lower Member. The Upper Member consisted of deposits from the surface down to Level 14. These deposits contained the vast majority of the small projectile points that he inferred to be arrow points (Forbis 1962:76). The Lower Member consisted of Levels 15 to 30. The projectile points were "comparatively large and heavy" and were inferred to be dart points (Forbis 1962:76). The continuous morphological change through time in the Upper Member of the Upper Pit point sequence was crucial in defining the Cayley Series projectile points (Peck 1996; Peck and Ives 2001). Pottery was recovered from Level 5 of the Upper Member of the Upper Pit. Byrne (1973:365) classified the pottery as Saskatchewan Basin Complex: Late Variant.

Seven radiocarbon dates were obtained from Layers 13 and above. For Layer 13, Forbis (1962:81) obtained two dates of ca. 1,100 BP. More recently, using Forbis' excavated material, two more dates were provided for Layer 13, ca. 1,120 BP and 910 BP; a date for Layer 7 of ca. 320 BP was provided; and two dates for Layer 3 were established, of ca. 270 BP and 180 BP (Table 25). The Upper Member of the Upper Pit (Layers 1 to 14) produced radiocarbon dates, Cayley Series points, and Saskatchewan Basin Complex: Late Variant pottery, indicating an Old Women's phase assignment.

Amber (EePi 1). The Amber site is located on the south floodplain of Arrowwood Creek, southwest of Mossleigh (Kirby and Justen 1974). In 1970, an initial excavation removed an eroding burial from the stream bank. In 1974, 54 m^2 of excavation recovered over two thousand artifacts from two components (Kirby and Justen 1974:11). The Upper Component contained Late Side-notched (Plains) points and pottery (n = 370 sherds). Separation between the Upper and Lower Components was problematic, but a single point attributed to the Lower Component was a Late Side-notched (Prairie) point. The Amber Burial was associated with the Lower Component (Kirby and Justen 1974:12). A single radiocarbon date of ca. 1,100 BP was produced for the Amber site (Table 25) (Brumley and Rushworth 1983:154; Morlan n.d.). The date was on bone although the context of the bone was not disclosed. The site appears to be an Old Women's campsite with an associated interment.

EgPm 82. EgPm 82 is located on the upper part of Beddington Creek along a seasonal drainage on the north side of Nose Hill in Calgary (Peach 2006). The site is a single-component Old Women's processing site with a diffuse historic component intermixed in the upper levels. It was mitigated as part of a transportation utility corridor expansion.

Sixteen Cayley Series projectile points and fragments were recovered in association with a hearth. Other tools included bifaces (n = 14), end scrapers (n = 24), retouched flakes (n = 22), cores (n = 5), and hammerstones (n = 2). The lithic debitage (n = 848) suggested that late-stage tool manufacturing occurred to some extent at the site (Peach 2006:62–63). The most common raw materials included coarse quartzite (31.3%), medium-fine quartzite (18.3%), and petrified wood (17.4%), although small amounts of Knife River flint, Avon chert, porcellanite, and obsidian were also present (Peach 2006:64). A single tibia shaft fragment with polish on its edge was interpreted as a skinning tool (Peach 2006:99). Pottery (n = 66) was rare at the site; most of the sherds were indeterminate vessel portions (n = 34) or vessel finish (n = 37) (Peach 2006:92). Textile-impressed and smoothed textile-impressed patterns were evident on fourteen of the sherds. Decorations included cord-wrapped object (n = 1), dentate (n = 2), and punctate (n = 2) impressions. Coarse grit, thick walls, and laminated paste suggest that this pottery is Saskatchewan Basin Complex: Late Variant pottery (Peach 2006:121–122).

The faunal assemblage (n = 21,081) consisted largely of unidentifiable large ungulate fragments (n = 19,189) and bison (n = 1,811) (Peach 2006:95). A minimum number of six bison were represented (Peach 2006:107). Sexing analysis suggested at least four females, one male, and one indeterminate adult animal were present in the assemblage. As well, a single ungulate fetal element was recovered (Peach 2006:112). The faunal assemblage was highly fragmented but, of the identifiable bone, most was low utility (73%). Two concentrations of low-utility bison bone occur within the southwest and northeast parts of the site. Seven cut marks on bone were observed. Two cut marks made with metal appear on bison bone while all others were made by stone or were indeterminate (Peach 2006:105). Some bird bone (n = 57) was also recovered but considered historic/intrusive or natural. Charred bone (n = 1,887) and calcine bone (n = 208) suggested burning of bone at the site. FBR (n = 2,445) was fairly common at the site; it was largely water fractured (98.9%). Two radiocarbon dates were obtained for the assemblage: ca. 890 BP and 970 BP (Table 25) (Peach 2006:114). The site is an Old Women's secondary processing site with activity areas indicating bone processing and hide working around a hearth.

Little Bow Site (EaPh 4). The Little Bow site is a campsite/processing site situated on the edge of a high bluff on the bank of the Little Bow River, east of Carmangay (Heitzmann 1985; Fedirchuk 1986:91–92). In 1985, a total of 78 m^2 was excavated in a block. Two components were observed in the upper 20 cm (Heitzmann 1985; Fedirchuk 1986:91). The distinctions between these two components were not always clear (Fedirchuk 1986:91–92). Both levels were Old Women's components. The site was mitigated prior to realignment of a roadway.

The Upper Component produced eight Cayley Series projectile points. A triangular piece of iron, probably reflecting a metal point blade, was also recovered at 4 cm BS and may be associated with this component. Other tools included bifaces (n = 14), end scrapers (n = 24), retouched flakes (n = 22), cores (n = 5), and hammerstones (n = 2). Lithic raw materials were mainly quartzite (45.4%), miscellaneous cherts (32.9%), and petrified wood (13.9%), with trace amounts of obsidian (1.5%) and Knife River Flint (0.6%) (Heitzmann 1985). Three ceramic vessels were found exclusively in this component (Vessels 2, 4, and 5), while three other vessels were found in both upper and lower components (Fedirchuk 1986:107). The fauna from this component was mainly bison (MNI = 2). Large lower-leg elements were represented, along with many unidentifiable pieces. An associated rock feature consisting of FBR and fire-reddened rock defied interpretation. A single radiocarbon date of roughly 700 BP was obtained for the component (Table 25).

The Lower Component produced seven Cayley Series points in association with a basin hearth and a number of bone pegs (Heitzmann 1985:89;

Fedirchuk 1986:109–110). Other lithic tools included a biface, a uniface, scrapers (n = 6), a spokeshave, edge retouched cobble spalls (n = 2), edge retouched flakes (n = 9), a wedge, a split pebble, a hammerstone, an abrader, and cores (n = 13). The lithic raw materials tended to be quartzite (55.7%), miscellaneous chert (23.7%), and petrified wood (12.9%), with some obsidian (1.9%), Montana chert (1.0%), and Knife River flint (0.8%) (Heitzmann 1985:91). Like the Upper Component, the emphasis on sharpening flakes indicated that maintenance of tools was a main activity at the site. Ceramic vessels 7 and 8 were associated with this component (Fedirchuk 1986:108). The fauna from this component was bison (MNI = 3). Fetal bone was recovered after a post-grading inspection of the site (Fedirchuk 1986:124). Other bone clustered around a basin-shaped hearth. Another feature included a line of four bone pegs about 50 cm apart; two more similar pegs were noted about 1 m apart, about 2 m north (Fedirchuk 1986:109–110). A single radiocarbon date of ca. 530 BP was obtained from this level (Table 25). Bone from directly beneath this level (20–30 cm BS) produced a date of ca. 1,000 BP (Table 25).

H.M.S. Balzac (EhPm 34). The H.M.S. Balzac site is discussed in the section on the Avonlea phase. In Block 2, Old Women's material occurred within Regisols 3 to 8 while Avonlea material occurred in Regisols 10–11 and 14 (and 12 by inference) (Head 1985). For Block 2, radiocarbon dates from Old Women's occupations were available for Regisols 4 and 6. Regisol 4 produced a modern date and Regisol 6 produced a date of ca. 320 BP (Table 25). These dates fall within the range expected for Old Women's occupations.

DjPm 100. DjPm 100 is a terrace tipi ring site in Warriner's Coulee on the Crowsnest River (Van Dyke 1994:232). Excavations totalling 63 m^2 were undertaken in four blocks at stone circles A–D, although the Old Women's component was recovered between 10 and 20 cm BS under both Stone Circles A and D (Van Dyke 1994:243). This excavation was part of the mitigation associated with the Oldman River Dam project.

Six projectile points and fragments were recovered. A Cayley Series point, a stem fragment, two triangular preforms, and two tips were associated with the two stone circles. In addition, rock-lined hearths and FBR concentrations were also associated. Other tools included bifaces (n = 7), end scrapers (n = 4), a uniface, a core, and retouched flakes (n = 10). A single metal buckle was recovered but not considered to be associated with the occupation (Van Dyke 1994:243). The raw materials were diverse but emphasized the use of quartzite, chalcedony, petrified wood, and Swan River chert, with small amounts of argillite, siltstone, black chert, Top-of-the-World chert, miscellaneous cherts, and obsidian (Van Dyke 1994:243). No pottery was recorded.

The faunal assemblage (n = 1,829) was highly fragmented, and included bison (MNI = 3), large canid, elk, and deer (Van Dyke 1994:245). A fetal bison specimen suggested a late winter/early spring occupation. A single radiocarbon date of roughly 930 BP was obtained for the compressed material (Table 25). This date correlates well with the morphology of the complete point. This material may correlate with kill deposits underlying Rings B and C, although this was not established.

Junction (DkPi 2). The Junction site is a bison kill and processing site located on the Oldman River, about 5 km upstream from Fort Macleod (Unfreed and Van Dyke 2005). The site consisted of two distinct topographic zones, an upper prairie and lower river terrace. Excavations focused on the lower terrace, as it contained bison kill and butchering/processing deposits. The sediments were divided into three components: Component III contained historic material while Component II and I contained Old Women's material. Component II was separated from Component I by fluvial sands. Based on thirty-four radiocarbon dates, an average age of about 800 BP was suggested for Component I and 500 BP for Component II (Unfreed and Van Dyke 2005). Artifacts recovered from the site include Cayley Series points (n = 394), bifaces, scrapers, choppers, wedges, cores, flakes, and numerous expedient tools. Bone and antler tools, shell ornaments, and ceramics were also recovered from the site. The ceramics were classified as Late Variant pottery of the Saskatchewan Basin complex.

Echo Creek (EhPv 78; 515R). The Echo Creek site is described in the section on the Sonota phase. The Old Women's material was recovered from Component 3 (Fedje 1986:54–55). Thirty-eight small side-notched projectile points and preforms were recovered. The points appeared to be very similar to the Cayley Series projectile points and were recovered in association with lithic heat treating/reduction areas, animal processing features, hearths, and FBR concentrations. The faunal assemblage included bison, elk, moose, mule deer, sheep, beaver, porcupine, canid, rabbit, coot, sucker, and trout/char (Fedje 1986:55–57). Four radiocarbon dates were associated with this material. Four dates suggested a rough age of ca. 700 BP (Table 25).

Many Snakes (DgOv 12). The Many Snakes site is located in Writing-on-Stone Provincial Park in the valley of the Milk River, east of the Milk River townsite (Getty 1971:1). The term *Many Snakes* was given to the site owing to three rattlesnakes the crew encountered during the excavation (Getty 1971:3). In 1968, parts of a human skeleton were noticed at the base of the sandstone cliffs by a Parks employee. The site was a primary human inhumation in a saucer-shaped, wind-eroded depression at the base of a 9-metre-high cliff. The body was in a flexed position, lying on its right side, with the head towards the east (Getty 1971:4). The skeleton was a male between 40 and 55 years of age and stood about 5' 7". The distal fifth digit phalanx of both hands was missing.

Twenty-four grave offerings were associated with the burial, including five early Cayley Series points and two preforms. Also included were bone flakers (n = 4), an antler hammer, bifaces (n = 3), a worked flake, a utilized flake, unmodified flakes (n = 5) and a shell bead. The initial discovery of the skeleton disturbed some artifacts, but the researchers involved indicated that the items came from the thoracic area. Artifacts from undisturbed context were all recovered from this area of the body, except for a single bone flake recovered beside the right ankle (Getty 1971:24). A date of ca. 780 BP was obtained for the site (Table 25).

Castle Forks Buffalo Jump (DjPm 126), Component 3. The Castle Forks Buffalo Jump is located on the south side of the Oldman River just upstream from its confluence from the Castle River (Landals 1993:226). The site location is known locally as the Castle Forks, hence the site name. The uppermost component is a Protohistoric period Old Women's bison jump (Landals 1993:226). This is underlain by Component 2, which is a sparse occupation lacking diagnostics. Component 3, of interest here, is an Old Women's campsite. The lowest component, 4, is another culturally sparse, non-diagnostic occupation. This site was mitigated as part of the Oldman Dam project.

A total of ten points or point fragments were recovered in association with two hearths, butchered bone, lithic debitage, red ochre fragments, and ceramic sherds (Landals 1993:254). Other tools recovered included bifaces (n = 2), an end scraper, a wedge, and flake tools (n = 13). The ceramic assemblage (n = 181) represented several vessels assigned to the Saskatchewan Basin Complex: Late Variant pottery. An antler tool found in association may have been used in pottery production or may be more of a marrow-scooping implement. The faunal assemblage was dominated by bison (MNI = 7). Most bone showed signs of butchering such as green fracture and spiral fracture. Two small pieces of fetal bone were recovered, suggesting a late winter/early spring occupation (Landals 1993:258). A high representation of limb elements and their consistent breakage was interpreted as marrow extraction supplementing a fat-reduced winter diet.

The two hearths are separated by 7 m but exhibited similar characteristics. One hearth was a surface hearth that yielded FBR, red ochre, bone fragments, ceramic sherds, and a Late Side-notched point (Landals 1993). The second feature is a well-constructed, rock-encircled basin hearth exhibiting long-term use. In the immediate vicinity were points, many retouch/resharpening flakes, retouched flakes, a biface fragment, an end scraper, red ochre, and numerous pottery sherds (Landals 1993:255). Neither hearth appeared to represent intensive food processing; instead they were likely hearths for roasting/boiling fresh meat, warmth, and/or light (Landals 1993:255). Two radiocarbon dates of ca. 460 BP and 710 BP were obtained from this component of the site (Table 25). The former is considered too late, given the dates from other levels, but the two dates do overlap at two standard deviations (Landals 1993:236).

Manyfingers (DhPj 31). The Manyfingers site is described in the section on the Avonlea phase. The site covers three terraces, with the second terrace containing two Old Women's components (Level B and C) overlying an Avonlea component (Level A). Component 2 (Level B) is a thin living floor about 3–7 cm thick and 50 cm BS. Component 3 (Level C) is a living floor scattered somewhat by rodent activity, at approximately 40 cm BS. Quigg (1974b:27) combined his discussion of these levels. Five late Cayley Series points and pottery sherds indicate these are Old Women's occupations (Quigg 1974b:27). The pottery was very fragmentary but some exhibited check-stamping, and was attributed to the Saskatchewan Basin Complex: Late Variant pottery (Byrne 1973:331; Quigg 1975a:57). FBR was not common although lithic debitage was present on both living floors. The debitage suggested that tools were both manufactured and resharpened at the site. The fauna consisted mainly of small bone fragments although bison, coyote, dog, and kit fox were identified (Quigg 1974b:47). Component 2 contained only bison while Component 3 contained all the species mentioned as well as fetal bison bone, suggesting a late winter/early spring occupation (Quigg 1974b:28). Two oval ash lenses were also noted but were not considered actual hearths (Quigg 1975a:57). Two radiocarbon dates of roughly 720 BP and 460 BP were obtained from Component 2 (Table 25). These dates both corroborate a late Old Women's occupation.

Ross (DlPd 3). The Ross site was excavated by the Glenbow Foundation in 1957 (Forbis 1960:119). The site is located in south-central Alberta on the south bank of the Oldman River, about 4 km upstream from its confluence with the Little Bow River (Forbis 1960:119). It exhibits three cultural levels: I, II, and III, from bottom to top. All levels produced Cayley Series projectile points and Saskatchewan Basin Complex: Late Variant pottery. Each level also yielded radiocarbon dates: Level III a date of ca. 615 BP, Level II a date of ca. 540 BP, and Level I a modern date. Importantly, an ammonite septum was recovered from Level III (Forbis 1960).

DjPm 84. DjPm 84 is a small campsite/processing site on the east bank of Todd Creek, just upstream from its confluence with the Crowsnest River (Van Dyke 1994:219). More than one Late Prehistoric component was differentiated but a single Old Women's component was presented as relatively discrete (Van Dyke 1994:222–223). A total of 18 m^2 was excavated.

Three late Cayley Series projectile points were recovered in association with a feature consisting of an anvil stone with fragmented bone and FBR. A single metal point was recovered, but was considered intrusive from the surface possibly from ploughing. Other tools recovered included a biface, a scraper, cores (n = 2), and retouched flakes (n = 5). The lithic debitage assemblage (n = 36) was small but reflected a reliance on miscellaneous cherts (Van Dyke 1994:223). The faunal assemblage indicated utilization of mainly bison (MNI = 3), although large canid, wolverine, freshwater shell, and a small ungulate (likely deer) were recovered. A single radiocarbon date of 530 BP was obtained (Table 25).

DjPl 13, Component C-5. DjPl 13 is a campsite/processing site on the north bank of the Oldman River (Van Dyke 1994:38). Block C (50 m^2) contained five components: two Bracken phase followed by two Besant phase and one Old Women's phase. Twelve points or point fragments were recovered from the Old Women's Component. Three specimens were classified as Plains or Prairie side-notched, one stem fragment was classified as possibly Besant, six other fragments were unclassified, and two triangular specimens were considered preforms (Van Dyke 1994:96). The Besant fragment may relate to underlying material, while the rest of the point assemblage fits within the Cayley Series points. Other tools included bifaces (n = 7), cores (n = 14), an end scraper, retouched flakes (n = 20), a drill, unifaces (n = 2), elongate pebbles (n = 4), and a side scraper (n = 4). Debitage and tools showed no patterned distribution. Raw materials showed a clear preference for chalcedony, black cherts, and Etherington chert, although a wide range of materials was present.

The faunal assemblage (n = 1,850) was mainly bison (MNI = 2) but also included nine freshwater shell fragments (Van Dyke 1994:96). Bison fetal bone was present. Bone was scattered throughout the site with burned bone concentrated south of the features. The features included a pit with FBR and bone, and an FBR concentration with cobbles adjacent to the pit (Van Dyke 1994:94–95). The pits and FBR suggested that processing of bone for marrow and grease occurred at the site. Two radiocarbon dates of ca. 500 BP and 470 BP were obtained for this component (Table 25). These dates fit well with the associated Cayley Series points. As well, this component yielded no diagnostic material but it was dated to 480 +/- 90 BP (AECV-1358C), and so stratigraphically correlates with DjPl 13, Component B-5.

Ellis (EcOp 4) Medicine Wheel. The Ellis site is a death lodge medicine wheel site overlooking the South Saskatchewan River on the Canadian Forces Base Suffield (Brumley 1985:180). The site is an interment of an individual during the Old Women's phase. In 1974, seven 2-×-2-m units (28 m^2) were excavated at the site. This was followed by mapping in 1980. The site consists of a boulder structure with a central stone circle from the edge of which eleven lines or spokes radiate, towards thirteen stone circles and two cairns (Brumley 1985:180). The apparent use of some of the stones from the surrounding stone circles in the spokes suggests that the former were created earlier than the latter (Brumley 1985:198, 192). Similarly, a gap in a spoke near a cairn suggests rock-robbing for the cairn construction at the later date.

Excavations within the central part of the medicine wheel recovered fragments of human skeletal material (n = 66), some small bone fragments of a large animal (likely bison), a Cayley Series projectile point, a marginally retouched stone tool, a piece of FBR, pieces of debitage (n=54), and decomposing wooden pegs (n=2). The better-preserved peg was determined to be white oak with a dye-like pigment on it containing barium sulphate. A radiocarbon date of ca. 450 BP was obtained from this item (Table 25).

Brumley (1985:204–205) provided a good argument for the contemporaneity of the medicine wheel, the human remains, the Cayley Series point, and the radiocarbon date. Brumley (1985) placed this research in context by noting that historic Blackfoot often interred prominent people in death lodges. Stone lines were often added to a death lodge as a sign of respect. While medicine wheels come in many forms, the Ellis format is found in a handful of medicine wheels, many of which are known in the historic Blackfoot's traditional territory (Brumley 1985:225; Peck 2007).

DgPl 68. DgPl 68 is a campsite/kill site near the valley entrance on the north side of Pass Creek in Waterton Lakes National Park (Reeves 1972:42). Three components were differentiated, with the lowest apparently containing one Scottsbluff and one Maple Leaf point (Reeves 1972, plate 18, nos. 9 and 24), the second component yielding Avonlea material, and the uppermost containing Old Women's material (Reeves 1972:77–78). In 1969, a total of seven 2-×-2-m units (28 m^2) was excavated. The upper component of the site was substantially disturbed but considered discrete enough to separate from the lower two components.

Two Plains side-notched, a preform, and two broken points were recovered (Reeves 1972:332). The high basal edges on the points suggested a late Old Women's affiliation for this material. Other tools recovered included a biface fragment, end scrapers (n=2), perforators (n=8), utilized flakes (n=10), a cobble chopper, and spall choppers (n=3) (Reeves 1972:332). Only small amounts of debitage (n=13) were recovered. Bone tools recovered included a leg bone side scraper, a side scraper, a splinter awl, and flakers (n=2). The faunal assemblage represented mainly bison (MNI=2). Bone was largely burned on its upper surface, indicating that the charring resulted from a forest fire (Reeves 1972:77). FBR was also present across the floor. A single radiocarbon date of ca. 330 BP was obtained for the component (Table 25).

Kenney (DjPk 1), Layer 4. The Kenney site is a multicomponent campsite on a low terrace of Pincher Creek, just west of Brocket, in southwest Alberta (Reeves 1983b:3). It appears to have been named after the geological terrace in which it is located (the second major terrace of the Oldman

River, the Kenney Terrace) (Reeves 1983b:10). Three major occupations were identified. The lower two occupations contained Besant material, while the upper occupation is represented by Old Women's material. In the summers of 1963 and 1964, a total of 187 m² was excavated (Reeves 1983b:23).

Seventeen late Cayley Series points, four preforms and four unclassifiable points were recovered from Layer 4. Other tools included gravers (n = 2), awls (n = 2), end scrapers (n = 12), side scrapers (n = 15), choppers (n = 7), polishing stones (n = 5), and a pipe fragment. The lithic assemblage emphasized miscellaneous chert and chalcedonies in the tools, and black chert, quartzite, and miscellaneous cherts and chalcedonies in its lithic debitage (Reeves 1983b:50). Bone tools included punches (n = 3), a notched bone, and a cut bone (Reeves 1983b:119–121). Eight rim sherds and 292 body sherds were recovered from Layer 4. Most of these (all but eight body sherds) were attributed to a single vessel. Reeves (1983b:123) considered the sherds to be Manitoba Corded Ware, although Byrne (1973:365) placed the sherds amongst local artisans of the Saskatchewan Basin Complex: Late Variant pottery.

The faunal assemblage included bison (MNI = 6), canids, mule deer, and beaver (Reeves 1983b:38). Mature, immature, and fetal bison were found in every level of the site, suggesting late winter/early spring occupations (Reeves 1983b:39). Heavy non-meaty bones are not common in the faunal assemblage while the elements are from meaty parts of the animal, suggesting that butchering units were being brought into the camp at some distance and low-utility bones were left behind. Elements that did make it to camp were highly processed, based on the degree of fragmentation for marrow and grease extraction (Reeves 1983b:49). Large FBR concentrations, five surface hearths, and two basin hearths attest to this interpretation of the fauna. A single radiocarbon date of roughly 350 BP was obtained for this occupation (Table 25).

Bodo Bison Skulls (FaOm 1). The Bodo Bison Skulls and FaOm 22 (immediately to the west) are two very large sites comprising numerous localities (Mann 2007). The sites are located just south of Eyehill Creek in Sounding Basin, within an area of stabilized sand dunes (Gibson 2001:2). The sites are bison kill, butchering, and processing areas (Mann 2007). The reason for the massive nature of the bison kill sites in this area is due to the topography and the environment. Bodo represents an oasis of tree cover that creates a "peninsula" in the Plains. In fall, as the bison were moving into their wintering grounds, the Bodo area was used as an intercept locale to pound the animals in large numbers. The trees provided wood for pounds and fuel to keep the people warm. The rolling hills provide the blinds for luring the animals to the pounds (Peck 2004).

Many Cayley Series points have been recovered in association with Saskatchewan Basin Complex: Late Variant pottery at Bodo. Material from Locality Pad 10-32 produced such an assemblage (Blaikie 2005). At Locality PL 1, however, Cayley Series points, apparently in association with Mortlach Group points, were recovered with unusual pottery possibly classifiable as Mortlach (Mann 2007). Mann (2007, 2009) suggested that the Bodo sites are located in a common area between three Late Prehistoric archaeological cultures. The Old Women's phase appears to be most strongly represented at Bodo and distributed to the southwest. The Mortlach phase appears to be represented by points and perhaps pottery at the Bodo sites. Mortlach material is known to be distributed to the southeast into Saskatchewan. A possible third archaeological culture in the Bodo area is the Selkirk Composite, adding complexity to sites' assemblages from the north (Mann 2007, 2009).

EfOw 26, Component 3. EfOw 26 is described in the sections on the Besant phase. The Old Women's component consisted of three late Cayley Series points recovered in association with three hearths and two micro-debitage clusters (Goldsmith 2005:76–78, 175). Other tools recovered included a biface, wedges (n = 2), bifacially and unifacially retouched tools (n = 4), marginally modified flakes (n = 8), utilized flakes (n = 3), bipolar cores (n = 2), and multidirectional cores (n = 4). The assemblage emphasized miscellaneous cherts, chalcedony, petrified wood, and quartzite (Goldsmith 2005:81). Small amounts of obsidian were recovered and sourced to Obsidian Cliff, Wyoming (Goldsmith 2005:172).

A number of pottery sherds (n = 323) were found associated with this component. Most of the sherds came from Component 3 but other components did contain some pottery. Most of the pottery conformed to Old Women's phase Ethridge Ware. One sherd exhibited wrapped-object-impressed chevron pattern, indicating a late Old Women's design (Goldsmith 2005:155).

The faunal assemblage (n = 2,130) included mainly bison (MNI = 3), with a deer bone and a small amount of shell (Goldsmith 2005:133). Evidence of impacts, cutting, and burning was observed (Goldsmith 2005). Many limb bone fragments were identified, indicating that meat sections were brought to the camp for consumption, with the bones being reduced for marrow extraction and grease production (Goldsmith 2005:136). Three hearth features were encountered at the site: two basin hearths and a surface hearth (Goldsmith 2005:193). Many small pieces of FBR showed signs of water fracturing. Shell was recovered in the form of three shell beads in Hearth Feature 4. Associated with this feature were two micro-debitage clusters, possibly suggesting a single workshop event (Goldsmith 2005:195). A single radiocarbon date of ca. 260 BP was obtained for this component (Table 25).

EgPn 230, Component 1. EgPn 230 is discussed in the section on the Country Hills phase. Component 1, the Old Women's component, consists of twenty projectile points or point fragments. Those complete enough to classify were considered Late Side-notched points (Vivian et al. 1998:27–33). All the specimens fit within the Cayley Series (Peck 1996; Peck and Ives 2001). Other tools included bifaces (n = 15), scrapers (n = 15), drills (n = 2), a wedge, choppers (n = 2), a maul, and retouched flakes (n = 17) (Vivian et al. 1998:27–47). Three bones exhibiting polish were also recovered (Vivian et al. 1998:47–48). A fragment of fossilized cretaceous clam shell was recovered and inferred to be ornamental (Vivian et al. 1998:48). The lithic raw materials emphasized locally available lithics including quartzite, siltstone, petrified wood, and miscellaneous cherts. Exotics such as obsidian, porcellanite, Knife River flint, and Top-of-the-World chert were also represented (Vivian et al. 1998:49). The range of debitage suggested that all stages of knapping (from decortication to sharpening) were being conducted, although emphasis was on the production of finished tools (Vivian et al. 1998:49).

The faunal assemblage (n = 12,283) was largely bison (MNI = 12) with a wolf-sized canid, a coyote-sized canid, and a deer-sized ungulate (Vivian et al. 1998:49). Bison fetal bone was recovered; based on the development of the bone, the researcher suggested a mid-February kill (Vivian et al. 1998:50). Three features were present at the site: a large hearth and associated bone feature, a small hearth, and a large pile of bone and FBR. The large hearth was about 80 cm in diameter with large concentrations of mainly unburned bone piled on a bed of FBR in a basin scooped out 10–15 cm into the ground. The small hearth consisted of a soil stain only 5 cm thick and a cluster of FBR and calcine bone. The large pile of bone (n = 1,400+) and FBR exhibited little evidence of burning and was interpreted as a refuse pile (Vivian et al. 1998:51). A single radiocarbon date of 440 BP was obtained for the site (Table 25).

EhPn 56. EhPn 56 is a small campsite, southwest of Calgary, in a steep bowl-shaped depression on the west side of a large coulee. In 2002, a total of 40 m² was excavated at the site to mitigate a subdivision development (Murphy 2003). Thirty-two of the units were in a contiguous block, with eight satellite units. Two components were recognized: a Lower Component lacking diagnostics and an Upper Component producing Old Women's material.

Three points or point fragments were recovered. The complete point is considered a Cayley Series side-notched point while the other two points consist of only the blades (Murphy 2003:61). Other tools recovered included a scraper, modified flakes (n = 3), unifacially retouched stone tools (n = 4), and cores (n = 3). Petrified wood (43.1%), quartzite (25.5%) and miscellaneous cherts (17.6%) were the most common raw materials in the assemblage; obsidian was sourced to Obsidian Cliff, Wyoming (Murphy 2003:86).

The faunal assemblage (n = 1,066) appeared to be almost entirely bison (MNI = 3). Heavier elements were not present at the site, suggesting that the main kill and processing activities may have occurred elsewhere (Murphy 2003:57–58). FBR (n = 365) was mainly small fragments (i.e., < 10 cm) of water-fractured rock. A stone-ringed, oval-shaped hearth surrounded by FBR, lithics, and bone was identified (Murphy 2003:66). A second feature consisted of a bone concentration and an alignment of stones and FBR. The points were close to this feature but the only interpretation presented was a possible disturbed hearth (Murphy 2003:68). A single radiocarbon date of roughly 310 BP was available for the component (Table 25).

DgPl 55. DgPl 55 is a campsite on a 3-metre-high terrace at the valley entrance on the north side of Pass Creek (Reeves 1972:40). In 1967, the site was excavated, focusing on two areas. A total of 52 m² was excavated in Area A along the edge of the creek while 30 m² was excavated in Area B, about 33 m to the north away from the creek (Reeves 1972:74). Historic artifacts were found intermixed with prehistoric materials although researchers felt confident they could be separated. The earliest occupation was an Old Women's campsite while the more recent historic occupation postdated to A.D. 1900.

Nine Plains side-notched points, one Prairie side-notched point, eight side-notched fragments, and five preforms were recovered (Reeves 1972:332). Other tools included asymmetrical triangular bifaces (n = 5), end scrapers (n = 2), side scrapers (n = 2), perforators (n = 10), retouched flakes (n = 5), utilized flakes (n = 10), cobble choppers (n = 3), and a core. Bone tools included a leg bone side scraper, a rib side scraper, bone knives (n = 6), cut bone (n = 2), a leg bone splinter awl, rib spatulas (n = 2), and flakers (n = 3). A shell pendant blank was also recovered (Reeves 1972:332). Sherds from what appeared to be a single Saskatchewan Basin complex: Late Variant pottery vessel were also recovered (Reeves 2003:108). The vessel was globular in form with a surface finish that was truncated cord-marked (Byrne 1973:129). The rim exhibited the same surface finish and sloped inward at a considerable angle, except for the last 1 cm, which rises vertically and is unthickened (Byrne 1973:134).

The occupation floor was littered with butchered bone and some small FBR. At least one bison and one deer were represented in the faunal material. Three small (40-cm diameter) surface hearths were recorded. An obsidian working area produced thirty-five obsidian flakes (Reeves 2003:108). A single radiocarbon date was available for the prehistoric component; it was modern. The recent date fits well with the late Cayley Series points and the pottery. Importantly, all of the historic material recovered at the site would postdate items expected in a Protohistoric period site. If the Old Women's material was Protohistoric in nature it would have been more appropriate to recover glass beads, metal points, tinkle cones, and such. The site appears to be an example of a very late Late Prehistoric period Old Women's campsite.

DgPl 1. DgPl 1 is a kill site/campsite on a terrace on the valley floor on the north side of the entrance to Pass Creek valley. The site consists of two areas: a kill site/campsite, and a kill site to the west on the hillside (Reeves 1972:41). During 1968–1969, a total of 104 m^2 was excavated at the kill site/campsite (Reeves 1972:53–54, 373). Five cultural levels were recognized. The lowest level, 1A, produced two Lusk points, with possible Early Middle Prehistoric period material found in Level 1B, McKean material in Level 1C, Hanna and Pelican Lake material in Level 2A, and Old Women's material in Level 2B.

Three Plains side-notched points, two flake points, and a preform were recovered from Level 2B (Reeves 1972:332).). Other tools recovered included asymmetrical triangular bifaces (n = 7), biface fragments (n = 2), end scrapers (n = 5), a split pebble scraper, cores (n = 3), pièce esquillées (n = 2), a retouched flake, utilized flakes (n = 31), choppers (n = 4), and flake choppers (n = 3). Bone tools included a bone knife, a piece of cut bone, a rib biface handle, a rib splint awl, a neural spine awl, rib spatulates (n = 3), and bone flakers (n = 3).

The living floor had a small, circular surface hearth (30 × 30 cm) with 1.5 cm of ash and burned bone associated with an arc of sandstone slabs and FBR. A second feature was a rock-filled surface hearth (90 × 70 cm and 5–10 cm thick). In addition, the floor exhibited a scatter of small FBR, bone fragments, and artifacts that tended to cluster around the hearths. An obsidian flake concentration, suggesting a chipping station, was observed near the hearths. The faunal assemblage consisted mainly of bison (MNI = 4) (Reeves 1972:338). A single radiocarbon date of ca. 220 BP was obtained for this level (Table 25).

Pigeon Mountain (EgPt 28), Upper Component. The Pigeon Mountain site is described with regards to the Sonota phase. The overlying Old Women's material was represented by eight points or point fragments: three were classified as Plains side-notched, one as Prairie side-notched, and one as similar to Avonlea side-notched or Head-Smashed-In corner-notched, with the remaining specimens too fragmentary to classify. All the points are well within the range of variability exhibited in the Cayley Series. Other tools recovered included bifaces (n = 7), a large biface or chithos, end scrapers (n = 5), a side scraper, marginally retouched flakes (n = 8), and a uniface (Clarke et al. 1998:89). The debitage was largely secondary flakes, retouch flakes, and shatter, indicating that tool production and maintenance took place (Clarke et al. 1998:99). Most of the lithic raw materials used at the site were local shales, miscellaneous cherts, and Swan River chert, along with small amounts of quartzite, basalt, porcellanite, siltstone, chalcedony, petrified wood, Top-of-the-World chert, and obsidian. Analysis of four obsidian samples indicated that they came from Bear Gulch, Idaho, and Obsidian Cliffs, Wyoming (Clarke et al. 1998:119–120). A single culturally modified elk antler tine exhibited use wear on its tip (Clarke et al. 1998:125)

The faunal assemblage (n = 6,621) was mainly bison. A minimum number of four bison were estimated from the sample, although elk, moose, deer, large canid, medium canid, fox, bear, beaver, muskrat, and hare/rabbit were also recovered (Clarke et al. 1998:129–134). Fetal bone was recovered, suggesting an early spring occupation (Clarke et al. 1998:155–160). Bones that bear substantial amounts of meat occur frequently at the site while lower-utility bones are rarer, suggesting that the former were transported to the site. The range of species recovered and the highly fragmented marrow bones also indicate a campsite where people returned with meat to process (Clarke et al. 1998:263). Bone tends to be associated with FBR features. FBR occurred in four small concentrations and one large concentration, and while associated with bone, it was not associated with pit features or substantial amounts of charcoal or ash. A small surface hearth about 30 cm in diameter and 3 cm thick was evidenced by some ash, charcoal, and an orange stain in the soil (Clarke et al. 1998:70–74).

Two radiocarbon dates were obtained from this component of the site: ca. 140 BP (Table 25) and a modern date (Beta-90061). The researchers noted that earlier flood deposits may have contaminated the bone proteins with bacteria, which might result in a later-than-actual date (Clark et al. 1998:264). While the recent dates corroborate the age estimate based on the point classification, it is noteworthy that no Euro-Canadian items were recovered within the same deposits.

Other sites. There are so many other Old Women's sites that have radiocarbon dates from good contexts that could be reviewed, they cannot all be addressed in this text. A few more Old Women's sites with unusual contents are briefly outlined below.

Two other subsurface interments that exhibit Old Women's material culture and date to the appropriate age are the Belly Burial (DhPj 69) and the Folkins Lake Burial (FeOm 1). The Belly Burial is located on the Belly River west of Cardston (Ball 1986a:207–210), and the Folkins Lake Burial is located on the northwest shore of Folkins Lake east of Chauvin (Ball and Beattie 1987).

The Blakiston site (DjPm 115) is a multicomponent stone circle site and buried campsite located on a terrace of the Crowsnest River valley (Dau 1993, 2005). Nine stone circles were identified and twelve block excavations, A–L, were undertaken. All the diagnostic lithic projectile points were considered assignable to the Old Women's phase (Dau 1993:117). Historic artifacts were recovered in association with some of the Old Women's occupations. The recovery of fetal bone supported the interpretation of the site as a winter campsite (Dau 1993).

EbPk 15 is a bison processing area near the north end of the Pine Coulee Reservoir (Hjermstad 1998). In the campsite/processing area three large block excavations contained a number of Old Women's occupations. In the second most recent occupation in the center block, a maul was recovered in situ with Cayley Series (i.e., Prairie and Plains side-notched) points

(Hjermstad 1998:252). A radiocarbon date of 640 +/- 90 BP (S-3987) was obtained for the level (Hjermstad 1998:247). Nearby, EaPk 201 represented a comparable Old Women's site that consists of a butchering/processing area towards the southwest end of the Pine Coulee Reservoir (Hjermstad 1998).

EgPn 656 and EgPn 661 are two sites that do not fall within the variability of the Old Women's phase despite dating to ca. 950 BP and being recovered from the valley's edge along the Elbow River. Some of the point specimens are somewhat reminiscent of Besant points but most are more stemmed with sharp shoulders (Vivian 2006b). It was suggested the material might represent the arrival of the Stoney in the area (Vivian 2006b).

Old Women's: Archaeological Evidence for the Prehistoric Blackfoot (Nitsitapii)

The Old Women's phase in Alberta first occurs on the Plains and in the parkland starting at approximately 1,100 BP. The Old Women's phase has two main diagnostics: the Cayley Series projectile points (Peck 1996; Peck and Ives 2001) and the Saskatchewan Basin Complex: Late Variant pottery (Byrne 1973). The Cayley Series points are morphologically varied side-notched points that exhibit time-transgressive changes. Similarly, the Saskatchewan Basin Complex: Late Variant pottery appears to have developed from Avonlea pottery (Byrne 1973; Quigg 1988b). Thick-walled, globular, coconut, and shouldered vessel forms dominate. Surface treatments include vertical cord impression, fabric impression, and smoothed, while decorative techniques made by a variety of tools are usually located on the lip, neck, or shoulder.

Lithic utilization focuses on local materials and is dominated by relatively large amounts of Montana cherts. Knife River flint and obsidian are much less common but are not absent. The main source of food for the Old Women's people was bison. Jumps (e.g., Head-Smashed-In), natural traps (e.g., Lower Kill), and pounds (e.g., Ramillies) were all used by the people of the Old Women's phase.

Other signatures of the Old Women's phase include the use of ammonites as Iniskim (buffalo charms) (Peck 2002; Reeves 1993). Based on ethnographic sources, the Iniskim is a Blackfoot item used in bundle ceremonies, in tobacco ceremonies, in sacred tipis, for personal power, for healing, and for calling buffalo to a jump. The recovery of ammonites not only provides some evidence for peoples' ceremonial practices in the past, but also suggests ethnic affiliation between the Old Women's phase and the Blackfoot

(Peck 2002). Similarly, some medicine wheels exhibiting tipi rings with spokes (e.g., Ellis) or cairns with spokes that have been examined contain human bone and Old Women's material. Ethnographically, the Blackfoot are known to have buried important people in such structures (Brumley 1985). Through a series of papers, Peck (1996, 2002, 2007; Peck and Hudecek-Cuffe 2003) has drawn connections between the Old Women's phase and the historic Blackfoot, suggesting that the foundation has been laid for an "archaeology of the prehistoric Blackfoot (Nitsitapii)." Peck (2007) framed this foundation on four main lines of evidence: (1) the coincidental distribution of the Old Women's phase (Cayley Series points and Saskatchewan Basin pottery) with historically known Blackfoot (Magne et al. 1987; Peck 1996; Peck and Ives 2001); (2) the direct link between archaeologically recovered ammonites at Old Women's sites and Blackfoot Iniskim (Peck 2002); (3) the recovery of Old Women's artifacts associated with human remains at medicine wheels of form similar to those documented as burials of the historic Blackfoot (Brumley 1988; Peck and Hudecek-Cuffe 2003); and (4) the distribution and identification of human boulder effigies on the plains and their likely ties to the Blackfoot trickster, Napi (Vickers 2008).

As the distribution of the aforementioned artifacts and features indicates, the Old Women's phase is not restricted to southern Alberta; there are numerous other Old Women's sites in southern Saskatchewan and northern Montana. In Saskatchewan most of the sites represent only the early part of the Old Women's phase (ca. 1,100–650 BP); however, a few sites along the western side of Saskatchewan occur during the late part of the Old Women's phase (ca. 650–250 BP).

The Lucky Strike site (FdNm 16) is a habitation locale just east of the South Saskatchewan River, near Rosthern (Wilson 1984). Two excavation blocks produced Prairie side-notched points (early Cayley Series) and Saskatchewan River Basin: Late Variant pottery (Wilson 1984:11–12, 21–23). The south block was dated to 1,020 +/- 90 BP (S-2281) while the north block was dated to 875 +/- 95 BP (S-8820) (Wilson 1984:24; Morlan n.d.). The two blocks appear to be functionally and temporally independent of each other, indicating successive occupations that represent different activities.

The Tschetter site (FbNr 1) is a bison pound and processing site in the Dunfermline Sand Hills, west of Saskatoon (Prentice 1983; Linnamae 1988). Prairie side-notched points (early Cayley Series) and Saskatchewan Basin Complex: Late Variant pottery were recovered in this single-component site. Radiocarbon dates supported the interpretation: 1,005 +/- 75 BP (S-669);

1,020 +/- 100 BP (S-1265); 915 +/- 45 BP (S-1631); and a modern date (NZA 15751) (Prentice 1983:34; Linnamae 1988:115).

The Garratt site (EcNj 7) is a multicomponent campsite along Moose Jaw Creek (Morgan 1979:74). The Old Women's material was recovered from Levels 1–2, although a single Prairie side-notched point was recovered in Level 4 (Morgan 1979:317). Pottery (n=254) conforming to the Saskatchewan Basin Complex: Late Variant was also recovered (Morgan 1979:294–317). Similarly, two Plains side-notched and nineteen Prairie side-notched points (early Cayley Series) were also recovered from Levels 1–2 (Morgan 1979:263). The lithic suite emphasized the use of Knife River flint, Sard chalcedony, and miscellaneous cherts (Morgan 1979:281). A date for the level was not obtained.

The Estuary site (EfOk 16) is a bison kill site at the head of a large coulee near Leader, southwestern Saskatchewan. Above an Avonlea–Old Women's transitional component was a component of Old Women's material. It consisted of Cayley Series (Prairie side-notched) points and was dated to 1,070 +/- 70 BP (S-640) (Adams 1977:142; Morlan n.d.).

The Gull Lake site (EaOd 1) is a bison kill site in southwestern Saskatchewan (Kehoe 1973). A long sequence of Prairie and Plains side-notched points (i.e., Cayley Series) was recovered, overlying a sequence of Avonlea material. Old Women's material was recovered from Layers 24 through 2. Layer 24 produced a radiocarbon date of 1,220 +/- 80 BP (S-149) and Layer 21 produced a radiocarbon date of 1,165+/- 80 BP (S-150) (Kehoe 1973:43; Morlan n.d.). The morphology of the most recent points suggested that the occupation persisted well into the late Old Women's phase.

In Montana, the vast majority of the Old Women's sites tend to fall within the late Old Women's phase (ca. 650–250 BP). The Boarding School Bison Drive site (24GL302) is located on the valley margin of Cut Bank Creek, north of Browning in northwestern Montana (Kehoe 1967). Many Plains and Prairie side-notched points were recovered, almost all above a layer dating to ca. 360 +/-75 BP (M-1066) (Kehoe 1967:42; Morlan n.d.). Of the 180 Plains side-notched specimens, thirty-eight were Paskapoo, sixty-four were Pekisko, ten were Buffalo Gap single-spur, three were Cut Bank jaw-notched, and sixty-five were Washita. At Gull Lake the numbers were very different for Plains side-notched points (n=102): Paskapoo (n=57), Pekisko (n=34), and Washita (n=11). Furthermore, there were no Cut Bank jaw-notched or Buffalo Gap single-spur varieties. Chalcedony (32%), obsidian (19%), and miscellaneous cherts (16%) comprised the main lithic materials in point manufacture at the Boarding School site. The numbers were similar for the Prairie side-notched points: 27 percent, 27 percent, and 13 percent, respectively (Kehoe 1967:43, 45). This unusual lithic utilization pattern might merely reflect the Old Women's phase's proximity to important lithic resources. The late date and the increased use of southern lithic raw materials, combined with the unusually high frequency of Washita, Buffalo Gap single-spur, and Cut Bank jaw-notched point varieties, however, possibly suggests a Highwood phase influence at the bison kill (see following section).

Bootlegger Trail (24TL1237) is a multicomponent spring bison kill on the Marias River in northwestern Montana (Roll and Deaver 1980). The researchers interpreted the site as containing two components while the radiocarbon dates suggest three components are present. In Area B, the stratigraphy clearly had a lower and upper component. In the lower component, cultural Level II, four radiocarbon dates were obtained: 760 +/- 80 BP (I-9204), 680 +/- 80 BP (I-9205), 580 +/- 115 BP (GX-4711), and 565 +/- 115 BP (GX-4713). These dates suggest a single occupation. The associated points exhibit high, flaring bases with angular corners (Roll and Deaver 1980:112, fig. 23b). Some pottery that exhibits unusual S-shaped rims and possible check-stamping was also recovered. This pottery is quite unlike the Saskatchewan Basin complex (Roll and Deaver 1980:138, fig. 45c).

In the upper component, four radiocarbon dates suggested that two components, rather than one, are present. The earlier two dates are 645+/- 80 BP (I-9202) and 640 +/- 135 BP (GX-4710), suggesting an age very close in time to cultural Level I. The other two dates are 260 +/- 75 BP (I-9203) and 185 +/- 120 BP (GX-4712), suggesting an age near the beginning of Protohistoric period. The point assemblage is mixed, showing straight basal edges, high bases, sharp-angled points, and more open-notched points with irregular basal edges that are more readily attributable to the Cayley Series. Most of the pottery in the site came from this level, and was concentrated in the southeast corner of the excavation. The vessels appear to have slightly constricted necks, as the profile is a very gentle S-curve, and the surface treatment is grooved paddle impressed or smooth. The researchers classified it as Saskatchewan Basin pottery (Roll and Deaver 1980:141, fig. 45a, b). The obsidian hydration measurements indicate that obsidian from Levels I and II is the same age, suggesting a single component.

This site might represent an initial occupation by Highwood peoples at ca. 650 BP (see next section). The flared-ear, sharp-based points, the unusual pottery, and the use of obsidian all support this inference. The uppermost occupation, in cultural Level I, is represented by the early dates of ca. 640 BP from this level. The recovered assemblage has some points with deep notches high on the lateral margins and amounts of obsidian dated to the same age as obsidian in cultural Level II. Steatite pipe fragments from cultural Levels I and II suggest a southern origin and support a Highwood phase cultural assignment (Roll and Deaver 1980:147), making the component a reoccupation by the Highwood phase. In addition, cultural Level I also produced dates relating to ca. 250 BP. These dates might be associated with the open-notched and irregular-based points (such as the Cayley Series) in possible association with the Saskatchewan Basin pottery. A piece of copper found in association with bone splinters supports a Protohistoric date for the component (Roll and Deaver 1980:148). Thus, part of cultural Level I may represent a late Old Women's campsite.

The Taft Hill site is a buffalo jump located west of Great Falls in northwestern Montana (Shumate 1967). A systematic excavation has not occurred at the site, however, numerous flared-base or basally notched points have been recovered. Many of the points exhibiting narrow notches high on the lateral margins were manufactured on obsidian while those with wide notches low on the lateral margins were rarely manufactured from obsidian (Shumate 1967:20–21). Steatite pipe fragments have been found at the kill, leading the researcher to speculate that the pipes were ceremonially fractured in some form of ritual (Shumate 1967:19, 22). As well, most of the pottery is attributable to Ethridge Ware (Saskatchewan Basin Complex: Late Variant pottery) with the exception of a small amount of flared-base, flat-bottomed potsherds from a single hearth (Shumate 1967:24–25). No historic material was found in the kill deposits or the campsite, while Washita points are found in the later kill deposits (Shumate 1967:30). As with the Bootlegger Trail site, this site might exhibit both an Old Women's component and a Highwood component. In this case, the Old Women's phase is replaced in the deposits by the Highwood phase presumably around 300–400 BP (see Shumate 1967:30)

The Risley Bison Kill site (24LC1003) is a kill and butchering site located on the Sun River near Augusta, west-central Montana (Keyser and Knight 1976). Four stratigraphic levels were observed. The projectile points recovered from the site resemble Cayley Series (see Keyser and Knight 1976, fig. 8a–g). Five of these came from the second lowest level. The site likely dates to the last few hundred years before the Protohistoric period.

In summary, despite a few early dates at EgPn 440 and possibly the initial Old Women's level at the Gull Lake Bison Drive, the Old Women's phase appears to begin at ca. 1,100 BP. The early distribution of the phase occurs on the plains of central Saskatchewan and across Alberta, with little or no infiltration into Montana. The late distribution, ca. 650 to the Protohistoric period, shifts the Old Women's phase to the western edge of the Saskatchewan plains, across southern Alberta, and well into north-central Montana.

HIGHWOOD PHASE (CA. 500 TO 300 BP)

The Highwood phase is a poorly understood phenomenon that is focused in central Montana (Brumley and Dau 1988:48; Brumley and Rennie 2005). The most recent definition of the phase was mainly based on materials recovered from the Highwood bison kill (for which the phase is named), the Morrow-Bateman bison kill (24CH234), and the Square Butte campsite (24CH395). These sites are located in the southern part of Choteau County to the south of the Missouri River (Brumley and Dau 1988:57; Brumley and Rennie 2005; Shumate 1950).

The diagnostic artifacts of the phase include Plains side-notched projectile points, commonly made on obsidian, porcellanite, and Madison Formation chert (Brumley and Rennie 1995:44). These points exhibit superior craftsmanship, often displaying spurs and basal notching (Brumley and Rennie 1995:57, 2005). As well, Intermountain tradition pottery (Mulloy 1958:196) has been used to characterise the Highwood phase (Brumley and Rennie 1995:43). These vessels are distinct from vessels common to the Alberta plains. They tend to be vase-like in shape with flat circular bases, no handles, and a general lack of decoration (Mulloy 1958:197). In addition, based on their recovery at the Morrow-Bateman kill site, heavy unifacial quartzite cobble cores that exhibit crushed and dulled platform edges, indicating heavy use, are also considered diagnostic of the phase (Brumley and Rennie 2005).

Brumley and Dau (1988:58) initially included the upper levels of the Boarding School Bison drive site (24GL302), the Beaver Creek Park site (24HL411), and the Buffalo Gap bison kill site (Brumley and Dau 1988:58) as Highwood sites north of the Missouri River. More recently, Brumley and Rennie (2005) have not acknowledged any Highwood sites north of the Missouri River, restricting their definition to materials recovered south of the Missouri River.

Originally, Brumley and Dau (1988:58) dated the Highwood phase between ca. 650–400 BP. Subsequently, Brumley and Rennie (1995:44) revised the dating of the phase by suggesting it begins at ca. 650 BP and possibly persists into the Protohistoric period. This is based on excavations at the Morrow-Bateman kill site, which produced ten bone layers yielding Buffalo Gap single-spur and Emigrant basal-notched points dating to ca. 650 BP (Brumley and Rennie 2005). Brumley and Rennie (1995:43, n.d.) equated the Highwood phase with historic Shoshonean groups, based on suggested relationships between basal-notched projectile points and/or Intermountain pottery with a historically known ethnic group (Mulloy 1958; Frison 1991a).

The Sites

In order to assess the various lines of thinking presented above, possible Highwood assemblages from Alberta are outlined below. These sites are used to critically evaluate the current view of the Highwood phase in terms of its presence in the province (see Plate 27 and Figure 28).

PLATE 27 Highwood points. Illustrated are projectile points from Head-Smashed-In Buffalo Jump (DkPj 1) (a–e); DjPm 114 (f); and EhPm 34 (g). Photo credit: Royal Alberta Museum (a–e); Alberta Culture and Community Spirit (f and g).

FIGURE 28
Highwood sites
within Alberta

(Old) Women's Buffalo Jump (EcPl 1). The (Old) Women's Buffalo Jump is the sine qua non of Old Women's sites. The Upper Member (Layers 1–14) of the Upper Pit produced a sequence of points that provided the backbone of the Cayley Series projectile point classification system. Still, the large amount of micro-variation within lithic assemblages is difficult to encapsulate into appropriate cultural patterns. Peck (1996; Peck and Ives 2001) has repeatedly suggested that more decipherable variation may be hidden within the Cayley Series assemblages. Projectile points of the Highwood phase may, in fact, be hidden among Late Prehistoric projectile point assemblages of southern Alberta.

In the four uppermost layers of the jump deposits, which date to the last 450 years, 216 points were recovered. Of these, fifteen were classified as Washita points with flaring basal edges, high base heights, and narrow-deep notches. They were manufactured on a wide range of lithic raw materials (Forbis 1962:96, fig. 12a–c). They exhibit features found in Highwood phase points. It is possible that Highwood material is represented as a discrete, inter-mixed, or contemporaneous assemblage within the Old Women's assemblages at the (Old) Women's Buffalo Jump.

Head-Smashed-In Buffalo Jump (DkPj 1). The possibility of Highwood assemblages being imbedded in the Late Prehistoric levels of the (Old) Women's Buffalo Jump site suggests that other sites may exhibit similar traits. At Head-Smashed-In Buffalo Jump, Old Women's material was recovered in Levels 1–7B (Reeves 1978). In Levels 1 and 2, Peck (1996) noted aberrantly high mean values for base height, shoulder height, and weight for all points, compared to earlier levels at other sites of the same age. This aberration in metric values might be detecting Highwood points. Reeves (1978, fig. 17.25) illustrated some projectile points recovered from Head-Smashed-In Buffalo Jump, although he did not depict them by level, and a few exhibit features attributable to Highwood points. For example, Specimen 20 (Reeves 1978, fig. 17.25) appears to have a spur and high base height although the raw material type cannot be discerned.

Crowsnest Valley Campsite (DjPp 8). DjPp 8 also exhibits the trend towards well-formed points that are recovered in the uppermost levels of the Late Side-notched point sequence. Type 10 points display well-defined, deep notches placed relatively high on the lateral margins (Driver 1983:14, fig. 10, nos. 26–29). The nature of the excavation made it impossible to determine whether the material represented a discrete occupation, a mixed occupation or a concurrent occupation.

DjPm 114. DjPm 114 is a multicomponent site on an isolated 10-metre-high bench on the south side of the Crowsnest River, upstream from its confluence with the Oldman River. Two areas, east and west, were examined at the site (Landals 1993:20). In the West Area, two buried Old Women's components were observed overlying a Bracken component. A total of 12 m² was excavated in the West Area to mitigate the development of the Oldman River Dam project.

A single triangular side-notched point was recovered that exhibited a right basal edge projecting as a sharp spur (Landals 1993:20). The point was associated with a diffuse scatter of lithics, FBR, and butchered bone. The lithics (n = 40) exhibited a range of material types including obsidian (n = 1), porcellanite (n = 2), Avon chert (n = 3), and Etherington chert (n = 8). The fauna was mainly bison (MNI = 5) but also included elk, deer, fox, and a medium-sized canid (Landals 1993:20). Fetal bone was recovered. The fetal bone and the site's open location suggested a spring occupation. A single radiocarbon date of 430 +/- 80 BP (AECV-696C) correlated well with the late-style side-notched point (Landals 1993:20). The spurred point with the diverse lithic suite showing ties to the south and the widely varied faunal assemblage are a deviation from typical Old Women's sites. This material may reflect a Highwood occupation.

Mosquito Creek (EbPi 73). The Mosquito Creek site is located on the Little Bow River. In the second-lowest level, Landals (2007) recovered grinding stones, parts of ground stone bowls with flat bases, and very plain, thin-walled pottery sherds with highly burnished black surfaces. Landals (2007) indicated that plain pottery and ground stone bowls with flat bottoms are often associated with the ancestors of the Shoshone. Lithic raw materials showed a marked increase in the amount and relative recovery of porcellanite and obsidian. Similarly, point morphology was noted to shift subtly to include spurred points (Landals 2007).

Gilchrist (DgOu 29). The Gilchrist site is a cache of exotic lithic artifacts found east of Writing-on-Stone Provincial Park. The cache of large obsidian flakes (n = 17), pieces of obsidian shatter (n = 3), chert flakes (n = 10), chert bifaces (n = 2), and one piece of chert shatter was found scattered down slope from a badger burrow (Brumley 1982). The obsidian was inferred to originate from Yellowstone National Park about 480 km to the south, and the chert was inferred to be Avon chert from quarries 280 km to the southwest. Hydration dates on four obsidian specimens produced a mean age of ca. 500 BP with all four dates falling within both the Highwood phase and the Old Women's phase established time spans (Brumley 1982:140). It is unclear to which, if either, of the two cultural entities the material is related. The answer would likely have bearing on whether the exotic materials were traded in or procured by travelling to the source quarries.

Other sites. Brumley and Dau (1988:58) originally indicated that evidence of Highwood sites in Alberta was illusive and consisted mainly of isolated recovery of projectile points manufactured with craftsmanship superior to that of the coeval Cayley Series points and made on key raw material types such as Madison Formation cherts, porcellanite, or obsidian. More recently, they have limited the Highwood phase's distribution to central Montana. Despite the redefinition of the phase, new opportunities to test for the presence of Highwood material in Alberta have occurred. For example, Wyman (2006) recovered a "Washita" point at EdPn 53. Washita points typically have high, flaring bases and deep-narrow notches not unlike points from the Highwood phase. Sites such as EdPn 53 will provide testing grounds for determining the existence of the Highwood phase in Alberta. As well, Brian Vivian (personal communication 2008) noted that EgPn 624, on the Paskapoo Slopes in Calgary, contained an obsidian tri-notched point from mixed context. Obsidian source analysis traced it to Timber Butte, Idaho, a source rarely found in Alberta obsidian recoveries.

Highwood: Shoshonean (Snake) Invaders in Southern Alberta

Very little is known about the Highwood phase. The trend in diagnostic projectile points towards higher bases, deep-narrow notches, and spurs might simply be an extension of trends that exist within the Cayley Series points. Similarly, an increase in obsidian and porcellanite in the lithic raw materials might be reflecting changes in trade patterns within the Old Women's phase. Whether a northern expression of the Highwood phase is observed in Alberta or whether the notion can be rejected will likely depend on a rigorous review of numerous well-stratified sites with a focus on the nature of micro-stylistic variability within projectile point and ceramic assemblages.

As well, the uncertain nature of the Highwood phase in Alberta is due, in part, to the paucity of materials recovered from Montana. Of the three sites that define the Highwood phase, the Square Butte site (24CO395) is the only site with published data available for review and evaluation (Johnson and Armstrong 1990; Brumley and Rennie 2005). The Square Butte site is a multicomponent site located in the Highwood Mountains east of Great Falls in west-central Montana (Johnson and Armstrong 1990). Intermountain Ware was recovered, including smooth, flat-bottom specimens. As well, substantial amounts of obsidian were recovered. A single projectile point was sourced to Yellowstone National Park (Johnson and Armstrong 1990:6). While Brumley and Rennie (2005) affiliated this material with the Highwood phase and the Shoshone, Johnson and Armstrong (1990:5) acknowledged the general tendency to associate Intermountain pottery with the Crow.

A few other sites in Montana exhibit the types of projectile points and pottery that make them possible contenders for the Highwood phase. As mentioned in the section on the Old Women's phase, the Boarding School Bison Drive site (24GL302) has produced many Plains and Prairie side-notched points, mainly postdating ca. 360 BP (Kehoe 1967:42; Morlan n.d.). Many of the specimens have been classified as Washita, Buffalo Gap single-spur, and Cut Bank jaw-notched points, while during the same period of time at the Gull Lake site they are almost absent. Furthermore, chalcedony (32%), obsidian (19%), and miscellaneous cherts (16%) comprise the main lithic materials utilized in point manufacture at the Boarding School site. To reiterate, the unusual morphological change in points and the change in lithic utilization may simply be reflecting continued change in the Old Women's phase. On the other hand, the unusual spurred points and increase in the use of southern lithic raw materials may indicate a Highwood phase influence.

The Taft Buffalo Jump provides a similar record to the Boarding School Bison Drive (Shumate 1967). A possible interpretation of the deposits at the Taft Buffalo Jump have the Old Women's occupants as the original people who ultimately co-occupy or are replaced at the site by the people of the Highwood phase, presumably around 300–400 BP (see Shumate 1967:30).

The significance of a possible late presence of the Highwood phase in southern Alberta relates to an historical account transcribed by David

Thompson and a story in Blackfoot oral tradition, which both tell of a time in the recent past when the "Snake" peoples pushed the Blackfoot north across the Bow River. For some time the Blackfoot were restricted to this area. About the time that European trade goods reached the Blackfoot and the horse reached the Snake, the Blackfoot were able to regain the lands to the south.

Based on the recollections of Blackfoot elders, Dempsey (1994) recounted the story of Scabby Round Robe. About A.D. 1690, the Blackfoot were at peace with the Cree to the east, Kootenays to the west, and the Beaver to the north. In the south, however, war arose because of Shoshone people drifting north into the mountain valleys. The Bow River was the acknowledged border between the two groups, with the Blackfoot going south of the Bow only when accompanied by the Shoshone. Blackfoot territory was north of the Bow River to the North Saskatchewan and east to the Eagle Hills. An incident during a child's game at a camp of the Shoshone and Blackfoot led to deaths and, ultimately, war. Time passed as the feud continued. On one of the many war parties, a scout reported finding the Shoshone camp at Ridge Under Water, a major crossing of the Bow River. The two forces lined up across the river from one another, knowing that the spring waters made it possible to cross along the narrow ridge only in single file. The Shoshone leader issued a challenge to face any man in single combat. Scabby Round Robe had sought a vision and attained great power from the beavers in the form of a short stick. Thus, Scabby Round Robe engaged the Chief of the Snake (i.e., Shoshone), with only his powerful stick, and defeated him. This marked the beginning of the return of the Shoshone to the mountains.

David Thompson's (1916) account of Saukamappee took place a few decades later. Saukamappee was a Cree (Nahathaways). About A.D. 1720–1730, some Peigan came to the camp of Saukamappee's father, asking for help against Snake (Shoshone) attacks. The Cree were armed mainly with iron-tipped lances and arrow quivers that had one in ten arrows tipped with iron, the rest being tipped with stone. The Snake were encamped on the plains of the Eagle Hill. About 350 warriors crossed the river (presumably the Red Deer or South Saskatchewan). Upon finding their foe, singing and dancing ensued before all the warriors took cover behind full body shields. The battle was a draw with only a few people being injured. A few years later, Peigan scouts again came to the Cree for support against the Snake. By this time the Cree had more guns and more iron arrow heads.

The Snake, however, had acquired horses. The encounter with the Snake was one-sided. They had not brought their horses, for at that time these were still rare, and the Cree guns were accurate enough to inflict substantial damage. A charge of the Snake battle line ensued, and a decisive victory was won. Because the Snake had no European traders amongst them, the Peigan (Blackfoot) were able to continue to advance through the plains of the Red Deer River.

It is tempting to link the Highwood materials with the Shoshone and Old Women's material with the Blackfoot. As such, the historically known late seventeenth-century presence of the Shoshone in southern Alberta and the temporary displacement of Blackfoot peoples to the north might be documented in the archaeological record.

7 Late Prehistoric to Historic Period Transition

Protohistoric Period

CA. 250 TO 200 BP

The Little Ice Age occurred between ca. 500 and 100 BP. Compared to the modern regime this was a period of wetter and cooler conditions on the Plains. Still, the Alberta plains experienced short periods of drought (Vance 1991:153). High abundance and dependability of plant and animal resources likely prevailed until Historic-period over-hunting and exploitation decimated bison herds and other natural wealth.

PROTOHISTORIC OLD WOMEN'S PHASE (CA. 250 TO 200 BP)

The Old Women's phase continues in the Protohistoric period in much the same way it did during the Late Prehistoric period. Both Cayley Series projectile points and Saskatchewan Basin Complex: Late Variant pottery continued exhibiting gradual changes through time. A new ceramic type, Cluny pottery, is added to many Old Women's assemblages (see One Gun section). In terms of material culture, the most obvious change to the Old Women's phase in the Protohistoric period is the introduction of European goods (Byrne 1973:503). Archaeological proof of European materials in Old

Women's sites includes direct evidence such as metal points, files, axes, assorted metal fragments, glass beads, clay pipe bowls, and horse bone, and indirect evidence such as cut marks purported to have been made by metal objects.

Little has been written about the subsistence and settlement patterns of the Old Women's phase during the Protohistoric period because there is little data (Vickers 1986). The usual range of site types occur during the Protohistoric Old Women's phase. The Saamis site is a campsite/processing site near Medicine Hat (Milne Brumley 1978). The Castle Forks bison jump, located along the Oldman River, is a multicomponent bison kill site (Landals 1993). The Blakiston site is a multicomponent campsite at the confluence of the Oldman River and the Crowsnest River (Giering and Peck 1998:20). Regarding site distributions, Landals (2004) noted that river valleys exhibit evidence of greater use in Protohistoric times, possibly relating to the adoption of the horse and all that horse husbandry entailed (see Van Dyke et al. 1990:60).

A certain amount of continuity can be claimed in the belief systems between the Late Prehistoric period and the Protohistoric period Old Women's phases. Sites such as the Majorville Medicine Wheel (Calder 1977), British Block Cairn (Wormington and Forbis 1965), and Grassy Lake Cairn (Forbis 1960:132, 157) continued to be used. Items of European origin that have been recovered in these sites include glass beads, copper pendants, copper rings with beads, and brass rings. Still, it is very difficult to determine the sentiment behind the placement of items in these structures.

Ammonites continue to be found in Protohistoric Old Women's sites. Two such fossils were recovered from the Saamis site (Milne Brumley 1978). As with such artifacts found in a Prehistoric period context, it is inferred that the items are Iniskim and were used in a fashion similar to historical accounts (Peck 2002). Rock art images also suggest cultural continuity. For example, for Writing-on-Stone, Magne and Klassen (1991) suggested prehistoric imagery such as shield-bearing warriors continued to be produced into the Protohistoric period. Although the same style was used, new subject matter is portrayed in the images, including horses, guns, and other items relating to influence from Europeans. They argued that the function of these images exhibited continuity; that is, their purpose was to contact the spiritual world and memorialize events (Magne and Klassen 1991).

The fate of the Old Women's phase is not only of scientific interest, it touches Native people living today. Reeves (1983a:20) believed the Old Women's phase could be "regionally and temporally segregated into variants which represent the various 'tribal' constituents — North Peigans, Blood, Atsina, and Gros Ventre." The inference is that the Old Women's phase geographically coincides to the well-documented historical First Nation groups who occupied the region at the time of contact with Europeans. Byrne (1973) considered linguistics, oral tradition, and historic accounts and argued that the Old Women's phase was most likely produced by ancestors of the Blackfoot. Similarly, Magne and contributors to the Saskatchewan-Alberta Dialogue (1987:220–232) produced a composite map of Aboriginal distributions at A.D. 1700, illustrating that the Blackfoot were roughly co-distributed with the Old Women's phase. Peck's (1996; Peck and Ives 2001) redefinition of the Old Women's phase strengthened the discreteness of the phase and further illustrated its co-distribution with the estimated Blackfoot distribution at A.D. 1700 (Magne et al. 1987:220–232). Peck (2002) further argued that the repeated association of ammonites with the archaeological material of the Old Women's phase, coupled with the evidence for the antiquity and pervasive traditional use of these fossils as Iniskim among the Nitsitapii (Blackfoot) supported the Nitsitapii–Old Women's phase correlation. As noted above, Peck's (2007) argument culminated by further noting documented use of death lodge medicine wheels (Brumley's Types 3 and 4) by historic Blackfoot, the association of archaeological versions of these medicine wheels with Old Women's material (Brumley 1988), and the identification of human boulder effigies on the Plains as the Blackfoot trickster, Napi (Vickers 2008), within the geographic distribution of the Old Women's phase. Peck argued that his series of presentations laid the groundwork for an "archaeology of the prehistoric Blackfoot (Nitsitapii)" (Peck 2007).

The Sites

The following presents Protohistoric period sites that exhibit later radiocarbon dates and/or clear associations with early European trade items. These sites are used to critically evaluate the current view of the Protohistoric Old Women's phase. (see Plate 28 and Figure 29).

DjOu 22. DjOu 22 is a stone circle in a draw within Forty Mile Coulee (Dau and Brumley 1987:126). In 1986, 10 m² were excavated at the site (Dau and Brumley 1987:126). Most of the recovered material was bone (n = 164). In addition, a single Old Women's phase (Cayley Series) point and nine glass fragments were recovered (Brumley and Dau 1988:238).

The glass fragments exhibited flake scars indicative of working. Some of the fragments were recovered at the same depth and in the same trench as the Cayley Series point (Brumley and Dau 1987:127). The researchers inferred that the materials were contemporaneous.

PLATE 28 Protohistoric Old Women's points. Illustrated are projectile points and trade items from EgPn 430 (a–h); and the Castle Forks site (DjPm 126) (i–l). Photo credit: Alberta Culture and Community Spirit.

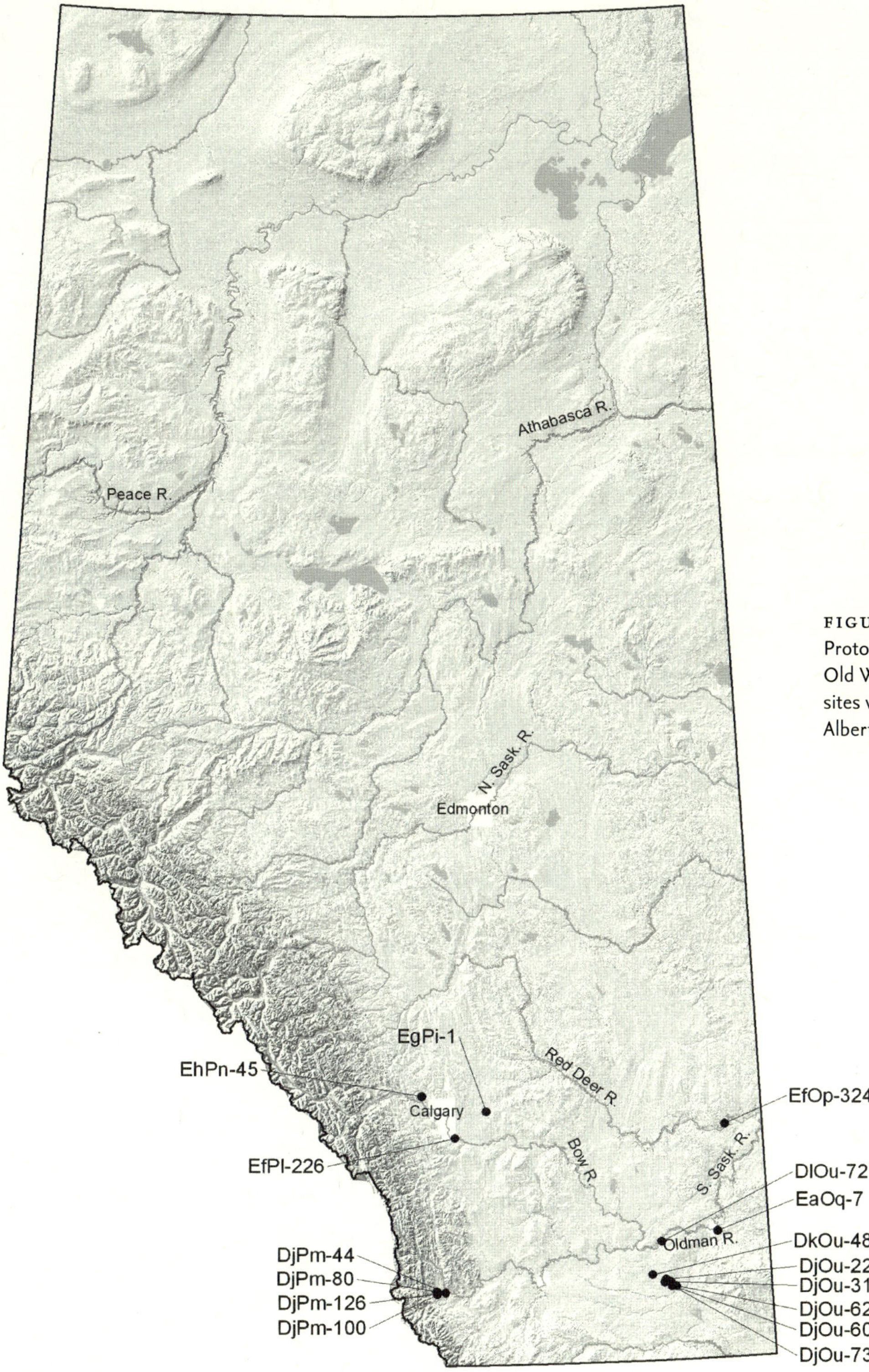

FIGURE 29 Protohistoric Old Women's sites within Alberta

DjOu 62. DjOu 62 is a site consisting of fourteen stone circles at the base of Forty Mile Coulee (Dau and Brumley 1987:342). In 1986, 88.96 m² of excavation and 9,360 m² of stripping were completed. Stone Circles 1–4, 7–8, 10–11, and 13–14 yielded mainly small bone and/or lithic assemblages. Stone Circle 5 contained a metal fragment (Dau and Brumley 1987:346). A pottery body sherd was recovered from Stone Circle 9 and was considered similar to the Saskatchewan Basin Complex: Late Variant pottery (Dau and Brumley 1987:349). Stone Circle 9 also yielded five Cayley Series side-notched points and six other pottery sherds possibly referable to the Saskatchewan Basin Complex: Late Variant pottery (Dau and Brumley 1987:353).

A number of dates were available from stone circles at the site. Stone Circle 7 produced a date of ca. 1,100 BP. Stone Circle 9 yielded a date of 250 BP. Stone Circle 11 produced a date of 230 BP. Lastly, Stone Circle 12 produced a date of ca. 470 BP (see Table 26). The evidence supports a late occupation at this site, and the association of metal with some of the stone circles entices one to think this site may be Protohistoric.

TABLE 26 Radiocarbon dates for Protohistoric Old Women's sites (calibrated by OxCal 3.10 [Ramsey 2005])

Site [LAB NO.]	Conventional ^{14}C Age	$^{13}C/^{12}C$ Ratio	Material	Calibration	Reference
DjPm 44 [AECV-1197C]	100 +/- 90	-19.1‰	collagen	A.D. 1660–1960 (p = 0.954)	Van Dyke 1994:208
DjOu 31 [BETA-19796]	470 +/- 150	-19.7‰	collagen	A.D. 1200–1850 (p = 0.942); A.D. 1900–2000 (p = 0.012)	Brumley and Dau 1988:241
DjOu 60, SC2 [BETA-19799]	430 +/- 90	?	collagen	A.D. 1300–1360 (p = 0.055) A.D. 1380–1660 (p = 0.899)	Brumley and Dau 1988:242
DjOu 60, SC9 [BETA-6710]	440 +/- 50	?	collagen	A.D. 1400–1530 (p = 0.791) A.D. 1550–1640 (p = 0.163)	Brumley and Dau 1988:242
DjOu 60, SC12 [BETA-6712]	320 +/- 60	?	collagen	A.D. 1440–1670 (p = 0.943) A.D. 1780–1800 (p = 0.011)	Brumley and Dau 1988:243
DjOu 60, SC12 [BETA-6711]	modern	?	collagen	n/a	Brumley and Dau 1988:243
DjOu 60, SC14 [BETA-19800]	modern	?	?	n/a	Brumley and Dau 1988:243

DjOu 62, SC7 [BETA-6715]	1,100 +/- 50	-20.0‰	collagen	A.D. 780–790 (p = 0.01) A.D. 800–1030 (p = 0.944);	Brumley and Dau 1988:243; Morlan n.d.
DjOu 62, SC9 [BETA-6716]	330 +/- 80	-20.0‰	collagen	A.D. 1400–1850 (p = 0.942) A.D. 1900–2000 (p = 0.013)	Brumley and Dau 1988:243; Morlan n.d.
DjOu 62, SC11 [BETA-19801]	230 +/- 90	-22.5‰	collagen	A.D. 1480–1960 (p = 0.954)	Brumley and Dau 1988:243; Morlan n.d.
DjOu 62, SC12 [BETA-19802]	470 +/- 70	-20.8‰	collagen	A.D. 1300–1370 (p = 0.115) A.D. 1380–1530 (p = 0.697) A.D. 1550–1640 (p = 0.942)	Brumley and Dau 1988:244; Morlan n.d.
DjPm 80, C2 [AECV-694C]	290 +/- 160	-20.5‰	collagen	A.D. 1400–2000 (p = 0.954)	Landals 1993; Morlan n.d.
DjPm 126, C1 [AECV-1238C]	260 +/- 90	-18.3‰	collagen	A.D. 1400–2000 (p = 0.954)	Landals 1993; Morlan n.d.
DjPm 126, C1 [AECV-699C]	670 +/- 100	-19.1‰	collagen	A.D. 1160–1440 (p = 0.954)	Landals 1993; Morlan n.d.
EaOq 7 [S-825]	165 +/- 75	-20.0‰	collagen	A.D. 1630–1960 (p = 0.954)	Milne Brumley 1978:33; Morlan n.d.
EaOq 7 [S-827]	210 +/- 80	-25.0‰	charcoal	A.D. 1490–1960 (p = 0.954)	Milne Brumley 1978:3); Morlan n.d.
EaOq 7 [S-824]	515 +/- 125	-20.0‰	collagen	A.D. 1250–A660 (p = 0.954)	Milne Brumley 1978:33; Morlan n.d.
EfOp 324 [I-9855]	450 +/- 80	?	charcoal	A.D. 1310–1360 (p = 065) A.D. 1380–1650 (p = 0.889)	Adams 1978
EfOp 324 [I-9856]	275 +/- 80	?	charcoal	A.D. 1400–2000 (p = 0.954)	Adams 1978
EfPl 226 [BETA-190211]	190 +/- 40	-19.6‰	collagen	A.D. 1640–1710 (p = 0.224) A.D. 1720–1820 (p = 0.483) A.D. 1830–1880 (p = 0.070) A.D. 1910–1960 (p = 0.177)	Turney 2004

NOTE: Radiocarbon dates for the past two hundred years are not reliable.

DjOu 73. DjOu 73 contained thirteen stone circles adjacent to the base of Forty Mile Coulee (Dau and Brumley 1987:443). In 1986, 55.55 m² were excavated at Stone Circles 3, 6, 8, 9, and 13 (Dau and Brumley 1987:444). Stone Circle 6 produced two small metal fragments and Stone Circle 13 produced four hundred sherds of pottery that could be classified as either Early or Late Variants of the Saskatchewan Basin pottery (Brumley and Dau 1988:244–245). The association of metal with the stone circle was the only reason for inferring any sort of Protohistoric period assignment to this site.

DkOu 48. DjOu 48 consisted of three well-buried stone circles and a cairn on the edge of Forty Mile Coulee (Dau and Brumley 1987:672). The site was not excavated although glass fragments were recovered from auger tests outside Stone Circle 3. As with DkOu 31 (see "Other Sites," below), the nature of the association between the glass fragments and the stone circle was unclear, making the interpretation of the site difficult.

DjPm 44, Component 4. DjPm 44 is discussed in the section on the Besant phase. The surface deposits that date to the Protohistoric period consisted of two spatially associated stone circles. The smaller of the two stone circles produced a single metal fragment interpreted as a decorative tinkler (Van Dyke 1994:206). This stone circle exhibited a central rock-ringed hearth about 70 × 50 cm in size. Numerous pieces of FBR (n = 45) and bone fragments (n = 285) were also recorded. The larger stone circle also had a rock-ringed central hearth about 100 × 100 cm (Van Dyke 1994:208). A small FBR concentration occurred along the northwest ring wall. Bone recovered from the concentration produced a date of 100 BP (Table 26). Historic items recovered from this stone circle included a metal file, a fragment of a saw blade, five pieces of metal scrap, two pony beads, and a possible metal point fragment. The file, saw blade, and a pony bead were recovered in good context associated with the hearth. Lithic tools recovered include Plains side-notched points (n = 2), core tools (n = 14), and retouched flakes (n = 9). A Besant point was recovered at the base of a unit and was thought to be associated with the underlying Besant occupation (Van Dyke 1994:208). Also recovered in this stone circle were numerous pieces of FBR (n = 194) and pieces of lithic debitage (n = 193). Bone (n = 741) was also recovered. The bison bone present suggested a least two animals (one adult and one fetal specimen) were recovered. A freshwater shell fragment, a canid tooth, and numerous small mammal bones were also recovered

(Van Dyke 1994:209). In view of the recovered historic material, the spatial association of the stone circles, the integrity of the deposits, the shallowness of burial, and a corroborating radiocarbon date, Van Dyke (1994) inferred that the two circles were of similar age and placed them in the Protohistoric period.

DjPm 100, Component 4. DjPm 100 is a terrace stone circle site located in Warriner's Coulee (Van Dyke 1994:232). The site is described in the section on the Old Women's phase. Of the four Late Prehistoric stone circles, the Protohistoric component consisted of two associated stone circles. Stone Circle B had a central rock-ringed hearth and a secondary hearth in the northwest part of the living floor (Van Dyke 1994:245). Stone Circle C also had a central hearth. Seven points were recovered, including four Plains side-notched, an unclassified corner-notched, and two Plains/Prairie side-notched (Cayley Series) points (Van Dyke 1994:246). Other tools included bifaces (n = 6), end scrapers (n = 6), core tools (n = 6), a hammerstone, an elongate pebble, and retouched flakes (n = 9). A bone awl was also recovered. Historic items recovered included a glass seed bead, bone buttons (n = 2), shell buttons (n = 4), a metal tinkler, a cartridge case, a metal projectile point, an axe head with four square nails in place, miscellaneous metal fragments (n = 4), and pottery specimens (n = 2). Additional historical material was recovered in the second component beneath Stone Circle C.

The fauna from the component was mainly bison (MNI = 4) although beaver, bird, large canid, small/medium canid, large ungulate, and small ungulate were also recovered (Van Dyke 1994:248). Presence of a fetal bison metapodial suggested a late-winter occupation. No dates were available for the component, although a date from the underlying component in Stone Circle B provided an age of ca. 310 +/- 120 BP (AECV 1194C). Van Dyke (1994:248) suggested that the early historic artifacts such as the glass bead, buttons, and metal points fit well with the recovery of late Plains side-notched (Cayley Series) material and support an Protohistoric Old Women's designation for the site.

Castle Forks Buffalo Jump (DjPm 126). The Castle Forks Buffalo Jump is described in the section on the prehistoric Old Women's phase. In the Protohistoric period component, nine projectile points were recovered, including eight late Plains side-notched (Cayley Series) specimens and one ferrous metal (iron) specimen (Landals 1993:238). The points were made on opaque brown chert (n = 6), glossy red chert (n = 2), and Swan River chert (n = 1). Other lithics included flakes (n = 3), cores (n = 3), and an elongate pebble/hammerstone (Landals 1993:240). Two shell beads were also recovered.

The faunal assemblage (n = 16,571) was mainly bison (MNI = 23), although deer and small and large canid were present. A late-term fetal bison humerus was also recovered. Cut marks from metal knives were observed on a number of ribs and vertebral fragments (Landals 1993:246). In addition, shear marks on several pelvis fragments and vertebral columns provided evidence that a metal axe was used to butcher parts of the carcasses (Landals 1993:246). Only three pieces of FBR were recovered. The assemblage was interpreted to represent a holistic approach to butchering. This type of butchering suggested that transportation was of little concern, normally implying that a camp was nearby. Landals (1993:249–251) suggested, however, that the Protohistoric period material might provide the option of horse transport of large amounts of bulk bison parts over distances. Thus, heavy butchering may have been conducted for high- and moderate-utility carcass parts to be transported by horse to relatively nearby camps.

Two dates were obtained for the bone bed, Component 1: ca. 260 BP and 670 BP (Table 26). The earlier date was rejected owing to its conflict with the diagnostic material and the dates from other levels (Landals 1993:237). The later date supports the Protohistoric age inferred for the site.

Saamis (EaOq 7). The Saamis site is located on a terrace of Seven Persons Creek, above its confluence with the South Saskatchewan River. The site was divided into five areas (A–E) based on geography and cultural activities (Milne Brumley 1978). The site is a multicomponent Protohistoric period Old Women's campsite from which 131 m² were excavated.

Two hundred fifty-nine points were recovered. All were classifiable as Cayley Series projectile points, with the exception of presumably intrusive McKean and Pelican Lake points. Both Saskatchewan Basin Complex: Late Variant pottery (97.8%) and Cluny pottery (2.2%) were recovered at the site (Milne Brumley 1978:109–126). The majority of the Cluny pottery was represented by check-stamped specimens. The site also yielded a metal trade point and five glass trade beads (Milne Brumley 1978:38). Two fossil ammonite septa were also recovered (Milne Brumley 1978:108). Three radiocarbon dates were obtained for the site: ca. 165 BP, 210 BP, and 515 BP (Table 26) (Milne Brumley 1978:33–37; Morlan n.d.). The lack of high consistency in the dates suggested reuse of the site, but the lack of superimposed features countered this idea. Alternatively, the normalized dates all overlap at about 250–300 BP, a time period that correlates well with the trade items in the assemblage. The actual number of occupations could not be determined.

EfOp 324. EfOp 324 is a stone circle site on a narrow bluff overlooking Alkali Creek (Adams 1978:32). Eight stone circles were positioned together on a flat bench. A total of 200 m^2 was excavated, exposing the floors of four stone circles and much of the intervening area. Trade items were found in three of the four stone circles, suggesting that this site represented a Protohistoric Old Women's campsite. The excavation was conducted as part of an archaeological study on the lower Red Deer River (Adams 1978:1).

Three projectile points were recovered. The points were assigned to the Old Women's (Cayley Series) (Adams 1978:45). One of the points exhibited the typical high base of very late side-notched points while the other two are less temporally diagnostic. Other tools recovered included bifaces (n = 4), end scrapers (n = 3), a bifacial retouched flake, unifaces (n = 28), and an elongate pebble. Historic artifacts recovered included large beads (n = 2), seed beads (n = 28), an 1866 Henry repeating rifle cartridge, a musket ball, a small piece of brass, a shotgun case, a brass tack head, a brass ring, a metal fragment, and several pieces of melted glass from a medicine bottle (Adams 1978:45).

Features, most notably hearths, were recovered inside and outside excavated Stone Circles 1 to 4. The hearth in Stone Circle 1 was 0.8 × 0.9 m and about 8 cm deep. The hearth (0.8 × 0.7 m) in Stone Circle 2 was associated with peg holes. Stone Circle 3 possessed a hearth (0.65 × 0.45 m) immediately adjacent to another hearth (0.3 × 0.3 m). The latter hearth contained seed beads. Similarly, the hearth in Stone Circle 4 contained seed beads. Two hearths were recorded outside the stone circles as well. The researcher identified evidence that suggested the site was occupied more than once. First, the occurrence of two hearths of different depths within a single stone circle is unusual. Second, the historic artifacts appeared to be associated with the shallow hearth stain while the lithic artifacts appeared to be associated with the deeper stain. Two radiocarbon dates were obtained from charcoal recovered from hearths at this site. However, the context of each sample was not disclosed. This is unfortunate, as the dates of ca. 450 BP and 275 BP (Table 26) appeared to support the researcher's interpretation of dual occupations.

Hartell Creek (EgPi 1). The Hartell Creek site is described in the section on the Sonota phase. In terms of Protohistoric period materials, Area B produced three Old Women's levels, with an upper layer (Level 5) yielding a metal point tip. A Pekisko point was recovered in Level 4. Levels 4 and 5 were organic bands about 20–32 cm BS. Artifacts from these levels were fairly scarce. Lithic artifacts from Level 5 included four utilized flakes and two retouched flakes, while Level 4 produced a utilized flake and a retouched flake (Murray et al. 1976:178). Bone was only recovered from Level 4; it included bison (MNI = 4), elk, canid, and Canada goose (Murray et al. 1976:172). Both levels were interpreted as small processing camps. Level 5 was estimated to have been occupied from about A.D. 1725 on, and Level 4 somewhat earlier (Murray et al. 1976:130).

DlOu 72. DlOu 72 is a multicomponent site on a prominent terrace on the east side of the South Saskatchewan River in the valley bottom, north of the town of Bow Island (Goldsmith 2003:57). Five components were identified in nine excavation blocks totalling 80 m^2 (Goldsmith 2003:59–63). The components show snapshots of Old Women's assemblages before and after trade items were introduced into southern Alberta (Goldsmith 2003:72–73).

Component 5, the oldest level, is a typical bison kill/primary processing site that produced a Plains side-notched point and a radiocarbon date of 180 +/- 40 BP (Beta-175619). Two small fragments of pottery lacking any evidence of surface treatment were also recovered from this level. Obsidian from this level was sourced to Obsidian Cliff, Wyoming. The next level, Component 4, represented the remains of an ephemeral campsite. Component 3, radiocarbon dated to 170 +/- 50 BP (Beta-175618), produced a Plains side-notched point in a small camp deposit. Component 2, the second-most recent level at the site, produced a glass bead and ribs that were apparently cut by a metal tool (Goldsmith 2003:130). Obsidian from this level was sourced to Big Southern Butte, Idaho (Goldsmith 2003:123). The most recent level, Component 1, contained the fewest lithic debitage and tools. A drilled tooth root bead and bone that appeared to have been cut with metal implements were found. The recovery of substantial amounts of antelope and medium-sized ungulates was interpreted as a culmination in an apparent shift in diet. Bison were still present in the faunal assemblage, but a more diverse exploitation pattern including antelope, beaver, fox, and perhaps bird was represented (Goldsmith 2003:130). This level was interpreted as a short-term Protohistoric Old Women's campsite that was occupied shortly before the demise of the bison and the arrival of European homesteaders near the end of the nineteenth century (Goldsmith 2003:130).

Flicka (EhPn 45). The Flicka site is a single-component bison kill site located on a northwest-oriented swale, northwest of Calgary (Vivian and Dow 2006:9). A total of 60 m² was excavated at the site prior to the construction of a subdivision (Vivian and Dow 2006:9).

Five points were recovered from the bone bed, including a flake point, three ferrous metal points, and a copper point (Vivian and Dow 2006:10–12). The only other tools recovered were two utilized flakes (Vivian and Dow 2006:12). The lithic raw materials included quartzite (n = 4), silicified siltstone (n = 2), Top-of-the-World Chert (n = 2), Montana chert (n = 1), and miscellaneous chert (n = 1) (Vivian and Dow 2006:12).

The faunal assemblage consisted mainly of bison bone (MNI = 24), although elements from what appeared to be a single horse were also recovered (Vivian and Dow 2006:17). The horse was interpreted as an accidental death, as part of the bison hunt. No canid bones were recovered at the site, possibly indicating that domestic dogs had been functionally replaced by the horse. The lack of fetal bone and the recovery of numerous male skeletons amongst the female and calf remains were interpreted as evidence for a late-summer/early-fall event (Vivian and Dow 2006:22). Preliminary inspection of the bone led the researchers to suggest that both stone and metal implements were used to butcher the animals (Vivian and Dow 2006:23). The site was compared to the Castle Forks site (above), with similarities in the bulk strategy of focusing on hindlimbs, the lack of a processing area, and the possibility of transportation of meat bundles by horse (Vivian and Dow 2006:40).

The recovery of metal trade points and a horse element places the site within the Protohistoric period. Pyszczyk (1999) has argued that trade points increase in length and neck width through time, and measurements from the Flicka site exceed the values for points made in the early nineteenth century (Vivian and Dow 2006:43). A mid-nineteenth century date for the site was suggested by the researchers. Although the cultural affiliation could fall amongst any of the groups known to have been in the area (i.e., Blackfoot, T'suu Tina, and Stoney), a Blackfoot affiliation was suggested owing to lithic raw materials that reflect traditional trade networks to Montana and British Columbia (Vivian and Dow 2006:43–44).

Other sites. Other Protohistoric period sites have been excavated but they do not provide evidence of their archaeological cultural affiliation. They may well be Protohistoric Old Women's sites, although they lack diagnostics. DjOu 23 is a deeply buried, single stone circle in the bottom of a draw within Forty Mile Coulee that yielded bone (n = 112), a metal can fragment, a glass fragment, and lithic debitage (n = 6) (Dau and Brumley 1987:132). DjOu 31 is a site consisting of six stone circles adjacent to the wall of Forty Mile Coulee. The site contained bone (n = 242), FBR (n = 42), and debitage (n = 36) along with eight pieces of glass from Stone Circle 3, and four pieces of glass and one piece of metal found inside and outside Stone Circle 5 (Dau and Brumley 1987:169). A radiocarbon date on bone recovered from Stone Circle 3 produced a date of ca. 470 BP (Table 26). DjOu 60 is a site consisting of seventeen stone circles along the west valley wall of Forty Mile Coulee. The stone circles produced small amounts of bone and/or lithics, with Stone Circle 17 yielding four small, thin metal fragments (Dau and Brumley 1987:241). DjOu 70 is a well-defined single stone circle that is deeply buried within the bottom of a draw near the wall in Forty Mile Coulee. It yielded a knife blade and a hinged metal handle outside the circle (Dau and Brumley 1987:427). DkOu 31 is stone circle site on the edge of the Forty Mile Coulee valley. Auger tests outside the stone circle produced glass fragments (Dau and Brumley 1987:618). Similarly, DjOu 48 consisted of three buried stone circles and a cairn on the edge of Forty Mile Coulee, with glass recovered from auger tests outside the circles (Dau and Brumley 1987:672).

DjPi 26 and DjPi 28 are located on a low bench of the McBride Lake Uplands, south of Fort Macleod (Reeves 2005). The sites consisted of horse travois trail segments and associated trail markers. At DjPi 26 the scars extend 200 m while at DjPi 28 there are two segments: a 200-metre-long trail segment associated with four cairns and two stone circles and a 200-metre-long trail segment associated with twenty-four cairns. Lichen growth on the cairns was minimal, suggesting that they were as recent as the 1800s (Reeves 2005:6). DjPl 100 is a stone feature site on a low terrace on the north bank of the Oldman River below the dam site. Here, a single glass trade bead was recovered below a cobble that formed part of the stone circle (Van Dyke 1994:103). EgPn 430, Area 6, is a very large multicomponent kill/processing site on the northwest slopes of the Paskapoo escarpment in west Calgary (Vivian et al. 2005, vol. 2:1). Eleven copper points, seven iron points, one iron knife, one iron file, one iron clasp, one brass button, and one glass bead were recovered. Only twenty-three stone tools were recovered in the excavation, including Pelican Lake points (n = 6), one Late Side-notched point, one McKean point, non-diagnostic point fragments (n = 5), bifaces (n = 2), one end scraper, retouched flakes (n = 4), a chopper, and a pebble core. An additional 172 pieces of lithic debitage were recovered. The faunal evidence suggested a summer kill (Vivian et al. 2005, vol. 38). In view of the large amount of European trade items recovered from the site, Vivian, Dow, and Reeves (2005, vol. 2:66) suggested that the event took place after direct contact with traders had been established. Pyszczyk (1999) established a sequence of chronological changes in metal points in Alberta. The EgPn 430, Area 6, points are most similar to those dating about A.D. 1830. Incidentally, Pyszczyk (1999) noted that the use of copper points falls off dramatically after A.D. 1834. Lastly, EhPl 27 is a small transitory campsite along Nose Creek north of Calgary (Vivian 2005). Six stone circles were found in proximity to each other, with one producing a metal point. Vivian (2005) suggested that the placement of the stone circles and the distribution of materials within each lodge reflected a well-defined social code.

Still other items from the Protohistoric period have been recovered. Metal projectile points have been found at a number of sites but their association with the other archaeological materials appears to be fortuitous. For example, at Head-Smashed-In Buffalo Jump, a metal point was recovered (Van Dyke 1994:223). Reeves (1978:166) noted that metal points and other trade goods were recovered from the latest component of the kill site, and inferred that the site was used until the mid-1800s. Metal points (n = 7) were also recovered from the upper two levels of the Morkin site (DlPk 2) (Byrne 1973:614). Byrne (1973:247) noted that these points were triangular in outline but appear to have been pounded from metal acquired in some other form and reshaped by Aboriginal people under the influence of European point forms. DgOv 94, a campsite along the Milk River in Writing-on-Stone Provincial Park, produced two metal points in association with a hearth (Brink 1979:41). The Little Bow site (EaPh 4) yielded a thin triangular piece of iron (likely a portion of a metal point) high in the stratigraphic profile of the site (Fedirchuk 1986:95–97, 111). The fragment may or may not be associated with the deeper Old Women's material. A metal trade point was recovered in a ploughed field at DjPm 36 in the area of the Snyder Locality (Van Dyke 1994:116). At the H.M.S. Balzac site (EhPm 34) a metal point was found in Regisol 2 of Block 2;

Old Women's points occurred in the next five regisols beneath the metal point (Head 1985:103). EgPn 506 is a large bison kill site and campsite on the Paskapoo Slopes in Calgary. Thirteen metal trade points were recovered in mixed association with Hanna, Avonlea, and Cayley Series projectile points (Vivian et al. 2003:89–121). One radiocarbon date (amongst many) produced an age of 200 +/-60 BP (Beta-151633), presumably dating the Protohistoric period material at the site (Vivian et al. 2003b:89). A metal point was recovered from the uppermost level at EfPm 27, a multicomponent bison kill site in Fish Creek Park (Crowe-Swords and Hanna 1980:48–51). EgPn 383 and EgPn 381 are surface scatters that produced a copper point each.

At DgOv 2, in Writing-on-Stone Provincial Park, excavation in front of rock art Panels 6 and 7 recovered glass seed beads from the surface and in the upper 10 cm BS (Brink 1979:20–22). A tinkle cone was recovered from a shovel test in a stone circle at the Pincher Creek Buffalo Jump (DjPl 1) (Ball 1987:27–28). A glass bead was found at EgPn 228; it is possibly in association with the Old Women's occupation (Vivian et al. 2006). At EgPn 430, Area 4, a trade bead and a possible gunflint were found in possible association with Old Women's material (Vivian and Reeves 2001).

A number of sites obtained "modern" or Protohistoric age radiocarbon dates but did not contain trade items to corroborate the age. For example, DjOu 42, DjOu 44, and DjOu 64 all yielded modern radiocarbon dates on material associated with a stone circle or an underlying occupation (Dau and Brumley 1987:238, 242). EfPl 226 is a multicomponent kill site on the north side of the Bow River, southeast of Calgary. The upper component contained numerous bones (n = 14,130), some FBR (n = 30), an antler tool, and a few pieces of debitage (n = 4). Two radiocarbon dates were associated with this material: 190 +/- 40 BP (Beta-190211) and a modern date (Beta-190212) (Turney 2004). Other sites dating to the Protohistoric Old Women's phase have unusual Protohistoric period artifacts in them. For example, EgPm 124 included, among other things, a shattered plate glass from which one piece had been worked into an end scraper (Vivian et al. 2005:95; Wilson 1977:42). The Blakiston site (DjPm 115) is known to have a substantial Protohistoric period component including metal points, iron fragments, musket balls, ceramic beads, glass, beads, and glass fragments, amongst other items (Dau 1993).

Protohistoric Old Women's: Continuity and Change

The Protohistoric period is a very brief segment of time in the archaeological record. Its brevity, however, is made up for in its enhanced archaeological visibility, as more sites are likely to have survived the short time since their deposition. Still, a recurring problem in interpreting Protohistoric sites rests in the ability to demonstrate a single unmixed occupation. The reoccupation of Old Women's sites by people with European trade goods might produce mixed assemblages difficult to differentiate from a "true" Protohistoric period site. Perhaps the only defence against this pitfall is the demonstration of unique but repeated patterns within Protohistoric sites. This would include patterns concerning how and when European artifacts were used by Aboriginal people and how these items influenced their movement on the landscape.

The former topic — landscape use after contact with Europeans — has long been an interest of Northern Plains archaeologists. Arguably, the largest single influence on landscape use of Aboriginal people on the Northern Plains in the Protohistoric period was the acquisition of the horse. Exactly when the horse arrived in Alberta is not known for certain. Dempsey's (1994:27) Blackfoot informants indicated that the horse arrived among their people about A.D. 1725 (see also Ewers 1955:18–19). Ewers (1955) placed the Blackfoot acquisition of the horse in the second quarter of the eighteenth century. Of course, the Blackfoot were aware of the horse (or Big Dog) immediately before this time period, as it was in the hands of their enemy, the Snake.

The apparent instantaneous adjustment to horses was remarkable. Landals (2004) presented some insights into the pros and cons of horse husbandry on the Northern Plains. In essence, she provided a discussion on the differences between horses and dogs in terms of their behavioural and physiological abilities with regard to transportation, traction, hunting efficiency, and raiding (see also Wissler 1914; Wilson 1924; Haines 1938; Ewers 1955; and Roe 1955). After a series of comparisons between horses and dogs, Landals (2004:246) summarized the horse-dog comparison by stating that pound for pound, horses are eight times more efficient than dogs; that is, they can move four times as much, twice as far. This ability comes at the cost of heavy water requirements and substantial husbandry knowledge. In terms of landscape use, she suggested that a shift favouring more intensive use of the river valleys and major coulee systems should accompany the transition to an equestrian lifeway (Landals 2004:250).

To a certain degree, Landals (2004:251–253) documented the equestrian shift in landscape use by comparing and contrasting the results of an upland 300-kilometre-long pipeline impact assessment study with those of three reservoir studies (Oldman, Little Bow, and Forty Mile Coulee). The reservoir projects all produced numerous Protohistoric period sites while the upland project produced only one Protohistoric period site. This was despite the fact that the pipeline project produced more sites than any one of the reservoir projects. Indeed, many Late Prehistoric sites were recorded during the pipeline project at locations that were many days from water (Landals 2004:253).

With regard to changes in hunting, the material at the Crowsnest River kill site suggests that mounted hunters drove bison over a precipice that would have otherwise been unorthodox. The Flicka site might represent a mounted surround. EgPn 430, Area 6, appears to have been an ambush at a spring. While the Castle Forks bison kill appears to be a more traditional jump with mounted participants mimicking driving lanes. Without a doubt, there was a wide range of bison procurement strategies being employed during the Protohistoric period.

The butchering process at these recent kill sites exhibited some divergent patterns from earlier times. At the Castle Forks bison kill and the Flicka site, arguments have been made that meat bundles and fetuses were being removed by horse to nearby camps. This removal of butchering units left a signature on the faunal assemblage at the site. This signature should be demonstrable when compared to earlier Old Women's faunal assemblages.

Large campsites such as Saamis and Blakiston are not particularly novel to Alberta's archaeological record, although they should take on different flavour in the Protohistoric period. The sites show signs of extended occupations. As predicted by Landals (2004), these sites are in sheltered valleys near rivers. Even small sites such as EhPl 27 and Hartell Creek are associated with flowing bodies of water. Despite the horse's utility, Landals (2004:252) asked an intriguing question: Did the horse extend the use of a favoured area or actually mandate the extended use?

The horse undoubtedly had an impact on Aboriginal people, but what of other European items? Pyszcyzyk (1997) argued that Native people of the Alberta plains, living in the indirect trade zone, acquired relatively few European goods and retained much of their traditional material culture during the Protohistoric period. In contrast, Ray (1974) suggested that fur trade middlemen, such as the Cree and Assiniboine, traded European goods inland a considerable distance to the Aboriginal people of southern Alberta as indirect trade. The high volume of indirect trade, he argued, would not show up in the archaeological record because of spatial diffusion of the material over a large trade area. Pyszczyk (1997:50–54) reviewed historic documents and illustrated that the material reaching the Alberta plains was minimal. As well, the dependence of Aboriginal people in southern Alberta on indirect trade was low; much of their traditional material culture was retained during the Protohistoric period (Pyszczyk 1997:53). Addressing how European materials entered Aboriginal material culture, Pyszczyk (1997:72–77) listed the types and quantities of European and traditional artifacts for Late Prehistoric, Protohistoric, and Historic sites, stating that "if Native people were simply replacing traditional articles with equivalent European goods, then the proportions of traditional goods should decrease in assemblages from the Protohistoric and Historic periods when compared to the Late Prehistoric period." In fact, he found that European goods did not initially replace traditional articles; rather, these goods may have been used for purposes beyond their originally intended utilitarian function. In other words, Aboriginal people were simply adding European goods to their traditional material (Pyszczyk 1997:77).

ONE GUN PHASE (CA. 200 BP)

The One Gun phase was named by Byrne (1973:478) in remembrance of a Blackfoot informant who originally showed archaeologists to the Cluny site. The One Gun phase is considered coeval with the Old Women's phase in the South Saskatchewan River Basin of Alberta during the Protohistoric period. It is apparently absent, however, to the south in the Milk River Basin and to the north in the North Saskatchewan Basin (Byrne 1973:366–367, 399; Vickers 1986:106). The phase is defined by projectile points of the Plains side-notched type (Byrne 1973:473–374; Forbis 1977:51–57; Kehoe 1966b), Cluny pottery (Byrne 1973:335–374), scapula squash knives, pitted handstones (nutstones), grinding slabs, and bell-shaped pits. The recovery of Cluny pottery from two sites, the Cluny site and the Morkin site, has provided the basis for defining the One Gun phase, although its recovery was noted at DkPj 2 (Level 1) and EaPk 17 (Byrne 1973:336).

The Cluny site (EePf 1) consists of a semicircular ditched area that presumably encircles a habitation zone, and is dated to the Protohistoric period. The Morkin site (DlPk 2) is an open-air campsite in the Porcupine Hills of southern Alberta (Byrne 1973:471–504). It is similar to most prehistoric campsites except for the recovery of a bell-shaped pit (Byrne 1973:20), some Cluny pottery, items reminiscent of scapula squash knives, and pitted handstones (Byrne 1978:254). Beyond the Cluny and Morkin sites, small quantities of Cluny pottery have been found in sites that are otherwise characterized by Old Women's material culture such as substantial amounts of Saskatchewan Basin Complex: Late Variant pottery (Byrne 1973:477).

Byrne (1973:335–338) defined the distinctive Cluny pottery. Vessels have relatively thin walls and are globular in shape with no flattened bases (Byrne 1973:337). "Necks are frequent and of two forms; 1) short and very sharply curved, producing external concave vertical profiles with arcs of 900 to 1300, and 2) long and shallow, curving gently out of the body area to form a tall, vertical-to-slightly-flaring section" (Byrne 1973:337). The interior of Cluny pottery is usually smooth with the exterior often paddled by a grooved object that left check or simple stamp impressions (Byrne 1973:336). In terms of decoration, linear dentate stamping is most common, as are impressions left by very fine-cord-wrapped objects while less common are punctates, fine-line incision, and plain impression. Byrne (1973:337–338) further stated that "Most motifs are fairly complex in composition, with oblique lines across the lip plus numerous closely spaced lines of horizontal or oblique orientation located just below the outer lip edge, on the collar, and/or in the neck region being a frequently seen combination."

While the pottery of the One Gun phase is very distinctive the same is not true for the projectile points. The projectile points associated with the One Gun phase were classified using the typology developed by Forbis (1962, 1977). Surprisingly, the points excavated from both the Cluny and Morkin sites cannot be distinguished from the Cayley Series projectile points. Peck (1996; Peck and Ives 2001) suggested that the brevity of the One Gun occupation may have permitted conflation of Cayley Series projectile points of the Old Women's phase with One Gun assemblages such that the assemblages representing the different phases cannot be stratigraphically separated.

In terms of other tools, Byrne (1973:479) noted a number of similarities between One Gun and Old Women's artifacts. He found correspondences between scrapers, drills, grooved shaft smoothers and mauls. With respect to bone artifacts Byrne (1973:479) found similarities among beads, pendants, punches, awls, quill flatteners, and hide grainers.

Concerning the origins of the One Gun phase, Forbis (1977) suggested that the materials derived from the Middle Missouri area. Byrne (1973:535) also suggested that "the One Gun phase probably represents the result of a migration of a group or groups from the area [Middle Missouri] through southern Saskatchewan to southern Alberta." Forbis and Byrne supported their claims by illustrating substantial similarity between the Cluny site structures, the Cluny pottery, and numerous tools and features (scapula squash knives, pitted handstones, grinding slabs, and bell-shaped pits) and their Middle Missouri counterparts.

Specifically, Byrne (1973:478) argued that Cluny pottery was much like contemporary Mortlach pottery in southern Saskatchewan. Vickers (1994), too, considered the possibility that the One Gun phase and the Mortlach phase might represent the most western extension of a movement out of the Middle Missouri area. In contrast, Kehoe and Kehoe (1968:33) disagreed with the suggestion that a strong similarity between Cluny and Mortlach pottery exists. Kooyman (1996) provided an analysis of the Cluny pottery largely based on the artifacts themselves and oral tradition. He noted that Cluny pottery is relatively unique. Dentate stamping is more common at Cluny than at other sites: Cluny (42%), Mortlach (10–12%), Hagen (3%), and Middle Missouri Wares (2%). Similarly, check-stamping is more frequent in Cluny pottery: Cluny (38%), Mortlach (6%), Hagen (6%), and Middle Missouri area (< 6%). He concluded that Cluny pottery is most like Mortlach pottery and material from the Hagen site. Further, Kooyman (1996) considered the nature of the ditch and palisade, noting similarities to Dakota and Ojibwa defensive structures in Manitoba (Historic Resources Branch 1997:9–11).

Bone and stone tools were also reviewed. Lithics were almost entirely local in origin and no digging implements were recovered, which would suggest horticulture (Kooyman 1996). The sparse remains suggested the occupation was very temporary. Kooyman (1996) suggested that the Cluny site represented a trading site of people of Mountain Crow or Hidatsa origin. Walde (2003:61–62, 2004:45) noted that Cluny ceramics and Mortlach ceramics were similar, but suggested that their resemblance was owing to a derivation from a common Woodland ceramic tradition. Rather than making direct comparisons to Mortlach ceramics in the east, he found more comparable materials to the south.

Peck (1996; Peck and Ives 2001) has demonstrated that a distinctive projectile point style (Mortlach Group) is associated with Mortlach assemblages in Saskatchewan. These points are not found in association with Cluny pottery, further supporting the suggestion that Mortlach and One

Gun materials are not directly related. Furthermore, the lithic raw materials used were all local in origin, again dissimilar from Mortlach phase use of lithic raw materials (Peck 1996; Peck and Ives 2001).

The fate of the One Gun phase is not well understood either. Forbis (1977:74), the original excavator of the Cluny site, outlined a number of possibilities. He suggested the Cluny peoples may have been decimated by disease or overrun by enemies, although he noted the lack of human skeletal remains does not support such interpretations (Forbis 1977:74). Alternatively, he suggested the Cluny inhabitants abandoned their distinctive culture and merged with the local Old Women's phase (Forbis 1977:74). Cluny pottery is known from a number of sites otherwise attributable to the Old Women's phase (Byrne 1973:477), providing support for this hypothesis. Finally, Forbis (1977:74) suggested the inhabitants of Cluny may have simply returned to the Middle Missouri area.

Since 2007, Dale Walde has operated the field school for the Department of Archaeology, University of Calgary, at the Cluny site. This is the first archaeological work at the site since Forbis' excavations. No doubt, the excavation will answer a number of questions and raise many more.

The Sites

One Gun sites exhibiting Cluny pottery are summarized below. These sites are used to critically evaluate the current view of the One Gun phase (see Plate 29 and Figure 30).

PLATE 29 One Gun points. Illustrated are nine projectile points from the Cluny site (EePf 1). Photo credit: Dale Walde.

FIGURE 30
One Gun sites within Alberta

Cluny (EePf 1). The Cluny site is located along the Bow River near Cluny, Alberta. It consists of a semicircular ditch (250 m long by 2.5 m wide by 1 m deep) that is bridged by three or four causeways. The ditch terminates at a terrace edge produced by a former position of the Bow River (Forbis 1977; Byrne 1978). Parallel to and inside the semicircular ditch is a series of 9–10 pits (ca. 3 m in diameter) about 20 m apart. These pits may be earthlodges or bastions inside a palisade. Around the pits lay a thin scattering of archaeological material and numerous storage pits (Byrne 1978:251). A few metres behind the pits, again parallel to the ditch, is a palisade constructed of poplar posts. Inside the palisade were a number of hearths possibly marking locations of skin tents (Forbis and Huscher 1961:102). Cluny pottery and numerous Late Side-notched projectile points were also recovered (Byrne 1973; Forbis 1977; Forbis and Huscher 1961). Bone tools included punches, awls, scapula knives, quill flatteners, grainers, and bone beads (Forbis 1977; Forbis and Huscher 1961). The site was dated to the Protohistoric period based on two pieces of brass slotted into ribs as knife blades, two horse bones, and an appropriately recent radiocarbon date of 60 +/- 70 BP (HAR-534).

Morkin (DlPk 2). The Morkin site is a multicomponent open-air campsite in the Porcupine Hills of southern Alberta (Byrne 1973:471–504). Five cultural levels were distinguished. Besant material was focused in the lowest level, 5. Avonlea was best represented in the overlying cultural Level 4. Levels 3 to 1 produced the most Late Side-notched material, with Levels 2 and 1 yielding Protohistoric period material.

The site is similar to a prehistoric campsite; it lacks the unique structural features of the Cluny site with the exception that it contains a bell-shaped pit similar in shape to those found in the Middle Missouri area (Byrne 1973:20). However, Morkin also contains some Cluny pottery. In addition, the site exhibits items reminiscent of scapula squash knives and pitted handstones also of the Middle Missouri area (Byrne 1978:254). As well, small quantities of Cluny pottery have also been found in sites that are otherwise characterized by Old Women's material culture; that is, they contain substantial amounts of Saskatchewan Basin Complex: Late Variant pottery (Byrne 1973:477).

One Gun: More Migrants from the Middle Missouri Area

There can be little doubt that the Cluny site represents an intrusive group, likely from the Middle Missouri area, into southern Alberta. Byrne (1978) used a number of lines of evidence to demonstrate a Middle Missouri movement of people to southern Alberta. The Cluny site exhibits numerous traits from the Middle Missouri area not found in the contemporary Old Women's material culture. The ditch with the associated palisade and large pits are unique in Alberta archaeology. The pottery most closely resembles pottery of the Middle Missouri type but is similar to Mortlach pottery. The bone tools are somewhat unusual including possible "scapula knives." The projectile points are all made of local materials and are classifiable as Cayley Series projectile points of the Old Women's phase. Not surprisingly, there is no consensus regarding the function of the site or the exact ethnic affiliation of the site.

The Morkin site has been considered to exhibit features similar to the Cluny site. These similarities include Cluny pottery, pitted handstones, and grinding slabs. Similarities that the Morkin site has to the Middle Missouri area are bell-shaped pits and possible scapula knives. With regard to the pottery, Kooyman (1996) outlined the distinctiveness of the Cluny pottery. Dentate stamping is more common at Cluny than other sites: Cluny (42%), Mortlach (10–12%), Hagen (3%), and Middle Missouri Wares (2%); and check-stamping is more frequent in Cluny pottery, with Cluny (38%), Mortlach (6%), Hagen (6%), and Middle Missouri area (< 6%). In contrast, at the Morkin site dentate stamping occurs at a rate of 30 percent in Level 2 and 33.3 percent in Level 1. Check or simple stamped pottery accounts for 7.7 percent of the pottery in level 2 and none in level 1 (Byrne 1973:628). Morkin does not appear to exhibit Cluny pottery; rather it exhibits traits common in Cluny pottery.

Understanding the One Gun phase must take into account a range of variables. First, there can be little doubt the Cluny site represents an intrusive group of people from the Middle Missouri area. These people brought with them a distinctive pottery as well as other implements. The Cluny site appears to be defensive in nature. The outer trench defines a perimeter. The "house pits" are very small and located on the outside of the palisade. Their vanguard position and size suggests they may have been defensive pits. In fact, post-moulds at the outward edge of the pits might represent "screens," reinforcing their interpretation as part of a defensive structure (Forbis 1977, fig. 21). Also, the palisade is behind the pits; it is not inside the walls. Importantly, the palisade often cuts across the interior margin of the pits, thus providing access into and out of the palisade. Within the palisade are the hearths, suggesting the location of daily life activities (Forbis and Huscher 1961:102). The projectile points found within the Cluny site itself are of local stone and classifiable as Cayley Series projectile points. Given the local stone and the defensive nature of the structure, it is possible to infer that the points were launched into the compound from the outside. Old Women's people would have defended their territory from intruders. Thus, excavations well outside the compound might find stylistically different arrow points or perhaps lead balls. The "rifle pits" suggest the use of muskets that required reloading in an upright position, with the use of a rod. Unless people reloading these weapons were safe within a pit, they would have had to stand and expose themselves to the line of fire. A reasonable date of ca. A.D. 1750 has been assigned to the site. The survivors of this confrontation with the people of the Old Women's phase would have been kept as slaves to carry out menial tasks. This provides a mechanism for Cluny pottery or traits from Cluny pottery to be found in Old Women's sites. Morkin might be an example of one such site.

Commentary 8

About 13,000 years ago, the people that produced the Clovis phase appeared in Alberta. Clovis material represents the first people to enter this vast, unpopulated land. The Clovis phase spread rapidly from the northwestern part of North America to cover most of the western half of the continent. This peopling event likely started within the Ice-free Corridor in the foothills of the Rocky Mountains, around the current border between British Columbia and Alberta. Since deglaciation had been underway for centuries, the corridor was likely quite wide and not a restrictive passage as often suggested. Currently in Alberta, the Clovis phase is known only from surface finds of its large fluted spear points. Further south in the United States, the people of the Clovis phase left evidence of their high mobility, curated toolkits, and a focus on large game for subsistence. Social groups consisted of family units with, perhaps, only few families residing together at any one time. A redundant land-use pattern by these pioneers reveals their unfamiliarity with the nuances of the new setting. This inexperience with the landscape is reflected in their lithic technology; it was designed for mobile people (i.e., large biface cores, macroblades, Clovis points) and ensured that good-quality lithic raw material was always at hand. These and other technological improvements in the hunting system would certainly help to explain how the Clovis people spread so far so fast. In fact, the change in relatively straight-sided Clovis specimens, commonly found in Alberta, to more excurvate-sided forms, found to the south, may reflect an evolution toward increased penetrating power of the Clovis point. As well, the traditional interpretation of Clovis as a thrusting spear has been challenged; some evidence suggests that Palaeoindian points are better understood as dart tips on unfletched darts launched from atlatls. Lastly, the high quality and regularity found in Clovis lithic craftsmanship suggests rigid organization in some aspect of these people's social structure, whether it be kinship, craft specialization, or sodalities. Of significance to Alberta's search for the Clovis material was the highly dynamic environment that likely destroyed or deeply buried much of the evidence of this early part of the province's human past.

Between about 12,800 and 12,200 years ago these same people continued to flourish in the western half of North America. Clovis technology changed and the subsequent material culture is called the Folsom phase. Overlap between the material remains of the Folsom phase with the ancestral Clovis phase is apparent in the continued use of large fluted points with highly curated toolkits designed for high mobility and a focus on large game for subsistence. These two phases geographically coincide over the western half of the continent. Unlike their Clovis ancestors, the Folsom people were restricted to bison hunting on the Plains, as mammoths and other large game animals had become extinct. Folsom kill sites provide evidence that Folsom people took advantage of the behaviour of numerous animals, utilizing natural traps. The regularity and exquisite form of Folsom points suggests that knowledge transmission within tight kin-groups or working with designated craft specialists was an intricate part of an individual's upbringing. Practices of stone conservation, the use of biface cores, multi-function stone tools, and Folsom point preforms as tools were all elegant adaptive responses to a highly mobile lifeway focused on hunting bison in stone-poor areas. Retooling at quarries would still have been necessary. The social unit remained small, with a few families gathering at any one time. There is evidence that such gatherings took place over substantial distances at predetermined locales, indicating increased familiarity with the landscape. In the eastern half of North America and in South America, the spread of this same population is seen in Folsom-like fluted points.

Regionalization within Alberta may have begun as early as 12,000 years ago with the Sibbald phase in northwestern North America, people that used basally thinned triangular points, not unlike short Clovis points, subsisted in the mountains and foothills on large game such as bison and bighorn sheep. Gone was the focus on exotic lithics and finely crafted tools within highly curated toolkits. Local lithic sources and less curation of toolkits predominated these assemblages. Small family groups continued to be the norm at this time. The relationship between Clovis, Northern Fluted points, and basally thinned triangular points is difficult to assess. Currently, it appears that all three groups of material were isolated in space and time. Thus, the practice of basal thinning is related to fluting, but is not the same, so basally thinned points are not simply resharpened Clovis points. Further, basally thinned material, in the Sibbald phase, appears to date more recently than Clovis material. The coinciding geographic distribution, the relationship between fluting and basal thinning, and the focus on large game provide overlap between the Sibbald people and the previous Clovis and Folsom people.

In contrast, on the plains and foothills about 12,000 to 11,500 years ago there were people employing a slightly different technology, represented by the Agate Basin/Hell Gap complex. The complex occurs over much of the same geographic area previously inhabited by people using Folsom material, but was contracted to the north (north of Colorado and Kansas). Arguments for and against deriving Agate Basin/Hell Gap projectile point technology from the preceding Folsom phase have been made. The focus on bison as the main subsistence animal continues from the preceding period. Small and large kill sites occur, usually in areas of natural traps. The use of lithic raw materials was more locally focused compared to the previous Folsom phase. Similarly, while the lithic craftsmanship was still very good during the Agate Basin/Hell Gap complex, it was not at the same exquisite standard as the Folsom phase. Social groups continued to be small, consisting of no more than a few families camped together at any one time. The overlap between the projectile point technologies of Folsom phase and Agate Basin/Hell Gap complex has not been established with certainty; however, the geographic distribution and subsistence strategy exhibits substantial continuity between the two cultural units.

People continued focusing their subsistence strategy on bison from 11,500 to 10,800 years ago. The material culture associated with these people is represented by the Alberta phase. Numerous lines of evidence indicate continuity between Agate Basin/Hell Gap and Alberta cultures. Researchers have inferred that the lanceolate shape of the Alberta point indicates that the phase originated from the preceding Agate Basin/Hell Gap complex. Alberta phase distribution coincides with the Agate Basin/Hell Gap complex. Evidence indicates that a sustained focus on bison, with kill sites indicating natural traps, continued to provide avenues for ambushing substantial numbers of animals. Lithic craftsmanship remained relatively high, with utilization of local raw lithic materials. Still, in Alberta, items manufactured on a dull red "jasper" at the Bayrock and Norquay sites should inspire interesting lines of research in terms of quarrying, exchange, seasonal movements, and group contact. Social groups remained small with known campsites representing a few family units camped together.

By 10,800 to 9,200 years ago, a subtle change in technology is evident in the archaeological record, represented by the Scottsbluff-Eden material culture. The material culture occurs in the same core area as the Alberta phase, but appears to have expanded to the surrounding lands, particularly western Ontario, Michigan, Wisconsin, Colorado, northeastern British Columbia, and northeastern Alberta. The Scottsbluff-Eden phase exhibits a strong reliance on bison for subsistence, especially when found on the Plains, but is also now known to exhibit a more diverse subsistence strategy both on the Plains and the Plains periphery. The frequent recovery of Knife River flint in many Scottsbluff-Eden sites suggests that these people either moved around substantially or had increased interactions with each other. Perhaps an expanding grassland allowed the Scottsbluff-Eden people to also increase in number. The diagnostic projectile points are strikingly similar in form to the preceding Alberta point. As well, the characteristic Cody knife was also present in the preceding Alberta phase. Overlap between Alberta phase and Scottsbluff-Eden phase is substantial, including the strikingly similar point morphologies, the continued presence of Cody knives, bison-focused subsistence, and coincidental geographic distributions.

Between 9,200 and 8,500 years ago, people that produced Plains/Mountain material thrived in the mountain/foothills/forest surrounding the Northern Plains, while people that produced Lusk material were on the Northern Plains. This period provides the early and good evidence for regionalization in Alberta's archaeological past. The origin of the Plains/Mountain complex will likely be resolved as data from the central Rocky Mountains and Northern Plains periphery increases. The Lovell Constricted material in Alberta and farther east to Manitoba is morphologically distinct from the original Lovell Constricted in the south. This spread of "northern" Lovell Constricted and Castle stemmed material across the Plains periphery may reflect the establishment of the southern extent of the northern forest after a more open environment during the Scottsbluff-Eden phase. Although evidence is limited, big-game subsistence continued as a focus despite the more forest-oriented nature of this phase. Large bison kills in natural traps and the transportation of butchered meat units to central locations indicates comfort with procuring large animals. On the Northern Plains, the Lusk complex continued the long tradition of lanceolate points. The adoption of new dart technology added innovation in the form of corner-notched projectile points to the hunting system repertoire. The smaller corner-notched points likely represent experimentation with the hunting system. The new points signify an attempt to fine-tune fletched darts, tipped with corner-notched points, to the atlatl. A focus on bison procurement and local lithic raw materials continued. The social groups continued to be small, with a few family units cooperating in subsistence activities. Although climatic changes may have forced the people of the Lusk complex to utilize waterways and the periphery of the Plains more, the complex still exhibits some continuity with the preceding Scottsbluff-Eden phase.

Lusk points continue to be found in the subsequent complex. By 8,500 to 8,000 years ago, Lusk points overlap with diagnostic artifacts in the Country Hills complex. This latter complex is defined by the recovery of Burmis barbed points. Bison kill and processing sites continued to be common around the periphery of the Plains during this phase. Some of these bison kill sites are relatively large. The earliest lithic artifacts from this phase are very finely crafted. The points exhibit ties to material recovered in Wyoming, suggesting a possible foothills/mountain origin for the phase. Up to this period in time, the archaeological record appears to represent settling-in of people. That is to say, the initial peopling of the region progressed to regionalization at an increasingly geographically restricted level. The geographic distribution or territory of each archaeological culture became increasingly smaller. The Country Hills complex appears to represent the first instance in which people from one area moved to another area. The finely crafted points in the Mummy Cave site appear slightly earlier in the archaeological record than the very similar Burmis barbed points in Alberta, suggesting a physical movement of people. The earliest Country Hills artifacts are finely crafted; however, craftsmanship within the lithic assemblage deteriorates through time. This change in aesthetics might reflect a move from a highly structured kinship to a generational kinship system with less structure, or a shift from craft specialization to more generalized modes of manufacture. The recovery of Country Hills sites almost exclusively around the periphery of the Plains suggests that the Hypsithermal conditions played a role in site establishment.

Around 8,000 to 7,700 years ago the Country Hills complex was replaced by the Mummy Cave complex. This is interpreted as a replacement of people rather than a change in technology. Similar assemblages are found in the foothills/plains areas of Wyoming, suggesting a possible movement of people from that area. At this time, finely crafted side-notched dart points (Bitterroot and Blackwater side-notched) appeared. This is the first appearance of side-notched projectile points in the archaeological record in Alberta. The quality and uniformity in craftsmanship suggests high fidelity of transmission with respect to lithic tool manufacturing. While bison was still a subsistence focus at this time period, there is evidence of a broader diet. Compared to earlier periods, bison kill sites are not particularly visible, or perhaps were not particularly common. This may be a product of increased aridity during the Hypsithermal interval, reducing bison numbers. Alternatively, sampling problems may have limited the number of sites found. Large bison kills may have been present during this period that have not been discovered. Social units continued to be quite small, with single family or extended family gatherings being common. The Mazama Ash fall event provided a massive blow to these people. There is little evidence of Mummy Cave complex for subsequent times.

There is a stretch of a few hundred years for which no or little archaeological material is recovered in the province, possibly owing to the devastation brought by the fallout of the Mt. Mazama eruption. It has not yet been determined whether people remained in southern Alberta after the Mazama Ash fall or returned once things were more amenable. This gap in the record may also be a product of sampling rather than the reality of the devastation of the eruption.

By about 7,300 to 6,200 years ago, the Maple Leaf complex was established throughout the Plains periphery in Alberta. The diagnostic projectile points, Salmon River fishtail, and Salmon River oval base, are mediocre in the quality of their manufacture. Bison procurement was still the focus of subsistence. Hunting strategies continued to focus on the use of natural traps, such as coulees and springs, which also provided trap or ambush locales of choice for these hunters. There might be evidence at Head-Smashed-In buffalo Jump for early use of this "natural trap," but further examination of the recovered artifacts would be required to confirm this idea; if verified, the Maple Leaf phase would represent the earliest use of the jump. This is interesting since the evidence continues to suggest the social group was quite small with a family or two cohabitating at sites. The evidence for the gathering of the numerous people required to conduct a jump has not been recovered from the archaeological record.

There is very little data available for the Gowen complex. It is not clear whether it represents an actual cultural entity in Alberta archaeology, although it appears as a consistent phenomenon in Saskatchewan. In Saskatchewan, it dates reliably to about 7,000 years ago. The limited data suggest that bison were the main subsistence animal. Hunting strategies included solitary stalking, with meat units being brought back to camp, and small kills at natural traps. The recovery of a single hearth or two hearths within sites encircled by camp detritus supports the notion that social groups were restricted to one or two family groups encamped together.

By 6,200 to 5,500 years ago the Calderwood complex was present on the Plains periphery. At this time, people were living through the end of the Hypsithermal interval. Projectile point diversity was substantial for this time, with as many as four types identifiable. Such heterogeneity represents a loosening of social filters concerning the manner in which things are made. The harsh reality of the Plains kept social groups smaller and more fluid. Less-rigid social controls presented more room for individual expression in the material culture. Pockets of uniformity in material culture arose where heritability was strongest, but isolation and fluidity created other areas where transmission of different ideas occurred. Despite the apparent increase in the fluidity of social structure during the Calderwood complex, bison jumping at Head-Smashed-In Buffalo Jump and the formation of the Majorville cairn began. Perhaps the waning of the Hypsithermal interval provided opportunities that pulled social groups together as well as circumstances that pushed them apart. In addition, the appearance of modern bison and modern bison behaviour may have occurred around 6,000–7,000 years ago. The congregation of large numbers of bison near Head-Smashed-In Buffalo Jump might have provided incentive for a people used to trapping small numbers of animals in natural traps to gather themselves in larger numbers for a larger operation. At the same time, the bison concentration would last only briefly before the animals moved on. The hunters would likely have had to break into small social groups and follow suite. The bison bone beds at Head-Smashed-In indicate jumps were not frequent compared with later times.

Bison jumping at Head-Smashed-In Buffalo Jump ceases after the Calderwood complex, as new people arrive in southern Alberta. Between 5,500 and 4,900 years ago, the Estevan phase appears to have replaced the

Calderwood materials. It is during this time period that certain areas across the Plains begin to be inhabited for the first time since the onset of the Hypsithermal interval. As well, the earliest evidence of stone boiling occurs with the Estevan phase, as large amounts of fire-broken rock (FBR) appear in the archaeological record for the first time. The oldest mauls are also recovered from this time period. These events are not coincidental, as stone boiling provides a means to extract grease from bone for preserving meat. Mauls would provide a way to smash bone, to increase its surface area for better grease extraction in the boiling pits. Preserved meat stocks would allow people to be bolder in the travels they undertake. Further evidence of this group's intrusiveness rests in their finely crafted and very regular Long Creek dart points, which have been recovered from a number of campsites as well as the Gray Burial site. The Long Creek point is strikingly similar in morphology to the Oxbow point in the subsequent phase. Similarly, Oxbow material predominates at the Gray Burial site. The overlap between the point forms and burial practice suggest heritable continuity between these phases. The movement of Estevan phase into Alberta was a tipping point in Alberta's prehistory. Until this point in time, movement of people onto the Alberta plains had occurred from populations in the mountainous west. After the Estevan phase, movement of people into Alberta comes exclusively from the east, with the exception of the McKean complex, which originated from the south. Population build-up in the east reached a threshold by about 6,000 years ago and people began looking for, or were force to move to, a new home. In many instances, people moved west onto the Plains. This scenario is especially well known from the Protohistoric and Historic periods.

Oxbow dates to between 4,900 and 4,400 years ago. The structured nature of the Estevan and Oxbow projectile points, the presence of a burial complex, with some exhibiting copper, and the use of stone boiling all indicate the movement of people into southern Alberta from elsewhere, likely from the east. The significance of the Gray Burial site should not be downplayed. The nature of the Oxbow burials and their associated grave goods is relatively consistent, and is not duplicated at other periods. As well, the site itself is centrally located within the distribution of the Oxbow phase. Oxbow burials aside from the Gray Burial site are located at the periphery of the Oxbow phase distribution, suggesting that the substantial effort to transport the individual to the central cemetery out-weighed the need to bury the body. Whether the Gray site was truly a hub of Oxbow phase lifeways is difficult to assess without further data. In terms of subsistence, solitary stalking and small kills predominated Oxbow bison procurement. Social units remained small, consisting of a few cooperating families. Circular distributions of artifacts suggest conical dwellings were being used at the time, but do not definitively indicate tipis.

By about 4,400 to 3,500 years ago, the McKean complex arrived in southern Alberta. The initial diagnostic projectile point is a lanceolate form that becomes increasingly "stemmed" through time. The earliest McKean lanceolate points are quite large and finely crafted with deep basal concavities. The spread of this material from the Big Horn Basin/Black Hills area to Saskatchewan and Alberta is fairly well documented. In the associated burial complex, the deceased were placed in the floors of living areas rather than cemeteries as in the preceding phases. Similarly, the people of the McKean phase used ambushes to capture prey, as opposed to use of solitary stalking of animals in Oxbow times. Once the McKean phase arrived in Alberta, Saskatchewan, Manitoba, northern North Dakota, and northern Montana, it was expressed as a regional variant from the material to the south. The southern material exhibits items such as grinding slabs, cobble-lined hearths, edge-ground cobbles, pit houses, and Mallory points, none of which appear in the north McKean record. Intensive processing tools are not noted. Instead of pit houses, at least one circular debris pattern indicated that conical structures were likely used for habitation, although evidence of a tie-down stake is absent. The data is scarce, but it suggests that McKean shows continuity within the McKean-Duncan-Hanna sequence although it is quite different from the preceding Estevan-Oxbow material.

The Hanna projectile point is the last diagnostic within the point manifestations of the McKean complex. Some scholars have argued that it represents the material link between the McKean complex and the Pelican Lake complex. Pelican Lake points, dating to between 3,500 to 3,000 years ago, are finely crafted dart points. In terms of morphology and craftsmanship, they are quite different from the stemmed and more crudely flaked McKean points. While there is evidence for ambushes and small kills of bison during McKean times, the Pelican Lake complex exhibits evidence for stalking bison and other prey individually. Pelican Lake material is distributed across the Canadian Plains (Alberta, Saskatchewan and Manitoba) and northern Montana, while McKean materials cover a greater area in their northern expression and an even greater area when their southern expression is considered. There is little overlap between the McKean and

Pelican Lake complexes. Social groups were small, with a couple of family groups cohabitating a site. Contemporaneous stone circles recovered from this period suggest that conical lodges were utilized. These may have been tipis, although tie-down stakes have not been found. The finely crafted Pelican Lake points are interpreted as evidence of a kinship system exhibiting multiple bonds between a limited array of relatives that were maintained through generations, or possibly craft specialization likely originating out of the east. Material similar to the Pelican Lake complex is known from Minnesota; this is a likely locale in which population pressure, among other forces, would have placed stress on groups, forcing them to move out on to the Plains proper.

Between 3,000 and 2,100 years ago the Bracken phase was well established on the Northern Plains. The large corner-notched diagnostic points are not unlike crude versions of the preceding Pelican Lake points. The form of the points became increasingly crude and heterogeneous through time, suggesting an increased fluidity within the social structure. At the same time, the burial complex associated with the Bracken phase is distinct. It is tempting to link the Bracken phase back to the Pelican Lake complex. The Highwood site might represent a late Pelican Lake burial rather than an early Bracken burial. The burial pattern is a mound of cobbles overlying the body. This is a burial pattern well known to the south and east, in which earth replaces the cobbles. Whether it arrived with the Pelican Lake complex or the Bracken phase is an important question because it seems unlikely to have developed in situ without any precedent. There are stone circles present in both archaeological units and they exhibit similar lithic assemblages. Large bison kill sites are lacking from the Pelican Lake subsistence repertoire, yet the development of large kills may have been brought on by later pressure from increasing eastern populations.

While the Pelican Lake complex occurred over Manitoba, Saskatchewan, Alberta and Montana, the Bracken phase failed to occur in Manitoba. The first large encampments of up to eighteen stone circles (possibly representing 100+ people) are known at this time. As well, industrialization of bison jumping and pounding occurs as kill sites are used repeatedly. The increased aggregation of people and escalation in subsistence pursuits are likely intertwined. The issue of whether people started aggregating more and thus required more food or whether the ability to produce more food allowed more aggregation to occur as a possible chicken-and-egg situation arises. Still, at this time, population pressure from the east continued to force the distribution of archaeological cultures increasingly farther west. The increased activity at bison kill sites provides the archaeological evidence for the strengthening in the population base on the Plains. Mixed into this story is the development of stone circles with tie-down stakes, which occur within the Bracken phase, suggesting that the true tipi was being utilized. The slow and gradual changes within the Bracken phase, however, seem to lead inevitably to the origin of the Besant phase.

Around 2,600 years ago, the Outlook and the Sandy Creek complexes appeared in scattered locations across the Northern Plains. The Outlook complex has large lanceolate points made on Knife River flint. The sites tend to emphasize bison procurement. The finely crafted points and their association with bison kill sites have all the hallmarks of an intrusive group. Further, the lithic assemblage associated with the complex strongly suggests ties to the Middle Missouri area. The faunal assemblages show few signs of intensive processing, which suggests a "gourmet" approach to carcass utilization. There can be little doubt that this complex represents archaeological evidence for Eastern pressure onto the western Plains. The Sandy Creek complex is more mysterious. In Alberta, some of this material may simply represent aberrant Bracken material culture, as Bracken projectile points are known to have become increasingly heterogeneous through time. Regardless, the Sandy Creek complex appears relatively consistent in Saskatchewan. The most interesting aspect of these archaeological cultures is that both the Outlook and Sandy Creek complexes are present on the Northern Plains during the tenure of the Bracken phase. The Bracken phase, of course, exhibits the first strong evidence in the archaeological record of dramatically increased social group size.

The Besant phase dates to between 2,100 and 1,500 years ago. Large Besant stone circle camps are known, as are bison jumps and pounds. A number of researchers have noted the overlap between the lithic assemblages of the Bracken and the Besant phases. The craftsmanship of the points is relatively crude and resembles a degenerated but homogenous form of Bracken points at the end of its tenure. The Besant phase appears to represent an in situ development from the preceding Bracken phase of a socially fluid people adapted to life on the Northern Plains. Like the Bracken phase before it, the Besant phase distribution was limited more to the west; it was geographically restricted to southwest Saskatchewan, southern Alberta, and northern Montana. The Sonota phase occupied the southeastern corner of Saskatchewan as pressure, presumably from increasing sedentism and agriculture from the east, continued to limit the distribution of archaeological cultures in the west.

By 1,500 to 1,350 years ago, the Sonota phase expanded into southern Alberta. Before 1,500 years ago, the Sonota phase co-existed with the Besant phase as a separate cultural entity around the Middle Missouri area. The Sonota phase exhibits large lanceolate dart points often manufactured on Knife River flint. This is in stark contrast to the short Besant points mainly manufactured on local lithic raw materials. As well, the Sonota phase utilized pottery, a technology not found in Besant sites. Sonota burial mounds are known along the Middle Missouri, but these are not found in Besant sites nor are they found in Sonota sites in Alberta. Most of the Sonota sites in Alberta are bison kill sites, suggesting a task-specific purpose to their foreign presence. Previous Sonota phase excursions into Wyoming suggest that this movement may have been part of a procurement or expansion strategy. The movement of the Sonota phase into southern Alberta, southwestern Saskatchewan, and Montana replaced the existing Besant phase. The Sonota phase likely shared direct ties to the preceding Outlook complex: both of these archaeological cultures exhibit traits of being intrusive onto the Canadian Plains from the Middle Missouri area.

As the Sonota phase moved into southern Alberta, the Avonlea phase was moving from northern Minnesota into south-central Saskatchewan. Climate for this period was wetter and cooler, providing a good environment for bison. A number of sites indicate that people of the Sonota and Avonlea phases co-occupied campsites in Manitoba, Saskatchewan, and ultimately Alberta. It is tempting to suggest that the Avonlea phase was "piggybacking" on the preceding Sonota phase movement. While Sonota people controlled the very southernmost Canadian plains, Avonlea people spread to the adjacent area and filled in the void left behind as Sonota moved west. The Avonlea phase was present in Alberta between 1,350 and 1,100 years ago. It produced small, finely crafted, side-notched arrow points. Lithic raw materials tended to be procured locally except when the Avonlea phase is found in association with the Sonota phase. In these instances, Avonlea points were often manufactured on Knife River flint. Subsistence is more generalized in the eastern sites with an increasing focus on bison in western sites. Avonlea pottery is limited in surface treatments (parallel grooved, net/fabric impressed, and plain) and is generally conoidal. Researchers have provided strong arguments that stylistically link it to pottery in Minnesota. Some of the most recent Avonlea pottery has shoulders, a trait common in

Old Women's pottery. The finely crafted points and restricted vessel forms suggest a highly structured kin system or craft specialization. Avonlea burials tend to be interments under cairns, harkening an eastern origin for the cultural pattern. The time-transgressive movement of Avonlea sites from east to west, the burial pattern, and the evidence for an eastern origin of the pottery leave little doubt of an eastern origin for the Avonlea phase.

About 1,100 years ago, a number of sites exhibit traits of both Avonlea and Old Women's sites. Avonlea and Cayley Series points co-occur in campsite and kill site deposits in southern Alberta, southern Saskatchewan, and north-central Montana. The shouldered pottery vessels that appeared in late Avonlea sites are common in Old Women's sites. The range of variability in Cayley Series points and Saskatchewan Basin Complex: Late Variant pottery is substantial. The strict filters that produced the structured Avonlea points and pottery broke down and came to be represented by the more heterogeneous Old Women's materials. The rigid social structures of the people of the Avonlea phase were slowly reconsidered in the face of the harsh Plains environment in favour of a more fluid band structure. The result was the in situ development of the Old Women's phase, which exhibits heterogeneous point and pottery forms. Interestingly, it was approximately 1,050 years ago that the cool and wet period that Avonlea enjoyed began to fail and a more unpredictable environment of drought and plenty was established for the next 1,000 years. This environmental change placed tremendous stress on the Avonlea phase in terms of its internal social relationships and subsistence practices.

The Old Women's phase existed on the southern Alberta plains between 1,100 and 250 years ago. Like their ancestors represented by the Avonlea phase, the people in the Old Women's phase continued a strong tradition of bison hunting, tipi camps, and utilization of local lithic raw materials. A number of features and artifacts attributed to the Old Women's phase are recognized as traditionally used by the Blackfoot. Iniskim or buffalo stones, burial lodge medicine wheels (types 3 and 4), and human boulder outline/Napi figures provide archaeological links between the Old Women's phase and the Blackfoot people. Given the Old Women's-Avonlea relationship, of particular importance are some linguistic studies that suggest the Blackfoot had their origins at the west end of the Great Lakes, which is roughly the area where the Avonlea phase originated. The Old Women's phase came under increasing pressure from the east by the time of the Mortlach phase; many scholars believe this latter archaeological entity was ancestral to the Assiniboine. There are increasing lines of evidence for linking historically known Native groups of people with archaeologically recorded sets of material culture.

At about five hundred years ago, intrusive people apparently arrived. The Highwood phase exhibits Late Side-notched points often manufactured on exotic raw materials such as porcellanite, obsidian, and Madison Formation cherts. These points are typically well crafted with unusual basal notches or spurs. Pottery associated with the phase is often flat-based and vase-like in form. Few sites of this kind are known from Alberta, but their age correlates well with oral tradition of the Blackfoot being forced north by the "Snake." A number of researchers have attributed Snake material to the Shoshone, based on its distribution and spread.

The overlap between the Old Women's phase and the Protohistoric Old Women's phase is undeniable. The projectile point and pottery forms remain the same. Trade items, however, are recovered from these otherwise Old Women's sites. Owing to the use of horses, the settlement pattern appears to concentrate more around water bodies than for the preceding period. Iniskim and burial lodges recovered from the Old Women's phase are also recovered from the Protohistoric Old Women's phase and overlap with traits known amongst the historic Blackfoot. The Blackfoot are a classic band-oriented society. The fluid nature of band structure is reflected in the heterogeneous point and pottery forms of the Old Women's phase.

Despite the presence of the Protohistoric Old Women's phase on the Alberta plains, the One Gun phase arrived about two hundred years ago. The One Gun phase is mainly represented by the Cluny fortified location along the Bow River. Researchers agree that the pottery exhibits traits similar to those found to the southeast. The settlement type and artifacts also suggest ties to the southeast. Again, population pressure, perhaps even the spread of disease with the arrival of Europeans, encouraged westward movement. In a few late Protohistoric Old Women's sites some of the pottery exhibits the traits observed at the Cluny site. The intruders were likely overwhelmed and wiped out by the local forces, with the survivors enculturated into the local group.

REFERENCES

AABERG, STEPHEN A., LESLIE B. DAVIS, GLEN G. FREDLUND, LINDA SCOTT CUMMINGS, AND KATHRYN PUSEMAN

1996 Barton Gulch Site Geochronology and Paleoecology. *Current Research in the Pleistocene* 13:85–87.

AABERG, STEPHEN A., WILLIAM P. ECKERLE, AND KENNETH P. CANNON

2003 Cree Crossing (24PH3396): The Cultural and Palaeoenvironmental Record. *Archaeology in Montana* 44(1):1–72.

ADAMS, GARY F.

1975 The Bakken-Wright Site: A Multicomponent Bison Kill in Southwestern Saskatchewan. In *Salvage Contributions: Prairie Provinces*, edited by Roscoe Wilmeth, pp. 133–199. Archaeological Survey of Canada Paper No. 33. National Museum of Man Mercury Series, National Museums of Canada, Ottawa.

1976 *Prehistoric Survey of the Lower Red Deer River, 1975*. Occasional Paper No. 3. Archaeological Survey, Provincial Museum of Alberta, Edmonton.

1977 *The Estuary Bison Pound Site in Southwestern Saskatchewan*. Archaeological Survey of Canada Paper No. 88. National Museum of Man Mercury Series, National Museums of Canada, Ottawa.

1978 *Tipi Rings in Southern Alberta: The Alkali Creek Sites*. Occasional Paper No. 9. Archaeological Survey of Alberta, Edmonton.

ADOVASIO, J.M., AND D.R. PEDLER

1997 Monte Verde and the Antiquity of Humankind in the Americas. *Antiquity* 71:573–80.

AGENBROAD, LARRY D.

1978a *The Hudson-Meng Site: An Alberta Bison Kill in the Nebraska High Plains*. University Press of America, Washington, D.C.

1978b Cody Knives and the Cody Complex in Plains Prehistory: A Reassessment. *Plains Anthropologist* 23(80):159–161.

AGOGINO, GEORGE A.

1969 The Midland Complex: Is It Valid? *American Anthropologist (new series)* 71(6):1117–1118.

AGOGINO, GEORGE A., AND AL PARRISH

1971 The Fowler-Parrish Site: A Folsom Campsite in Eastern Colorado. *Plains Anthropologist* 16(52):111–114.

AGOGINO, GEORGE A., AND EUGENE GALLOWAY

1965 The Sister's Hill Site: A Hell Gap Site in North-central Wyoming. *Plains Anthropologist* 10(29):190–195.

AHLER, STANLEY A., AND MICHAEL MCGONIGAL

2001 Agate Basin at Beacon Island, North Dakota. *Current Research in the Pleistocene* 18:1–3.

AHLER, STANLEY A., AND PHIL R. GEIB

2000 Why Flute? Folsom Point Design and Adaptation. *Journal of Archaeological Science* 27:799–820.

AMICK, DANIEL S.

1996 Regional Patterns of Folsom Mobility and Land Use in the American Southwest. *World Archaeology* 27(3):411–426.

AMUNDSON, LESLIE J.

1986 The Amisk Site: A Multicomponent Campsite in South-central Saskatchewan. Unpublished Master's thesis, Department of Anthropology and Archaeology, University of Saskatchewan, Saskatoon.

AMUNDSON, LESLIE J., AND DAVID MEYER

2003 Late-Plano Occupation at the St. Louis Site (FfNk 7), Central Saskatchewan. *Current Research in the Pleistocene* 20:1–2.

APLAND, B.C.

1981 *Historical Resources Impact Mitigation of Sites EeOu-5 and EeOm-15 Along the Alaska Highway Gas Pipeline (Alberta Zone 6, the Eastern Leg): Final Report, Permit 80-139*. Archaeological Survey of Alberta. Permit No. 80-139. Copies available from Archaeological Survey of Alberta, Edmonton.

ARNOLD, THOMAS G.

1985 A Comparison of Plano Complexes. Unpublished Master's thesis, Department of Archaeology, University of Calgary, Calgary.

BALL, BRUCE F.

1986a Radiocarbon Dates from the Belly Burial Site (DhPj-69). In *Archaeology in Alberta 1985*, edited by J. Ives, pp. 207–210. Occasional Paper No. 29. Archaeological Survey of Alberta, Edmonton.

1986b Site Classification and Prehistoric Settlement Systems in the Upper Athabasca River Valley. In *Eastern Slopes Prehistory: Selected Papers*, edited by Brian Ronaghan, pp. 133–159. Occasional Paper No. 30. Archaeological Survey of Alberta, Edmonton.

1987 The Pincher Creek Buffalo Jump: A Late Prehistoric Bison Kill Site. In *Archaeology in Alberta 1986*, edited by Martin Magne, pp. 31–43. Occasional Paper No. 31. Archaeological Survey of Alberta, Edmonton.

BALL, BRUCE F., AND OWEN BEATTIE

1987 *The Folkins Lake Burial Site (FeOm-1), Permit 86-057*. Archaeological Survey of Alberta. Permit No. 86-057. Copies available from Archaeological Survey of Alberta, Edmonton.

BAMFORTH, DOUGLAS B.

1991a Flintknapping Skill, Communal Hunting, and Paleoindian Projectile Point Typology. *Plains Anthropologist* 36(137):309–322.

1991b Population Dispersion and Paleoindian Technology at the Allen Site. In *Raw Material Economies Among Prehistoric Hunter-Gatherers*, edited by Anta Montet-White and Steven Holen, pp. 357–374. Publications in Anthropology No. 19. University of Kansas, Lawrence.

BARBOUR, E.H., AND C. BERTRAND SCHULTZ

1932 *The Scottsbluff Bison Quarry and Its Artifacts*. Bulletin 34, Vol. 1, Nebraska State Museum, Lincoln.

BARRY, PATRICIA S.

1991 *Mystical Themes in Milk River Rock Art*. University of Alberta Press, Edmonton.

BEAUDOIN, ALWYNNE B.

1987 Alberta Radiocarbon Dates, 1982–1986. In *Archaeology in Alberta 1986*, edited by Martin Magne, pp. 197–213, Occasional Paper No. 31. Archaeological Survey of Alberta, Edmonton.

BEAUDOIN, ALWYNNE B., AND DONALD S. LEMMEN

2000 Late Quaternary History and Geoarchaeology of Southeastern Alberta and Southwestern Saskatchewan. Field-trip Guidebook No. 3. GeoCanada, Calgary.

BEAUDOIN, ALWYNNE B., AND GERALD A. OETELAAR

2003 The Changing Ecophysical Landscape of Southern Alberta During the Late Pleistocene and Early Holocene. *Plains Anthropologist* 48(187):187–207.

2006 The Day the Dry Snow Fell: The Record of a 7,627-Year-Old Disaster. In *Alberta Formed, Alberta Transformed*, edited by Michael Payne, Donald Wetherell, and Catherine Cavanaugh, pp. 37–53. University of Calgary Press, Calgary.

BEAUDOIN, ALWYNNE, MILT WRIGHT, AND BRIAN RONAGHAN

1996 Late Quaternary Landscape History and Archaeology in the "Ice-free Corridor": Some Recent Results from Alberta. *Quaternary International* 32:113–126.

BEMENT, LELAND C.

1997 The Cooper Site: A Stratified Folsom Bison Kill in Oklahoma. In *Southern Plains Bison Procurement and Utilization from Paleoindian to Historic*, edited by Leland C. Bement and Kent J. Buehler. Memoir 29, *Plains Anthropologist* 42(159):85–100.

References

BENEDICT, J.B., AND B.L. OLSON

1973 Origin of the McKean Complex: Evidence from Timberline. *Plains Anthropologist* 18(61):323–327.

BEREZIUK, DARRYL A.

2001 The Smuland Creek Site and Implications for Palaeoindian Site Prospection in the Peace Region of Northwestern Alberta. In *Sovremeniye Problemiy Evraziyskovo Paleolitovedeniya*, edited by A.P. Derevianko and G.I. Medvedev, pp. 382–402. Institute of Archaeology and Ethnology, Novosibirsk, Russia.

BILLECK, WILLIAM T.

1998 Fluted Point Distribution in the Loess Hills of Southwestern Iowa. *Plains Anthropologist* 43(166):401–409.

BLACK, KEVIN D.

1991 Archaic Continuity in the Colorado Rockies: The Mountain Tradition. *Plains Anthropologist* 36(133):1–29.

BLACKMAR, JEANETTE M.

2001 Regional Variability in Clovis, Folsom, and Cody Land Use. *Plains Anthropologist* 46(175):65–94.

BLACKMAR, JEANETTE M., AND JACK L. HOFMAN

1997 Cody-Complex Artifacts in Oklahoma. *Current Research in the Pleistocene* 14:9–11.

BLAKESLEE, DONALD J.

1994 Reassessment of Some Radiocarbon Dates from the Central Plains. *Plains Anthropologist* 39(148):203–210.

BLAIKIE, KURTIS

2005 Investigations at FaOm-1: The Bodo Bison Skulls Site. Unpublished Master's thesis, Department of Anthropology, University of Alberta, Edmonton.

BLISS, WESLEY L.

1950 Birdshead Cave: A Stratified Site in Wind River Basin, Wyoming. *American Antiquity* 3:187–196.

BOLDURIAN, ANTHONY T.

1990 Lithic Technology at the Mitchell Locality of Blackwater Draw: A Stratified Folsom Site in Eastern New Mexico. Memoir 24, *Plains Anthropologist* 35(130):1–105.

1991 Folsom Mobility and Organization of Lithic Technology: A View from Blackwater Draw, New Mexico. *Plains Anthropologist* 36(137):281–295.

BOLDURIAN, ANTHONY T., AND SUSANNE M. HUBINSKY

1994 Preforms in Folsom Lithic Technology: A View from Blackwater Draw, New Mexico. *Plains Anthropologist* 39(150):445–464.

BONNICHSEN, B. ROBSON, AND JAMES D. KEYSER

1982 Three Small Points: A Cody Complex Problem. *Plains Anthropologist* 27(96):137–144.

BONNICHSEN, B. ROBSON, MARVIN BEATTY, MORT D. TURNER, JOANNE TURNER, AND DIANE DOUGLAS

1992 Paleoindian Lithic Procurement at the South Fork of Everson Creek, Southwestern Montana. In *Ice Age Hunters of the Rockies*, edited by Dennis J. Stanford and Jane S. Day, pp. 285–322. Denver Museum of Natural History and University Press of Colorado, Niwot.

BOYD, MATTHEW

2000 Changing Physical and Ecological Landscapes in Southwestern Manitoba in Relation to Folsom (11,000–10,000) and McKean (4,000–3,000) Site Distributions. *Prairie Forum* 25(1):23–44.

BOYD, MATTHEW, GARRY LEONARD RUNNING IV, AND KAREN HAVHOLM

2003 Paleoecology and Geochronology of Glacial Lake Hind During the Pleistocene-Holocene Transition: A Context for Folsom Surface Finds on the Canadian Prairies. *Geoarchaeology: An International Journal* 18(6):538–607.

BRADLEY, BRUCE A.

1993 Paleo-Indian Flaked Stone Technology in the North American High Plains. In *From Kostenki to Clovis: Upper Paleolithic—Paleo-Indian Adaptations*, edited by Olga Soffer and N.D. Praslov, pp. 251–262. Plenum Press, New York.

BRADLEY, BRUCE A., AND GEORGE C. FRISON

1987 Projectile Points and Specialized Bifaces from the Horner Site. In *The Horner Site: The Type Site of the Cody Cultural Complex*, edited by George C. Frison and Lawrence Todd, pp. 199–231. Academic Press, New York.

BRADLEY, BRUCE A., AND DENNIS STANFORD

1987 The Claypool Study. In *The Horner Site: The Type Site of the Cody Cultural Complex*, edited by George C. Frison and Lawrence Todd, pp. 405–434. Academic Press, New York.

BRADY, TAMI

2004 *Historical Resources Impact Assessment, EOG Resources Canada Inc., Rattlesnake 2004 Pipeline, Township 12, Range 10, W4M: Final Report. Permit 04-423.* Archaeological Survey of Alberta. Permit No. 04-423. Copies available from Alberta Archaeological Survey, Edmonton.

BREWER, GARY, REBECCA BALCOM, AND TOM HOFFERT

1995 *Pine Coulee Reservoir Historical Resources Impact Mitigation, Vol. 1: Final Report, Permit 93-083.* Archaeological Survey of Alberta. Permit No. 93-083. Copies available from Archaeological Survey of Alberta, Edmonton.

BRINK, JACK

1979 Excavations at Writing-On-Stone. In *Archaeology in Southern Alberta*. Occasional Paper No. 12. Archaeological Survey of Alberta, Edmonton.

BRINK, JACK, AND STUART J. BALDWIN

1988 The Highwood River Site: A Pelican Lake Phase Burial from the Alberta Plains. *Canadian Journal of Archaeology* 12:109–136.

BRINK, JACK, AND ROBERT DAWE

1989 *Final Report of the 1985 and 1986 Field Season at Head-Smashed-In Buffalo Jump, Alberta.* Manuscript Series No. 16. Archaeological Survey of Alberta, Edmonton.

BRINK, J., M. WRIGHT, B. DAWE, AND D. GLAUM

1986 *Final Report of the 1984 Season at Head-Smashed-In Buffalo Jump, Alberta.* Manuscript Series No. 9. Archaeological Survey of Alberta, Edmonton.

BRINK, JACK, ROBERT J. DAWE, AND SUSAN E. MARSHALL

1987 Preliminary Report on the 1986 Field Season at Head-Smashed-In and Calderwood Buffalo Jumps. In *Archaeology in Alberta 1986*, edited by Martin Magne, pp. 44–78. Occasional Paper No. 31. Archaeological Survey of Alberta, Edmonton.

BROWN, R.M., H.R. ANDREWS, G.C. BALLS, N. BURN, Y. IMAHORI, AND J.C.D. MILTON

1983 Accelerator ^{14}C Dating of the Taber Child. *Canadian Journal of Archaeology* 7(2):233–237.

BRUMLEY, JOHN H.

1972 *The 1972 Suffield Military Reserve: Preliminary Results.* Archaeological Survey of Alberta. CRM 17. Copies available from Archaeological Survey of Alberta, Edmonton.

1974 Report on Test Excavations at the DesRosier Site (24ME1002). *Archaeology in Montana* 15(3):1–21.

1975 *The Cactus Flower Site in Southeastern Alberta: 1972–1974 Excavations.* Archaeological Survey of Canada Paper No. 46. National Museum of Man Mercury Series, National Museums of Canada, Ottawa.

1976 *Ramillies: A Late Prehistoric Bison Kill and Campsite Located in Southeastern Alberta, Canada.* Archaeological Survey of Canada Paper No. 55. National Museum of Man Mercury Series, National Museums of Canada, Ottawa.

1978 McKean Complex Subsistence and Hunting Strategies in the Southern Alberta Plains. In *Bison Procurement and Utilization: A Symposium*, edited by Leslie B. Davis and Michael Wilson. Memoir 14, *Plains Anthropologist* 23(82, pt. 2):175–193.

1981 *Results of Salvage Excavations at the Southridge Site, EaOq 17, Permit 79-151*. Archaeological Survey of Alberta. Permit No. 79-151. Copies available from Archaeological Survey of Alberta, Edmonton.

1982 A Description and Discussion of the Gilchrist Site, DgOu 29, in Writing-On-Stone Locality of South Central Alberta. In *Archaeology in Alberta 1981*, edited by Jack Brink, pp. 123–149. Occasional Paper No. 19. Archaeological Survey of Alberta, Edmonton.

1985 The Ellis Site (EcOp 4): A Late Prehistoric Burial Lodge/Medicine Wheel Site in Southeastern Alberta. In *Contributions to Plains Prehistory*, edited by David Burley, pp. 180–232. Occasional Paper No. 26. Archaeological Survey of Alberta, Edmonton.

1988 *Medicine Wheels on the Northern Plains: A Summary and Appraisal*. Manuscript Series No. 12. Archaeological Survey of Alberta, Edmonton.

1990 Investigations at Herdegen's Birdtail Butte Site (24BL1152). *Archaeology in Montana* 31(1):17–86.

1991 Investigations at the Meissner Ranch Site (24HL188). *Archaeology in Montana* 32(1):39–54.

1995 *Prehistoric Settlement and Subsistence in the Plains of Southern Alberta and Northern Montana: The Seasonality Evidence*. Archaeological Survey of Alberta. Consultants Report (Ethos Consulting Ltd.) for Alberta Publics Works, Supply and Services. Copies available from Archaeological Survey of Alberta, Edmonton.

BRUMLEY, JOHN H., AND BARRY J. DAU

1987 *Historical Resource Investigations Within the Forty Mile Coulee Reservoir: Data Summaries, Part 1 of 4*. Archaeological Survey of Alberta. Permit No. 86-020. Copies available from Archaeological Survey of Alberta, Edmonton.

1988 *Historical Resource Investigations Within the Forty Mile Coulee Reservoir*. Manuscript Series No. 13. Archaeological Survey of Alberta, Edmonton.

BRUMLEY, JOHN H., BARRY J. DAU, AND L. HEIKKILA

1983 *1976 to 1980 Salvage Investigations on the Suffield Military Reserve, Alberta*. 3 vols. Archaeological Survey of Alberta. Submitted for the Alberta Energy Company, Inc. CRM 23. Archaeological Survey of Alberta, Edmonton.

BRUMLEY, JOHN H., AND PATRICK J. RENNIE

1995 A Culture History Model for the Plains of Northern Montana and Surrounding Regions. Manuscript on file, Ethos Consulting, Havre, Montana.

1999 The King Site Along the Eastern Margin of the Little Rocky Mountains. *Archaeology in Montana* 40(1):31–106.

2005 Chasing Ancient Shadows: A Culture History Model for the Northwestern Plains. Manuscript on file, Ethos Consulting, Havre, Montana.

BRUMLEY, JOHN H., AND CAROL RUSHWORTH

1983 A Summary and Appraisal of Alberta Radiocarbon Dates. In *Archaeology in Alberta 1982*, edited by D. Burley, pp. 142–160. Occasional Paper No. 21. Archaeological Survey of Alberta, Edmonton.

BRUMLEY, JOHN H., AND GORDON K. WILLIS

1977 *An Archaeological Inventory of the Suffield Military Reserve, Alberta*. CRM 19. Copies available from Archaeological Survey of Alberta, Edmonton.

BRYAN, ALAN

2000 *The Lindoe Site, Southeastern Alberta*. Non-permit. Archaeological Survey of Alberta, Edmonton.

BRYAN, ALAN, AND RUTH GRUHN

2007 A Revised Chronology for the Varsity Estates Sites, Calgary, Alberta. *Canadian Journal of Archaeology* 31:79–103.

BRYANT, LAUREEN MARIE

2002 A Reanalysis of the Long Creek Site: Forty-five Years After the Excavation. Unpublished Master's thesis, Department of Anthropology and Archaeology, University of Saskatchewan, Saskatoon.

2007 *Reanalysis of the Long Creek Site: Forty-five Years After the Excavation.* Occasional Papers of the Archaeological Society of Alberta No. 8. Archaeological Society of Alberta, Calgary.

BUBEL, SHAWN

2007 *Interim Report, Permits 2004-123 and 2006-153, for the Fincastle Bison Kill Site (DlOx 5), Southwestern Alberta.* Archaeological Survey of Alberta. Permit Nos. 2004-123 and 2006-153. Copies available from Archaeological Survey of Alberta, Edmonton.

BUCHANAN, BRIGGS

2002 Folsom Lithic Procurement, Tool Use, and Replacement at the Lake Theo Site, Texas. *Plains Anthropologist* 47(181):121–146.

BUCHANAN, BRIGGS, AND MARK COLLARD

2007 Investigating the Peopling of North America Through Cladistic Analyses of Early Palaeoindian Projectile Points. *Journal of Anthropological Archaeology* 26:366–393.

BUCHNER, ANTHONY P.

1979 *The 1978 Caribou Lake Project, Including a Summary of the Prehistory of East-central Manitoba.* Papers in Manitoba Archaeology, Final Report No. 8. Department of Cultural Affairs and Historical Resources, Historic Resources Branch, Winnipeg.

1981a *Sinnock: A Palaeolithic Camp and Kill Site in Manitoba.* Papers in Manitoba Archaeology, Final Report No. 10. Department of Cultural Affairs and Historical Resources, Historic Resources Branch, Winnipeg.

1981b The Oxbow Complex and the Anomalous Winter Hypothesis. *Canadian Journal of Archaeology* 5:137–144.

1988 The Geochronology of the Lockport Site. *Manitoba Archaeology Quarterly* 12(2):27–31.

BUCKMASTER, M.M., AND J.R. PAQUETTE

1988 The Gorto Site: Preliminary Report on a Late Paleo-Indian Site in Marquette County, Michigan. *The Wisconsin Archaeologist* 69(3):101–124.

BUPP, SUSAN L.

1981 The Willow Springs Bison Pound: 48AB130. Unpublished Master's thesis, Department of Anthropology, University of Wyoming, Laramie.

BUTLER, B. ROBERT

1968 *A Guide to Understanding Idaho Archaeology, 2nd (Revised) Edition.* A Special Publication of the Idaho State University Museum, Pocatello, Idaho.

BYRNE WILLIAM J.

1973 *The Archaeology and Prehistory of Southern Alberta as Reflected by Ceramics.* Archaeological Survey of Canada Paper No. 14. National Museum of Man Mercury Series, National Museums of Canada, Ottawa.

1978 A Demonstration of Migration on the Northern Great Plains. In *Archaeological Essays in Honor of Irving B. Rouse*, edited by Robert C. Dunnell and Edwin S. Hall Jr., pp. 247–273. Mouton Publishers, New York.

CALDER, JAMES M.

1977 *The Majorville Cairn and Medicine Wheel Site, Alberta.* Archaeological Survey of Canada Paper No. 62. National Museum of Man Mercury Series, National Museums of Canada, Ottawa.

CAMPBELL, JOHN MARTIN

1956 A Folsom Site in Idaho. *Plains Anthropologist* 6:1–2.

CARLSON, GAYLE F., JOHN R. BOZELL, TERRY L. STEINACHER, MAJORIE BROOKS LOVVORN, AND GEORGE W. GILL

1999 The Sidney Burial: A Middle Plains Archaic Mortuary Site from Western Nebraska. *Plains Anthropologist* 44(168):105–119.

CARLSON, MURIEL

1993 *Collections Can Speak for Themselves: A Regional Profile of Paleo-Indian Lithics from West-Central Saskatchewan, as Viewed from Local Collections, Permit #89-10.* Saskatchewan Heritage Branch. Permit No. 1989-10. Copies available from Saskatchewan Heritage Branch, Regina.

CARLSON, ROY L.

1991 Clovis from the Perspective of the Ice-Free Corridor. In *Clovis: Origins and Adaptations*, edited by Robson Bonnichsen and Karen Turnmire, pp. 81–90. Center for the Study of the First Americans, Department of Anthropology, University of Oregon, Corvallis.

1994 Early Cultural Traditions in British Columbia West of the Rocky Mountains. *Current Research in the Pleistocene* 11:123–125.

CARLSON, ROY L, AND MARTIN P.R. MAGNE (EDITORS)

2008 *Projectile Point Sequences in Northwestern North America*. Publication No. 35. Archaeology Press, Simon Fraser University, Burnaby, British Columbia.

CASSELLS, E. STEVE

1986 *Prehistoric Hunters of the Black Hills*. Johnson Publishing Company, Boulder, Colorado.

CHISHOLM, BRIAN, JONATHAN DRIVER, SYLVAIN DUBE, AND HENRY P. SCHWARCZ

1986 Assessment of Prehistoric Bison Foraging and Movement Patterns via Stable-carbon Isotopic Analysis. *Plains Anthropologist* 31(113):193–205.

CHLACHULA, JIRI

1994a Varsity Estates: A Palaeo-American Site in Southwestern Alberta, Canada (1990–1992 Investigation). *Anthropologie* XXXII(2):101–127.

1994b A Paleo-American (Pre-Clovis) Settlement in Alberta. *Current Research in the Pleistocene* 11:21–23.

1996 Geology and Quaternary Environments of the First Preglacial Palaeolithic Sites Found in Alberta, Canada. *Quaternary Science Review* 15:285–313.

CHLACHULA, JIRI, AND LOUISE LESLIE

2001 Preglacial Archaeological Evidence at Grimshaw, the Peace River Area, Alberta: Reply. *Canadian Journal of Earth Sciences* 38:875–878.

CHOMKO, STEPHEN A.

1990 Chronometric Dates from Eagle Shelter, Big Horn County, Wyoming. *Archaeology in Montana* 31(2):51–58.

CINQ-MARS, JEAN

1979 Bluefish Cave I: A Late Pleistocene Eastern Beringian Cave Deposit in the Northern Yukon. *Canadian Journal of Archaeology* 3:1–32.

CLARK, DONALD W.

1984 Northern Fluted Points: Paleo-Eskimos, Paleo-Arctic, or Paleo-Indian. *Canadian Journal of Anthropology* 4(1):65–81.

CLARK, DONALD W., AND MCFADYEN CLARKE

1983 Paleo-Indians and Fluted Points: Subarctic Alternatives. *Plains Anthropologist* 28(102): 283–292.

CLARKE, GERALD R., AND MICHAEL WILSON

1981 The Ayers-Frazier Bison Trap (24PE30): A Late Middle Period Bison Kill on the Lower Yellowstone River. *Archaeology in Montana* 22(1):23–77.

CLARKE, GRANT M.

1995 The Hartley Site (FaNp 19): Interpreting a Transitional Avonlea/Old Women's Faunal Assemblage. Unpublished Master's thesis, Department of Archaeology, University of Saskatoon, Saskatoon.

2000 *Alberta Ethane Gathering System (AEGS), East Leg, Historical Resources Impact Mitigation, Permit 99-122*. Archaeological Survey of Alberta. Permit No. 1999-122. Copies available from Archaeological Survey of Alberta, Edmonton.

CLARKE, GRANT, BEN HJERMSTAD, REBECCA BALCOM, TOM HOFFERT, AND JAMES LIGHT

1998 *Historical Resources Impact Mitigation of EgPs 63 and EgPt 28, the Pigeon Mountain Site, Permit #95-077*. Archaeological Survey of Alberta. Permit No. 1995-077. Copies available from Archaeological Survey of Alberta, Edmonton.

CLOUTIER, RIEL

2004 Testing Contemporaneity: The Avonlea and Besant Complexes on the Northern Plains. Unpublished Master's thesis, Department of Archaeology, University of Saskatchewan, Saskatoon.

CORBEIL, MARCEL

1995 The Archaeology and Taphonomy of the Heron Eden Site, Southwestern Saskatchewan. Unpublished Master's thesis, Department of Anthropology and Archaeology, University of Saskatchewan, Saskatoon.

CROWE-SWORDS, D.B., AND MARGARET G. HANNA

1980 *EfPm 27: Report on the 1979 Excavations*. Archaeological Survey of Alberta. Permit No. 1979-55. Copies available from Archaeological Survey of Alberta, Edmonton.

DAMKJAR, ERIC

1995 *Final Report of the 1991 and 1992 Mitigative Excavations at Head-Smashed-In Buffalo Jump (DkPj-1) and Dersch Site (DkPj 35)*. Archaeological Survey of Alberta. Permit No. 1992-022. Copies available from Archaeological Survey of Alberta, Edmonton.

DAU, BARRY J.

1993 *Oldman River Dam Prehistoric Archaeology Mitigation Programme, Technical Series No. 3: Stone Features Study, ASA Permits 88-34, 89-42, 90-18*. Archaeological Survey of Alberta. CRM 110. Copies available from Archaeological Survey of Alberta, Edmonton.

2005 *Oldman River Dam Stone Features Study, Prehistoric Archaeology Mitigation Programme, Technical Series*. Occasional Papers of the Archaeological Society of Alberta No. 6. Archaeological Society of Alberta, Calgary.

DAU, BARRY J., AND JOHN H. BRUMLEY

1987 *Historical Resource Investigations Within the Forty Mile Coulee Reservoir*. Archaeological Survey of Alberta. Permit No. 1986-020. Copies available from Archaeological Survey of Alberta, Edmonton.

DAVIS, LESLIE B.

1966 Avonlea Point Occurrence in Northern Montana and Canada. *Plains Anthropologist* 11:100–116.

1976 The Dodge Site (24RB1225): A McKean Phase Lithic "Cache" in the Tongue River Valley. *Archaeology in Montana* 17(1 and 2):35–51.

1986 Age and Source Analysis for Obsidian Hell Gap Complex Artifacts in the Montana Rockies. *Current Research in the Pleistocene* 3:27–28.

1988 Paleoindian Tradition Fluted Points in Montana. *Current Research in the Pleistocene* 5:25–27.

1993 Paleo-Indian Archaeology in the High Plains and Rocky Mountains of Montana. In *From Kostenki to Clovis: Upper Paleolithic — Paleo-Indian Adaptations*, edited by Olga Soffer and N.D. Praslov, pp. 263–277. Plenum Press, New York.

DAVIS, LESLIE B., JOHN P. ALBANESE, LINDA SCOTT CUMMINGS, AND JOHN W. FISHER, JR.

1991 Reappraisal of the MacHaffie Site Paleoindian Occupational Sequence. *Current Research in the Pleistocene* 8:17–20.

DAVIS, LESLIE, AND STEPHEN A. AABERG

1988 Early Paleoindian Site Reconnaissance in the Lower Yellowstone Badlands Area, Southwestern Montana. *Current Research in the Pleistocene* 5:7–8.

DAVIS, LESLIE, STEPHEN A. AABERG, WILLIAM P. ECKERLE, JOHN W. FISHER, JR., AND SALLY T. GREISER

1989 Montane Paleoindian Occupation of the Barton Gulch Site, Ruby Valley, Southwestern Montana. *Current Research in the Pleistocene* 6:7–9.

DAVIS, LESLIE B., AND MARK F. BAUMLER

2000 Clovis and Folsom Occupations at Indian Creek. *Current Research in the Pleistocene* 17:17–19.

DAVIS, LESLIE B., AND JOHN W. FISHER, JR.

1988 Avonlea Predation on Wintering Plains Pronghorns. In *Avonlea Yesterday and Today:*

Archaeology and Prehistory, edited by Leslie Davis, pp. 101–118. Saskatchewan Archaeological Society, Saskatoon.

DAVIS, LESLIE, B., JOHN W. FISHER, JR., MICHAEL C. WILSON, STEPHEN A. CHOMKO, AND RICHARD E. MORLAN

2000 Avonlea Phase Winter Fare at Lost Terrace, Upper Missouri River Valley of Montana: The Vertebrate Fauna. In *Pronghorn Past and Present: Archaeology, Ethnology, and Biology*, edited by Jana V. Pastor and Patrick M. Lubinski. Memoir 32, *Plains Anthropologist* 45(174):53–69.

DAVIS, LESLIE B., AND SALLY GREISER

1992 Indian Creek Paleoindians: Early Occupation of the Elkhorn Mountains' Southeast Flank, West-Central Montana. In *Ice Age Hunters of the Rockies*, edited by Dennis J. Stanford and Jane S. Day, pp. 225–284. Denver Museum of Natural History and University Press of Colorado, Niwot.

DAVIS, LESLIE B., AND EMMETT STALLCOP

1965 *The Keaster Site (24PH401): A Stratified Bison Kill Occupation in the Missouri Breaks Area of North Central Montana*. Montana Archaeological Society Memoir No. 2.

1966 *The Wahkpa Chu'gn Site (24HL101): Late Hunters in the Milk River Valley, Montana*. Montana Archaeological Society Memoir No. 3.

DAVIS, LESLIE B., AND CHARLES D. ZEIER

1978 Multi-Phase Late Period Bison Procurement at the Antonsen Site, Southwestern Montana. In *Bison Procurement and Utilization: A Symposium*, edited by Leslie B. Davis and Michael C. Wilson. Memoir 14, *Plains Anthropologist* 23(82, pt. 2):222–235.

DAWE, ROBERT J.

1987 The Triangular Projectile Point in Plains Prehistory: A Preform Trade Hypothesis. In *Archaeology in Alberta 1986*, edited by Martin Magne, pp. 150–162. Occasional Paper No. 31. Archaeological Survey of Alberta, Edmonton.

1997 A Unique Fluted Point from the Grande Prairie Region. *Alberta Archaeological Review* 25:12–14.

2004 The Cody Complex in Alberta. Manuscript on file, Royal Alberta Museum, Edmonton.

DAWSON, SHEILA M., AND ERNEST G. WALKER

1988 The Bethune Site: An Avonlea Burial from Saskatchewan. *Saskatchewan Archaeology* 9:3–14.

DE GUZMAN, MARGARITA

2008 Excavations at EhPo 78: A Multicomponent Campsite within the Cochrane Ranche Provincial Historic Resource Site. *Alberta Archaeological Review* 48:6–9.

DELLING, MARILYN POWELL

1966 A Folsom Point from Boone County, Missouri. *Plains Anthropologist* 11(33):235.

DE MILLE, CHRISTY, AND THOMAS HEAD

2001 *Final Report, Historical Resources Mitigation, Stonepine Residential Community Development Portions of NE Sec. 1 and SE Sec. 12, Township 24, Range 3, W5M, ASA Permit No. 98-052*. Archaeological Survey of Alberta. Permit No. 1998-052. Copies available from Archaeological Survey of Alberta, Edmonton.

DEMPSEY, HUGH A.

1956 Stone Medicine Wheels — Memorials to Blackfoot War Chiefs. *Journal of the Washington Academy of Sciences* 46(6):177–182.

1994 *The Amazing Death of Calf Shirt and Other Blackfoot Stories*. Fifth House Publishers, Saskatoon.

DOLL, MAURICE F.V.

1982 *The Boss Hill Site (FdPe 4) Locality 2: Pre-Archaic Manifestations in the Parkland of Central Alberta, Canada*. Occasional Paper No. 2. Human History, Provincial Museum of Alberta, Edmonton.

DORMAAR, JOHN F., AND ALWYNNE B. BEAUDOIN

1991 Application of Soil Chemistry to Interpret Cultural Events at the Calderwood Buffalo Jump (DkPj 27), Southern Alberta, Canada. *Geoarchaeology: An International Journal* 6(1):85–98.

DRIVER, JONATHAN C.

1976 *Report of Excavations and Survey, Crowsnest Pass 1975, Permit 75-024.* Archaeological Survey of Alberta. Permit No. 1975-024. Copies available from Archaeological Survey of Alberta, Edmonton.

1978 Holocene Man and Environments in the Crowsnest Pass, Alberta. Unpublished PhD dissertation, Department of Archaeology, University of Calgary, Calgary.

1982 Early Prehistoric Killing of Bighorn Sheep in the Southeastern Canadian Rockies. *Plains Anthropologist* 27(98, pt. 1):265–271.

1983 *DjPp-8: A Prehistoric Campsite on the Continental Divide.* Archaeological Survey of Alberta. Permit No. 1976-043. Copies available from Archaeological Survey of Alberta, Edmonton.

2001 Preglacial Archaeological Evidence at Grimshaw, the Peace River Area, Alberta: Discussion. *Canadian Journal of Earth Sciences* 38:871–874.

DUKE, PHILIP G.

1985 The Pelican Lake Phase in the Crowsnest Pass: A Locational Analysis. *Archaeology in Montana* 26 (1):1–35.

1988 Models of Cultural Process During the Avonlea Phase. In *Avonlea Yesterday and Today: Archaeology and Prehistory*, edited by Leslie B. Davis, pp. 265–271. Saskatchewan Archaeology Society, Saskatoon.

1991 *Points in Time: Structure and Event in a Late Northern Plains Hunting Society.* University Press of Colorado, Niwot.

DYCK, IAN

1970 Two Oxbow Settlement Types in Central Saskatchewan. *Napao* 2(2):1–29.

1977 The Harder Site: A Middle Period Bison Hunter's Campsite in the Northern Great Plains. Archaeological Survey of Canada Paper No. 67. National Museum of Man Mercury Series, National Museums of Canada, Ottawa.

1983 The Prehistory of Southern Saskatchewan. In *Tracking Ancient Hunters: Prehistoric Archaeology in Saskatchewan*, edited by Henry T. Epp and Ian Dyck, pp. 63–139. Saskatchewan Archaeological Society, Saskatoon.

DYCK, IAN, AND RICHARD E. MORLAN

1995 *The Sjovold Site: A River Crossing Campsite in the Northern Plains.* Mercury Series Paper No. 151. Archaeological Survey of Canada, Canadian Museum of Civilization, Hull, Quebec.

EBELL, S. BIRON

1980 *The Park Hill Site: An Agate Basin Surface Collection in South Central Saskatchewan.* Pastlog No. 4. Saskatchewan Culture and Youth, Regina.

1982 Three Paleo-Indian Bifaces from Saskatchewan. *Saskatchewan Archaeology* 3(1 and 2): 53–64.

1988 The Dunn Site. *Plains Anthropologist* 33(122):505–530.

EDMUNDS, F.H., J.L. JACKSON, J.W.T. SPINKS, AND V.A. VIGFUSSON

1938 Some Skeletal Remains in Saskatchewan. *American Antiquity* 3:244–246.

EGGAN, FRED

1955a The Cheyenne and Arapaho Kinship System. In *Social Anthropology of North American Tribes*, edited by Fred Eggan, pp. 35–95. University of Chicago Press, Chicago.

1955b Social Anthropology: Methods and Results. In *Social Anthropology of North American Tribes*, edited by Fred Eggan, pp. 483–551. University of Chicago Press, Chicago.

EPP, HENRY T.

1988 Ways of the Migrant Herds: Dual Dispersion Strategy Among Bison. *Plains Anthropologist* 33(21):309–320.

EWERS, JOHN C.

1955 *The Horse in Blackfoot Indian Culture with Comparative Material from Other Western Tribes.* Bureau of American Ethnology Bulletin 159. Smithsonian Institution Press, Washington, D.C.

FARDOE, BRIAN

1977 Initial Perceptions on Three Sites in the Oak Lake Locality Through the Orville Raymer Collection of Projectile Points. *Archae-Facts* 4(4):1–17.

FEDIRCHUK, GLORIA

1986 Two Late Prehistoric Ceramic Components at the Little Bow Site, EaPh-4. In *Archaeology in Alberta 1985*, edited by John W. Ives, pp. 91–129. Occasional Paper No. 29. Archaeological Survey of Alberta, Edmonton.

1991 *The Dersch Locality, DkPj-35, Besant Adjunct to Head-Smashed-In, Permit 89-086.* Archaeological Survey of Alberta. Permit No. 1989-086. Copies available from Archaeological Survey of Alberta, Edmonton.

FEDIRCHUK, GLORIA J, E.J. MCCULLOUGH, L.R. GORHAM, W.J. UNFREED, B.J. KULLE, E.M. GRYBA, AND L.V. HILLS

1998 *Historical Resources Impact Assessment Report, Alliance Pipeline Limited Partnership, Alliance Pipeline Project, Alberta, Permit 96-063.* Archaeological Survey of Alberta. Permit No. 1996-063. Copies available from Archaeological Survey of Alberta, Edmonton.

FEDJE, DARYL

1985 *Archaeological Investigations in Banff National Park: 1983.* Research Bulletin No. 236. Parks Canada, Ottawa.

1986 Banff Archaeology, 1983–1985. In *Eastern Slopes Prehistory: Selected Papers*, edited by Brian Ronaghan, pp. 25–62. Occasional Paper No. 30. Archaeological Survey of Alberta, Edmonton.

1988 *The Norquay and Eclipse Sites: Trans-Canada Highway Twinning Mitigation in Banff National Park.* Microfiche Report Series 395. Environment Canada, Parks Service, Ottawa.

FIEDEL, STUART J.

2000. The Peopling of the New World: Present Evidence, New Theories, and Future Directions. *Journal of Archaeological Research* 8(1):39–103.

FINNIGAN, JAMES T., AND ELDON JOHNSON

1984 The Elma Thompson Site: A Besant Phase Tipi Ring in the West-central Saskatchewan Plains. *Saskatchewan Archaeology* 5:27–35.

FLADMARK, KNUT R., JONATHAN C. DRIVER, AND DIANA ALEXANDER

1988 The Paleoindian Component at Charlie Lake Cave (HbRf 39), British Columbia. *American Antiquity* 53(2):371–384.

FORBIS, RICHARD G.

1960 *Some Late Sites in the Oldman River Region, Alberta.* National Museums of Canada Bulletin 162, pp. 119–164. Contributions to Anthropology, 1957. National Museums of Canada, Ottawa.

1962 The Old Woman's Buffalo Jump, Alberta. National Museums of Canada Bulletin 180, Contributions to Anthropology, Part I. National Museums of Canada, Ottawa.

1966 A Report on Archaeological Investigations on the Three Proposed Reservoir Basins in South-western Alberta During 1965. Manuscript on file. National Museum of Man, Ottawa.

1968a Fletcher: A Paleo-Indian Site in Alberta. *American Antiquity* 33(1):1–10.

1968b Alberta. In *The Northwestern Plains: A Symposium*, edited by Warren Caldwell, pp. 37–44. Occasional Paper No. 1. The Center for Indian Studies, Rocky Mountain College, Billings, Montana.

1970 *A Review of Alberta Archaeology to 1964.* National Museum of Man Publications in Archaeology No. 1, pp. v–49. National Museum of Man, Ottawa.

1977 *Cluny: An Ancient Fortified Village in Alberta.* Occasional Paper No. 4. Department of Archaeology, University of Calgary, Calgary.

1992 The Mesoindian (Archaic) Period in the Northern Plains. *Journal of American Archaeology* 5:27–70.

FORBIS, RICHARD G., AND H.A. HUSCHER

1961 A Brief Account of Excavations at the Cluny Earthlodge Village. *Plains Anthropologist* 6(12, pt. 2):101–102.

FORBIS, RICHARD G., AND JOHN D. SPERRY

1952 An Early Man Site in Montana. *American Antiquity* 2:127–133.

FOSHA, MICHAEL, AND FREDERIC SELLET

2000 The Ghost Site: A Folsom/Goshen Locality in South Dakota. *Current Research in the Pleistocene* 17:26–27.

FRALEY, DAVID C.

1988 Avonlea and Besant in Eastern Montana: Archaeological Distributions in the Lower Yellowstone Region. In *Avonlea Yesterday and Today: Archaeology and Prehistory*, edited by Leslie Davis, pp. 129–136. Saskatchewan Archaeological Society, Saskatoon.

FRALEY, DAVID, AND ANN M. JOHNSON

1981 Ceramics and Cultural Affiliation at the Goheen Site, 24WX30. *Archaeology in Montana* 22(1):1–22.

FREDLUND, LYNN B.

1988 Distribution and Characteristics of Avonlea South of the Yellowstone River in Montana. In *Avonlea Yesterday and Today: Archaeology and Prehistory*, edited by Leslie Davis, pp. 171–182. Saskatchewan Archaeological Society, Saskatoon.

FREDLUND, LYNN B., DALE HERBORT, AND GENE MUNSON

1985 Investigations at a Besant Stone Ring Site (32OL270) in Central North Dakota. In *Contributions to Plains Prehistory*, edited by David Burley, pp. 116–154. Occasional Paper No. 26. Archaeological Survey of Alberta, Edmonton.

FREEMEN, ANDREA K.L.

2006 Radiocarbon Age Estimates from the SCAPE Project, 2000-2005. *Plains Anthropologist* 51(199):451–486.

FRISON, GEORGE C.

1962 Wedding of the Waters Cave: A Stratified Site in the Bighorn Basin of Northern Wyoming. *Plains Anthropologist* 7(18):246–265.

1968 Daugherty Cave, Wyoming. *Plains Anthropologist* 13(42):253–295.

1970 The Kobold Site, 24BH406: A Post-Altithermal Record of Buffalo-Jumping for the Northwestern Plains. *Plains Anthropologist* 15(47):1–35.

1971 The Buffalo Pound in North-Western Plains Prehistory: Site 48CA302, Wyoming. *American Antiquity* 36(1):77–95.

1974 *The Casper Site: A Hell Gap Bison Kill on the High Plains*. Academic Press, New York.

1976 The Chronology of Paleo-Indian and Altithermal Cultures in the Bighorn Basin, Wyoming. In *Cultural Change and Continuity: Essays in Honor of James Bennett Griffin*, edited by Charles E. Cleland, pp. 147–173. Academic Press, New York.

1983 The Lookingbill Site, Wyoming: 48FR308. *Tebiwa* 20:1–16.

1984 The Carter/Kerr-McGee Paleoindian Site: Cultural Resource Management and Archaeological Research. *American Antiquity* 49(2):288–314.

1988 Avonlea and Contemporaries in Wyoming. In *Avonlea Yesterday and Today: Archaeology and Prehistory*, edited by Leslie Davis, pp. 155–170. Saskatchewan Archaeological Society, Saskatoon.

1991a *Prehistoric Hunters of the High Plains* (2nd Edition). Academic Press, Toronto.

1991b The Goshen Paleoindian Complex: New Data for Paleoindian Research. In *Clovis: Origins and Adaptations*, edited by Robson Bonnichsen and Karen L. Turnmire, pp. 133–151. Center for the Study of the First Americans, Department of Anthropology, Oregon State University, Corvallis.

1992 The Foothills-Mountains and the Open Plains: The Dichotomy in Paleoindian Subsistence Strategies Between Two Ecosystems. In *Ice Age Hunters of the Rockies*, edited by Dennis J. Stanford and Jane S. Day, pp. 323–342. Denver Museum of Natural History and University Press of Colorado, Niwot.

1993a The North American Paleoindian: A Wealth of New Data but Still Much to Learn. *Plains Anthropologist* 1993:5–16.

1993b North American High Plains Paleo-Indian Hunting Strategies and Weaponry Assemblages. In *From Kostenki to Clovis: Upper Paleolithic—Paleo-Indian Adaptations*, edited by Olga Soffer and N.D. Praslov, pp. 237–249. Plenum Press, New York.

FRISON, GEORGE C., AND DONALD C. GREY

1980 Pryor Stemmed: A Specialized Late Paleo-Indian Ecological Adaptation. *Plains Anthropologist* 25(87):27–46.

FRISON, GEORGE C., DAVID SCWAB, L. ADRIEN HANNUS, PETER WINHAM, DAVID WALTER, AND ROBERT C. MAINFORT

1996 Archaeology of the Northwestern Plains. In *Archaeological and Bioarchaeological Resources of the Northern Plains: A Volume in the Central and Northern Plains Archaeological Overview*, edited by George C. Frison and Robert C. Mainfort, pp. 8–40. Arkansas Archaeological Survey Research Series No. 47. Arkansas Archaeological Survey, Fayetteville.

FRISON, GEORGE C., AND DENNIS J. STANFORD

1982 *The Agate Basin Site: A Record of the Palaeoindian Occupation of the Northwestern High Plains*. Academic Press, New York.

FRISON, GEORGE C., AND LAWRENCE C. TODD (EDITORS)

1987 *The Horner Site: The Type Site of the Cody Cultural Complex*. Academic Press, New York.

GEBHARD, PAUL H.

1949 An Archaeological Survey of the Blowouts of Yuma County, Colorado. *American Antiquity* 2:132–143.

GETTY, RONALD

1971 *The Many Snakes Burial (DgOv 12): A Primary Inhumation from Southern Alberta*. Department of Archaeology, University of Calgary, Calgary.

GIBSON, TERRANCE H.

1981 Remnant Oxbow on the Northern Plains. *Canadian Journal of Archaeology* 5:131–136.

2001 *Management Summary of Archaeological Work Undertaken in the South Bodo Oilfield (FaOm 1) for Murphy Oil Company in 2000, Permit 2000-116*. Archaeological Survey of Alberta. Permit No. 2000-116. Copies available from Archaeological Survey of Alberta, Edmonton.

GIBSON, TERRANCE H., AND PEGGY MCKEAND

1992 Excavation of the Crane Site, DiMv 93. Draft copy, manuscript on file. Western Heritage Services, Saskatoon.

GIERING, KAREN L., AND TREVOR R. PECK

1998 A Ceramic Vessel from the Blakiston Site (DjPm 115), S.W. Alberta. *Alberta Archaeological Review* 28:20–24.

GILL, G.W.

1984 The Partial Skeleton of a Child from Dead Indian Creek. In *Dead Indian Creek Site: An Archaic Occupation in the Absaroka Mountains of Northeastern Wyoming*, edited by George C. Frison and Danny N. Walker, pp. 11–122. *The Wyoming Archaeologist* 27(1 and 2).

GILLESPIE, JASON D.

2002 Archaeological and Geological Evidence for the First Peopling of Alberta. Unpublished Master's thesis, Department of Archaeology, University of Calgary, Calgary.

2003 Rethinking Taxonomy on the Northern Plains: A Comment on Yellowhorn's "Regarding the American Paleolithic." *Canadian Journal of Archaeology* 27:309–313.

2007 Enculturing an Unknown World: Caches and Clovis Landscape Ideology. *Canadian Journal of Archaeology* 31(2):171–189.

GILLESPIE, JASON D., ANDREA FREEMAN, AND EUGENE GRYBA

2002 Early-Paleoindian Projectile Point Distribution in Alberta, Canada. *Current Research in the Pleistocene* 19:25–27.

GILLESPIE, JASON D., SUSAN TUPAKKA, AND CHRISTINE CLUNEY

2004 Distinguishing Between Naturally and Culturally Flaked Cobbles: A Test Case from Alberta, Canada. *Geoarcheology: An International Journal* 19(7):615–633.

GOEBEL, TED, W. ROGER POWERS, AND NANCY BIGELOW

1991 The Nenana Complex of Alaska and Clovis Origins. In *Clovis: Origins and Adaptations*, edited by Robson Bonnichsen and Karen L. Turnmire, pp. 49–80. Center for the Study of the First Americans, Department of Anthropology, Oregon State University, Corvallis.

GOEBEL, TED, W. ROGER POWERS, NANCY H. BIGELOW, AND ANDREW S. HIGGS

1996. Walker Road. In *American Beginnings: The Prehistory and Palaeoecology of Beringia*, edited by Frederick Hadleigh West, pp. 356–362. University of Chicago Press, Chicago.

GOLDSMITH, SEAN

2003 *Final Report, Historical Resource Impact Mitigation, Inter Pipeline Fund Husky Tie-In 6-26-11-11-W4M to 7-28-11-12-W4M, Mitigation of DlOu 71, 72, and 73 (Permit #2002-110)*. Archaeological Survey of Alberta. Permit No. 2002-110. Copies available from Archaeological Survey of Alberta, Edmonton.

2005 *Final Report, Historical Resource Impact Mitigation, Alberta Transportation Deadfish Dam Rehabilitation Project (Permit #2003-100)*. 2 vols. Archaeological Survey of Alberta. Permit No. 2003-100. Copies available from Archaeological Survey of Alberta, Edmonton.

2007a *Final Report, Historical Resource Impact Mitigation, Arcus Developments Inc., Bow Ridge Subdivision in Cochrane, Alberta (ASA Permit #2006-624)*. Archaeological Survey of Alberta. Permit No. 2006-624. Copies available from Archaeological Survey of Alberta, Edmonton.

2007b Excavations at EhPp 74: Summary Report. *Alberta Archaeological Review* 46(Spring):3–6.

GRASPOINTER, ANDREAS

1980 *Archaeology and Ethno-history of the Milk River in Southern Alberta*. Western Publishers, Calgary.

GRAYSON, DONALD K., AND DAVID J. MELTZER

2002 Clovis Hunting and Large Mammal Extinction: A Critical Review of the Evidence. *Journal of World Prehistory* 16(4):313–359.

GREAVES, SHEILA

1982 *Upon the Point: A Preliminary Investigation of Ethnicity as a Source of Metric Variation in Lithic Projectile Points*. Archaeological Survey of Canada Paper No. 109. National Museum of Man Mercury Series, National Museums of Canada, Ottawa.

1994 The Cultural-Historical and Technological Implications of Selected Components at the Echo Creek Site (515R), Banff National Park. Manuscript on file, Parks Canada, Contract 2872B04, Parks Canada, Western Region.

GREEN, D'ARCY CLARKE

2000 *Historical Resources Impact Assessment, AEC Suffield Gas Pipeline Inc., North Suffield Project, Alberta Portion (Section 3-19-9-W4M to Section 1-20-1-W4M), Permit 2000-063*. Archaeological Survey of Alberta. Permit No. 2000-063. Copies available from Archaeological Survey of Alberta, Edmonton.

2005 *A Re-evaluation of the Oxbow Dam Site (DhMn 1): Middle Holocene Cultural Continuity on the Northern Plains*. Occasional Papers of the Archaeological Society of Alberta No. 5. Archaeological Society of Alberta, Calgary.

GREGG, MICHAEL L.

1986 *An Overview of the Prehistory of Western and Central North Dakota*. Cultural Resources Series No. 1, Bureau of Land Management, Montana.

GREGG, MICHAEL L. (EDITOR)

1987 *Archaeological Excavation at the Naze Site (32SN246)*. National Technical Information Service, Operations Division, Springfield, Virginia.

GREGG, MICHAEL L., AND FERN E. SWENSON

1987 Naze Site Structure and Cultural Deposits. In *Archaeological Excavation at the Naze Site (32SN246)*, edited by Michael Gregg, pp. 64–88. National Technical Information Service, Operations Division, Springfield, Virginia.

GREISER, SALLY T.

1986 Artifact Collections from Ten Sites at Canyon Ferry Reservoir. *Archaeology in Montana* 27 (1 and 2):1–190.

1988 Lost Terrace Avonlea Material Culture. In *Avonlea Yesterday and Today: Archaeology and Prehistory*, edited by Leslie Davis, pp. 119–128. Saskatchewan Archaeological Society, Saskatoon.

1994 Late Prehistoric Cultures on the Montana Plains. In *Indian Cultures of the Great Plains, A.D. 500–1500*, edited by Karl Schlesier, pp. 34–68. University of Oklahoma Press, Norman.

GREISER, SALLY T., T. WEBER GREISER, AND SUSAN M. VETTER

1985 Middle Period Adaptations and Palaeoenvironment in the Northwestern Plains: The Sun River Site. *American Antiquity* 50(4):849–877.

GRUHN, RUTH

1969 *Preliminary Report on the Muhlbach Site: A Besant Bison Trap in Central Alberta.* National Museums of Canada Bulletin 232:128–156.

1981 *Archaeological Research at Calling Lake, Northern Alberta.* Archaeological Survey of Canada Paper No. 99. National Museum of Man Mercury Series, National Museums of Canada, Ottawa.

GRYBA, EUGENE

1966 A Possible Midland Point from the Swan Valley of Manitoba. *Plains Anthropologist* 11(33):238.

1968 A Possible Palaeo-Indian and Archaic Site in the Swan Valley, Manitoba. *Plains Anthropologist* 13(41):218–227.

1975 The Stampede Site, DjPn 26, Cypress Hills Provincial Park, June 1975. Manuscript on file, Parks Planning Division, Parks Branch, Alberta Department of Parks, Recreation, and Wildlife.

1976 The Early Side-notched Component at Site DjOn 26. In *Archaeology in Alberta 1975*, edited by J. Michael Quigg and W.J. Byrne, pp. 92–107. Occasional Paper No. 1. Archaeological Survey of Alberta, Edmonton.

1983 *Sibbald Creek: 11,000 Years of Human Use of the Alberta Foothills.* Occasional Paper No. 22. Archaeological Survey of Alberta, Edmonton.

1985 Evidence of the Fluted Point Tradition in Alberta. In *Contributions to Plains Prehistory*, edited by David Burley, pp. 22–38. Occasional Paper No. 26. Archaeological Survey of Alberta, Edmonton.

1988 An Inventory of Fluted Point Occurrences in Alberta, Vols. 1 and 2. Archaeological Survey of Alberta. CRM 151. Copies available from Archaeological Survey of Alberta, Edmonton.

2001 Evidence of the Flute Point Tradition in Western Canada. In *On Being First: Cultural Innovation and Environmental Consequence of First Peopling*, edited by Jason Gillespie, Susan Tupakka, and Christy de Mille, pp. 251–284. Proceedings of the 31st Annual Chacmool Conference, Chacmool Archaeology Association, University of Calgary, Calgary.

GRYBA, EUGENE M., AND CHARLES GRYBA, JR.

1980 A Clovis Occurrence Near Invermay, Saskatchewan. *Plains Anthropologist* 25(88, pt. 2): 171–172.

HABERMAN, THOMAS W.

1986 Comments on McKean Plant Food Utilization. *Plains Anthropologist* 31(113):237–240.

HAINES, FRANCIS

1938 The Northward Spread of Horses Among the Plains Indians. *American Anthropologist* (new series) 40:429–437.

HALEY, S.D., B.M. NEWTON, AND G.J. FEDIRCHUK

1982 *Historical Resource Investigations, Merland Explorations Limited, Canard Sales Lines, ASA* Permit 82-38. Archaeological Survey of Alberta. Permit No. 1982-38. Copies available from Archaeological Survey of Alberta, Edmonton.

HAMILTON, MARCUS J., AND BRIGGS BUCHANAN

2007 Spatial Gradients in Clovis-age Radiocarbon Dates Across North America Suggest Rapid Colonization from the North. *Proceedings of the National Academy of Science* 104(40):15625–15630.

HANNA, DON

2002 *Historical Resources Mitigation, Speargrass Golf Course and Residential Subdivision, Carseland Parts of 5-22-25-W4M and 32-21-25-W4M: Final Report, ASA Permit 2001-032.* Archaeological Survey of Alberta. Permit No. 2001-032. Copies available from Archaeological Survey of Alberta, Edmonton.

HANNA, DON, AND THOMAS HEAD

2000 *Final Report, Historical Resources Impact Assessment and Mitigation, Excavations Astley Properties (Pt. W1/2 of 1-25-3-W5M), Permit 97-111.* Archaeological Survey of Alberta. Permit No. 97-111. Copies available from Archaeological Survey of Alberta, Edmonton.

HANNA, MARGARET G.

1986 An Examination of Vessels from the Avonlea Type Site EaNg 1. *Saskatchewan Archaeology* 7:33–37.

HANNA, SHARON, AND BARBARA NEAL

1992 *Final Report, Historical Resources Mitigation, North Lateral Extension Loop #2, Sullivan Lake Section, ASA Permit 90-69.* Archaeological Survey of Alberta. Permit No. 1990-069. Copies available from Archaeological Survey of Alberta, Edmonton.

HANNUS, L. ADRIEN, AND TIMOTHY R. NOWAK

1988 Avonlea: A Point Industry Surfaces in South Dakota, or Archers on the March. In *Avonlea Yesterday and Today: Archaeology and Prehistory*, edited by Leslie Davis, pp. 183–190. Saskatchewan Archaeological Society, Saskatoon.

HASPEL, H.L., AND D.L. WEDEL

1985 A Middle Plains Archaic Child Burial from the McKean Site in Northeastern Wyoming In *McKean/Middle Plains Archaic: Current Research*, edited by M. Kornfeld and L.C. Todd, pp. 105–108. Occasional Papers on Wyoming Archaeology No. 4, Wyoming Recreation Commission, Cheyenne.

HAUG, JAMES K.

1975 The 1974 End-of-Season Field Report on the Cherry Point Site Excavations, Southwestern Manitoba. *Archae-Facts* 2(2 and 3):2–20.

1981 *Analysis of a Paleo-Indian Occupation Floor at the Duck River Site, ElMb 10, Manitoba.* Papers in Manitoba Archaeology, Miscellaneous Paper No. 11. Department of Cultural Affairs and Historical Resources, Historical Resources Branch, Winnipeg.

HAYNES, JR., C. VANCE

1987. Clovis Origin Update. *The Kiva* 52(2):83–93.

1993 Clovis-Folsom Geochronology and Climate Change. In *From Kostenki to Clovis: Upper Paleolithic—Paleo-Indian Adaptations*, edited by Olga Soffer and N.D. Praslov, pp. 219–236. Plenum Press, New York.

HAYNES, JR., C. VANCE, ROELF P. BEUKENS, A.J.T. JULL, AND OWEN K. DAVIS

1992 New Radiocarbon Dates for Some Old Folsom Sites: Accelerator Technology. In *Ice Age Hunters of the Rockies*, edited by Dennis Stanford and Jane S. Day, pp. 83–100. Denver Museum of Natural History and University Press of Colorado, Niwot.

HEAD, THOMAS

1985 Northern Plains Prehistory: The Late Prehistoric Period as Viewed from the H.M.S. Balzac Site (EhPm 34). In *Contributions to Plains Prehistory*, edited by David Burley, pp. 100–115. Occasional Paper No. 26. Archaeological Survey of Alberta , Edmonton.

1986 Springtime at H.M.S. Balzac: Two Millennia of Bison Processing at a Stratified Campsite on the Alberta Plains. Unpublished Master's thesis, Department of Archaeology, University of Calgary, Calgary.

HEAD, THOMAS, AND MARGARET A. KENNEDY

1994 Historical Resources Impact Mitigation, the Frank Zinc Smelter, DjPo-122, NPS 42, Western Alberta System Mainline Upgrade (Crowsnest Section) and St. Pierre Site (DjPn-127), NPS 42, Western Alberta System Mainline Loop (Lundbreck Section). Permit 93-030. Archaeological Survey of Alberta. Permit No. 1993-030. Copies available from Archaeological Survey of Alberta, Edmonton.

HEAD, THOMAS, BRENT MURPHY, AND THAYER SMITH

2002 Historical Resources Impact Mitigation, EgPn 111, ASA Permit No. 2000-097 (Incorporating Work from ASA Permit 1998-024). Archaeological Survey of Alberta. Permit No. 1998-024. Copies available from Archaeological Survey of Alberta, Edmonton.

HEAD, THOMAS, LES GORHAM, AND WENDY UNFREED

2003 *Saahkomaapina (Boy Chief): EeOv-68*. Occasional Papers of the Archaeological Society of Alberta No. 1. Archaeological Society of Alberta, Calgary.

HEITZMAN, ROD

1985 Historical Resource Mitigation, Little Bow River Crossing, EaPh 4 and EaPh 5, ASA Permits 84-38 and 84-49. Archaeological Survey of Alberta. Permit Nos. 1984-038 and 1984-049. Copies available from Archaeological Survey of Alberta, Edmonton.

HESTER, THOMAS ROY

1968 Folsom Points from Southwest Texas. *Plains Anthropologist* 13(40):117.

HELMICK, TROY C.

1984 Cody Complex Artifacts in the Townsend Basin. *Archaeology in Montana* 25(1):31–34.

HILL, JR., MATTHEW E., AND JACK. L. HOFMAN

1997 The Waugh Site: A Folsom-age Bison Bonebed in Northwestern Oklahoma. In *Southern Plains Bison Procurement and Utilization from Paleoindian to Historic*, edited by Leland C. Bement and Kent J. Buehler. Memoir 29, *Plains Anthropologist* 42(159):63–83.

HIMOUR, BRADLEY

2002 Final Report, Historical Resources Impact Assessment for Real Resources Inc., Atlee Well Sites, Access Roads and Pipeline Tie-in Program, Permit #2001-038. Archaeological Survey of Alberta. Permit No. 2001-038. Copies available from Archaeological Survey of Alberta, Edmonton.

HISTORIC RESOURCES BRANCH

1997 *The Dakota Fortified Camps of the Portage Plains*. Historic Resources Branch, Province of Manitoba, Winnipeg.

HJERMSTAD, BENJAMIN E.

1996 The Fitzgerald Site: A Besant Pound and Processing Area on the Northern Plains. Unpublished Master's thesis, Department of Anthropology and Archaeology, University of Saskatchewan, Saskatoon.

1998 The Pine Coulee Reservoir Historical Resources Impact Mitigation: Final Report, Permit 96-041. Archaeological Survey of Alberta. Permit No. 1996-041. Copies available from Archaeological Survey of Alberta, Edmonton.

HOFFECKER, JOHN F.

1996 Moose Creek. In *American Beginnings: The Prehistory and Palaeoecology of Beringia*, edited by Frederick Hadleigh West, pp. 363–365. University of Chicago Press, Chicago.

2001 Late Pleistocene–Early Holocene Sites in the Nenana River Valley, Central Alaska. *Arctic Anthropology* 38(2):139–153.

HOFFECKER, JOHN F., W. ROGER POWERS, AND NANCY H. BIGELOW

1996 Dry Creek. In *American Beginnings: The Prehistory and Palaeoecology of Beringia*, edited by Frederick Hadleigh West, pp. 343–352. University of Chicago Press, Chicago.

HOFFECKER, JOHN F., W. ROGER POWERS, AND PETER G. PHIPPEN

1996 Owl Ridge. In *American Beginnings: The Prehistory and Palaeoecology of Beringia*, edited by Frederick Hadleigh West, pp. 353–355. University of Chicago Press, Chicago.

HOFMAN, JACK L.

1994 The Occurrence of Folsom Points in Kansas. *Current Research in the Pleistocene* 11:37–39.

HOFMAN, JACK L., DANIEL S. AMICK, AND RICHARD O. ROSE

1990 Shifting Sands: A Folsom-Midland Assemblage from a Campsite in Western Texas. *Plains Anthropologist* 35(129):221–253.

HOFMAN, JACK L., AND ERIC INGBAR

1988 A Folsom Hunting Overlook in Eastern Wyoming. *Plains Anthropologist* 33(121):337–350.

HOLDER, PRESTON, AND JOYCE WIKE

1949 The Frontier Culture Complex: A Preliminary Report on a Prehistoric Hunters' Camp in Southwestern Nebraska. *American Antiquity* 4:260–266.

HOLMES, CHARLES E.

1996a Broken Mammoth. In *American Beginnings: The Prehistory and Palaeoecology of Beringia*, edited by Frederick Hadleigh West, pp. 312–318. University of Chicago Press, Chicago.

1996b Swan Point. In *American Beginnings: The Prehistory and Palaeoecology of Beringia*, edited by Frederick Hadleigh West, pp. 319–323. University of Chicago Press, Chicago.

HOWARD, CALVIN D.

1988 Fluting Technology at the Lincoln Hills Site. *Plains Anthropologist* 33(121):395–397.

1990 The Clovis Point: Characteristics and Type Description. *Plains Anthropologist* 35(129):255–262.

HOWARD, EDGAR B.

1939 Folsom and Yuma Points from Saskatchewan. *American Antiquity* 3:277–279.

HOY, JUDY

1973 Six Bison Kill Sites in Phillips County, Montana. *Archaeology in Montana* 14(3):1–33.

HUDECEK, CAROLINE R.

1989 Avonlea/Old Women's: A Study of Culture Change on the Northern Plains Through the Analysis of Lithic and Ceramic Assemblages. Unpublished Master's thesis, Department of Anthropology, University of Alberta, Edmonton.

HUDECEK-CUFFE, CAROLINE R.

1992 Aspects of Culture Change in the Late Prehistoric Period on the Northwestern Plains. *North American Archaeologist* 13(4):317–331.

1998 *Final Report, Department of Anthropology, University of Alberta, Archaeological Fields School, Jasper National Park, July 15–August 20, 1997, Permit No. WRA 97-03.* Parks Canada. Permit WRA 97-03. Parks Canada, Canadian Heritage, Western Region, Calgary.

HUGHES, SUSAN S.

1981 Projectile Point Variability: A Study of Point Curation at a Besant Kill Site, Southcentral Wyoming. Unpublished Master's thesis, Department of Anthropology, University of Wyoming, Laramie.

1991 Division of Labor at a Besant Hunting Camp in Eastern Montana. In *Approaches to Gender Processes on the Great Plains*, edited by Marcel Kornfeld. Memoir 26, *Plains Anthropologist* 36(134):25–49.

1998 Getting to the Point: Evolutionary Change in Prehistoric Weaponry. *Journal of Archaeological Method and Theory* 5(4):345–403.

HURT, W.R.

1966 The Altithermal and the Prehistory of the Northern Plains. *Quaternia* 8:101–114.

HUSTED, WILFRED M.

1965 Early Occupations in Bighorn Canyon, Montana. *Plains Anthropologist* 10(27):7–13.

1969 *Bighorn Canyon Archaeology*. Smithsonian Institution River Basin Surveys, Publications in Salvage Archaeology No. 12. Lincoln, Nebraska.

HUSTED, WILFRED M., AND ROBERT EDGAR

2002 *The Archaeology of Mummy Cave, Wyoming: An Introduction to Shoshonean Prehistory*. Special Report No. 4, Technical Reports Series No. 9, National Park Service, Midwest Archaeological Center and Southeast Archaeological Center, Lincoln, Nebraska.

HUTCHINGS, WALLACE KARL

1997 Paleoindian Point: Dart or Spear Armature? The Identification of Paleoindian Delivery

Technology Through the Analysis of the Lithic Fracture Velocity. Unpublished PhD dissertation, Simon Fraser University, Burnaby, British Columbia.

IRWIN, HENRY T., AND H. MARIE WORMINGTON

1970 Paleo-Indian Tool Types in the Great Plains. *American Antiquity* 35(1):24–34.

IRWIN-WILLIAMS, CYNTHIA, HENRY WILLIAMS, GEORGE AGOGINO, AND C. VANCE HAYNES

1973 Hell Gap: Paleo-Indian Occupation on the High Plains. *Plains Anthropologist* 18(59):40–53.

JEPSON, GLENN L.

1953 Ancient Buffalo Hunters of Northwestern Wyoming. *Southwestern Lore* 19(2):19–23.

JERDE, TOM R.

1981 Eight Paleo-Indian Period Site Locations in Northeastern Montana. *Archaeology in Montana* 22(2):21–38.

JODRY, MARGARET A., AND DENNIS J. STANFORD

1992 Stewart's Cattle Guard Site: An Analysis of Bison Remains in a Folsom Kill-Butchery Campsite. In *Ice Age Hunters of the Rockies*, edited by Dennis J. Stanford and Jane S. Day, pp. 101–168. Denver Museum of Natural History and University Press of Colorado, Niwot.

JODRY, MARGARET, MORT D. TURNER, VINCE SPERO, JOANNE C. TURNER, AND DENNIS STANFORD

1996 Folsom in the Colorado High Country: The Black Mountain Site. *Current Research in the Pleistocene* 13:25–27.

JOHNSON, ELDON A.

1983 EdOh 23: A Besant Site in the Great Sand Hills. *Saskatchewan Archaeology* 4:41–44.

JOHNSON, ANN M.

1977 Woodland and Besant in the Northern Plains: A Perspective. *Archaeology in Montana* 18(1):27–41.

1988 Parallel Grooves Ceramics: An Addition to Avonlea Material Culture. In *Avonlea Yesterday and Today: Archaeology and Prehistory*, edited by Leslie Davis, pp. 137–144. Saskatchewan Archaeological Society, Saskatoon.

JOHNSON, ANN M., AND HENRY L. ARMSTRONG

1990 Square Butte: A Multicomponent Campsite in Central Montana. *Archaeology in Montana* 31(1):1–6.

JONES, TIM

1997 On the Appropriateness of the Term "Pre-Contact." *Saskatchewan Archaeological Society Newsletter* 18(3):63–65.

JOYES, DENNIS C.

1970 The Culture Sequence at the Avery Site at Rock Lake. In *Ten Thousand Years: Archaeology in Manitoba*, edited by Walter M. Hlady, pp. 209–222. Manitoba Archaeological Society. D.W. Friesen and Sons Ltd., Altona, Manitoba.

1984 Review of *Culture Change in the Northern Plains 1000 B.C.–A.D. 1000*, by Brian O.K. Reeves. *Plains Anthropologist* 29(104):167–170.

1988 A Summary and Evaluation of Avonlea in Manitoba. In *Avonlea Yesterday and Today: Archaeology and Prehistory*, edited by Leslie Davis, pp. 227–236. Saskatchewan Archaeological Society, Saskatoon.

2000 Cody Technology at the McLeod Site, Saskatchewan, Canada. *Current Research in the Pleistocene* 17:47–49.

KASSTAN, STEVEN C.

2004 Lithic Technology at the Below Forks Site, FhNg 25: Stratagems of Stone Tool Manufacture. Unpublished Master's thesis, Department of Archaeology, University of Saskatoon, Saskatoon.

KEHOE, THOMAS F.

1960 *Stone Tipi Rings in North-Central Montana and the Adjacent Portion of Alberta, Canada: Their Historical, Ethnological, and Archaeological Aspects*. Anthropological Papers No. 62. Smithsonian Institution, Bureau of American Ethnology Bulletin 173, pp. 417–473.

1964 Middle Woodland Pottery of Saskatchewan. *Plains Anthropologist* 9:51–53.

1965 Research Report, 1965. *Saskatchewan Archaeology* 11:1.

1966a The Distribution and Implications of Fluted Points in Saskatchewan. *American Antiquity* 31(4):530–539.

1966b The Small Side-notched Point System of the Northern Plains. *American Antiquity* 31(6):827–841.

1967 The Boarding School Bison Drive Site. Memoir 4, *Plains Anthropologist* 12(35):1–165.

1973 *The Gull Lake Site: A Prehistoric Bison Drive Site in Southwestern Saskatchewan*. Publications in Anthropology and History No. 1. Milwaukee Pubic Museum, New Berlin, Wisconsin.

1974 The Large Corner-notched Point System of the Northern Plains and Adjacent Woodlands. In *Aspects of Upper Great Lakes Anthropology: Papers in Honor of Lloyd A. Wilford*, edited by Elden Johnson, pp. 103–114. Minnesota Historical Society, St. Paul.

1988 The Avonlea Point: A History of the Concept. In *Avonlea Yesterday and Today: Archaeology and Prehistory*, edited by Leslie Davis, pp. 7–10. Saskatchewan Archaeological Society, Saskatoon.

KEHOE, THOMAS F., AND ALICE KEHOE

1968 Saskatchewan. In *The Northwestern Plains: A Symposium*, edited by Warren W. Caldwell and Stuart W. Conner, pp. 21–35. Occasional Paper No. 1. The Center for Indian Studies Rocky Mountain College, Billings, Montana.

KEHOE, THOMAS F., AND BRUCE A. MCCORQUODALE

1961 The Avonlea Point: Horizon Marker for the Northwestern Plains. *Plains Anthropologist* 6(13):179–188.

KEHOE, THOMAS F., BRUCE A. MCCORQUODALE, AND ALICE KEHOE

1988 1984 Excavations at the Avonlea Type Site. In *Avonlea Yesterday and Today: Archaeology and Prehistory*, edited by Leslie Davis, pp. 11–24. Saskatchewan Archaeological Society, Saskatoon.

KELLY, DAVID

1986 The Newo Asiniak Site: A Multicomponent Bison Procurement Site in Central Saskatchewan. Unpublished Master's thesis, Department of Anthropology and Archaeology, University of Saskatchewan, Saskatoon.

KELLY, ROBERT, AND LAWRENCE C. TODD

1988 Coming into the Country: Early Paleo-Indian Hunting and Mobility. *American Antiquity* 53(2):231–244.

KEYSER, JAMES D.

1979 Late Prehistoric Period Bison Procurement on the Milk River in North-Central Montana. *Archaeology in Montana* 20(1):i-241.

1982 A Comparative Analysis of Two McKean Phase Occupations in the Grand River Drainage. *Journal of the North Dakota Archaeological Association* 1:31–41.

1986 The Evidence for McKean Complex Plant Utilization. *Plains Anthropologist* 31(113):225–234.

KEYSER, JAMES D., AND C.M. DAVIS

1984 Lightning Spring: 4000 Years of Pine Parkland Prehistory. *Archaeology in Montana* 25(2 and 3):1–64.

KEYSER, JAMES D., AND JOHN L. FAGAN

1993 McKean Lithic Technology at Lightning Spring. *Plains Anthropologist* 38(145):37–51.

KEYSER, JAMES D., AND GEORGE C. KNIGHT

1976 The Risley Bison Kill: West-Central Montana. *Plains Anthropologist* 21(74): 291–300.

KIRBY, FOSTER B., AND ANN B. JUSTEN

1974 *The Amber Burial EePi-1: Preliminary Report, Permit 74-024*. Archaeological Survey of Alberta. Permit No. 1974-024. Copies available from Archaeological Survey of Alberta, Edmonton.

KLASSEN, MICHAEL A.

1995 Icons of Power, Narrative of Glory: Ethnic Continuity and Cultural Change in the Contact Period Rock Art of Writing-On-Stone. Unpublished Master's thesis, Department of Anthropology, Trent University, Peterborough, Ontario.

2003 Spirit Images, Medicine Rocks: The Rock Art of Alberta. In *Archaeology in Alberta: A View from the New Millennium*, edited by Jack W. Brink and John F. Dormaar, pp. 154–186. Archaeological Society of Alberta, Medicine Hat.

KLIMKO, OLGA

1985 New Perspectives on Avonlea: A View from the Saskatchewan Forest. In *Contributions to Plains Prehistory*, edited by David V. Burley, pp. 64–81. Occasional Paper No. 26. Archaeological Survey of Alberta, Edmonton.

KLIMKO, OLGA, AND MARGARET HANNA

1988 The Avonlea Type Site Revisited: A Report on Excavations and Ceramic Analysis. In *Avonlea Yesterday and Today: Archaeology and Prehistory*, edited by Leslie Davis, pp. 25–42. Saskatchewan Archaeological Society, Saskatoon.

KOOYMAN, BRIAN P.

1996 Cluny as Seen Through Archaeology and Oral Tradition. Manuscript on file, Siksika Nation and Canadian Parks Service.

2000a *1994 Excavations at the Spring Kill Site (EgPs 51) Near Exshaw Alberta, Permit Number 94-034*. Archaeological Survey of Alberta, Permit No. 1994-034. Copies available from Archaeological Survey of Alberta, Edmonton.

2000b *Understanding Stone Tools and Archaeological Sites*. University of Calgary Press, Calgary.

KOOYMAN, BRIAN P., MARGARET E. NEWMAN, CHRISTINE CLUNEY, MURRAY LOBB, SHAYNE TOLMAN, PAUL MCNEIL, AND LEN V. HILLS

2001 Identification of Horse Exploitation by Clovis Hunters Based on Protein Analysis. *American Antiquity* 66(4):686–691.

KOZAKAVICH, STACY C.

2001 *Historical Resources Impact Mitigation, AEC Gas Pipeline Inc., North Suffield Project Sites EeOm 50 and EeOm 51, Permits 2000-179 and 2001-053*. Archaeological Survey of Alberta. Permit Nos. 2000-179 and 2001-053. Copies available from Archaeological Survey of Alberta, Edmonton.

KULLE, BARBARA, AND BARBARA NEAL

1998 *Historical Resources Mitigation, Cardinal River Coals Ltd., Cheviot Mine Project Sites FfQh-27 and FfQh-32, Permit 97-115*. Archaeological Survey of Alberta. Permit No. 1997-115. Copies available from Archaeological Survey of Alberta, Edmonton.

LAHREN, LARRY

1976 The Myers-Hindman Site: An Exploratory Study of the Human Occupation Patterns in the Upper Yellowstone Valley from 7000 B.C. to A.D. 1200. Unpublished PhD dissertation, Department of Archaeology, University of Calgary, Calgary.

LAHREN, LARRY A., AND ROBSON BONNICHSEN

1974 Bone Foreshafts from a Clovis Burial in Southwestern Montana. *Science* 186:147–150.

LANDALS, ALISON

1986 The Maple Leaf Site: An Interpretation of Prehistoric Hunting and Butchering Strategies in the Southern Alberta Rockies. Unpublished Master's thesis, Department of Archaeology, University of Calgary, Calgary.

1993 *Oldman River Dam Prehistoric Archaeology Mitigation Program Kill Site Study* (Permits 88-38, 89-32, 90-27). Archaeological Survey of Alberta. CRM 109. Copies available from Archaeological Survey of Alberta, Edmonton.

1995 The Miniota and Broadview Sites: Two Avonlea Loci on the Northeastern Plains. *Manitoba Archaeological Journal* 5(1):1–27.

2004 Horse Heaven: Change in Late Precontact to Contact Period Landscape Use in Southern Alberta. In *Archaeology on the Edge: New Perspectives from the Northern Plains*, edited by Brian Kooyman and Jane Kelley, pp. 231–262. University of Calgary Press, Calgary.

2007 At the Confluence: Terminal Precontact Period and Early Contact Period Interactions at the Little Bow Reservoir. Paper presented at the 2007 meeting of the Alberta Archaeological Association, Calgary.

2008 The Lake Minnewanka Site: Patterns in Late Pleistocene Use of the Alberta Rocky Mountains. Unpublished PhD dissertation, Department of Archaeology, University of Calgary, Calgary.

LANDALS, ALISON, BARB KULLE, AND DIANE COCKLE

2004 *The Miniota Site: An Avonlea Component in Southwestern Manitoba.* Occasional Papers of the Archaeological Society of Alberta No. 3. Archaeological Society of Alberta, Calgary.

LINNAMAE, URVE

1988 The Tschetter Site: A Prehistoric Bison Pound in the Parklands. In *Out of the Past: Sites, Digs, and Artifacts in the Saskatoon Area,* edited by Urve Linnamae and Tim E.H. Jones, pp. 91–115. Saskatoon Archaeological Association, Saskatoon.

LINNAMAE, URVE, AND ELDON JOHNSON

1999 An Analysis of the Lithic Collection from the Heron Eden Site: A Cody Complex Manifestation in Saskatchewan. *Saskatchewan Archaeology* 20:14–32.

LOBDELL, JOHN E.

1974 The Scoggin Site: A Study in McKean Typology. *Plains Anthropologist* 19(64):123–128.

LOVESETH, BEATRICE

1980 The Crowsnest Lake Dancehall Site (DjPp 3): Interpretation Based on Lithic Artifact and Type Analyses. Unpublished Master's thesis, Department of Archaeology, University of Calgary, Calgary.

1981 *Final Report, EiPl 12 Test and Area L Excavations, 1980 Gulf Canada Limited* (ASA Permit 80-60). Archaeological Survey of Alberta. Permit No. 1980-060. Copies available from Archaeological Survey of Alberta, Edmonton.

1983 *Historical Resources Impact Assessment and Archaeological Conservation Studies, Sundance Oil Canada Limited, 1981 Oil Gathering System Expansion and Alterations, Wintering Hills, Alberta* (ASA Permit 81-83). Archaeological Survey of Alberta. Permit No. 1981-083. Copies available from Archaeological Survey of Alberta, Edmonton.

1984 *Final Report, Archaeological Conservation Studies at EhPc 88, EhPd 55, EhPd 60, Sundance Oil Canada Limited, Gas Lease Road Development* (ASA Permit 82-94). Archaeological Survey of Alberta. Permit No. 1982-094. Copies available from Archaeological Survey of Alberta, Edmonton.

LOY, THOMAS H., AND E. JAMES DIXON

1998 Blood Residues on Fluted Points from Eastern Beringia. *American Antiquity* 63(1):21–46.

LYMAN, R. LEE, AND MICHAEL J. O'BRIEN

2006 *Measuring Time with Artifacts: A History of Methods in American Archaeology.* University of Nebraska Press, Lincoln.

LYMAN, R. LEE, MICHAEL J. O'BRIEN, AND VIRGIL HAYES

1998 A Mechanical and Functional Study of Bone Rods from the Richey-Roberts Clovis Cache, Washington, U.S.A. *Journal of Archaeological Science* 25:887–906.

MCCORMAC, F.G., A.G. HOGG, PAUL G. BLACKWELL, CAITLIN E. BUCK, T.F.G. HIGHMAN, AND PAULA J. REIMER

2004 SHCAL04 Southern Hemisphere Calibration, 0–11.0 CAL KYR BP. *Radiocarbon* 46(3):1087–1092.

MCCULLOUGH, EDWARD J.

1980 *Historical Resources Inventory and Assessment, Husky Oil Ltd., Cold Lake to Lloydminster Pipeline,* ASA Permit 80-44. Archaeological Survey of Alberta. Permit No. 1980-044. Copies available from Archaeological Survey of Alberta, Edmonton.

MCCULLOUGH, EDWARD J., AND GLORIA J. FEDIRCHUK

1983 *Archaeological Investigations Eastern Slopes Region: Sites EdPp 21, EdPp 22, EfPq 5, EfPq 6,*

ASA Permit 82-128. Archaeological Survey of Alberta. Permit No. 1982-128. Copies available from Archaeological Survey of Alberta, Edmonton.

MCCULLOUGH, EDWARD J., AND ALISON J. LANDALS

1995 CFD *Wainwright Baseline Archaeological Inventory*. Permit 94-073. Archaeological Survey of Alberta. Permit No. 1994-073. Copies available from Archaeological Survey of Alberta, Edmonton.

MCINTYRE, MICHAEL

1975 *Archaeological Salvage Investigations, Alberta Highways and Transport, Construction Projects, Highway 1A, Secondary Highway SR 901, Bow River Crossing*, Permit 74-028. Archaeological Survey of Alberta. Permit No. 1974-028. Copies available from Archaeological Survey of Alberta, Edmonton.

1978 *Studies in Archaeology, Highway 1A Coal Creek*. Occasional Paper No. 7. Archaeological Survey of Alberta, Edmonton.

MCNERNEY, MICHAEL

1970 A Description of Chipped Stone Artifacts from Northeastern South Dakota. *Plains Anthropologist* 15(50):291–296.

MAGNE, MARTIN P., AND CONTRIBUTORS TO THE SASKATCHEWAN-ALBERTA DIALOGUE

1987 Distribution of Native Groups in Western Canada, A.D. 1700 to A.D. 1850. In *Archaeology in Alberta 1986*, edited by Martin Magne, pp. 220–232. Occasional Paper No. 31. Archaeological Survey of Alberta, Edmonton.

MAGNE, MARTIN P., AND MICHAEL A. KLASSEN

1991 A Multivariate Study of Rock Art Anthropomorphs at Writing-On-Stone, Southern Alberta. *American Antiquity* 56(3):389–418.

MALASIUK, JORDYCE

2007 *Historical Resources Mitigation of EhPm 113 for the Panorama North Lands Neighborhood in SE-33-25-1 W5M (Permit 07-316): Final Report*. Archaeological Survey of Alberta. Permit No. 2007-316. Copies available from Archaeological Survey of Alberta, Edmonton.

MANN, ELIZABETH H.

2007 Preliminary Evaluation of Precontact Pottery Recovered from the University of Alberta Field School near Bodo, East-Central Alberta. Paper presented at the 2007 meeting of the Canadian Archaeological Association, St. John's, Newfoundland.

2009 *Final Report, University of Alberta Field School, 2002, at FaOm 1, the Bodo Bison Skulls Site (Permit 2002-113)*. Archaeological Survey of Alberta. Permit No. 2002-113. Copies available from Archaeological Survey of Alberta, Edmonton.

MARSHALL, SUSAN E.

1988 The Calderwood Buffalo Jump: Bison Procurement in the Porcupine Hills of Southern Alberta. Unpublished Master's thesis, Department of Anthropology, Trent University, Peterborough, Ontario.

MEYER, DANIEL A., NANCY SAXBERG, BRAD SOMER, JASON ROE, AND CARMEN OLSON

2007 *Historical Resources Impact Mitigation, Elk Valley Coal Corporation, Cardinal River Operations, Cheviot River Operations, Cheviot Mine 2005 Mitigation Excavations: Final Report*, Permit 2005-396. Archaeological Survey of Alberta. Permit No. 2005-396. Copies available from Archaeological Survey of Alberta, Edmonton.

MEYER, DAVID

1985 A Component in the Scottsbluff Tradition: Excavations at the Niska Site. *Canadian Journal of Archaeology* 9(1):1–37.

1988 The Old Women's Phase on the Saskatchewan Plains: Some Ideas. In *Archaeology in Alberta 1987*, edited by Martin Magne, pp. 55–63. Occasional Paper No. 32. Archaeological Survey of Alberta, Edmonton.

MEYER, DAVID, OLGA KLIMKO, AND JAMES T. FINNIGAN

1988 Northernmost Avonlea in Saskatchewan. In *Avonlea Yesterday and Today: Archaeology and Prehistory*, edited by Leslie B. Davis, pp. 33–42. Saskatchewan Archaeological Society, Saskatoon.

MEYER, DAVID, AND HENRI LIBOIRON

1990 A Paleoindian Drill from the Niska Site in Southern Saskatchewan. *Plains Anthropologist* 35(129):299–302.

MEYER, JAY

1992 Plains Woodland Ceramics of Wyoming: Vessel Morphology as an Indicator of Subsistence. Unpublished Master's thesis, Department of Anthropology, University of Wyoming, Laramie.

MICHLOVIC, MICHAEL G., AND DEAN T. SATHER

2005 Lithic Artifacts from the Early Archaic Component. In *Archaeology and Paleoenvironment at the Rustad Site (32RI775)*, edited by Michael G. Michlovic and Garry L. Running IV. Memoir 37, *Plains Anthropologist* 50(196):135–158.

MILLAR, J.F.V.

1978 *The Gray Site: An Early Plains Burial Ground*. 2 vols. Manuscript Report No. 304. Parks Canada, Ottawa.

MILLAR, J.F.V., H. EPP, T.W. FOSTER, J.S. WILSON, AND G. ADAMS

1971 The Southwestern Saskatchewan Archaeological Project, Preliminary Report, 1971. *Napao* 3(2):1–39.

MILLER, MARK E., AND BRIAN R. WAITKUS

1989 The Butler-Rissler Site: Plains Woodland Occupation Along the North Platte River, Wyoming. *The Wyoming Archaeologist* 32(1 and 2):1–37.

MILLER, MARK E., BRIAN R. WAITKUS, AND DAVID G. ECKLES

1987 A Woodland-Besant Occurrence in Central Wyoming. *Plains Anthropologist* 32(118):420–423.

MILNE, LAURIE ANN

1988 The Larson Site (DlOn 3) and the Avonlea Phase in Southeastern Alberta. In *Avonlea Yesterday and Today: Archaeology and Prehistory*, edited by Leslie B. Davis, pp. 43–66. Saskatchewan Archaeological Society, Saskatoon.

MILNE BRUMLEY, LAURIE ANN

1971 The Narrows Site in Waterton Lakes National Park, Alberta. In *Aboriginal Man and Environments of the Plateau of Northwest America*, edited by Arnoud H. Stryd and Rachel A. Smith, pp. 73–115. University of Calgary Archaeological Association, Calgary.

1978 *The Saamis Site: A Late Prehistoric-Protohistoric Campsite in Medicine Hat, Alberta*. Archaeological Survey of Canada Paper No. 79. National Museum of Man Mercury Series, National Museums of Canada, Ottawa.

MILNE BRUMLEY, LAURIE ANN, AND JOHN H. BRUMLEY

1977 *Report on Evaluation Excavations Conducted at 7 Sites Along the Highway 41:12 Construction Project, New Brigden, East-Central Alberta*. Archaeological Survey of Alberta. Permit No. 1976-022. Copies available from Archaeological Survey of Alberta, Edmonton.

MOFFATT, E.A., AND I.N.M. WAINWRIGHT

1983 Protein Concentrations in the Taber Child Skeleton: Probable Evidence for a Late Chronology. *Canadian Journal of Archaeology* 7(2):223–231.

MORGAN, R. GRACE

1979 *An Ecological Study of the Northern Plains as Seen Through the Garratt Site*. Occasional Paper in Anthropology No. 1. Department of Anthropology, University of Regina, Regina, Saskatchewan.

1980 Bison Movement Patterns on the Canadian Plains: An Ecological Analysis. *Plains Anthropologist* 25(88):143–160.

MORLAN, RICHARD E.

1988 Avonlea and Radiocarbon Dating. In *Avonlea Yesterday and Today: Archaeology and*

Prehistory, edited by Leslie B. Davis, pp. 291–309. Saskatchewan Archaeological Association, Saskatoon.

1994 Oxbow Bison Procurement as Seen from the Harder Site, Saskatchewan. *Journal of Archaeological Science* 21:757–777.

n.d. Canadian Archaeological Radiocarbon Database. Record on file, Canadian Museum of Civilization, Gatineau, Quebec.

MORLAN, RICHARD E., R. MCNEELY, S.A. WOLFE, AND B.T. SCHREINER

2002 *Quaternary Dates and Vertebrate Faunas in Saskatchewan*. Geological Survey of Canada, Open File 38888, Natural Resources Canada, Ottawa.

MULLOY, WILLIAM

1954 The McKean Site in Northeastern Wyoming. *Southwestern Journal of Anthropology* 10:432–461.

1958 *A Preliminary Historical Outline for the Northwestern Plains*. Continuation of University of Wyoming Publications in Science, Vol. 22 (1 and 2), Laramie.

MUNSON, PATRICK J.

1990 Folsom Fluted Projectile Points East of the Great Plains and Their Biogeographical Correlates. *North American Archaeologist* 11(3):255–272.

MURPHY, BRENT

2003 *Final Report, Historical Resource Mitigation, Westminster Glen Country Residential Subdivision NW 114, Sec. 12-26-03-W5M* (ASA Permit 02-045). Archaeological Survey of Alberta. Permit No. 2002-045. Copies available from Archaeological Survey of Alberta, Edmonton.

MURRAY, E.M., THAYER SMITH, AND BRIAN O.K. REEVES

1976 *Archaeological Salvage Investigations, Alberta Highways and Transportation Construction Projects, Hwy. 1, Hartell Creek Site*. Archaeological Survey of Alberta. Permit No. 1974-027. Copies available from Archaeological Survey of Alberta, Edmonton.

NANCE, JACK D.

1972 Classification and Analysis of Artifacts. Unpublished PhD dissertation, Department of Archaeology, University of Calgary, Calgary.

NERO, ROBERT W.

1997 An Oxbow Occupation Site Near Elm Creek, Manitoba. *Manitoba Archaeological Journal*. 7(2):50–64.

NERO, ROBERT W., AND BRUCE A. MCCORQUODALE

1958 Report of an Excavation at the Oxbow Dam Site. *The Blue Jay* 16 (2):82–90.

NEUMAN, ROBERT W.

1975 *The Sonota Complex and Associated Sites on the Northern Great Plains*. Nebraska State Historical Society Publications in Anthropology No. 6. Nebraska State Historical Society, Lincoln.

NEWTON, BARRY

1991 Bow Corridor Project: Summary of the 1988–1989 Research. In *Archaeology in Alberta 1988 and 1989*, edited by Martin Magne, pp. 113–125. Occasional Paper No. 33. Archaeological Survey of Alberta, Edmonton.

NICHOLSON, BEVERLY A.

1985 The Kain Cache Site (DiLw 12): A Functional Explanation of a Boulder Structure on the Northern Plains / Parkland Interface. *Canadian Journal of Archaeology* 9(2):173–181.

1994 Cultural Stratigraphy at the Kain Site (DlLw 11). *Manitoba Archaeological Quarterly* 12(1):31–48.

NICHOLSON, BEVERLY, AND SCOTT HAMILTON

1997 Preliminary Report on the Middle Precontact Occupations at the Vera Site in the Makotchi-Ded Dontipi Locale. *Manitoba Archaeological Journal* 7(2):37–50.

NICHOLSON, BEVERLY, AND TOMASIN PLAYFORD

2009 The Atkinson Site: A 6,400-Year-Old Gowen (Mummy Cave) Occupation Near Lauder, Manitoba. *Plains Anthropologist* 54(209):29–48

NOVECOSKY, BRAD

2002a Archaeological Investigations in the Quill Lakes Region, East Central Saskatchewan. Unpublished Master's thesis, Department of Anthropology and Archaeology, University of Saskatchewan, Saskatoon.

2002b The Haskey Area: A Cody Complex Site from the Quill Lakes Region, Saskatchewan, Canada. *Current Research in the Pleistocene* 19:73–74.

NOWATZYK, GABRIELE

1983 Archaeological Investigations at the Cremer Site (24SW264). *Archaeology in Montana* 24(2):59–91.

O'BRIEN, PATRICIA

1984 The Tim Adrian Site (14NT604): A Hell Gap Quarry in Norton County, Kansas. *Plains Anthropologist* 29(103)41–55.

OETELAAR, GERALD

1998 *Interim Report on the 1997 Archaeological Excavations at Tuscany (Permit 97-045).* Archaeological Survey of Alberta, Permit No. 1997-045. Copies available from Archaeological Survey of Alberta, Edmonton.

2004a Six Meters Below Surface and Beyond: Yet New Opportunities and Challenges at the Stampede Site, Cypress Hills, Alberta. Paper presented at the 62nd Annual Plains Anthropological Conference, Billings, Montana.

2004b Landscape Evolution and Human Occupation During the Archaic Period on the Northern Plains. *Canadian Journal of Earth Sciences* 41:725–740.

OSBORN, GERALD, LIONEL JACKSON JR., RENE BARENDREGT, RANDOLPH ENKIN, ROBERT YOUNG, AND PAUL WILSON

2000 Geological Constraints on Archaeological Interpretations of a Late Wisconsinan Site at Varsity Estates, Calgary, Alberta. *Quaternary International* 68(71):209–215.

PAULSON, LLOYD

1980 The Richards Site: A Sonota Site in South-Central Manitoba. *Archae-Facts* 7(3 and 4):1–39.

PAYETTE, JACQUELINE M., LYNELLE A. PETERSON, AND EDWIN HAJIC

2006 Investigations at the Vestal Site (24FR760): An Avonlea Bison Processing Site. *Archaeology in Montana* 47(1):1–96.

PEACH, KATE

2006 *Historical Resources Mitigation, Alberta Transportation, Stoney Trail Expansion, Component A, Stage I, Mitigation of Sites EgPn 667 and EhPm 85; Stage I and II, Mitigation of Site EgPm 82: Final Report,* Permit 2004-184. Archaeological Survey of Alberta. Permit No. 2004-184. Copies available from Archaeological Survey of Alberta, Edmonton.

PECK, TREVOR R.

1996 Late Side-notched Projectile Points on the Northwestern Plains. Unpublished Master's thesis, Department of Anthropology, University of Alberta, Edmonton.

2002 Archaeologically Recovered Ammonites: Evidence for Long-term Continuity in Nitsitapii Ritual. *Plains Anthropologist* 47(181): 147–164.

2004 *Bison Ethology and Native Settlement Patterns During the Old Women's Phase on the Northwestern Plains.* BAR International Series 1278. Archaeopress, Oxford, England.

2005 A Refinement of "Mummy Cave Complex" Projectile Point Systematics on the Alberta Plains. Paper presented at the 63rd Annual Plains Anthropological Conference, Edmonton.

2006 A Note on Boss Hill Corner-notched Projectile Points. *Alberta Archaeological Review* 44:20–23.

2007 Ammonites, Death Lodges, and Effigies: Archaeological Evidence for the Prehistoric Nitsitapii (Blackfoot). Paper presented to the Department of Anthropology, University of Alberta, Edmonton.

PECK, TREVOR R., JASON GILLESPIE, AND SHAWN BUBEL

2006 *The Purple Springs Site (DlOx 6): A Possible Palaeoindian Site Near Taber, Alberta: Permit*

2004-382, *Final Report*. Archaeological Survey of Alberta. Permit No. 2004-382. Copies available from Archaeological Survey of Alberta, Edmonton.

PECK, TREVOR R., AND CAROLINE R. HUDECEK-CUFFE

2003 Archaeology on the Alberta Plains: The Last Two Thousand Years. In *Archaeology in Alberta: A View from the New Millennium*, edited by Jack W. Brink and John F. Dormaar, pp. 72–103. Archaeological Society of Alberta, Medicine Hat.

PECK, TREVOR R., AND JOHN W. IVES

2001 Late Side-notched Projectile Points on the Northern Plains. *Plains Anthropologist* 46(176):115–232.

PENDREE, WAYNE R.

1981 Surface Finds: A Discussion of Harris Sand Hills Materials. *Saskatchewan Archaeological Society Newsletter* 2(1):25–27.

PETTIPAS, LEO F.

1970 Early Man in Manitoba. In *Ten Thousand Years: Archaeology in Manitoba*, edited by Walter M. Hlady, pp. 5–28. Manitoba Archaeological Society. D. W. Friesen and Sons Ltd., Altona, Manitoba.

1971 Possible Early Man Artifacts from Manitoba. *Saskatchewan Archaeology Newsletter* 32:6–17.

1976 A Clovis Point from Near Manitou, Manitoba. *Archae-Facts* 3(2 and 3):4–14.

1980 The Little Gem Complex. *Saskatchewan Archaeology* 1(2):3–81.

1982 A Reconsideration of Late Paleo-Indian (Plano) Prehistory. *Manitoba Archaeological Quarterly* 6(4):44–77.

1985 Recent Developments in Palaeo-Indian Archaeology in Manitoba. In *Contributions to Plains Prehistory*, edited by David Burley, pp. 39–63, Occasional Paper No. 26. Archaeological Survey of Alberta, Edmonton.

1996a *Aboriginal Migrations: A History of Movements in Southern Manitoba*. Manitoba Museum of Man and Nature, Winnipeg.

1996b Manitoba Plano: A Theory Revisited. *Manitoba Archaeological Journal* 6(1):86–99.

PERTTULA, TIMOTHY K.

1993 New Folsom Point Finds from Eastern Texas. *Plains Anthropologist* 38(143):199–202.

PITULKO, V.V., P.A. NIKOLSKY, E. YU. GIRYA, A.E. BASILYAN, V.E. TUMSKOY, S.A. KOULAKOV, S.N. ASTAKHOV, E. YU. PAVLOVA, AND M.A. ANISIMOV

2004 The Yana RHS Site: Humans in the Arctic Before the Last Glacial Maximum. *Science* 303:52–56.

PLAYFORD, TOMASIN M.

1996 Two Thousand Years of Occupation at Nahastewin: A Sacred Site in Southwestern Manitoba. Unpublished Bachelor's thesis, Department of Anthropology, Brandon University, Brandon, Manitoba.

POLLOCK, JOHN W.

1981 Plains Archaic Complexes in the Alberta Parkland and Boreal Forest. *Canadian Journal of Archaeology* 5:145–153.

PRENTICE, JEAN

1983 The Tschetter Site: A Study of a Late Prehistoric Bison Kill. Unpublished Master's thesis, Department of Anthropology and Archaeology, University of Saskatchewan, Saskatoon.

PYSZCZYK, HEINZ

1997 The Use of Fur Trade Goods by Plains Indians, Central and Southern Alberta, Canada. *Canadian Journal of Archaeology* 21(1):45–84.

1999 Historic Metal Projectile Points and Arrows, Alberta, Canada: A Theory for Aboriginal Arrow Design on the Great Plains. *Plains Anthropologist* 44(168):165–187.

QUIGG, J. MICHAEL

1974a St. Mary Salvage Project. In *Archaeological Salvage Projects 1973*, edited by William J. Byrne, pp. 100–104. Archaeological Survey of Canada Paper No. 26. National Museum of Man Mercury Series, National Museums of Canada, Ottawa.

1974b *The Belly River: Prehistoric Population Dynamics in a Northwestern Plains Transitional Zone.* Archaeological Survey of Canada Paper No. 23. National Museum of Man Mercury Series, National Museums of Canada, Ottawa.

1975a Preliminary Investigation of the St. Mary and Belly River Regions: 1973. In *Salvage Contributions: Prairie Provinces*, edited by R. Wilmeth, pp. 44–74. Archaeological Survey of Canada Paper No. 33. National Museum of Man Mercury Series, National Museums of Canada, Ottawa.

1975b Preliminary Description and Interpretation of the S.S. Burmis Site (DjPn 62):1974, In *Salvage Contributions: Prairie Provinces*, edited by R. Wilmeth, pp. 75–94. Archaeological Survey of Canada Paper No. 33. National Museum of Man Mercury Series, National Museums of Canada, Ottawa

1976 A Note on the Fletcher Site. In *Archaeology in Alberta 1975*, edited by J. Quigg and W. Byrne, pp. 108–110. Occasional Paper No. 1. Archaeological Survey of Alberta, Edmonton.

1984 A 4,700-Year-Old Tool Assemblage from East-central Alberta. *Plains Anthropologist* 29(104):151–159.

1986 *Ross Glen: A Besant Stone Circle Site in Southeastern Alberta.* Manuscript Series No. 10. Archaeological Survey of Alberta, Edmonton.

1988a A Ceramic-Bearing Avonlea Component in Southwestern Alberta. In *Avonlea Yesterday and Today: Archaeology and Prehistory*, edited by Leslie B. Davis, pp. 67–80. Saskatchewan Archaeological Society, Saskatoon.

1988b A New Avonlea Ceramic Style from North-central Montana. In *Avonlea Yesterday and Today: Archaeology and Prehistory*, edited by Leslie B. Davis, pp. 145–154. Saskatchewan Archaeological Society, Saskatoon.

RAMSAY, ALLYSON M.

1991 The Melhagen Site: A Besant Bison Kill in South-central Saskatchewan. Unpublished Master's thesis, Department of Anthropology and Archaeology, University of Saskatchewan, Saskatoon.

RAMSAY, CHARLES L.

1993 The Redtail Site: A McKean Habitation in South Central Saskatchewan. Unpublished Master's thesis. Department of Anthropology and Archaeology, University of Saskatchewan, Saskatoon.

2005 *Interim Report, Alberta Infrastructure and Transportation and the City of Calgary, Stoney Trail and Crowchild Trail Interchange HRM Study at EgPn 677 (Permits 2005-121 and 2005-520).* Archaeological Survey of Alberta. Permit Nos. 2005-121 and 2005-520. Copies available from Archaeological Survey of Alberta, Edmonton.

RAMSEY, BRONK

2005 OxCal Version 3.10.

RAY, ARTHUR

1974 *Indians in the Fur Trade.* University of Toronto Press, Toronto.

REEVES, BRIAN O.K.

1969 The Southern Alberta Paleo-Cultural–Paleo-Environmental Sequence. In *Post-Pleistocene Man and His Environment on the Northern Plain*, edited by R.G. Forbis, L.B. Davis, O.A. Christensen, and G. Fedirchuk, pp. 6–46. University of Calgary Archaeological Association, Calgary.

1970 Culture Change in the Northern Plains, 1000 B.C.–A.D. 1000. Unpublished PhD dissertation, Department of Archaeology, University of Calgary, Calgary.

1972 *The Archaeology of Pass Creek Valley, Waterton Lakes National Parks.* National Historic Sites Service. Manuscript Report No. 61. National and Historic Parks Branch, Department of Indian Affairs and Northern Development.

1973 The Concept of an Altithermal Cultural Hiatus in Northern Plains Prehistory. *American Anthropologist* 75:1221–1253.

1974 EfPs-3, A 6,500-Year-Old Campsite in the Kananaskis Valley. Archaeological Survey of Alberta. CRM 046. Copies available from Archaeological Survey of Alberta, Edmonton.

1975 Archaeological Investigations, Village of Bellvue, Sewer and Water System, 1974, Permit No. 74-001. Archaeololgical Survey of Alberta. Permit No. 1974-001. Copies available from Archaeological Survey of Alberta, Edmonton.

1976 Archaeological Salvage Investigations, Alberta Highways and Transport Construction Projects, Hwy. 3: West of Coleman and Bellevue/Maple Leaf Area, Permit 75-020. Archaeological Survey of Alberta. Permit No. 1975-020. Copies available from Archaeological Survey of Alberta, Edmonton.

1977a Archaeological Salvage Investigations, Alberta Highways and Transport Construction Projects, Prehistoric Sites DjPo-9 and 46, Permit No. 76-23. Archaeological Survey of Alberta. Permit No. 1976-023. Copies available from Archaeological Survey of Alberta, Edmonton.

1977b Historical Site Report, Dome Petroleum Limited, Empress–Red Deer Ethane Pipeline. Archaeological Survey of Alberta. Permit No. 1976-065. Copies available from Archaeological Survey of Alberta, Edmonton.

1978 Head-Smashed-In: 5,500 Years of Bison Jumping in the Alberta Plains. Plains Anthropologist 14 (2):151–174.

1983a Culture Change in the Northern Plains: 1000 B.C.–A.D. 1000. Occasional Paper No. 20. Archaeological Survey of Alberta, Edmonton.

1983b The Kenney Site: A Stratified Campsite in Southwestern Alberta. Archaeology in Montana 24(1):1–135.

1990 Communal Bison Hunters of the Northern Plains. In Hunters of the Recent Past, edited by L.B. Davis and B.O.K. Reeves, pp. 168–194. Unwin Hyman, London.

1993 Iniskim: A Sacred Nitsitapii Religious Tradition. In Kunaitupii: Coming Together on Native Sacred Sites, edited by Brian O.K. Reeves and Margaret Kennedy, pp. 194–259. Proceedings of the First Joint Meeting of the Archaeological Society of Alberta and the Montana Archaeological Society, Waterton Lakes National Park, Alberta.

2003 Mistakis: The Archaeology of Waterton-Glacier International Peace Park, Archaeological Inventory and Assessment Program, 1993–1996. Manuscript on file, Archaeological Survey of Alberta, Edmonton, Alberta.

2005 Historical Resources Impact Assessment, Vision Quest Windelectric Inc., Blue Trail Wind Farm Project: Final Report (Permit 2004-196). Archaeological Survey of Alberta. Permit No. 2004-196. Copies available from Archaeological Survey of Alberta, Edmonton.

REEVES, BRIAN O.K., CLAIRE BOURGES, CARMEN OLSON, AND AMANDA DOW

2000 City of Calgary Native Archaeological Site Inventory. Vols. 1 and 2. Manuscript on file, Archaeological Survey of Alberta, Edmonton.

REEVES, BRIAN O.K., AND JOHN F. DORMAAR

1972 A Partial Holocene Pedological and Archaeological Record from the Southern Alberta Rocky Mountains. Arctic and Alpine Research 4(4):325–336.

REEVES, BRIAN O.K., AND JONATHAN C. DRIVER

1978 Archaeological Investigations, Crowsnest Pass Site DjPo-47, 1977 Field Season, Permit 77-068. Archaeological Survey of Alberta. Permit No. 1977-068. Copies available from Archaeological Survey of Alberta, Edmonton.

REEVES, BRIAN O.K., AND MARGARET KENNEDY

1980 DjPo 25, Archaeological Investigations in the Crowsnest Pass: Final Report. Report prepared for the Social Sciences and Humanities Research Council, Ottawa.

ROBERTS, FRANK H.H.

1935 A Folsom Complex: A Preliminary Report on Investigations at the Lindenmeier Site in Northern Colorado. Smithsonian Miscellaneous Collections 94(4):1–35.

1942 A New Site. American Antiquity 8(1):300.

ROBERTS, ARTHUR

1984 Ice Free Corridor Paleoindian Survey. Current Research in the Pleistocene 1:15–17.

ROE, FRANK GILBERT

1955 *The Indian and the Horse*. University of Oklahoma Press, Norman.

ROLL, TOM E.

1988 Focus on a Phase: Expanded Geographical Distribution and Resultant Taxonomic Implications for Avonlea. In *Avonlea Yesterday and Today: Archaeology and Prehistory*, edited by Leslie B. Davis, pp. 237–250. Saskatchewan Archaeological Society, Saskatoon.

ROLL, TOM E., STEPHEN A. AABERG, AND MIKE BERGSTROM

1994 The Seline Site (24DW250): A Late-Middle Period Bison Kill Near Glendive, Montana. *Archaeology in Montana* 35(1):1–53.

ROLL, TOM E., AND KEN DEAVER

1980 *The Bootleger Trail Site: A Late Prehistoric Spring Bison Kill*. Heritage Conservation and Recreation Service, Interagency Archaeological Services, Denver.

RONAGHAN, BRIAN

1986 Radiocarbon Dates on Pre-Mazama Ashfall Occupations in the Crowsnest Pass. In *Archaeology in Alberta 1985*, edited by J. Ives, p. 206. Occasional Paper No. 29. Archaeological Survey of Alberta, Edmonton.

1992 *An Archaeological Assessment of the Burmis Lundbreck Corridor, Southern Alberta Foothills, Permit 85-043*. Archaeological Survey of Alberta. Permit No. 1985-043. Copies available from Archaeological Survey of Alberta, Edmonton.

1993 The James Pass Project: Early Holocene Occupation in the Front Ranges of the Rocky Mountains. *Canadian Journal of Archaeology* 17:85–91.

RONAGHAN, BRIAN, AND ROBERT DAWE

1998 An Early Holocene Occupation of James Pass, Alberta. Paper presented at the 31st Annual Canadian Archaeological Association Conference, Victoria, British Columbia.

RONAGHAN, BRIAN, AND ALISON LANDALS

1983 *Final Report, Historical Resources Impact Assessment and Conservation Excavation Studies, Douglasdale Estates* (ASA Permit No. 81-038). Archaeological Survey of Alberta. Permit No. 1981-038. Copies available from Archaeological Survey of Alberta, Edmonton.

RONAGHAN, BRIAN, AND BRIAN O.K. REEVES

1980 *Conservation Archaeological Excavations, Calgary Power Ltd., Lethbridge, Magrath 138 KV Transmission Line: Final Report, Permits 80-013 and 80-071*. Archaeological Survey of Alberta. Permit Nos. 1980-013 and 1980-071. Copies available from Archaeological Survey of Alberta, Edmonton.

ROOT, MATTHEW J.

1998 Dating a Cody-Complex Occupation in the Knife River Flint Quarries. *Current Research in the Pleistocene* 15:62–64.

ROOT, MATTHEW J., DOUGLAS MACDONALD, AND ALICE M. EMERSON

1996 The Bobtail Wolf Site: An Update on Recent Excavations. *Current Research in the Pleistocene* 13:38–40.

ROOT, MATTHEW J., W.P. MILLER, AND DENNIS L. TOOM

2001 Stone Tools and Flake Debris. In *Besant-Sonota on the Little Missouri River: The Doaks Butte Site (32BO222), Bowman County, North Dakota*, edited by Dennis L. Toom, pp. 9.1–9.66. Report Submitted to Montana State Office, U.S. Bureau of Land Management, Billings, Montana.

ROOT, MATTHEW J., JEB TAYLOR, JERRY D. WILLIAM, AND LISA K. SHIFRIN

1999 Gearing Up and Moving Out: Folsom Settlement in Western North Dakota. *Current Research in the Pleistocene* 16:67–69.

RUEBELMANN, GEORGE N.

1988 The Henry Smith Site: An Avonlea Bison Procurement and Ceremonial Complex in Northern Montana. In *Avonlea Yesterday and Today: Archaeology and Prehistory*, edited by Leslie B. Davis, pp. 191–202. Saskatchewan Archaeological Society, Saskatoon.

RUTHERFORD, A.A., JUERGEN WITTENBERG, AND ROSCOE WILMETH
1981 University of Saskatchewan Radiocarbon Dates IX. *Radiocarbon* 23(1):94–135.

SAXBERG, NANCY, AND BRIAN O.K. REEVES
2003 The First Two Thousand Years of Oils Sands History: Ancient Hunters at the Northwest Outlet of Glacial Lake Agassiz. In *Archaeology in Alberta: A View from the New Millennium*, edited by Jack Brink and John Dormaar, pp. 290–323. Archaeological Society of Alberta, Medicine Hat.

SAYLOR, STAN
1975 DhLb 1: Early Period Occupation Near Glacial Lake Agassiz, Southeast Manitoba. *Plains Anthropologist* 20(70):241–252.
1978 Test Excavations at a Manitoba Clovis Site, EdLw 1. *Archae-Facts* 5(4):1–7.

SCHLESIER, KARL J. (EDITOR)
1994 *Plains Indians, A.D. 500–1500: The Archeological Past of Historic Groups*. University of Oklahoma Press, Norman.

SCHNEIDER, FRED, AND JEFF KINNEY
1978 Evans: A Multicomponent Site in Northwestern North Dakota. *Archaeology in Montana* 19(1 and 2):2–39.

SCHROEDL, A.R., AND E.G. WALKER
1978 A Preliminary Report on the Gowen Site: An Early Middle Prehistoric Site on the Northwestern Plains. *Napao* 8(1 and 2):1–5.

SCRIBE, BRIAN
1997 *Nistam Ka-ke Askihkokechik Puskwaw-askihk*: An Assessment of Besant-Sonota Pottery on the Canadian Plains. Unpublished Master's thesis, Department of Archaeology, University of Saskatoon, Saskatoon.

SCRIBE, BRIAN, AND BEVERLY NICHOLSON
1994 Excavations at the Middle Woodland *Pinew Watchi* and *Wapiti Sakihtaw* Sites on the Big Tiger Geoform: A First Nation Training Project. *Manitoba Archaeological Journal* 4(1 and 3):113–128.

SELLARDS, E. H.
1952 *Early Man in America: A Study in Prehistory*. Texas Memorial Museum Publication. University of Texas Press, Austin.

SELLET, FREDERIC
2001 A Changing Perspective on Paleoindian Chronology and Typology: A View from the Northwestern Plains. *Arctic Anthropology* 38(2):48–63.

SELLET, FREDERIC, AND MICHAEL FOSHA
2000 Distribution of Folsom and Goshen Artifacts in South Dakota. *Current Research in the Pleistocene* 17:74–75.

SHEEHAN, MICHAEL S.
1995 Cultural Response to the Altithermal or Inadequate Sampling? *Plains Anthropologist* 40(153):261–270.

SHELLEY, PHILLIP H., AND GEORGE AGOGINO
1983 Agate Basin Technology: An Insight. *Plains Anthropologist* 28(99):115–118.

SHIFRIN, LISA K., AND JERRY D. WILLIAM
1996 Investigations at Young-Man-Chief, a Folsom Site in North Dakota. *Current Research in the Pleistocene* 13:42–44.

SHORTT, MACK
1993 The Happy Valley Bison Kill. Unpublished Master's thesis, Department of Archaeology, University of Calgary, Calgary.

SHUMATE, MAYNARD
1950 *The Archaeology of the Vicinity of Great Falls, Montana*. Anthropology and Sociology Papers No. 2. Montana State University, Missoula.

1967 The Taft Hill Buffalo Jump. *Archaeology in Montana* 8(4):12–34.

1976 Two Former Besant Pounds Along the Sun River. *Archaeology in Montana* 17(1 and 2):11–31.

1984 Surface Finds from Missouri Valley Blowouts Between Tunis and Loma, Montana. *Archaeology in Montana* 25(1):17–24.

SIEGFRIED, EVELYN V.

2002 Paleoethnobotany on the Northern Plains: The Tuscany Archaeological Site (EgPn-377), Calgary, Alberta. Unpublished PhD dissertation, Department of Archaeology, University of Calgary, Calgary.

SIMON, A.

1979 Pottery Manufacture Analysis: Experimental Assessment of Technological Continuity in the Altamont Region. *Archaeology in Montana* 20(2):1–78.

SMITH, BRIAN J., AND ERNEST G. WALKER

1988 Evidence for Diverse Subsistence Strategies in an Avonlea Component. In *Avonlea Yesterday and Today: Archaeology and Prehistory*, edited by Leslie B. Davis, pp. 81–88. Saskatchewan Archaeological Society, Saskatoon.

SMITH, CRAIG S., AND LANCE M. MCNEES

1990 Rattlesnake Pass Site: A Folsom Occupation in South-central Wyoming. *Plains Anthropologist* 35(129):273–289.

SMITH, MARC B.

1981 Archaeological Investigations in the Deep Creek/French Creek Locality; Deer Lodge County, Montana. *Archaeology in Montana* 22(2):39–87.

SMITH, THAYER, AND BRIAN O.K. REEVES

1978 *Archaeological Investigations, Alberta Gas Ethylene Water Intake Area, Red Deer River, Joffre, Alberta (Permit No. 77-42)*. Archaeological Survey of Alberta. Permit No. 1977-042. Copies available from Archaeological Survey of Alberta, Edmonton.

SPEIDEL, PAUL

1996 A Parallel-Grooved Avonlea Vessel from the Forks, Winnipeg (DlLg 33). *Manitoba Archaeological Journal* 6(2):72–81.

SPICER, GARETH

2007a *Final Report, Historical Resources Impact Assessment, TransCanada Pipelines Limited, Nevis to Gadsby Crossover Pipeline, RoW Townships 40–42, Ranges 16–23, W4M, and Historical Resources Impact Mitigation, the Henry James Site (FcPc 35) (ASA Permit 2006-085)*. Archaeological Survey of Alberta. Permit No. 2006-085. Copies available from Archaeological Survey of Alberta, Edmonton.

2007b The Henry James Site (FcPc 35): A Multicomponent Pre-Contact Archaeological Site Near Stettler, Alberta. *Alberta Archaeological Review* 46:10–12.

SPURLING, BRIAN E., AND BRUCE F. BALL

1981 On Some Distributions of the Oxbow "Complex." *Canadian Journal of Archaeology* 5:89–102.

STANFORD, DENNIS

1978a The Jones-Miller Site: An Example of Hell Gap Bison Procurement Strategy. In *Bison Procurement and Utilization: A Symposium*, edited by Leslie B. Davis and Michael Wilson. Memoir 14, *Plains Anthropologist* 23(82, pt. 2):90–97.

1978b Some Clovis Points. Paper presented at the 5th Biennial Meeting of the American Quaternary Association, Edmonton.

1996 Foreshaft Sockets as Possible Clovis Hafting Devices. *Current Research in the Pleistocene* 13:44–46.

STORCK, PETER L.

1973 A Description of Some Paleo-Indian and Archaic Projectile Points and Knives from Saskatchewan, Manitoba, and Alberta in Collections of the Royal Ontario Museum, Toronto. *Saskatchewan Archaeology Newsletter* 41:1–28.

STRONG, WILLIAM DUNCAN

1935 An Introduction to Nebraska Archaeology. *Smithsonian Miscellaneous Collection*, Vol. 93, No. 10.

STUART, G.

1988 *Archaeological Investigations at the Wells Site and Anderson Site in Alberta's Parkland, Permit 87-034*, Fedirchuk McCullough and Associates Ltd. Archaeological Survey of Alberta. Permit No. 1987-034. Copies available from Archaeological Survey of Alberta, Edmonton.

SWANSON, JR., EARL H.

1962 Early Cultures in Northwestern America. *American Antiquity* 28(2):151–158.

SWANSON, JR., EARL H., B. ROBERT BUTLER, AND ROBSON BONNICHSEN

1964 *Birch Creek Papers No. 2: Natural and Cultural Stratigraphy in the Birch Creek Valley of Eastern Idaho*. Occasional Papers of the Idaho State University Museum No. 14. Pocatello, Idaho.

SWANSON, JR., EARL H., AND PAUL G. SNEED

1966 *Birch Creek Papers No. 3: The Archaeology of the Shoup Rockshelters in East Central Idaho*. Occasional Papers of the Idaho State University Museum No. 17. Pocatello, Idaho.

SYMS, E. LEIGH

1970 The McKean Complex in Manitoba. In *Ten Thousand Years: Archaeology in Manitoba*, edited by Walter M. Hlady, pp. 123–138. Manitoba Archaeological Society. D.W. Friesen and Sons Ltd., Altona, Manitoba.

1974 An Assessment of the Archaeological Resources of the Cherry Point Site in Southwestern Manitoba. *Archae-facts* 1(3–4):10–23.

1977 *Cultural Ecology and Ecological Dynamics of the Ceramics Period in Southwestern Manitoba*. Memoir 12, *Plains Anthropologist* 22(76, pt. 2):1–160.

TAYLOR, JEB

2006 *Projectile Points of the High Plains*. Jeb Taylor Artifacts Inc., Buffalo, Wyoming.

THOMPSON, DAVID

1916. *David Thompson's Narrative of His Explorations in Western America, 1784–1812*, edited by J.B. Tyrrell. Publication No. 12. Champlain Society, Toronto.

TIBESAR, WILLIAM

1980 An Intra-site Discussion of Grayrocks Archaeological Site: 48PL65. Unpublished Master's thesis, Department of Anthropology, University of Wyoming, Laramie.

TISCHER, JENNIFER C.

2000 EgPn-440: A Late Prehistoric Bison Pound on the Northwestern Plains. Unpublished Master's thesis, University of Calgary, Calgary.

TOLMAN, M. SHAYNE

2001 DhPg 8: From Mammoths to Machinery: An Overview of 11,000 Years Along the St. Mary River. Unpublished Master's thesis. University of Calgary, Calgary.

TOMPKINS, C.N.

1993 Classifying Clovis Points: A Study in Metric Variability. Unpublished Master's thesis, Department of Anthropology, University of Arizona, Tucson.

TOOM, DENNIS L. (EDITOR)

2001 *Besant-Sonota on the Little Missouri River: The Doaks Butte Site (32BO222), Bowman County, North Dakota*. Report submitted to the Montana State Office, U.S. Bureau of Land Management, Billings, Montana.

TOOM, DENNIS L., AND MICHAEL A. JACKSON

2001 Discussion and Conclusions. In *Besant-Sonota on the Little Missouri River: The Doaks Butte Site (32BO222), Bowman County, North Dakota*, edited by Dennis L. Toom, pp. 14.1–14.8. Report submitted to the Montana State Office, U.S. Bureau of Land Management, Billings, Montana.

TRATEBAS, ALICE, AND ANN M. JOHNSON

1988 Three Avonlea Bison Kill Sites in the Milk River Drainage of Northeastern Montana. In *Avonlea Yesterday and Today: Archaeology and Prehistory*, edited by Leslie B. Davis, pp. 89–100. Saskatchewan Archaeological Society, Saskatoon.

TURNEY, MICHAEL

2004 Final Report, Historical Resources Impact Mitigation, Lafarge Canada Inc., Gravel Extraction Facility Mitigation of EfPl 226 (ASA Permit 2003-253). Archaeological Survey of Alberta. Permit No. 2003-253. Copies available from Archaeological Survey of Alberta, Edmonton.

UNFREED, WENDY J., AND STANLEY VAN DYKE

2005 *Archaeological Investigations at the Junction Site (DkPi 2).* Occasional Papers of the Archaeological Society of Alberta No. 4. Archaeological Society of Alberta, Calgary.

VAN DYKE, STANLEY

1982 Archaeological Conservation Studies at EfPm-104, the Bow Bottom Site, and EfPm-103: Final Report, Permit 80-064. Archaeological Survey of Alberta. Permit No. 1980-064. Copies available from Archaeological Survey of Alberta, Edmonton.

1993 Archaeological Site Mitigation, Pt. S.E. 4-26-4-W5M, EhPo-54 and EhPo-55, Archaeological Survey: Final Report, Permit 93-012. Archaeological Survey of Alberta. Permit No. 1993-012. Copies available from Archaeological Survey of Alberta, Edmonton.

1994 Oldman River Dam Prehistoric Archaeology Mitigation Program, Technical Series No. 1: Campsites Study, 1988–1991 (Permits 88-39, 89-25, 90-25, 91-50). Archaeological Survey of Alberta. CRM 100. Copies available from Archaeological Survey of Alberta, Edmonton.

1997 Final Report, Historical Resources Impact Assessment and Conservation of DjPn- 132, Villa-Vega Acres (Phase 2) Subdivision, Bison Historical Services Ltd., Permit 97-016. Archaeological Survey of Alberta. Permit No. 1997-016. Copies available from Archaeological Survey of Alberta, Edmonton.

VAN DYKE, STANLEY, SHARON HANNA, WENDY UNFREED, AND BARB NEAL

1990 Section 3.0, 1989 Oldman River Dam Prehistoric Archaeological Mitigation Program, Campsites Component: Final Report, Bison Historical Services Limited, Permit 89-025. Vols. 1–3. Archaeological Survey of Alberta. Permit No. 1989-025. Copies available from Archaeological Survey of Alberta, Edmonton.

VAN DYKE, STANLEY, AND SALLY STEWART

1985 *Hawkwood Site (EgPm 179): A Multicomponent Historic Campsite on Nose Hill.* Manuscript Series No. 7, Archaeological Survey of Alberta, Edmonton.

VAN DYKE, STANLEY, AND WENDY UNFREED

1992 Section 1.0, 1990 Oldman River Dam Prehistoric Archaeology Mitigation Project: Campsites Programme, Bison Historical Services Limited, Permit 90-025. Archaeological Survey of Alberta. Permit No. 1990-025. Copies available from Archaeological Survey of Alberta, Edmonton.

VANCE, ROBERT E.

1991 A Paleobotanical Study of Holocene Drought Frequency in Southern Alberta. Unpublished PhD dissertation, Department of Biological Sciences, Simon Fraser University, Burnaby, British Columbia.

VANCE, ROBERT E., ALWYNNE B. BEAUDOIN, AND BRIAN H. LUCKMAN

1995 The Paleoecological Record of 6 KA BP Climate in the Canadian Prairie Provinces. *Géographie Physique et Quaternaire* 49(1):81–98.

VARSAKIS, IRENE

2006 Besant Revisited: The Fincastle Site (DlOx 5) and Archaeological Cultures on the Northwestern Plains, 2500 BP–1250 BP. Unpublished Master's thesis, Department of Geography, University of Lethbridge, Lethbridge, Alberta.

VARSAKIS, IRENE, AND TREVOR R. PECK

2005 Pelican Lakes and Sandy Creeks: The Late Middle Prehistoric Period on the Alberta Plains. Paper presented at the 63rd Annual Plains Anthropological Conference, Edmonton.

VICKERS, J. RODERICK

1986 *Alberta Plains Prehistory: A Review.* Occasional Paper No. 27. Archaeological Survey of Alberta, Edmonton.

1994 Cultures on the Northwestern Plains: From the Boreal Forest Edge to the Milk River. In *Plains Indians, A.D. 500–1500: The Archeological Past of Historic Groups*, edited by Karl H. Schlesier, pp. 3–33. University of Oklahoma Press, Norman.

2008 Anthropomorphic Effigies of the Plains. *Plains Anthropologist* 53(206):199–221.

VICKERS, J. RODERICK, AND ALWYNNE BEAUDOIN

1989 A Limiting AMS Date for the Cody Complex Occupation at the Fletcher Site, Alberta. *Plains Anthropologist* 34(125):261–264.

VIVIAN, BRIAN C.

2002 *Historical Resource Conservation Excavations, Valley Ridge Golf Course, EgPn 220 (Permits 91-028 and 98-013).* Archaeological Survey of Alberta. Permit Nos. 1991-028 and 1998-013. Copies available from Archaeological Survey of Alberta, Edmonton.

2005 *Historical Resources Mitigative Excavations at Genesis Land Development Corp.'s North Calgary Commercial Campus at Balzac: Final Report (Permit 2004-153).* Archaeological Survey of Alberta. Permit No. 2004-153. Copies available from Archaeological Survey of Alberta, Edmonton.

2006a *Historical Resource Mitigative Excavations, EfPm 266: Final Report (ASA Permit 2006-162).* Archaeological Survey of Alberta. Permit No. 2006-162. Copies available from Archaeological Survey of Alberta, Edmonton.

2006b *Historical Resource Mitigative Excavations at Genesis Land Development Corp.'s Grandview Estates: Final Report (Permit 2005-173).* Archaeological Survey of Alberta. Permit No. 2005-173. Copies available from Archaeological Survey of Alberta, Edmonton.

2007a *Historical Resource Conservation Studies of the Tuscany Stage 9 Subdivision Development Sites EgPn 700, EgPn 701, and EgPn 702 (Permit 2006-163).* Archaeological Survey of Alberta. Permit No. 2006-163. Copies available from Archaeological Survey of Alberta, Edmonton.

2007b *Historical Resources Mitigative Excavations at Genesis Land Development Corp.'s Symons Valley Development: Final Report (Permit 2006-404).* Archaeological Survey of Alberta. Permit No. 2006-404. Copies available from Archaeological Survey of Alberta, Edmonton.

VIVIAN, BRIAN C., AND JANET BLAKEY

2009 *Historical Resource Mitigative Studies, Crestmont Stage 4 Development Area (SW-31-24-2-W5M and NW-30-24-2-W5M): Final Report (Permit 2008-159).* Archaeological Survey of Alberta. Permit No. 2008-159. Copies available from Archaeological Survey of Alberta, Edmonton.

VIVIAN, BRIAN C., K. BOSCH, AND BRIAN O.K. REEVES

1997 *Archaeological Investigations, EePn-86, Turner Valley Sewage Transfer Line: Final Report (Permit 96-053).* Archaeological Survey of Alberta. Permit No. 1996-053. Copies available from Archaeological Survey of Alberta, Edmonton.

1998 *Historical Resource Conservation Excavations, EgPn 230: Final Report (Permit 97-83).* Archaeological Survey of Alberta. Permit No. 1997-083. Copies available from Archaeological Survey of Alberta, Edmonton.

VIVIAN, BRIAN C., AND AMANDA DOW

2006 *Historical Resource Conservation Excavations at EhPn 44 and EhPn 45: Final Report (Permit 2002-046).* Archaeological Survey of Alberta. Permit No. 2002-046. Copies available from Archaeological Survey of Alberta, Edmonton.

VIVIAN, BRIAN C., AMANDA DOW, AND BRIAN O.K. REEVES

2003a *Historical Resources Impact Assessment and Conservation Excavations at Cougar Ridge, Off-site Sewer Services: Final Report (Permit 00-032).* Archaeological Survey of Alberta. Permit No. 2000-032. Copies available from Archaeological Survey of Alberta, Edmonton.

2003b *Historical Resource Impact Assessment and Conservation Excavations, Valley Ridge Subdivision Phase 17: Final Report (Permit 2002-119).* Archaeological Survey of Alberta. Permit No. 2002-119. Copies available from Archaeological Survey of Alberta, Edmonton.

2005 *Historical Resources Conservation Excavations, EgPn 430, Vol. 1: Areas Two and Three: Final Report (Permit 2003-097).* Archaeological Survey of Alberta. Permit No. 2003-097. Copies available from Archaeological Survey of Alberta, Edmonton.

2006 *Historical Resource Conservation Excavations, EgPn-228A, EgPn-286, and EgPn-139C, Valley Ridge Estates (Permit 98-012).* Archaeological Survey of Alberta. Permit No. 1998-012. Copies available from Archaeological Survey of Alberta, Edmonton.

VIVIAN, BRIAN C., AND BRIAN O.K. REEVES

1999 *Historical Resource Conservation Excavations, EgPn 428, Crestmont Estates: Final Report (Permit 97-30, 98-131).* Archaeological Survey of Alberta. Permit Nos. 1997-030 and 1998-131. Copies available from Archaeological Survey of Alberta, Edmonton.

2001 *Historical Resources Conservation Excavations, EgPn 430, Area 4: A Precontact Processing Camp (Permit 2000-033): Final Report.* Archaeological Survey of Alberta. Permit No. 2000-033. Copies available from Archaeological Survey of Alberta, Edmonton.

2002 *Historical Resource Impact Assessment of the Genesis Lands, Symons Valley (Permit 2001-257): Final Report.* Archaeological Survey of Alberta. Permit No. 2001-257. Copies available from Archaeological Survey of Alberta, Edmonton.

VIVIAN, BRIAN C., JASON ROE, AND JANET BLAKEY

2009 *Historical Resources Mitigative Studies, Crestmont Stage 3 Development Area (NE Section 30-24-2-W5M): Final Report, Vol. 1 (Permit 2007-141).* Archaeological Survey of Alberta. Permit No. 2007-141. Copies available from Archaeological Survey of Alberta, Edmonton.

WALDE, DALE

2003 *The Mortlach Phase.* Occasional Papers of the Archaeological Society of Alberta No. 2. Archaeological Society of Alberta, Calgary.

2004 Mortlach and One Gun: Phase to Phase. In *Archaeology on the Edge: New Perspectives from the Northern Plains*, edited by Brian Kooyman and Jane Kelley, pp. 39–51. University of Calgary Press, Calgary.

2006a Avonlea and Athabaskan Migrations: A Reconsideration. *Plains Anthropologist* 51(198): 185–197.

2006b Sedentism and Pre-contact Tribal Organization on the Northern Plains: Colonial Imposition or Indigenous Development? *World Archaeology* 38(2):291–310.

WALDE, DALE, AND DAVID MEYER

2003 Pre-contact Pottery in Alberta: An Overview. In *Archaeology in Alberta: A View from the New Millennium*, edited by Jack W. Brink and John F. Dormaar, pp. 132–152. Archaeological Society of Alberta, Medicine Hat.

WALDE, DALE, DAVID MEYER, AND WENDY UNFREED

1995 The Late Period on the Canadian and Adjacent Plains. *Journal of American Archaeology* 9:7–66.

WALKER, DANNY N.

1982 Early Holocene Vertebrate Fauna. In *The Agate Basin Site: A Record of the Paleoindian Occupation of the Northwestern Plains*, edited by George Frison and Dennis Stanford, pp. 274–308. Academic Press, New York.

WALKER, ERNEST G.

1981 The Greenwater Lake Site (FcMv 1): An Archaic Burial From Saskatchewan. *Napao* 11(1 and 2):8–12.

1982 The Bracken Cairn: A Late Middle Archaic Burial from Southwestern Saskatchewan. *Saskatchewan Archaeology* 3 (1 and 2):8–35.

1984a The Graham Site: McKean Cremation from Southern Saskatchewan. *Plains Anthropologist* 29(104):139–150.

1984b A Late Prehistoric Burial from South-central Saskatchewan. *Saskatchewan Archeology* 5:37–41.

1986 Appendix A: Human Skeletal Remains from the Crown Site. In *The Crown Site (FhNa 86) Excavation Results. Nipawin Reservoir Heritage Study, Vol. 8*, edited by David Meyer, pp. 247–261. Publication No. E-903-7-E-86, Saskatchewan Research Council, Saskatoon.

1992 *The Gowen Sites: Cultural Responses to Climatic Warming on the Northern Plains (7500–5000 BP).* Mercury Series Paper No. 145. Archaeological Survey of Canada, Canadian Museum of Civilization, Hull, Quebec.

WATERS, MICHAEL R., AND THOMAS W. STAFFORD, JR.

2007 Redefining the Age of Clovis: Implications for the Peopling of the Americas. *Science* 315:1122–1126.

WEBSTER, SEAN MICHAEL

2004 A Re-evaluation of the McKean Series on the Northern Plains. Unpublished Master's thesis, Department of Archaeology, University of Saskatoon, Saskatoon.

WEST, FREDERICK HADLEIGH

1996 Beringian and New World Origins: The Archaeological Evidence. In *American Beginnings: The Prehistory and Palaeoecology of Beringia*, edited by Frederick Hadleigh West, pp. 537–559. University of Chicago Press, Chicago.

WETTLAUFER, BOYD

1955 *The Mortlach Site in the Besant Valley of Central Saskatchewan.* Anthropological Series No. 1. Department of Natural Resources, Regina, Saskatchewan.

WETTLAUFER, BOYD, AND WILLIAM J. MAYER-OAKES

1960 *The Long Creek Site.* Anthropological Series No. 2. Saskatchewan Museum of Natural History. Department of Natural Resources. Regina, Saskatchewan.

WHEELER, RICHARD PAGE

1952 A Note of the "McKean Lanceolate Point." *Plains Archeological Conference Newsletter* 4(4):45–50.

1954 Two New Point Types: Duncan and Hanna Points. *Plains Anthropologist* 1:7–14.

WHEAT, JOE BEN

1967 A Paleo-Indian Bison Kill. *Scientific American* 216:44–52.

1972 The Olsen-Chubbuck Site: A Paleo-Indian Bison Kill. Memoirs of the Society for American Archaeology No. 26. *American Antiquity* 37(1, pt. 2).

1979 The Jurgens Site. Memoir 15, *Plains Anthropologist* 24(84, pt. 2):1–153.

WILLEY, GORDON R., AND PHILIP PHILLIPS

1958 *Method and Theory in American Archaeology.* University of Chicago Press, Chicago.

WILMETH, ROSCOE

1968 A Fossilized Bone Artifact from Southern Saskatchewan. *American Antiquity* 33(1):100–101.

WILCOX, DAVID R.

1988 Avonlea and Southern Athapascan Migrations. In *Avonlea Yesterday and Today: Archaeology and Prehistory*, edited by Leslie B. Davis, pp. 273–280. Saskatchewan Archaeological Society, Saskatoon.

WILSON, GILBERT L.

1924 *The Horse and the Dog in Hidatsa Culture.* Anthropological Papers of the American Museum of Natural History 15, pt. 2. American Museum Press, New York.

WILSON, IAN

1987 The Pink Mountain Palaeo-Indian Site. In *Archaeology in Alberta 1986*, edited by Martin Magne, pp 217–219. Occasional Paper No. 3, Archaeological Survey of Alberta, Edmonton.

WILSON, JAMES S.

1984 The Lucky Strike Site: A Late Prehistoric Campsite in the Aspen Parkland. *Saskatchewan Archaeology* 5:5–26.

WILSON, MICHAEL C.

1977 *Archaeological Studies in the Longview-Pekisko Area of Southern Alberta, Permit 75-016.* Archaeological Survey of Alberta. Permit No. 1975-016. Copies available from Archaeological Survey of Alberta, Edmonton.

1980 *Archaeological Excavations Mount Royal Village (Mona Lisa site, EgPm-3, Locality C), Calgary, Alberta, Permit 78-019.* Archaeological Survey of Alberta. Permit No. 1978-019. Copies available from Archaeological Survey of Alberta, Edmonton.

1983 Canid Scavengers and Butchering Patterns: Evidence from a 3,600-Year-Old Bison Bone Bed in Alberta. In *Carnivores, Human Scavengers, and Predators: A Question of Bone Technology*, edited by

Genevieve M. LeMoine and A. Scott MacEachern, pp. 95–139. Proceedings of the 15th Annual Chacmool Conference, Chacmool Archaeology Association, University of Calgary, Calgary.

WILSON, MICHAEL C., DAVID W. HARVEY, AND RICHARD G. FORBIS

1983 Geoarchaeological Investigation of the Age and Context of the Stalker (Taber Child) Site, DlPa 4, Alberta, *Canadian Journal of Archaeology* 7(2):179–207.

WILSON-MEYER, DIANE, AND MURIEL I. CARLSON

1985 The Yellowsky (FjOd 2): An Avonlea Campsite in West-central Saskatchewan. *Saskatchewan Archaeology* 6:19–32.

WISSLER, CLARK

1914 The Influence of the Horse in the Development of Plains Culture. *American Anthropologist* 16:1–25.

WOLFE, STEPHEN A., JEFF OLLERHEAD, DAVID J. HUNTLEY, AND OLAV B. LIAN

2006 Holocene Dune Activity and Environmental Change in the Prairie Parkland and Boreal Forest, Central Saskatchewan, Canada. *The Holocene* 16(1):17–29.

WOOD, W. RAYMOND, AND ANN M. JOHNSON

1973 High Butte, 32ME13: A Missouri Valley Woodland-Besant Site. *Archaeology in Montana* 14(3):35–83.

WORMINGTON, H. MARIE

1957 *Ancient Man in North America*, 4th Edition. Popular Series No. 4, Denver Museum of Natural History, Denver, Colorado.

WORMINGTON, H. MARIE, AND RICHARD G. FORBIS

1965 *An Introduction to the Archaeology of Alberta, Canada*. Proceedings No. 11, Denver Museum of Natural History, Denver, Colorado.

WOWCHUK, GARY

1990 A Cody Complex Site in the Swan River Valley. *Manitoba Archaeological Newsletter*, series 2, 2(3).

WRIGHT, BRUCE W.

1983 *Historical Resources Impact Mitigation, EgPn 146, Calgary: Final Report, Permit 82-007*. Archaeological Survey of Alberta. Permit No. 1982-007. Copies available from Archaeological Survey of Alberta, Edmonton.

WYCKOFF, DON G.

1992 The Cody Complex in Eastern Oklahoma's Arkansas Basin. *Current Research in the Pleistocene* 9:47–49.

WYMAN, DANIEL

2006 *Historical Resource Impact Mitigation, Double D Development Ltd., Gateway of Turner Valley, EdPn-47 and EdPn 53, Stage 1 HRIM (ASA Permit 2006-559): Final Report*. Archaeological Survey of Alberta. Permit No. 2006-559. Copies available from Archaeological Survey of Alberta, Edmonton.

YELLOWHORN, ELDON

2003 Regarding the American Paleolithic. *Canadian Journal of Archaeology* 27:62–73.

YOUNG, ROBERT R., R. BRUCE RAINS, AND GERALD OSBORN

1998 Comment on "Geology and Quaternary Environments of the First Preglacial Palaeolithic Sites Found in Alberta Canada," by Jiri Chlachula. *Quaternary Science Reviews* 17:449–453.

ZDANOWICZ, C.M., G.A. ZIELINSKI, AND M.S. GERMANI

1999 Mount Mazama Eruption: Calendrical Age Verified and Atmospheric Impact Assessed. *Geology* 27(7):621–624.

ZEIER, CHARLES D.

1983 Besant Projectile Points from the Antonsen Site (24GA660), Gallatin County, Montana: Within-sample Variance. *Archaeology in Montana* 24(3):1–57.

ZURBURG, SUZANNE C.

1991 The Norby Site: A Mummy Cave Complex Bison Kill on the Northern Plains. Unpublished Master's thesis, Department of Archaeology, University of Saskatoon, Saskatoon.

INDEX

Page numbers in grey refer to illustrations.

A

B

C

D

E

F

G

H

I

J

K

S

Y

Z

Trevor R. Peck is the plains archaeologist at the Archaeological Survey, Ministry of Culture and Community Spirit, with the Alberta Government. He received his MA from the University of Alberta and his PhD from the University of Calgary. The author of numerous articles and monographs, Dr. Peck's research interests include the prehistory of the northern plains, public archaeology, and archaeological theory.

This book was printed on 60lb Rolland Opaque in Cream. The cover stock is Wausau Paper Astroparche in Ancient Gold. The text face is LTC Kaatskill, designed by Frederic Goudy and Jim Rimmer. The sanserif face is FF Seria, designed by Martin Majoor.